Microsoft® QuickPascal:

An Introduction to Structured and Object-Oriented Programming

David I. Schneider
University of Maryland

DELLEN PUBLISHING COMPANY
San Francisco

COLLIER MACMILLAN PUBLISHERS
London

Divisions of Macmillan, Inc.

On the Cover: The untitled drawing on the cover was executed by Robert Hudson, who lives and works in Cotati, California. Hudson does both painting and sculpture using strong geometric forms and primary colors. Frequently Hudson incorporates found objects in both his two- and three-dimensional work.

Hudon's work is represented by Dorothy Goldeen Gallery in Santa Monica, California and Allan Frumkin Gallery in New York City, New York. His work may also be seen in the permanent collections of the Los Angeles County Museum, the Museum of Modern Art in San Francisco, the Oakland Museum, the Whitney Museum and the Museum of Modern Art in New York City, the Boston Museum of Fine Arts, and the Chicago Art Institute.

Photography: John Drooyan
Interior Design and Composition: Rebecca Evans & Associates
Laser Art: F. E. Harrington, Rebecca Evans & Associates

Photo/Illustration Credits: page 12, Courtesy of International Business Machines Corporation; page 327, Courtesy of Hammond Incorporated; page 443, Courtesy of Hammond Incorporated; page 446, Courtesy of Resorts International Hotel Casino.

© Copyright 1990 by Dellen Publishing Company, a division of Macmillan, Inc.

Printed in the United States of America.

Permissions: Dellen Publishing Company
                    400 Pacific Avenue
                    San Francisco, California 94133

Orders: Macmillan Publishing Company
                    Front and Brown Streets
                    Riverside, New Jersey 08075

Collier Macmillan Canada, Inc.

Library of Congress Cataloging in Publication Data

Schneider, David I.
    Microsoft QuickPascal : an introduction to structured and object
-oriented programming / by David I. Schneider.
        p.   cm.
    ISBN 0-02-407595-7
    1. Pascal (Computer program language) 2. Microsoft QuickPascal
(Computer program) I. Title
QA76.73.P2S337 1990
005.13'3—dc20
                                              90-3178
                                              CIP

Printing: 1 2 3 4 5 6 7 8   Year: 0 1 2 3

Table of Contents

Preface

This text provides an introduction to programming in Microsoft® QuickPascal on the IBM PC and IBM PC-compatible computers.

My objectives when writing this text were as follows:

1. To develop focused chapters. Rather than cover many topics superficially, I concentrate on important subjects and cover them thoroughly.

2. To use examples and exercises that students can relate to, appreciate, and be comfortable with. Real data is used frequently. Examples do not have so many embellishments that students are distracted from the programming technique being illustrated.

3. To produce compact text that students will find both readable and informative. The main points of each topic are discussed first and then the peripheral details are presented as comments.

4. To teach good programming practices that are in step with modern programming methodology. Problem solving techniques and structured programming are discussed early and used throughout the book.

5. To provide insights into the major applications of computers.

The book is organized into 13 chapters:

1. An Introduction to Computers and QuickPascal

2. Problem Solving

3. Fundamentals of Programming in QuickPascal

4. Procedures and Functions

5. Selection Structures

6. Looping

7. User-Defined Data Types

8. Arrays

9. Files

10. Graphics

11. Random Numbers

12. Advanced Topics

13. Object-Oriented Programming

Chapters 1 through 8 provide the foundations of programming; Chapters 9, 10, and 11 explore three major applications of computers; and Chapters 12 and 13 delve into modern and challenging aspects of programming. Chapters 1 and 2 provide both an introduction and a preview of coming attractions. Students learn about the computer as a problem-solving tool and get a glimpse of the diverse contributions that led to the current state of computing. Chapter 3 gives the student confidence by showing what QuickPascal can do and providing a solid base for the different means of inputting and outputting data. Chapters 4 through 8 present essential tools for processing data. The final five chapters permit the course to be customized to the audience.

Unique and Distinguishing Features

Exercises for most Sections. Each section that teaches QuickPascal programming has an exercise set. The exercises both reinforce the key ideas of the section and challenge the student to explore applications. Most of the exercise sets require the student to trace programs, find errors, and write programs. The answers to all odd-numbered exercises in Chapters 2 through 8 and selected odd-numbered exercises from Chapters 9 through 13 are given at the end of the text.

Practice Problems. Practice problems are located at the end of each section, just before the exercise set. Complete solutions are given following the exercise set. The practice problems often focus on points that are potentially confusing or are best appreciated after the student has worked on them. The reader should attempt the practice problems and study their solutions before moving on to the exercises.

Programming Projects. Beginning with Chapter 3, every chapter contains programming projects. The programming projects not only reflect the variety of ways that computers are used in the business and engineering communities, but also present some games and general interest topics. The large number and range of difficulty of the programming projects provide the flexibility to adapt the course to the interests and abilities of the students. Some of the programming projects in Chapters 9 through 13 can be assigned as end-of-the-semester projects.

Comments at the End of each Section. Extensions and fine points of new topics are reserved for the "Comments" portion at the end of each section so that they will not interfere with the flow of the presentation.

Case Studies. The five case studies focus on important programming applications. The problems are analyzed and the programs are developed with top-down charts and pseudocode.

Chapter Summary. In Chapters 3 through 13, the key results are stated and the important terms are highlighted.

Procedures and Functions. The early introduction of procedures and functions in Chapter 4 allows structured programming to be used in simple situations before being applied to complex problems. Some material from this chapter can easily be postponed.

Files. Chapter 9 presents a detailed introduction to files. The opportunity to introduce files earlier is provided with the optional (and elementary) discussion of text files in Section 6.3.

Appendix on Debugging.   The placement of the discussion of QuickPascal's sophisticated debugger in an appendix allows the instructor flexibility in deciding when to cover this topic.

Reference Manual Built into Appendices.   Appendices F and G describe all QuickPascal procedures, functions, and keywords, not just the ones covered in this text. These appendices replace the on-line help from the commercial version of QuickPascal 1.0.

Help With Error Messages.   Appendices B and C explain the run-time and compiler error messages in terms understandable to beginning programmers. These appendices replace the on-line help from the commercial version of QuickPascal 1.0.

Thorough Discussion of Environment.   In addition to the sections on getting started and using DOS, the text is supplemented with Appendices E and H on using the editor and an optional mouse. Appendix J describes the tasks in the menu bars.

Solutions Manual.   A manual containing the solution to every exercise and programming project is available for the instructor.

Case Studies.   A diskette containing the source code for the case studies and the longer programs in the book is available to the instructor.

QuickPascal Diskettes.   Each book contains the Textbook Edition of Microsoft QuickPascal 1.0 on two 5¼-inch diskettes. The Textbook Edition contains the same compiler and debugger as the commercial version. Programs compile to stand-alone EXE files and as many as nine programs can be present in memory at once. The files present on the two diskettes are listed on the inside front cover of the book. A complete copy of the commercial version of Microsoft QuickPascal, including all documentation, is available to each instructor. The primary difference between the two versions is that help with syntax and error messages is available on-line with the commercial version. Instead, this book contains extensive printed help in appendices customized for beginning Pascal students.

Acknowledgments

Many talented instructors, students, and programmers provided helpful comments and thoughtful suggestions at each stage in the preparation of this text. I extend my gratitude for their contributions to the quality of the book to Gerardo Ayzanoa, University of Maryland; Eric Berger; Eric Boesch, University of Maryland; Sid Brounstein, Montgomery College; Helen Casey, Sam Houston State University; Mark Ellis, MIT; O. R. Evans, Stephen F. Austin State University; Christine Kay, DeVry Institute of Technology; Jim Henry, Northern Illinois University; Shelly Langman, Bellevue Community College; J. X. McEnerney, United States Naval Academy; John Milligan, Onondaga Community College; Frederick Mosher; Steve Nameroff; Walter Nissen; Theresa Phinney; Texas A & M University; Peter Rosenbaum, Framingham State College; Brooke Stephens, University of Maryland; Brian Turnquist, University of Maryland; Greg Voss; Walter Wadycki, University of Illinois at Chicago; Michael Willis, Montgomery College.

Sheryl L. Harris did a meticulous job of copy editing the manuscript, John Drooyan contributed creative photographs and artwork, and Rebecca Evans did a superb job of managing the editing and production of the book.

I extend an extra special thanks to Don Dellen, president of Dellen Publishing Company, for his help in planning and executing this text. His partnership and friendship have added a warm, personal dimension to the writing process.

1

An Introduction to Computers and QuickPascal

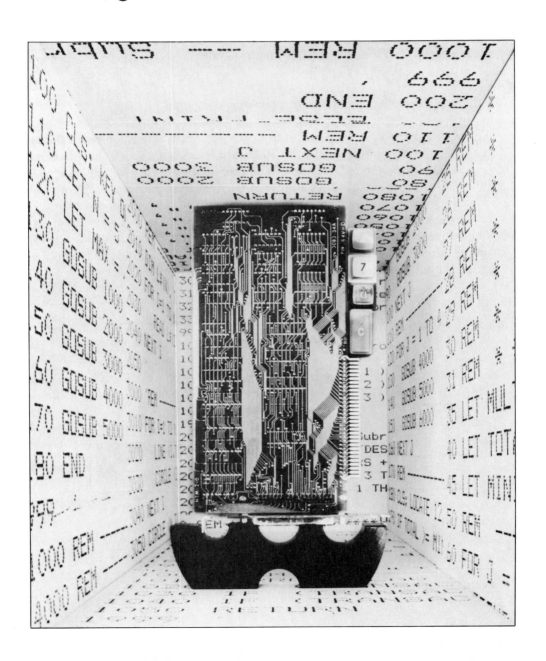

1.1 AN INTRODUCTION TO COMPUTERS

Microsoft QuickPascal: An Introduction to Structured and Object-Oriented Programming is a book about problem solving with computers. The programming language used is Pascal, but the principles taught apply to many modern structured programming languages. The examples and exercises present a sampling of the ways that computers are used in society.

Computers are so common today that you certainly have seen them in use and heard some of the terminology applied to them. Here are some of the questions that you might have about computers and programming.

Question: What is meant by *personal computer?*

Answer: The word *personal* does not mean that the computer is intended for personal, as opposed to business, purposes. Rather, it indicates that the machine is operated by one person at a time instead of by many people.

Question: What are the main components of a personal computer?

Answer: The visible components are shown in Figure 1.1. Instructions are entered into the computer by typing them on the **keyboard** or reading them from a **diskette** in a **diskette drive**. Characters normally appear on the **monitor** as they are typed. Information processed by the computer can be displayed on the monitor, printed on the **printer**, or recorded on a diskette in the diskette drive. Hidden from view inside the **system unit** are the microprocessor and the memory of the computer. The **microprocessor**, which can be thought of as the brain of the computer, carries out all computations. The **memory** stores the instructions and data that are processed by the computer.

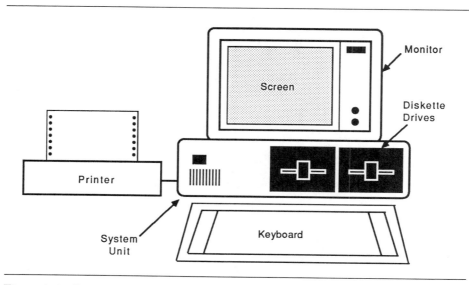

Figure 1.1 Components of a Personal Computer

Question: What are some uses of computers in our society?

Answer: Whenever we make a phone call, a computer determines how to route the call and calculates the cost of the call. Banks store all customer transactions on computers and process this data to revise the balance for each customer. Airlines record all reservations into computers. This information, which is said to form a database, can be accessed to determine the status of any flight. NASA uses computers to calculate the trajectories of satellites. Business analysts use computers to create pie and bar charts that give visual impact to data.

Question: What are some topics covered in this text that students can use immediately?

Answer: Computer files can be created to hold lists of names, addresses, and phone numbers, which can be alphabetized and printed out in entirety or selectively. Line graphs and attractive tables can be created to enhance the data in a term paper. Mathematical computations can be carried out for science, business, and engineering courses. Personal financial transactions, such as bank deposits and loans, can be recorded, organized, and analyzed.

Question: How do we communicate with the computer?

Answer: There are many languages that are used to communicate with the computer. At the lowest level, there is *machine language*, which is understood directly by the microprocessor, but is awkward for humans. Pascal is an example of a higher-level language. It consists of instructions to which people can relate, such as Write, Read, and Repeat. QuickPascal contains a file, called the **compiler**, that translates Pascal programs into machine language programs.

Question: How do we get computers to perform complicated tasks?

Answer: Tasks are broken down into a sequence of simple instructions that can be communicated by a computer language. (This text uses the language Pascal.) The sequence of instructions is called a **program**. Programs range in size from two or three instructions to tens of thousands of instructions. Instructions are typed on the keyboard and stored in the computer's memory. (They also can be stored permanently on a diskette.) The process of executing the instructions is called **running the program**.

Question: Are there certain features that all programs have in common?

Answer: Most programs do three things: take in data, manipulate it, and give desired information. These operations are referred to as **input, processing,** and **output**. The input data might be held in a portion of the program, reside on a diskette, or be provided by the computer operator in response to requests made by the computer while the program is running. The processing of the input data takes place inside the computer and can take from a fraction of a second to many hours. The output data is either displayed on the screen, printed on the printer, or recorded onto a diskette. As a simple example, consider a program that computes sales tax. The input data is the cost of the item. The processing consists of multiplying the cost by a certain percentage. The output data is the resulting product, the amount of sales tax to be paid.

Question: What are the meanings of the terms *hardware* and *software?*

Answer: The term **hardware** refers to the physical components of the computer, including all peripherals, data terminals, disk drives, and all mechanical and electrical devices. Programs are referred to as **software**.

Question: What are the meanings of the terms *programmer* and *user?*

Answer: A **programmer** is a person who solves problems by writing programs on a computer. After analyzing the problem and developing a plan for solving it, he or she writes and tests the program that instructs the computer how to carry out the plan. The program might be run many times, either by the programmer or by others. A **user** is any person who uses a program. While working through this text, you will function both as a programmer and a user.

Question: What is meant by *problem solving?*

Answer: Problems are solved by carefully reading them to determine what data are given and what data are requested. Then a step-by-step procedure is devised to process the given data and produce the requested data. This procedure is called an **algorithm**. Finally, a computer program is written to carry out the algorithm. Algorithms are discussed in Section 2.2.

Question: What types of problems are solved in this text?

Answer: Carrying out business computations, creating and maintaining records, alphabetizing lists, simulating games, and drawing line graphs are some of the types of problems we will solve.

Question: What is the difference between *standard Pascal* and *QuickPascal?*

Answer: Pascal is a language developed in 1971 by Nicklaus Wirth. After the language became widely used, a committee composed formal rules for the language. These rules are referred to as **standards**, and the language adhering to these standards is called **standard Pascal**. QuickPascal is a version of Pascal that was written by the Microsoft Corporation to take advantage of the capabilities of personal computers. QuickPascal has most of the features of standard Pascal, as well as many enhancements.

1.2 GETTING STARTED

If this is your first session using the diskettes supplied with this book, refer to Appendix I for directions on installing and invoking QuickPascal. Figure 1.2 shows the initial display for QuickPascal.

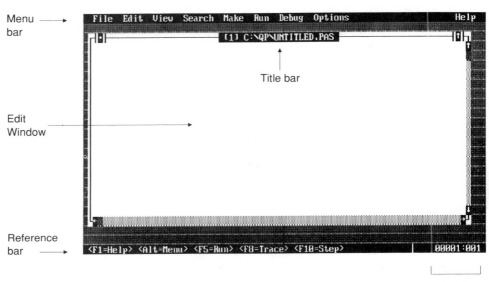

Figure 1.2 Screen after QuickPascal is Invoked

The blinking dash is called the **cursor**. Each character you type will appear at the cursor. The QuickPascal screen is divided into four parts. The part containing the cursor is called the **Edit window**. It is the most important part of the screen since programs are typed into this window.

The **Menu bar** at the top of the screen is used to call up menus and lists of tasks. QuickPascal is a rich programming language that serves both beginning and advanced programmers. Many of the tasks accessed through the Menu bar are only needed by advanced programmers. Later, we will examine the tasks that are most important for beginners.

The small **Title bar** just below the Menu bar holds the file name associated with the program in the Edit window. This file name is used to identify the program after it is recorded on a diskette or hard disk. Until the program is given a file name, the default name is "UNTITLED.PAS." The name is preceded by the disk location of the file. (In Figure 1.2, the symbols "C:\QP\" indicate that the program will be recorded in a portion of the hard disk known as the QP directory. The number in brackets is of no importance to us now and is discussed in Comment 6.)

The bottom line of the screen briefly contains a copyright message and then appears as in Figure 1.2. The information displayed in the bar will vary. In Figure 1.2, the display 00001:001 informs us that the cursor is located on the first line and on the first column of that line.

Programs are created from the keyboard in much the same way that they would be written with a typewriter. Writing and modifying a program is called **editing** the program; the part of QuickPascal used to create and alter programs is called the **editor**. Before discussing the editor, we first examine the workings of the keyboard.

There are several styles of keyboards. Figure 1.3 contains a typical keyboard. The keyboard is divided into three parts. The center portion functions like an ordinary typewriter keyboard. The left-hand portion consists of 10 keys, labeled from F1 through F10, called the **function keys**. (On some keyboards, the function keys are located across the top. Also, some keyboards have more than 10 function keys.) These keys are used to perform certain tasks with a single keystroke. For instance, pressing the function key F5 causes the displayed program to be run. (The commands associated with other function keys will be discussed later in this section.) The right-hand portion of the keyboard, called the **numeric keypad**, is used either to move the cursor or to enter numbers. Press the **Num Lock key** a few times and notice the letter N appearing and disappearing in the right part of the Reference bar. When the letter N is present, the numeric keypad produces numbers; otherwise, it moves the cursor. The Num Lock key is called a **toggle key** since it "toggles" between two states. When the numeric keypad is in the cursor-moving state, the four arrow keys move the cursor one space.

Figure 1.3   IBM PC Keyboard

Two very important keys are located at the right side of the main portion of the keyboard. The **Backspace key** is the gray key with the left-pointing arrow. It moves the cursor one space to the left and erases any character in that location. The **Enter key** is the key with the hooked arrow located below the Backspace key. It is used to execute commands or to enter lines in a program.

After QuickPascal has been invoked, the following routine will introduce you to the keyboard.

1. Use the right and left cursor-moving keys on the numeric keypad to move the cursor. Notice that the cursor position number at the lower right corner of the screen changes each time one of these keys is pressed.

2. Press the **Home key** to move the cursor back to the beginning of the line. In general, the Home key moves the cursor to the beginning the line on which it currently is located.

3. Type some letters using the central "typewriter" portion of the keyboard. The **Shift keys**, marked with the symbol ⇧, are used to obtain uppercase letters or the upper character of keys showing two characters.

4. Press the **Caps Lock key** and then type some letters. The letters will appear in uppercase. We say that the computer is in uppercase mode. To toggle back to lowercase mode, press the Caps Lock key again. Only alphabetic keys are affected by Caps Lock. (**Note:** When the editor is in the uppercase state, the letter C appears in the right part of the Reference bar.)

5. Hold down the **Ctrl key** (Ctrl stands for "Control") and press the Y key. This combination erases the line containing the cursor. We describe this combination as **Ctrl+Y**.

6. Type some letters and then press the Backspace key a few times. It will erase letters one at a time. Another method of deleting a letter is to move the cursor to the letter and press the **Del** (Delete) key. The backspace key erases the character to the left of the cursor, and the Del key erases the character at the cursor.

7. Type a few letters and use the appropriate cursor-moving key to move the cursor under one of the letters. Now type any letter and notice that it is inserted at the cursor position and that the letters following it move to the right. This is because **insert mode** is active. The **overwrite mode**, in which a typed letter overwrites the letter located at the cursor position, is invoked by pressing the **Ins key** (Insert). Pressing this toggle key again reinstates insert mode. The cursor size indicates the active mode; a large cursor means overwrite mode.

8. Type some letters and move the cursor left a few spaces. Now press the **End key** (on the numeric keypad). The cursor will move to the end of the line.

9. The key to the left of the Q key is called the **Tab key**. It is marked with a pair of arrows, the top one pointing to the left and the lower one pointing to the right. Pressing the Tab key has the same effect as pressing the space bar several times.

10. Type more characters than can fit on one line of the screen. Notice that the leftmost characters scroll off the screen to make room for the new characters. Although QuickPascal allows up to 128 characters to appear on a line, we will not exceed the limits of the Edit window.

11. The Enter key is used to begin a new line on the screen in much the same way that the carriage return lever is used on a manual typewriter.

12. The **Alt key** activates the Menu bar. Then pressing one of the highlighted letters, such as F, E, or V, selects a menu. A specific item from a menu is selected by pressing yet another highlighted letter. Selections also can be made by using the cursor-moving keys to highlight the choice and then pressing the Enter key.

13. The **Esc key** (Escape) is used to return to the Edit window.

A Programming Walkthrough

The following walkthrough introduces you to the mechanics of creating and running a program. Just follow the directions and observe the results. The QuickPascal instructions used here will be explained later in the text.

1. Use the cursor-moving keys and the combination Ctrl+Y to clear the Edit window.

2. Type the line

```
PROGRAM First;
```

and then press the Enter key. On many monitors, the word PROGRAM will appear in a different color or intensity than the word First. PROGRAM is an example of a **keyword** or **reserved word**. Keywords have special meanings to QuickPascal. The keyword PROGRAM is always the first word of the first line of a Pascal program. In this case, the name of the program is "First." There are 52 keywords in QuickPascal. Semicolons are used to separate various parts of programs. The above line also could have been written

```
PROGRAM
First;
```

4. Type additional lines to create the display shown below. This is an example of a QuickPascal program. It consists of a sequence of instructions that tell the computer to perform certain tasks. This program causes the word "Hello" to be displayed 100 times.

```
PROGRAM First;

USES Crt;

VAR i : Integer;

BEGIN
  ClrScr;
  FOR i := 1 TO 100 DO
    Write('Hello   ')
END.
```

5. To compile the program (that is, translate it from QuickPascal into machine language), press and release Alt, then press and release M, and then press C. (This key combination is abbreviated as Alt/M/C. It moves the cursor to the Menu bar, opens the Make menu, and selects the option "Compile File.") A compilation box informs you of the number of lines that were compiled. Your disk will whirl during this process. (In the event that a message containing the word "error" appears on the screen, see Step 11.) The compilation box disappears when compilation is complete.

6. To execute the program, press the F5 key. (**Note:** Pressing the F5 key is denoted later in the book by **[run]**.)

7. When the program runs, the **Output screen** appears. After the program finishes, the last line on the screen gives the time required for the execution

of the compiled program. The statement "Program returned(0)" indicates that the program ran correctly.

8. Press any key to return to the Edit window, as instructed by the message at the bottom of the screen.

9. Press F4 to see the Output screen again. This key toggles between the Edit and Output windows.

10. Press F5 to run the program again if you so desire.

11. Sometimes errors are found in the program as it is compiling. To see an example of this, move the cursor to the word FOR in the program and delete the letter O from the word. When the program compiles, a dialog box with the message "Unknown identifier" appears. (See Figure 1.4.) The dialog box can be removed by pressing the Esc key or the Enter key. After the dialog box is removed, the cursor is near the offending word. Correct the error by changing the word back to FOR.

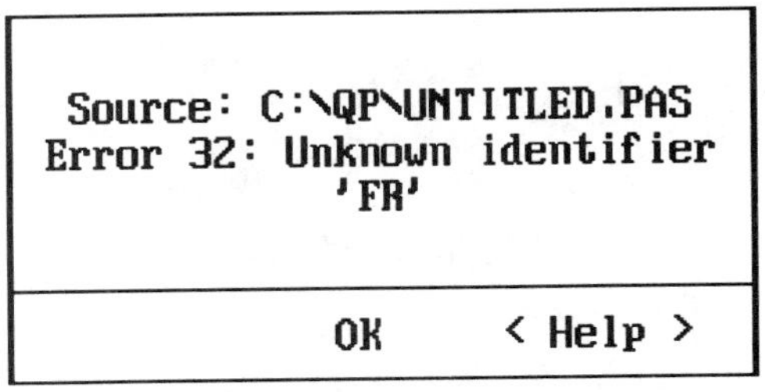

```
Source: C:\QP\UNTITLED.PAS
Error 32: Unknown identifier
          'FR'

          OK        < Help >
```

Figure 1.4   Compiler Dialog Box

12. Modify the program by inserting the line

```
Writeln('One Hundred Greetings');
```

after the ClrScr line. To create space for the line, move the cursor to the end of the ClrScr line and press the Enter key. (Alternately, move the cursor to the beginning of the FOR line, press the Enter key, and move the cursor up one line.) Now type in the new line.

13. To perform another modification to the program, move the cursor to the first apostrophe in the Write statement and type the letter i, followed by a comma and a space. The line will now read

```
Write(i, 'Hello   ')
```

14. Compile and run the new program. The display now will be titled and each *Hello* will be numbered.

15. Press any key to return to the Edit window.

16. You can store the program on a diskette or hard disk so you can run it later without having to retype it. To save the program press Alt/F/A (press Alt, then F, and then A). A dialog box will appear and ask you for a file name. Type in a name containing at most eight letters and digits (no spaces) and

then press the Enter key. For instance, you might type MYPROG1 as the file name. The program will then be stored. This process is called **saving** the program. QuickPascal automatically adds a period and the suffix PAS to the name. Therefore, the complete file name is MYPROG1.PAS on the diskette or hard disk and in the Title bar. If the program is later modified, it can be saved again with its current name simply by pressing Alt/F/S.

17. Suppose you want to write a new program. To clear MYPROG1.PAS from the Edit window, hold down the Ctrl key and press F4 (abbreviation: press Ctrl+F4). (**Note:** In the event you press Ctrl+F4 before saving the previous program, a dialog box will appear to give you another chance to save it before it is removed. Use the Tab key to move the highlight to the desired item and press Enter.) Press Alt/F/N to obtain a clear Edit window for the new program.

18. You can restore MYPROG1.PAS as the program in the Edit window by pressing Alt/F/O instead of Alt/F/N in Step 17, typing MYPROG1 at the prompt, and then pressing the Enter key. Alternately, instead of typing and Entering MYPROG1, you can press the Tab key, move the cursor bar to MYPROG1, and press Enter.

A Walkthrough of Menus

1. Press the Alt key to activate the Menu bar.

2. Press F to "pull down" the File menu. Notice that the task "New" is high-lighted.

3. Press the cursor-down key to highlight other items in the File menu.

4. Press the cursor-right key to move to the other menus. Information on the items in the menus appears in Appendix J.

5. Press Esc one or two times to return to the Edit window.

Comments:

1. The key sequences discussed in this section have the form key1+key2 or key1/key2. The plus sign instructs you to hold down key1 while pressing key2. The slash symbol (/) tells you to release key1 before pressing key2.

2. Here are other useful key combinations:
   (a) Ctrl+Home: moves the cursor to the beginning of the program
   (b) Ctrl+End: moves the cursor to the end of the program
   (c) Alt/F/P/Enter: prints a copy of the current program on the printer
   (d) Alt/F/X: exits QuickPascal and returns to DOS

3. When the Edit window is completely filled with program lines, the program scrolls upwards to accommodate additional lines. The lines that scrolled off the top can be viewed again by pressing PgUp. The PgDn key moves down the program.

4. There are two methods to clear the Edit window. You can either erase the lines one at a time with Ctrl+Y or erase all lines simultaneously with Ctrl+F4. With the second method, a dialog box may query you about saving the

current program. In this case, use Tab to select the desired option and press Enter.

5. The QuickPascal editor supports many of the tasks of word processors, such as search and block operations; however, these features need not concern us presently. (See Appendix E for details.)

6. The QuickPascal editor can hold up to nine programs at one time. The programs are identified by a number appearing in brackets in the title bar. (For instance, [1], [2], . . ., [9].) To type in a new program, you usually press Ctrl+F4 to remove the current program from memory. If instead you press Alt/F/N, the current program will remain in memory and a new Edit window, identified by a new bracketed number, will appear on the screen. The previous window still exists in memory even though it is not displayed on the screen. Pressing Alt+n makes Edit window [n] the currently displayed Edit window. This allows you to change between Edit windows as desired. Compile commands or run commands apply to the program in the currently displayed Edit window.

7. There are many uses of dialog boxes. For instance, they pop up to report errors in a program and to allow you to assign a file name to a program. The Tab key moves around in a dialog box and the Enter key makes a selection. Although dialog boxes often have a cancel rectangle, the Esc key also can be used to remove the dialog box from the screen.

8. There are two names associated with a program: the name following the word PROGRAM and the name appearing in the Title bar. The name following the word PROGRAM must begin with a letter or an underline character and can consist of any sequence of at most 63 letters and digits. The name in the Title bar identifies the program on a diskette or hard disk. This name must conform to certain file-naming conventions, discussed in Section 1.3. The PROGRAM name and the name in the Title bar need not be the same. The PROGRAM name is also called the "internal" name, and the name in the Title bar is also called the "external" name.

9. In the demonstration program, the active tasks are performed by the statements contained within the keywords BEGIN and END, where END is followed by a period. This portion of the program is called the "statement part" or "main body" of the program. The line beginning with the word PROGRAM is called the "heading" and the remaining portion of the program is called the "declaration part." The heading must precede the declarations part which, in turn, must precede the statement part.

10. The statement "ClrScr;" in the demonstration program clears the screen. Executing this statement requires code from the file CRT.QPU, the Crt Unit, found on the Utilities Diskette. The statement "USES Crt;" tells the compiler to incorporate the Crt Unit in the program. All the program examples in this text include the "USES Crt;" declaration and the ClrScr statement; however, these lines are sometimes omitted from programs in the Exercises and Solutions sections of the text.

11. When the program with file name MYPROG1 is compiled, the compiled version is stored on a diskette or hard disk and given the file name

MYPROG1.EXE. When the program is saved, the text in the Edit window is stored on the diskette or hard disk and given the file name MYPROG1.PAS. MYPROG1.PAS is commonly called **source code** and MYPROG1.EXE is called **executable code**. (Actually, the compiler also creates a file named MYPROG1.QDB required by the QuickPascal debugger.)

12. Appendices B, C, and F at the back of this text provide help on the interpretation of error messages and the syntax of statements. All the QuickPascal error messages and statements are included, not just the ones covered in the text. Take a few minutes to familiarize yourself with these appendices. (**Note:** QuickPascal has an on-line help system that is normally accessed by pressing F1; however, this feature is not present on the version of QuickPascal provided with this text.)

13. A mouse can be used to access items from menus and move the cursor. See Appendix H for details.

PRACTICE PROBLEMS 1.2

(Solutions to Practice Problems always follow the exercises.)

1. What QuickPascal keyword appears in the first line of the program in the walkthrough?

2. Programs appearing in Examples in this text are usually followed by "[run]" and then the output of the program. What does "[run]" mean?

EXERCISES 1.2

1. What is the name of the window in which a program is written?

2. What information is given by the two numbers on the right side of the Reference bar?

3. What is the difference between the backspace and delete keys?

4. What QuickPascal statement clears the screen?

5. By what name is a program known before a file name is specified?

6. What is the name of the small blinking dash and what is its purpose?

7. What follows the word PROGRAM?

8. Name three toggle keys.

Figure 1.5 shows many of the special keys on the keyboard. In Exercises 9 through 34, select the key (or key combination) that performs the task.

9. Erase the line containing the cursor.

10. Toggle between insert mode and overwrite mode.

11. Erase the character preceding the cursor.

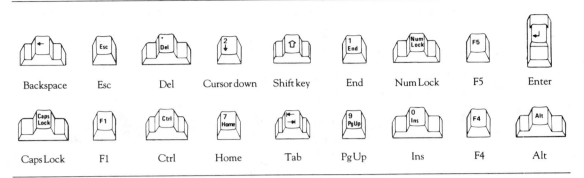

Figure 1.5   Some Special Keys

12. Toggle the numeric keypad between states.

13. Erase the character at the cursor.

14. Toggle the case of alphabetic characters.

15. Move the cursor to the beginning of the line containing the cursor.

16. Move the cursor to the end of the line containing the cursor.

17. Compile the program in the Edit window.

18. Cause the upper character of a double-character key to be displayed.

19. Move the cursor up one line.

20. Print a copy of the current program on the printer.

21. Exit QuickPascal and return to DOS.

22. Move the cursor to the beginning of the program.

23. Move the cursor to the end of the program.

24. Delete the current line.

25. Cancel a dialog box.

26. Move from the Menu bar to the Edit window.

27. Move from one option rectangle of a dialog box to another rectangle.

28. Clear the current program from the Edit window and start a new program.

29. Insert a blank line in the middle of a program.

30. With the cursor at the end of a line, begin a new line.

31. Remove a pull-down menu from the screen.

32. Look at the Output screen.

33. Create a new Edit window without removing the current program from memory.

34. Switch from the currently displayed Edit window to Edit window [1].

In Exercises 35 through 42, perform the task and/or answer the question.

35. How can the program in the programming walkthrough be changed so it does not clear the screen prior to displaying the Hello's?

36. Remove the line "PROGRAM First;" from the program in the walkthrough and compile the program. Does an error occur? Explain. *No*

37. Change the word "Write" to the word "Writeln" in the programming walkthrough. Compile and run the program. What is different in the output?

38. Remove the "END." statement from the program in the programming walkthrough. Compile the program. What error occurs?

39. Clear Edit window [1] and enter the word "one" in it. Without removing Edit window [1], create a new Edit window [2] and enter the word "two" in it. Continue in this way until there are five Edit windows in memory. Now, move directly to Edit window [2] and remove it from memory without saving its contents. What is the number of the Edit window that appears after window [2] is removed?

40. Use the Open command from the File menu to load the program written during the walkthrough.

41. Open the file containing the program from the programming walkthrough so it appears in the Edit window. Move the cursor to the end of the program. Go to the file menu and select the Merge option. Enter the file name of the program in the programming walkthrough as if it were being opened for the first time. What happens in the Edit window?

42. Enter, run, and save the following program. (Give the program the name HAPPY.PAS when saving it.) If a printer is available, print a copy of the program.

```
PROGRAM Second;

USES Crt;

BEGIN
  ClrScr;
  Write('Happy Birthday')
END.
```

In Exercises 43 through 46, explain the error in the task or program.

43. Attempt to save a program with the file name MYPROGRAM.

44. Pressing and releasing Ctrl and then pressing F4 to remove the current Edit window.

45.
```
USES Crt;

PROGRAM SaySomething;

BEGIN
  ClrScr;
  Writeln('Something')
END.
```

46.
```
PROGRAM ET;

BEGIN
  ClrScr;
  Writeln('Phone home.')
END.
```

SOLUTIONS TO PRACTICE PROBLEMS 1.2

1. The heading begins with the keyword PROGRAM. In QuickPascal, the heading can be omitted; however, it is required in many versions of Pascal and should be included for good programming style. All the programs appearing as examples in this text have headings, although headings are sometimes omitted in exercises and solutions.

2. "[run]" means to compile and run the program. The program is compiled by pressing Alt/M/C and is run by pressing F5. If F5 is pressed before the program has been compiled, a message box might display "Source file(s) have been modified. Rebuild?." Answering "Yes" causes the program to both compile and run.

1.3   USING DOS

Each computer comes with a set of DOS (Disk Operating System) diskettes. The DOS programs carry out diskette operations.

If the computer has a hard disk, the contents of the DOS diskettes are usually placed on the hard disk when the computer is first readied for use. Then, every time the computer is turned on, a program containing the most basic DOS procedures is copied into memory.

For systems without a hard disk, the DOS Startup diskette should be placed in the A drive before the computer is turned on. Then, the core DOS program will automatically be copied into memory when the computer is turned on.

After the computer has been turned on with access to DOS, we say that the computer is in the DOS environment. After QuickPascal has been invoked, we say that the computer is in the QuickPascal environment. To return to DOS from QuickPascal, execute the Exit command from the File menu by pressing Alt/F/X. (For systems without a hard disk, the computer may prompt you to place the DOS diskette in the A drive.)

DOS Commands

Some commands that can be executed in DOS are FORMAT, DIR, COPY, DISKCOPY, ERASE, and RENAME.

FORMAT

The first time a blank diskette is used, it must be formatted for the computer. The formatting process is analogous to preparing graph paper by drawing grid lines. The procedure for formatting a diskette using a system with two drives is presented below. (Comment 6, later in this section, gives the procedure for other configurations.)

To format a diskette:

1. Place the DOS Startup diskette in drive A.

2. Type

    ```
    FORMAT B:
    ```

after the prompt A>, and press the Enter key.

3. The computer will respond with

```
Insert a new diskette for drive B:
and strike any key when ready
```

(The message instead might specify that you strike the Enter key.)

4. Place the blank diskette in drive B, press the Enter key, and wait. The light on the B drive will go on, the blank diskette will spin, and the message "Formatting . . ." will appear on the screen.

5. After about one minute, the message "Format complete" will appear on the screen, the light will go out, and the spinning will stop. Also, you will be informed of the amount of space on the diskette. (Some recent versions of DOS also request a volume label. You can decline by pressing the Enter key.)

6. The statement "Format another (Y/N)?" will then be displayed. Answer the question by pressing either the Y or N key and then the Enter key. If the answer is N, the DOS prompt will appear and await your next command. If the answer is Y, steps 3 to 6 will be repeated.

Caution: Formatting a floppy or hard disk destroys all of its existing files. The hard disk is formatted when the computer is first readied for use, so never enter FORMAT C:.

DIR

Let us assume that the DOS diskette is still in the A drive and the cursor is next to the prompt A>. Type DIR and press the Enter key. A long list of names, numbers, dates, and times will scroll by on the screen. Enter DIR again but this time press Ctrl+Break before the screen has filled. The first few lines of the screen will be similar to Figure 1.6. Each line corresponds to a program.

```
A> DIR

    Volume in drive A has no label
    Directory of  A:\

    COMMAND  COM    37557  12-19-88  12:00a
    ANSI     SYS     9105  10-06-88  12:00a
    FORMAT   COM    22875  04-07-89  12:00a
    CHKDSK   COM    17787  11-06-88  12:00a
```

Figure 1.6   Effect of Entering the DIR Command

Diskettes hold not only programs but also collections of data located in **data files**. The term **file** is used to refer to either a program or a data file. The word DIR is an abbreviation of "directory," which is a list of all the files on a diskette. (To obtain a listing of the files on the diskette in drive B, enter DIR B:.)

COMMAND COM, the first file appearing in Figure 1.6, is a key program that DOS uses to coordinate its tasks. The name "COMMAND COM" is referred to as a **file name**. The three entries following the file name give the amount of space (in bytes) that the program occupies on the diskette and the date and time it was created. Every program has a file name of one or two parts. The first part, which consists of up to eight characters, is called the **base name**. The optional second part, which consists of up to three characters, is called the **extension**. When a file name is specified, a period should be added to separate the base name and the extension. For instance, we would type the first file name in Figure 1.6 as COMMAND.COM.

COPY

The command COPY is used to make a second copy of a file. The command

```
COPY A:filename B:
```

will copy the specified file from the diskette in drive A to the diskette in drive B. The combination of the drive letter followed by a colon and the file name is called the **filespec**, an abbreviation of "file specification." (If you have only one diskette drive, Enter COPY A:*filename* B: and then follow the directions displayed on the screen. The computer will tell you when to insert the proper diskette. You will have to insert and remove each diskette one or more times.) The diskette from which the file is copied is called the "source diskette" and the other diskette is called the "target" diskette. The command COPY C:*filename* A: will copy a file from the hard disk to the diskette in drive A.

DISKCOPY

The command DISKCOPY is used to duplicate an entire diskette. It formats the new diskette and copies all the files onto it. With the DOS diskette in drive A, the command

```
DISKCOPY A: B:
```

produces a message instructing that the diskette to be copied be placed in drive A, a blank diskette be placed in drive B, and the Enter key be pressed. (On a one-diskette system, issue the same command and switch diskettes as instructed.)

ERASE

The command

```
ERASE filespec
```

removes the specified file from the diskette. For instance, the command ERASE B:ACCOUNTS.PAS deletes the file ACCOUNTS.PAS from the diskette in drive B.

RENAME

The command

```
RENAME filename1 filename2
```

changes the name of the file identified as *filename1* to the new name *filename2*. The new name must be different from the name of any file currently on the diskette.

Directories (of hard disks)

Since a hard disk is capable of storing thousands of files, locating a specific file can be time consuming. Therefore, DOS allows related files to be grouped into directories.

Think of a hard disk as a large envelope, called the **root** envelope, which contains several smaller envelopes, each with its own name. (The naming of envelopes follows the same rule as the naming of files.) Each of these smaller envelopes can contain yet other named envelopes. Each envelope is identified by listing the successively smaller envelopes that contain it, separated by backslashes. Such a sequence is called a **path**. For instance, a possible path is \SALES\NY.90\JULY.

Think of a file name as written on a slip of paper that can be placed into either the root envelope or any of the smaller envelopes. At any time, we can select one of the envelopes. The selected envelope is called the **current** envelope. All commands to place a slip of paper into an envelope or list the contents of an envelope refer to the current envelope unless a path leading to another envelope is specified. In the language of directories, the root envelope is the root directory and the other envelopes are subdirectories.

When DOS is first invoked, the root directory is the current directory. (The root directory does not have a name.) The command

```
CD pathName
```

tells DOS to change the current directory to the directory at the end of the named path.

The command

```
DIR
```

tells DOS to display all of the files in the current directory. Also, all of the immediate subdirectories in the current directory are displayed.

The command

```
MD directoryName
```

tells DOS to create a new subdirectory with the specified name in the current directory.

The command

```
RD directoryName
```

tells DOS to remove the specified subdirectory from the current directory. A subdirectory can only be removed if it has no files or subdirectories. The current directory cannot be removed.

Comments:

1. File names can consist of digits, letters of the alphabet, and the characters & ! _ @ ' ` ~ ( ) { } – # % $. Spaces are not allowed in file names.

2. Neither DOS nor QuickPascal distinguishes between upper and lowercase letters in file names. For instance, the names COSTS89.PAS, Costs89.Pas, and costs89.pas are equivalent. DOS always displays file names with uppercase characters.

3. If the name of a QuickPascal program is not given an extension when it is saved, QuickPascal automatically adds the extension PAS. This extension can be omitted when opening the program in QuickPascal, but must be used when deleting or renaming the program in DOS.

4. Although QuickPascal does not have a DIR command, the QuickPascal environment provides a list of the programs on a diskette at appropriate times. For instance, pressing Alt/F/O to open a program produces a dialog box similar to the one in Figure 1.7. The file to be retrieved from the diskette can either be typed into the narrow rectangle at the top or selected from the list of QuickPascal programs in the lower rectangle. To make a selection from the listed programs, press Tab to move to the lower rectangle, use the cursor-moving keys to highlight the desired program, and then press the Enter key.

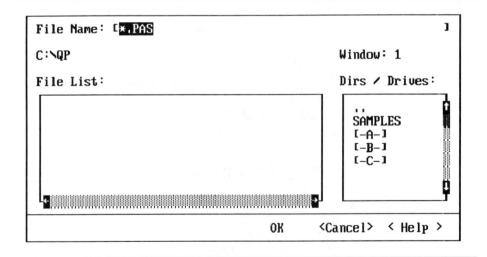

Figure 1.7 Dialog Box for Opening a File

5. At any time, one of the drives, called the **current drive** or **default drive**, is given preferential treatment. Commands that omit a drive specification, such as DIR or ERASE COSTS89.PAS, apply to files on the current drive. When DOS is first invoked from a diskette, the prompt A> appears and the A drive is the current drive. To change the current drive to B, enter B:. The prompt will change to B>. In a hard disk system, the current drive is usually C.

6. To format a diskette using a hard disk system, select the directory on the hard disk containing the DOS file FORMAT. (The FORMAT file will most likely be in a directory named DOS.) Enter FORMAT A: and then follow the directions displayed on the screen.

7. To duplicate a diskette using a hard disk system, select the directory on the hard disk containing the DOS file DISKCOPY. (The DISKCOPY file will most likely be in a directory named DOS.) Enter DISKCOPY A: B: and then follow the directions displayed on the screen. The computer will tell you when to insert the proper diskette. You may have to insert and remove each diskette several times. (The disk being copied is called the "source diskette" and the blank disk is called the "target" diskette.)

8. The command CD \ makes the root directory the current directory.

9. The command DIR *path* lists the files and immediate subdirectories of the directory specified by the path.

10. The commands RD *subDirectoryName* and MD *subDirectoryName* can be given in the forms RD *path* and MD *path*, respectively.

11. Each directory except the root directory contains two entries ". <Dir>" and ".. <Dir>." These refer to the current and **parent** directories, respectively, and are automatically created by DOS. For instance, if the current directory is \QP\PROGRAMS, then the command CD .. changes to the parent directory, \QP.

12. The command

```
COPY *.PAS A:
```

copies all the QuickPascal source files from the current drive or subdirectory to the diskette in drive A. The command ERASE *.PAS removes the QuickPascal source files. Replacing PAS with EXE or QDB in these commands causes the same tasks to be performed on the files having extensions EXE or QDB, respectively.

PRACTICE PROBLEMS 1.3

1. What is the purpose of the DOS diskettes?

2. Suppose that you saved a QuickPascal program with the name MYPROG and want to erase the program from within DOS. You execute the command ERASE MYPROG from DOS program and receive the error message "File not found." What is wrong?

EXERCISES 1.3

In Exercises 1 through 7, give the DOS command that accomplishes the stated task.

1. Reproduce a file on another diskette.

2. Delete a file from a diskette.

3. Change the name of a file.

4. Prepare a new diskette for use.

5. List all the files on a diskette.

6. Change the current disk drive to drive B.

7. Copy an entire diskette.

8. What might you do if you are storing your QuickPascal programs on a Working Utility Diskette and the diskette becomes full?

9. How much space does the program "FORMAT COM" (shown in Figure 1.6) occupy on the DOS diskette?

10. Give a command that erases all the files with extension QDB from a diskette in drive B.

SOLUTIONS TO PRACTICE PROBLEMS 1.3

1. The DOS diskettes contain commands to carry out disk operations. DOS is also needed to boot the computer.

2. Since an extension was not specified when the program was saved, QuickPascal added the extension PAS. The proper command to erase the program is ERASE MYPROG.PAS.

1.4 BIOGRAPHICAL HISTORY OF COMPUTING

The following people made important contributions to the evolution of the computer and the principles of programming.

1800s

George Boole: A self-taught British mathematician; devised an algebra of logic that later became a key tool in computer design. The logical operators presented in Section 5.1 are also known as Boolean operators.

Charles Babbage: A British mathematician and engineer; regarded as the father of the computer. Although the mechanical "analytical engine" that he conceived was never built, it influenced the design of modern computers. It had units for input, output, memory, arithmetic, logic, and control. Algorithms were intended to be communicated to the computer via punched cards and numbers were to be stored on toothed wheels.

Augusta Ada Byron: A mathematician and colleague of Charles Babbage; regarded as the first computer programmer. She encouraged Babbage to modify the design based on programming considerations. Together they developed the concepts of decision structures, loops, and a library of procedures. Decision structures, loops, and procedures are presented in Chapters 5, 6, and 4 of this text respectively.

Herman Hollerith: The founder of a company that was later to become IBM; at the age of 20 he devised a computer that made it possible to process the data for the U.S. Census of 1890 in one-third of the time required for the 1880 census. His electromagnetic "tabulating machine" passed metal pins through holes in punched cards and into mercury-filled cups to complete an electronic circuit. Each location of a hole corresponded to a characteristic of the population.

1930s

Alan Turing: A gifted and far-sighted British mathematician; made fundamental contributions to the theory of computer science, assisted in the construction of some of the early large computers, and proposed a test for detecting intelligence within a machine. His theoretical "Turing machine" laid the foundation for the development of general purpose programmable computers. He changed the course of the second world war by breaking the German "Enigma" code, thereby making secret German messages comprehensible to the Allies.

John V. Atanasoff: A mathematician and physicist at Iowa State University; declared by a federal court in Minnesota to be the inventor of the first electronic digital special-purpose computer. Designed with the assistance of his graduate assistant, Clifford Berry, this computer used vacuum tubes (instead of the less efficient relays) for storage and arithmetic functions.

1940s

Howard Aiken: A professor at Harvard University; built the Mark I, a large-scale digital computer functionally similar to the "analytic engine" proposed by Babbage. This computer, which took five years to build and used relays for storage and computations, was technologically obsolete before it was completed.

Grace M. Hopper: Retired in 1986 at the age of 79 as a rear admiral in the United States Navy; wrote the first major subroutine (a procedure used to calculate sin x on the Mark I computer) and one of the first assembly languages. In 1945 she found that a moth fused into an electrical relay of the Mark I was causing the computer to malfunction, thus the origin of the term "debugging" for correcting errors. As an administrator at Remington Rand in the 1950s, Dr. Hopper pioneered the development and use of COBOL, a programming language for the business community written in English-like notation.

John Mauchley and J. Presper Eckert: Electrical engineers working at the University of Pennsylvania; built the first large-scale electronic digital general-purpose computer to be put into full operation. The ENIAC used 18,000 vacuum tubes for storage and arithmetic computations, weighed 30 tons, and occupied 1500 square feet. It could perform 300 multiplications of two 10-digit numbers per second, whereas the Mark I required three seconds to perform a single multiplication. Later they designed and developed the UNIVAC I, the first commercial electronic computer.

John von Neumann: A mathematical genius and member of the Institute of Advanced Studies in Princeton, New Jersey; developed the stored program concept used in all modern computers. Prior to this development, instructions were programmed into computers by manually rewiring connections. Along with Hermann H. Goldstein, he wrote the first paper on the use of flowcharts.

Stanislaw Ulam: American research mathematician and educator; pioneered the application of random numbers and computers to the solution of problems in mathematics and physics. His techniques, known as Monte Carlo methods or computer simulation, are used in Chapter 11 to determine the likelihoods of various outcomes of games of chance and to analyze business operations.

Maurice V. Wilkes: An electrical engineer at Cambridge University in England and student of von Neumann; built the EDSAC, the first computer to use the stored program concept. Along with D.J. Wheeler, and S. Gill, he wrote the first computer programming text, *The Preparation of Programs for an Electronic Digital Computer* (Addison-Wesley, 1951), that dealt in depth with the use and construction of a versatile subroutine library.

John Bardeen, Walter Brattain, and William Shockley: Physicists at Bell Labs; developed the transistor, a miniature device that replaced the vacuum tube and revolutionized computer design. It was smaller, lighter, more reliable, and generated less heat than the vacuum tube.

1950s

John Backus: A programmer for IBM; in 1953 headed a small group of programmers who wrote the most extensively used early interpretive computer system, the IBM 701 Speedcoding System. An interpreter translates a high-level language program into machine language one statement at a time as the program is executed. In 1957, Backus and his team produced the compiled language Fortran, which soon became the primary academic and scientific language. A compiler translates an entire program into efficient machine language *before* the program is executed. QuickPascal combines the best features of compiled and interpreted languages. It has the power and speed of a compiled language and the ease of use of an interpreted language.

Donald L. Shell: In 1959, the year that he received his Ph.D. in mathematics from the University of Cincinnati, published an efficient algorithm for ordering (or sorting) lists of data. Sorting has been estimated to consume nearly one-quarter of the running time of computers. The Shell sort is presented in Chapter 8 of this text.

1960s

Corrado Bohm & Guiseppe Jacopini: Two European mathematicians; proved that any program can be written with the three structures discussed in Section 2.1: sequence, decision, and loop. This result led to the systematic methods of modern program design known as structured programming.

Edsger W. Dijkstra: Stimulated the move to structured programming with the publication of a widely read article, "Go To Statement Considered Harmful." In that article he proposes that GOTO statements be abolished from all high-level languages such as BASIC. The modern programming structures available in QuickPascal do away with the need for GOTO statements.

Harlan B. Mills: IBM Fellow and Professor of Computer Science at the University of Maryland; has long advocated structured programming. In 1969, Mills was asked to write a program creating an information database for the *New York Times*, a project that was estimated to require 30 man-years with traditional programming techniques. Using structured programming techniques, Mills single-handedly completed the project in six months. The methods of structured programming are used throughout this text.

Donald E. Knuth: Professor of Computer Science at Stanford University; is generally regarded as the pre-eminent scholar of computer science in the world. He is best known for his monumental series of books, *The Art of Computer Programming*, the definitive work on algorithms. The algorithm presented in Exercise 25 of Section 11.1 of this text is an example of the programming gems that appear in Knuth's books.

Ted Hoff, Stan Mazer, Robert Noyce, and Federico Faggin: Engineers at the Intel Corporation; developed the first microprocessor chip. Such chips, which serve as the central processing units for microcomputers, are responsible for the extraordinary reduction in the size of computers. A computer with greater power than the ENIAC can now be held in the palm of the hand.

Kristen Nygaard and Ole-Johan Dahl: Norwegian computer scientists; developed Simula, the first programming language to use the structure type *object*. Object-oriented programming allows large programs to be broken down into logical objects that manage their own behavior and hide internal complexity. Objects are discussed in Chapter 13 of this text.

1970s

Niklaus Wirth: Professor of Computer Science at the Eidgenössische Technishe Hochshule in Zurich, Switzerland; developed Pascal in 1971. His intention was "to make available a language suitable to teach programming as a systemic discipline based on certain fundamental concepts clearly and naturally reflected by the language." In addition, the language was to be "both reliable and efficient on presently available computers." Pascal is now the teaching language of choice in most college computer science departments in the United States.

Paul Allen and Bill Gates: Cofounders of Microsoft Corporation, the company that developed QuickPascal and the operating system for the IBM PC. The operating system, known as MS-DOS, is a collection of programs that manage the operation of the computer. In 1974, Gates dropped out of Harvard after one year, and Allen left a programming job with Honeywell to write software together. Their initial project was a version of BASIC for the Altair, the first microcomputer. Microsoft is one of the most highly respected software companies in the United States and a leader in the development of programming languages.

Alan Kay: Computer scientist at the Xerox Palo Alto Research Center; developed Smalltalk, the first language designed with objects as the centerpiece. Microsoft QuickPascal is the first version of Pascal for IBM compatible PCs to incorporate objects.

Stephen Wozniak and Stephen Jobs: Cofounders of Apple Computer Inc.; started the microcomputer revolution. The two had met as teenagers while working summers at Hewlett-Packard. Another summer, Jobs worked in an orchard, a job that inspired the names of their computers. Wozniak designed the Apple computer in Jobs' parents' garage and Jobs promoted it so successfully that the company was worth hundreds of millions of dollars when it went public. Both men resigned from the company in 1985.

Dan Bricklin and Dan Fylstra: Cofounders of Software Arts; wrote VisiCalc, the first electronic spreadsheet program. An electronic spreadsheet is a worksheet divided into rows and columns that analysts use to construct budgets and estimate costs. A change made in one number results in the updating of all numbers derived from it. For instance, changing a person's housing expenses will immediately produce a change in his total expenses. Bricklin got the idea for an electronic spreadsheet after watching one of his professors at the Harvard Business School struggle while updating a spreadsheet at the blackboard. VisiCalc became so popular that many people bought personal computers just so they could run the program. A simplified spreadsheet is developed as a case study in Section 8.4 of this text.

Robert Barnaby: A dedicated programmer; best known for writing WordStar, one of the most popular word processors. Word processing programs account for 30 percent of all software sold in the United States. The QuickPascal editor uses WordStar-like commands.

1980s

William L. Sydnes: Manager of the IBM Entry Systems Boca engineering group; headed the design team for the IBM Personal Computer. Shortly after its introduction in 1981, the IBM PC dominated the microcomputer field. QuickPascal runs on all IBM Personal Computers and compatibles.

Mitchell D. Kapor: Cofounder of Lotus Corporation; wrote the business software program 1-2-3, the most successful piece of software for personal computers. Lotus 1-2-3 is an integrated program consisting of a spreadsheet, a database manager, and a graphics package. Databases are studied in Chapter 9 of this text and graphics in Chapter 10.

2

Problem Solving

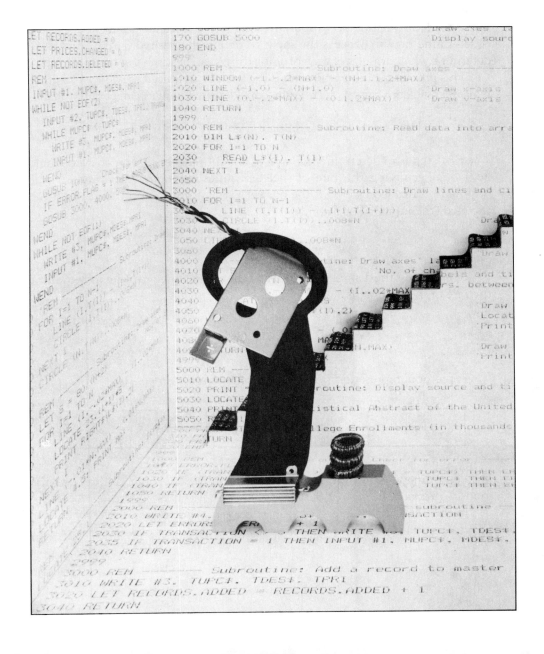

2.1 PROGRAM DEVELOPMENT CYCLE

We learned in the first chapter that hardware refers to the machinery in a computer system (such as the monitor, keyboard, and CPU) and software refers to a collection of instructions, called a program, that directs the hardware. Programs are written to solve problems or perform tasks on a computer. Programmers translate the solutions or tasks into a language the computer can understand. As we write programs, we must keep in mind that the computer will only do what we instruct it to do. Because of this, we must be very careful and thorough with our instructions.

Designing a Computer Program

The first step in designing a program is to determine what the **output** of the program should be, that is, exactly what the program should produce. The second step is to identify the data, or **input**, necessary to obtain the output. The last step is determine how to **process** the input to obtain the desired output, that is, to determine what formulas or ways of doing things can be used to obtain the output.

This problem-solving approach is the same as that used to solve word problems in an algebra class. For example, consider the following algebra problem:

How fast is a car traveling if it goes 50 miles in 2 hours?

The first step is to determine the type of answer requested. The answer should be a number giving the rate of speed in miles per hour (the output). The information needed to obtain the answer is the distance and time the car has traveled (the input). The formula

$$rate = distance / time$$

is used to process the distance traveled and the time elapsed in order to determine the rate of speed. That is,

$$rate = 50 \text{ miles} / 2 \text{ hours}$$
$$= 25 \text{ miles} / \text{hour}$$

A pictorial representation of this problem solving process is

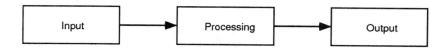

We determine what we want as output, get the needed input, and process the input to produce the desired output.

In the following chapters, we discuss how to write programs to carry out the above operations. But first, we look at the general process of writing programs.

Program Planning

A recipe provides a good example of a plan. The ingredients and the amounts are determined by what is to be baked. That is, the *output* determines the *input* and the *processing*. The recipe, or plan, reduces the number of mistakes you might make if you tried to bake with no plan at all. While it's difficult to imagine an architect building a bridge or a factory without a detailed plan, many program-mers (particularly students in their first programming course) frequently try to write programs without first making a careful plan. The more complicated the problem, the more complex the plan must be. You will spend much less time working on a program if you first devise a carefully thought out, step-by-step plan and test it before actually writing the program.

Many programmers plan their programs using a sequence of steps referred to as the **program development cycle**. The following step-by-step procedure will help you design a program that produces the desired output and enables you to use your time efficiently.

1. *Analysis:* Define the problem.

   Be sure you understand what the program should do, that is, what the output should be. Have a clear idea of what data (or input) is given and the relationship between the input and the desired output.

2. *Design:* Plan the solution to the problem.

   Find a logical sequence of precise steps that solve the problem. Such a sequence of steps is called an **algorithm.** Every detail, including obvious steps, should appear in the algorithm. In the next section, we discuss three popular methods used to develop the logical plan: flowcharts, pseudocode, and top-down charts. These tools help the programmer break a problem into a sequence of small tasks the computer can perform to solve the problem.

   Planning also involves using representative data to test the logic of the algorithm by hand to ensure that it is correct.

3. *Coding:* Translate the algorithm into a programming language.

   Coding is the technical word for writing the program. During this stage, the program is written in QuickPascal and entered into the computer. The programmer uses the algorithm devised in step 2 along with a knowledge of QuickPascal.

4. *Testing and debugging:* Locate and remove any errors in the program.

   Testing is the process of finding errors in a program and **debugging** is the process of correcting errors found during the testing process. (An error in a program is called a **bug**.) QuickPascal's compiler points out certain types of program errors. Other errors will be detected by QuickPascal when the program is executed; however, many errors due to typing mistakes, flaws in the algorithm, or incorrect usages of the QuickPascal language rules can only be uncovered and corrected by careful detective work. An example of such an error would be using addition when multiplication was the proper operation.

5. *Completing the documentation:* Organize the material that describes the program.

Documentation is intended to allow another person, or the programmer at a later date, to understand the program. Internal documentation consists of statements in the program that are not executed, but point out the purposes of various parts of the program. Documentation might also consist of a detailed description of what the program does and how to use the program (for instance, what type of input is expected). For commercial programs, documentation includes an instruction manual. Other types of documentation are the flowchart, pseudocode, and top-down chart that were used to construct the program. Although documentation is listed as the last step in the program development cycle, it should take place as the program is being coded.

2.2 PROGRAMMING TOOLS

This section discusses some specific algorithms and develops three tools used to convert algorithms into computer programs: flowcharts, pseudocode, and top-down charts.

You use algorithms every day to make decisions and perform tasks. For instance, whenever you mail a letter, you must decide how much postage to put on the envelope. One rule of thumb is to use one stamp for every five sheets of paper or fraction thereof. Suppose a friend asks you to determine the number of stamps to place on an envelope. The following algorithm will accomplish the task.

1. Request the number of sheets of paper, call it Sheets. *(input)*

2. Divide Sheets by 5. *(processing)*

3. Round the quotient up to the next highest whole number, call it Stamps. *(processing)*

4. Reply with the number Stamps. *(output)*

The algorithm above takes the number of sheets (Sheets) as input, processes the data, and produces the number of stamps needed (Stamps) as output. We can test the algorithm for a letter with 12 sheets of paper.

1. Request the number of sheets of paper, Sheets = 12.

2. Dividing 5 into 12 gives 2.4.

3. Rounding 2.4 up to 3 gives Stamps = 3.

4. Reply with the answer, 3 Stamps.

This problem-solving example can be pictured by

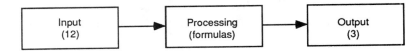

Of the program design tools available, the three most popular are the following:

Flowcharts: Graphically depicts the logical steps of the program and shows how the steps relate to each other.

Pseudocode: Uses English-like phrases with some QuickPascal terms to outline the program.

Top-down charts: Shows how the different parts of a program relate to each other.

Flowcharts

A flowchart consists of special geometric symbols connected by lines. Within each symbol is a phrase presenting the activity at that step. The shape of the symbol indicates the type of operation that is to take place. For instance, the parallelogram denotes input or output. The lines connecting the symbols, called **flowlines**, show the progression in which the steps take place. Although the symbols used in flowcharts are standardized, no standards exist for the amount of detail required within each symbol. Below is a table of the flowchart symbols adopted by the American National Standards Institute (ANSI). Figure 2.1 contains the flowchart for the Postage Stamp problem.

Symbol	Name	Meaning
⟶	*Flowline*	Used to connect symbols and indicate the flow of logic.
⬭	*Terminal*	Used to represent the beginning (Start) or the end (End) of a program.
▱	*Input/Output*	Used for input and output operations, such as reading and printing. The data to be read or printed are described inside.
▭	*Processing*	Used for arithmetic and data-manipulation operations. The instructions are listed inside the symbol.
◇	*Decision*	Used for any logic or comparison operations. Unlike the input/output and processing symbols, which have one entry and one exit flowline, the decision symbol has one entry and two exit paths. The path chosen depends on whether the answer to a question is "yes" or "no."

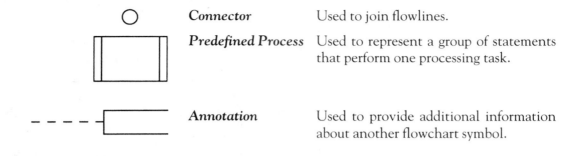

○	**Connector**	Used to join flowlines.
	Predefined Process	Used to represent a group of statements that perform one processing task.
	Annotation	Used to provide additional information about another flowchart symbol.

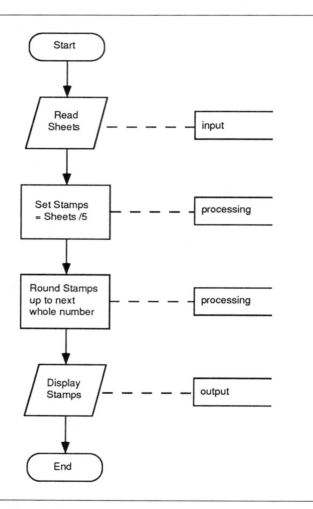

Figure 2.1 Flowchart for the Postage Stamp Problem

The main advantage of using a flowchart to plan a program is that it provides a pictorial representation of the program, which makes the program logic easier to follow. We can clearly see every step of the program and how each step connects to the next. The major disadvantage with flowcharts is that when a program is very large, the flowcharts may continue for many pages, making them hard to follow and modify.

Pseudocode

Pseudocode is an abbreviated version of actual computer code (hence *pseudo-code*). The geometric symbols used in flowcharts are replaced by English-like statements that outline the program. As a result, pseudocode looks more like a program than does a flowchart. Pseudocode allows the programmer to focus on the steps required to solve a problem rather than on how to use the computer language. The programmer can describe the algorithm in QuickPascal-like form without being restricted by the rules of QuickPascal. When the pseudocode is completed, it can be easily translated into the QuickPascal language.

The following is pseudocode for the Postage Stamp problem.

Program: Determine the proper number of stamps for a letter
Read Sheets   (*input*)
Compute the number of stamps   (*processing*)
Round the number of stamps to the next whole number   (*processing*)
Display the number of stamps   (*output*)

Pseudocode has several advantages. It is compact and probably will not extend for many pages as flowcharts commonly do. Also, the plan looks like the code to be written and so is preferred by many programmers.

Top-Down Chart

The last programming tool we'll discuss is the top-down chart, which shows the overall program structure. Top-down charts are also called hierarchy charts, HIPO (Hierarchy plus Input-Process-Output) charts, structure charts, or VTOC (Visual Table of Contents) charts. These names refer to planning diagrams that are similar to a company's organization chart.

Top-down charts depict the organization of a program but omit the specific processing logic. They describe what each part, or **module**, of the program does and they show how the modules relate to each other. The details on how the modules work, however, are omitted. The chart is read from top to bottom and from left to right. Each module may be subdivided into a succession of sub-modules that branch out under it. Typically, after the activities in the succession of submodules are carried out, the module to the right of the original module is considered. A quick glance at the top-down chart reveals each task performed in the program and where it is performed. Figure 2.2 contains a top-down chart for the Postage Stamp problem.

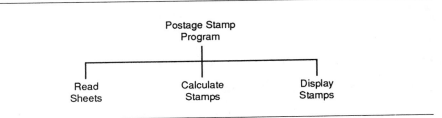

Figure 2.2 Top-Down Chart for the Postage Stamp Problem

The main benefit of top-down charts is in the initial planning of a program. We break down the major parts of a program so we can see what must be done in general. From this point, we can then refine each module into more detailed plans using flowcharts or pseudocode. This process is called the **divide and conquer** method.

The Postage Stamp problem was solved by a series of instructions to read data, perform calculations, and display results. Each step was in a sequence; that is, we moved from one line to the next without skipping over any lines. This kind of structure is called a **sequence structure**. Many problems, however, require a decision to determine whether a series of instructions should be executed. If the answer to a question is "Yes," then one group of instructions is executed. If the answer is "No," then another group is executed. This structure is called a **decision structure**. Figure 2.3 contains the flowchart and pseudocode for a decision structure.

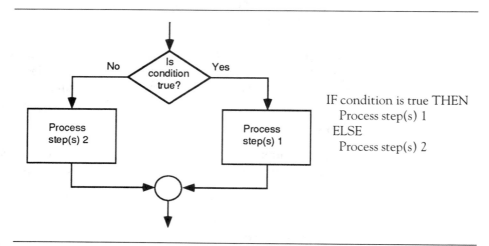

Figure 2.3   Flowchart and Pseudocode for a Decision Structure

The sequence and decision structures are both used to solve the following problem.

Direction of Numbered New York Streets Algorithm

Problem: Given a street number of a one-way street in New York City, decide the direction of the street, either eastbound or westbound.

Discussion: There is a simple rule to tell the direction of a numbered one-way street in New York City: Even-numbered streets run eastbound.

Input: Street number

Processing: Decide if street number is divisible by 2.

Output: "Eastbound" or "Westbound"

Figures 2.4 through 2.6 contain the flowchart, pseudocode, and top-down chart for the New York City Numbered Streets problem.

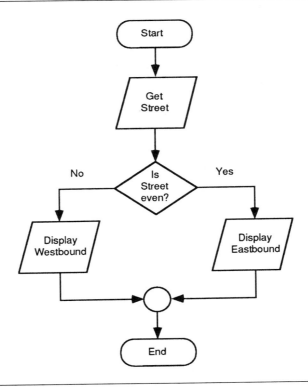

Figure 2.4 Flowchart for the New York City Numbered Streets Problem

Program: Determine the direction of a numbered NYC street
Get Street
IF Street is even THEN
    Display Eastbound
ELSE
    Display Westbound

Figure 2.5 Pseudocode for the New York City Numbered Streets Problem

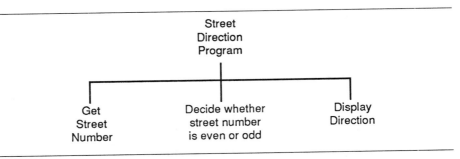

Figure 2.6 Top-down Chart for the New York City Numbered Streets Problem

The solution to the next problem requires the repetition of a series of instructions. A programming structure that executes instructions one or more times is called a **loop structure**.

We need a test (or decision) to tell when the loop should end. Without an exit condition, the loop would repeat endlessly (an infinite loop). One way to control the number of times a loop repeats (often referred to as the number of passes or iterations) is to check a condition before each pass through the loop and continue executing the loop so long as the condition is true.

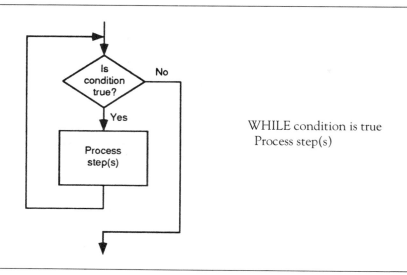

WHILE condition is true
Process step(s)

Figure 2.7   Flowchart and Pseudocode for a Loop

Class Average Algorithm

Problem: Calculate and report the grade-point average for a class.

Discussion: The average grade equals the sum of all grades divided by the number of students. We need a loop to read and then add (accumulate) the grades for each student in the class. Inside the loop we also need to total (count) the number of students in the class. See Figures 2.8 through 2.10.

Input: Student grades

Processing: Find the sum of the grades; count the number of students; calculate average grade = sum of grades / number of students.

Output: Average grade

Comments:

1. Tracing a flowchart is like playing a board game. We begin at the Start symbol and proceed from symbol to symbol until we reach the End symbol. At any time we will be at just one symbol. In a board game, the path taken depends on the result of spinning a spinner or rolling a pair of die. The path taken through a flowchart depends on the input.

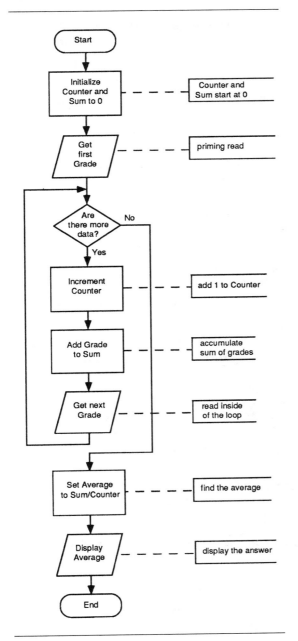

Figure 2.8 Flowchart for the
Class Average Problem

Program: Determine the average grade of a class
Initialize Counter and Sum to 0
Get the first Grade
WHILE there is more data
  Add the Grade to the Sum
  Increment the Counter
  Get the next Grade
Compute Average = Sum / Counter
Display Average

Figure 2.9 Pseudocode for the
Class Average Problem

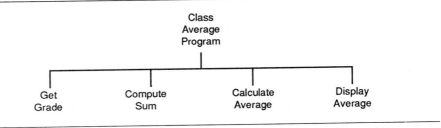

Figure 2.10 Top-Down Chart for the Class Average Problem

2. The algorithm should be tested at the flowchart stage before being coded into a program. Different data should be used as input and the output checked. This process is known as **desk-checking**. The test data should include nonstandard data as well as typical data.

3. Flowcharts, pseudocode, and top-down charts are universal problem-solving tools. They can be used to construct programs in any computer language, not just QuickPascal.

4. Flowcharts are used throughout this text to provide a visualization of the flow of certain programming tasks and QuickPascal control structures. Major examples of pseudocode and top-down charts appear in the five case studies.

5. There are four primary logical programming constructs: sequence, decision, loop, and unconditional branch. Unconditional branching, which appears in some languages as a GOTO statement, involves jumping from one place in a program to another. Structured programming uses the first three constructs, but forbids the fourth. One advantage of pseudocode over flowcharts is that pseudocode has no provision for unconditional branching and thus forces the programmer to write structured programs.

6. Flowcharts are time consuming to write and update. For this reason, professional programmers are more likely to favor pseudocode and top-down charts. Since flowcharts so clearly illustrate the logical flow of programming techniques they are a valuable tool in the education of programmers.

7. There are many styles of pseudocode. Some programmers use an outline form, whereas others use a form that looks almost like a programming language. The pseudocode appearing in the case studies of this text focuses on the primary tasks to be performed by the program and leaves many of the routine details to be completed during the coding process. Several QuickPascal keywords, such as IF, THEN, ELSE, and WHILE, are used extensively in the pseudocode appearing in this text.

8. Many people draw rectangles around each item in a top-down chart. In this text, rectangles are omitted to encourage the use of top-down charts by making them easier to draw.

3

Fundamentals of Programming in QuickPascal

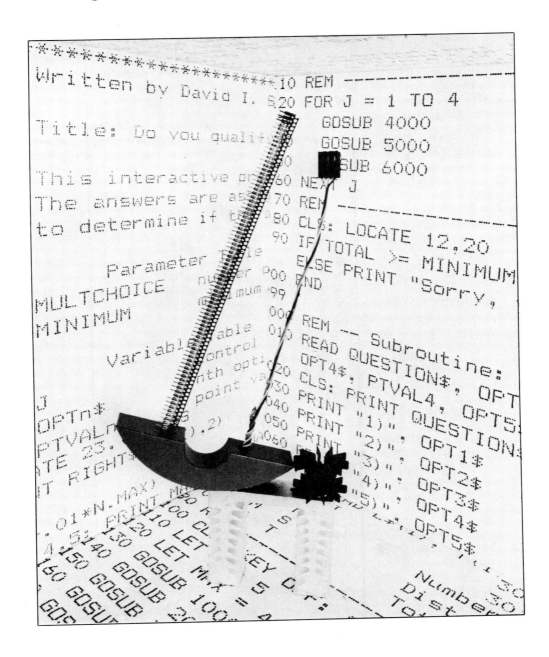

3.1 NUMBERS

Much of the data processed by computers consists of numbers. In "computerese," numbers are often called **numeric literals**. This section discusses the operations that are performed with numbers and the ways numbers are displayed.

Two types of numbers are recognized by all versions of Pascal: integers and real numbers. Mathematically, the integers are the numbers $0, \pm 1, \pm 2, \pm 3, \ldots$ and the real numbers consist of *all* the numbers on the real line. In Pascal, the words "integer" and "real" have specialized meanings. We capitalize the first letters of the Pascal types to distinguish them from the mathematical types. After explaining Integers and Reals separately, we will discuss their use together.

Integers

In QuickPascal, the Integers consist of the mathematical integers from -32768 to 32767. The four primary arithmetic operations are addition, subtraction, multiplication, and division. Addition and subtraction are denoted in Pascal by the standard symbols + and −. The notation for multiplication differs from the customary mathematical notation. In QuickPascal, the product of a and b is written $a * b$.

In Pascal, Integer division is carried out with the method you used in the third grade: long division. Namely, dividing the Integer m by the Integer n produces an Integer quotient and a remainder. For instance, dividing 5 into 32 produces the quotient 6 and the remainder 2.

$$
\begin{array}{r}
6 \\
5\overline{\smash{)}32} \\
\underline{30} \\
2
\end{array}
$$

The quotient and remainder are written m DIV n and m MOD n, respectively. For instance, 32 DIV 5 is 6 and 32 MOD 5 is 2. In general,

$$
\begin{array}{r}
m\ \mathrm{DIV}\ n \\
n\ \overline{\smash{)}\ m} \\
\cdot \\
\overline{} \\
\cdot \\
\cdot \\
\overline{m\ \mathrm{MOD}\ n}
\end{array}
$$

If n is any Integer, then the statement

```
Writeln(n)
```

displays n on the screen. When the parentheses contain a combination of numbers and arithmetic operators, Writeln carries out the calculation and displays the result.

EXAMPLE 1   The following program applies the arithmetic operations to the numbers 3 and 2 and then evaluates an expression. (**Note:** The notation [run] indicates that Alt/M/C is pressed to compile the program and then F5 is pressed to execute the program.)

```
PROGRAM DemoIntegers;

USES Crt;

BEGIN
  ClrScr;
  Writeln(3 + 2);
  Writeln(3 - 2);
  Writeln(3 * 2);
  Writeln(3 DIV 2);
  Writeln(3 MOD 2);
  Writeln(2 * (3 + 2))
END.

[run]
5
1
6
1
1
10
```

Variables

In applied mathematics problems, quantities are referred to by names. Consider the following elementary algebra problem: How many eggs can 95 egg cartons hold? Also, how many cartons can be completely filled with 100 eggs? Here's a computer program to solve this problem:

```
PROGRAM CalculateEggsAndCartons;

USES Crt;

VAR cartons, eggs : Integer;

BEGIN
  ClrScr;
  cartons := 95;
  eggs := 12 * cartons;
  Writeln(eggs);
  eggs := 100;
  cartons := eggs DIV 12;
  Writeln(cartons)
END.

[run]
1140
8
```

The first line is the heading of the program. The third line declares that the words *cartons* and *eggs* represent Integer quantities. The statement part of the program follows the word BEGIN. The second statement assigns the value 95 to *cartons* and the third statement multiplies the value for *cartons* by 12 and assigns this product to *eggs*. The fourth statement displays the answer to the first question. The following three statements similarly calculate and display the answer to the second question.

The names *cartons* and *eggs*, which hold Integers, are called **Integer variables**. Consider the variable *cartons*. In the second statement its value was set to 95. In the sixth statement its value was changed as the result of a computation.

In general, a variable is a name that refers to data. The value assigned to the variable may change during the execution of the program. In QuickPascal, variable names can be up to 23 characters long, must begin with a letter or an underline character, and may consist of letters, digits, or the underline character. (The shortest variable names consist of a single letter.) QuickPascal does not distinguish between upper and lowercase letters used in variable names. Some examples of variable names are *total*, *numberOfCars*, *taxRate_1990*, and *n*. As a convention, we will keep variable names in lowercase letters except for the first letters of additional words (as in *numberOfCars*). Pascal reserves certain words, such as PROGRAM and VAR, for its own use. Such words are called **keywords** and cannot be used as variable names. (See Comment 20.)

The portion of the program beginning with the word VAR is called the **variable declaration part** of the program. Each variable appearing in the program must be listed in the variable declaration part, with its type specified. Both of the variables in the program above hold Integer values and, therefore, have the type Integer.

The program above contains two kinds of statements: assignment statements and output statements. The four containing ":=" are assignment statements and the two beginning with "Writeln" are output statements.

If *intVar* is an Integer variable and *num* is a numeric literal, then the statement

```
intVar := num
```

assigns the number *num* to the variable *intVar*. The computer sets aside a location in memory with the name *intVar* and places the number *num* in it. The statement

```
Writeln(intVar)
```

looks into this memory location for the value of the variable, displays the value on the screen, and moves the cursor to the beginning of the next line.

A combination of literals, variables, and arithmetic operations that can be evaluated to yield a number is called a **numeric expression**. Expressions are evaluated by replacing each variable by its value. Some examples of expressions are 2 * cartons + 7, n + 1, and (a + b) MOD 3. Formally, a numeric expression is anything that can be evaluated to yield a number. For instance, an individual variable or literal is an expression. If *expr* is an expression, the statement

```
Writeln(expr)
```

displays the value of *expr*.

If *intVar* is a variable, then the statement

```
intVar := expression
```

first evaluates the expression on the right and *then* assigns its value to the variable. For instance, in the program CalculateEggsAndCartons, the expression 12 * *cartons* is evaluated to 1140 and then this value is assigned to the variable *eggs*.

Since the expression in an assignment statement is evaluated before an assignment is made, a statement such as

```
t := t + 1
```

is meaningful. It first evaluates the expression on the right (that is, it adds 1 to the original value of the variable *t*), and then assigns this sum to the variable *t*. The effect is to increase the value of the variable *t* by 1. In terms of memory locations, the statement reads the value of *t* from *t*'s memory location, uses it to compute *t* + 1, and then places the sum back into *t*'s memory location.

Writeln and Write Statements

When a sequence of Writeln statements is used to display numbers, the numbers will appear left-justified as in Figure 3.1 (a). Pascal also can produce the right-justified form shown in Figure 3.1(b), which is usually preferred.

6	6
23	23
1234	1234
(a)	(b)

Figure 3.1   Left- and Right-Justified Columns of Numbers

The statement

```
Writeln(expr:n)
```

right-justifies the value of *expr* in a field of *n* spaces. That is, *n* spaces are set aside to hold the value of *expr*, and the number is displayed in these spaces with the units digit occupying the rightmost space. (If *n* spaces are not sufficient to hold the value of *expr*, then the statement has the same effect as Writeln(*expr*).)

EXAMPLE 2   The following program segment produces the right-justified column of Figure 3.1(b):

```
BEGIN
  Writeln(6:4);
  Writeln(23:4);
  Writeln(1234:4)
END.
```

The Writeln statements considered so far only display one number per line. After displaying a number, the cursor moves to the leftmost position and down a line for the next display. Borrowing some typewriter terminology, we say the computer performs a carriage return and a line feed after each number is displayed. The carriage return and line feed, however, can be suppressed by using the statement Write instead of Writeln. The statement

```
Write(exp)
```

displays the value of *exp* and leaves the cursor at the space just to the right of the displayed value. The statement

```
Write(exp:n)
```

right-justifies the value of *exp* in a field of *n* spaces and leaves the cursor at the space just to the right of the displayed value. Although *n* is usually a numeric literal, it can be any Integer expression.

EXAMPLE 3 The following program illustrates the effect of colons in Write and Writeln statements.

```
PROGRAM ColonDemo;

USES Crt;

VAR num : Integer;

BEGIN
  ClrScr;
  Write(123:4);
  Write(56:6);
  num := 5;
  Writeln(22:num);
  Write((num * num):7)
END.
[run]
 123    56   22
     25
```

Commas can be used with Write and Writeln statements to condense several statements into one. The statement

```
Write(a, b, c)
```

has the same effect as the sequence of statements

```
Write(a);
Write(b);
Write(c)
```

and the statement

```
Writeln(a, b, c)
```

has the same effect as the sequence of statements

```
Write(a);
Write(b);
Writeln(c)
```

That is, both display the values of a, b, and c one after the other. With Write(a, b, c), the cursor is left at the space immediately following the displayed value of c. With Writeln(a, b, c), a carriage return and line feed are performed after c is displayed. Actually, the number of items separated by commas can be as many as the length of the line will allow. Also, the items can consist of any expressions, with or without colons.

Real Numbers

Let us first review powers of 10 and scientific notation. Our method of decimal notation is based on a systematic use of exponents.

$$10^1 = 10 \qquad 10^{-1} = 1/10 = .1$$
$$10^2 = 100 \qquad 10^{-2} = .01$$
$$10^3 = 1000 \qquad 10^{-3} = .001$$
$$\vdots \qquad \vdots$$
$$10^n = 1000\ldots0 \qquad 10^{-n} = .000\ldots01$$

$$\underbrace{}_{n \text{ zeros}} \qquad \underbrace{}_{n \text{ digits}}$$

Scientific notation provides a convenient way of writing numbers by using powers of 10 to stand for zeros. Numbers are written in the form $b \cdot 10^r$ where b is a number from 1 up to (but not including) 10, and r is an integer. For example, it is much more convenient to write the diameter of the sun (1,400,000,000 meters) in scientific notation: $1.4 \cdot 10^9$ meters. Similarly, rather than writing .0000003 meters for the diameter of a bacterium, it is simpler to write $3 \cdot 10^{-7}$ meters.

In QuickPascal, $b \cdot 10^r$ usually is written as bEr. (The letter E is an abbreviation for *exponent*.) The following forms of the numbers mentioned above are equivalent:

```
1.4 * 10⁹     1.4E+0009    1.4E+9    1.4E9    1400000000.0
3 * 10⁻⁷      3E-00007     3E-7      3E-07    0.0000003
```

QuickPascal displays r as a four-digit number, preceded by a plus sign if r is positive and a minus sign if r is negative.

QuickPascal can display numbers in either standard or scientific notation. Figure 3.2 shows some equivalences between the two.

Standard	Scientific
123.45	1.23450000000000E+0002
0.0123	1.23000000000000E−0002
−3.0	−3.00000000000000E+0000

Figure 3.2   Standard Vs. Scientific Notation

The Real numbers in QuickPascal essentially consist of the numbers from $-1.7 \cdot 10^{38}$ to $1.7 \cdot 10^{38}$ with, at most, 12 significant digits. Any acceptable number can be entered into the computer in either standard or scientific notation. Pascal normally displays Real numbers in scientific notation in a field of 23 spaces as in the right column of Figure 3.2. Positive numbers have a leading space on the left.

Colons are used to tell QuickPascal to display numbers in standard notation and to specify the number of decimal places. If a is a Real number and m and n are Integers, then the statement

```
Writeln(a:m:n)
```

displays the value of a in standard notation, right-justified in a field of m spaces and containing n decimal places. (If $:n$ is omitted, then the number is displayed in scientific notation in a field of m spaces.) A literal in standard notation is a Real number if it has a decimal point and at least one digit on each side of the decimal point. For instance, 12.3, 2.0, and 0.2 are valid Real numbers. Figure 3.3 shows the displays resulting from various Writeln statements. (The digits at the top of the right-hand column serve to number the positions of the field.)

Statement	12345678901234567890123
`Writeln(2.456789)`	2.45678900000000E+0000
`Writeln(-24567890.12)`	-2.45678901200000E+0007
`Writeln(12345.0:15:3)`	12345.000
`Writeln(-23.4567:15:3)`	-23.457
`Writeln(2.4E+5:15:3)`	240000.000
`Writeln(-123.55555:10:2)`	-123.56
`Writeln(-24.0:10)`	-2.4E+0001
`Writeln(24.0:10)`	2.4E+0001
`Writeln(24.0:15)`	2.400000E+0001

Figure 3.3   Displaying Real Numbers

A variable is declared as a Real variable by listing it in the variable declaration part of the program followed by a colon and the word Real. If *realVar* is a Real variable, and *expr* is any expression that evaluates to a number, then the assignment statement

```
realVar := expr
```

assigns the value of the expression to the variable.

Constants

A variable is an example of a **data structure**; it is a device that holds data. At any time, the latest value assigned to a variable can be read or altered. Pascal has another type of data structure called a **constant**. Constants are similar to variables. They have the same type of names as variables, are assigned Integer or Real values, and can be used in expressions; however, there are three important differences. First, values are assigned at the same time the constants are declared. Second, the assignment is made with an equal sign, in the constant declaration part of the program. Finally, values assigned to constants cannot be altered. The program in Example 4 uses both variables and constants.

EXAMPLE 4   The following program calculates successive balances in a savings account where $1000 is deposited at 6 percent interest for two years beginning in 1990.

```
PROGRAM AccountBalance;

USES Crt;

CONST InterestRate = 0.06;
      Year        = 1990;
      Principal   = 1000.00;

VAR balance : Real;

BEGIN
  ClrScr;
  balance := Principal;
  Writeln(Year, balance:10:2);
  balance := (1 + InterestRate) * balance;
  Writeln(Year + 1, balance:10:2);
  balance := (1 + InterestRate) * balance;
  Writeln(Year + 2, balance:10:2)
END.

[run]
1990    1000.00
1991    1060.00
1992    1123.60
```

Imagine that the statement part of the program in Example 4 was elaborate and performed many calculations involving a year, an interest rate, and a principal amount of money. We can easily change the values of these three items to consider a different interest rate, year, or principal without having to modify the statement part of the program. This benefit of using constants will be appreciated even more when we discuss the modular design of programs.

Errors

There are three types of programming errors:

1. *Compiler:* detected by the compiler

2. *Run-time:* undetected by the compiler, but pointed out by QuickPascal during the execution of the program

3. *Logic:* undetected by the compiler or at run-time, but might produce incorrect output

Appendix C lists various compiler errors. The most common compiler error involves **syntax**, that is, computer grammar, such as misspelling a word or omitting a semicolon from the end of a variable declaration. Some kinds of syntax errors are shown below. When the compiler discovers an error, compilation terminates, an error message appears, and the cursor moves to a point in the program just beyond the location of the error.

Syntax Error	Reason for Error
PROGRM	Misspelling of a keyword
Writeln(2 +)	Operator with missing operand
VAR 9W : Integer;	9W is not a valid variable name

Appendix B describes the most common run-time errors. Run-time errors usually terminate execution of the program. For example, suppose that num is a Real variable. Then the pair of statements

```
num := 1.0E+38;
num := num * num
```

causes QuickPascal to terminate execution of the program and display the message "Program terminated on run-time error (205)." Appendix B tells us a "Real overflow" has occurred, that is, num * num is outside the valid range for a Real variable.

Errors in logic are the most difficult to detect. One example is adding when you meant to multiply. Of course, QuickPascal could not possibly detect such an error. The QuickPascal debugger, discussed in Appendix D, is helpful in uncovering logic errors.

Comments:

1. The names of constants and variables can be written with any mixture of uppercase and lowercase letters. In this text we use lowercase letters except for the first letters of constants. For names such as InterestRate, however, we capitalize the first letter of the second word to improve readability. Whatever your convention, try to be consistent with capitalization.

2. Variables are assigned values with :=, a colon and an equals sign, whereas constants are declared and given their values solely with an equals sign. (Some people think of the := symbol as an arrow pointing to the left. This stresses the fact that the value on the right is assigned to the variable on the left.)

3. The three variables *a*, *b*, and *c* can be declared as Integers with the declaration

```
VAR a : Integer;
    b : Integer;
    c : Integer;
```

The single line

```
VAR a, b, c : Integer;
```

is a compact alternative. Commas also can be used with Real declarations.

4. When a variable is first assigned a value, we say the variable is **initialized**. Variables that have not been assigned values have unpredictable values. All variables should be initialized before being used, even if the initial value assigned is zero.

5. Numbers must not contain commas, dollar signs, or percent signs. Also, mixed numbers, such as 8 1/2, are not allowed.

6. Parentheses should be used when necessary to clarify the meaning of an expression. When there are no parentheses, the arithmetic operations are performed in the following order: multiplications and divisions (including DIV and MOD), additions and subtractions. In the event of ties, the leftmost operation is carried out first. (See Table 3.1.)

( )	Inner to outer
* / DIV MOD	Left to right in expression
+ -	Left to right in expression

Table 3.1 Level of Precedence for Arithmetic Operations

7. The omission of the asterisk to denote multiplication is a common error. For instance, the expression *a(b + c)* is not valid. It should read *a * (b + c)*.

8. Real numbers can be combined with Integers; the result is always a Real number. For instance, the statement Writeln(3.0 + 2) produces the output 5.00000000000000E+0000.

9. Any Real or Integer value can be assigned to a Real variable, but only Integer values can be assigned to Integer variables. For instance, if *n* is an Integer variable and *r* is a Real variable, then

```
n := 5.0  and   r := 5;
                n := r
```

are not valid, but

```
n := 5;
r := n
```

is valid.

✗ **10.** Two Integers can be divided with the operator /, but Pascal treats the result as a Real number, even if the first is a multiple of the other. Therefore, the result cannot be assigned to an Integer variable.

✗ **11.** Pascal has two built-in constants named Pi and MaxInt. Pi is a Real constant and has as its value the area of a circle of radius one, 3.14159265.... MaxInt is an Integer constant whose value is the largest Integer, 32767.

12. QuickPascal has additional numerical variables other than Integer and Real. To see their names and ranges, look at Supporting Topic [1] at the end of Appendix F. These additional variables are not part of standard Pascal.

13. Scientific and regular notations are also known as **floating point** and **fixed point** notations, respectively.

14. When scientific notation is used, a Real literal can be written without a decimal point and the digit following the decimal point. Also, the plus sign in the exponent is optional. For instance, the following representations are equivalent: 1E+20, 1E20, 1.E20, 1.0E20, 0.1E21.

✗ **15.** The pair of statements

```
a := 1.0E38;
Writeln(a)
```

produce the output 9.99999999999918E+0037, whereas the statement Writeln(1.0E38) produces the expected output 1.0000000000000E+0038. The first output is a consequence of the way Real values are stored. (Real variables can store only 12 significant digits.) Had colons been used to specify a shorter field, both outcomes would have been as expected.

16. When Writeln(r:m:n) is used to display the number r, QuickPascal displays the number of decimal places specified by n even if the field specified by m is too small. In this situation, QuickPascal ignores m and extends the field.

17. Table 3.2 shows that a number represented in scientific notation requires a field of at least 10 spaces. If Writeln(r:m) is used to display r, and m is too small to accommodate all of r's digits, then r will be rounded to fit into a field of m or 10 spaces (whichever is larger).

	Spaces
Leading space or minus sign	1
Digit preceding decimal point	1
Decimal point	1
Digit following decimal point	1
E±xxxx	6
Total	10

Table 3.2 Minimum Number of Spaces for Output of Writeln(r:m), r Real

18. Pascal does not have an operator for exponentiation, that is, raising a number to a power. Section 3.4 gives a method for exponentiation.

19. You might wonder why Pascal allows for both Integers and Reals, since any Integer can be written as a Real. The reasons concern memory space and computation time. Real numbers require three times as much memory space to store and more time to add and multiply.

20. Words such as PROGRAM, USES, CONST, VAR, BEGIN, and END have specific meanings in QuickPascal and are called **keywords**. They cannot be used as the name of any variable, constant, or process. Pascal does not distinguish between the cases used for keywords. In this text, we always write keywords with capital letters. A list of keywords can be found in Appendix G. Keywords appear in a special color on a color monitor.

21. Semicolons play an important role in Pascal. A semicolon must follow the program heading and each declaration. In the statement part of the program, semicolons are used to separate statements. Therefore, the last statement of a program does not require a semicolon. Also, two statements can be written on the same line, provided they are separated by a semicolon; however, this practice should be avoided because it makes programs difficult to read.

22. A program consists of three sections: heading, declarations, and statements. The heading consists of the word PROGRAM followed by the name of the program. The declarations section consists of several parts, the unit declarations part, constant declarations part, and variable declarations part. (Later we introduce three additional parts.) The heading and each declaration is followed by a semicolon. The statement part of the program is sometimes called the **main body** of the program. It begins with the word BEGIN and ends with the word END followed by a period.

23. If num is an Integer variable, then the statement

    ```
    num := 32768;
    ```

    produces a compiler "Out-of-range" error message; however, the pair of statements

    ```
    num := 32767;
    num := num + 1
    ```

    will be compiled. These statements will not even generate a run-time "Overflow" message. Instead, the variable num will assume an unintended value. Forewarned is forearmed.

PRACTICE PROBLEMS 3.1

1. Evaluate 2 + 3 * 4.

2. Complete the table by filling in the value of each variable after each line of the program is executed.

    ```
    VAR a, b, c : Integer;
    ```

Statement Part	a	b	c
BEGIN			
a := 3;	3	–	–
b := 4;	3	4	–
c := a + b;			
a := c * a;			
Write(a - b);			
b := b * b			
END.			

EXERCISES 3.1

In Exercises 1 through 24, evaluate the numeric expression.

1. 3 * 4

2. 7 DIV 2

3. 7 MOD 2

4. -2 * -5

5. 14 DIV 5

6. 12 MOD 3

7. 3 + (5 DIV 3)

8. (5 - 3) * 4

9. (6 + 9) MOD 5

10. (8 DIV 4) - 1

11. -3 * (2 + 5)

12. (2 * 3) MOD 7

13. 5 * ((37 - 3) DIV 4)

14. 2 * ((9 - 1) MOD 3)

15. 2 * 3 + 4

16. 2 - 3 * 4

17. -(2 + 3)

18. -2 + 3

19. 2 * 5 MOD 3

20. 2 + 5 MOD 3

21. 4 + (-2) * 6

22. (15 MOD 4) DIV 2

23. (13 DIV 2) MOD 3

24. 10 * 3 MOD 6 - 5 + 7 DIV 2

In Exercises 25 through 30 convert the numbers from scientific to standard notation for reals. (For instance, 1.00000000000000E+0000 would be converted to 1.0.)

25. 1.00000000000000E+0002

26. -1.00000000000000E+0003

27. 3.50000000000000E-0002

28. 1.20000000000000E-0001

29. -5.01230000000000E+0005

30. 3.00456000000000E+0000

In Exercises 31 through 51, determine the output of the following Writeln statements.

31. Writeln(3)

32. Writeln(3.0)

33. Writeln(25.3)

34. Writeln(20)

35. Writeln(-7.0)   **36.** Writeln(-0.02)

37. Writeln(2001.0)   **38.** Writeln(49.0)

39. Writeln(0.0001492)   **40.** Writeln(5 + 2)

41. Writeln(32 MOD 5)   **42.** Writeln(14 DIV 3)

43. Writeln(50 * 30)   **44.** Writeln(21 MOD 2)

45. Writeln(5 + 1.0)   **46.** Writeln(2 * 1.5)

47. Writeln(2 / 2)   **48.** Writeln(3 / 2)

49. Writeln(-5 * -1.0)   **50.** Writeln(2 + 0.0)

In Exercises 51 through 62, determine whether or not the name is a valid variable name.

51. Number9   **52.** room&board

53. 1stName   **54.** home_team

55. hourlywage   **56.** x

57. one.two   **58.** 1990Costs

59. _digit   **60.** my friend

61. DATE   **62.** $Price

In Exercises 63 through 66, determine the proper value of _m_ to produce the output shown on the right. (The number 12345678901234567890 serves as a spacing guide.)

	12345678901234567890
63. Writeln(123:_m_)	123
64. Writeln(1492:_m_)	1492
65. Writeln(-123:_m_)	-123
66. Writeln(1 + 3:_m_)	4

In Exercises 67 through 72, determine the proper values of _m_ and _n_ to produce the output shown on the right.

	12345678901234567890
67. Writeln(2.034:_m_:_n_)	2.03
68. Writeln(12.35:_m_:_n_)	12.4
69. Writeln(-123.2228:_m_:_n_)	-123.223
70. Writeln(Pi:_m_:_n_)	3.1416
71. Writeln(100 / 3:_m_:_n_)	33.333333
72. Writeln(2 * 8.0:_m_:_n_)	16.00

In Exercises 73 through 78, determine the proper value of *m* to produce the output shown on the right.

	12345678901234567890
73. Writeln(1.2:*m*)	1.2E+0000
74. Writeln(1.2:*m*)	1.200E+0000
75. Writeln(-1.2:*m*)	-1.200E+0000
76. Writeln(-3.24:*m*)	-3.240000E+0000
77. Writeln(0.00751:*m*)	7.510000E-0003
78. Writeln(-0.0123:*m*)	-1.230000E-0002

In Exercises 79 and 80, complete the table by filling in the value of each variable after each line of the program is executed. If a variable has not been initialized put a "–" in the blank.

79. VAR m, n : Integer;

Statement Part	m	n
BEGIN		
m := 2;		
n := 3 * m;		
m := n + 5;		
Writeln(m + 4);		
n := n + 1		
END.		

80. VAR bal, inter, withDr : Real;

Statement Part	bal	inter	withDr
BEGIN			
bal := 100;			
inter := 0.05;			
withDr := 25;			
bal := bal + inter * bal;			
bal := bal - withDr			
END.			

In Exercises 81 through 86, determine the output of the program. The PROGRAM headings have been omitted to save space.

81.
```
VAR amount : Integer;

BEGIN
  amount := 10;
  Writeln(amount - 4)
END.
```

82.
```
VAR a, b : Integer;

BEGIN
  a := 4;
  b := 5 * a;
  Writeln(a + b);
  Writeln(a - b)
END.
```

83.
```
BEGIN
  Write(1:2, 2:2);
  Write(3:2, 4:2);
  Writeln(5 + 6:2)
END.
```

84.
```
VAR number : Integer;

BEGIN
  number := 5;
  number := 2 * number;
  Writeln(number)
END.
```

85.
```
VAR unitPrice, tax : Real;
    number        : Integer;

BEGIN
  tax := 0.05;
  unitPrice := 3.55;
  number := 4;
  Writeln((number * unitPrice) * (1 + tax):0:2)
END.
```

86.
```
VAR divisor, dividend, quotient, remainder : Integer;

BEGIN
  dividend := 23;
  divisor := 7;
  quotient := 23 DIV 7;
  remainder := 23 MOD 7;
  Writeln(quotient:4, remainder:4)
END.
```

In Exercises 87 through 94, identify the errors.

87.
```
VAR j, k, m : Integer;

BEGIN
  j := 2;
  k := 3;
  j + k := m;
  Writeln(m)
END.
```

88.
```
VAR r, s, t, u : Real;

BEGIN
  r := 2.0;
  s := 3.0;
  t := r + s + r;
  Writeln(r(s + t))
END.
```

89.
```
VAR balance, deposit : Real;

BEGIN
  balance := $1,234.00;
  deposit := $100.00;
  Writeln(balance + deposit:0:2)
END.
```

90.
```
VAR balance, interest : Real;

BEGIN
  interest := 5.0%;
  balance := 800.00;
  Writeln(interest * balance)
END.
```

91.
```
CONST Num = 2.0;

VAR anotherNum : Integer;

BEGIN
  anotherNum := Num;
  Writeln(anotherNum, Num)
END.
```

92.
```
VAR r, s, t : Real;

BEGIN
  r := 33;
  s := 10;
  t := r DIV s;
  Writeln(t)
END.
```

93.
```
VAR one = Integer;

BEGIN
  two := one
END.
```

94.
```
VAR one, two : Integer;

BEGIN
  one := 6;
  two := one / 2;
  Writeln(one / 2)
END.
```

95. Rewrite the following program to use a constant to hold the value of the earth's radius.
```
PROGRAM EarthConstants;

VAR diameter, circumference, volume : Real;

BEGIN
  diameter := 2 * 6.378E06;
  circumference := diameter * Pi;
  volume := (4 / 3) * Pi * 6.378E06 * 6.378E06 * 6.378E06;
  Writeln(diameter:10:5, circumference:10:5, volume:10:5)
END.
```

96. Which of the following declarations are equivalent?

(a) `VAR hits, homeRuns, atBats, errors : Integer;`

(b)
```
VAR hits,
    homeRuns,
    atBats,
    errors : Integer;
```

(c)
```
VAR    hits : Integer;
    homeRuns : Integer;
      atBats : Integer;
      errors : Integer;
```

In Exercises 97 through 102, write a program to solve the problem. The program should use constants and variables for the quantities as appropriate.

97. Suppose each acre of farmland produces 18 tons of corn. How many tons of corn can be produced on a 30-acre farm?

98. Suppose a ball is thrown straight up in the air with an initial velocity of 50 feet per second and an initial height of 5 feet. How high will the ball be after 3 seconds? (**Note:** The height after t seconds is given by the expression $-16t^2 + v_0t + h_0$, where v_0 is the initial velocity and h_0 is the initial height.)

99. If a car left Washington, D.C. at two o'clock and arrived in New York at seven o'clock, what was its average speed? (**Note:** New York is 233 miles from Washington.)

100. A motorist wants to determine her gas mileage. At 23,340 miles (on the odometer), the tank is filled with 12.6 gallons and at 23,695 miles, the tank is filled with 14.1 gallons. How many miles per gallon did the car average between the two fillings?

101. A U.S. geological survey showed that Americans use an average of 1600 gallons of water per person per day, including industrial use. How many gallons of water are used each year in the United States? (**Note:** The current population of the U.S. is about 240 million people.)

102. According to FHA specifications, each room in a house should have a window area equal to at least 10 percent of the floor area of the room. What is the minimum window area for a 14-foot by 16-foot room?

SOLUTIONS TO PRACTICE PROBLEMS 3.1

1. 14. Multiplications are performed before additions. If the intent is for the addition to be performed first, the expression should be written (2 + 3) * 4.

2.

Statement Part	a	b	c
BEGIN			
a := 3;	3	–	–
b := 4;	3	4	–
c := a + b;	3	4	7
a := c * a;	21	4	7
Write(a - b);	21	4	7
b := b * b	21	16	7
END.			

Each time an assignment statement is executed, only one variable has its value changed (the variable to the left of ":=").

3.2 CHARACTERS AND STRINGS

The two types of data presented in Section 3.1 are Integers and Reals. This section considers two additional data types: characters and strings. A **character** is a single symbol and a **string** is a sequence of symbols.

QuickPascal uses a set of 256 symbols. The 94 most common symbols are the letters (both upper and lowercase) of the alphabet, digits, punctuation marks, and characters that can be generated by the typewriter portion of the computer keyboard. The remaining symbols will be discussed later. The 256 symbols are called **character literals**. In Pascal, a character literal is written as a symbol surrounded by single quote marks ('). [The single quote mark is located on the same key as the standard double quotation mark (").]

A character variable is specified with a declaration of the form

```
VAR variable : Char;
```

and a value is assigned to a variable with a statement of the form

```
variable := 's'
```

where s is a symbol. A character constant is specified and assigned a value with a declaration of the form

```
CONST Constant = 's';
```

A **string**, or string literal, is a sequence of symbols that is treated as a single item. Sentences, phrases, words, names, phone numbers, addresses, and dates are all examples of strings. A string also can consist of a single symbol. Like characters, string literals are written surrounded by single quote marks. Declarations and assignments for string constants and variables are carried out with declarations and statements such as

```
(a) CONST Constant = 'Popcorn';
(b) VAR variable : STRING;
(c) variable := 'Fence';
```

Character and string variables have the same kinds of names as numeric variables. Like numeric variables, they correspond to locations in memory. Also, literals and the values of variables can be displayed with Write and Writeln statements. Strings are displayed without leading or trailing spaces. Character and string literals used in Write, Writeln, and assignment statements must be surrounded by single quotes, but names of string constants and variables are never surrounded by quote marks.

EXAMPLE 1 The following program shows how character and string variables and constants are declared, assigned values, and displayed. Each of the Writeln statements uses a string consisting of a single space.

```
PROGRAM CharAndStringDemo;

USES Crt;

CONST MaxGrade = 'A';
      Resource = 'will';

VAR en    : Char;
    phrase : STRING;

BEGIN
  ClrScr;
  en := 'n';
  phrase := 'there is a';
  Writeln('Where ', phrase, ' ', Resource, ',');
  Writeln(phrase, en, ' ', MaxGrade, '.')
END.

[run]
Where there is a will,
there is an A.
```

As with numbers, colons can be used with strings in Write and Writeln statements to display strings in specified fields. The string appears right-justified in the field. If the string is too long for the designated field, QuickPascal ignores the field. Figure 3.4 shows a piece of a program and the corresponding output.

```
stVar := '1234567890';    [run]
Writeln(stVar);           1234567890
Writeln('abc':5);              abc
Writeln('abcde':3);       abcde
Writeln('ab', 'cd');      abcd
Writeln('ab', 'cd':3)     ab cd
```

Figure 3.4   Fields Used to Display Strings

EXAMPLE 2   The following program has strings and numbers occurring together in a Writeln statement. The last statement uses a field of length 1 to force the number to follow a dollar sign immediately.

```
PROGRAM DemoMixingDataTypes;

USES Crt;

VAR intRate, prin : Real;
```

```
BEGIN
  ClrScr;
  intRate := 0.0655;
  prin := 100.00;
  Writeln('After one year,');
  Writeln('the balance is $', ((1 + intRate) * prin):1:2)
END.

[run]
After one year,
the balance is $106.55
```

Concatenation

Two strings can be combined to form a new string consisting of the strings joined together. The joining operation is called **concatenation** and is represented by a plus sign (+). For instance, 'good' + 'bye' is 'goodbye'. A combination of strings and plus signs that can be evaluated to form a string is called a **string expression**. Assignment, Write, and Writeln statements evaluate expressions before assigning them to variables or displaying them. Figure 3.5 shows a program segment and the corresponding output.

```
stVar := 'potato,';                          [run]
Writeln('One ' + stVar);                     One potato,
Writeln('Two', ' ' + stVar);                 Two potato,
Writeln('Three ', stVar + ' four.');         Three potato, four.
stVar2 := 'Five ' + stVar;
Writeln(stVar2)                              Five potato,
```

Figure 3.5 Examples of Concatenation

Strings of Bounded Lengths

If *s* is a string, then the value of

```
Length(s)
```

is the number of symbols in the string. For instance, Length('perhaps') is 7, Length('*ab cd*') is 5, and Length(' *ab* ') is 4. If stVar is a string variable with the value 'one', then Length(stVar) is 3.

A string can have a length of 255 at most. Whenever a string variable is declared, the compiler sets aside space for the maximum number of symbols. This is wasteful for string variables that will only hold short strings. The declaration

```
VAR stVar : STRING[n];
```

sets aside just *n* spaces for the value of stVar. Then, only string constants and literals of length at most *n* can be assigned to stVar. If stVar2 is an ordinary string variable of length at least *n*, then the statement

```
      stVar := stVar2
```

assigns the first *n* symbols of stVar2 to stVar.

EXAMPLE 3   The following program demonstrates bounded-length strings.

```
PROGRAM DemoBoundedLength;

USES Crt;

VAR city : STRING;
    town : STRING[10];

BEGIN
  ClrScr;
  city := 'San Francisco';
  town := city;
  Writeln(city);
  Writeln(town);
  Writeln('city has length ', Length(city));
  Writeln('town has length ', Length(town));
  town := 'Boston';
  Writeln('Boston has length ', Length(town))
END.

[run]
San Francisco
San Franci
city has length 13
town has length 10
Boston has length 6
```

ASCII Table

Each of the 47 keys in the center typewriter portion of a standard IBM keyboard can produce two characters, for a total of 94 characters. Adding 1 for the space character produced by the space bar makes 95 characters, but many more characters can be displayed.

Appendix A shows the complete table of characters, numbered 0 to 255, that the computer recognizes. (The number assigned to each character is called its **ASCII value**.) The keyboard characters are numbered 32 through 126. Figures 3.6 to 3.9 show some different types of characters. The box-drawing characters in Figure 3.7 are grouped to show how they fit together. The characters in these figures are referred to by their ASCII values. If *n* is a number between 0 and 255, then

```
      Chr(n)
```

is the character with ASCII value *n*. For instance, Chr(227) is the Greek letter *pi*.

Figure 3.6 Foreign Language Characters (128 to 168)

Figure 3.7 Box-drawing Characters (179 to 218)

Figure 3.8 Greek Letters and Mathematical Symbols (224 to 254)

Figure 3.9 Miscellaneous Characters

EXAMPLE 4 The following program demonstrates the use of Chr to produce strings:

```
PROGRAM ChrDemo;

USES Crt;

VAR queenOfHearts, area : STRING[10];

BEGIN
  ClrScr;
  Writeln(Chr(227));
  queenOfHearts := 'Q' + Chr(3);
  Writeln(queenOfHearts);
  area := Chr(227) + Chr(114) + Chr(253);
  Writeln('The area of a circle of radius r is ', area)
END.
```

```
[run]
π
Q♥
The area of a circle of radius r is πr²
```

Extracting Characters From Strings

If strVar is a string variable and *n* is between 1 and the length of strVar, then the value of strVar[n] is the *n*th character of the value of strVar. This feature can be used to extract or alter a character in a string.

```
VAR quote : STRING;

BEGIN
  quote := 'Truth is shorter than fiction.';
  Write(quote[2]);
  Write(quote[3]);
  Writeln(quote[21]);
  quote[23] := 'F';
  Writeln(quote)
END.

[run]
run
Truth is shorter than Fiction.
```

If the value of *n* is greater than the length of the string, then either the compiler will point out the error or the result will be unpredictable.

Comments:

1. Assigning strings to numeric variables or numbers to string variables are common errors.

Valid	Not Valid
intVar := 5	intVar := '5'
stVar := '5'	stVar := 5

   The string '5' is different than the number 5 and cannot be used in arithmetic calculations.

2. In the declaration

   ```
   CONST Letter = 'L';
   ```

   the constant *Letter* can be considered to be either of type character or string. It can be assigned to either a character or a string variable.

3. The amount of space in memory that stores one symbol is called a **byte**. A byte holds the ASCII value of a symbol. The number of bytes required to store a string is one more than the number of symbols in the string. The additional byte tells the length of the string. See Figure 3.10.

Figure 3.10   Representation of a String

4. The word *string* is a keyword in QuickPascal, but *char* is not. Therefore, we only write STRING with uppercase letters.

5. The **empty string** is the string of length zero and is written ''. It is different from ' ' and Chr(0), which are characters.

6. If stVar is a string variable and chVar is a character variable, then the assignment statement

    stVar := chVar

is valid; however, the statement

    chVar := stVar

is not valid. Even when stVar holds a string of length one, it cannot be assigned to a character variable. (Recall that a string of length one is stored in two bytes, whereas a character is stored in one byte.)

7. A variable declared as STRING[1] does not have type Char.

8. The single quote symbol can be placed into a string by preceding it with another quote symbol. For instance, the output of Write('Don''t touch that dial') is Don't touch that dial.

9. The same rules apply to naming constants, variables, and the program headings. These names are called **identifiers**.

10. The characters in the ASCII table also can be displayed on the screen by using the Alt key and the numeric keypad. If you hold down the Alt key, press 227 on the numeric keypad, and then release the Alt key, the Greek letter *pi* will appear on the screen. Most of the ASCII characters can be displayed in this manner. (The exceptions are character 127 and the characters with ASCII values less than 32.) This technique is used to place characters not found on the keyboard into strings.

11. Characters numbered 7, 9 through 13, and 28 through 31 in the ASCII table are called **control characters**. For these numbers, the statement Write(Chr(n)) produces the stated effect. For instance, the statement Write(Chr(31)) moves the cursor down one line. The character with ASCII value 12 can be used with Write(Lst, . . .) to advance the paper to the top of the next sheet.

12. Chr gives the ASCII character associated with a number. The reverse of this information can be found with Ord. If *s* is a symbol, then the value of Ord('s') is the ASCII number of the symbol *s*. For instance, Ord('A') is 65.

13. QuickPascal allows Chr(n) to be abbreviated as #n. For example, the statement Writeln(#81, #80) displays QP.

14. The statement Writeln, with no parentheses, simply skips a line on the screen.

15. The QuickPascal editor can process up to 128 characters on a single line of the screen. Also, program statements need not reside on a single line of the screen. For instance, the last two statements in Example 2 can be written as

```
Writeln('After one year, the balance is $', ((1 +
        intRate) * prin):1:2)
```

Statements should not be split in the middle of a string literal. For instance, the statement

```
Write('Today is the first day of the rest of your life.')
```

can be split as

```
Write('Today is the first day of the rest ',
      'of your life.')
```

or

```
Write('Today is the first day of the rest ' +
      'of your life.')
```

but not as

```
Write('Today is the first day of the rest
      of your life.')
```

16. With color monitors, the QuickPascal editor displays string literals in a special color. This helps distinguish literals from variables and deters the common error of omitting the quote mark following a string literal.

PRACTICE PROBLEMS 3.2

1. What is the difference in the outputs of the following two statements: Write('isn''t') and Write('isn', Chr(96), 't')?

2. Suppose the variable, stVar, has the value *'ab'*. Give four ways to use Write and stVar to obtain the display

```
ab c
```

EXERCISES 3.2

In Exercises 1 through 10, determine the output of the Writeln statements.

1. Writeln('Tom and Jerry')   **2.** Writeln('cat and mouse')

3. Writeln('That''s life.')   **4.** Writeln('"Ain''t" ain''t a word.')

5. Writeln('Moscow,', ' USSR')   **6.** Writeln('4', 'ever', '&', 'ever')

7. Writeln(10, ' plus ', '10')   **8.** Writeln(90, 'minus', 90)

9. Writeln('con' + 'cat' + 'enation')

10. Writeln('ten' + 'twenty = ', 30)

In Exercises 11 through 18, determine the output of the Writeln statements.

11. `Writeln('Q: How long is a mile?', '  A: ', Length('a mile'))`

12. `Writeln(Length('The fog comes on little cat feet'))`

13. `Writeln(Chr(73), Chr(3), Chr(78), Chr(89))`

14. `Writeln(Chr(1), ' Have a nice day ', Chr(2))`

15. `Writeln(Chr(Length('The answer to the universe is 43.') + 30))`

16. `Writeln(Length(Chr(19)))`

17. `Writeln('The ASCII value of ''B'' is ', Ord('B'))`

18. `Writeln(Chr(Ord('B')))`

In Exercises 19 through 22, determine the proper value of *m* to produce the output shown on the right. (The number 12345678901234567890 serves as a spacing guide.)

```
                                  12345678901234567890
19. Writeln('elephant':m)             elephant
20. Writeln('10 +' + ' 10':m)       10 + 10
21. Writeln(3, '''s a crowd':m)     3 's a crowd
22. Writeln('34th', 'Street':m)     34th    Street
```

In Exercises 23 through 38, determine the output of the program.

23.
```
BEGIN
  Writeln('Hello');
  Writeln('12' + '34')
END.
```

24.
```
BEGIN
  Writeln('Welcome, friend.');
  Writeln('Welcome ', 'friend.')
END.
```

25.
```
BEGIN
  Writeln('12', 12, 'Twelve')
END.
```

26.
```
BEGIN
  Writeln(Chr(104) + Chr(105))
END.
```

27.
```
VAR r, s : STRING[10];

BEGIN
  r := 'A ROSE';
  s := ' IS ' ;
  Writeln(r, s, r, s, r)
END.
```

28.
```
VAR a, b, c : Char;

BEGIN
  a := 'a';
  b := Chr(Ord('a') + 1);
  c := Chr(Ord('b') + 1);
  Writeln(a, b, c)
END.
```

29.
```
VAR houseNum : Integer;
    street   : STRING;

BEGIN
  houseNum := 10;
  street := ' Downing Street';
  Writeln(houseNum, street)
END.
```

30.
```
VAR prefix       : STRING[4];
    word1, word2 : STRING;

BEGIN
  prefix := 'fore';
  word1 := 'warned';
  word2 := 'armed';
  Write(prefix, word1, ' is ');
  Writeln(prefix, word2)
END.
```

31.
```
VAR person, quote : STRING;
    qMark         : Char;

BEGIN
  person := 'Lily Tomlin';
  quote := 'We''re all in this alone.';
  qMark := Chr(34);
  Writeln(qMark + quote + qMark + '  ' + person);
  Writeln(qMark, quote, qMark, '  ', person)
END.
```

32.
```
VAR longStr  : STRING;
    shortStr : STRING[4];

BEGIN
  longStr := 'antidisestablishmentarianism';
  shortStr := longStr;
  Writeln(shortStr)
END.
```

33.
```
CONST Alphabet = 'abcdef';

BEGIN
  Writeln(Alphabet:3);
  Writeln(Alphabet:8);
  Writeln(Alphabet, Alphabet:7)
END.
```

34.
```
VAR a, b, c, d : Char;

BEGIN
  a := 'a';
  b := 'b';
  c := 'c';
  d := 'd';
  Write(a:1, b:2);
  Writeln(c:3, d:4)
END.
```

35.
```
VAR dogType : STRING;

BEGIN
  dogType := 'Irish setter';
  Writeln(dogType[1], dogType[6], dogType[2], dogType[6], dogType[7])
END.
```

36. `VAR alphabet : STRING;`

```
   BEGIN
     Writeln('What did Old Mother Hubbard say at her cupboard?');
     alphabet := 'abcdefghijklmnopqrstuvwxyz';
     Write(alphabet[15], alphabet[9], alphabet[3], alphabet[21]);
     Writeln(alphabet[18], alphabet[13], alphabet[20])
   END.
```

37. `VAR quote1, quote2 : STRING[30];`
`       quote        : STRING[60];`

```
   BEGIN
    quote1 := 'The ballgame isn''t over, ';
    quote2 := 'until it''s over.';
    quote := quote1 + quote2;
    Writeln(quote + '   Yogi Berra')
   END.
```

38. `VAR phrase: STRING[30];`

```
   BEGIN
     phrase := 'win or lose that counts.';
     Writeln('It''s not whether you ', phrase);
     Writeln('It''s whether I ', phrase)
   END.
```

39. Determine which of the following are valid.

(a) `Writeln('Oysters are not good in a month that hath`
`            not an R in it.')`

(b) `Writeln('Oysters are not good in a month that hath ',`
`            'not an R in it.')`

(c) `Writeln('Oysters are not good in a month that hath' + ' ' +`
`            'not an R in it.')`

In Exercises 40 through 46, identify the errors.

40. `VAR evenPrime : Integer;`
`       two       : STRING[10];`

```
   BEGIN
     evenPrime := 2;
     two := evenPrime;
     Writeln(two)
   END.
```

41. `VAR letterA : STRING[1];`
`       letterB : Char;`

```
   BEGIN
     letterA := 'a';
     letterB := 'b';
     letterA := letterB;
     letterB := letterA;
     Writeln(letterA, letterB)
   END.
```

42. `CONST Friend := 'me.';`

```
VAR question, answer : STRING;

BEGIN
  question := 'Who''s your friend?';
  answer := Friend;
  Writeln(question);
  Writeln(answer)
END.
```

43. `VAR quote : STRING;`

```
BEGIN
  quote := "I came to Casablanca for the waters.";
  Writeln(quote, '  Bogart')
END.
```

44. `CONST Number = '5';`

```
VAR fivePlusFive : Integer;

BEGIN
  fivePlusFive := Number + Number;
  Writeln(fivePlusFive)
END.
```

45. `CONST Anyword = 'wonderful';`

```
BEGIN
  Writeln('The fifth letter of "wonderful" is ', Anyword[5])
END.
```

46. `CONST Phrase = 'A penny saved is worth nothing.';`

```
VAR myString : STRING;
    myChar   : Char;

BEGIN
  myString := Phrase;
  myString := myString[4];
  myChar := myString;
  Writeln(myChar)
END.
```

In Exercises 47 and 48, write the given string in the form Chr(m) + Chr(n) + ...

47. München

48. $\sqrt{4} = 2$

In Exercises 49 and 50, write a program to solve the problem. The program should use variables for each of the quantities and display the outcome with a complete explanation, as in Example 4.

49. If the radius of the earth is 6170 kilometers, what is the volume of the earth? (**Note:** The volume of a sphere of radius r is $(4/3) * \text{Pi} * r^3$.)

50. How many pounds of grass seed are needed to seed a lawn 40 feet by 75 feet if 40 ounces are recommended for 2000 square feet? (**Note:** There are 16 ounces in a pound.)

SOLUTIONS TO PRACTICE PROBLEMS 3.2

1. There is no difference.

2. ```
Write(stVar, ' ', 'c')
Write(stVar + ' ', 'c')
Write(stVar, 'c':2)
Write(stVar, ' ' + 'c')
```

---

# 3.3 INPUT AND OUTPUT

So far we have relied on the assignment statement to assign values to variables. Data also can be supplied by the user in response to a request by an input statement.

### Readln Statement

The person executing a program is called the **user**. QuickPascal has the capability of interactive programming in which the user supplies data in response to a request by the program. The statement

```
Readln(varbl)
```

causes the execution of the program to pause until the user types in a literal of the appropriate type and presses the Enter key. The entered value is then assigned to the variable *varbl*.

EXAMPLE 1 The following program computes social security taxes. The response, 200, is entered by the user after "Enter taxable earnings: " appears. The user's response is underlined. (**Note:** The tax rate was 7.65 percent in 1990.)

SOLUTION
```
PROGRAM SocSecTax;

USES Crt;

VAR earnings, tax : Real;
```
```

```
BEGIN
  ClrScr;
  Write('Enter taxable earnings: ');
  Readln(earnings);
  tax := 0.0765 * earnings;
  Writeln('Your social security tax is $', tax:1:2)
END.
```

```
[run]
Enter taxable earnings: 200
Your social security tax is $15.30
```

The prompting string in the Write statement told the user what response was requested. Without the Write statement, the program would have paused and the user wouldn't have the foggiest idea what to do.

A single Readln statement can request values for several numeric variables. If so, the variables must be separated by commas in the Readln statement and the values must be separated by spaces in the user's response.

EXAMPLE 2 Write a program to request an employee's hourly wage, number of hours worked, and name and then report his name and earnings.

SOLUTION Since the three pieces of data supplied will be two numbers and a string, the three variables in the Readln statements must be of these types.

```
PROGRAM WeeklyWages;

USES Crt;

VAR wage, hrs : Real;
    name       : STRING;

BEGIN
  ClrScr;
  Write('Enter name: ');
  Readln(name);
  Write('Enter hourly wage, hrs worked: ');
  Readln(wage, hrs);
  Writeln(name, ', your earnings are $', (hrs * wage):1:2)
END.
```

```
[run]
Enter name: Mike Jones
Enter hourly wage, hrs worked: 7.35  35
Mike Jones, your earnings are $257.25
```

Readln statements also can assign values to character variables. When the values are assigned to several character variables by the same Readln statement, any space appearing is treated like a character. For instance, if the statement

```
Readln(chVar1, chVar2, chVar3)
```

receives the response

```
2 B
```

then the value chVar2 will be a space and the values of chVar1 and chVar3 will be 2 and B, respectively.

When values for a mixture of several different types of variables are to be requested, the safest way to proceed is to use a separate Readln statement for each variable.

The Placement of Output on the Screen

So far, the location of output on the screen was controlled by the Clrscr, Write, and Writeln statements, and the use of colons. The Clrscr statement allowed output to be displayed at the top of the screen. Each item was displayed immediately following or on the next line following the previous item, depending on whether the previous item was displayed with Write or Writeln, respectively. Colons were used to right-justify or prettify displayed items.

A common type of output consists of two columns, a left-justified column of strings and a right-justified column of numbers. The following example uses the Length function to obtain such output.

EXAMPLE 3   The following program displays the cities projected to have the greatest populations in the year 2000. The populations are shown in millions. Twenty positions in each row of output are occupied by a city, its population, and intervening spaces.

```
PROGRAM Cities;

USES Crt;

VAR city : STRING;
    pop  : Real;

BEGIN
  ClrScr;
  city := 'Mexico City';
  pop := 26.3;
  Writeln(city, pop:20 - Length(city):1);
  city := 'Sao Paulo';
  pop := 24.0;
  Writeln(city, pop:20 - Length(city):1);
  city := 'Tokyo';
  pop := 17.1;
  Writeln(city, pop:20 - Length(city):1)
END.

[run]
Mexico City    26.3
Sao Paulo      24.0
Tokyo          17.1
```

The GotoXY statement can be used to display items anywhere on the screen. The screen can display 25 lines of text, with each line holding up to 80 characters. We think of the screen as subdivided into 25 rows (numbered 1 to 25 from the top of the screen) and 80 columns (numbered 1 to 80 starting at the left of the screen). In Figure 3.11 we see that the position in the *c*th column, *r*th row is obtained by moving *c* units to the right and then *r* units down. We say that the position has text coordinates *c*, *r*.

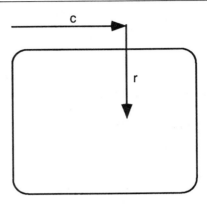

Figure 3.11   Position *c*, *r*

The statement

```
GotoXY(c, r)
```

moves the cursor to the position with coordinates *c*, *r*. The next Write or Writeln statement will then begin displaying output at this position. For instance, the pair of statements

```
GotoXY(10, 3);
Writeln(stVar)
```

displays the value of the variable stVar in the 10th column of the third row of the screen. The pair of statements

```
GotoXY((80 - Length(stVar)) DIV 2, 3);
Writeln(stVar)
```

centers the value of stVar in the third row of the screen.

Output to the Printer

There are three ways to obtain a printed copy of the output of a program. (Make sure the printer has paper, is turned on, and is set to ON LINE before trying these methods.)

   1. After a program has executed, pressing the key combination Shift+Print Screen causes the contents of the screen to be printed on the printer.

2. When the word *Lst* is inserted as the first item inside the parentheses of a Write or Writeln statement, the output of these statements is sent to the printer instead of being displayed on the screen. For instance, the statement Writeln(Lst, 'Hello') causes the printer to print the word *Hello*; however, the USES portion of the program must contain the term "Printer" and the Printer unit must be on the disk.

3. When a program is compiled, a file having the same base name as the program and the extension EXE is created on disk. This version of the program can be executed directly from DOS by entering the base name. If the program has no Readln statements, the output can be sent to the printer instead of the screen by adding " > PRN" after the base name. Suppose a program with no input statements and MYPROG in the title bar has been compiled. A file with the name MYPROG.EXE will have been created on the disk by the compiler. DOS can be invoked either by exiting QuickPascal with the key combination Alt/F/X or "shelling" to DOS with the key combination Alt/F/D. Then the command

```
MYPROG > PRN
```

executes the program and sends the output to the printer instead of the screen. (**Note:** If you shelled to DOS, enter EXIT to return to QuickPascal.)

Documentation

Now that we have the capability to write more complicated programs, we must concern ourselves with program documentation. **Program documentation is the inclusion of comments that specify the intent of the program, the purpose of the variables, the nature of the data to be input by the user, and the tasks performed by individual portions of the program.** Comments are surrounded by braces and can be placed anywhere in a program. Comments are completely ignored by the compiler but appear whenever the program is displayed or printed.

EXAMPLE 4   Document the program in Example 2.

SOLUTION   In the following program, the first comment describes the entire program and the second set of comments gives the meanings of the variables.

```
PROGRAM WeeklyWages;
{ Compute weekly wages. Requests worker's name, hourly wage, and
  hours worked as input and then displays the name and the week's
  wages. Earnings for the week are calculated as (number of hours
  worked) * (hourly wage) }

USES Crt;

VAR wage,        { hourly wage }
    hrs  : Real;  { number of hours worked during the week }
    name : STRING; { worker's name }
```

```
BEGIN
  ClrScr;
  Write('Enter name: ');
  Readln(name);
  Write('Enter hourly wage, hrs worked: ');
  Readln(wage, hrs);
  Writeln(name, ', your earnings are $', (hrs * wage):1:2)
END.
```

Some of the benefits of documentation are:

1. Other people can more easily comprehend the program.

2. The program can be understood when read later.

3. Long programs are easier to read since the purposes of individual pieces can be determined at a glance.

Comments:

1. The Readln statement provides a whole new dimension to the capabilities of a program. The user, rather than the programmer, can provide the data to be processed. Also, as we will see in Chapter 5, Readln allows the user to select from a menu the tasks to be performed.

2. If a Readln statement expects a string and receives a number, it will treat the number as a string; however, providing a string to a request for a number results in a run-time error:

```
VAR stVar  : STRING;
    intVar : Integer;

BEGIN
  Write('Enter a string: ');
  Readln(stVar);
  Writeln(stVar);
  Write('Enter an integer: ');
  Readln(intVar);
  Writeln(intVar)
END.

[run]
Enter a string: 12.34
12.34
Enter an integer: one
[Run-time error 106]
```

3. If a Readln statement expects a Real number and receives an Integer, it will convert the Integer to a Real. For example, if num is a Real variable, then the request Readln(num) will accept 2 as a response; however, if an Integer is expected, the response cannot be a Real.

4. The values of c and r in a GotoXY statement must be Integers. For instance, the compiler will reject the statement GotoXY(5, 6 / 3).

5. There is no limit to the number of items given in response to a single Readln statement, provided the total number of characters (including spaces) does not exceed 255.

6. Any item given in response to an input request must be a literal. It *cannot* be a variable or an expression. For instance, 1 / 2 or 2 + 3 are not acceptable numeric responses to a Readln statement.

7. If a Readln statement requests several values and fewer than the requested number are entered, the program will wait until the remaining values are supplied. When the lines in the following program segment were executed, the user entered just one value. The pressing of the Enter key caused the cursor to move to the next line to await the second value.

```
Write('Enter two integers: ');
Readln(intVar1, intVar2);
Writeln(intVar1, ' ', intVar2)

[run]
Enter two integers: 1
2
1  2
```

8. If a Readln statement requests several values and more than the requested number are entered, the program discards the excess values.

9. If the Enter key is pressed in response to the request by a statement of the form Readln(*strVar*), then the empty string will be assigned to the variable and the program will continue execution. Numeric and character values cannot be assigned values in this manner.

10. The Readln statement without parentheses can be used to pause a program until the user is ready to continue. For example, suppose a program displays many screens full of text. If the computer reaches

```
Write('Press the Enter key to continue.');
Readln;
ClrScr;
```

after 20 or so lines are displayed on the screen, the user can read the block of text at leisure. After the Enter key is pressed, the ClrScr statement is executed and the next block of text can be displayed.

11. The programs in this text are commented in the following ways:
  (a) The program heading is followed by a comment describing the purpose of the program.
  (b) Variables have descriptive names and are accompanied by comments when they are declared.
  (c) Certain computations are explained with comments.

12. Large programs or programs to be submitted to a supervisor or instructor should have additional documentation at the top of the program that identifies the author, the project, and the date.

13. With a color monitor, QuickPascal displays comments in a special color.

14. So far, the only type of input has been from the keyboard and the only type of output has been to the screen or printer. Input and output also can be provided by files on a disk. This topic is addressed in Chapter 9.

15. Pascal also has an input statement named Read. Read is similar to Readln. The main difference is that if more data is supplied than is requested, Read does not discard the extraneous data but instead, causes it to be saved for the next request of data. The following program segment illustrate how Read differs from Readln:

```
Write('Enter an Integer: ');
Read(intVar1);
Write('Enter an Integer: ');
Read(intVar2);
Writeln(intVar1, ' ', intVar2)

[run]
Enter an Integer: 1   2
Enter an Integer: 1   2
```

In the above output, the program did not pause when the second Read statement was encountered; the values 1 and 2 in the second line of output were displayed by the Writeln statement. If the Read statements are changed to Readln, the program *will* pause after the second Readln statement and the output will be

```
[run]
Enter an Integer: 1   2
Enter an Integer: 3
1   3
```

16. The GotoXY statement requires that "USES Crt" appear in the declarations part of the program.

17. When a program requires a large amount of keyboard input, debugging time can be shortened by responding initially with simple substitute names and numbers. For instance, if the program asks for three names of Presidents, the names A, B, and C could be entered during the early debugging stage.

18. The braces surrounding comments can be replaced by parentheses and asterisks. For instance, the comment

```
{ hourly wage }
```

also can be written as

```
(* hourly wage *)
```

19. The output of a program also can be sent to the printer by opening the printer as a file. (See Section 9.1.)

PRACTICE PROBLEMS 3.3

1. Why did QuickPascal generate a run-time error when 1/2 was entered? How should it be entered?

```
VAR weight : Real;

BEGIN
  Write('Enter weight of item in pounds:  ');
  Readln(weight);
  Writeln('The weight in ounces is ', 16 * weight)
END.

[run]
Enter weight of item in pounds? 1/2
Run-time error 106
```

2. Write a program that requests the current year and a person's age. Then calculate that person's age in the year 2000 and output it to the screen.

EXERCISES 3.3

In Exercises 1 through 8, determine the output of the program for the given user input.

1.
```
VAR n : Integer;

BEGIN
  Readln(n);
  Writeln(n * n)
END.
```
(User response: 4)

2.
```
VAR years, dogYears : Integer;

BEGIN
  Write('How old is your dog? ');
  Readln(years);
  dogYears := years * 7;
  Write('That''s ', dogYears, ' in dog years.')
END.
```
(User response: 5)

3.
```
VAR m : Integer;

BEGIN
  m := 3;
  Writeln(m);
  Readln(m);
  Writeln(m);
  Readln(m);
  Writeln(m)
END.
```
(User response: 5, 2)

4.
```
VAR num : Integer;

BEGIN
  num := 10;
  Writeln(num);
  Readln(num);
  num := num - 5 * 2;
  Writeln(num)
END.
```
(User response: 12)

5.
```
VAR adjective : STRING;

BEGIN
  Readln(adjective);
  adjective := 'un' + adjective;
  Writeln(adjective)
END.
```
(User response: bearable)

6.
```
VAR firstN, middleN, lastN : STRING;
    monogram               : STRING[3];

BEGIN
  Readln(lastN);
  Readln(firstN);
  Readln(middleN);
  monogram := firstN[1] + lastN[1] + middleN[1];
  Writeln(monogram)
END.
```
(User response: Kane, Charles, and Foster)

7.
```
VAR mentalAge, chronAge : Integer;
    iq                  : Real;

BEGIN
  Write('Enter subject''s mental age, chronological age  ');
  Readln(mentalAge, chronAge);
  iq := (mentalAge / chronAge) * 100;
  Writeln('IQ is ', iq:3:0)
END.
```
(User response: 24 20)

8.
```
VAR hourlyWage, hoursWorked : Real;

BEGIN
  Readln(hourlyWage, hoursWorked);
  Writeln('Earned: $', hourlyWage * hoursWorked:4:2)
END.
```
(User response: 4.68 40)

In Exercises 9 and 10, replace assignment statements with Writeln and Readln statements to request and read data from the user.

9.
```
VAR num : Integer;

BEGIN
  num := 3;
  Writeln(num, ' cubed is ', num * num * num)
END.
```

10.
```
VAR favColor, favAnimal : STRING;      { favorite color and animal }
    favNumber           : Integer;   { favorite number }

BEGIN
  favColor := 'yellow';
  favAnimal := 'cat';
  favNumber := 2;
  Writeln('Then would you like to have ', favNumber, ' ', favColor,
          ' ', favAnimal, 's?')
END.
```

In Exercises 11 through 14, identify the errors.

11.
```
VAR myVar : STRING;

BEGIN
  Readln(myVar + myVar);
  Writeln(myVar)
END.
```

12.
```
VAR name, rank, serialNum : STRING;

BEGIN
  Write('What is your name, rank, and serial number? ');
  Readln(name rank serialNum)
END.
```

13.
```
USES Crt;

VAR screenPos : Integer;
    saying    : STRING;

BEGIN
  ClrScr;
  saying := 'Normality is overrated.';
  GotoXY((80 - Length(saying)) / 2, 12);
  Writeln(saying)
END.
```

14.
```
CONST Number = 5;

VAR halfNumber : Real;

BEGIN
  Writeln(Number);
  Readln(Number);
  halfNumber := Number / 2;
  Writeln(halfNumber)
END.
```

15. If n is the number of seconds between lightning and thunder, then the storm is $n/5$ miles away. Write a program that requests the number of seconds between lightning and thunder and reports the distance of the storm. (Test the program for the case where there are one and a quarter seconds between the lightning and thunder.)

16. Write a program to request the name of a baseball team, the number of games won, and the number of games lost as input. Then the percentage of games won should be displayed. (Execute the program with the data Kansas City, 91, 71.)

17. The number of calories burned per hour by bicycling, jogging, and swimming are 200, 475, and 275 respectively. A person loses 1 pound of weight for each 3500 calories burned. Write a program that allows the user to input the number of hours spent at each activity, and then calculates the number of pounds worked off. (Test the program for a triathalon participant who bicycles 2 hours, jogs 3 hours, and swims 1 hour.)

18. The American College of Sports Medicine recommends you maintain your *training heart rate* during an aerobic workout. Your training heart rate is computed as $0.7 * (220 - a) + 0.3 * r$ where a is your age and r is your resting heart rate (your pulse when you first awaken). Write a program to request a person's age and resting heart rate and then calculate the training heart rate. (Test the program with an age of 20 and a resting heart rate of 70. Then determine your training heart rate.)

In Exercises 19 and 20, write a program from the given flowchart.

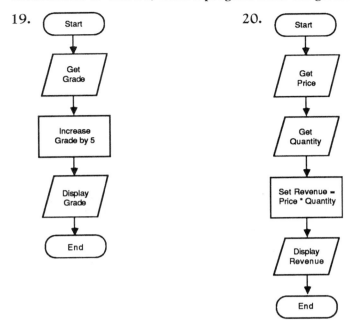

19.

20.

SOLUTIONS TO PRACTICE PROBLEMS 3.3

1. The response, 1/2, was an expression. The correct response should have been 0.5.

2. ```
VAR age, year : Integer;

BEGIN
  Write('What is your age? ');
  Readln(age);
  Write('What is the current year? ');
  Readln(year);
  Writeln('You will be ', 2000 - year + age, ' in the year 2000.')
END.
```

---

# 3.4 BUILT-IN FUNCTIONS

QuickPascal has a number of built-in functions that greatly extend its capabilities. These functions perform such varied tasks as taking the square root of a number, counting the number of characters in a string, and capitalizing letters. Functions associate with one or more values, called the input, a single value called the output. The function is said to **return** the output value. The two functions considered below have numeric input and output.

### Two Numeric Functions: Round, Sqrt

The function Round rounds a number to the nearest Integer. The function Sqrt calculates the square root of a number. The inputs to these functions may be
```

Integer or Real values. Round returns Integer values and Sqrt returns Real values. Some examples are:

Round(3.4) is 3.	Sqrt(900) is 3.00000000000000E+0001
Round(3.7) is 4.	Sqrt(0) is 0.00000000000000E+0000
Round(3) is 3.	Sqrt(2.0) is 1.41421356237310E+0000

The terms inside the parentheses can be either numbers (as above), constants, variables, or expressions. Expressions are evaluted first to produce the input.

EXAMPLE 1 The following program demonstrates the use of functions.

```
PROGRAM FunctionDemo;
{ Demonstrate the different ways functions are evaluated }

USES Crt;

CONST C = 4;

VAR m, n : Integer;
    r    : Real;

BEGIN
  ClrScr;
  Write(Round(5.5));
  m := 16;
  r := Sqrt(m);
  Writeln(r, Sqrt(r));
  Writeln(Sqrt(2 * m + C));
  Write(Round(Sqrt(2)))
END.

[run]
6 4.00000000000000E+0000 2.00000000000000E+0000
 6.00000000000000E+0000
 1
```

EXAMPLE 2 The following program shows an application of the Sqrt function.

```
PROGRAM SqrtDemo;
{ Find the length of the hypotenuse of a right triangle }

USES Crt;

VAR leg1, leg2, hyp : Real;
```

```
BEGIN
  ClrScr;
  Write('Enter length of one leg: ');
  Readln(leg1);
  Write('Enter length of other leg: ');
  Readln(leg2);
  hyp := Sqrt(leg1 * leg1 + leg2 * leg2);
  Write('The length of the hypotenuse is ', hyp:1:2)
END.

[run]
Enter length of one leg: 3
Enter length of other leg: 4
The length of the hypotenuse is 5.00
```

EXAMPLE 3 The following program uses the function Round to round an amount of money to dollars and cents. The interest is rounded to two decimal places by multiplying the number by 100, rounding to the nearest integer, and then dividing by 100. For instance, applying this process to 3.458 results in 345.8, then 346, and finally 3.46.

```
PROGRAM CalculateBalance;
{ Determine the balance when money earns 5% interest }

USES Crt;

CONST InterestRate = 0.05;

VAR principal, interest, roundedInterest, balance : Real;

BEGIN
  ClrScr;
  Write('Enter an amount of money: ');
  Readln(principal);
  interest := InterestRate * principal;
  Writeln('Interest = ', interest:1:4);
  roundedInterest := Round(100 * interest) / 100;
  Writeln('Rounded interest = ', roundedInterest:1:4);
  balance := principal + roundedInterest;
  Writeln('Balance = ', balance:1:2)
END.

[run]
Enter an amount of money: 123.45
Interest = 6.1725
Rounded interest = 6.1700
Balance = 129.62
```

A String and a Character Function: Length, UpCase

The function Length accepts a string as input and returns the length of the string. The function UpCase accepts a character as input and returns the uppercase version of the character if meaningful. Otherwise, it returns the character itself.

Some examples are

Length('Pascal') is 6.	UpCase('a') is 'A'.
Length('IBM PC ') is 7.	UpCase('A') is 'A'.
Length('') is 0.	UpCase('5') is '5'.

The terms inside the parentheses can be either literals (as above), variables, or expressions.

EXAMPLE 4 The following program demonstrates the use of Length and UpCase.

```
PROGRAM FunctionDemo;
{ Demonstrate the different ways functions are evaluated }

USES Crt;

CONST C = 't';

VAR x : STRING;
    d : Char;

BEGIN
  ClrScr;
  Write(Length('Hello'));
  Write(UpCase('r'):3);
  x := 'beep';
  Write(Length(x):3);
  d := 'n';
  Write(UpCase(d):3);
  Write(Length(x + x):3);
  Writeln(UpCase(UpCase(C)):3)
END.

[run]
5 R 4 N 8 T
```

Functions With Multiple Inputs: Copy and Pos

One string is said to be a substring of position m in a second string if the first string appears (as consecutive characters) beginning with the mth character of the second string. For instance, 'eric' is a substring of position 3 in 'America'.

The function Copy accepts a string and two Integers, call them m and n, as input and returns the substring of position m having length n. The function Pos accepts two strings as input and returns either 0 (if the first string is not a substring of the second) or the position of the first string in the second.

Some examples are:

Copy('abcdefg', 4, 2) is 'de'.   Pos('de', 'abcdefg') is 4.
Copy('Hi There', 3, 4) is ' The'.   Pos('bx', 'abc') is 0.

The terms inside the parentheses can be either literals (as above), variables, or expressions. The following program presents an application of Copy and Pos.

EXAMPLE 5   Write a program to request two sentences in a single input statement and separate the sentences.

SOLUTION   Assume the sentences are separated by a single space. The length of the second sentence can be found by subtracting the length of the first sentence from the length of the two sentences and then subtracting one for the space between them.

```
PROGRAM Separate;
{ Separate a pair of sentences }

USES Crt;

VAR sentences,
    firstSentence,
    secondSentence : STRING;
    firstLength,                  { Length of first sentence. }
    secondLength   : Integer;     { Length of second sentence. }

BEGIN
  ClrScr;
  Writeln('Enter two sentences separated by a space.');
  Readln(sentences);
  Writeln;
  firstLength := Pos('.', sentences);
  firstSentence := Copy(sentences, 1, firstLength);
  Writeln('The first sentence is "', firstSentence, '"');
  secondLength := Length(sentences) - firstLength - 1;
  secondSentence := Copy(sentences, firstLength + 2, secondLength);
  Writeln('The second sentence is "', secondSentence, '"')
END.

[run]
Enter two sentences separated by a space.
I like life. It's something to do.

The first sentence is "I like life."
The second sentence is "It's something to do."
```

Two Useful Numeric Functions: Exp and Ln

Pascal does not have an exponentiation operator; however, numbers can be raised to powers with the aid of the mathematical functions Exp and Ln.

An exponential function is a function of the form b^x, where b is a constant and x is a variable. The number b is called the base of the function. The most important exponential function in advanced mathematics is the one having as base a special number known as "e". The value of "e" to 12 significant digits is 2.71828182846. For any number x, Exp(x) has the value e^x. Exp is the **natural exponential function**.

The function Ln, called the **natural logarithm function**, is closely related to the natural exponential function. If x is any positive number, then the value of Ln(x) is the power to which e must be raised in order to get x.

Properties of the natural exponential and logarithm functions are derived in algebra and calculus courses. For our purposes, the most important property of these functions is the identity that allows Pascal to raise numbers to powers,

$$b^x = \text{Exp}(x * \text{Ln}(b)).$$

EXAMPLE 6 When P dollars is deposited in the bank at interest rate r, compounded annually, the balance after n years is $P(1 + r)^n$. Write a program to request P, r, and n as input and display the balance.

```
PROGRAM FutureValue;
{ Calculate the future value of an investment }

USES Crt;

VAR principal,
    intRate,
    balance    : Real;
    years      : Integer;

BEGIN
  ClrScr;
  Write('Enter the amount deposited: ');
  Readln(principal);
  Write('Enter the interest rate (such as 0.05 for 5%): ');
  Readln(intRate);
  Write('Enter the number of years on deposit: ');
  Readln(years);
  balance := principal * Exp(years * Ln(1 + intRate));
  Writeln('The balance is $', balance:1:2)
END.

[run]
Enter the amount deposited: 1000
Enter the interest rate (such as 0.05 for 5%): 0.065
Enter the number of years on deposit: 12
The balance is $2129.10
```

Other Useful Numeric Functions: Abs, Sqr, Trunc, Frac

The function Abs strips the minus signs from negative numbers while leaving other numbers unchanged. The function Sqr returns the square of a number. The functions Trunc and Frac split a Real number into its Integer and decimal parts, respectively.

Some examples are:

Abs(−3) is 3.   Abs(0) is 0.   Abs(3.2) is 3.20000000000000E+0000.
Sqr(3) is 9.   Sqr(−2) is 4.   Sqr(2.5) is 6.25000000000000E+0000.
Trunc(3.2) is 3.   Frac(3.2) is 2.00000000000000E−0001.
Trunc(3) is 3.   Frac(3) is 0.00000000000000E+0000.
Trunc(−3.2) is −3.   Frac(−3.2) is −2.00000000000000E−0001.

The functions Abs and Sqr, which accept either Integer or Real input, return a value of the same type as the input. Trunc and Frac accept any numeric input and return Integer and Real values, respectively.

Comments:

1. If Sqrt is asked to compute the square root of a negative number, no value is returned and the message "Runtime error 207" appears.

2. Recall that the function Copy has the form Copy(*str*, *m*, *n*) and returns the substring of *str* starting with position *m* and having length *n*. QuickPascal does its best to please for unexpected values of *m* and *n*. If *m* is greater than the length of the string or *n* is 0, then the empty string is returned. Copy(*string*, 0, *n*) has the same value as Copy(*string*, 1, *n*). If *m* + *n* is greater than the length of the string, then Copy(*string*, *m*, *n*) is the righthand part of the string beginning with the *m*th character. For instance, the value of Copy('abcdef', 3, 9) is 'cdef', a string of length 4.

3. Some QuickPascal functions that have not been mentioned are Cos, Sin, Tan, ArcTan, and Int. The first four are standard trigonometric functions. Int is similar to Trunc, except that it returns a Real value. For instance, Int(3.2) is 3.00000000000000E+0000.

4. The definition of "expression" can now be extended to include functions. For instance, 2 + 5 * Round(3.2) and Sqrt(Sqr(x) + Sqr(y)) are expressions.

PRACTICE PROBLEMS 3.4

1. What is the value of Pos('E', 'Computer')?

2. What is the value of Sqrt(12 * Length('WIN'))?

3. Suppose *myVar* is greater than or equal to 0 and less than 1. What are the possible values of Trunc(6 * myVar) + 1?

EXERCISES 3.4

In Exercises 1 through 28, find the value of the given expressions (express real numbers in standard notation).

1. Round(9.7)

2. Sqrt(64)

3. Sqrt(0.25)

4. Round(-14.6)

5. Sqrt(3 * 12)

6. Length('U S A')

7. UpCase('z')

8. Round(0.7)

9. Length('"hello"')

10. UpCase('$')

11. Length(' ')

12. Pos('h', 'shoe')

13. Pos('f', 'shoe')

14. Copy('harp', 1, 2)

15. Trunc(9 - 2)

16. Copy('ABCD', 2, 2)

17. Copy('shoe', 4, 1)

18. Trunc(9.5 - 2)

19. Frac(12.5)

20. Trunc(10.75)

21. Sqr(4)

22. Frac(3.1415)

23. Abs(-45.0)

24. Sqr(2)

25. Abs(-101)

26. Int(10.75)

27. Int(7.5)

28. Copy('borderline', Pos('l', 'borderline'), 4)

In Exercises 29 through 44, find the value of the given function where $m = 5$, $n = 3$, aVar = 'Lullaby', and bVar = 'lab'.

29. Length(bVar)

30. Sqrt(4 + m)

31. Trunc(-n / 2)

32. Sqr(m + n)

33. Sqr(m - n)

34. Round(n * 0.5)

35. Copy(aVar, m, 3)

36. Copy(bVar, 1, n - 2)

37. Pos(bVar, aVar)

38. Pos('r', aVar)

39. Pos(aVar, bVar)

40. Sqr(Pos('a', aVar))

41. Copy(aVar, 1, Length(bVar))

42. Length(aVar + Copy(bVar, 1, 2))

43. Copy(aVar, m - n, 2 * m)

44. UpCase(bVar[2])

In Exercises 45 through 50, evaluate the expression. Express real numbers in standard notation. Recall, $b^x = Exp(x * Ln(b))$.

45. Exp(4 * Ln(2))

46. Exp(2 * Ln(3))

47. Exp(2 * Ln(0.5))

48. Exp(0 * Ln(0.25))

49. Exp(1 * Ln(0.33))   **50.** Exp(9 * Ln(1))

In Exercises 51 through 59, determine the output of the program.

51. VAR num1, num2 : Real;

```
BEGIN
  num1 := 3.67;
  num2 := 7.345;
  Writeln(Round(10 * num2) DIV 10);
  Writeln(Round(10 * num1) DIV 10)
END.
```

52. VAR weekDay : STRING;
        index   : Integer;

```
BEGIN
  weekDay := 'SunMonTueWedThuFriSat';
  Write('Day of week (1 to 7): ');
  Readln(index);
  Writeln('Today is ', Copy(weekDay, 3 * index - 2, 3))
END.
```
(User response: 5)

53. VAR date : STRING;

```
BEGIN
  Write('Enter date (mm/dd/yy): ');
  Readln(date);
  Writeln('The year is 19' + Copy(date, 7, 2))
END.
```
(User response: 08/23/90)

54. VAR anyWord : STRING;

```
BEGIN
  Write('Enter a word: ');
  Readln(anyWord);
  Writeln(Copy(anyWord, Length(anyWord), 1))
END.
```
(User response: Hello)

55. VAR names : STRING;

```
BEGIN
  Write('Enter your first name and last name: ');
  Readln(names);
  Writeln(Copy(names, 1, 1) + Copy(names, Pos(' ', names), 2))
END.
```
(User response: James Cash)

56.
```
VAR answer : STRING;
    num    : Integer;

BEGIN
  Write('Do you like jazz (yes or no)? ');
  Readln(answer);
  num := Round(Pos(Copy(answer, 1, 1), 'YyNn') / 2);
  answer := Copy('yesno', 3 * num - 2, 3);
  Writeln('I guess your answer is ', answer)
END.
```
(User response: yup)

57.
```
VAR pizzaCost, yourShare : Real;
    numFriends           : Integer;

BEGIN
  numFriends := 3;
  pizzaCost := 15.25;
  yourShare := Round(100 * (pizzaCost / numFriends)) / 100;
  Writeln('You each owe ', yourShare:1:2)
END.
```

58.
```
VAR base, exponent : Real;

BEGIN
  Write('Enter a non-negative base and an exponent:');
  Readln(base, exponent);
  Writeln(base, ' raised to the power ', exponent);
  Writeln('  is: ', Exp(exponent * Ln(base)):6:1)
END.
```
(User response: 2.5 3)

59.
```
VAR phrase1, phrase2 : STRING;

BEGIN
  phrase1 := 'Quick as ';
  phrase2 := 'a wink.';
  Writeln(Copy(phrase1, 1, 7));
  Writeln(Copy(phrase1 + phrase2, 7, 6));
  Writeln('The average ', Copy(phrase2, 3, 4), ' lasts .1 seconds.')
END.
```

In Exercises 60 through 63, determine the errors.

60.
```
VAR aWord : STRING;

BEGIN
  aWord := 'Thank you';
  Writeln(Pos(k, aWord))
END.
```

61.
```
VAR yob : Integer;

BEGIN
  Write('Enter your year of birth:');
  Readln(yob);
  Writeln(Copy(yob, 3, 2))
END.
```

62.
```
VAR num1, num2 : Integer;

BEGIN
  num1 := 7;
  num2 := 5;
  Writeln(Sqrt(num1 - num2 * 2))
END.
```

63.
```
VAR num1, num2 : Integer;

BEGIN
  num1 := 3;
  num2 := 5;
  num1 := Int(2 * num1 / num2);
  Writeln(num2:1, num1:2)
END.
```

64. Write a program that requests a number of inches and converts it to feet and inches. (Try the program with 72, 53, and 8.4 inches.)

65. Write a program that requests a number and the number of decimal places to which the number should be rounded, and then displays the rounded number.

66. Write a program that requests a letter, converts it to uppercase and gives its first position in the sentence "THE QUICK BROWN FOX JUMPS OVER A LAZY DOG." A typical output is:

```
[run]
Letter? b
B is letter 11 in the sentence.
```

67. Write a program that requests an amount of money and gives the number of quarters to be used when making that amount of change. (Try each of the amounts 0.85, 9.57, and 15.0 as input.)

68. Write a program that requests a day of the week (Sun, Mon, . . ., Sat) and gives the numerical position of that day in the week. A possible outcome is:

```
[run]
Day of week? Wed
Wed is day 4 in the week.
```

69. Write a program that converts a length of time in decimal hours to an equivalent length of time in hours and (nearest) minute.

```
[sample run]
Enter a time in decimal hours: 5.75
5 hours, 45 minutes
```

70. Write a program that requests a sentence, a word in the sentence, and another word, and then displays the sentence with the first word replaced by the second. A possible outcome is:

```
[run]
Sentence? What you don't know won't hurt you.
Word to find? know
Replace with? owe
What you don't owe won't hurt you.
```

SOLUTIONS TO PRACTICE PROBLEMS 3.4

1. 0. There is no uppercase letter E in the string "Computer". Pos distinguishes between upper and lowercase.

2. 6. Length('WIN') is 3, 12 * 3 is 36, and Sqrt(36) is 6. This expression is an example of function **composition**. The inner function will be evaluated first.

3. 1, 2, 3, 4, 5, or 6. Since $0 \leq$ myVar < 1, then $0 \leq (6 *$ myVar$) < 6$, and therefore Trunc(6 * myVar) is 0, 1, 2, 3, 4, or 5. Adding 1 gives the stated result.

Chapter 3
Summary

1. A program consists of three parts: the *program heading*, the *declaration section*, and the *statement part*.

2. Three parts of the declaration section are indicated by the words USES, CONST, and VAR.
   (a) The USES part lists the units needed by the program.
   (b) Literals of the data types Integer, Real, STRING, and Char can be assigned to constants.
   (c) Variables of the data types Integer, Real, STRING, and Char can be declared in the VAR part.

3. The statement part (or main body) of the program starts with the word BEGIN and concludes with the word END followed by a period. The individual statements are separated by semicolons.

4. The name of the program (as given in the program heading) and the names of constants and variables are called **identifiers**.

5. The arithmetic *operations* are +, −, *, /, DIV, and MOD. The only string operation is +, concatenation. An *expression* is a combination of constants, variables, functions, and operations that can be evaluated.

6. Variables obtain their values from assignment statements or the input statements *Readln* and *Read*. String literals appearing on the right side of assignment statements must be surrounded by single quote marks. String literals entered from the keyboard as input do not require quote marks.

7. *Write* and *Writeln* statements display data on the screen or send it to the printer. *Colons* can be used to format the data and *GotoXY* allows items to be placed anywhere on the screen.

8. *Functions* can be thought of as accepting data as input and returning numbers or strings as output.

Function	Input	Output
Abs	Integer (Real)	Integer (Real)
Chr	Integer	Char
Copy	String,Integer,Integer	String
Exp	Real	Real
Frac	Real	Real
Length	String	Integer
Ln	Real	Real
Pos	String,String	Integer
Round	Real	Integer
Sqr	Integer (Real)	Integer (Real)
Sqrt	Real	Real
Trunc	Real	Integer
UpCase	Char	Char

Chapter 3
Programming Projects

1. The weight of an object (measured in newtons) is the gravitational force exerted on it by the earth and is given by the formula,

```
weight = mass * Gravity
```

where *mass* is the mass of the object in kilograms and *Gravity* is a constant acceleration due to gravity (9.8). Write a program that requests the mass of an object in kilograms and displays its weight in newtons. Use constants where appropriate.

2. Figure 3.12 shows a simplified bill for long-distance phone calls. (The items in the third and fourth columns are the rates for the first minute and each additional minute.) Write a program to produce this bill. The data for the date, destination, and the number of minutes should be input with Readln statements; and the rates should be stored in constants. The program should compute the amounts and the total. (**Note:** [amount] = [rate for first min] + [rate for each additional minute] * ([number of minutes] − 1).)

Date	To	1st Min	Addl. Min	Mins	Amount
JUN 16	BOSTON	0.4698	0.3740	17	6.45
JUN 23	SAN FRANCI	0.5330	0.4158	5	2.20
				Total:	8.65

Figure 3.12   Bill for Long-Distance Calls

3. Suppose automobile repair customers are billed at the rate of $35 per hour for labor. Also, costs for parts and supplies are subject to a 5 percent sales tax. Write a program to print out a simplified bill. The customer's name, the number of hours of labor, and the cost of parts and supplies should be entered into the program with Readln statements. The computer should display the customer's name (indented) and the three costs shown in the sample run below.

```
[run]
Customer? John Doe
Hours of labor? 3.5
Cost of parts (and supplies)? 23.55

      John Doe
Labor cost    $122.50
Parts cost    $ 24.73
Total cost    $147.23
```

4. Write a program to generate the personalized form letter shown below. The person's name and address should be entered with Readln statements.

```
Mr. John Jones
123 Main Street
Juneau, Alaska  99803

Dear Mr. Jones,

    The Jones family has been selected as the
first family on Main Street to have the opportunity
to purchase an Apex solar-powered flashlight. Due to limited
supply, only 1000 of these amazing inventions will be available
in the entire state of Alaska. Don't delay. Order today.

                    Sincerely,
                    Cuthbert J. Twillie
```

5. Table 3.3 gives the distribution of the U.S. population (in thousands) by age group and sex. Write a program to produce the table that is partially shown in Figure 3.13. Use a constant to hold each of the six numbers. For each age group, the column labeled %Males gives the percentage of the males in that age group, similarly for the column labeled %Females. The last column gives the percentage of the total population in each age group.

Age Group	Males	Females
Under 18	32,079	30,611
18 - 64	71,858	74,094
Over 64	11,299	16,741

Table 3.3   U.S. Population (1984)

U.S. Population					
Age Group	Males	Females	%Males	%Females	%Total
Under 18	32079	30611	51.2	48.8	26.5
18 - 64	71858	74094			
Over 64	11299	16741			

Figure 3.13   Partial Output of Programming Project 5

4

Procedures and Functions

4.1   PROCEDURES

Structured program design requires that large problems be broken into small problems to be solved one at a time. Pascal has two devices, procedures and functions, that are used to break problems into manageable chunks. Procedures and functions also eliminate repetitive code, they can be reused by other programs, and allow a team of programmers to work separately on a single program.

In this section, we show how procedures are defined and used. The programs in this section are designed to demonstrate procedures rather than to accomplish sophisticated programming tasks. Subsequent chapters of the book use procedures for more substantial programming efforts.

A **procedure** is a part of a program that performs one or more related tasks, has its own name, is written as a separate part of the program, and is accessed by having its name appear as a statement. The simplest type of procedure has the form

```
PROCEDURE ProcedureName;
  BEGIN
    Statement(s)
  END;
```

Consider the following program that calculates the sum of two numbers. This program will be revised to incorporate procedures.

```
PROGRAM Addition;
{ Display the sum of two numbers }

USES Crt;

VAR a, b : Integer;

BEGIN
  ClrScr;
  Writeln('This program displays a sentence');
  Writeln('identifying two numbers and their sum.');
  Writeln;
  a := 2;
  b := 3;
  Writeln('The sum of ', a, ' and ', b, ' is ', a + b)
END.

[run]
This program displays a sentence
identifying two numbers and their sum.

The sum of 2 and 3 is 5
```

The tasks performed by this program can be summarized as follows:

Explain purpose of program.
Display numbers and their sum.

Procedures allow us to write the program in such a way that we focus first on the tasks and later on how to accomplish each task.

EXAMPLE 1 The following program uses a procedure to accomplish the first task of the program above. Procedures are placed in the declaration portion of the program, just before the statement part. As before, execution begins with the first statement in the statement part, in this case ClrScr. When ExplainPurpose is reached, execution jumps to the procedure. The lines between BEGIN and END are executed, and then execution continues with the line following ExplainPurpose in the statement part.

```
PROGRAM Addition;
{ Display the sum of two numbers }

USES Crt;

VAR a, b : Integer;

PROCEDURE ExplainPurpose;
{ Explain the task performed by the program }
  BEGIN
    Writeln('This program displays a sentence');
    Writeln('identifying two numbers and their sum.');
    Writeln
  END;

BEGIN
  ClrScr;
  ExplainPurpose;
  a := 2;
  b := 3;
  Writeln('The sum of ', a, ' and ', b, ' is ', a + b)
END.
```

Procedures make the program easy to read, modify, and debug. The statement part of the program gives an unencumbered description of what the program does and the procedures fill in the details.

In a certain sense, procedures are self-contained programs that are accessed by the statement part. Accessing a procedure is referred to as **calling** the procedure.

The second task performed by the addition program also can be handled by a procedure. The values of the two numbers, however, must be transmitted to the procedure. This transmission is called **passing**.

EXAMPLE 2 The following revision of the program in Example 1 uses a procedure to accomplish the second task. The statement Add(2, 3) causes execution to jump to the procedure Add and assigns the number 2 to *a* and the number 3 to *b*. After the lines of the procedure are executed, execution continues with the line following the Add(2, 3) statement. The variables *a* and *b* appearing in the procedure Add are called **parameters**. Just like the variables in the declaration part of a program, the types of the parameters must be specified.

```
PROGRAM Addition;
{ Display the sum of two numbers }

USES Crt;

PROCEDURE ExplainPurpose;
{ Explain the task performed by the program }
  BEGIN
    Writeln('This program displays a sentence');
    Writeln('identifying two numbers and their sum.');
    Writeln
  END;

PROCEDURE Add (a, b : Integer);
{ Display numbers and their sum }
  BEGIN
    Writeln('The sum of ', a, ' and ', b, ' is ', a + b)
  END;

BEGIN
  ClrScr;
  ExplainPurpose;
  Add(2, 3)
END.
```

One of the benefits of procedures is that they can be called several times during the execution of the program. This feature is especially efficient when there are many statements in the procedure.

EXAMPLE 3 The following extension of the program in Example 2 displays several sums.

```
PROGRAM Addition;
{ Display the sums of several pairs of numbers }

USES Crt;

PROCEDURE ExplainPurpose;
{ Explain the task performed by the program }
  BEGIN
    Writeln('This program displays sentences');
    Writeln('identifying pairs of numbers and their sums.');
    Writeln
  END;
```

```
PROCEDURE Add (a, b : Integer);
{ Display numbers and their sum }
  BEGIN
    Writeln('The sum of ', a, ' and ', b, ' is ', a + b);
  END;

BEGIN
  ClrScr;
  ExplainPurpose;
  Add(2, 3);
  Add(4, 6);
  Add(7, 8)
END.

[run]
This program displays sentences
identifying pairs of numbers and their sums.

The sum of 2 and 3 is 5
The sum of 4 and 6 is 10
The sum of 7 and 8 is 15
```

The parameters in the procedure Add are merely temporary placeholders for the numbers passed to the procedure; their names are not important. The only essentials are their type, quantity, and order. In this case, the parameters must be Integer variables and there must be two of them. For instance, the procedure could have been written

```
PROCEDURE Add (num1, num2 : Integer);
{ Display numbers and their sum }
  BEGIN
    Writeln('The sum of ', num1, ' and ', num2, ' is ', num1 + num2)
  END;
```

A procedure has virtually all of the features of a program. It may contain a declaration part and has a statement part enclosed between BEGIN and END. The declaration part may even declare other procedures. One difference between a procedure and a program is that a procedure's terminating END statement is followed by a semicolon instead of a period.

EXAMPLE 4 The following program passes a string and two real numbers to a procedure. When the procedure is first called, the string parameter *state* is assigned the string 'Hawaii', and the real parameters *pop* and *area* are assigned the numbers 1062000 and 6450, respectively. The procedure then uses these parameters to carry out the task of producing the population density of Hawaii. The second calling assigns different values to the parameters.

```
PROGRAM PopulationDensity;
{ Calculate the population density of a state }

USES Crt;

PROCEDURE ProduceDensity (state : STRING; pop, area : Real);
{ The density (number of people per square mile)
  will be rounded to a whole number }
  VAR density : Integer;
  BEGIN
    density := Round(pop / area);
    Writeln('The density of ', state, ' is ', density,
            ' people per square mile.')
  END;

BEGIN
  ClrScr;
  ProduceDensity('Hawaii', 1062000, 6450);
  ProduceDensity('Alaska', 534000, 586412)
END.
```

```
[run]
The density of Hawaii is 165 people per square mile.
The density of Alaska is 1 people per square mile.
```

The parameters in the density program can have any names, as did the parameters in the addition program of Example 3. The only restriction is that the first parameter be a string variable and the last two parameters be real variables. For instance, the procedure could have been written

```
PROCEDURE ProduceDensity (x : STRING; r, s : Real);
{ The density (number of people per square mile)
  will be rounded to a whole number }
  VAR density : Integer;
  BEGIN
    density := Round(r / s);
    Writeln('The density of ', x, ' is ', density,
            ' people per square mile.')
  END;
```

Variables and Expressions as Arguments

The items appearing in the parentheses of a procedure-calling statement are known as **arguments**. These should not be confused with parameters, which appear in the heading of the procedure. In Example 3, the arguments of the Add statements were numbers. These arguments also could have been variables or expressions. For instance, the following variable declarations could have been made and the statement part written as follows:

```
      VAR a, b, c : Integer;

      BEGIN
        ClrScr;
        ExplainPurpose;
        a := 2;
        b := 3;
        Add(a, b);
        Add(a + 2, 2 * b);
        c := a;
        Add(c, c + 1)
      END.
```

This feature allows values obtained from Readln statements to be passed to a procedure.

EXAMPLE 5   The following variation of the addition program requests the two numbers as input from the user. Notice that the names of the arguments, m and n, are different than the names of the parameters. The names of the arguments and parameters may be the same or different; what matters is the order, number, and types of the arguments and parameters.

```
PROGRAM Addition;
{ Display the sum of two numbers }

USES Crt;

VAR m, n : Integer;

PROCEDURE ExplainPurpose;
{ Explain the task performed by the program }
  BEGIN
    Writeln('This program requests two numbers and');
    Writeln('displays the two numbers and their sum.');
    Writeln
  END;

PROCEDURE Add (a, b : Integer);
{ Display numbers and their sum }
  BEGIN
    Writeln('The sum of ', a, ' and ', b, ' is ', a + b)
  END;

  BEGIN
    ClrScr;
    ExplainPurpose;
    Write('Enter two numbers: ');
    Readln(m, n);
    Add(m, n)
  END.
```

```
[run]
This program requests two numbers and
displays the two numbers and their sum.

Enter two numbers: 2  3
The sum of 2 and 3 is 5
```

EXAMPLE 6   The following variation of Example 4 obtains its input from the user. The second calling statement uses different variable names for the arguments to show that using the same argument names is not necessary.

```
PROGRAM PopulationDensity;
{ Calculate the population density of a state }

USES Crt;

VAR state1, state2          : STRING;
    pop1, area1, pop2, area2 : Real;

PROCEDURE ProduceDensity (state : STRING; pop, area : Real);
{ The density (number of people per square mile)
  will be rounded to a whole number }
  VAR density : Integer;
  BEGIN
    density := Round(pop / area);
    Writeln('The density of ', state, ' is ', density,
            ' people per square mile.')
  END;

BEGIN
  ClrScr;
  Write('Enter state: ');
  Readln(state1);
  Write('Enter population, area: ');
  Readln(pop1, area1);
  ProduceDensity(state1, pop1, area1);
  Writeln;
  Write('Enter state: ');
  Readln(state2);
  Write('Enter population, area: ');
  Readln(pop2, area2);
  ProduceDensity(state2, pop2, area2)
END.

[run]
Enter state: Hawaii
Enter population, area: 1062000  6450
The density of Hawaii is 165 people per square mile.

Enter state: Alaska
Enter population, area: 534000  586412
The density of Alaska is 1 people per square mile.
```

Arguments and parameters also can be used to pass values from procedures back to the calling statement. This important property of procedures is explored in detail in the next section.

Nested Procedures

A procedure declared in the declaration part of another procedure is said to be nested inside the original procedure. A sequence of nested procedures is called a **chain of nested procedures**.

EXAMPLE 7 Specify all of the chains of nested procedures in the following program outline:

```
PROGRAM Baseball;
{ Illustrate chains of nested procedures }

VAR n1 : Integer;

PROCEDURE NationalLeague;
  VAR n2 : Integer;
  BEGIN
    Statement(s)
  END;

PROCEDURE AmericanLeague;
  VAR n3 : Integer;
  PROCEDURE AmLeagueWest;
    VAR n4 : Integer;
    BEGIN
      Statement(s)
    END;
  PROCEDURE AmLeagueEast;
    VAR n5 : Integer;
    PROCEDURE Orioles;
      VAR n6 : Integer;
      BEGIN
        Statement(s)
      END;
    BEGIN
      Statement(s)
    END;
  BEGIN
    Statement(s)
  END;

BEGIN
  Statement(s)
END.
```

SOLUTION   There are four nested chains of procedures.

(1) AmericanLeague, AmLeagueWest
(2) AmericanLeague, AmLeagueEast
(3) AmericanLeague, AmLeagueEast, Orioles
(4) AmLeagueEast, Orioles

Comments:

1. The rules for naming procedures are identical to the rules for naming variables. The names should describe the task performed by the procedure.

2. In this text, we begin procedure names with uppercase letters in order to distinguish them from variable names. Like variable names, however, they can be written with any combination of uppercase and lowercase letters.

3. In this text, the first line inside a procedure is often a comment describing the task performed by the procedure.

4. A procedure can call another procedure preceding it in the declarations part of the program. After the called procedure is executed, execution continues with the line following the calling statement in the first procedure. Section 12.4 presents a method for a procedure to call a procedure that follows it in the list of declarations.

5. Procedures allow programmers to first focus on the main flow of the program and defer the details of accomplishing the secondary tasks. Modern programs use procedures liberally. The statement part of the program acts as a supervisor, delegating tasks to the procedures. This method of program construction is known as **modular** or **top-down** design.

6. As a general rule, a procedure should perform only one task, or several closely related tasks, and should be kept relatively small.

PRACTICE PROBLEMS 4.1

1. What will be the output of the following program?

```
PROGRAM ProcCallsProc;
{ Demonstrate procedures calling other procedures }

PROCEDURE Second;
  BEGIN
    Write(2:2)
  END;

PROCEDURE First;
  BEGIN
    Write(1);
    Second;
    Write(3:2)
  END;
```

```
BEGIN
  First;
  Write(4:2)
END.
```

2. What is wrong with the following program?

```
PROGRAM AgeNextCentury;
{ Determine a person's age in the year 2000 }

VAR name : STRING;
    yob  : Integer;

PROCEDURE AgeIn2000(name : STRING; yob : Integer);
  VAR age : Integer;
  BEGIN
    age := 2000 - yob;
    Writeln(name, ', at the turn of the century you will be ', age)
  END;

BEGIN
  Write('What is your year of birth? ');
  Readln(yob);
  Write('What is your name? ');
  Readln(name);
  AgeIn2000(yob, name)
END.
```

EXERCISES 4.1

In Exercises 1 through 34, determine the output of the program.

1.
```
PROGRAM KermitQuotation;

PROCEDURE Quotation;
{ Display a quotation }
  BEGIN
    Writeln('It isn''t easy being green.')
  END;

BEGIN
  Quotation;
  Writeln('          Kermit the frog')
END.
```

2.
```
PROGRAM DeepThought;

PROCEDURE Day;
  BEGIN
    Write('is the first day ')
  END;
```

```
      BEGIN
        Write('Today ');
        Day;
        Writeln('of the rest of your life.')
      END.
```

3.
```
PROGRAM WhyClockwise;

      PROCEDURE Question;
        BEGIN
          Writeln('Why do clocks run clockwise?')
        END;

      PROCEDURE Answer;
        BEGIN
          Writeln('Because they were invented in the northern');
          Writeln('hemisphere where sundials move clockwise.')
        END;

      BEGIN
        Question;
        Answer
      END.
```

4.
```
PROCEDURE TitleAndName;
        VAR title, name : STRING;
        BEGIN
          Write('what is your title? ');
          Readln(title);
          Write('What is your first name? ');
          Readln(name);
          Write(title, ' ', name, ', ')
        END;

      BEGIN
        Write('Hello, ');
        TitleAndName;
        Writeln('how are you today?')
      END.
```
   (User response: Sir, Arthur)

5.
```
PROGRAM AddTwoNumbers;
      VAR num1, num2 : Integer;

      PROCEDURE AddEm (num1, num2 : Integer);
        VAR total : Integer;
        BEGIN
          total := num1 + num2;
          Writeln(total)
        END;
```

```
BEGIN
  num1 := 2;
  num2 := 5;
  AddEm(num1, num2)
END.
```

6. `PROGRAM DeepThoughtII;`

```
PROCEDURE Rose;
  BEGIN
    Write(', is a rose')
  END;

BEGIN
  Write('A rose');
    Rose;
    Rose;
    Writeln('.')
  END.
```

7. `PROGRAM GoodAdvice;`
   `{ Good advice to follow }`

```
PROCEDURE Source;
  BEGIN
    Writeln('Source: A jar of mayonnaise.')
  END;

PROCEDURE Advice;
  BEGIN
    Writeln('Keep cool, but don''t freeze.');
    Source
  END;

BEGIN
  Advice
END.
```

8. `PROGRAM Karnac;`

```
PROCEDURE Question;
{ Note: 'Wagner' is pronounced 'Vagner' }
  BEGIN
    Writeln;
    Writeln('Do you spell your name with a V, Mr. Wagner?')
  END;

PROCEDURE Answer;
  BEGIN
    Writeln('The answer is 9W.');
    Writeln('What is the question?')
  END;
```

```
     BEGIN
       Answer;
       Question
     END.
```

9. PROGRAM HowManyKeys;

```
   VAR blackKeys, whiteKeys : Integer;

   PROCEDURE TotalKeys (blackKeys, whiteKeys : Integer);
     VAR pianoKeys : Integer;
     BEGIN
       pianoKeys := blackKeys + whiteKeys;
       Writeln(pianoKeys)
     END;

   BEGIN
     blackKeys := 36;
     whiteKeys := 52;
     TotalKeys(blackKeys, whiteKeys)
   END.
```

10. PROGRAM MobyDick;

```
   PROCEDURE FirstLine (name : STRING);
     { Display first line }
     BEGIN
       Writeln('Call me ', name)
     END;

   BEGIN
     FirstLine('Ishmael')
   END.
```

11. PROGRAM TaleOfTwoCities;

```
   PROCEDURE Times (word : STRING);
   { Display first line }
     BEGIN
       Writeln('It was the ', word, ' of times.')
     END;

   BEGIN
     Times('best');
     Times('worst')
   END.
```

12. PROGRAM CountPotato;

```
   PROCEDURE Potato (quantity : Integer);
     BEGIN
       Write(quantity, ' potato, ')
     END;
```

```
  BEGIN
    Potato(1);
    Potato(2);
    Potato(3);
    Writeln(4)
  END.
```

13. PROGRAM NameAnalysis;

```
VAR name : STRING;

PROCEDURE AnalyzeName (name : STRING);
{ Display length and first letter }
BEGIN
  Writeln('Your name has ', Length(name), ' letters.');
  Writeln('The first letter is ', Copy(name, 1, 1))
END;

BEGIN
  name := 'Gabriel';
  AnalyzeName(name)
END.
```

14. PROGRAM SaySomethingNice;

```
VAR color : STRING;

PROCEDURE Flattery (color : STRING);
  BEGIN
    Writeln('You look dashing in ', color)
  END;

BEGIN
  Write('What is your favorite color? ');
  Readln(color);
  Flattery(color)
END.
```
(User response: blue)

15. PROGRAM GetALetter;

```
VAR num : Integer;

PROCEDURE Alphabet (num : Integer);
  VAR n : Integer;
  BEGIN
    n := num;
    Writeln(Copy('abcdefghijklmnopqrstuvwxyz', 1, n))
  END;
```

```
BEGIN
  Write('Give a number from 1 to 26: ');
  Readln(num);
  Alphabet(num)
END.
```
(User response: 5)

16. PROGRAM Representatives;

```
VAR size : Integer;

PROCEDURE House (size : Integer);
  BEGIN
    Write(size, ' members in the House ')
  END;

BEGIN
  size := 435;
  House(size);
  Writeln('of Representatives')
END.
```

17. PROGRAM GrossMessage;

```
VAR num : Integer;

PROCEDURE Gross (amount : Integer);
  BEGIN
    Writeln(amount, ' items in a gross')
  END;

BEGIN
  num := 144;
  Gross(num)
END.
```

18. PROGRAM Conversion;

```
PROCEDURE Acres (numMiles : Integer);
  CONST AcresPerMile = 640;
  BEGIN
    Writeln('There are ', numMiles * AcresPerMile, ' acres in ',
            numMiles, ' square miles.')
  END;

BEGIN
  Acres(10)
END.
```

19. PROGRAM Census;

```
VAR candy : STRING;

PROCEDURE Brown (fraction : Real; item : STRING);
  BEGIN
    Writeln(Round(fraction * 100), '% of ', item, ' are brown.')
  END;

BEGIN
  candy := 'M&M''s Plain Chocolate Candies';
  Brown(0.3, candy)
END.
```

20. PROGRAM Savings;

```
VAR annualRate : Real;

PROCEDURE Balance (r : Real);
  VAR p : Real;
  BEGIN
    Write('What is the principal? ');
    Readln(p);
    Writeln('The balance after 1 year is ', (1 + r) * p)
  END;

BEGIN
  annualRate := 0.08;
  Balance(annualRate)
END.
```
(User response: 100)

21. PROGRAM Conversion;

```
VAR hours : Integer;

PROCEDURE Minutes (num : Integer);
  BEGIN
    Writeln(num, ' minutes in a day')
  END;

BEGIN
  hours := 24;
  Minutes(60 * hours)
END.
```

22. PROGRAM Griffin;

```
VAR a, b : STRING;

PROCEDURE Display (aWord : STRING);
  BEGIN
    Writeln(aWord)
  END;
```

```
BEGIN
  a := 'United States';
  b := 'acorn';
  Display(Copy(a, 1, 3) + Copy(b, 2, 4))
END.
```

23. PROGRAM FindT;

```
VAR word : STRING;

PROCEDURE T (num : Integer);
  BEGIN
    Writeln('t is the ', num, 'th letter of the word.')
  END;

BEGIN
  Write('Enter a word: ');
  Readln(word);
  T(Pos('t', word))
END.
```
(User response: computer)

24. PROGRAM SenateFact;

```
VAR states, senators : Integer;

PROCEDURE Senate (num : Integer);
  BEGIN
    Writeln('The number of members of the U.S. Senate is ', num)
  END;

BEGIN
  states := 50;
  senators := 2;
  Senate(states * senators)
END.
```

25. PROGRAM PopularLanguages;

```
PROCEDURE DisplaySource;
  BEGIN
    Writeln(
      'According to a poll in the May 31, 1988 issue of PC Magazine,');
    Writeln(
      '75% of the people polled write programs for their companies.');
    Writeln('The four most popular languages used are as follows.')
  END;

PROCEDURE Language(name : STRING; users : Integer);
  BEGIN
    Writeln(users, '% of the respondents use ', name)
  END;
```

```
BEGIN
  DisplaySource;
  Language('BASIC', 22);
  Language('Assembler', 16);
  Language('C', 15);
  Language('Pascal', 13)
END.
```

26.
```
PROGRAM SatisfactoryProgress;

VAR num          : Integer;
    things, where : STRING;

PROCEDURE Phrase (num : Integer; things, where : STRING);
  BEGIN
    Writeln(num, things, where)
  END;

BEGIN
  num := 2;
  things := ' steps';
  where := ' forward';
  Phrase(num, things, where);
  num := 1;
  where := ' back.';
  Phrase(num, things, where)
END.
```

27.
```
PROGRAM YourBirthYear;

VAR name      : STRING;
    year, age : Integer;

PROCEDURE BirthYear (name : STRING; year, age : Integer);
  BEGIN
    Writeln(name, ', you were born in ', year - age)
  END;

BEGIN
  Write('Name: ');
  Readln(name);
  Write('Year is: ');
  Readln(year);
  Write('Your age at the end of ' , year, ': ');
  Readln(age);
  BirthYear(name, year, age)
END.
```

(User response: Yoko Izumi, 1990, and 25)

```
28. PROGRAM Substring;

    VAR aWord : STRING;
        num   : Integer;

    PROCEDURE FirstPart (term : STRING; num : Integer);
      BEGIN
        Writeln('The first ', num, ' letters are ', Copy(term, 1, num))
      END;

    BEGIN
      Write('Enter a word: ');
      Readln(aWord);
      Write('Enter a number from 1 to ', Length(aWord),': ');
      Readln(num);
      FirstPart(aWord, num)
    END.
```
(User response: QuickPascal, 5)

```
29. PROGRAM DisplayWeight;

    VAR thing  : STRING;
        weight : Integer;

    PROCEDURE HowHeavy (what : STRING; weight : INTEGER);
      BEGIN
        Writeln(what, ' weighs ', weight, ' tons')
      END;

    BEGIN
      Write('Object: ');
      Readln(thing);
      Write('Wt in tons: ');
      Readln(weight);
      HowHeavy(thing, weight)
    END.
```
(User response: The Statue of Liberty, 250)

```
30. PROGRAM Oxymoron;

    VAR aWord : STRING;

    PROCEDURE SayOxymoron (aWord : STRING);
      BEGIN
        Writeln('Un', aWord, 'ly ', aWord)
      END;

    BEGIN
      aWord := 'world';
      SayOxymoron(aWord)
    END.
```

31. PROGRAM Degree;

```
VAR age, years : Integer;
    major      : STRING;

PROCEDURE Graduation (num : Integer; letter : STRING);
  BEGIN
    Writeln('You will receive a B', letter, ' degree at age ', num)
  END;

BEGIN
  Write('How old are you? ');
  Readln(age);
  Write('In how many years will you graduate? ');
  Readln(years);
  Write('What type of major do you have (Arts or Sciences)? ');
  Readln(major);
  Graduation(age + years, Copy(major, 1, 1))
END.
```

(User response: 19, 3, and Arts)

32. PROGRAM Delicacy;

```
PROCEDURE What (num : Integer);
  BEGIN
    Write(num, ' blackbirds')
  END;

PROCEDURE HowMany (num : Integer);
  BEGIN
    What(num);
    Write(' baked in ')
  END;

BEGIN
  HowMany(24);
  Writeln('a pie.')
END.
```

33. PROGRAM Shakespeare;

```
PROCEDURE PrintWell;
  BEGIN
    Write(' well')
  END;

PROCEDURE PrintWords (words : STRING);
  BEGIN
    Write(words);
    PrintWell
  END;
```

```
    BEGIN
      Write('All''s');
      PrintWell;
      PrintWords(' that ends');
      Writeln('.')
    END.
```

34.
```
PROGRAM NestingDemo;

VAR radius : Real;

PROCEDURE AreaAndVol (radius : Real);
  PROCEDURE AreaCircle (radius : Real);
    BEGIN
      Writeln('Circle Area: ', Pi * radius * radius:5:1)
    END;
  PROCEDURE VolSphere (radius : Real);
    VAR radiusCubed : Real;
    BEGIN
      radiusCubed := radius * radius * radius;
      Writeln('Sphere Volume: ', ((4 / 3) * Pi * radiusCubed):5:1)
    END;
  BEGIN
    AreaCircle(radius);
    VolSphere(radius)
  END;

BEGIN
  radius := 3.5;
  AreaAndVol(radius)
END.
```

In Exercises 35 through 38, find the errors.

35.
```
PROGRAM Letters;

VAR n : Integer;

PROCEDURE Alphabet (n : Integer);
  BEGIN
    Writeln(Copy('abcdefghijklmnopqrstuvwxyz', 1, n))
  END;

BEGIN
  n := 5;
  Alphabet
END.
```

36. PROGRAM SaySeven;

```
VAR word    : STRING;
    number : Integer;

PROCEDURE Display (num : Integer; term : STRING);
BEGIN
  Writeln(num:7, term)
END;

BEGIN
  word := 'seven';
  number := 7;
  Display(word, number)
END.
```

37. PROGRAM LetterCount;

```
VAR who : STRING;

PROCEDURE LengthName (name : STRING);
  VAR name : STRING;
  BEGIN
    Writeln('Your name is ', Length(name), ' characters long.')
  END;

BEGIN
  Readln(who);
  LengthName(who)
END.
```

38. PROGRAM FamousSong;

```
VAR num : Integer;

PROCEDURE Tea4 (num : Integer);
  BEGIN
    Write('Tea for ', num, ' and ');
    Two4('tea')
  END;

PROCEDURE Two4 (drink : STRING);
  BEGIN
    Writeln('two for ', drink, '.')
  END;

BEGIN
  num := 2;
  Tea4(num)
END.
```

In Exercises 39 through 42, rewrite the program so that the output is performed by procedures.

39. PROGRAM ShowLuckyNum;

```
VAR num : Integer;

BEGIN
  num := 7;
  Writeln(num, ' is a lucky number.')
END.
```

40. PROGRAM GreetSomebody;

```
VAR name : STRING;

BEGIN
  name := 'Jack';
  Writeln('Hi, ', name)
END.
```

41. PROGRAM TreeInfo;

```
VAR tree   : STRING;
    height : Integer;

BEGIN
  Readln(height, tree);
  Writeln('The tallest ', tree, ' in the U.S. is ', height, ' feet.');
  Readln(height, tree);
  Writeln('The tallest ', tree, ' in the U.S. is ', height, ' feet.')
END.
```

42. PROGRAM PowerDemo;
```
  { NOTE: Write the procedure to perform the calculation and output the
          result }

VAR base, exponent : Real;

BEGIN
  Write('Enter a valid base and exponent: ');
  Readln(base, exponent);
  Writeln(base, ' to the ', exponent, ' is ',
          Exp(exponent * Ln(base)))
END.
```

In Exercises 43 through 46, write a program to produce the output shown. The last two lines of the output should be displayed by one or more procedures using data passed by variables.

43. [run]
```
According to a 1986 survey of college freshmen
taken by the Higher Educational Research Institute:

26 percent said that they intend to major in business
2 percent said that they intend to major in computer science
```

44. [run] (Assume the current date is 12/31/90.)
```
What is your year of birth? 1971
You are now 19 years old.
You have lived for more than 6935 days.
```

45. [run]
```
What is your favorite number? 7
The sum of your favorite number with itself is 14
The product of your favorite number with itself is 49
```

46. [run]
```
In the year 1986,
411,300 college students took a course in Spanish
275,300 college students took a course in French
```

47. Write a program to display verses of *Old McDonald Had a Farm*. The primary verse, with variables substituted for the animals and sounds, should be contained in a procedure; the animal and sound should be entered by the user. For example, if the user enters **lamb** and **baa**, the output should be

```
Old McDonald had a farm. Eyi eyi oh.
And on his farm he had a lamb. Eyi eyi oh.
With a baa baa here and a baa baa there.
Here a baa, there a baa, everywhere a baa baa.
Old McDonald had a farm. Eyi eyi oh.
```

48. Write a program to display the word WOW vertically in large letters. Each letter should be drawn in a procedure. For instance, the procedure for the letter W is shown below.

```
PROCEDURE DrawW;
{ Draw the letter W }
  BEGIN
    Writeln('**          **');
    Writeln(' **        **' );
    Writeln('  ** ** **' );
    Writeln('   **    **'  );
    Writeln
  END;
```

SOLUTIONS TO PRACTICE PROBLEMS 4.1

1. 1 2 3 4

After the procedure Second is called, execution continues with the remaining statements in the procedure First before returning to the main body of the program. (**Note:** This program would have produced a compiler error if the procedure First had been declared before the procedure Second.)

2. The arguments in the calling statement AgeIn2000(yob, name) have the same types as the parameters in the procedure AgeIn2000, but are in the wrong order. The calling statement should be changed to AgeIn2000(name, yob).

4.2 PROCEDURES (PASSING BY VALUE AND REFERENCE)

The previous section introduced the concept of a procedure, but left a major question unanswered. How do procedures pass values back to the statement part of the program?

Passing Values from Procedures Back to the Program

Suppose a variable, call it *arg*, appears as an argument in a procedure call and its corresponding parameter in the PROCEDURE declaration is *par*. After the procedure is executed, *arg* will have the same value it had originally.

EXAMPLE 1 The following program will lead to valuable insights into the passing of values to procedures.

```
PROGRAM DemoPassing;
{ Demonstrate that arguments retain their values after calls. }

USES Crt;

VAR amt : Integer;

PROCEDURE Triple (num : Integer);
  BEGIN
    num := 3 * num;
    Write(num:7)
  END;

BEGIN
  ClrScr;
  amt := 2;
  Write(amt);
  Triple(amt);
  Writeln(amt:7)
END.

[run]
2      6       2
```

Two memory locations are involved. Initially, the main program allocates a memory location to store the value of amt (Figure 4.1(a)). When the procedure is called, a temporary second memory location for the parameter num is set aside for the procedure's use and the value of amt is copied into this location. (Figure 4.1(b)). When the value of num is tripled, the value of num becomes 6 (Figure 4.1(c)). After the completion of the procedure, num's memory location disappears (Figure 4.1(d)). Since only the value in the procedure's memory location is tripled, the value of the variable amt in the main program remains the same.

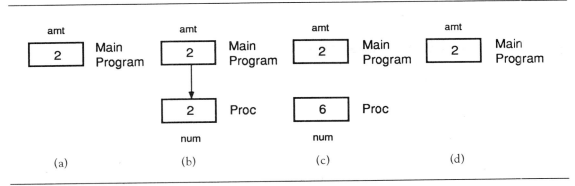

Figure 4.1   Passing a Variable to a Procedure by Value

The variable argument amt is said to be **passed by value**. When the procedure is exited, the memory location for num is released and the variable num is forgotten. Had the line Writeln(num) been added to the statement part of the program, a compiler error would have occurred.

The outcome of the program in Example 1 would be the same even if the parameter in the procedure also was named amt. There would still be two memory locations when the procedure was called, one for the argument amt and the other for the parameter amt.

Pascal provides an alternate way for parameters to interact with their corresponding argument variables. If the word VAR is placed before the parameter, then the corresponding argument will assume the value of the parameter after the procedure is exited. For instance, if the first line of the procedure Triple is changed to

```
PROCEDURE Triple (VAR num : Integer);
```

then the output of the program in Example 1 will be as follows.

```
[run]
2    6    6
```

Only one memory location is involved. Initially, the main program allocates a memory location to store the value of amt (Figure 4.2(a)). When the procedure is called, the parameter num becomes the procedure's name for this memory location. (Figure 4.2(b)). When the value of num is tripled, the value in this memory location becomes 6 (Figure 4.2(c)). After the completion of the procedure, the parameter num is forgotten; however, its value lives on in amt

(Figure 4.2(d)). The variable amt is said to be **passed by reference**. (**Note:** As with passing by value, naming the parameter amt produces the same result.)

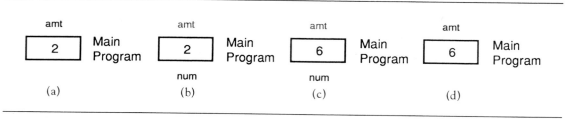

Figure 4.2   Passing a Variable to a Procedure by Reference

Passing by reference has a wide variety of uses. In Example 2, it is used as a vehicle to transport a value from a procedure back to the statement part of the program.

EXAMPLE 2   The following variation of Example 1 uses the procedure GetInput to acquire input. The variable amt is passed, with no preassigned value, for the sole purpose of carrying back a value from the procedure.

```
PROGRAM Demo;
{ Demonstrate that arguments can be altered by procedures. }

USES Crt;

VAR amt : Integer;

PROCEDURE GetInput (VAR num : Integer);
  BEGIN
    Write('Enter an integer: ');
    Readln(num)
  END;

PROCEDURE Triple (num : Integer);
  BEGIN
    num := 3 * num;
    Writeln(num)
  END;

BEGIN
  ClrScr;
  GetInput(amt);
  Triple(amt)
END.

[run]
Enter an integer: 5
15
```

EXAMPLE 3   The following variation of the Addition program of the previous section allows the statement part of the program to be written in the input-process-output style. The word VAR in the procedure InputNumbers applies to both num1 and num2.

```
PROGRAM SumNumbers;
{ This program requests two numbers and
  displays the two numbers and their sum. }

USES Crt;

VAR n1, n2, addition : Integer;

PROCEDURE InputNumbers (VAR num1, num2 : Integer);
{ Request two numbers as input from the user }
  BEGIN
    Write('Enter two numbers: ');
    Readln(num1, num2)
  END;

PROCEDURE CalculateSum (num1, num2 : Integer; VAR sum : Integer);
{ Add the values of num1 and num2 and assign the value to sum }
  BEGIN
    sum := num1 + num2
  END;

PROCEDURE DisplayResult (num1, num2, sum : Integer);
{ Display a sentence giving the two numbers and their sum }
  BEGIN
    Writeln;
    Writeln('The sum of ', num1, ' and ', num2, ' is ', sum)
  END;

BEGIN
  ClrScr;
  InputNumbers(n1, n2);
  CalculateSum(n1, n2, addition);
  DisplayResult(n1, n2, addition)
END.

[run]
Enter two numbers: 2  3

The sum of 2 and 3 is 5
```

Scope

The constants, variables, and procedures appearing in the declaration part of a program or procedure are said to be **declared** within the program or procedure. The parameters of a procedure also are said to be declared within the procedure.

Earlier we introduced the term "identifier" to refer to the name of a constant or variable. We now extend the meaning to include the names of procedures and parameters. An identifier is said to be **referenced** whenever it appears in the statement part of a program or procedure.

The scope rules for identifiers resolve questions such as the following:

1. Clearly, an identifier declared in a procedure can be referenced in that procedure. Where else can it be referenced?

2. Suppose the same identifier is declared in two different procedures. Is this legitimate? What happens when the identifier is referenced?

For purposes of stating the scope rules, we use the word "procedure" to refer to either the program or a procedure. The scope of an identifier is determined by the two scope rules:

1. An identifier can be referenced in any chain of nested procedures beginning with the procedure in which the identifier is declared.

2. The same identifier can be declared in two or more different procedures; Pascal regards them as distinct entities. Any referencing of the identifier applies to the closest declaration.

(**Note:** Of course, an identifier must be declared before it can be referenced.)

EXAMPLE 4 Consider the program outline below. Determine the procedures that can reference each of the following identifiers:

(a) r   (b) v   (c) t   (d) Two   (e) Four

```
PROGRAM IllustrateScope;

VAR r : Real;

PROCEDURE One (s : Real);
  VAR t : Real;
  PROCEDURE Two (u : Real);
    BEGIN
      Statement(s)
    END;
  PROCEDURE Three (v : Real);
    BEGIN
      Statement(s)
    END;
  BEGIN
    Statement(s)
  END;

PROCEDURE Four (w : Real);
  PROCEDURE Five (x : Real);
    BEGIN
      Statement(s)
    END;
  BEGIN
    Statement(s)
  END;
```

```
BEGIN
  Statement(s)
END.
```

SOLUTION   (a) The identifier r is declared by the program and therefore can be referenced by any procedure of the program.
(b) Procedure Three only.
(c) Procedures One, Two, and Three.
(d) Since procedure Two is declared in procedure One, it can be called by procedures One and Three. (It also can call itself, provided special precautions are taken. This is called recursion and is discussed in Section 12.4.)
(e) The statement part of the program. (Also, Four can call itself.) Since the declaration of procedure Four follows the statement part of procedure One, the note above tells us that procedure One cannot call procedure Four.

The identifiers declared in a procedure cease to have any meaning after the procedure is exited to the calling level. In a certain sense, they cease to exist. For this reason, the identifiers are said to be **local** to the procedure. For instance, in the program outline of Example 4, the identifiers t, Two, and Three are local to procedure One. Therefore, statements such as $t := 5.0$ or $One(5.0)$ cannot appear in the statement part of the program. The following example uses the concept of a local variable to demonstrate the consequences of the duplication of a variable name:

EXAMPLE 5   Determine the output of the following program:

```
PROGRAM DemoDuplication;
{ Demonstrate the scope of a variable appearing twice }

USES Crt;

VAR x : Integer;

PROCEDURE First;
  VAR x : Integer;
  BEGIN
    x := 1;
    Write(x)
  END;

BEGIN
  ClrScr;
  x := 2;
  First;
  Write(x:3)
END.
```

SOLUTION   The variable x declared in procedure First is local to that procedure. Pascal considers it to be a different entity from the other variable of the same name. From Pascal's viewpoint, their names might just as well be x_First and x_Program. Table 4.1 shows the variables referenced by each statement and the values of the variables after the statements are executed; therefore, the output of the program is:

```
[run]
1   2
```

Statement	Variable Referred To	x_First	x_Program
x := 2;	x_Program	undeclared	2
x := 1;	x_First	1	2
Write(x)	x_First	1	2
Write(x:3)	x_Program	undeclared	2

Table 4.1   Distinguishing Between Two Variables of the Same Name

Comments:

1. An argument passed by reference must be a variable and must be of the same type as the receiving parameter. Such is not the case for arguments passed by value. For instance, numeric expressions and Integer variables both can be passed by value to Real parameters; however, Real variables and literals can never be passed to Integer parameters.

2. Commas can be used to reduce the number of occurrences of the word VAR. For instance, the heading

```
PROCEDURE First (VAR x : Real; VAR y : Real);
```

can be abbreviated to

```
PROCEDURE First (VAR x, y : Real);
```

3. In addition to the reasons presented earlier, some other reasons for using procedures are:
   (a) Programs with procedures are easier to debug. Each procedure can be checked individually before being placed into the program.
   (b) The task performed by a procedure might be needed in another program. The procedure can be reused with some minor changes. Programmers refer to the collection of their most universal procedures as a **library** of procedures.
   (c) Often, programs are written by a team of programmers. After a problem has been broken into distinct and manageable tasks, each programmer is assigned a single procedure to write.
   (d) Procedures make large programs easier to understand. Some programming standards insist that the statement part of the program not exceed two pages. Similarly, each procedure should be at most two pages long.
   (e) Procedures permit the following program design, which provides a built-in outline of the program. A reader can focus on the main flow of the program first, and then go into the specifics of accomplishing the secondary tasks.

```
PROGRAM DEMO;
{ A program written entirely as procedures }

  BEGIN
    FirstProcedure;      { Perform first task }
    SecondProcedure;     { Perform second task }
    ThirdProcedure       { Perform third task }
  END.
```

4. Not all the variables referenced by a procedure are local to the procedure. For instance, a variable declared by the program itself can be referenced in any procedure without being passed. These nonlocal (global) variables should be used sparingly, if at all. Their use negates several of the advantages of procedures listed in Comment 3. The use of a nonlocal variable can lead to an unintended change in the value of the variable; such a change is called a **side effect**.

5. Constants and variables declared inside a procedure are always local to the procedure. Although they might have the same name as identifiers appearing in the main program, these names are treated as different while the procedure executes. They cease to exist after the procedure is exited.

6. Like variables, the parameters of a procedure can be displayed on separate lines. This style adds clarity when comments are included. For instance, the declaration

```
PROCEDURE ShowBalance (p, i : Real; n : Integer);
```

can be written in the style

```
PROCEDURE ShowBalance (p, i : Real;      { principal, interest }
                       n   : Integer);   { number of years }
```

7. Parameters to which values are passed by reference are known as **VAR parameters**, **variable parameters**, or **reference parameters**.

8. Arguments also are known as **actual parameters**.

PRACTICE PROBLEMS 4.2

1. What is the output of the following program?

```
PROGRAM Rhymer;

VAR a, b, c : Integer;

PROCEDURE Rhyme (VAR x : Integer; y : Integer);
  BEGIN
    Writeln(x, ' ', y, ' buckle my shoe.');
    x := 3;
    y := 4
  END;
```

```
BEGIN
  b := 1;
  c := 2;
  Rhyme(b, c);
  Writeln(b, c:2)
END.
```

2. What is the output of the following program?

```
PROGRAM SquareANumber;

VAR num : Integer;

PROCEDURE SquareIt (num : Integer);
  BEGIN
    num := num * num
  END;

BEGIN
  num := 5;
  SquareIt(num);
  Writeln(num)
END.
```

3. We know a parameter passed by value cannot pass a value back to its calling statement; however, when a variable is passed by reference, how do we know if its role is solely to transmit values to the procedure, pass a value back to the calling statement, or both?

EXERCISES 4.2

In Exercises 1 through 20, determine the output of the program.

1.
```
VAR num : Integer;

PROCEDURE AddTwo (VAR num : Integer);
  BEGIN
    num := num + 2
  END;

BEGIN
  num := 7;
  AddTwo(num);
  Writeln(num)
END.
```

2.
```
VAR term : STRING;

PROCEDURE Plural (VAR aWord : STRING);
  BEGIN
    aWord := aWord + 's'
  END;
```

```
      BEGIN
        term := 'auto';
        Plural(term);
        Writeln(term)
      END.
```

3. `VAR dance : STRING;`

```
      PROCEDURE Twice (VAR dance : STRING);
        BEGIN
          dance := dance + dance
        END;

      BEGIN
        dance := 'Can ';
        Twice(dance);
        Writeln(dance)
      END.
```

4. `VAR alphabet : STRING;`

```
      PROCEDURE CutInHalf(VAR alphabet : STRING);
        BEGIN
          alphabet := Copy(alphabet, 1, Length(alphabet) DIV 2)
        END;

      BEGIN
        alphabet := 'abcdefghijklmnopqrstuvwxyz';
        CutInHalf(alphabet);
        CutInHalf(alphabet);
        CutInHalf(alphabet);
        Writeln(alphabet)
      END.
```

5. `VAR a : Integer;`

```
      PROCEDURE Square (num : Integer);
        BEGIN
          num := num * num
        END;

      BEGIN
        a := 5;
        Square(a);
        Writeln(a)
      END.
```

6. `VAR state : STRING;`

```
      PROCEDURE Abbreviate (VAR a : STRING);
        BEGIN
          a := Copy(a, 1, 2)
        END;
```

```
   BEGIN
     state := 'WISCONSIN';
     Abbreviate(state);
     Writeln(state)
   END.
```

7. `VAR aWord : STRING;`

```
   PROCEDURE GetWord (VAR aWord : STRING);
     VAR temp : STRING;
     BEGIN
       temp := 'Sir Thomas More';
       temp := Copy(temp, Pos('M', temp), 4);
       aWord := temp
     END;

   BEGIN
     GetWord(aWord);
     Writeln('Less is ', aWord)
   END.
```

8. `VAR hourlyWage, annualWage : Real;`

```
   PROCEDURE CalculateAnnualWage (VAR hWage, aWage : Real);
     BEGIN
       aWage := 2080 * hWage
     END;

   BEGIN
     hourlyWage := 10;
     CalculateAnnualWage(hourlyWage, annualWage);
     Writeln('Approximate Annual Wage: ', annualWage:10:2)
   END.
```

9. `VAR name : STRING;`
`     yob  : Integer;`

```
   PROCEDURE InputVita (VAR name : STRING; VAR yob : Integer);
     BEGIN
       Write('Enter your name: ');
       Readln(name);
       Write('Enter your year of birth: ');
       Readln(yob)
     END;

   BEGIN
     InputVita(name, yob);
     Writeln(name, ' was born in the year ', yob)
   END.
```

(User response: Gabriel and 1980)

10.
```
VAR word1, word2 : STRING;

PROCEDURE Sentence (word1, word2 : STRING);
  BEGIN
    Writeln(word1, ' to ', word2)
  END;

PROCEDURE SwapStr (VAR word1, word2 : STRING);
  VAR temp : STRING;
  BEGIN
    temp := word1;
    word1 := word2;
    word2 := temp
  END;

BEGIN
  word1 := 'fail';
  word2 := 'plan';
  Write('If you ');
  Sentence(word1, word2);
  SwapStr(word1, word2);
  Write('then you ');
  Sentence(word1, word2)
END.
```

11.
```
VAR state : STRING;

PROCEDURE Team;
  VAR state : STRING;
  BEGIN
    state := 'Cleveland'
  END;

BEGIN
  state := 'Ohio';
  Team;
  Writeln(state, ' Buckeyes')
END.
```

12.
```
VAR number : Integer;

PROCEDURE Multiply (VAR num : Integer);
  BEGIN
    num := 11;
    Writeln(num * num)
  END;

BEGIN
  number := 5;
  Multiply(number);
  Writeln(number * 7)
END.
```

13.
```
VAR number : Integer;

    PROCEDURE Multiply (num : Integer);
      BEGIN
        num := 11;
        Writeln(num * num)
      END;

    BEGIN
      number := 5;
      Multiply(number);
      Writeln(number * 7)
    END.
```

14.
```
VAR name : STRING;

    PROCEDURE Hello (name : STRING);
      VAR temp : STRING;
      BEGIN
        temp := name;
        name := 'Bob';
        Writeln('Hello ', name, ' and ', temp)
      END;

    BEGIN
      name := 'Ray';
      Hello(name);
      Writeln(name)
    END.
```

15.
```
VAR num : Integer;

    PROCEDURE Amount (total : Integer);
      BEGIN
        total := total + 1;
        Writeln(total)
      END;

    BEGIN
      num := 0;
      Amount(num);
      Amount(num)
    END.
```

16.
```
VAR river : STRING;

    PROCEDURE Another;
      VAR river : STRING;
      BEGIN
        river := 'Yukon';
        Writeln(river)
      END;
```

```
    BEGIN
      river := 'Wabash';
      Another;
      Writeln(river);
      Another
    END.
```

17.
```
VAR explorer : STRING;

    PROCEDURE Place (name : STRING);
      BEGIN
        Writeln(name, ' discovered Florida')
      END;

    BEGIN
      explorer := 'de Leon';
      Place(explorer)
    END.
```

18.
```
VAR tax, price, total : Real;

    PROCEDURE InputPrice (item : STRING; VAR price : Real);
      BEGIN
        Write('What is the price of a ', item, '?  ');
        Readln(price)
      END;

    PROCEDURE ProcessItem (price, tax : Real; VAR total : Real);
      BEGIN
        total := (1 + tax) * price
      END;

    PROCEDURE DisplayResult (total : Real);
      BEGIN
        Write('With tax, the price is ', total:6:2)
      END;

    BEGIN
      tax := 0.05;
      InputPrice('bicycle', price);
      ProcessItem(price, tax, total);
      DisplayResult(total)
    END.
```
(Assume the cost of the bicycle is $200.)

19.
```
PROGRAM AddTwoNumbers;

    VAR num1, num2, total : Integer;

    PROCEDURE AddEm (num1, num2, total : Integer);
      BEGIN
        total := num1 + num2;
        Writeln(total)
      END;
```

```
    BEGIN
      num1 := 2;
      num2 := 5;
      total := 0;
      AddEm(num1, num2, total);
      Writeln(total)
    END.
```

20. `PROGRAM SatisfactoryProgress;`

```
    VAR num          : Integer;
        things, where : STRING;

    PROCEDURE Phrase1 (num : Integer; things, where : STRING);
      BEGIN
        num := num + num;
        where := ' forward';
        Writeln(num, things, where)
      END;

    PROCEDURE Phrase2 (num : Integer; things, where : STRING);
      BEGIN
        Writeln(num, things, where)
      END;

    BEGIN
      num := 1;
      things := ' steps';
      where := ' back';
      Phrase1(num, things, where);
      Phrase2(num, things, where)
    END.
```

In Exercises 21 and 22, find the errors.

21. `VAR var1, var2 : Integer;`

```
    PROCEDURE Sum (var1, var2 : Integer; VAR var3 : Real);
      BEGIN
        var3 := var1 + var2
      END;

    BEGIN
      var1 := 1;
      var2 := 2;
      Sum(var1, var2, var3);
      Writeln('The sum is', var3)
    END.
```

22.
```
VAR aWord : STRING;

    PROCEDURE Capitalize (VAR aWord : STRING);
      BEGIN
        aWord := UpCase(aWord[1]) + Copy(aWord, 2, Length(aWord))
      END;

    BEGIN
      aWord := 'january';
      Capitalize(aWord);
      Writeln(aWord);
      Capitalize('february');
      Writeln(aWord)
    END.
```

In Exercises 23 through 26, rewrite the program so that input, process, and output are each performed by procedures.

23.
```
{ Calculate sales tax }
VAR price, tax, cost : Real;

BEGIN
  Write('Enter the price of the item: ');
  Readln(price);
  tax := 0.05 * price;
  cost := price + tax;
  Writeln('Price: ', price:10:2);
  Writeln('Tax: ', tax:12:2);
  Writeln('      ----------');
  Writeln('Cost: ', cost:11:2)
END.
```

24.
```
{ Letter of acceptance }
VAR name, firstName : STRING;
    spacePos        : Integer;

BEGIN
  Write('What is your full name: ');
  Readln(name);
  spacePos := Pos(' ', name);
  firstName := Copy(name, 1, spacePos - 1);
  Writeln('Dear ', firstName, ',');
  Writeln('We are proud to accept you to Gotham College.')
END.
```

25.
```
{ Determine the area of a rectangle }
VAR length, width, area : Real;

BEGIN
  Write('Enter the length and width: ');
  Readln(length, width);
  area := length * width;
  Writeln('The area of the rectangle is ', area)
END.
```

26. ```
{ Convert feet and inches to centimeters }
VAR feet, inches, totalInches, centimeters : Real;

BEGIN
  Write('Give the length in feet and inches: ');
  Readln(feet, inches);
  totalInches := 12 * feet + inches;
  centimeters := 2.54 * totalInches;
  Writeln('The length in centimeters is ', centimeters)
END.
```

**In Exercises 27 through 32, write a program to perform the stated task. The input, processing, and output should be performed by procedures.**

**27.** Request a person's first name and last name as input and display his initials in uppercase separated by spaces.

**28.** Request the amount of a restaurant bill as input and display that amount, the tip (15 percent), and the total amount.

**29.** Request the cost and selling price of an item of merchandise as input and display the percentage markup. (**Note:** The percentage markup is ((selling price − cost) / cost) * 100. Test the program with a cost of $4 and a selling price of $6.)

**30.** Request the number of students in public colleges (8.2 million) and private colleges (2.5 million), and display the percentage of college students attending public colleges.

**31.** Request a baseball player's name, times at bat, and hits. Display his name and batting average. (Test the program with the data: Gwynn, 589,218.)

**32.** Request three numbers as input and then calculate and display the average of the three numbers.

---

SOLUTIONS TO PRACTICE PROBLEMS 4.2

**1.** [run]
```
1 2 buckle my shoe.
3 2
```

This program illustrates the difference between passing by value and passing by reference. The change to the value of *y* is not passed back to the variable *b* since VAR does not precede it in the procedure's parameter list.

**2.** 5. Again, since num is passed by value, changing its value in the procedure does not affect the value of num in the main program. Although they have the same name and initially have the same value, num in the procedure and num in the main program are stored in different memory locations.

**3.** One cannot determine this by simply looking at the arguments and the parameters. The code of the procedure must be examined.

---
```

4.3 USER-DEFINED FUNCTIONS

QuickPascal has many built-in functions. In some respects, functions are like miniature programs. They use input, they process the input, and they have output. Some functions we encountered earlier are listed in Table 4.2.

Function	Example	Input	Output
Round	Round(2.6) is 3	Real	Integer
Chr	Chr(65) is 'A'	Integer	Char
Length	Length ('perhaps') is 7	String	Integer
Copy	Copy ('perhaps', 4, 2) is 'ha'	String, Integer,Integer	String
Pos	Pos('b', 'to be') is 4	String, String	Integer

Table 4.2 Some QuickPascal Built-In Functions

Although the input can involve several values, <u>the output always consists of</u> a single value. The items inside the parentheses can be literals (as above), constants, variables, or expressions.

In addition to using built-in functions, we can define functions of our own. These new functions, called **user-defined functions**, are declared in much the same way as procedures and are used in the same way as built-in functions. Like built-in functions, user-defined functions have a single output of a specific data type. User-defined functions can be used in expressions in exactly the same way as built-in functions. Programs use them by referring to them as if they were constants, variables, or expressions.

An example of a user-defined function is:

```
FUNCTION FirstName (fullName : STRING) : STRING;
{ Extract the first name from a full name }
  VAR firstSpace : Integer;
  BEGIN
    firstSpace := Pos(' ', fullName);
    FirstName := Copy(fullName, 1, firstSpace - 1)
  END;
```

The parenthesis following the parameter list is followed by a colon and the type of the output. When this function is called, its variables are declared and the statement part of the function is executed. The value is assigned to the function FirstName by the statement

```
FirstName := Copy(fullName, 1, firstSpace - 1)
```

Functions can be declared anywhere a procedure can be declared. They look like procedures except that the word PROCEDURE is replaced by the word FUNCTION and the top line ends with a colon and a variable type. A typical form for a function is:

```
FUNCTION FunctionName (par1 : Type1; par2 : Type2) : Type;
  Declaration(s);
  BEGIN
    Statement(s);
    FunctionName := expression;
    Statement(s)
  END;
```

Arguments are passed to a parameter by value unless the parameter is preceded by the word VAR; however, functions rarely have VAR parameters. In those cases where a VAR parameter appears to be needed, the function probably should be replaced by a procedure.

Function names, like constant, variable, parameter, and procedure names, are identifiers; therefore, functions are subject to the same rules for acceptable names and scope as other identifiers. The declaration part of a function is identical to the declaration part of a procedure. It may declare constants, variables, procedures, and functions.

EXAMPLE 1   The following program uses the function FirstName.

```
PROGRAM GivenName;
{ Determine a person's first name }

USES Crt;

VAR name : STRING;

FUNCTION FirstName (name : STRING) : STRING;
{ Extract the first name from a full name }
  VAR firstSpace : Integer;
  BEGIN
    firstSpace := Pos(' ', name);
    FirstName := Copy(name, 1, firstSpace - 1)
  END;

BEGIN
  ClrScr;
  Write('Enter full name: ');
  Readln(name);
  Writeln('The first name is ', FirstName(name))
END.

[run]
Enter full name: Thomas Woodrow Wilson
The first name is Thomas
```

The input of a user-defined function can consist of one or more values. Two examples of functions with several parameters are shown below. One-letter variable names have been used so that the mathematical formulas will look familiar and be readable. Since the names are not descriptive, the meanings of these variables are carefully stated in the comment describing the function.

EXAMPLE 2 The following program uses the function Hypotenuse:

```
PROGRAM Triangle;
{ Calculate the length of the hypotenuse of a right triangle }

USES Crt;

VAR a, b : Real;

FUNCTION Hypotenuse (a, b : Real) : Real;
{ Calculate the hypotenuse of the right
  triangle having sides of lengths a and b }
  BEGIN
    Hypotenuse := Sqrt(Sqr(a) + Sqr(b))
  END;

BEGIN
  ClrScr;
  Write('Enter lengths of two sides of a right triangle: ');
  Readln(a, b);
  Writeln('The hypotenuse has length ', Hypotenuse(a, b):1:2)
END.

[run]
Enter lengths of two sides of a right triangle: 3  4
The hypotenuse has length 5.00
```

EXAMPLE 3 The following program uses the future value function. With the responses shown, the program computes the balance in a savings account when $100 is deposited for 5 years at 8 percent interest compounded quarterly. Interest is earned 4 times per year at the rate of 2 percent per interest period. There will be 4 * 5 or 20 interest periods.

```
PROGRAM Balance;
{ Find the future value of a bank deposit }

USES Crt;

VAR p,           { principal, the amount deposited }
    r  : Real;   { annual rate of interest }
    c,           { # of times interest compounded per year }
    n  : Integer; { # of years }
```

```
PROCEDURE InputData (VAR p, r : Real; VAR c, n : Integer);
  BEGIN
    Write('Amount of bank deposit: ');
    Readln(p);
    Write('Annual rate of interest: ');
    Readln(r);
    Write('Number of times interest compounded per year: ');
    Readln(c);
    Write('Number of years: ');
    Readln(n)
  END;

FUNCTION Power (b, p : Real) : Real;
{ Raise the base b to the exponent p }
  BEGIN
    Power := Exp(p * Ln(b))
  END;

FUNCTION FutureValue (p, r : Real; c, n : Integer) : Real;
{ Find the future value of a bank savings account }
  VAR i : Real;      { interest per period }
      m : Integer;   { number of times interest is compounded }
  BEGIN
    i := r / c;
    m := c * n;
    FutureValue := p * Power(1 + i, m)
  END;

PROCEDURE DisplayResult (p, r : Real; c, n : Integer);
  BEGIN
    Write('The balance is ', FutureValue(p, r, c, n):1:2)
  END;

BEGIN
  ClrScr;
  InputData(p, r, c, n);
  DisplayResult(p, r, c, n)
END.

[run]
Amount of bank deposit: 100
Annual rate of interest: 0.08
Number of times interest compounded per year: 4
Number of years: 5
The balance is 148.59
```

There are many reasons for employing user-defined functions.

1. User-defined functions are consistent with the modular approach to program design. Once we realize a particular function is needed, we can give it a name but save the task of figuring out the computational details until later.

2. Sometimes a single formula must be used several times in a program. Specifying the formula as a function saves repeated typing of the same formula, improves readability, and simplifies debugging.

3. Functions written for one program can be used in other programs. Programmers maintain a collection, or library, of frequently used functions.

Comments:

1. Functions can perform the same tasks as procedures. For instance, they can request data and display text; however, they are primarily used to calculate a single value. Normally, procedures are used to carry out several tasks.

2. Functions differ from procedures in the way they are accessed. Procedures are invoked with statements, whereas functions are invoked by placing them where you would otherwise expect to find a constant, variable, or expression.

3. The built-in function Sqr can return both Integer and Real values. For instance the statement Write(Sqr(2)) and Write(Sqr(2.0)) have the outputs 4 and 4.00000000000000E+0000, respectively. User-defined functions, however, always return the same type of value.

4. Functions, like procedures, need not have any parameters. The following program uses a "parameterless" function.

```
PROGRAM FavoriteSaying;
{ Request and display a saying }

USES Crt;

FUNCTION Saying : STRING;
{ Retrieve a saying from the user }
  BEGIN
    Write('Enter your favorite saying: ');
    Readln(Saying)
  END;

BEGIN
  ClrScr;
  Writeln(Saying)
END.

[run]
Enter your favorite saying: Less is more.
Less is more.
```

PRACTICE PROBLEMS 4.3

1. Why is the following function heading invalid?

```
FUNCTION Value (VAR num1 : Integer; num2 : Real);
```

2. What is the output of the following program, if the first response is 3 and the second response is 9?

```
PROGRAM GallonsOfAppleCider;

VAR gallonsPerBushel, apples : Integer;

PROCEDURE InputData (VAR gallonsPerBushel, apples : Integer);
  BEGIN
    Write('How many gallons of cider will 1 bushel of apples make? ');
    Readln(gallonsPerBushel);
    Write('How many bushels of apples do you have? ');
    Readln(apples)
  END;

FUNCTION Cider (g, x : Integer) : Integer;
  BEGIN
    Cider := g * x
  END;

PROCEDURE DisplayNumOfGallons (galPerBu, apples : Integer);
  BEGIN
    Writeln('You can make ', Cider(galPerBu, apples),
            ' gallons of cider.')
  END;

BEGIN
  InputData(gallonsPerBushel, apples);
  DisplayNumOfGallons(gallonsPerBushel, apples)
END.
```

EXERCISES 4.3

In Exercises 1 through 10, determine the output of the program.

1.
```
PROGRAM ConvertToLowCase;

VAR aWord : STRING;

FUNCTION DnCase (anyChar : Char) : Char;
  BEGIN
    DnCase := Chr(Ord(anyChar) + 32)
  END;

BEGIN
  aWord := 'PUP';
  aWord[1] := DnCase(aWord[1]);
  aWord[2] := DnCase(aWord[2]);
  aWord[3] := DnCase(aWord[3]);
  Writeln(aWord)
END.
```

2.
```
PROGRAM FahrenheitToCentigrade;
{ Convert Fahrenheit to centigrade }

VAR temp : Real;
```

```
FUNCTION FtoC (t : Real) : Real;
  BEGIN
    FtoC := (5 / 9) * (t - 32)
  END;

BEGIN
  Write('Temperature in Fahrenheit: ');
  Readln(temp);
  Writeln(FtoC(temp))
END.
```
(User response: 20)

3. PROGRAM CarPark;

```
VAR acres : Integer;

FUNCTION Cars (x : Integer) : Integer;
{ Parking cars }
  BEGIN
    Cars := 100 * x
  END;

BEGIN
  Write('How many acres is your parking lot? ');
  Readln(acres);
  Writeln('You can park about ', Cars(acres), ' cars.')
END.
```
(User response: 5)

4. PROGRAM BankAccount;
{ Rule of 72 }

```
VAR p : Integer;

FUNCTION DoublingTime (x : Integer) : Integer;
{ Estimate time required for a population to double
  at a growth rate of x percent }
  BEGIN
    DoublingTime := Round(72 / x)
  END;

BEGIN
  Write('Population growth as a percent: ');
  Readln(p);
  Writeln('The population will double in ', DoublingTime(p), ' years.')
END.
```
(User response: 3)

5. PROGRAM MaxHeight;
{ Calculate max. ht. of a ball thrown straight up in the air }

```
VAR initVel, initHt : Integer;
```

```
FUNCTION MaximumHeight (v, h : Integer) : Integer;
  BEGIN
    MaximumHeight := h + (v * v) DIV 64
  END;

BEGIN
  Write(
  'Enter the initial velocity (ft/sec) and height (ft) of ball: ');
  Readln(initVel, initHt);
  Writeln(MaximumHeight(initVel, initHt))
END.
```
(User response: 96 256)

6.
```
PROGRAM CylinderArea;

VAR r, h : Integer;

FUNCTION Area (r : Integer) : Real;
  BEGIN
    Area := Pi * r * r
  END;

PROCEDURE DisplayVolume (r, h : Integer);
  BEGIN
    Writeln('Volume of cylinder having base area ', Area(r):1:5,
            ' and height ', h, ' is ', (h * Area(r)):1:5)
  END;

BEGIN
  Write('What are the radius and the height? ');
  Readln(r, h);
  DisplayVolume(r, h);
  r := r * 2;
  h := h * 2;
  DisplayVolume(r, h)
END.
```
(User response: 1 2)

7.
```
PROGRAM Weekday;
{ Determine the day of the week from its number }

VAR days : STRING; { Will contain 3-letter abbreviations of weekdays }
    num  : Integer; { Day of week by number }

FUNCTION DayOfWeek (x : STRING; n : Integer): STRING;
  VAR position : Integer;
  BEGIN
    position := 3 * n - 2;    {Starting position of desired day in x}
    DayOfWeek := Copy(x, position, 3)
  END;
```

```
    BEGIN
      days := 'SunMonTueWedThuFriSat';
      Write('Enter the number of the day: ');
      Readln(num);
      Writeln('The day is ', DayOfWeek(days, num))
    END.
```
(User response: 4)

8. PROGRAM LocalVariableDemo;

```
    VAR aWord : STRING;

    FUNCTION TypeOfTrain : STRING;
      VAR aWord : STRING;
      BEGIN
        aWord := aWord + aWord;
        TypeOfTrain := aWord + 'train'
      END;

    BEGIN
      aWord := 'Choo ';
      Writeln(TypeOfTrain)
    END.
```

9. PROGRAM TripleNum;

```
    VAR num : Integer;

    FUNCTION Triple (x : Integer) : Integer;
      BEGIN
        Triple := 3 * x
      END;

    BEGIN
      num := 5;
      Writeln(Triple(num));
      Writeln(num)
    END.
```

10. VAR someWord : STRING;

```
    FUNCTION AddA (someWord : STRING) : STRING;
      BEGIN
        AddA := 'a' + someWord
      END;

    PROCEDURE Negative (someWord : STRING);
      BEGIN
        Writeln(someWord, ' has the negative ', AddA(someWord))
      END;
```

```
BEGIN
  someWord := 'moral';
  Negative(someWord);
  someWord := 'political';
  Negative(someWord)
END.
```

In Exercises 11 and 12, identify the errors.

11. `PROGRAM SelectGreeting;`

```
VAR answer : Integer;

FUNCTION Greeting (x : Integer);
  BEGIN
    Greeting := Copy('hellohi ya', 5 * x - 4, 5)
  END;

BEGIN
  Write('Enter 1 or 2: ');
  Readln(answer);
  Writeln(Greeting(answer))
END.
```

12. `PROGRAM DoubleLength;`

```
VAR aWord : STRING;

FUNCTION Twice (w : STRING) : STRING;
{ Compute twice the length of a String }
  BEGIN
    Twice := 2 * Length(w)
  END;

BEGIN
  Write('What is your favorite word? ');
  Readln(aWord);
  Write('When the word is written twice, ', Twice(aWord),
        ' letters are used.')
END.
```

In Exercises 13 through 18, construct user-defined functions to carry out the primary task(s) of the program.

13. To convert temperatures from centigrade to Fahrenheit, multiply the centigrade temperature by (9/5) and add 32. Write a program that requests a temperature in centigrade as input and gives the corresponding temperature in Fahrenheit.

14. According to Plato, a man should marry a woman whose age is half his age plus seven years. Write a program that requests a man's age as input and gives the ideal age of his wife.

15. Write a program that accepts a Real number m and a small positive Integer *n* as input and rounds *m* to *n* decimal places.

16. In order for exercise to be beneficial to the cardiovascular system, the heart rate (number of heart beats per minute) must exceed a value called the training heart rate, THR. A person's THR can be calculated from their age and resting heart rate (pulse when first awakening) as follows:

(a) Calculate the maximum heart rate as 220 – age.

(b) Subtract the resting heart rate from the maximum heart rate.

(c) Multiply the result in step (b) by 60 percent and then add the resting heart rate.

Write a program to request a person's age and resting heart rate as input and display their THR. (Test the program with an age of 20 and a resting heart rate of 70, then determine your training heart rate.)

17. The three ingredients for a serving of popcorn at a movie theater are popcorn, butter substitute, and a bucket. Write a program that requests the cost of these three items and the price of the serving as input and then displays the profit. (Test the program where popcorn costs 5 cents, butter substitute costs 2 cents, the bucket costs 25 cents, and the selling price is $2.)

18. Rewrite the population density program from Example 4 of Section 4.1 using a function to calculate the population density.

19. A function, Max(num1, num2), that returns the greater of its two arguments, can be defined in the following manner:

```
FUNCTION Max (num1, num2 : Integer) : Integer;
  BEGIN
    Max := (num1 + num2 + Abs(num1 - num2)) DIV 2
  END;
```

(a) Write another function, Min(num1, num2), that returns the lesser of its two arguments. (You may wish to use Max in your definition of Min.)

(b) Write a procedure, Order(num1, num2), that gives num1 the value Min(num1, num2) and gives num2 the value Max(num1, num2).

(c) Using Order, write a program that requests three Integers and then outputs them in order from smallest to largest.

SOLUTIONS TO PRACTICE PROBLEMS 4.3

1. The heading must specify the type of value returned by the function. For instance, a proper heading might be

```
FUNCTION Value (VAR num1 : Integer; num2 : Real) : Real;
```

The VAR parameter appearing in the heading is legal; however, its use is unusual since functions normally pass back only one value—the function value.

2. You can make 27 gallons of cider. In this program, the function was used by a procedure rather than by the main body.

4.4 MODULAR DESIGN

Top-Down Design

Large problems usually require large programs. One method programmers use to make a large problem more understandable is to divide it into smaller, less complex subproblems. Repeatedly using a "divide-and-conquer" approach to break up a large problem into smaller subproblems is called **stepwise refinement**. Stepwise refinement is part of a larger methodology of writing programs known as **top-down design**. Top-down design and structured programming emerged as techniques to enhance programming productivity. Their use leads to programs that are easier to read and maintain. They also produce programs containing fewer initial errors, and these errors are easier to find and correct. When such programs are later modified, there is a much smaller likelihood of introducing new errors.

The goal of top-down design is to break a problem into individual tasks, or modules, that can easily be transcribed into pseudocode, flowcharts, or a programming language. First, a problem is restated as several simpler problems depicted as modules. Any modules that remain too complex are broken down further. The process of refining modules continues until the smallest modules can be coded directly. Each stage of refinement adds a more complete specification of what tasks must be performed. The main idea in top-down design is to go from the general to the specific. This process of dividing and organizing a problem into tasks can be pictured using a top-down chart showing a hierarchy of the modules. The term top-down refers to the fact that the more general modules occur near the top of the design and modules representing their refinement occur below. When using top-down design, certain factors are important:

1. The design should be easily readable and emphasize small module size.

2. Modules proceed from general to specific as you read down the chart.

3. The modules, as much as possible, should be single-minded. That is, they should only perform a single, well-defined task.

4. Modules should be as independent of each other as possible, and any relationships among modules should be specified.

This process is illustrated with the following example.

EXAMPLE 1 Write a top-down chart for a program that gives certain information about a car loan. The amount of the loan, the duration (in years), and the interest rate should be input. The output should consist of the monthly payment and the amount of interest paid during the first month.

SOLUTION In the broadest sense, the program calls for obtaining the input, making calculations, and displaying the output. Figure 4.3 shows these tasks as the first row of a top-down chart.

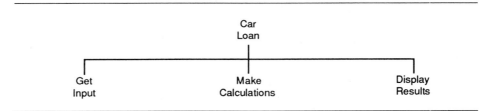

Figure 4.3 Beginning of a Top-Down Chart for the Car Loan Program

Each of these tasks can be refined into more specific subtasks. (See Figure 4.4 for the final top-down chart.) Most of the subtasks in the second row are straightforward and so do not require further refinement. For instance, the first month's interest is computed by multiplying the amount of the loan by one-twelfth of the annual rate of interest. The most complicated subtask, the computation of the monthly payment, has been broken down further. This task is carried out by applying a standard formula found in finance books; however, the formula requires the number of payments.

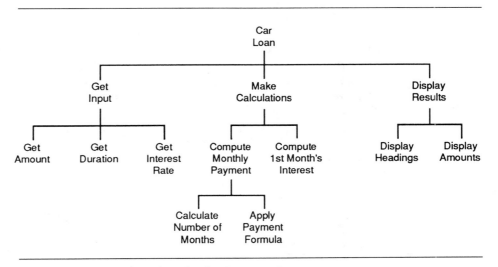

Figure 4.4 Top-Down Chart for the Car Loan Program

It is clear from the top-down chart that the top modules manipulate the modules beneath them. While the higher-level modules control the flow of the program, the lower-level modules do the actual work. By designing the top modules first, specific processing decisions can be delayed.

Structured Programming

A program is said to be **structured** if it meets modern standards of program design. Although there is no formal definition of the term *structured program*, computer scientists are in uniform agreement that such programs should have modular design and use only the three types of logical structures discussed in Chapter 2: sequence, decision, and looping.

Sequence: Statements are executed one after another.

Decision: One of two blocks of program code is executed based on a test for some condition.

Looping (iteration): One or more statements are executed as long as a specified condition is true.

Chapters 5 and 6 are devoted to decision and looping respectively.

One major shortcoming of the earliest programming languages was their reliance on the GOTO statement. This statement was used to branch (that is, jump) from one line of a program to another. It was common for a program to be composed of a convoluted tangle of branchings that produced confusing code referred to as *spaghetti code*. At the heart of structured programming is the assertion of E. W. Dijkstra that GOTO statements should be eliminated entirely since they lead to complex and confusing programs. Two Italians, C. Bohm and G. Jacopini, were able to prove that GOTO statements are not needed and that any program can be written using only the three types of logic structures discussed above.

Structured programming requires all programs to be written using sequence, decision, and looping. Nesting of such statements is allowed. All other logical constructs, such as GOTOs, are not allowed. The logic of a structured program can be pictured using a flowchart that flows smoothly from the top to the bottom without unstructured branching (GOTOs). The portion of a flowchart shown in Figure 4.5(a) contains the equivalent of a GOTO statement and, therefore, is not structured. A correctly structured version of the flowchart in which the logic flows from the top to the bottom appears in Figure 4.5(b).

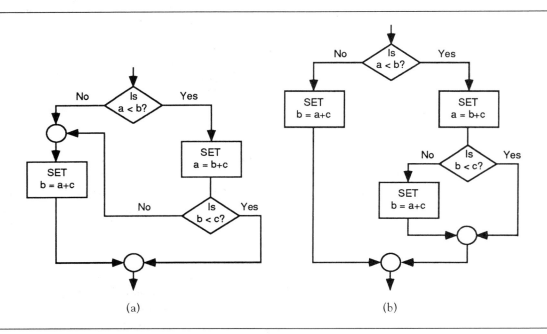

(a)   (b)

Figure 4.5   Flowcharts Illustrating the Removal of a GOTO Statement

Advantages of Structured Programming

The goal of structured programming is to create correct programs that are easy to write, understand, and change. Let us now take a closer look at the way modular design, along with a limited number of logical structures, contributes to attaining these goals.

1. *Easy to write*

   Modular design increases the programmer's productivity by allowing him or her to look at the big picture first and focus on the details later. During the actual coding, the programmer is working with a manageable chunk of the program and does not have to think about an entire complex program.

   Several programmers can work on a single large program, each taking responsibility for a specific module.

   Studies have shown structured programs require significantly less time to write than standard programs.

   Often, subprograms written for one program can be reused in other programs requiring the same task. Not only is time saved in writing the program, but reliability is enhanced since the subprogram will have already been tested and debugged. A subprogram that can be used in many programs is said to be **portable**.

2. *Easy to debug*

   Since each subprogram is specialized to perform just one task, a subprogram can be checked individually to determine its reliability. A dummy program, called a **driver**, is set up to test the actual subprogram. The driver contains the minimum definitions needed to call the subprogram to be tested. For instance, if the subprogram to be tested is a function, the driver program assigns diverse values to the arguments and then examines the corresponding function values. The arguments should contain both reasonable and unreasonable values.

   The QuickPascal editor facilitates testing by allowing a subprogram to be written and tested with a driver in a secondary window. When testing is complete, the driver can be erased and the subprogram merged into the program in the main window.

   The main module can be tested and debugged as it is being designed with a technique known as **stub programming**. In this technique, the main module and perhaps some of the smaller modules are coded first. Dummy modules, or stubs, are written for the remaining modules. Initially, a stub procedure might consist of a Writeln statement to indicate the procedure has been called, and thereby confirm that the procedure was called at the right time. Later, a stub might simply display values passed to it in order to confirm not only that the procedure was called, but also that it received the correct values from the calling procedure. A stub also can assign new values to one or more of its parameters to simulate either input statements or computations. This provides greater control of the conditions being tested. The stub procedure is always simpler than the actual procedure it represents. Although the stub program is only a skeleton of the final program, the program's structure can still be debugged and tested at this point.

Old-fashioned unstructured programs consist of a sequence of instructions that are not grouped for specific tasks. The logic of such a program can be cluttered with details and therefore difficult to follow. Needed tasks are easily left out and crucial details easily neglected. Tricky parts of the program cannot be isolated and examined. Bugs are difficult to locate since they might be present in any part of the program.

3. *Easy to understand*

The interconnections of the procedures reveal the modular design of the program.

The procedure names, along with relevant comments, identify the tasks performed by the modules.

The meaningful variable names help the programmer to recall the purpose of each variable.

4. *Easy to change*

Since a structured program is self-documenting, it can easily be deciphered by another programmer.

Modifying a structured program often amounts to inserting or altering a few subprograms rather than revising an entire complex program. The programmer does not even have to look at most of the program. This is in sharp contrast to the situation with unstructured programs that requires an understanding of the entire logic of the program before any changes can be made with confidence.

Object-Oriented Programming

In recent years, structured programming has seen some new developments. In an effort to increase program modularity, a powerful programming tool called an **object** has been introduced and implemented in several programming languages, including QuickPascal. Objects have both data and programming statements; as with subprograms, objects are used in a main program to maintain and manipulate these data in an organized manner; however, objects can take advantage of similarites occurring in dealing with data that procedures are forced to treat separately. This capability reduces the number of modules needed to complete a task and coincides with many of the ideals of structured programming discussed already. Objects are discussed in detail in Chapter 13.

Units

A **unit** is the compiled form of a collection of QuickPascal declarations and procedures. An application program that wants to use a precompiled unit simply adds the USES statement followed by the name of the unit immediately following the PROGRAM statement. This book contains many programs using the standard unit Crt.

Programmers can create their own units in QuickPascal. A unit resembles an ordinary program with the following exceptions:

1. Units begin with the keyword UNIT rather than PROGRAM. A unit is compiled just like any other QuickPascal program; however, a compiled unit has the file extension .QPU (rather than .EXE).

2. Units have a "public" section that begins with the keyword INTERFACE. This section contains USES, TYPE, CONST, and VAR declarations as well as forward references for functions and procedures that are defined later.

3. Units have a "private" section that begins with the keyword IMPLEMENTATION. This section contains definitions of every function or procedure whose forward reference is contained in the INTERFACE section. In addition, this section may contain new definitions of variables, types, and auxiliary procedures. The point is that all of this is hidden from the user of the unit.

Chapter 4
Summary

1. *Procedures* and *functions* are defined in the declaration part of a program and are accessed by the statement part or other procedures or functions. Collectively they are referred to as *subprograms*.

2. Procedures are defined in blocks beginning with the word PROCEDURE and look like minature programs. They are accessed by using the name of the procedure as a statement.

3. Functions are defined in blocks beginning with the word FUNCTION and look like minature programs. They can be used in any context where an expression might appear.

4. In any subprogram, the arguments appearing in the calling statement must match the parameters in the subprogram heading in number, type, and order. They need not match in name.

5. The parameters in a procedure or function heading are identified as either *value* or *reference* parameters. Reference parameters are preceded with the word VAR and pass their value back to the corresponding argument variable when the procedure or function terminates.

6. A variable declared in a procedure or function is *local* to the procedure. A variable with the same name appearing in another part of the program is treated as a different variable. Also, the values of these variables are not retained between calls.

7. Structured programming uses modular design to refine large problems into smaller subproblems. Programs are coded using the three logical structures of sequence, decision, and looping.

Chapter 4
Programming Projects

1. The numbers of calories per gram of carbohydrate, fat, and protein are 4, 9, and 4, respectively. Write a program that requests the nutritional content of a 1-ounce serving of food and displays the number of calories in the serving. The input and output should be handled by procedures and the calories computed by a function. The following output corresponds to a typical breakfast cereal.

```
[run]
Enter grams of carbohydrate: 24
Enter grams of fat: 1
Enter grams of protein: 1

The serving contains 109 calories.
```

2. Two million PCs were sold in 1987. Table 4.3 gives the market share for the three largest vendors. Write a program that displays the number of computers sold by each of the Big Three. The input and output should be handled by procedures and the number of computers calculated by a function.

Company	Market Share
Apple	20.2%
Compaq	15.4%
IBM	37.4%

Table 4.3   Market Shares of Leading PC Companies

3. Table 4.4 gives the percentages of workers with desk-top PCs in several industries. The figures for 1990 are projections. Write a program that displays the percentage growth for each occupational group. Procedures should be used for input and output and the percentage growth should be computed with a function. (**Note:** The percentage growth is 100 * ([1990 percentage] − [1985 percentage]) / [1985 percentage].)

Occupational Group	Percentage of Workers with Desk-Top Computers	
	1985	1990
Technical	55.9%	76.2%
Managerial	36.5%	64.4%
Professional	39.2%	63.7%
Armed Forces	20.3%	40.0%

Table 4.4   Computers in the Work Force

4. A fast-food vendor sells pizza slices ($1.25), fries ($1.00), and soft drinks ($.75). Write a program to compute a customer's bill. The program should request the quantity of each item ordered in a procedure, calculate the total cost with a function, and use a procedure to display an itemized bill. A sample output is shown in Figure 4.6.

```
[run]
How many pizza slices? 3
How many fries? 4
How many soft drinks? 5
```

Item	Quantity	Price
pizza slices	3	$ 3.75
fries	4	$ 4.00
soft drinks	5	$ 3.75
Total		$11.50

Figure 4.6 Sample Output of Programming Project 4

5. Some metals are easier to heat than others. The *specific capacity* of a metal (for instance, aluminum has a specific capacity = 0.217) can be used to calculate the amount of heat needed to raise the temperature of a metal object by a certain amount. If m is the mass of an object, c is the specific capacity of the metal, and the initial and final temperatures are $T1$ and $T2$ (respectively), then the heat, Q, required to raise the object from $T1$ to $T2$ is given by

$$Q = m * c * (T2 - T1)$$

Write a program that requests the values of m, $T1$, and $T2$ and calculates the amount of heat required to raise an aluminum object of mass m from $T1$ to $T2$. Use a procedure to obtain the input and a function to compute Q.

5

Selection Structures

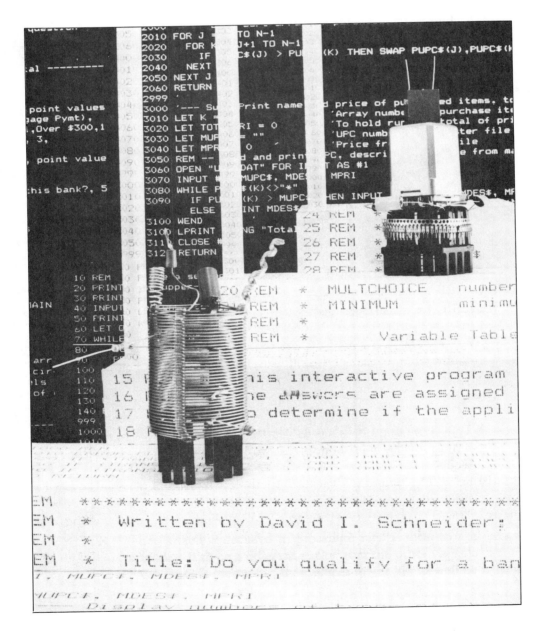

5.1   RELATIONAL AND LOGICAL OPERATORS

A **condition** is an expression involving relational operators (such as < and =) that is either true or false when evaluated. Conditions also may incorporate logical operators (such as AND, OR, and NOT).

The relational operator *less than* (<) can be applied to numbers, strings, and characters. The number a is said to be less than the number b if a lies to the left of b on the number line. For instance, $2 < 5$, $-5 < -2$, and $0 < 3.5$.

The string a is said to be less than the string b if a precedes b when using the ASCII table to alphabetize their values. For instance, 'c' < 'dog', 'cat' < 'dog', 'cart' < 'cat', and 'cat' < 'catalog'. The ASCII table in Appendix A shows the order of individual characters. Digits precede uppercase letters, which precede lowercase letters. Two strings are compared working from left to right, character by character, to determine which one should precede the other. Therefore, '9W' < 'bat', 'Dog' < 'cat', and 'Sales-89' < 'Sales-retail'. For purposes of comparison, characters are regarded as strings of length 1.

Table 5.1 shows the different mathematical relational operators, their representations in Pascal, and their meanings.

Mathematical Notation	Pascal Notation	Numeric Meaning	String or Character Meaning
=	=	equal to	identical to
≠	<>	unequal to	different from
<	<	less than	precedes alphabetically
>	>	greater than	follows alphabetically
≤	<=	less than or equal to	precedes alphabetically or is identical to
≥	>=	greater than or equal to	follows alphabetically or is identical to

Table 5.1   Relational Operators

EXAMPLE 1   Determine whether each of the following conditions is true or false.

(a) 1 <= 1   (c) 'car' < 'cat'
(b) 1 < 1   (d) 'Cat' < 'cat'

SOLUTION
(a) True. The notation <= means "less than *or* equal to." That is, the condition is true provided at least one of the two circumstances holds. The second one (equal to) holds.

(b) False. The notation < means "strictly less than" and no number can be strictly less than itself.

(c) True. The characters of the string are compared one at a time working from left to right. Since the first two match, the third character decides the order.

(d) True. The first character of 'Cat' precedes the first character of 'cat' in the ASCII table.

Conditions also can involve variables, numeric operators, and functions. To determine whether a condition is true or false, first compute the numerical values and then decide if the resulting assertion is true or false.

EXAMPLE 2   Suppose the values of a, b, c, and d are 4, 3, 'hello', and 'bye', respectively. Are the following conditions true or false?

(a) $(a + b) < (2 * a)$
(b) $(\text{Length}(c) - b) = (a / 2)$
(c) $c < ('good' + d)$

SOLUTION   (a) The value of $a + b$ is 7 and the value of $2 * a$ is 8. Since $7 < 8$, the condition is true.
(b) True, since the value of Length$(c) - b$ is 2, the same as $(a / 2)$.
(c) The condition 'hello' < 'goodbye' is false since h follows g in the ASCII table.

Logical Operators

Programming situations often require more complex conditions than those considered so far. For instance, suppose we would like to state that the value of an integer variable, n, is strictly between 2 and 5. The proper Pascal statement is:

$$(2 < n) \text{ AND } (n < 5)$$

The condition $(2 < n)$ AND $(n < 5)$ is a combination of the two conditions $2 < n$ and $n < 5$ with the logical operator AND.

The three main logical operators are AND, OR, and NOT. If *cond1* and *cond2* are conditions, then the condition

```
cond1 AND cond2
```

is true if both *cond1* and *cond2* are true. Otherwise, it is false. The condition

```
cond1 OR cond2
```

is true if either *cond1* or *cond2* (or both) is true. Otherwise, it is false. The condition

```
NOT cond1
```

is true if *cond1* is false, and is false if *cond1* is true.

EXAMPLE 3   Suppose n has the value 4 and *ans* has the value 'Y'. Determine whether each of the following conditions is true or false.

(a) $(2 < n)$ AND $(n < 6)$
(b) $(2 < n)$ OR $(n = 6)$
(c) NOT $(n < 6)$
(d) $(ans = 'Y')$ OR $(ans = 'y')$

(e) (ans = 'Y') AND (ans = 'y')
(f) NOT (ans = 'y')
(g) ((2 < n) AND (n = 5 + 1)) OR (ans = 'No')
(h) ((n = 2) AND (n = 7)) OR (ans = 'Y')
(i) (n = 2) AND ((n = 7) OR (ans = 'Y'))

SOLUTION
(a) True, since the conditions (2 < 4) and (4 < 6) are both true.
(b) True, since the condition (2 < 4) is true. The fact that the condition (4 = 6) is false does not affect the conclusion. The only requirement is that at least one of the two conditions must be true.
(c) False, since (4 < 6) is true.
(d) True, since the first condition becomes ('Y' = 'Y') when the value of ans is substituted for ans.
(e) False, since the second condition is false. Actually, this compound condition is false for every value of ans.
(f) True, since ('Y' = 'y') is false.
(g) False. In this logical expression, the compound condition ((2 < n) AND (n = 5 + 1)) and the simple condition (ans = 'No') are joined by the logical operator OR. Since both of these conditions are false, the total condition is false.
(h) True, since this second clause is true.
(i) False. Comparing (h) and (i) shows the necessity of using parentheses to specify the intended grouping.

Boolean Type

In addition to the four data types presented so far (Integer, Real, Char, and String), QuickPascal has a fifth data type called Boolean. The Boolean type has two possible values: True and False. In addition, the values of conditions are considered to have the type Boolean. Hence, statements such as Writeln(x < y) display the value TRUE or FALSE. Table 5.2 shows the parallels between the Booleans and Integers.

	Type Integer	Type Boolean
Possible values	. . . −2, −1, 0, 1, 2 . . .	False, True
Constant declaration	CONST MoonWalk = 1969;	CONST Whatever = True;
Variable declaration	VAR i1, i2 : Integer;	VAR b1, b2 : Boolean;
Order	1 < 2, etc.	False < True
Operators	+, −, *, DIV, MOD	AND, OR, NOT
	<, >, =, <=, >=	<, >, =, <=, >=
Variable assignments		
Simple	i1 := 3;	b1 := False;
Complex	i2 := i1 * 5 + 4;	b2 := b1 AND (i2 > 3);

Table 5.2 Parallels Between Integer and Boolean Types

If *v1* and *v2* are Boolean values, then *v1* AND *v2*, *v1* OR *v2*, and NOT *v1* are as expected. For instance, *v1* AND *v2* has the value True if both *v1* and *v2* have the value True. Otherwise, it has the value False. Therefore, in the last expression in Table 5.2, if *b1* has the value False and *i2* has the value 19, then (*i2* > 3) has the value True and *b1* AND (*i2* > 3) has the value False.

EXAMPLE 4   The following program demonstrates a use of the Boolean type.

```
PROGRAM ExactFactor;
{ Determines whether either of two nonzero numbers
  divides the other exactly }

USES Crt;

VAR a, b     : Integer;
    divisors : Boolean;

FUNCTION Divides (a, b : Integer) : Boolean;
{ Returns the value True if a divides b exactly
  and False otherwise }
  BEGIN
    Divides := (b MOD a = 0)
  END;

BEGIN
  ClrScr;
  Write('Enter two nonzero integers: ');
  Readln(a, b);
  divisors := Divides(a, b) OR Divides(b, a);
  Writeln;
  Writeln(a, ' divides ', b, ' OR ', b, ' divides ', a);
  Writeln('is a ', divisors, ' statement.')
END.

[run]
Enter two nonzero integers: 7  35

7 divides 35 OR 35 divides 7
is a TRUE statement.
```

Comments:

1. A condition involving numeric variables is different from an algebraic result. The assertion (*a* + *b*) < (2 * *a*), considered in Example 2, is not a valid algebraic result since it isn't true for all values of *a* and *b*; however, when encountered in a Pascal program, it will be considered true if it is correct for the current values of the variables.

2. The expressions considered in this section are called **Boolean expressions** since their values are of Boolean type.

3. QuickPascal has several built-in Boolean functions, that is, functions that return True or False. A useful one is Odd(x), which tells if the integer x is an odd number. For instance, Odd(5) is True and Odd(6) is False.

4. Readln statements cannot be used to assign values to Boolean variables.

5. The Boolean constants True and False are different from the string literals 'True' and 'False'.

6. A condition such as $2 < n < 5$ will generate a compiler error. The correct condition is $(2 < n)$ AND $(n < 5)$.

7. A common error is to replace the condition NOT $(2 < 3)$ by the condition $(3 > 2)$. The correct form is $(3 >= 2)$.

8. Parentheses determine the order in which the different operations (arithmetic, relational, and logical) are carried out during the evaluation of an expression. In the absence of parentheses, Pascal uses an operator hierarchy. First, NOT is evaluated. Then the leftmost occurrence of *, /, DIV, MOD, or AND is evaluated, followed by the next one these operators, and so on. Next, the operators +, −, and OR, are evaluated working from left to right. Finally, the operators =, <>, <, <=, >, and >= are evaluated working from left to right. (See Table 5.3.) Most programmers do not rely on the hierarchy rules and use parentheses generously to make their programs easy to read.

( )	Inner to outer
NOT	
* / DIV MOD AND	Left to right in expression
+ − OR	Left to right in expression
= <> < <= > >=	Left to right in expression

Table 5.3   Level of Precedence for Expressions

9. When evaluating a compound condition of the form

```
cond1 AND cond2
```

QuickPascal first evaluates cond1 and, if it is false, regards the compound condition to be false. The condition cond2 is not evaluated. For instance, if the variables num and den have the values 1 and 0, respectively, the statement

```
okay := (den <> 0) AND (num / den <> 20)
```

will not cause a division-by-zero error.

10. Since most Real values are not stored exactly, comparisons of Real quantities can be unreliable. For instance, the Boolean expression Sqr(Sqrt(2)) = 2 is False and should be replaced by an expression such as Abs(Sqr(Sqrt(2)) − 2) < 0.0000001 to produce the desired result.

11. There is an additional relational operator, IN, relating to sets. It will be introduced in Chapter 7.3.

PRACTICE PROBLEMS 5.1

1. Is the condition ' Hello ' = 'Hello' True or False?

2. Complete Table 5.4.

cond1	cond2	cond1 AND cond2	cond1 OR cond2	NOT cond2
True	True	True		
True	False		True	
False	True			False
False	False			

Table 5.4 Truth Values of Logical Operators

EXERCISES 5.1

In Exercises 1 through 12, determine whether the condition is True or False. Assume $m = 2$ and $n = 3$.

1. $3 * m = 2 * n$

2. $(5 - m) * n < 7$

3. $n <= 3$

4. $m - n = n - m$

5. $m * (5 - 2) > 7$

6. $3E{-}02 < 0.01 * m$

7. $(m < n)$ OR $(n < m)$

8. $(m * m < n)$ OR NOT $(m * m < m)$

9. NOT $((m < n)$ AND $(m < (n + m)))$

10. NOT $(m < n)$ OR NOT $(m < (n + m))$

11. $((m = n)$ AND $(m * m < n * n))$ OR $((n < m)$ AND $(2 * m < n))$

12. $((m = n)$ OR NOT $(n < m))$ AND $((m < n)$ OR $(n = m + 1))$

In Exercises 13 through 24, determine whether the Boolean expression is valid or not. Assume m, n and k are integer variables and b is a Boolean variable. State the error in the expression if it is invalid.

13. $4 < m < 7$

14. $m + n <= 6$

15. $(m * k = n)$ OR b

16. b AND NOT $(n > k)$

17. $((n >= m + k)$ AND $b)$ OR $((2 * n) < m)$

18. $(n + k)$ OR NOT b

19. $(4 < m)$ AND $(m < 7)$

20. NOT $($NOT $((m + n) < k)$ AND $(2 * k > n)$ OR $b)$

21. NOT (n MOD m = (k OR b))

22. ((Sqrt(m) + k) <= n) OR b

23. b AND ((n * m) <= k) AND (2 * m > 6)

24. (6 * m = n) AND b OR NOT (b > k + m)

In Exercises 25 through 37, determine whether the condition is True or False.

25. '9W' <> '9w'

26. 'Inspector' < 'gadget'

27. 'Car' < 'Train'

28. 'J' >= 'J'

29. '99' > 'ninety-nine'

30. 'B' > '?'

31. ('Duck' < 'pig') AND ('pig' < 'big')

32. 'Duck' < 'Duck' + 'Duck'

33. NOT (('B' = 'b') OR ('Big' < 'big'))

34. NOT ('B' = 'b') AND NOT ('Big' < 'big')

35. (('Ant' < 'hill') AND ('mole' > 'hill')) OR NOT (NOT ('Ant' < 'hill') OR NOT ('Mole' > 'hill'))

36. NOT ('C' = UpCase('c')) OR True

37. ('A' >= 'a' + 'A') OR ('Bad' = 'Good') OR ('' > ' ')

In the Exercises 38 through 47, determine whether or not the two conditions are equivalent, that is, whether they will be True or False for exactly the same values of the variables appearing in them.

38. a <= b; (a < b) OR (a = b)

39. NOT (a < b); a > b

40. (a = b) AND (a < b); a <> b

41. NOT ((a = b) OR (a = c)); (a <> b) AND (a <> c)

42. (a < b) AND ((a > d) OR (a > e));
    ((a < b) AND (a > d)) OR ((a < b) AND (a > e))

43. NOT ((a = b + c) OR (a = b)); (a <> b) OR (a <> b + c)

44. (a < b + c) OR (a = b + c); NOT ((a > b) OR (a > c))

45. NOT (a >= b); (a <= b) OR NOT (a = b)

46. NOT (a >= b); (a <= b) AND NOT (a = b)

47. (a = b) AND ((b = c) OR (a = c)); (a = b) OR ((b = c) AND (a = c))

In Exercises 48 through 54, write a condition equivalent to the negation of the given condition. (For example, *a <> b* is equivalent to the negation of *a = b*.) In Exercises 53 and 54, *b1* and *b2* are Boolean variables.

48. a > b

49. (a = b) OR (a = d)

50. (a < b) AND (c <> d)

51. NOT ((a = b) OR (a > b))

52. (a <> ") AND (a < b) AND (Length(a) < 5)

53. (NOT b1) = (NOT b2)

54. b1 = (NOT b2)

55. *Implication: cond1* **implies** *cond2* if either *cond2* is True or *cond1* is False. Write a Boolean-valued function, *Implies*, that takes two Boolean values as arguments and has the value True if the first Boolean value implies the second.

56. Write a Boolean-valued function, Letter, that determines whether a value of type Char is a letter of the alphabet.

SOLUTIONS TO PRACTICE PROBLEMS 5.1

1. False. The first string has seven characters, whereas the second has five. Two strings must be 100 percent identical to be considered equal.

2.

cond1	cond2	cond1 AND cond2	cond1 OR cond2	NOT cond2
True	True	True	True	False
True	False	False	True	True
False	True	False	True	False
False	False	False	False	True

5.2 IF STATEMENTS

IF statements allow a program to decide on a course of action based on whether a certain condition is true or false. A statement of the form

```
IF condition THEN
    action1                  { IF clause }
ELSE
    action2                  { ELSE clause }
```

causes the program to take *action1* if *condition* is true and *action2* if *condition* is false. (An **action** can consist of either a single statement or, as we soon will see, several statements surrounded by BEGIN and END.) Note that *action1* is not followed by a semicolon.

After an action is taken, execution continues with the line after the IF statement. Figure 5.1 contains the pseudocode and flowchart for an IF statement.

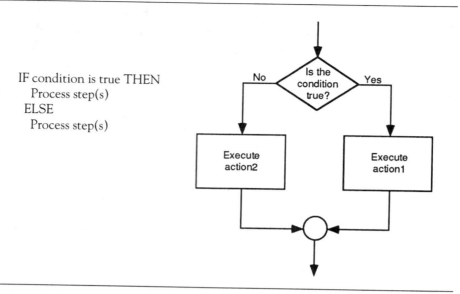

IF condition is true THEN
    Process step(s)
ELSE
    Process step(s)

Figure 5.1   Pseudocode and Flowchart for an IF Statement

EXAMPLE 1   Write a program to find the larger of two numbers input by the user.

SOLUTION   In the following program, the condition is num1 > num2 and each action consists of a single assignment statement. With the input 3 and 7, the condition is false and so the second action is taken.

```
PROGRAM LargerNumber;
{ Find the larger of two numbers }

USES Crt;

VAR num1, num2, bigger : Integer;

BEGIN
  ClrScr;
  Write('First number: ');
  Readln(num1);
  Write('Second number: ');
  Readln(num2);
  IF num1 > num2 THEN
      bigger := num1
    ELSE
      bigger := num2;
  Writeln('The larger number is ', bigger)
END.

[run]
First number: 3
Second number: 7
The larger number is 7
```

EXAMPLE 2 In 1990, social security taxes (FICA) are paid at the rate of 7.65 percent on the first $50,400 of earnings in a year. Write a program to calculate an employee's social security tax for a specific paycheck.

SOLUTION In the following program, the ELSE clause of the initial IF statement consists of another IF statement.

```pascal
PROGRAM SocialSecurityTax;
{ Calculate Social Security Tax }

USES Crt;

CONST TaxRate = 0.0765;
      MaxEarn = 50400;        {Annual maximum taxable earnings}

VAR yearToDateEarnings, currentEarnings : Real;

FUNCTION FICA (yearToDateEarnings,
               currentEarnings      : Real) : Real;
{ Calculate social security tax for a single pay period }
  BEGIN
    IF (yearToDateEarnings + currentEarnings < maxEarn) THEN
       FICA := TaxRate * currentEarnings
    ELSE
       IF yearToDateEarnings >= MaxEarn THEN
          FICA := 0
       ELSE
          FICA := TaxRate * (MaxEarn - yearToDateEarnings)
  END;

PROCEDURE GetWageInfo (VAR yearToDateEarnings,
                           currentEarnings    : Real);
{ Input two pieces of data needed to calculate FICA tax }
  BEGIN
    Writeln('Enter this year''s total earnings prior');
    Write('to the current pay period: ');
    Readln(yearToDateEarnings);
    Writeln;
    Write('Enter your earnings for the current pay period: ');
    Readln(currentEarnings)
  END;

BEGIN
  ClrScr;
  GetWageInfo(yearToDateEarnings, currentEarnings);
  Write('Your current social security tax is $',
        FICA(yearToDateEarnings,currentEarnings):1:2)
END.
```

```
[run]
Enter this year's total earnings prior
to the current pay period: 12345.67

Enter your earnings for the current pay period: 543.21
Your current social security tax is $41.56
```

Compound Statements

Pascal has a construct that allows an IF or ELSE clause to contain several statements. A **compound statement** consists of several statements preceeded with BEGIN and terminating with END. The statements between BEGIN and END are separated by semicolons and there is no period after END. The following program contains two compound statements.

EXAMPLE 3   Rewrite Example 1 so both the larger and the smaller of the two values are displayed.

```
PROGRAM OrderNumbers;
{ Order two numbers }

USES Crt;

VAR num1, num2, bigger, smaller : Integer;

BEGIN
  ClrScr;
  Write('First number: ');
  Readln(num1);
  Write('Second number: ');
  Readln(num2);
  IF num1 > num2 THEN
      BEGIN
        bigger := num1;
        smaller := num2
      END
    ELSE
      BEGIN
        bigger := num2;
        smaller := num1
      END;
  Writeln('The larger number is ', bigger);
  Writeln('The smaller number is ', smaller)
END.

[run]
First number: 3
Second number: 7
The larger number is 7
The smaller number is 3
```

EXAMPLE 4 The IF statement in the following program has a logical operator in its condition.

```
PROGRAM Quiz;

USES Crt;

VAR answer : Real;

BEGIN
  ClrScr;
  Write('How many gallons does a "ten-gallon" hat hold? ');
  Readln(answer);
  IF (answer > 0.5) AND (answer < 1.25) THEN
      Write('Good, ')
    ELSE
      Write('No, ');
  Writeln('it holds about 3/4 of a gallon.')
END.

[run]
How many gallons does a "ten-gallon" hat hold? 1
Good, it holds about 3/4 of a gallon.
```

The ELSE part of an IF statement can be omitted. In its absence, a false condition causes execution to continue with the statement after the IF statement. This important type of IF statement appears in the next example.

EXAMPLE 5 The following program offers assistance to the user before presenting a quotation.

```
PROGRAM Quotation;
{ Display a quotation with a possible preceding explanation }

USES Crt;

VAR answer : Char;

PROCEDURE ExplainSkittles;
{ Describe the game skittles }
  BEGIN
    Writeln('Skittles is an old form of bowling ',
            'in which a wooden');
    Writeln('disk is used to knock down ',
            'nine pins arranged in a square.');
    Writeln
  END;
```

```
BEGIN
  ClrScr;
  Write('Before we procede, ');
  Write('do you know what "skittles" is (Y/N)? ');
  Readln(answer);
  IF answer = 'N' THEN        { A semicolon is added since }
    ExplainSkittles;          { there is no ELSE clause }
  Write('Life ain''t all beer and skittles. ');
  Writeln('- Du Maurier (1894)')
END.
```

```
[run]
Before we proceed, do you know what "skittles" is (Y/N)? Y
Life ain't all beer and skittles. - Du Maurier (1894)
```

EXAMPLE 6   IF statements are useful in defining functions that are not determined by a formula. The function Sgn is used to identify values as either positive, negative or zero.

```
FUNCTION Sgn (num : Real) : Integer;
{ Sgn(+) is 1, Sgn(-) is -1, Sgn(0) is 0 }
  BEGIN
    IF num < 0.0 THEN
        Sgn := -1
      ELSE
        IF num > 0.0 THEN
            Sgn := 1
          ELSE
            Sgn := 0
  END;
```

Care should be taken to make IF statements easy to understand. For instance, in Figure 5.2, the statement on the left can be more clearly written as the statement on the right.

```
IF cond1 THEN              IF cond1 AND cond2 THEN
    IF cond2 THEN              action
        action
```

Figure 5.2   A Confusing IF Statement and an Improvement

Constructs in which an IF statement is contained inside another IF statement are referred to as **nested** IF statements. Interpreting nested IF statements requires care in pairing up each ELSE clause with the proper IF. In the statement in Figure 5.3(a), the ELSE corresponds to the second IF. (Pascal is not influenced by the programmer's attempt to use indentation to tie the ELSE to the first IF.) In general, when BEGIN and END enclosures are not used, the first ELSE is associated with the closest preceding IF and each subsequent ELSE is associated with the closest unassigned preceding IF. In Figure 5.3(b), BEGIN and END are used to associate the ELSE with the first IF. The statement shown in (c) shows the simplest way to rewrite the middle statement.

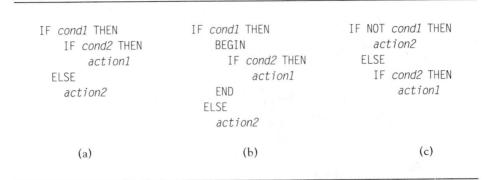

```
IF cond1 THEN              IF cond1 THEN              IF NOT cond1 THEN
    IF cond2 THEN              BEGIN                          action2
        action1                   IF cond2 THEN          ELSE
    ELSE                              action1                IF cond2 THEN
        action2                   END                            action1
                              ELSE
                                  action2

        (a)                       (b)                        (c)
```

Figure 5.3   Clarifying the Intent of a Nested IF Statement

The difficulty in Figure 5.3(a) arises because an IF statement appears as an IF clause. This situation should be avoided when possible. If unavoidable, the inner IF clause should be surrounded by BEGIN and END to improve readability or, as in this case, to correct the code by terminating the inner IF. (**Note:** IF statements used as ELSE clauses do not usually cause confusion.)

EXAMPLE 7   Rewrite the following IF statement in a clearer style.

```
IF cond1 THEN
    IF cond2 THEN
        action1
    ELSE
        action2
ELSE
    action3
```

SOLUTION   According to Pascal's rule for associating ELSEs with IFs, the first ELSE corresponds to the second IF and the second ELSE to the first IF; therefore, the statement is more clearly written as

```
IF cond1 THEN
    BEGIN
        IF cond2 THEN
            action1
        ELSE
            action2
    END
ELSE
    action3
```

The statement also can be written more compactly as

```
IF NOT cond1 THEN
    action3
  ELSE
    IF cond2 THEN
        action1
      ELSE
        action2
```

Comments:

1. The term "statement" refers to either a simple statement or a compound statement.

2. In IF statements, the use of multiple lines and indentation is solely for readabilty. Pascal doesn't even care if the IF statement of Example 1 is written

```
    IF num1
> num2 THEN bigger :=
num1 ELSE bigger := num2;
```

   However, a block form with indentation, such as that used in this text, is regarded as good programming style and should be used.

3. Some programs call for selecting among many possibilities. Although such tasks can be accomplished with complicated nested IF statements, the CASE statement (discussed in the next section) is a better alternative when it can be applied.

4. Semicolons should never precede nor follow the keywords THEN and ELSE.

PRACTICE PROBLEMS 5.2

1. Fill in the IF statement so that the program below either will display the message "Number can't be negative" or will display the square root of the number.

```
PROGRAM RobustSquareRoot;
{ Checks reasonableness of data. ("Robust" means error-resistant.) }

VAR num : Real;

BEGIN
  Write('Enter number of which to take square root: ');
  Readln(num);
  IF

END.
```

2. Improve the statement

```
IF a < b THEN
    IF c < 5 THEN
        Writeln('hello')
```

EXERCISES 5.2

In Exercises 1 through 14, determine the output of the program.

1. ```
VAR num : Integer;

BEGIN
  num := 4;
  IF num <= 9 THEN
      Writeln('Less than ten')
    ELSE
      IF num = 4 THEN
          Writeln('Equal to four')
END.
```

**2.** ```
VAR gpa : Real;

BEGIN
  Readln(gpa);
  IF gpa >= 3.5 THEN
      Write('Honors ');
  Writeln('Student')
END.
```
(User response: 3.59)

3. ```
VAR num : Integer;

BEGIN
  num := 5;
  IF 3 * num - 4 < 9 THEN
      Writeln('Remember, ');
  Writeln('Tomorrow is another day.')
END.
```

**4.** ```
VAR change :  Integer;     { Amount of change (in cents) }

BEGIN
  change := 356;
  IF change >= 100 THEN
      Writeln('The change contains ', change DIV 100, ' dollars.')
    ELSE
      Writeln('The change contains no dollars.')
END.
```

5.
```
VAR var1, var2, var3 : Integer;

BEGIN
  var1 := 2;
  var2 := 3;
  var3 := 5;
  IF var1 * var2 < var3 THEN
      var2 := 7
    ELSE
      var2 := var3 - var1;
  Writeln(var2)
END.
```

6.
```
VAR var1, var2 : Integer;

BEGIN
  Readln(var1, var2);
  IF var1 > var2 THEN
      var1 := var1 + 1
    ELSE
      var2 := var2 + 1;
  Writeln(var1, var2:var1 - 3)
END.
```
(User response: 7 11)

7.
```
PROGRAM LongDistance;
{ Cost of phone call from NY to LA }

VAR len : Real;

PROCEDURE InputLength (VAR len : Real);
{ Request the length of a phone call }
  BEGIN
    Write('What is the duration of the call in minutes? ');
    Readln(len)
  END;

FUNCTION Cost (len : Real) : Real;
  BEGIN
    IF len < 1 THEN
        Cost := 0.46
      ELSE
        Cost := 0.46 + (len - 1) * 0.36
  END;

PROCEDURE DisplayCost (len : Real);
{ Display the cost of a call }
  BEGIN
    Writeln('The cost of a call is $', Cost(len):1:2)
  END;
```

```
BEGIN
  InputLength(len);
  DisplayCost(len)
END.
```
(User response: 31)

8.
```
PROGRAM Alphabet;

VAR letter : Char;

PROCEDURE DisplayAmessage;
  BEGIN
    Writeln('A, my name is Alice.')
  END;

PROCEDURE DisplayBmessage;
  BEGIN
    Writeln('To be or not to be.')
  END;

PROCEDURE DisplayCmessage;
  BEGIN
    Writeln('Oh, say can you see.')
  END;

BEGIN
  Write('Enter A, B, or C: ');
  Readln(letter);
  IF letter = 'A' THEN
      DisplayAmessage
    ELSE
      IF letter = 'B' THEN
          DisplayBmessage
        ELSE
          IF letter = 'C' THEN
              DisplayCmessage
            ELSE
              Writeln('Not a valid letter')
END.
```
(User response: B)

9.
```
PROGRAM AnalyzeLetters;

VAR vowels : Integer;      { Number of vowels }
    aWord  : STRING;

PROCEDURE ExamineLetter (VAR vowels : Integer; c : Char);
  BEGIN
    IF (c='A') OR (c='E') OR (c='I') OR (c='O') OR (c='U') THEN
        vowels := vowels + 1
  END;
```

```
     BEGIN
       vowels := 0;
       aWord := 'OIL';
       ExamineLetter(vowels, aWord[1]);
       ExamineLetter(vowels, aWord[2]);
       ExamineLetter(vowels, aWord[3]);
       Writeln('The number of vowels is ', vowels)
     END.
```

10.
```
VAR num : Integer;

     BEGIN
       num := 5;
       IF (num > 2) AND ((num = 3) OR (num < 7)) THEN
           Writeln('Hi')
     END.
```

11.
```
VAR num : Integer;

     BEGIN
       num := 5;
       IF num < 0 THEN
           Writeln('negative')
         ELSE
           IF num = 0 THEN
               Writeln('zero')
             ELSE
               Writeln('positive')
     END.
```

12.
```
VAR message : STRING;
       age     : Integer;

     BEGIN
       message := 'You are eligible to vote';
       Write('Enter your age: ');
       Readln(age);
       IF age >= 18 THEN
           Writeln(message)
         ELSE
           Writeln(message, ' in ', 18 - age, ' years.')
     END.
```
(User response: 16)

13.
```
VAR b : Boolean;

     PROCEDURE DoIt (VAR b : Boolean);
       VAR myStr : STRING;
       BEGIN
         Readln(myStr);
         IF b THEN
             Writeln(myStr);
         b := NOT b
       END;
```

```
BEGIN
  b := True;
  DoIt(b);
  DoIt(b);
  DoIt(b)
END.
```
(Assume the responses are: One, Two, and Three)

14.
```
PROGRAM AllVowels;

VAR myWord : STRING;

PROCEDURE GetAWord (VAR anyWord : STRING);
  BEGIN
    Write('Enter a word: ');
    Readln(anyWord)
  END;

FUNCTION CheckWord (anyWord : STRING) : Boolean;
  BEGIN
    CheckWord := (Pos('a', anyWord) <> 0) AND
                 (Pos('e', anyWord) <> 0) AND
                 (Pos('i', anyWord) <> 0) AND
                 (Pos('o', anyWord) <> 0) AND
                 (Pos('u', anyWord) <> 0)
  END;

BEGIN
  GetAWord(myWord);
  IF CheckWord(myWord) THEN
      Writeln(myWord, ' contains all of the vowels.')
    ELSE
      Writeln(myWord, ' doesn''t have all of the vowels.')
END.
```
(User response: facetious)

In Exercises 15 through 22, identify the error in each program segment.

15.
```
num := 2;
IF (1 < num < 3) THEN
    Writeln('Number is between 1 and 3.')
```

16.
```
num := 6;
IF (num > 5 AND < 9) THEN
    Writeln('Yes')
  ELSE
    Writeln('No')
```

17.
```
IF major = 'Business' OR 'Computer Science' THEN
    Writeln('Yes')
```

18.
```
IF num1 <> num2 THEN
    Writeln('Numbers are not equal.');
  ELSE
    Writeln('Numbers are equal.');
```

19.
```
n := 'Seven';
Readln(num);
num := num + 1;
IF num < n THEN
    Writeln('Less than')
  ELSE
    Writeln('Greater than')
```

20.
```
{ Change switch from 'on' to 'off', or from 'off' to 'on' }
Readln(switch);
IF switch = 'off' THEN
    switch := 'on';
IF switch = 'on' THEN
    switch := 'off'
```

21.
```
{ Display 'OK' if either j or k equals 4 }
j := 4;
k := 3;
IF (j OR k = 4) THEN
    Writeln('OK')
```

22.
```
x := 0;
IF (x < 0) OR (1 / x > 5) THEN
    Writeln('x is in desired range.')
```

In Exercises 23 through 28, simplify the code.

23.
```
IF a = 2 THEN
    a := 3 + a
  ELSE
    a := 5
```

24.
```
IF NOT (answer <> 'y') THEN
    Writeln('YES')
  ELSE
    IF (answer = 'y') OR (answer = 'Y') THEN
        Writeln('YES')
```

25.
```
IF j = 7 THEN
    b := 1
  ELSE
    IF j <> 7 THEN
        b := 2
```

26.
```
IF a < b THEN
    IF b < c THEN
        Writeln(b, ' is between ', a, ' and ', c)
```

```
27. Write('Is Alaska bigger than Texas and California combined? ');
    Readln(answer);
    IF answer[1] = 'Y' THEN
        answer := 'YES';
    IF answer = 'YES' THEN
        Writeln('Correct' )
      ELSE
        Writeln('Wrong');
    answer := ''
```

```
28. Write('How tall (in ft.) is the Statue of Liberty? ');
    Readln(feet);
    IF feet <= 141 THEN
        Writeln('Nope');
    IF feet > 141 THEN
        IF feet < 161 THEN
            Writeln('Close')
          ELSE
            Writeln('Nope');
    Writeln('The Statue of Liberty is 151.08 ft from base to torch.')
```

In Exercises 29 through 40, write a Pascal expression for each paragraph. Assume j, k, m and n are integer variables, d and c are character variables, s and t are string variables, and b is a Boolean variable.

29. If j times 2 is greater than 7, then assign n plus 2 to m.

30. If s is not equal to 'carrot', output 'fruit'; otherwise assign 'vegetable' to t.

31. Assign the sum of j and k to n if m is greater than or equal to 5 or d is less than 'H'; otherwise assign False to b.

32. If m doubled is three times greater than j, then output s; otherwise if the sum of j and m is not a third of k, then output t.

33. If d is equal to '#' and b is False, then add 1 to j.

34. If d equals 'C' and t is greater than 'Andrew', then if j is less than half of n, assign 'Fred' to s; otherwise if j is greater than or equal to half of n, assign 'Bob' to s.

35. If j is greater than k, two times c is equal to m, and d is equal to 'L', then output c; otherwise output d.

36. If t is less than or equal to 'Red' and m is greater than half of n, then assign m plus 1 to n and output m; otherwise output n.

37. If the sum of j and m is greater than n and c equals d, then assign s to t and output c; otherwise assign j squared to n.

38. If b is False then output 'False'. If m is less than or equal to 6, then assign 5 to n and output c.

39. If *d* is greater than 'M', *m* is greater than 5, and *n* equals 7 then assign True to *b*; otherwise, if *n* is less than 7, then assign 8 to *n*.

40. If *c* does not equal 'R' and *j* is greater than twice *k*, then assign 'f' to *d* and output *d*; otherwise output *j* and add 1 to *k*.

41. Write a program to determine how much to tip the bartender in a fine restaurant. The tip should be 15 percent of the check with a minimum of $1.

42. Write a quiz program to ask "Who was the first Ronald McDonald?" The program should display "Correct" if the answer is Willard Scott and otherwise should display "Nice try."

43. A computer store sells diskettes at $1 each for small orders or at 70 cents apiece for orders of 25 diskettes or more. Write a program that requests the number of diskettes ordered and displays the total cost. (Test the program for purchases of 5, 1, 25, and 35 diskettes.)

44. A copying center charges 5 cents per copy for the first 100 copies and 3 cents per copy for each additional copy. Write a program that requests the number of copies as input and displays the total cost. (Test the program with the quantities 25 and 125.)

45. Write a program to handle a savings account withdrawal. The program should request the current balance and the amount of the withdrawal as input and then display the new balance. If the withdrawal is greater than the original balance, the program should display "Withdrawal denied." If the new balance is less than $150, the message "Balance below $150" should be displayed.

46. Write a program that requests three scores as input and displays the average of the two highest scores. The input and output should be handled by procedures and the average should be determined by a function.

47. A lottery drawing produces three digits. Write a program that requests the three digits as input and then displays "Lucky seven" if two or more of the digits are 7.

48. Federal law requires hourly employees be paid "time-and-a-half" for work in excess of 40 hours in a week. For example, if a person's hourly wage is $4 and he works 60 hours in a week, his gross pay should be

    $$(40 \times 4) + (1.5 \times 4 \times (60 - 40)) = 280.$$

    Write a program that requests as input the number of hours a person works in a given week and his hourly wage, and then displays his gross pay.

49. Write a program that requests a word (with lowercase letters) as input and translates the word into pig latin. The rules for translating a word into pig latin are:
    (a) If the word begins with a consonant, move the first letter to the end of the word and add *ay*. For instance, *chip* becomes *hipcay*.
    (b) If the word begins with a vowel, add *way* to the end of the word. For instance, *else* becomes *elseway*.

50. The current calendar, called the Gregorian calendar, was introduced in 1582. Every year divisible by 4 was declared to be a leap year with the exception of the years ending in 00 (that is, those divisible by 100) and not divisible by 400. For instance, the years 1600 and 2000 are leap years, but 1700, 1800, and 1900 are not. Write a program that requests a year as input and states whether or not it is a leap year. (Test the program on the years 1987, 1988, 1900, and 2000.)

51. The flowchart in Figure 5.4 calculates New Jersey state income tax. Write a program corresponding to the flowchart. (Test the program with taxable incomes of $15,000, $30,000, and $60,000.)

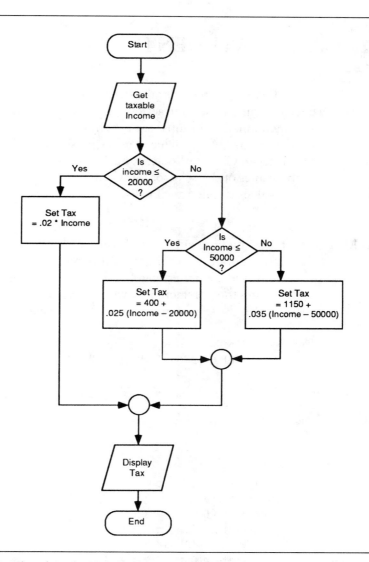

Figure 5.4 Flowchart for New Jersey State Income Tax Program

SOLUTIONS TO PRACTICE PROBLEMS 5.2

1. IF num < 0 THEN
       Writeln('Number can''t be negative.')
     ELSE
       Writeln(Sqrt(num))

2. The Writeln statement will be executed when a < b is True and c < 5 is also True. That is, it will be executed when both of these two conditions are True. The clearest way to write the IF statement is

IF (a < b) AND (c < 5) THEN
    Writeln('hello')

5.3 CASE STATEMENTS

A CASE statement is an efficient decision-making structure that simplifies choosing among several actions. It avoids complex nested IF constructs. IF statements make decisions based on the truth value of a condition; CASE choices are determined by the value of an expression called a **selector**, which can have type Integer, Char, or Boolean. Each of the possible actions is preceded by a set of the values of the selector for which the action should be taken. Each of the sets of values is called a **value list**.

EXAMPLE 1   The following program converts the finishing position in a horse race into a descriptive phrase. After the variable *position* is assigned a value by the Readln statement, the computer searches for the first value list containing that value and executes the statement following the colon. If the value of position is greater than 5, then the statement following ELSE is executed.

```
PROGRAM HorseRaceResults;
{ Describe finishing positions in a horse race. }

USES Crt;

VAR position : Integer;

BEGIN
  ClrScr;
  Write('Enter finishing position (1, 2, 3, etc.): ');
  Readln(position);
  CASE position OF
    1    : Writeln('Win');
    2    : Writeln('Place');
    3    : Writeln('Show');
    4, 5 : Writeln('You almost placed in the money.')
    ELSE   Writeln('Out of the money.')
  END
END.
```

```
[run]
Enter finishing position (1, 2, 3, etc.): 2
Place

[run]
Enter finishing position (1, 2, 3, etc.): 5
You almost placed in the money.
```

EXAMPLE 2   In the following program, the value lists specify ranges of values. The first value list provides another way to specify the numbers 1, 2, and 3. It is read "1 through 3." The second value list covers all numbers from 4 on.

```
PROGRAM HorseRace;
{ Describe finishing positions in a horse race. }

USES Crt;

VAR position : Integer;

BEGIN
  ClrScr;
  Write('Enter finishing position (1, 2, 3, etc.): ');
  Readln(position);
  CASE position OF
    1..3     : BEGIN
                  Writeln('In the money.');
                  Writeln('Congratulations.')
               END;
    4..MaxInt : Writeln('Not in the money.')
  END
END.

[run]
Enter finishing position (1, 2, 3, etc.): 4
Not in the money.
```

The general form of the CASE statement is

```
CASE selector OF
  valuelist1 : action1;
  valuelist2 : action2;


  valuelistn : actiom
  ELSE actionElse
END
```

where each value list contains one or more of the following types of items separated by commas:

1. A literal, that is, an Integer, character, or Boolean value (such as 5, 'X', or True)

2. A constant

3. An expression using literals, constants, and built-in functions, but not variables

4. A range expressed in the form x..y, where x and y are of the types given in 1 through 3 and in ascending order.

Different items appearing in the same list must be separated by commas. The actions are often compound statements, as in the first case of the preceding example. After the selector is evaluated, the computer looks for the first value list item containing the value of the selector and carries out its associated statement. Figure 5.5 contains the flowchart for a CASE statement. The pseudocode for a CASE statement is the same as for the equivalent IF statement.

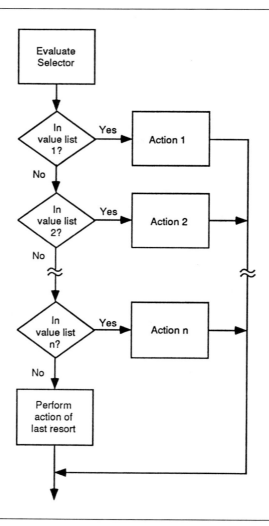

Figure 5.5   Flowchart for a CASE Statement

EXAMPLE 3 The following program illustrates several different types of value lists. With the response shown, the first action was selected because the value of Y − X is 1.

```
PROGRAM NurseryRhyme;
{ One, Two, Buckle My Shoe }

USES Crt;

CONST X = 2;
      Y = 3;

VAR num : Integer;

BEGIN
  ClrScr;
  Write('Enter a number from 1 to 10: ');
  Readln(num);
  CASE num OF
    Y - X, X         : Writeln('Buckle my shoe');
    3..4             : Writeln('Shut the door');
    (X + Y)..(X * Y) : Writeln('Pick up sticks');
    7, 8             : Writeln('Lay them straight')
    ELSE               Writeln('Start all over again')
  END
END.

[run]
Enter a number from 1 to 10: 1
Buckle my shoe
```

In each of the three preceding examples, the selector was a numeric variable; however, the selector can be a character or Boolean value as well.

EXAMPLE 4 The following program has the character variable *name* as a selector. A question is asked either four times or until the correct answer is given.

```
PROGRAM Quiz;

USES Crt;

VAR correct : Boolean;

PROCEDURE ShowChoices;
  BEGIN
    Writeln('What was President Wilson''s first name? ');
    Writeln('  (a) Woodrow');
    Writeln('  (b) President');
    Writeln('  (c) Thomas');
    Writeln('  (d) Other')
  END;
```

```
PROCEDURE GetResponse (VAR correct : Boolean);
{ If the correct answer has not been given, ask for a guess }
  VAR name : Char;
  BEGIN
    IF NOT correct THEN
        BEGIN
          Writeln;
          Write('Enter your response: ');
          Readln(name);
          CASE UpCase(name) OF
            'A' : Writeln('That was his middle name.');
            'B' : Writeln('Are you for real?');
            'C' : BEGIN
                    Writeln('Correct');
                    correct := True
                  END;
            'D' : Writeln('Nice try, but no cigar.')
            ELSE  Writeln('Not a letter from a to d.')
          END
        END
  END;

BEGIN
  ClrScr;
  ShowChoices;
  correct := False;
  GetResponse(correct);
  GetResponse(correct);
  GetResponse(correct);
  GetResponse(correct);
  IF NOT correct THEN
      Writeln('His full name was Thomas Woodrow Wilson.')
END.
```

EXAMPLE 5 The following program has a character value as selector. In the sample run, only the first action was carried out even though the value of the selector was in both of the first two value lists. The computer stops looking as soon as it finds the value of the selector.

```
PROGRAM CharacterType;
{ Analyze the first character of a string }

USES Crt;

VAR anyChar : Char;
```

```
BEGIN
  ClrScr;
  Write('Enter any string: ');
  Readln(anyChar);
  Write('The string begins with ');
  CASE UpCase(anyChar) OF
    'S', 'Z'    : Writeln('a sibilant.');
    'A'..'Z'    : Writeln('a nonsibilant.');
    '0'..'9'    : Writeln('a digit.');
    Chr(0)..'0' : BEGIN
                    Writeln('a character having ASCII');
                    Writeln('value less than 48 ',
                            '(e.g. +, &, #, or %).')
                  END
  END
END.

[run]
Enter any string: Sam Spade
The string begins with a sibilant.
```

EXAMPLE 6   CASE is useful in defining functions that are not determined by a formula. The following program assumes the current year is not a leap year.

```
PROGRAM MonthDays;
{ Determine the number of days in a month }

USES Crt;

VAR month : Integer;

PROCEDURE InputMonth (VAR month : Integer);
{ Request a number from 1 to 12 }
  BEGIN
    Write('Enter a month (1 - 12): ');
    Readln(month)
  END;

FUNCTION NumDays (month : Integer) : Integer;
{ Look up the number of days in a given season }
  BEGIN
    CASE month OF
      4, 6, 9, 11 : NumDays := 30;
      2           : NumDays := 28;
      1..12       : NumDays := 31
    END
  END;
```

```
BEGIN
  ClrScr;
  InputMonth(month);
  Writeln('Month #', month, ' has ', NumDays(month), ' days.')
END.
```

```
[run]
Enter a month (1 - 12): 10
Month #10 has 31 days.
```

Comments:

1. Some programming languages do not allow a value to appear in two different value lists; QuickPascal does. If a value appears in two different value lists, the action after the first value list will be carried out. If the value of the selector is not in any value list and there is no ELSE clause, no action will be taken.

2. The cases do not have to be indented; however, since indenting improves the readability of the statement, it is regarded as good programming style. As soon as you see the words CASE, your eyes can easily scan down the statement to find the matching END statement. You then immediately know the number of different value lists under consideration.

3. The value of b must be less than or equal to the value of c in a clause of the form $b..c$.

4. The notation $b..c$ indicates a range of values. In Section 7.1, this same notation is used to represent a user-defined data type known as a subrange type.

5. Every CASE statement can be replaced by an IF statement. CASE is preferable to an IF statement when there are many possible choices.

6. In a CASE statement, there is no semicolon following OF and preceding ELSE; and no colon following ELSE.

PRACTICE PROBLEMS 5.3

Suppose the selector of a CASE statement is the Integer variable num. Determine whether each of the following value lists is valid.

1. 1, 4, 2

2. 2, num * num

3. 2, 1..5

EXERCISES 5.3

In Exercises 1 through 8, determine the output of the program for each of the user responses shown below.

1. ```
VAR age, price : Real;

BEGIN
  Readln(age);
  CASE Trunc(age) OF
    0..5 : price := 0;
    6..17 : price := 3.75
    ELSE   price := 5.00
  END;
  Writeln(price:0:2)
END.
```
(User responses: 6.5; 17)

2. ```
VAR num : Integer;

BEGIN
  Readln(num);
  CASE num OF
    5    : Writeln('case 1');
    5..7 : Writeln('case 2');
    7..12 : Writeln('case 3')
  END
END.
```
(User responses: 7; 5; 11)

3. ```
VAR aWord : STRING;

BEGIN
  Readln(aWord);
  CASE aWord[1] OF
    'A'..'Z' : Writeln('Begins with an uppercase letter.');
    'a'..'z' : Writeln('Begins with a lowercase letter.')
    ELSE   Writeln('Does not begin with a letter.')
  END
END.
```
(User responses: apple; Zebra; ?anonymous? )

4. ```
VAR year : Integer;

PROCEDURE AskQuestion (VAR year : Integer);
  { Ask question and obtain answer }
  BEGIN
    Write('In what year was the ENIAC computer completed? ');
    Readln(year)
  END;
```

```
PROCEDURE ProcessAnswer (year : Integer);
  { Respond to answer }
  BEGIN
    CASE year OF
      1945      : Writeln('Correct');
      1943..1947 : Writeln('Close, 1945.');
      0..1943   :
        Writeln('Sorry, 1945. Work on the ENIAC began in June 1943.')
      ELSE       Writeln('No, 1945. By then IBM had built ',
                         'a stored program computer.')
    END
  END;

BEGIN
  AskQuestion(year);
  ProcessAnswer(year)
END.
```
(User responses: 1940; 1945; 1950)

5.
```
PROGRAM StateQuotation;

CONST Con = 3;

VAR num : Integer;

BEGIN
  Readln(num);
  CASE 2 * num - 1 OF
    Sqr(Con) : Writeln('Less is more.');
    Con + 2  : Writeln('Time keeps everything from ',
                       'happening at once.')
    ELSE       Writeln('The less things change, ',
                       'the more they remain the same.')
  END
END.
```
(User responses: 2; 3; 5)

6.
```
VAR whatever : Integer;

BEGIN
  Readln(whatever);
  CASE whatever OF
    7 : Writeln('lucky')
    ELSE  Writeln('Hi')
  END
END.
```
(User responses: 7; −1)

7.
```
VAR someNum : Integer;

BEGIN
  Readln(someNum);
  CASE someNum * someNum < 9 OF
    True  : Writeln('True.');
    False : Writeln('False.')
  END
END.
```
(User responses: 0; 3)

8.
```
PROGRAM BlueSuedeShoes;

VAR howMany : Integer;

BEGIN
  Readln(howMany);
  CASE howMany OF
    1 : Writeln('for the money..');
    2 : Writeln('for the show..');
    3 : Writeln('to get ready..')
    ELSE
      BEGIN
        Writeln;
        Writeln('Don''t step on my blue suede shoes')
      END
  END
END.
```
(User responses: 2; 5)

In Exercises 9 through 16, identify the errors.

9.
```
six := 6;
num := 2;
CASE num * num OF
  0..six : Writeln('Zero to six')
END
```

10.
```
CASE 5 OF
  3..10   : Writeln('Between 3 and 10');
  7..5, 6 : Writeln('Near 5')
END
```

11.
```
CASE num OF
  4              : Writeln('Near 5');
  3 <= num <= 10 : Writeln('Between 3 and 10')
END
```

12.
```
a := '1';
CASE a OF
  0..9 : Writeln('is a digit')
END
```

13.
```
word := 'hello';
CASE Copy(word, 1, 1) OF
  'h' : Writeln('Begins with h')
END
```

14.
```
Write('Enter a word from the United States motto: ');
Readln(word);
CASE word[1] OF
  'E'             : Writeln('This is the first word of the motto.');
  word[1] = 'P'   : Writeln('The second word is PLURIBUS.');
  ELSE            Writeln('The third word is UNUM.')
END
```

15.
```
num := 5;
CASE num OF
  5, 0..MaxInt : Writeln('Five');
  6..MaxInt    : Writeln('Greater than 5')
END
```

16.
```
CASE purchase OF
  0..99.95    : Writeln('Five dollars per item.');
  99.96..999  : Writeln('Four dollars per item.');
  1000..3000  : Writeln('Three dollars per item.')
END
```

In Exercises 17 through 22, suppose the selector of a CASE statement, *myChar*, is of type Char. Determine whether the value list is valid.

17. 'u'

18. UpCase('u'), 'V'

19. '0'..'9'

20. myChar <> 'N'

21. Ord(MyChar)

22. Copy('abc', 1, 1)

In Exercises 23 through 26, rewrite the code using CASE statements.

23.
```
IF num = 1 THEN
    Writeln('one')
ELSE
  IF num > 5 THEN
      Writeln('two')
```

24.
```
IF num < 5 THEN
    IF num = 9 THEN
        Writeln('yes')
    ELSE
        Writeln('no')
  ELSE
    IF num = 9 THEN
        Writeln('maybe')
```

25.
```
IF num = 1 THEN
  Writeln('lambs');
IF (num = 3) OR (num = 4) THEN
  Writeln('eat');
IF (num = 5) OR (num > 7) THEN
  Writeln('ivy')
```

26.
```
IF num = 3 THEN
  num := 1;
IF num = 2 THEN
  num := 3;
IF num = 1 THEN
  num := 2
```

27. Table 5.5 gives the terms used by the National Weather Service to describe the degree of cloudiness. Write a program that requests the percentage of cloud cover as input and then displays the appropriate descriptor.

Percentage of Cloud Cover	Descriptor
0-30	clear
31-70	partly cloudy
71-99	cloudy
100	overcast

Table 5.5 Cloudiness Descriptors

28. Table 5.6 shows the location of books in the library stacks according to their call numbers. Write a program that requests the call number of a book as input and displays the location of the book.

Call Numbers	Location
100 to 199	basement
200 to 500 and over 900	main floor
501 to 900 except 700 to 750	upper floor
700 to 750	archives

Table 5.6 Location of Library Books

29. Figure 5.6 shows some geometric shapes and formulas for their areas. Write a menu-driven program that asks the user to select one of the shapes (by giving the first letter of the shape), requests the appropriate lengths, and then gives the area of the figure. Input and output should be handled by procedures, and the areas should be computed by functions.

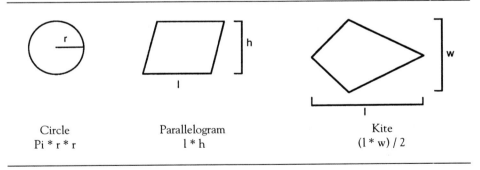

Circle	Parallelogram	Kite
Pi * r * r	l * h	(l * w) / 2

Figure 5.6 Areas of Geometric Shapes

30. Write an interactive program that requests an exam score and assigns a letter grade with the scale 90-100 (A), 80-89 (B), 70-79 (C), 60-69 (D), 0-59 (F). The input should be accomplished by a procedure and the computation carried out in a function. (Test the program with the grades 84, 100, and 57.)

31. IRS informants are paid cash awards based on the value of the money recovered. If the information was specific enough to lead to a recovery, the informant receives 10 percent of the first $75,000, 5 percent of the next

$25,000, and 1 percent of the remainder, up to a maximum award of $50,000. Write a program that requests the amount of the recovery as input (in thousands of dollars) and displays the award. (**Note:** The source of this formula is *The Book of Inside Information*; Boardroom Books, 1982; test the program on the amounts $10,000, $125,000, and $10,000,000.)

SOLUTIONS TO PRACTICE PROBLEMS 5.3

1. Valid. The elements of a value list do not need to be specified in order of magnitude.

2. Not valid. Items in a value list cannot be specified by variables; however, it would be valid if num were a constant.

3. Valid. These items are redundant since 2 is just a special case of 1..5; however, this makes no difference in QuickPascal.

5.4 A CASE STUDY: WEEKLY PAYROLL

This case study processes a weekly payroll. Table 5.7 shows typical data used by a company's payroll office. These data are processed to produce the information in Table 5.8 that is supplied to each employee along with his or her paycheck. The program should request the data from Table 5.7 for an individual as input and produce output similar to that in Table 5.8.

The items in Table 5.8 should be calculated as follows:

Current Earnings: Hourly wage times hours worked (with time and a half after 40 hours)

Year to Date Earnings: Previous year-to-date earnings plus current earnings

FICA Tax: 7.65 percent of first $50,400 of earnings

Federal Income Tax Withheld: Subtract $39.42 from the current earnings for each withholding exemption and use Table 5.9 or Table 5.10, depending on marital status

Check Amount: [Current earnings] − [FICA taxes] − [Income tax withheld]

Name	Hourly Wage	Hours Worked	Withholding Exemptions	Marital Status	Previous Year to Date Earnings
Al Johnson	26.25	38	4	MARRIED	$49,665.00
Ann Jones	14.00	35	3	MARRIED	$21,840.50
John Smith	7.95	50	1	SINGLE	$12,900.15
Sue Williams	27.50	43	2	SINGLE	$41,890.50

Table 5.7 Employee Data

Name	Current Earnings	Yr. to Date Earnings	FICA Taxes	Income Tax Wh.	Check Amount
Al Johnson	997.50	50662.50	56.23	135.83	805.44

Table 5.8 Payroll Information

Adjusted Weekly Income	Income Tax Withheld
$0 to $23	0
Over $23 to $397	15% of amount over $23
Over $397 to $928	$56.10 + 28% of amount over $397
Over $928 to $2121	$204.78 + 33% of amount over $928
Over $2121	$598.47 + 28% of amount over $2121

Table 5.9 1990 Federal Income Tax Withheld for a Single Person

Adjusted Weekly Income	Income Tax Withheld
$0 to $65	0
Over $65 to $689	15% of amount over $65
Over $689 to $1573	$93.60 + 28% of amount over $689
Over $1573 to $3858	$341.12 + 33% of amount over $1573
Over $3858	$1095.17 + 28% of amount over $3858

Table 5.10 1990 Federal Income Tax Withheld for a Married Person

Designing the Weekly Payroll Program

After the data for an employee has been requested as input, the program must compute the five items appearing in Table 5.8 and then display the payroll information. The five computations form the basic tasks of the program.

1. Compute current earnings.

2. Compute year-to-date earnings.

3. Compute FICA tax.

4. Compute Federal Income Tax withheld.

5. Compute paycheck amount (that is, take-home pay).

Tasks 1, 2, 3, and 5 are fairly simple. Each involves applying a formula to given data. (For instance, if hours worked is at most 40, then Current Earnings = Hourly Wage times Hours Worked.) Thus, we won't break these tasks down any further. Task 4 is more complicated, so we continue to divide it into smaller subtasks.

4. *Compute Federal Income Tax withheld.* First the employee's pay is adjusted for exemptions, and then the amount of income tax to be withheld is computed. The computation of the income tax withheld differs for married and single individuals. Task 4 is, therefore, divided into the following subtasks:

4.1 Compute pay adjusted by exemptions.
4.2 Compute income tax withheld for single employee.
4.3 Compute income tax withheld for married employee.

The top-down chart in Figure 5.7 shows the stepwise refinement of the problem.

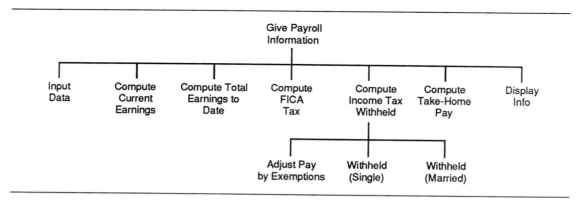

Figure 5.7 Top-Down Chart for the Weekly Payroll Program

Pseudocode for the Weekly Payroll Program

Get employee data (Procedure InputData)
COMPUTE CURRENT GROSS PAY (Procedure ComputePay)
COMPUTE TOTAL EARNINGS TO DATE (Procedure ComputeTotalPay)
COMPUTE FICA TAX (Procedure ComputeFICATax)
IF total pay <= 50400 THEN
   ficatax := .0765 * current gross pay
 ELSE
   ficatax := .0765 * (50400 – previous total earnings)
COMPUTE FEDERAL TAX (Procedure ComputeFedTax)
Adjust pay for exemptions
IF employee is single THEN
   COMPUTE INCOME TAX WITHHELD from adjusted pay using tax brackets for single taxpayers (Function TaxSingle)
 ELSE
   COMPUTE INCOME TAX WITHHELD using tax brackets for married taxpayers (Function TaxMarried)
COMPUTE CHECK (Procedure ComputeCheck)
Display payroll information (Procedure ShowInformation)

Writing the Weekly Payroll Program

The main module of the program calls a sequence of seven subprograms. Table 5.11 shows the tasks and the procedures and functions that perform the tasks.

Task	Subprogram
0. Read employee data.	ReadData
1. Compute current earnings.	ComputePay
2. Compute year-to-date earnings.	ComputeTotalPay
3. Compute FICA tax.	ComputeFICATax
4. Compute federal income tax withheld.	ComputeFedTax
4.1 Compute adjusted pay.	ComputeFedTax
4.2 Compute amount withheld for single employee.	TaxSingle
4.3 Compute amount withheld for married employee.	TaxMarried
5. Compute paycheck amounts.	ComputeCheck
6. Display payroll information.	ShowInformation

Table 5.11 Tasks and Their Subprograms

```
PROGRAM Payroll;
{ Program to compute employees' weekly payroll }

USES Crt;

VAR mStatus,             { Marital status (SINGLE or MARRIED) }
    name      : STRING; { Employee name }
    exemptions,          { Number of of exemptions }
    fedTax,              { Federal income tax withheld this week }
    ficaTax,             { Social Security tax for this week }
    hrsWorked,           { Hours worked this week }
    hrWage,              { Hourly wage }
    pay,                 { This week's pay before taxes }
    payCheck,            { Paycheck this week (take-home pay) }
    prevPay,             { Total pay for year excluding this week }
    totalPay   : Real;   { Total pay for year including this week }

PROCEDURE InputData (VAR name, mStatus     : STRING;
                     VAR hrWage, hrsWorked,
                         exemptions, prevPay : Real);
{ Get payroll data for employee }
  BEGIN
    Write('Name: ');
    Readln(name);
    Write('Hourly wage: ');
    Readln(hrWage);
    Write('Number of hours worked: ');
    Readln(hrsWorked);
    Write('Number of exemptions: ');
    Readln(exemptions);
    Write('Marital status SINGLE/MARRIED: ');
    Readln(mStatus);
    Write('Total pay prior to this week: ');
    Readln(prevPay)
  END;
```

```
PROCEDURE ComputePay (      hrWage,
                            hrsWorked : Real;
                       VAR pay       : Real);
{ Compute weekly pay before taxes }
  BEGIN
    IF hrsWorked <= 40 THEN
        pay := hrsWorked * hrWage
      ELSE
        pay := 40 * hrWage + (hrsWorked - 40) * 1.5 * hrWage
  END;

PROCEDURE ComputeTotalPay (     prevPay, pay : Real;
                           VAR totalPay      : Real);
{ Compute total pay before taxes }
  BEGIN
    totalPay := prevPay + pay
  END;

PROCEDURE ComputeFICATax (     pay, prevPay,
                               totalPay    : Real;
                          VAR ficaTax      : Real);
{ Compute social security tax }
  BEGIN
    IF totalPay <= 50400 THEN
        ficaTax := 0.0765 * pay
      ELSE
        IF prevPay < 50400 THEN
            ficaTax := 0.0765 * (50400 - prevPay)
          ELSE
            ficaTax := 0
  END;

PROCEDURE ComputeFedTax (     pay, exemptions : Real;
                              mStatus         : STRING;
                         VAR fedTax           : Real);
{ Compute federal tax }
  VAR withhold, adjPay : Real;
  FUNCTION TaxSingle (adjPay : Real) : Real;
  { Compute federal tax for single person based on adjusted pay }
    BEGIN { Function TaxSingle }
      { CASE does not work with Reals }
      CASE Trunc(adjPay) OF
        0..22     : TaxSingle := 0;
        23..396   : TaxSingle := 0.15 * (adjPay - 23);
        397..927  : TaxSingle := 56.10 + 0.28 * (adjPay - 397);
        928..2120 : TaxSingle := 204.78 + 0.33 * (adjPay - 928);
        ELSE        TaxSingle := 598.47 + 0.28 * (adjPay - 2121)
      END
    END; { Function TaxSingle }
```

```
FUNCTION TaxMarried (adjPay : Real) : Real;
{ Compute federal tax for married person based on adjusted pay }
  BEGIN { Function TaxMarried }
    CASE Trunc(adjPay) OF
       0..64      : TaxMarried := 0;
       65..688    : TaxMarried := 0.15 * (adjPay - 64);
       689..1572  : TaxMarried := 93.60 + 0.28 * (adjPay - 689);
       1573..3857 : TaxMarried := 341.21 + 0.33 * (adjPay - 1573);
       ELSE         TaxMarried := 1095.17 + 0.28 * (adjPay - 3858)
    END
  END; { Function TaxMarried }
BEGIN { Procedure ComputeFedTax }
  withhold := 39.42 * exemptions;
  adjPay := pay - withhold;
  IF adjPay < 0 THEN
      adjPay := 0;
  IF mStatus = 'SINGLE' THEN
      fedTax := TaxSingle(adjPay)
    ELSE
      fedTax := TaxMarried(adjPay)
END; { Procedure ComputeFedTax }


PROCEDURE ComputeCheck (    pay, ficaTax,
                            fedTax        : Real;
                        VAR payCheck      : Real);
{ Compute amount of money given to employee }
  BEGIN
    payCheck := pay - ficaTax - fedTax
  END;


PROCEDURE ShowInformation (name              : STRING;
                           pay, totalPay,
                           ficaTax, fedTax,
                           payCheck          : Real);
{ Display headings and information for paycheck }
  BEGIN
    Writeln;
    Writeln;
    Writeln('                Current   Yr. to date  FICA     Income',
          '   Check');
    Writeln('Name            Earnings  Earnings     Taxes   Tax Wh.',
          '   Amount');
    Writeln;
    Writeln(name, pay:21 - Length(name):2, totalPay:11:2, ficaTax:10:2,
          fedTax:10:2, payCheck:8:2)
  END;
```

```
BEGIN  { Payroll }
  ClrScr;
  InputData(name, mStatus, hrWage, hrsWorked, exemptions, prevPay);
  ComputePay(hrWage, hrsWorked, pay);
  ComputeTotalPay(prevPay, pay, totalPay);
  ComputeFICATax(pay, prevPay, totalPay, ficaTax);
  ComputeFedTax(pay, exemptions, mStatus, fedTax);
  ComputeCheck(pay, ficaTax, fedTax, payCheck);
  ShowInformation(name, pay, totalPay, ficaTax, fedTax, payCheck)
END.   { Payroll }
```

Comments:

1. In ComputeFICATax, care has been taken to avoid taxing income in excess of $50,400 per year. The logic of the program ensures that an employee whose income crosses the $50,400 threshold during a given week is only taxed on the difference between $50,400 and his previous year-to-date income.

2. The two functions TaxMarried and TaxSingle use CASE to incorporate the tax brackets given in Tables 5.9 and 5.10 for the amount of Federal Income Tax withheld. The upper limit of each CASE clause was made one less than the limit used in the pseudocode. This ensured fractional values for adjPay, such as $23.50 in the ComputeSingle procedure, would be properly treated as part of the higher salary range.

Chapter 5
Summary

1. The *relational operators* are <, >, =, <>, <=, and >=.

2. The *logical operators* are AND, OR, and NOT.

3. A *condition* or *Boolean expression* is an expression involving constants, variables, functions, and operators (arithmetic, relational, and/or logical) that evaluates to either True or False.

4. An IF statement decides what action to take depending upon the truth value of a condition. To allow several courses of action, the IF and ELSE parts of an IF statement can contain other IF statements.

5. A CASE statement selects one of several actions depending on the value of an expression, called the *selector*. The selector must evaluate to one of the types Integer, Char, or Boolean. The entries in each *value list* must be written in terms of constants or literals (such as 5, 'x', or False) corresponding to the type of the selector.

Chapter 5
Programming Projects

1. Table 5.12 gives the 1989 Federal Income Tax rate schedule for single taxpayers, where the value of E is 2000 * (number of exemptions). Write a program that requests the taxable income and number of exemptions of a single taxpayer and calculates the Federal Income Tax. Use a procedure for the input and a function to calculate the tax.

Taxable Income Over –	But Not Over –	Your Tax Is –	Of Amount Over –
$0	$18,550	15%	$0
$18,550	$44,900	$ 2,782.50 + 28%	$18,550
$44,900	$93,130	$10,160.50 + 33%	$44,900
$93,130	$93,130 + 5.6 * E	$26,076.40 + 33%	$93,130
$93,130 + 5.6 * E		.28 * (taxable income + E)	

Table 5.12 1989 Federal Income Tax Rate Schedule for Single Taxpayers

2. Write a program to determine the real roots of the quadratic equation $ax^2 + bx + c = 0$ (where $a <> 0$) after requesting the values of a, b, and c. Use a subprogram to ensure a is nonzero. (**Note:** The equation has 2, 1, or 0 solutions depending upon whether the value of $b * b - 4 * a * c$ is positive, zero, or negative. In the first two cases the solutions are given by the quadratic formula $(-b \pm Sqrt(b * b - 4 * a * c)) / (2 * a)$.)

3. Table 5.13 contains seven proverbs and their truth values. Write a program that presents these proverbs one at a time and asks the user to evaluate them as true or false. The program should then tell the user how many questions were answered correctly and display one of the following evaluations: Perfect (all correct), Excellent (5 or 6 correct), You might consider taking Psychology 101 (less than 5 correct).

Proverb	Truth Value
The squeaky wheel gets the grease.	True
Cry and you cry alone.	True
Opposites attract.	False
Spare the rod and spoil the child.	False
Actions speak louder than words.	True
Familiarity breeds contempt.	False
Marry in haste, repent in leisure.	True

Table 5.13 Seven Proverbs
Source: "You Know What They Say . . .", by Alfie Kohn, *Psychology Today*, April 1988.

4. Write a program to find the day of the week for any date after 1582, the year our current calendar was introduced. The program should:

(a) Request the year and the number of the month as input.

(b) Determine the number of days in the month. (**Note:** All years divisible by 4 are leap years, with the exception of those years divisible by 100 and not by 400. For instance, 1600 and 2000 are leap years, but 1700, 1800, and 1900 are not.)

(c) Request the number of the day as input. The prompt should list the possible range for the number.

(d) Determine the day of the week with the following algorithm.

    (1) Treat January as the 13th month and February as the 14th month of the previous year. For example 1/23/1986 should be converted to 13/23/1985 and 2/6/1987 should be converted to 14/6/1986.

    (2) Denote the number of the day, month, and year by d, m, and y. Compute

$$w = d + 2 * m + \text{Trunc}(0.6 * (m + 1)) + y + \text{Trunc}(y / 4) \\ - \text{Trunc}(y / 100) + \text{Trunc}(y / 400) + 2$$

    (3) The remainder when w is divided by 7 is the day of the week of the given date, with Saturday as the zeroth day of the week, Sunday the first day of the week, Monday the second, and so on.

Some sample outputs of the program are:

```
[run]
Year (xxxx)? 1776
Month (1 - 12)? 7
Day of Month (1 - 31)? 4
The day of the week was Thu

[run]
Year (xxxx)? 1987
Month (1 - 12)? 2
Day of Month (1 - 28 )? 28
The day of the week was Sat
```

Test the program with the following memorable dates in the history of the U.S. space program.

On Tuesday, February 20, 1962, John Glenn became the first American to orbit the earth.

On Sunday, July 20, 1969, Neil Armstrong became the first person to set foot on the moon.

On Saturday, June 18, 1983, Sally Ride became the first American woman to travel in space.

6

Looping

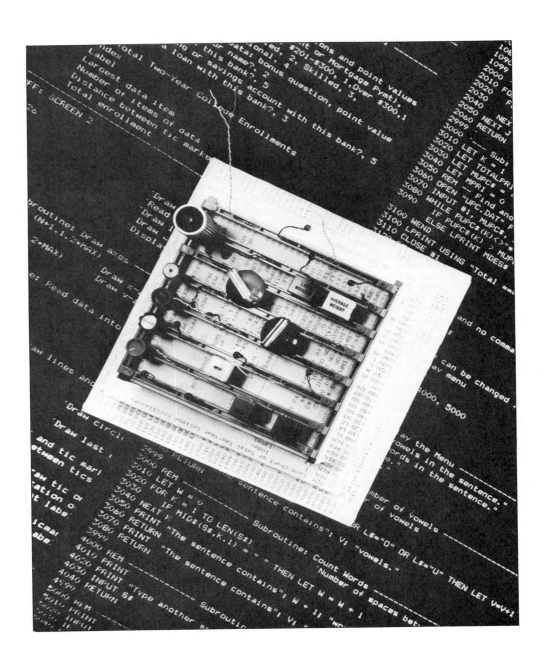

6.1   WHILE AND REPEAT LOOPS

A **loop**, one of the most important structures in Pascal, is used to repeat a statement a number of times. The WHILE loop repeats a statement as long as a certain condition is true. The REPEAT loop repeats a sequence of statements until a certain condition is true.

When Pascal executes a loop of the form

```
WHILE condition DO
    statement
```

where *statement* is either a simple or compound statement, it first checks the truth value of *condition*. If *condition* is false, then the statement inside the loop is not executed and the program continues with the next line of the program. If *condition* is true, the statement inside the loop is executed. Afterward, the process is repeated beginning with the testing of *condition*. In other words, the statement inside the loop is repeatedly executed as long as the condition is true. Figure 6.1 contains the pseudocode and flowchart for this loop.

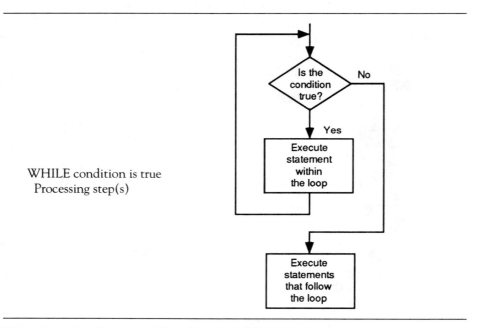

WHILE condition is true
Processing step(s)

Figure 6.1   Pseudocode and Flowchart for a WHILE Loop

EXAMPLE 1   Write a program that displays the numbers from 0 through 9.

SOLUTION   The condition in the WHILE loop is num <= 9.

```
PROGRAM ShowDigits;
{ Display the numbers from 0 to 9 }

USES Crt;

VAR num : Integer;
```

```
BEGIN
  ClrScr;
  num := 0;
  WHILE num <= 9 DO
    BEGIN
      Write(num:3);
      num := num + 1
    END
END.
```

```
[run]
  0  1  2  3  4  5  6  7  8  9
```

(**Note:** Each execution of a loop is called a **pass**. The variable num in Example 1 is called a **counter**. It keeps track of the number of passes through the loop.)

EXAMPLE 2   Suppose you deposit $100 into a savings account and let it accumulate at 7 percent interest compounded annually. The following program determines when you will be a millionaire:

```
PROGRAM Millionaire;
{ Compute years required to become a millionaire }

USES Crt;

VAR balance  : Real;
    numYears : Integer;

BEGIN
  ClrScr;
  balance := 100.0;
  numYears := 0;
  WHILE balance < 1000000.0 DO
    BEGIN
      balance := balance + 0.07 * balance;
      numYears := numYears + 1
    END;
  Writeln('In ', numYears, ' years you will have a million dollars.')
END.
```

```
[run]
In 137 years you will have a million dollars.
```

In Examples 1 and 2, the condition was checked at the top of the loop, that is, before the statements were executed. Alternately, the condition can be checked at the bottom of the loop. When Pascal encounters a loop of the form

```
REPEAT
  statement(s)
UNTIL condition
```

it executes the statements inside the loop and then checks the truth value of *condition*. If *condition* is True, then the program continues with the line after UNTIL. If *condition* is False, then the entire process repeats beginning with the REPEAT statement. In other words, the statements inside the loop are executed at least once and then are repeatedly executed until the condition is True. Figure 6.2 shows the pseudocode and flowchart for the REPEAT loop.

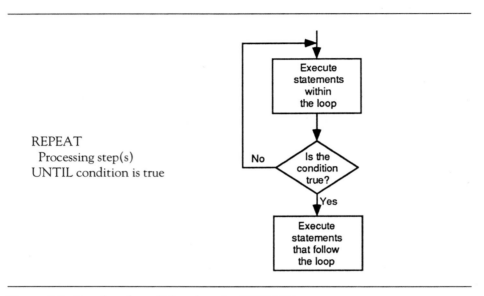

REPEAT
  Processing step(s)
UNTIL condition is true

Figure 6.2   Pseudocode and Flowchart for REPEAT loop

EXAMPLE 3   The following program uses a REPEAT loop to repeat a question until the correct answer is given.

```
PROGRAM Quiz;
{ Pose a multiple-choice question }

USES Crt;

PROCEDURE AskQuestion;
{ Show question and possible responses }
  BEGIN
    Writeln('What is the last line of the movie ',
            'Gone with the Wind?');
    Writeln;
    Writeln('1. Oh, Auntie Em, there''s no place like home.');
    Writeln('2. It wasn''t the airplanes, ',
               'it was beauty that killed the beast.');
    Writeln('3. Th-that''s all folks!');
    Writeln('4. After all, tomorrow is another day.');
    Writeln
  END;
```

```
PROCEDURE ProcessResponse;
{ Process the response }
  VAR num : Integer;
  BEGIN
    REPEAT
      Write('Enter a number from 1 to 4: ');
      Readln(num);
      IF num <> 4 THEN
          Writeln('No, try again.')
    UNTIL num = 4;
    Writeln('Correct.')
  END;

BEGIN
  ClrScr;
  AskQuestion;
  ProcessResponse
END.

[run]
What is the last line of the movie Gone with the Wind?

1. Oh, Auntie Em, there's no place like home.
2. It wasn't the airplanes, it was beauty that killed the beast.
3. Th-that's all folks!
4. After all, tomorrow is another day.

Enter a number from 1 to 4: 2
No, try again.
Enter a number from 1 to 4: 4
Correct.
```

EXAMPLE 4 The following program has the computer guess a number from 1 to 100 chosen by the user. Each guess is the middle number in the range of possible numbers.

```
PROGRAM GuessMyNumber;
{ Guess my number game }

USES Crt;

PROCEDURE AnnounceRules;
{ Display rules }
  BEGIN
    Writeln('Think of a number from 1 to 100. ',
            'After each guess I make,');
    Writeln('tell me whether my guess is ',
            'too high, too low, or correct.');
    Writeln
  END;
```

```
PROCEDURE GuessNumber;
{ Computer tries to guess number }
  VAR response            : Char;
      guess, lowerBound,
      upperBound, numTries : Integer;
  BEGIN
    lowerBound := 1;
    upperBound := 100;
    numTries := 0;
    REPEAT
      guess := (lowerBound + upperBound) DIV 2;
      numTries := numTries + 1;
      Writeln('My guess is ', guess);
      Write('Enter H (too high), L (too low), ',
            'or C (correct): ');
      Readln(response);
      response := UpCase(response);
      CASE response OF
        'H' : upperBound := guess - 1;
        'L' : lowerBound := guess + 1;
        'C' : Writeln('I guessed your number after ',
                    numTries, ' attempts.')
      END
    UNTIL response = 'C'
  END;

BEGIN
  ClrScr;
  AnnounceRules;
  GuessNumber
END.

[run]
  Think of a number from 1 to 100. After each guess I make,
  tell me whether my guess is too high, too low, or correct.

  My guess is 50
  Enter H (too high), L (too low), or C (correct): L
  My guess is 75
  Enter H (too high), L (too low), or C (correct): H
  My guess is 62
  Enter H (too high), L (too low), or C (correct): C
  I guessed your number after 3 attempts.
```

(**Note:** On each execution of the loop, the range of possible values of the number was halved. The number will be found after, at most, seven guesses. This efficient method is known as a **binary search** and will be explored further in Chapter 8.)

Since a statement appearing inside a loop can be of any kind, it also can be another loop. In this case, the two loops are called **nested loops**. The following variation of Example 2 uses nested loops to perform several calculations.

EXAMPLE 5 Suppose you deposit $100 into a savings account. The following program determines the lengths of time required to become a millionaire for several different interest rates.

```
PROGRAM Millionaire;
{ Compare years required to become a millionaire for
  different interest rates }

USES Crt;

VAR balance, interestRate : Real;
    numYears              : Integer;
    response              : Char;

BEGIN
  ClrScr;
  REPEAT
    balance := 100.0;
    numYears := 0;
    Write('What is the percent interest rate? ');
    Readln(interestRate);
    WHILE balance < 1000000 DO
      BEGIN
        balance := balance + balance * (interestRate / 100);
        numYears := numYears + 1
      END;
    Writeln('In ', numYears, ' years you will be a millionaire.');
    Writeln;
    Write('Do you want to continue (Y/N)? ');
    Readln(response)
  UNTIL UpCase(response) = 'N'
END.
```

```
[run]
What is the percent interest rate? 12
In 82 years you will be a millionaire.

Do you want to continue (Y/N)? Y
What is the percent interest rate? 25
In 42 years you will be a millionaire.

Do you want to continue (Y/N)? n
```

Comments:

1. Be careful to avoid so-called "infinite loops," that is, loops that are never exited. The following loop is infinite since the condition num = 0 will always be false. (**Note:** The process can be terminated by pressing Ctrl+Break.)

```
{ An infinite loop }
num := 7;
REPEAT
  num := num - 2;
  Write(num:8)
UNTIL num = 0
```

Notice that this slip-up can be avoided by changing the last line to UNTIL num <= 0.

2. All variables appearing in the condition of a WHILE loop should be assigned values prior to the execution of the loop.

3. The statements in a REPEAT loop are not enclosed with BEGIN and END. The words REPEAT and UNTIL serve to identify the beginning and end of the loop.

4. WHILE loops are said to be "tested at the top" and execute as long as the condition is True. REPEAT loops are said to be "tested at the bottom" and execute as long as the condition is False. They are also referred to as "pretest" and "post-test" loops, respectively.

PRACTICE PROBLEMS 6.1

1. How should one decide whether to use a WHILE loop or a REPEAT loop?

2. Change the following loop so it will be executed at least once.

```
WHILE answer = 'Y' DO
  BEGIN
    Write('Do you want to continue (Y or N)? ');
    Readln(answer)
  END
```

EXERCISES 6.1

In Exercises 1 through 8, determine the output of the program.

1.
```
VAR quota : Integer;

BEGIN
  quota := 3;
  WHILE quota < 15 DO
    quota := 2 * quota - 1;
  Writeln(quota)
END.
```

2.
```
VAR balance, interest : Real;
    yrs               : Integer;       { Number of years }

BEGIN
  balance := 1000;
  interest := 0.30;
  yrs := 0;
  REPEAT
    balance := (1 + interest) * balance;
    yrs := yrs + 1
  UNTIL balance > 2000;
  Writeln(yrs)
END.
```

3.
```
{ Display a message }
VAR num : Integer;
    mes : STRING;

BEGIN
  num := 4;
  REPEAT
    CASE num OF
      1 : BEGIN
            mes := 'al';
            num := -1
          END;
      2 : BEGIN
            mes := 'rsh';
            num := 7 - num
          END;
      3 : BEGIN
            mes := 'atme';
            num := 19 - 12 * num DIV 2
          END;
      4 : BEGIN
            mes := 'wo';
            num := num DIV (6 - num)
          END;
      5 : BEGIN
            mes := 'ip o';
            num := num - 2
          END
    END;
    Write(mes)
  UNTIL num = -1
END.
```

```
4. { Computer-assisted instruction }
   VAR year : Integer;

   BEGIN
     REPEAT
       Write('In what year was the IBM PC first produced? ');
       Readln(year);
       CASE year OF
         1981      : BEGIN
           Writeln('Correct. The computer was an instant success. By the');
           Writeln('end of 1981, there was such a backlog of orders that');
           Writeln('customers had a three-month waiting period.')
                     END;
         0..1980   : BEGIN
           Writeln('Later than that. The Apple II computer, which');
           Writeln('preceded the IBM PC, appeared in 1977.')
                     END;
         1981..2054 : BEGIN
                     Writeln('Earlier than that. The first successful IBM');
                     Writeln('PC clone, the Compaq, appeared in 1983.')
                     END
       END;
       Writeln
     UNTIL year = 1981
   END.
```

(Suppose the first response was 1980 and the second response was 1981.)

```
5. PROGRAM LongDivide;
   { Calculate the remainder in long division }

   FUNCTION Remainder (divisor, dividend : Integer) : Integer;
     VAR sum : Integer;
     BEGIN
       sum := 0;
       WHILE sum <= dividend DO
         sum := sum + divisor;
       Remainder := dividend - sum + divisor
     END;

   BEGIN
     Writeln(Remainder(3, 17))
   END.
```

6. { Simulate POS, search for the letter t }

```
VAR aWord    : STRING;
    counter : Integer;
    foundT  : Boolean;

BEGIN
  aWord := 'Potato';
  counter := 0;
  foundT := False;
  WHILE (NOT foundT) AND (counter <= Length(aWord)) DO
    BEGIN
      counter := counter + 1;
      IF aWord[counter] = 't' THEN
          BEGIN
            Writeln(counter);
            foundT := True
          END
    END;
  IF NOT foundT THEN
    Writeln(0)
END.
```

7. PROGRAM FlipCase;

```
VAR aWord : STRING;
    index : Integer;

FUNCTION DnCase (anyChar : Char) : Char;
  BEGIN
    DnCase := Chr(Ord(anyChar) + 32)
  END;

BEGIN
  aWord := '23 Skidoo';
  index := 1;
  WHILE index <= Length(aWord) DO
    BEGIN
      CASE aWord[index] OF
        'a'..'z' : aWord[index] := UpCase(aWord[index]);
        'A'..'Z' : aWord[index] := DnCase(aWord[index])
      END;
      index := index + 1
    END;
  Writeln(aWord)
END.
```

8. VAR myWord : STRING;

```
PROCEDURE ShiftAndRotate (VAR aStr : STRING);
  VAR temp  : STRING;
      index : Integer;
  BEGIN
    temp := aStr[Length(aStr)];
    index := 2;
    WHILE index <= Length(aStr) DO
      BEGIN
        temp := temp + aStr[index - 1];
        index := index + 1
      END;
    aStr := temp
  END;

BEGIN
  myWord := 'Texas';
  Writeln(myWord);
  ShiftAndRotate(myWord);
  Writeln(myWord);
  ShiftAndRotate(myWord);
  Writeln(myWord)
END.
```

In Exercises 9 through 12, identify the errors.

9.
```
q := 1.0;
WHILE q > 0 DO
  BEGIN
    q := 3 * q - 1;
    Write(q:8)
  END
```

10.
```
{ Display the numbers from 1 to 5 }
WHILE num <> 5 DO
  BEGIN
    num := 1;
    Write(num);
    num := num + 1
  END
```

11.
```
{ Repeat until a "yes" response is given }
REPEAT
  Write('Did you chop down the cherry tree (Y/N)?');
  Readln(answer)
WHILE answer <> 'Y'
```

12.
```
{ Repeat as long as desired }
Write('Do you want to continue (Y/N)? ');
Readln(answer);
REPEAT
  n := n + 1;
  Writeln(n);
  Write('Do you want to continue (Y/N)? ');
  Readln(answer)
UNTIL answer = 'N';
```

In Exercises 13 and 14, write a simpler and clearer program segment that performs the same task as the given segment.

13.
```
Readln(num);
Write(num);
Readln(num);
Write(num);
Readln(num);
Write(num)
```

14.
```
loopNum := 0;
REPEAT
  IF loopNum >= 1 THEN
      BEGIN
        Write('Do you want to continue (Y/N)? ');
        Readln(answer)
      END
    ELSE
      answer := 'Y';
  IF (answer = 'Y') OR (loopNum = 0) THEN
      BEGIN
        loopNum := loopNum + 1;
        Writeln(loopNum)
      END
UNTIL answer <> 'Y'
```

15. Write a program that requests a temperature between 0 and 100 degrees Celsius and converts the temperature to Fahrenheit. If the response is not between 0 and 100, the request should be repeated until a proper response is given. (**Note:** The formula $f = (9 / 5) * c + 32$ converts Celsius to Fahrenheit.)

16. Write a program that repeats the question "D'you know the capital of Alaska?" until the correct answer is given. The program should display the hint, "It rhymes with D'you know." when an incorrect answer is given.

17. Write a program that asks the user to enter positive numbers into the computer until the product of the numbers exceeds 400. The program should then display the highest number entered.

18. Write a program to display all of the numbers between 1 and 100 that are perfect squares (a perfect square is an integer that is the square of another integer; 1, 4 and 16 are example of perfect squares).

19. The population of Mexico City is currently 14 million people and growing at the rate of 3 percent each year. Write a program to determine when the population will reach 20 million.

20. Write a program to solve the equation $a * x + b = c$, where the numbers a, b, and c are supplied by the user. Allow for the case where a is 0. If so, there will either be no solution, or every number will be a solution. After solving each equation, ask the user if he wants another equation solved.

21. Write a program that requests a word containing the two letters r and n as input and determines which of the two letters appears first. If the word does not contain both of the letters, the program should keep requesting words until one does. (Test the program with the words *colonel* and *merriment*.)

22. The coefficient of restitution of a ball, a number between 0 and 1, specifies how much energy is conserved when a ball hits a rigid surface. A coefficient of .9, for instance, means a bouncing ball will rise to 90 percent of its initial height after each bounce. Write a program to input a coefficient of restitution and a height in meters and report how many times a ball bounces before it rises to a height of less than 10 centimeters. Also report the total distance traveled by the ball before this point. The coefficients of restitution of a tennis ball, basketball, super ball, and softball are .7, .75, .9, and .3, respectively.

In Exercises 23 through 26, write a program to solve the stated problem.

23. *Savings Account.* $15,000 is deposited into a savings account paying 5 percent interest and $1000 is withdrawn from the account at the end of each year. Approximately how many years are required for the savings account to be depleted?

24. Rework Exercise 23 for the case where the amount of money deposited initially is input by the user and the program computes the number of years required to deplete the account. (**Note:** Be careful to avoid infinite loops.)

25. $1000 is deposited into a savings account, and an additional $1000 is deposited at the end of each year. If the money earns interest at the rate of 8 percent, how long will it take before the account contains at least $1 million?

26. A person born in 1980 can claim "I will be x years old in the year x squared." Write a program to determine the value of x.

In Exercises 27 and 28, write a program corresponding to the flowchart.

27. The flowchart in Figure 6.3 requests an integer greater than 1 as input and factors it into a product of prime numbers. (**Note:** A number is prime if its only factors are 1 and itself; test the program with the numbers 660 and 139.)

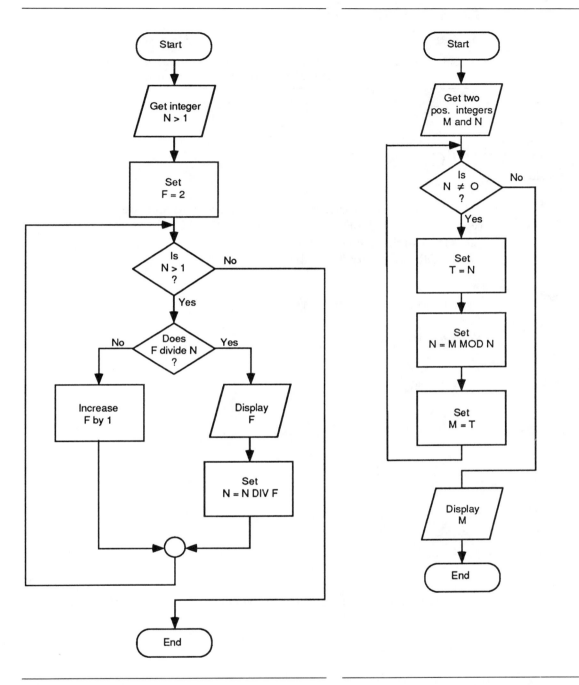

Figure 6.3 Prime Factors

Figure 6.4 Greatest Common Divisor

28. The flowchart in Figure 6.4 finds the greatest common divisor of two positive integers entered by the user. (The greatest common divisor of two positive integers is the largest integer that divides both of the numbers.) Write a program that corresponds to the flowchart.

SOLUTIONS TO PRACTICE PROBLEMS 6.1

1. A REPEAT loop is used if the loop should be executed at least once.

2. Either precede the loop with the statement answer := 'Y', or change the first line to REPEAT, delete BEGIN and replace the END statement with UNTIL answer <> 'Y'.

6.2 FOR LOOPS

When we know exactly how many times a loop should be executed, a special type of loop, called a FOR loop, can be used. A FOR loop has a counter that keeps track of the number of iterations through the loop. The following program uses a FOR loop to display a table.

```
PROGRAM Squares;
{ Display a table of the first 5 numbers and their squares }

CONST Lo = 1;
      Hi = 5;

VAR num : Integer;

BEGIN
  FOR num := Lo TO Hi DO
    Writeln(num, Sqr(num):4)
END.

[run]
1   1
2   4
3   9
4  16
5  25
```

The statement part of an equivalent program written with a REPEAT loop is as follows.

```
BEGIN
  IF lo <= hi THEN
     BEGIN
       num := lo;
       REPEAT
         Writeln(num, Sqr(num):4);
         num := num + 1
       UNTIL num = hi;
       Writeln(num, Sqr(num):4)
     END
END.
```

If i is an Integer variable, then a portion of a program of the form

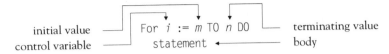

initial value ———   For i := m TO n DO   ——— terminating value

control variable ———   statement ←   ——— body

constitutes a FOR loop. If $m \leq n$, then i is assigned the values $m, m + 1, m + 2,$ ..., n in order and the body is executed once for each of these values. If $m > n$, then execution continues with the statement after the FOR loop and no value is assigned to i. The pseudocode for a FOR loop is

```
FOR i := m TO n
  Processing step(s)
```

EXAMPLE 1   Suppose the population of a city is 300,000 in the year 1990 and is growing at the rate of 3 percent per year. Write a program to display the projected population each year until 1994.

SOLUTION

```
PROGRAM ProjectedPopulations;
{ Display population from 1990 to 1994 }

USES Crt;

VAR pop  : Real;
    year : Integer;

BEGIN
  ClrScr;
  Writeln('Year', 'Population':15);
  pop := 300000.0;
  FOR year := 1990 TO 1994 DO
    BEGIN
      Writeln(year, pop:15:0);
      pop := pop + 0.03 * pop
    END
END.

[run]
Year      Population
1990         300000
1991         309000
1992         318270
1993         327818
1994         337653
```

The initial and terminating values can be constants, variables, or expressions, but they must always match the type of the control variable. In most cases the control variable will be Integer; however, it also can be of type Char or Boolean. Char type values are compared and incremented based on the ASCII table.

EXAMPLE 2   Display the letters of the alphabet as they would appear in a handwriting chart.

```
PROGRAM Letters;

USES Crt;

CONST FirstChar = 'a';
      LastChar  = 'z';

VAR letter : Char;

BEGIN
  FOR letter := FirstChar TO LastChar DO
    Write(UpCase(letter), letter)
END.

[run]
AaBbCcDdEeFfGgHhIiJjKkLlMmNnOoPpQqRrSsTtUuVvWwXxYyZz
```

EXAMPLE 3   The following user-defined function is an extension of the built-in function UpCase. The function UpCaseString accepts a string as input and converts its letters to uppercase.

SOLUTION
```
FUNCTION UpCaseString (str : STRING) : STRING;
  VAR charNum : Integer;
  BEGIN
    FOR charNum := 1 TO Length(str) DO
      str[charNum] := UpCase(str[charNum]);
    UpCaseString := str
  END;
```

In the examples considered so far, the control variable was incremented until the terminating value was reached. If the word TO in the FOR statement is changed to DOWNTO, the control variable is decremented instead of incremented. The loop repeats until the variable's value equals that of the terminating value.

EXAMPLE 4   Compose a program to accept a word as input and display it backwards.

SOLUTION   A FOR loop is used to print the letters starting with the last one and ending with the first.

```
PROGRAM Backwards;
{ Write a word backwards }

USES Crt;

VAR word    : STRING;
    charNum : Integer;
```

```
BEGIN
  ClrScr;
  Write('Enter a word: ');
  Readln(word);
  FOR charNum := Length(word) DOWNTO 1 DO
    Write(word[charNum])
END.
```

```
[run]
Enter a word: SUEZ
ZEUS
```

FOR loops can be nested just like the WHILE and REPEAT loops of Section 6.1. The program in Example 5 contains nested FOR loops.

EXAMPLE 5   Write a program to display the products of the numbers from 1 through 4.

SOLUTION   In the following program, i denotes the left factors of the products and j denotes the right factors. Each factor takes on values from 1 to 4. The values are assigned to i in the outer loop and to j in the inner loop. Initially, i is assigned the value 1 and then the inner loop is traversed 4 times to produce the first row of products. At the end of these 4 passes, the value of i will still be 1 and the value of j will have been incremented to 4. The Writeln statement just before the END of the outer loop guarantees no more products will be displayed in that row. The first execution of the outer loop is now complete. Then, the value of i increments to 2. The statement beginning FOR j is then executed. It resets the value of j to 1. The second row of products is displayed during the next 4 executions of the inner loop, and so on.

```
PROGRAM MultiplicationTable;
{ Display the products of the numbers from 1 through 4 }

USES Crt;

VAR i, j : Integer;

BEGIN
  ClrScr;
  FOR i := 1 TO 4 DO
    BEGIN
      FOR j := 1 TO 4 DO
        Write(i, ' x ', j, ' = ', i * j : 2, '    ');
      Writeln
    END
END.
```

outer loop / inner loop

Left factor ── / ── Right factor

```
[run]
1 x 1 =  1    1 x 2 =  2    1 x 3 =  3    1 x 4 =  4
2 x 1 =  2    2 x 2 =  4    2 x 3 =  6    2 x 4 =  8
3 x 1 =  3    3 x 2 =  6    3 x 3 =  9    3 x 4 = 12
4 x 1 =  4    4 x 2 =  8    4 x 3 = 12    4 x 4 = 16
```

FOR loops can be used to write compact programs to display truth values of Boolean expressions. False is considered to be less than True and can be incremented to True using a FOR loop.

EXAMPLE 6   Write a program to evaluate (*a* OR *b*) AND *c* for all values of the Boolean variables *a*, *b*, and *c*.

```
PROGRAM TruthTable;
{ Displays truth values for a condition of three variables }

USES Crt;

VAR a, b, c : Boolean;

BEGIN
  ClrScr;
  Writeln('a':5, 'b':9, 'c':9, '(a OR b) AND c':18);
  Writeln;
  FOR a := False TO True DO
    FOR b := False TO True DO
      FOR c := False TO True DO
        Writeln(a:5, b:9, c:9, ((a OR b) AND c):18)
END.

[run]
     a         b         c     (a OR b) AND c

 FALSE     FALSE     FALSE          FALSE
 FALSE     FALSE      TRUE          FALSE
 FALSE      TRUE     FALSE          FALSE
 FALSE      TRUE      TRUE           TRUE
  TRUE     FALSE     FALSE          FALSE
  TRUE     FALSE      TRUE           TRUE
  TRUE      TRUE     FALSE          FALSE
  TRUE      TRUE      TRUE           TRUE
```

Comments:

1. Consider a loop beginning with FOR $i := m$ TO n. The loop will not be executed at all if m is greater than n, and i will not be assigned a value. Similarly, a loop beginning with FOR $i := m$ DOWNTO n will not be executed if m is less than n. Either form of FOR loop will be executed exactly once if m equals n.

2. Pascal evaluates the limits of a FOR loop only once, before the body is ever executed, and stores these values; therefore, the program fragment

```
i := 5;
FOR i := 1 TO i + 1 DO
  Write(i:2)
```

produces the output

```
1 2 3 4 5 6
```

instead of repeating forever.

3. The following program fragment illustrates that changing the values of the limits in the body cannot alter the number of times the loop is executed.

```
n := 3;
FOR i := 1 TO n DO
  BEGIN
    n := 5;
    Write(i:2)
  END
```

produces the output

```
1 2 3
```

4. Altering the value of the control variable in the body of a FOR loop is considered poor programming practice and can lead to disastrous consequences. For instance, the program fragment

```
FOR i := 1 TO 10 DO
  BEGIN
    i := i + 3;
    Write(i:4)
  END
```

results in an infinite loop with the output

```
4   8  12  16  20  24  28 . . .
```

PRACTICE PROBLEMS 6.2

1. Why won't this statement work as intended?

```
FOR i := 15 TO 1 DO
  Writeln(i)           { Count down }
```

2. When is a FOR loop more appropriate than a WHILE or REPEAT loop?

EXERCISES 6.3

In Exercises 1 through 12, determine the output of the program.

1. ```
VAR i : Integer;

BEGIN
  FOR i := 1 TO 4 DO
    Writeln('Pass #', i)
END.
```
```

```
2. VAR countdown : Integer;

   BEGIN
     FOR countdown := 10 DOWNTO 1 DO
       Write(countdown:3);
     Writeln(' blastoff')
   END.

3. VAR i, num : Integer;

   BEGIN
     num := 5;
     FOR i := num TO 2 * num + 3 DO
       Write(i:4)
   END.

4. VAR i : Integer;

   BEGIN
     FOR i := 3 TO 6 DO
       Writeln(2 * i);
     FOR i := 12 TO 20 DO
       Write(i / 4:6:2);
     Writeln(i:4)
   END.

5. VAR i, j : Integer;

   BEGIN
     FOR i := 0 TO 2 DO
       BEGIN
         FOR j := 0 TO 3 DO
           Write(i + 3 * j + 1:5);
         Writeln
       END
   END.

6. VAR i, j : Integer;

   BEGIN
     FOR i := 1 TO 5 DO
       BEGIN
         FOR j := 1 TO i DO
           Write('*');
         Writeln
       END
   END.
```

7. ```VAR total, i, score : Integer;```

```pascal
BEGIN
  total := 0;
  FOR i := 1 TO 4 DO
    BEGIN
      Readln(score);
       total := total + score
    END;
  Writeln('Average = ', (total / 4):1:2)
END.
```
(Assume the responses are: 89, 85, 88, and 98)

8. ```VAR aWord : STRING;```
```
     num   : Integer;
```

```pascal
PROCEDURE Asterisks (num : Integer);
  { Display num asterisks }
  VAR i : Integer;
  BEGIN
    FOR i := 1 TO num DO
      Write('*')
  END;

BEGIN
  Write('Enter a word: ');
  Readln(aWord);
  num := (80 - Length(aWord)) DIV 2;
  Asterisks(num);
  Write(aWord);
  Asterisks(num)
END.
```
(Assume the response is Hooray.)

9. ```PROGRAM Letters;```

```pascal
VAR myWord : STRING;
    index  : Integer;

PROCEDURE DisplayFive (letter : Char);
{ Display letter five times  }
  VAR i : Integer;
  BEGIN
    FOR i := 1 TO 5 DO
      Write(letter)
  END;
```

```
     BEGIN
       myWord := 'Data';
       FOR index := 1 TO Length(myWord) DO
         BEGIN
           DisplayFive(myWord[index]);
           Writeln                        { Move to next line }
         END
     END.
```

10. VAR b : Boolean;

```
     BEGIN
       FOR b := False TO True DO
         Write((NOT b):6)
     END.
```

11. VAR c : Char;

```
     BEGIN
       FOR c := 'a' TO 'e' DO
         Write(UpCase(c))
     END.
```

12. VAR anyChar : Char;
        someBool : Boolean;

```
     BEGIN
       FOR someBool := False TO True DO
         FOR anyChar := 'a' TO 'c' DO
           IF someBool THEN
               Write(anyChar)
             ELSE
               Write(UpCase(anyChar))
     END.
```

In Exercises 13 through 16, identify the errors in the program segments.

13. FOR ch := 'a' TO 'B' DO
      Writeln(ch)

14. FOR i := Sqrt(4) TO Sqrt(25) DO
      FOR j := Sqrt(25) DOWNTO Sqrt(4) DO
        Write(i / j)

15. FOR b := False TO True DO
      IF b THEN
          b := NOT b
        ELSE
          Write(b:6)

16. FOR i := 10 DOWNTO 0 DO
      Writeln(55 / i)

In Exercises 17 and 18, rewrite the segment using a FOR loop.

17.
```
num := 1;
WHILE num <= 10 DO
  BEGIN
    Writeln(num);
    num := num + 1
  END
```

18.
```
Writeln('hello');
Writeln('hello');
Writeln('hello');
Writeln('hello')
```

In Exercises 19 through 37, write a program to complete the stated task. Use procedures and functions where appropriate.

19. Display a row of 10 stars (asterisks).

20. Request a number from 1 to 80 with a Readln statement and display a row of that many stars (asterisks).

21. Display a 10-by-10 square of stars.

22. Request a number with a Readln statement and call a subprogram to display a square having that number of stars on each side.

23. Find the sum 1 + 1/2 + 1/3 + 1/4 + . . . + 1/100.

24. According to researchers at Stanford Medical School (as cited in *Medical Self Care*), the ideal weight for a woman is found by multiplying her height in inches by 3.5 and subtracting 108. The ideal weight for a man is found by multiplying his height in inches by 4 and subtracting 128. Request a lower and upper bound for heights and then produce a table giving the ideal weights for women and men in that height range. One possible outcome of the program is shown in Figure 6.5.

```
Enter lower bound: 62
Enter upper bound: 65

Height    Wt - Women    Wt - Men
62          109.0          120
63          112.5          124
64          116.0          128
65          119.5          132
```

Figure 6.5 Output for Exercise 24

25. Request a sentence and display the number of sibilants (that is, letters S or Z) in the sentence. The counting should be carried out in a function and the total number should be displayed by the main body of the program.

26. Request a number, *n*, from 1 to 30 and one of the letters *S* or *P*. Then calculate the sum or product of the numbers from 1 to *n* depending upon whether *S* or *P* was selected. The calculations should be carried out with functions.

27. Suppose $800 is deposited into a savings account earning 7 percent interest compounded annually, and $100 is added to the account at the end of each year. Calculate the amount of money that will be in the account at the end of 10 years. (Determine a formula for computing the balance at the end of one year based on the balance at the beginning of the year. Then write a program that starts with a balance of $800 and makes 10 passes through a loop containing the formula to produce the final answer.)

28. A TV set is purchased with a loan of $563 to be paid off with 5 monthly payments of $116. The interest rate is 1 percent per month. Display a table giving the balance on the loan at the end of each month.

29. *Radioactive Decay.* Cobalt 60, a radioactive form of cobalt used in cancer therapy, decays or dissipates over a period of time. Each year, 12 percent of the amount present at the beginning of the year will have decayed. If a container of cobalt 60 initially contains 10 grams, determine the amount remaining after 5 years.

30. *Supply and Demand.* This year's level of production and price for most agricultural products greatly affects the level of production and price next year. Suppose the current crop of soybeans in a certain country is 80 million bushels and that experience has shown for each year,

$$[\text{price this year}] = 20 - 0.1 * [\text{quantity this year}]$$
$$[\text{quantity next year}] = 5 * [\text{price this year}] - 10$$

where quantity is measured in units of millions of bushels. Generate a table to show the quantity and price for each of the next 12 years.

31. Request a number greater than 3 with an Readln statement and display a hollow rectangle of stars (asterisks) with each outer row and column having that many stars. Do not use the GotoXY statement. (See Figure 6.6a.)

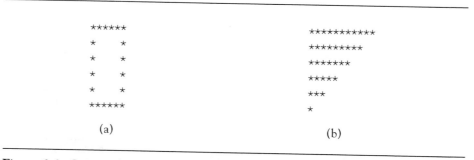

(a)   (b)

Figure 6.6 Outputs for Exercises 31 and 32.

32. Request an odd number with an Readln statement and display a triangle similar to the one in Figure 6.6b with the input number of stars in the top row.

33. Allow any two integers, m and n, between 2 and 12 to be input with a Readln statement and then generate an m by n multiplication table. Figure 6.7 shows the output when m is 5 and n is 7.

```
1    2    3    4    5    6    7
2    4    6    8   10   12   14
3    6    9   12   15   18   21
4    8   12   16   20   24   28
5   10   15   20   25   30   35
```

Figure 6.7 Output for Example 33

34. Write a program to create the histogram in Figure 6.8. The user should enter the years and percentages.

```
1982 *************************** 27
1983 ************************************** 38
1984 **************************************************** 51
          Percent of Entering College Freshmen Who Have
          Written a Computer Program within the Past Year
```

Figure 6.8 Histogram

35. In Section 4.3, user-defined functions, a function called Power was defined. It provides an approximate value of b^x for any positive value of b. Write a similar function called IntPower(*base, exponent*) which uses a FOR loop to calculate the result exactly for any integer *base* and nonnegative integer *exponent*. Let IntPower return the value 1 whenever *exponent* is zero.

36. To determine if a number n is a multiple of 9, one can use the following method:
    (a) Replace the value of n with the sum of the digits of n.
    (b) If n is still greater than 9, repeat part (a).
    (c) If the final value is nine, then the original value of n is a multiple of 9.

    For example, if n originally is 7958, then n becomes 7+9+5+8 = 29 after one step, 2+9 = 11 after another, and finally 2. Therefore, 7958 is not a multiple of 9, but instead leaves a remainder of 2 when divided by 9. (Much of numerology is indirectly based on division by 9.)

    Write a program that will accept a very long number (such as 98,998,998,998,998,998,998,998) in the form of a string, and, using the method explained above, continually reduce the number to determine its remainder when divided by 9. It should report the value that results after each step of the process. To determine the numeric value of individual digits in the string, the built-in Val function can be used; the Str function should be used to convert the resulting sum back to a string. (See Appendix F.) To test your program, the value listed above can be used; it yields a remainder of 1. (Be sure to leave out the commas when you enter it or write a procedure to remove them.)

37. Write a program that uses two FOR loops to list potential two-letter words. All combinations of letters that include at least one vowel (a, e, i, o, u, or y) should be produced.

SOLUTIONS TO PRACTICE PROBLEMS 6.2

1. There is no error as far as the compiler is concerned, that is, the program will run without producing an error message. However, the loop will never be executed since 15 is greater than 1. The intended first line might have been

   ```
   FOR i := 15 DOWNTO 1 DO
   ```

   or

   ```
   FOR i := 1 TO 15 DO
   ```

2. Generally, a FOR loop is best whenever:

   (a) the exact number of repetitions of the loop is known in advance, and
   (b) the control variable needs to be incremented or decremented by only one during each step.

   If either (a) or (b) is not true in a given situation, it is usually best to use a WHILE or REPEAT loop.

6.3   APPLICATIONS OF LOOPS

Processing Lists

One of the main applications of programming is the processing of lists of data. There are several devices that facilitate working with lists. **Counters** calculate the number of elements in lists, **accumulators** sum numerical values in lists, **flags** record whether or not a certain event has occurred, and **trailer values** indicate the ends of lists. The following program uses each of these devices.

EXAMPLE 1   Write a program to calculate the average of exam grades input by the user. The program also should indicate whether any student received a perfect score.

SOLUTION   The following program uses the variable numScores as a counter, the variable sum as an accumulator, the variable perfectScore as a flag, and the trailer value −1.

```pascal
PROGRAM FindAverageScore;

USES Crt;

VAR numScores, sum : Integer;
    perfectScore    : Boolean;

PROCEDURE ShowInstructions;
{ Display instructions }
  BEGIN
    Writeln('Enter the scores one at a time. ',
            'After all of the');
    Writeln('scores have been reported, ',
            'enter the number -1.')
  END;

PROCEDURE InputScores (VAR numScores, sum : Integer;
                       VAR perfectScore   : Boolean);
{ Input scores from the user }
  VAR score : Integer;
  BEGIN
    numScores := 0;
    sum := 0;
    perfectScore := False;
    Write('Enter a score: ');
    Readln(score);
    WHILE score <> -1 DO
      BEGIN
        numScores := numScores + 1;
        sum := sum + score;
        IF score = 100 THEN
            perfectScore := True;
        Write('Enter a score: ');
        Readln(score)
      END
  END;

PROCEDURE ComputeAverage (numScores, sum : Integer);
{ Compute and display average }
  VAR average : Real;
  BEGIN
    IF numScores >= 1 THEN
        BEGIN
          average := sum / numScores;
          Writeln('The average score is ', average:1:2)
        END
  END;
```

```
PROCEDURE Perfection (perfectScore : Boolean);
{ Tell whether a perfect score was achieved }
  BEGIN
    IF perfectScore THEN
        Writeln('A perfect score was achieved.')
      ELSE
        Writeln('There was no perfect score.')
  END;

BEGIN
  ClrScr;
  ShowInstructions;
  InputScores(numScores, sum, perfectScore);
  ComputeAverage(numScores, sum);
  Perfection(perfectScore)
END.

[run]
Enter the scores one at a time. After all of the
scores have been reported, enter the number -1.
Enter a score: 80
Enter a score: 90
Enter a score: 82
Enter a score: 88
Enter a score: -1
The average score is 85.00
There was no perfect score.
```

(**Note:** The value of the counter, numScores, was initially 0 and changed on each execution of the loop to 1, 2, 3, and finally 4. The accumulator, sum, initially had the value 0 and increased with each execution of the loop to 80, 170, 252, and finally 340. The flag, perfectScore, was initialized to False and never changed. After the loop was terminated, the average was calculated by dividing 340 by 4. The variables numScores, sum, and perfectScore were first used to retrieve values from a procedure and then used to pass these values to other procedures.)

Trailer Values

In this chapter, the data are entered in response to Readln statements. Trailer values (also known as *sentinels*) allow the user to indicate that all of the data has been entered. A literal used as a trailer value must not be a possible response. Commonly used trailer values are −1 and EOD. EOD stands for End Of Data.

The program in Example 1 illustrates the proper way to process a list of data having a trailer value. A WHILE loop, rather than a REPEAT loop, should be used. The first item of data should be obtained before the WHILE statement and used to determine whether the loop should be entered. The loop begins by processing the data and then requests the next piece of data just before the END statement. This method of processing a list assures the loop will not be entered if there are no items in the list and guarantees the trailer value will not be processed. Figure 6.9 contains the pseudocode and flowchart for this technique.

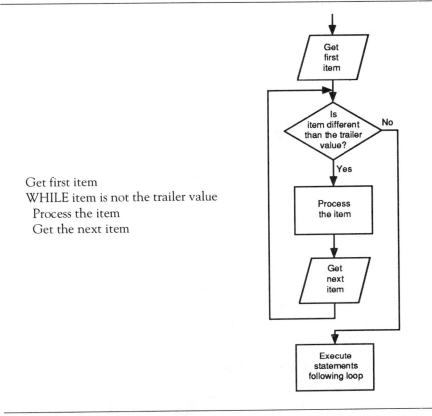

Get first item
WHILE item is not the trailer value
  Process the item
  Get the next item

Figure 6.9 Pseudocode and Flowchart for Processing a List With a Trailer Value

Counters, Accumulators, and Flags

A **counter** is an Integer variable that keeps track of the number of items that have been processed. An **accumulator** is a numeric variable that totals numbers. A **flag** is a Boolean variable that keeps track of whether a certain event has occurred. It is used within a loop to provide information that will be used after the loop has terminated. The flag also can be used to terminate a loop as in the next example.

EXAMPLE 2   Write a program that gives the user five chances to guess the country where Panama hats are made.

SOLUTION
```
PROGRAM Quiz;
{ Answer a question in five tries }

USES Crt;

VAR tries     : Integer;
    correctFlag : Boolean;
    country   : STRING;
```

```
BEGIN
  ClrScr;
  tries := 0;
  REPEAT
    Write('In what country are Panama hats made? ');
    Readln(country);
    tries := tries + 1;
    correctFlag := (country = 'Ecuador')
  UNTIL correctFlag OR (tries >= 5);
  IF correctFlag THEN
      Writeln('Correct')
    ELSE
      Writeln('Panama hats are made in Ecuador.')
END.
```

```
[run]
In what country are Panama hats made? Panama
In what country are Panama hats made? Mexico
In what country are Panama hats made? Spain
In what country are Panama hats made? Italy
In what country are Panama hats made? England
Panama hats are made in Ecuador.
```

Loops in Mathematics

Suppose the mathematical function $f(x)$ is defined and continuous on the interval $[a, b]$, and $f(a)$ has a different sign than $f(b)$. (See Figure 6.11.) Then the equation $f(x) = 0$ must have a solution between a and b. That is, there must exist a number c between a and b with $f(c) = 0$. Such a number c is called a *zero* of the function. The flowchart in Figure 6.10 describes an algorithm, known as the bisection method, for finding c. At each iteration, the length of the subinterval containing c is halved. Due to roundoff error, looking for a value of c with $f(c)$ exactly equal to zero might lead to an infinite loop; therefore, we are content to find a value of c for which $f(c)$ is very small, say less than .00001 in absolute value.

EXAMPLE 3   Write a program to find a zero of the function $e^x - x - 4$. This function is graphed in Figure 6.10.

```
PROGRAM BisectionMethod;
{ Find a zero of a function f(x) between two known values,
  a and b, where f(a) and f(b) have different signs }

USES Crt;

CONST Tolerance = 0.00001;

VAR a, b, middle, approx : Real;

FUNCTION F (x : Real) : Real;
  BEGIN
    F := Exp(x) - x - 4
  END;
```

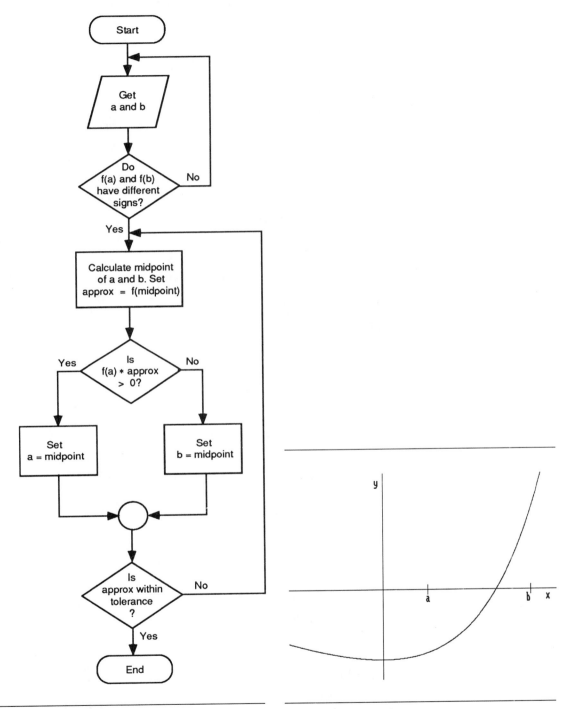

Figure 6.10   Flowchart for the Bisection Method

Figure 6.11   A Function with a Zero in the Interval [a, b]

```
PROCEDURE GetAandB (VAR a, b : Real);
  VAR badInput : Boolean;
  BEGIN
    REPEAT
      Write('Enter the values of a and b: ');
      Readln(a, b);
      badInput := (F(a) * F(b) >= 0);
      IF badInput THEN
          Writeln('f(a) and f(b) must have different signs.')
    UNTIL NOT badInput
  END;

FUNCTION SplitDistance (a, b : Real) : Real;
  BEGIN
    SplitDistance := a + (b - a) / 2
  END;

PROCEDURE AdjustAorB (VAR a, b          : Real;
                          middle, approx : Real);
  BEGIN
    IF F(a) * approx > 0 THEN
        a := middle
      ELSE
        b := middle
  END;

BEGIN
  ClrScr;
  GetAandB(a, b);
  REPEAT
    middle := SplitDistance(a, b);
    approx := F(middle);
    AdjustAorB(a, b, middle, approx);
  UNTIL Abs(approx) <= Tolerance;
  Writeln(middle:1:5, ' is a zero of the function.')
END.

[run]
Enter the values of a and b: 2  3
f(a) and f(b) must have different signs.
Enter the values of a and b: 1  2
1.74903 is a zero of the function
```

Accessing Text Files

Inputting data from the keyboard is not practical for a large collection of data. Instead, the data are usually stored on a disk in a form that can be pulled into a program in much the same way data are entered from the keyboard. The simplest type of disk file is called a **text file**. Since text files normally store a large, possibly unknown, quantity of data, loops are essential for reading all of the information.

Section 9.1 presents a detailed discussion of text files; however, to enable you to input data from a file *now*, we present here simple techniques for creating and accessing a text file. You can use these methods until you study text files in detail.

For illustrative purposes, assume the data needed by your program consists of a sequence of names of colleges and their student enrollments.

How to Create the Text File

1. Press Alt/F/New to open a new file.

2. Type the name of the first college on the first line.

3. Type its student enrollment on the following line.

4. Type the name of the second college on the next line.

5. Type its student enrollment on the following line.

6. Continue in this manner until all of the colleges and their enrollments have been typed in. (Do not press the Enter key after typing in the last enrollment number.) Figure 6.12 shows how your screen might look.

```
Ohio State
53669
Stanford
13224
USC
29590
```

Figure 6.12   Colleges and Their Student Enrollments

7. Press Alt/F/S to save the file to disk. When prompted for a name, enter ENROLL.DAT.

How to Input Data From the Text File

Suppose the college information was to be input from the keyboard in a program that computes the average enrollment of a collection of colleges. The following program would accomplish this task.

```
PROGRAM AverageEnrollments;

USES Crt;

VAR counter  : Integer;
    num, sum : Real;
    college  : STRING;
```

```
BEGIN
  ClrScr;
  counter := 0;
  sum := 0;
  Writeln('Enter EOD when finished entering data.');
  Write('Enter the name of a college: ');
  Readln(college);
  WHILE college <> 'EOD' DO
    BEGIN
      Write('Enter the student enrollment of the college: ');
      Readln(num);
      sum := sum + num;
      counter := counter + 1;
      Write('Enter the name of a college: ');
      Readln(college)
    END;
  Writeln('Number of colleges is ', counter);
  IF counter <> 0 THEN
    Writeln('Average enrollment is ', sum / counter:1:2)
END.
```

When the data is stored in a text file on a disk, there is no need to prompt with Write statements or to prime the loop with a query that might be answered with EOD. The Readln statements have an extra argument identifying the file. The following program does the job. The Assign statement specifies that the file ENROLL.DAT will be known as collegeFile during the execution of the program. The condition in the WHILE statement is read "WHILE the End of the file collegeFile has not been reached, DO." The Close statement announces that there is no further need for the file.

```
PROGRAM AverageEnrollments;

USES Crt;

VAR counter    : Integer;
    num, sum   : Real;
    college    : STRING;
    collegeFile : Text;
```

```
BEGIN
  ClrScr;
  Assign(collegeFile, 'ENROLL.DAT');
  Reset(collegeFile);          { Prepare file for reading }
  counter := 0;
  sum := 0;
  WHILE NOT Eof(collegeFile) DO
    BEGIN
      Readln(collegeFile, college);
      Readln(collegeFile, num);
      sum := sum + num;
      counter := counter + 1
    END;
  Close(collegeFile);
  Writeln('Number of colleges is ', counter);
  IF counter <> 0 THEN
    Writeln('Average enrollment is ', (sum / counter):1:2)
END.

[run]
Number of colleges is 3
Average enrollment is 32161.00
```

PRACTICE PROBLEMS 6.3

1. Determine the output of the following program.

```
{ Find the sum of a collection of bowling scores }
VAR sum, score : Integer;

BEGIN
  sum := 0;
  WHILE score <> -1 DO
    BEGIN
      Readln(score);
      sum := sum + score
    END;
  Writeln(sum)
END.
```
(Assume the responses are 150, 200, 300, and −1)

2. Why didn't the program above produce the intended output?

3. Correct the program above so it has the intended output.

EXERCISES 6.3

In Exercises 1 through 10, determine the output of the program for the input in parentheses. (Do not include the response to the request for input.)

1.
```
VAR total, num : Integer;

BEGIN
  total := 0;
  Readln(num);
  WHILE num > 0 DO
    BEGIN
      total := total + num;
      Readln(num)
    END;
  Writeln(total)
END.
(5, 2, 6, -1)
```

2.
```
VAR name : STRING;

BEGIN
  Readln(name);
  WHILE name <> 'EOD' DO
    BEGIN
      Writeln(name);
      Readln(name)
    END
END.
(Bo, Liz, EOD)
```

3.
```
{ Display list of desserts }
VAR dessert : STRING;

BEGIN
  REPEAT
    Readln(dessert);
    Writeln(dessert)
  UNTIL dessert = 'EOD'
END.
(pie, cake, melon, EOD)
```

4.
```
VAR city : STRING;
    pop  : Real;

BEGIN
  Readln(city);
  WHILE city <> 'EOD' DO
    BEGIN
      Readln(pop);
      IF pop >= 7 THEN
          Writeln(city:20, pop:8:1);
      Readln(city)
    END
END.
(San Francisco, 5.6, Boston, 4, Chicago, 8, New York, 17.7, EOD)
```

5.
```
VAR fruit       : STRING;
    firstLetter : Char;

BEGIN
  Readln(fruit);
  WHILE fruit <> 'EOD' DO
    BEGIN
      firstLetter := fruit[1];
      Writeln('   ', firstLetter);
      WHILE fruit[1] = firstLetter DO
        BEGIN
          Writeln(fruit);
          Readln(fruit)
        END;
      Writeln
    END
END.
(Apple, Apricot, Avocado, Banana, Blueberry, Grape, Lemon, Lime, EOD)
```

6.
```
{ Display list of numbers }
VAR num : Integer;

BEGIN
  Readln(num);
  WHILE num <> -1 DO
    BEGIN
      Writeln(num)
      Readln(num);
    END
END.
(2, 3, 8, 5, -1)
```

7.
```
CONST LastScore = -1;

VAR hiScore, score : Integer;

PROCEDURE GetScore (VAR score : Integer);
  BEGIN
    Write('Enter the score: ');
    Readln(score)
  END;

BEGIN
  hiScore := 0;
  REPEAT
    GetScore(score);
    IF hiScore < score THEN
        hiScore := score
  UNTIL score = LastScore;
  Writeln(hiScore)
END.
(76, 90, 87, 74, -1)
```

```
8. PROGRAM WriteSentence;

   VAR sentence : STRING;

   PROCEDURE Duplicate30 (sentence : STRING);
     VAR loopDone : Boolean; { True if while loop has been executed }
     BEGIN
       loopDone := False;
       WHILE Length(sentence) < 30 DO
         BEGIN
           loopDone := True;
           sentence := sentence + sentence
         END;
       IF loopDone THEN
           Writeln(sentence)
       ELSE
           Writeln('While loop not executed')
     END;

   BEGIN
     Readln(sentence);
     Duplicate30(sentence);
     Readln(sentence);
     Duplicate30(sentence)
   END.
   (Input 1: I think I can.)
   (Input 2: We're off to see the wizard, the wonderful wizard of OZ.)

9. VAR aWord, cWord : STRING;

   BEGIN
     Readln(aWord);
     WHILE aWord <> 'EOD' DO
       BEGIN
         IF aWord[1] = 'c' THEN
             cWord := aWord;
         Readln(aWord)
       END;
     Writeln(cWord)
   END.
   (time, is, a, child, idly, moving, counters, in, a, game, --Heraclitus,
    EOD)
```

10. `VAR value, rowmax, max : Integer;`

```
BEGIN
  max := 0;
  Readln(value);
  WHILE value <> -1 DO
    BEGIN
      rowMax := 0;
      value := 0;
      WHILE value <> -2 DO
        BEGIN
          IF value > rowMax THEN
              rowMax := value;
          Readln(value)
        END;
      Writeln(rowMax);
      IF rowMax > max THEN
          max := rowMax;
      Readln(value)
    END;
  Writeln(max)
END.
(5, 7, 3, -2, 10, 12, 6, 4, -2, 1, 9, -2, -1)
```

In Exercises 11 through 14, identify the errors in the program segment.

11.
```
WHILE price <> -1 DO
    BEGIN
      Readln(price);
      total := total + price;
      Writeln(price:10:2)
    END
(72.87, 16.50, 0.23, -1)
```

12.
```
flag := False;
WHILE NOT flag DO
    BEGIN
      Readln(num);
      IF Sqr(num) < 0 THEN
          flag := True
    END
```

13.
```
{ Display names of some U.S. Presidents }
REPEAT
    Readln(name);
    Writeln(name)
UNTIL name = 'EOD'
```

14.
```
Readln(num);
WHILE 1 < num < 5 DO
  BEGIN
    Writeln(num);
    Readln(num)
  END
```

15. Write an interactive program to find the average (rounded to an integer) of a collection of positive numbers. The user should be prompted to provide numbers until the response −1 is given. At that time, the average should be displayed. (Test the program with the collection of numbers 89, 77, 95, and 86.)

16. Write an interactive program that asks the user to enter a distance in miles and converts it to kilometers. The process should be repeated until the user signs off by entering −1. (**Note:** 1 mile is approximately 1.6 kilometers; test the program with the values 3 and 0.625.)

17. Table 6.1 shows the different grades of eggs and the minimum weight required for each classification. Write an interactive program in which the user repeatedly inputs the weight of an egg and obtains the appropriate grade. The user should enter a negative number to terminate the process. (**Note:** Eggs weighing less than 1.5 ounces cannot be sold in supermarkets.) Figure 6.13 shows a typical output of the program.

Grade	Weight (in ounces)
Jumbo	2.5
Extra Large	2.25
Large	2
Medium	1.75
Small	1.5

Table 6.1   Grades of Eggs

```
Weight of egg in ounces? 2.3
The grade is Extra Large.

Weight of egg in ounces? 1.4
Send it to the bakery.

Weight of egg in ounces? −1
```

Figure 6.13   Output for Exercise 17

18. Table 6.2 contains the meanings of some abbreviations doctors often use for prescriptions. Write a program that repeatedly requests an abbreviation and gives its meaning. The user should be informed if the meaning is not in the table.

Abbreviation	Meaning
ac	before meals
ad lib	freely as needed
bid	twice daily
gtt	a drop
hs	at bedtime
gid	four times a day

Table 6.2   Physicians' Abbreviations

19. Write a program to request a positive integer less than 400 as input and carry out the following algorithm. If the number is even, divide it by 2. Otherwise, multiply the number by 3 and add 1. Repeat this process with the resulting number and continue repeating the process until the number 1 is reached. After the number 1 is reached, the program should display how many passes through the algorithm were required. (Test the program with the numbers 9, 21, and 27.)

20. Write a program that allows the user 10 tries to answer the question "Which U.S. President was born on July 4?" After three incorrect guesses the program should give the hint "He once said, 'If you don't say anything, you won't be called upon to repeat it.'" After seven incorrect guesses the program should give the hint "His nickname was 'Silent Cal.'" (**Note:** Calvin Coolidge was born on July 4, 1872.)

21. Table 6.3 gives the U.S. Census Bureau projections for the populations (in millions) of the states predicted to be the most populous in the year 2000. Write a program that requests the current population of each of these states as input (one at a time) and then computes the percentage population growth for each state and the average percentage population growth for the five states. The percentage growth is calculated as

100 * (projected pop. − current pop.) / current pop.

(Test the program with the 1989 populations: CA, 29.1; TX, 17.7; NY, 17.7; FL, 12.5; and IL, 11.6.)

State	Population in 2000		
California	33.5	Light bulbs	2.65
Texas	20.2	Soda	3.45
New York	18.0	Soap	1.15
Florida	15.4		
Illinois	11.6	Sum	1.75
		Tax	0.36
		Total	7.61

Table 6.3 State Populations in Year 2000   **Figure 6.14** Output for Exercise 22

22. Write a program to produce a sales receipt. The items and their prices should be entered one at a time and displayed. After all of the entries have been made, the program should display the sum of the prices, the sales tax (5 percent of total), and the total amount to be paid. Figure 6.14 shows a typical output of the program.

23. Write a program that requests a list of scores and then displays the two highest scores.

24. Write a program to compute a student's grade point average. A procedure should request the grade and semester hours credit for each course, and then a function should compute the grade point average. Another procedure should display the GPA and then display one of two messages. A student with a GPA of 3 or more should be informed that he has made the honor roll. Otherwise, he should be congratulated on having completed the semester. In either case, he should be wished a merry vacation.

25. Write a program to do the following. (The program should use a flag.)
    (a) Ask the user to input a sentence possibly with one pair of parentheses.
    (b) Display the sentence with the parentheses and their contents removed.

    Test the program with the following sentence as input: PASCAL (named for the philosopher Blaise Pascal) is the world's most widely used teaching language.

SOLUTIONS TO PRACTICE PROBLEMS 6.3

1. 649

2. The trailer value was inadvertently added to the scores.

3.
```
VAR sum, score : Integer;

BEGIN
  sum := 0;
  Readln(score);
  WHILE score <> -1 DO
    BEGIN
      sum := sum + score;
      Readln(score)
    END;
  Writeln(sum)
END.
```

6.4 A CASE STUDY: ANALYZE A LOAN

This case study develops a menu-driven program to analyze a loan. Assume the loan is repaid in equal monthly payments and interest is compounded monthly. The program should request the amount (principal) of the loan, the annual rate of interest, and the number of years over which the loan is to be repaid. The four options in the menu are:

1. Calculate the monthly payment. The formula for the monthly payment is

$$\text{payment} = p * r / (1 - \text{Power}(1 + r, -n))$$

where p is the principal of the loan, r is the monthly interest rate (annual rate divided by 12) given as a number between 0 (for 0 percent) and 1 (for 100 percent), n is the number of months over which the loan is to be paid off, and Power is a user-defined function that raises a number to a power (in this case, it represents "$(1 + r)$ to the $-n$th power").

2. Display an amortization schedule, that is, a table showing the balance on the loan at the end of each month for the duration of the loan. Also show how

much of each monthly payment goes toward interest and how much is used to repay the principal. Finally, display the total interest paid over the duration of the loan. The balances for successive months are calculated with the formula

$$\text{balance} = (1 + r) * b - m$$

where r is the monthly interest rate (annual rate / 12, a fraction between 0 and 1), b is the balance for the preceding month (amount of loan left to be paid), and m is the monthly payment.

3. Show the effect of changes in the interest rate. Display a table giving the monthly payment for each interest rate from 1 percent below to 1 percent above the specified annual rate in steps of one-eighth of a percent.

4. Quit

Designing the Analyze a Loan Program

In addition to the tasks described in options 1 to 3 above, the basic tasks of this program include inputting the particulars of the loan to be analyzed and presenting a menu to the user. Thus, the first division of the problem is into the following tasks:

1. Input principal, interest, duration.

2. Present menu and get choice.

3. Calculate monthly payment.

4. Calculate amortization schedule.

5. Display the effects of interest rate changes.

6. Quit.

Tasks 1 and 2 are basic input operations and task 3 involves applying the formula given in step 1; therefore, these tasks need not be broken down any further. The demanding work of the program is done in tasks 4 and 5, which can be divided into smaller subtasks.

4. *Calculate amortization schedule.* This task involves simulating the loan month by month. First, the monthly payment must be computed. Then, for each month, the new balance must be computed together with a decomposition of the monthly payment into the amount paid for interest and the amount going toward repaying the principal. That is, task 4 is divided into the following subtasks:

    4.1 Calculate monthly payment.
    4.2 Calculate new balance.
    4.3 Calculate amount of monthly payment for interest.
    4.4 Calculate amount of monthly payment for principal.

5. *Display the effects of interest rate changes.* A table is needed to show the effects of changes in the interest rate on the size of the monthly payment. First the

interest rate is reduced by one percentage point and the new monthly payment is computed. Then the interest rate is increased by regular increments until it reaches one percentage point above the original rate, with new monthly payment amounts computed for each intermediate interest rate. The subtasks for this task are then:

5.1 Reduce interest rate by 1 percent.
5.2 Calculate monthly payment.
5.3 Increase interest rate by (1/8) percent.

The top-down chart in Figure 6.15 shows the stepwise refinement of the problem.

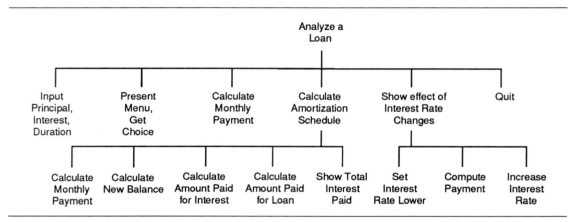

Figure 6.15 Top-Down Chart for the Analyze a Loan Program

Pseudocode for the Analyze a Loan Program

```
Get LOAN DATA (Procedure InputData)
REPEAT
  PRESENT MENU AND GET CHOICE (Procedure ShowMenu)
  IF choice is Calculate monthly payment THEN
    COMPUTE MONTHLY PAYMENT (Function Payment)
    DISPLAY MONTHLY PAYMENT (Procedure ShowPayment)
  IF choice is Display amortization schedule THEN
    DISPLAY AMORTIZATION SCHEDULE (Procedure ShowAmortSched)
    Compute monthly interest rate
    COMPUTE MONTHLY PAYMENT (Function Payment)
    Display amortization table
    Display total interest paid
  IF choice is Show change of interest rate table THEN
    Decrease annual rate by 0.01
    REPEAT
      Compute monthly interest rate
      COMPUTE MONTHLY PAYMENT (Function Payment)
      Increase annual rate by 0.00125
    UNTIL annual rate > original annual rate + 0.01
UNTIL choice is Quit
```

Writing the Analyze a Loan Program

Table 6.4 shows each task discussed above and the procedure or function that carries out the task.

Task	Subprogram
1. Input principal, interest, duration.	InputData
2. Present menu and get choice.	ShowMenu
3. Calculate monthly payment.	ShowPayment
4. Calculate amortization schedule.	ShowAmortSched
4.1 Calculate monthly payment.	Payment
4.2 Calculate new balance.	Balance
4.3 Calculate amount paid for loan.	ShowAmortSched
4.4 Calculate amount paid for interest.	ShowAmortSched
5. Show effect of interest rate changes.	ShowInterestChanges
5.1 Reduce interest rate.	ShowInterestChanges
5.2 Compute new monthly payment.	Payment
5.3 Increase interest rate.	ShowInterestChanges

Table 6.4 Tasks and Their Subprograms

```
PROGRAM LoanAnalysis;

USES Crt;

VAR choice,               { User's main menu choice (1 to 4) }
    numMonths  : Integer; { Number of months to pay loan }
    principal,            { Amount of loan }
    yearlyRate : Real;    { Yearly interest rate }

PROCEDURE InputData (VAR principal, yearlyRate : Real;
                     VAR numMonths             : Integer);
{ Input the loan amount, yearly rate of interest, and duration }
  VAR numYears      : Integer;
      percentageRate : Real;
  BEGIN
    Write('Amount of the loan: ');
    Readln(principal);
    Write('Annual percentage rate of interest: ');
    Readln(percentageRate);
    yearlyRate := percentageRate / 100;
    Write('Number of years of the loan: ');
    Readln(numYears);
    numMonths := numYears * 12
  END;
```

```
PROCEDURE GetChoice (VAR choice : Integer);
{ Display options and request that user make a selection }
  BEGIN
    ClrScr;
    Writeln('1. Calculate monthly payment');
    Writeln('2. Display amortization schedule');
    Writeln('3. Display interest rate change table');
    Writeln('4. Quit');
    Writeln;
    Write('Choice: ');
    Readln(choice)
  END;

PROCEDURE WaitForUser;
{ Pause until user hits Enter key }
  BEGIN
    Writeln;
    Write('Press Enter key to continue...');
    Readln
  END;

FUNCTION Power (base, exponent : Real) : Real;
  BEGIN
    Power := Exp(exponent * ln(base))
  END;

FUNCTION Payment (principal, monthlyRate, numMonths : Real) : Real;
  BEGIN
    Payment := principal * monthlyRate /
               (1 - Power(1 + monthlyRate, -numMonths))
  END;

PROCEDURE ShowPayment (principal, yearlyRate : Real;
                       numMonths             : Integer);
{ Display monthly payment amount }
  VAR monthlyRate : Real;
  BEGIN
    monthlyRate := yearlyRate / 12;
    Writeln('The monthly payment for a $', principal:1:2, ' loan at');
    Writeln((yearlyRate * 100):1:2, '% annual interest rate for ',
            numMonths DIV 12, ' years is $',
            Payment(principal, monthlyRate, numMonths):1:2);
    WaitForUser
  END;
```

```
PROCEDURE PauseIfNecessary (VAR lineCount : Integer);
{ Pause if screen is full }
{ lineCount records the number of lines of display on the screen }
  BEGIN
    lineCount := lineCount + 1;
    IF lineCount >= 22 THEN
        BEGIN
          WaitForUser;
          lineCount := 0
        END
  END;

FUNCTION Balance (monthlyPayment, principal, monthlyRate : Real) : Real;
{ Compute balance at end of month }
  BEGIN
    Balance := (1 + monthlyRate) * principal - monthlyPayment
  END;

PROCEDURE ShowAmortSched (principal, yearlyRate : Real;
                          numMonths : Integer);
{ Display amortization schedule }
  VAR lineCount,                         { number of lines displayed }
      monthNum                            : Integer;
      monthlyRate, monthlyPayment, totalInterest : Real;
      oldBalance, newBalance, principalPaid    : Real;
      interestPaid                        : Real;
  BEGIN
    { Amounts paid for principal and interest, balance at month's end }
    Writeln('Amount Paid':23, 'Amount Paid':18, 'Balance at':18);
    Writeln('Month', 'for Principal':18, 'for Interest':18,
            'End of Month':18);
    lineCount := 2;
    monthlyRate := yearlyRate / 12;
    monthlyPayment := Payment(principal, monthlyRate, numMonths);
    totalInterest := 0;
    oldBalance := principal;
    FOR monthNum := 1 TO numMonths DO
      BEGIN
        newBalance := Balance(monthlyPayment, oldBalance, monthlyRate);
        principalPaid := oldBalance - newBalance;
        interestPaid := monthlyPayment - principalPaid;
        totalInterest := totalInterest + interestPaid;
        Writeln(monthNum:5, principalPaid:18:2, interestPaid:18:2,
                newBalance:18:2);
        PauseIfNecessary(lineCount);
        oldBalance := newBalance
      END;
    Writeln;
    Writeln('Total interest paid is $', totalInterest:1:2);
    IF lineCount <> 0 THEN
        WaitForUser
  END;
```

```
        PROCEDURE ShowInterestChanges (principal, yearlyRate : Real;
                                       numMonths :  Integer);
    { Display effect of interest changes }
        CONST Tolerance = 0.000001;        { Counterbalance round-off error }
        VAR newRate, monthlyRate : Real;
        BEGIN
          Writeln('   Annual');
          Writeln('Interest rate', 'Monthly Payment':28);
          newRate := yearlyRate - 0.01;
          WHILE newRate <= yearlyRate + 0.01 + Tolerance DO
            BEGIN
              monthlyRate := newRate / 12;
              Writeln(newRate * 100:12:3, '%',
                      Payment(principal, monthlyRate, numMonths):28:2);
              newRate := newRate + 0.00125;
            END;
          Writeln;
          WaitForUser
        END;

    BEGIN { LoanAnalysis }
        ClrScr;
        InputData(principal, yearlyRate, numMonths);
        REPEAT
          GetChoice(choice);
          ClrScr;
          CASE choice OF
            1 : ShowPayment(principal, yearlyRate, numMonths);
            2 : ShowAmortSched(principal, yearlyRate, numMonths);
            3 : ShowInterestChanges(principal, yearlyRate, numMonths)
          END
        UNTIL choice = 4
    END. { LoanAnalysis }
```

Comments:

1. In the main module, the procedure ShowMenu is called repeatedly until a valid menu option is chosen by the user. Once an acceptable choice has been made, CASE is used to transfer control to the appropriate procedure.

2. Tasks 4.1 and 4.2 are performed by functions. Using functions to compute these quantities simplifies the computations in ShowAmortSched.

3. If the number of years over which the loan is to be repaid is more than one, then the amortization table produced by ShowAmortSched might fill more than one screen. Two procedures are used to produce a pause once the screen is filled. PauseIfNecessary keeps track of the amount of the screen that has been used and calls WaitForUser to produce a pause if the screen is full.

4. A subtle but important point should be noticed in the procedure ShowInterestChanges. What should be a simple comparison like

$$newRate <= yearlyRate + 0.01$$

is complicated by the fact that newRate and yearlyRate are Real variables. Each time the statements in the WHILE loop are executed, 0.125 percent is added to newRate. Thus, if the original value of newRate is 5, the successive values *should* be 5.125, 5.250, 5.375, . . ., 6.000. But due to round-off error, each number actually has an extremely small fraction of a percent added to it. At the final comparison in the WHILE loop, the total amount of error added to newRate is sufficient to make newRate just *slightly more* than yearlyRate + 0.01. This situation prevents the loop from executing for the final interest rate. For this reason, a small Tolerance constant is added to the condition so that newRate will be just slightly smaller than the expression on the right. That is,

$$newRate <= yearlyRate + 0.01 + Tolerance$$

will evaluate to True and the loop will execute for the required final interest rate.

Chapter 6
Summary

1. A WHILE loop repeatedly executes a statement as long as a certain condition is true. The condition is checked at the top of the loop.

2. A REPEAT loop repeatedly executes a statement or statements until a certain condition is true. The condition is checked at the bottom of the loop.

3. Input data are often followed by *trailer values*, or *sentinels*, that can be used by WHILE or REPEAT loops to terminate repetitions after all of the data have been read.

4. As various items of data are processed by a loop, a *counter* can be used to keep track of the number of items and an *accumulator* can be used to sum numerical values.

5. A *flag* is a variable used to indicate that a certain event has occurred.

6. A FOR loop repeats a statement or statement block a fixed number of times. The *control variable* assumes an initial value and increments (or decrements) by one after each pass through the loop.

Chapter 6
Programming Projects

1. The Rule of 72 is used to make a quick estimate of the time required for prices to double due to inflation. If the inflation rate is r percent, then the Rule of 72 estimates prices will double in $72/r$ years. For instance, at an inflation rate of 6 percent, prices double in about 72/6 or 12 years. Write a program to test the accuracy of this rule. The program should display a table showing, for

each value of r from 1 to 20, the rounded value of $72/r$ and the actual number of years required for prices to double at an r percent inflation rate. (Assume prices increase at the end of each year.) Figure 6.16 shows the first few rows of the output.

Interest Rate (%)	Rule of 72	Actual
1	72	70
2	36	36
3	24	24

Figure 6.16 Rule of 72

2. Write a menu-driven program to provide information on the height of a ball thrown straight up into the air. The program should request the initial height, h feet, and the initial velocity, v feet per second, as input. The four options are:

(a) Determine the maximum height of the ball. (**Note:** The ball will reach its maximum height after $v/32$ seconds.)

(b) Determine approximately when the ball will hit the ground. (**Hint:** Calculate the height after every .1 seconds and observe when the height is no longer a positive number.)

(c) Display a table showing the height of the ball every quarter second for 5 seconds, or until it hits the ground.

(d) Quit.

The formula for the height of the ball after t seconds, $h + v*t - 16*Sqr(t)$, should be specified in a user-defined function. (Test the program with $v = 148$ and $h = 0$. This velocity is approximately the top speed that has been clocked for a ball thrown by a professional baseball pitcher.)

3. *Depreciation to a Salvage Value of 0.* For tax purposes an item may be depreciated over a period of several years, n. With the *straight-line* method of depreciation, each year the item depreciates by 1/nth of its original value. With the *double-declining* balance method of depreciation, each year the item depreciates by 2/nths of its value at the *beginning* of that year. (In the last year it is depreciated by its value at the beginning of the year.) Write a program that

(a) Requests a description of the item, the year of purchase, the cost of the item, the number of years to be depreciated (estimated life), and the method of depreciation. The method of depreciation should be chosen from a menu.

(b) Displays a depreciation schedule for the item similar to the schedule shown in Figure 6.17.

Depreciation Schedule

Description: IBM-PC
Year of purchase: 1988
Cost: $2000.00
Estimated life: 5
Method of depreciation: Double-declining balance

Year	Value at Beg of Yr	Amount Deprec During Year	Total Depreciation to End of Year
1988	2000.00	800.00	800.00
1989	1200.00	480.00	1280.00
1990	720.00	288.00	1568.00
1991	432.00	172.80	1740.80
1992	259.20	259.20	2000.00

Figure 6.17   Depreciation Schedule

4. After the engine of a moving motorboat is turned off, the speed of the boat decreases as it continues to move across the water. If the boat's speed in miles/hour when the motor is turned off is *initSpeed*, then its *speed* after moving *distance* feet is given by:

$$speed = initSpeed * Exp(-2 * (5280 / distance))$$

(a) Write a function that accepts a boat's initial speed and the distance it has traveled since the motor was turned off as input, and computes its speed at that distance.

(b) Suppose to safely ground a boat on the beach, it should be moving between 2 and 5 miles/hour. Use the function in (a) to write a program that requests the initial speed of a boat and outputs the distance from the beach the motor should be turned off in order to drift safely to the beach. (**Hint:** Use a REPEAT loop to increase the distance until the function yields a value in the desired range.)

7

User-Defined Data Types

7.1 ENUMERATED AND SUBRANGE TYPES

The data types Integer, Real, String, and Character are predefined and always available. In addition, several other data types can be defined by the programmer.

An enumerated data type consists of a list of items created with a declaration of the form

```
TYPE ListName = (item1, item2, item3, ... );
```

where *ListName*, *item1*, *item2*, *item3*, . . . are identifiers. Some examples are

```
TYPE Day = (monday, tuesday, wednesday, thursday, friday, saturday);

TYPE Sport = (football, baseball, soccer, tennis, golf);
```

A variable is created with an enumerated data type by a declaration of the form

```
VAR enumVar : ListName;
```

For instance, the declarations

```
VAR date        : Day;
    game, hobby : Sport;
```

create variables of types Day and Sport.

The items comprising an enumerated data type are identifiers and, therefore, subject to the same naming rules as variables. Also, a specific item can appear in only one enumerated data type, and should not be the name of any variable or other visible entity appearing in the program.

EXAMPLE 1　Determine whether each of the following declarations is legal.

(a) `TYPE LuckyNumbers = (7, 11);`
(b) `TYPE Virtues = (faith, hope, charity, justice, prudence, temperance,`
`    fortitude);`
`    Departments = (Treasury, State, Justice, Agriculture, Defense,`
`    Interior, Health and Human Services);`
(c) `TYPE Rank = (Private, Corporal, Sergeant, Colonel, General);`
`    VAR colonel : STRING;`
(d) `TYPE Vowels = (a, e, i, o, u);`

SOLUTION　(a) Illegal. The items are identifiers and, therefore, must begin with a letter or an underscore and consist solely of letters, digits, and the underscore character.

(b) Illegal. The item "justice" appears in both enumerated types. Since identifiers are case insensitive, "justice" and "Justice" are the same. Also, "Health and Human Services" is not a valid identifier since it contains spaces.

(c) Illegal. The variable name "colonel" also appears in the list of items.
(d) Legal. The items are valid identifiers. At first glance, they look like characters; however, characters are written surrounded by single quotes. The declaration

```
TYPE Vowels = ('a', 'e', 'i', 'o', 'u');
```

is illegal.

The items of an enumerated data type acquire an ordering from the sequence in which they are listed. For instance, in the type Sport, football < baseball, baseball < soccer, . . ., tennis < golf. Also, the items are regarded as numbered 0, 1, 2, ... These numbers are called the **ordinal numbers** associated with the data type. For instance, football is the zeroth item, baseball is the first, . . ., and golf is the fourth.

Pascal has five functions related to order: Ord, Succ, Pred, First, and Last. Ord(item) is the ordinal number of the item, Succ(item) is the next item in the type list, and Pred(item) is the preceding item in the type list. [Succ and Pred are not defined for the last and zeroth items, respectively.] For instance, with type Sport, Ord(soccer) is 2, Succ(soccer) is tennis, and Pred(soccer) is baseball. For any ordinal variable, ordVar, or ordinal type, ordType, the value of First(ordVar) and First(ordType) is the first value of the data type. Similarly, the value of Last(ordVar) and Last(varType) is the last item of the data type.

Items in enumerated types are similar to Integers in many ways. They can be assigned to variables, used in expressions or conditions, and serve as indices of FOR loops. Items in enumerated types, however, cannot be read with Read and Readln or displayed with Write and Writeln.

EXAMPLE 2   The following program requests the number of a month and displays the number of days in that month. The WHILE loop uses the month's number to assign the name of the month to the variable thisMonth.

SOLUTION

```
PROGRAM MonthDays;

USES Crt;

TYPE Month = (Jan, Feb, Mar, Apr, May, Jun, Jul, Aug, Sep, Oct, Nov, Dec);

VAR num      : Integer;
    thisMonth : Month;
```

```
BEGIN
  ClrScr;
  Write('Enter the number of this month: ');
  Readln(num);
  Write('This month has ');
  thisMonth := Jan;
  WHILE Ord(thisMonth) < num - 1 DO
    thisMonth := Succ(thisMonth);
  CASE thisMonth OF
    Sep, Apr, Jun, Nov : Writeln('30 days.');
    Feb                : Writeln('28 or 29 days.')
    ELSE                 Writeln('31 days.')
  END
END.
```

```
[run]
Enter the number of this month: 5
This month has 31 days.
```

EXAMPLE 3   Modify the program in Example 2 so it displays the number of each month and the number of days in the month.

SOLUTION
```
BEGIN
  ClrScr;
  Writeln('Month  Number of Days');
  FOR thisMonth := Jan TO Dec DO
    BEGIN
      Write((Ord(thisMonth) + 1):5, '  ');
      CASE thisMonth OF
        Sep, Apr, Jun, Nov : Writeln('30 days');
        Feb                : Writeln('28 or 29 days')
        ELSE                 Writeln('31 days')
      END
    END
END.
```

```
[run]
Month  Number of Days
    1  31 days
    2  28 or 29 days
    3  31 days
    4  30 days
    5  31 days
    6  30 days
    7  31 days
    8  31 days
    9  30 days
   10  31 days
   11  30 days
   12  31 days
```

Enumerated types, along with Integer, Character, and Boolean types are known as **ordinal types**. The functions Ord, Succ, and Pred can be applied to any ordinal data type.

Subrange Types

If itemA and itemB are items of the same ordinal type and itemA ≤ itemB, the declaration

```
TYPE SubRangeType = itemA..itemB;
```

specifies a data type consisting of the items of the ordinal type between itemA and itemB inclusive.

Some examples are

```
TYPE SingleDigitNums = 0..9;
```

```
TYPE CapitalLetters = 'A'..'Z';
```

```
TYPE Day     = (monday, tuesday, wednesday, thursday, friday, saturday);
     Weekday = monday..friday;
```

A variable is created with a subrange data type by a declaration of the form

```
VAR subRangeVar : SubRangeType;
```

For instance, the declarations

```
VAR firstLottoNumber : SingleDigitNums;
    middleInitial    : CapitalLetters;
    washDay          : Weekday;
```

create variables of types SingleDigitNums, CapitalLetters, and Weekday.

EXAMPLE 4 The following program uses enumerated and subrange types to count the number of states founded before 1640. The data type Original13 consists of the original 13 states of the United States in the order founded. Delaware was founded in 1638 and North Carolina in 1660.

```
PROGRAM InitialStates;
{ Count number of states founded before 1640 }

USES Crt;

TYPE Original13 = (VA, NY, MA, NH, MD, CT, RI, DE, NC, NJ, SC, PA, GA);
     Before1640 = VA..DE;

VAR numStates : Integer;
```

```
BEGIN
  ClrScr;
  numStates := Ord(Last(Before1640)) + 1;
  Writeln(numStates, ' states were founded before 1640.')
END.

[run]
8 states were founded before 1640.
```

Shorthand Specification of Enumerated and Subrange Types

Enumerated and subrange types for variables can be specified directly in the VAR part of a program by following the variable name with a colon and a description of the type. For instance, in the program of Example 4, the TYPE declaration part can be eliminated and the VAR part given as

```
VAR originalStates : (VA, NY, MA, NH, MD, CT, RI,
                       DE, NC, NJ, SC, PA, GA);
    earlyStates    : VA..DE;
    numStates      : Integer;
```

Although this shorthand method of specifying types for variables eliminates the need for a type name, it has a serious limitation. Parameters of procedures and functions cannot have their types specified by a shorthand method. Since subprograms serve a major role in structured programming, this text favors the longhand TYPE method of declarations.

Compatibility of Data Types

Standard Pascal has strict rules governing when variables of different types can be assigned to one another and when an argument can be passed to a parameter of another type. QuickPascal is more permissive in this regard. In QuickPascal, two variables are considered to be of the same type if they consist of the same collection of values. For instance, in the declarations

```
TYPE LowNum = 1..3;

VAR firstFew : LowNum;
    trio     : 1..3;
```

firstFew and trio have the same type.

Suppose two variables or an argument and a parameter are of the same type or are subranges of the same type. Then, in QuickPascal, either variable can be assigned to the other, and the argument can be passed to the parameter by value. In addition, Integer and Char variables can be assigned to Real and String variables, respectively. Also, Integer and Char variables can be passed by value to Real and String parameters, respectively.

The rules governing passing by reference are more restrictive, but difficult to formulate. In this text, we only pass arguments by reference to parameters of the same type.

Comments:

1. QuickPascal does not normally do extensive range checking. For instance, following the declaration

   ```
   VAR intVar : Integer;
       lowNum : 1..5;
   ```

   the statements

   ```
   intVar := 7;
   lowNum := intVar;
   ```

   will generate neither a compiler nor a run-time error. QuickPascal provides for range checking with a special instruction to the compiler called a **compiler directive**. When {$R+} is added to the top of the program, the compiler generates extra code which performs range checking. In this case, the above program statements produce a run-time error. Normally, the compiler directive is used only while debugging to identify places where values might not be within the proper range. The programmer should add extra range-checking code in these areas.

2. Subrange types make a program easy to follow by precisely clarifying the values a variable can assume. Also, as discussed in Comment 1, they are useful in debugging.

3. A function can return a value from an enumerated type.

   ```
   FUNCTION IdentifyState (num : Integer) : Original13;
   { Identify a state given its position in Original13 }
     VAR counter : Integer;
         state   : Original13;
     BEGIN
       counter := 1;
       state := First(state);
       WHILE counter < num DO
         BEGIN
           state := Succ(state);
           counter := counter + 1
         END;
       IdentifyState :=  state
     END;
   ```

4. The DOWNTO option for FOR loops also is permitted for enumerated and subrange types. For instance, the FOR loop in Example 3 could have been written

   ```
   FOR thisMonth := Dec DOWNTO Jan DO
   ```

5. Constants of enumerated or subrange types can be defined. In addition, constants can be used to define subrange types. The declaration part of a QuickPascal program can contain more than one CONST section.

```
TYPE Colors = (blue, red, green, yellow, brown, white, black);

CONST MyFavorite = blue;

VAR primaryColors : MyFavorite..green;
    shade         : (light, medium, dark);

CONST MyShade = dark;
```

6. The Boolean type is similar to the enumerated type. The only difference is that the values of Boolean variables can be displayed with Write and Writeln, whereas enumerated variables cannot.

7. Since the items in an enumerated list are identifiers, they are case insensitive. For instance, in the type Sport, baseball can be written Baseball or BASE-BALL.

PRACTICE PROBLEMS 7.1

1. What is the output of the following program?

```
PROGRAM ListSeasons;

TYPE MonthType  = (jan, feb, mar, apr, may, jun,
                   jul, aug, sep, oct, nov, dec);

VAR month : MonthType;

BEGIN
  month := jan;
  WHILE month <= dec DO
    BEGIN
      CASE month OF
        jan..mar : Writeln('Winter');
        apr..jun : Writeln('Spring');
        jul..sep : Writeln('Summer');
        oct..dec : Writeln('Autumn')
      END;
      month := Succ(month);
      month := Succ(month);
      month := Succ(month)
    END
END.
```

2. Suppose *month* has been declared as in Practice Problem 1. What will be its value after each of the following statements is executed?
   (a) month := Pred(Last(month))
   (b) month := Pred(Last(MonthType))

3. How can the items of an enumerated data type be displayed on the screen?

EXERCISES 7.1

In Exercises 1 through 8, determine whether each of the following definitions is legal.

1. TYPE Voltage = (-1, 0 , 1);

2. TYPE Girls = (Shirley, Betty, Jennifer, Chris, Karla);
      Boys = (Charles, Chris, Mark, David, Tom);

3. TYPE Directions = (N, S, E, W);
      TranscriptGrades = (A, B, C, D, F, W, I);

4. TYPE SomePrimes = (2, 3, 5, 7, 11, 13, 17, 19);

5. TYPE Military = (Army, Navy, Air Force, Marines);

6. TYPE Const = (e, Pi, sqrtOF2);

7. TYPE Sibilants = ('s', 'z');

8. TYPE FamousFunction = (cos, sin, tan, square, square root);

In Exercises 9 through 20, use the following definition and declaration to determine the value of the expression.

```
TYPE ZodiacSigns = (Aries, Taurus, Gemini, Cancer, Leo, Virgo,
                    Libra, Scorpio, Sagittarius, Capricorn,
                    Aquarius, Pisces);

VAR mySign : ZodiacSigns;
```

9. Last(mySign)

10. Last(ZodiacSigns)

11. Succ(First(ZodiacSigns))

12. Pred(Last(mySign))

13. Succ(Pred(Last(mySign)))

14. Pred(Pred(Pred(Last(mySign))))

15. Succ(Succ(First(mySign)))

16. First(ZodiacSigns)

17. Ord(First(mySign))

18. Ord(Pred(Last(ZodiacSigns)))

19. Ord(Succ(First(mySign)))

20. Ord(Succ(Pred(Last(mySign))))

In Exercises 21 through 24, list the elements specified by the subrange definition.

21. SomeChars = 'a'..'f'

22. SymbolType = '!'..'&'

23. FileLabels = 'A'..'H'

24. RankLabels = '0'..'8'

In Exercises 25 through 30, write a TYPE statement to define an enumerated type for the collection. Think of a meaningful name for the type, and list the elements in order where appropriate.

25. the months having 31 days

26. the vowels

27. the planets in our solar system   **28.** the oceans

29. the four compass directions   **30.** the continents

In Exercises 31 and 32, determine the output of the program.

31.
```
TYPE ColorType = (red, orange, yellow, green, blue, indigo, violet);

    VAR color : ColorType;

    BEGIN
      FOR color := violet DOWNTO red DO
        Write(Ord(color):2)
    END.
```

32.
```
TYPE ChoiceList = (no, doubtIt, hmm, maybe, yes);

    VAR choice : ChoiceList;
        count  : Integer;

    PROCEDURE Change (VAR choice : ChoiceList);
      VAR index : Integer;
      BEGIN
        FOR index := 1 TO 3 DO
          IF choice = Last(ChoiceList) THEN
              choice := First(ChoiceList)
            ELSE
              choice := Succ(choice)
      END;

    BEGIN
      choice := First(ChoiceList);
      count := 0;
      WHILE choice <> Last(ChoiceList) DO
        BEGIN
          Change(choice);
          count := count + 1
        END;
      Writeln(count)
    END.
```

In Exercises 33 through 36, find the errors.

33.
```
TYPE LowCase    = 'a'..'z';
     SomeLetters = (c, k, m, p);

    VAR aLetter : SomeLetters;
        oneChar : LowCase;
        aWord   : STRING[25];
```

```
BEGIN
  aLetter := c;
  aWord := 'conundrum';
  oneChar := aWord[1];
  IF aLetter = oneChar THEN
      Writeln('Okee Dokee')
END.
```

34. `TYPE humorsAre = (choleric, sanguine, melancholic, phlematic);`

```
VAR personality : humorsAre;
    person      : STRING;

BEGIN
  Readln(person);
  Readln(personality);
  Writeln(person, ' has a ', personality, ' disposition.')
END.
```

35.
```
VAR anyString : STRING;
    first     : Char;

BEGIN
  Write('Enter any string of symbols: ');
  Readln(anyString);
  first := anyString[1];
  CASE first OF
    'a'..'Z' : Writeln('The first symbol is a letter or a symbol ' +
                       'between 91 and 97 in ASCII value.');
    '0'..'9' : Writeln('The first symbol is a digit.')
  END
END.
```

36. `TYPE SomeLetters = (c, e, h, i, l, o, p, r, t);`

```
VAR aLetter : SomeLetters;
    index   : Integer;
    myWord  : STRING;

BEGIN
  myWord := 'helicopter';
  FOR index := 1 TO Length(myWord) DO
    BEGIN
      aLetter := myWord[index];
      Write(aLetter)
    END
END.
```

37. Consider the TYPE Original13 from Example 4. Write a Boolean function to accept a variable of type Original13 as input and return True if the value of the variable is one of the New England states (MA, CT, RI, NH).

38. Modify Example 3 to display the name of each month and the number of days. The program should use a function that accepts a variable of type Month as input and returns the name of the month as a string.

39. In the child's game "Rock, Paper, Scissors," each of two children call out one of the three words. If they both call out the same word then the game is a tie. Otherwise, "Paper" beats "Rock" (since paper can cover a rock), "Scissors" beats "Paper" (since scissors can cut paper), and "Rock" beats "Scissors" (since a rock can break a pair of scissors). Write a program that requests the responses of the two players (R, P, S) as input and uses the enumerated type (Rock, Paper, Scissors) to determine the outcome.

40. Suppose a local pizza emporium has a special two-topping price for its pizzas. A customer can choose any *two* of the following toppings: Sausage, Pepperoni, Olives, Onions, Green Peppers. Write a program that outputs a list of all possible combinations one might have of these toppings. The program should use an enumerated type for the six toppings, nested FOR loops to tabulate the combinations, and a function to convert each topping to a string.

SOLUTIONS TO PRACTICE PROBLEMS 7.1

1. Winter
Spring
Summer
Autumn

At the end of the fourth pass, the third assignment statement increments the variable *month* past its last defined value, dec. This does not produce an error. Rather, QuickPascal assigns *month* the ordinal number 12 even though there is no item following dec in the enumerated type. The new ordinal value of *month* is therefore greater than the ordinal value of dec, 11, and terminates the WHILE loop. If a fourth Succ statement were executed after exiting the WHILE loop, *month* would have the ordinal value 13.

2. (a) nov. The value of Last(month) is the last item in the enumerated type, that is, dec. The value of Pred(Last(month)) is the item immediately preceding Last(month) in the enumerated type, that is, nov.

(b) nov. Last(month) and Last(MonthType) return the same value.

3. The items can be displayed with a CASE statement.

```
PROGRAM DisplaySeasons;

TYPE Seasons = (winter, spring, summer, autumn);

VAR time : Seasons;

BEGIN
  FOR time := winter TO autumn DO
    CASE time OF
      winter : Writeln('winter');
      spring : Writeln('spring');
      summer : Writeln('summer');
      autumn : Writeln('autumn')
    END
END.
```

7.2 RECORDS

A **record** is a user-defined data type that provides a convenient way of packaging as a single unit several related variables of different types.

Figure 7.1 shows an index card that can be used to hold data about colleges. The three pieces of data, name, state, and year founded, are called **fields**. Each field functions like a variable in which information can be stored and retrieved. The three fields hold a string, a string of length 2, and an Integer, respectively. The layout of the index card can be identified by a name such as CollegeData, which is represented in Pascal as a **record type**.

```
Name: _____

State: ____

Year Founded: _____
```

Figure 7.1 An Index Card Having Three Fields

For programming purposes, the layout of the record is declared by the block of statements

```
TYPE CollegeData = RECORD
                name        : STRING;
                state       : STRING[2];
                yearFounded : Integer
              END;
```

A **record** variable capable of holding the data for a specific college is declared by a statement such as

```
VAR college : CollegeData;
```

Each of the fields is accessed by giving the name of the record variable and the field, separated by a period. For instance, the three fields of the record variable *college* are accessed as college.name, college.state, and college.yearFounded. Figure 7.2 shows a representation of the memory location for the record variable college.

Figure 7.2 Record Variable with Values Assigned to the Fields

EXAMPLE 1   The following program illustrates the record data type.

```
PROGRAM CollegeAges;
{ Demonstration of records }

USES Crt;

TYPE CollegeData = RECORD
                      name        : STRING;
                      state       : STRING[2];
                      yearFounded : Integer
                   END;

VAR college          : CollegeData;
    age, currentYear : Integer;

BEGIN
  ClrScr;
  college.name := 'Montgomery College';
  college.state := 'MD';
  college.yearFounded := 1946;
  Write('Enter the current year: ');
  Readln(currentYear);
  age := currentYear - college.yearFounded;
  Write(college.name, ' was founded ', age, ' years ago in ',
       college.state, '.')
END.

[run]
Enter the current year: 1990
Montgomery College was founded 44 years ago in MD.
```

In general, a record type is created by a TYPE declaration of the form

```
TYPE RecordType = RECORD
                     fieldVariableName1 : Type1;
                     fieldVariableName2 : Type2;
                              .
                              .
                   END;
```

where *RecordType* is the name of the user-defined data type. A record variable is declared to be of that type by a statement of the form

```
VAR recordVar : RecordType;
```

A record can be assigned to another record of the same type, all fields at once, with a statement of the form

```
recordVar1 := recordVar2;
```

EXAMPLE 2 The following program assigns the value of an individual field of one record to a field of another record and also assigns an entire record to another record.

```
PROGRAM RoseBowlWinners;
{ Display the winners and their state from 1984 to 1986 }

USES Crt;

TYPE CollegeData = RECORD
                     name  : STRING;
                     state : STRING[2]
                   END;

VAR winner84, winner85, winner86 : CollegeData;

BEGIN
  ClrScr;
  winner84.name := 'UCLA';
  winner84.state := 'CA';
  winner85.name := 'USC';
  winner85.state := winner84.state;
  winner86 := winner84;
  Writeln('Year  Team  State');
  Writeln(1984, winner84.name:6, winner84.state:4);
  Writeln(1985, winner85.name:6, winner85.state:4);
  Writeln(1986, winner86.name:6, winner86.state:4)
END.

[run]
Year  Team  State
1984  UCLA  CA
1985   USC  CA
1986  UCLA  CA
```

Although an entire record can be transferred with a single assignment statement, statements of the forms

```
Writeln(recordVar)
Readln(recordVar)
```

will not display or read an entire record. In Writeln and Readln statements, each field must be specified explicitly.

EXAMPLE 3 The following modification of the statement part of Example 1 allows the user to supply the college information.

```
BEGIN
  ClrScr;
  Write('Enter name of college: ');
  Readln(college.name);
  Write('Enter state: ');
  Readln(college.state);
  Write('Enter year founded: ');
  Readln(college.yearFounded);
  Writeln(college.name, ' was founded in ',
          college.yearFounded, ' in ', college.state, '.')
END.

[run]
Enter name of college: Harvard
Enter state: MA
Enter year founded: 1636
Harvard was founded in 1636 in MA.
```

WITH Statement

The WITH statement spares the programmer the task of writing the record name and period when referring to a field. A block of the form

```
WITH recordName DO
  statement
```

specifies that any field mentioned in the statement will automatically be assumed to be a field of the named record.

EXAMPLE 4 The first three lines of the statement part of Example 2 can be replaced by the following code:

```
ClrScr;
WITH winner84 DO
  BEGIN
    name  := 'UCLA';
    state := 'CA'
  END;
```

A single WITH statement can specify several different records. For instance, the block

```
WITH record1, record2 DO
  statement
```

specifies that any field mentioned in the statement will automatically be assumed to be a field of one of the named records. If the field happens to be in both records, then the last mentioned record, record2, is used.

EXAMPLE 5   The following program contains a WITH statement listing multiple records.

```
PROGRAM RoseBowl87;
{ Display some information about the 1987 winners }

USES Crt;

TYPE CollegeData       = RECORD
                            name  : STRING;
                            state : STRING[2]
                         END;
     NicknameAndColors = RECORD
                            name   : STRING;
                            colors : STRING
                         END;

VAR winner87 : CollegeData;
    victor87 : NicknameAndColors;

BEGIN
  ClrScr;
  winner87.name := 'Arizona State';
  winner87.state := 'AZ';
  victor87.name := 'Sun Devils';
  victor87.colors := 'Maroon & Gold';
  WITH winner87, victor87 DO
    BEGIN
      Writeln(state);
      Writeln(colors);
      Writeln(name)
    END
END.

[run]
AZ
Maroon & Gold
Sun Devils
```

Nested Records

A field of a record can be any data type, even another record. A WITH statement can specify both the record variable and the name of a record field in order to access a field of the inner record. In the absence of a WITH statement, two periods are needed to access the field.

EXAMPLE 6   In the following program, the field teamID in the record type TeamData is a
record of type NicknameAndColors.

```
PROGRAM RoseBowl;

USES Crt;

TYPE NicknameAndColors = RECORD
                              nickname : STRING;
                              colors   : STRING
                           END;
     TeamData          = RECORD
                            name   : STRING;
                            teamID : NicknameAndColors
                         END;

VAR winner87 : TeamData;

BEGIN
  ClrScr;
  winner87.name := 'Arizona State';
  winner87.teamID.nickname := 'Sun Devils';
  winner87.teamID.colors := 'Maroon & Gold';
  WITH winner87, teamID DO
    BEGIN
      Writeln(name);
      Writeln(nickname);
      Writeln(colors)
    END;
END.

[run]
Arizona State
Sun Devils
Maroon & Gold
```

Passing Records to Subprograms

Parameters of procedures and functions can be of the type RECORD. The type
of the argument in the calling statement must be the same as the type of the
corresponding parameter.

EXAMPLE 7   The following program passes the record from Example 6 to a procedure.

```
PROGRAM TeamName;
{ Display the full name of a football team }

USES Crt;
```

```
TYPE NicknameAndColors = RECORD
                             nickname : STRING;
                             colors   : STRING
                         END;
     TeamData = RECORD
                  name   : STRING;
                  teamID : NicknameAndColors
                END;

VAR winner87 : TeamData;

PROCEDURE JoinFields (team : TeamData);
{ Concatenate the fields  of a record }
  BEGIN
    Writeln(team.teamID.colors + ' ' + team.name + ' ' +
            team.teamID.nickname)
  END;

BEGIN
  ClrScr;
  WITH winner87, teamID DO
    BEGIN
      name := 'Arizona State';
      nickname := 'Sun Devils';
      colors := 'Maroon & Gold'
    END;
  JoinFields(winner87)
END.

[run]
Maroon & Gold Arizona State Sun Devils
```

Comments:

1. Functions cannot return record values. That is, a heading of the form

   ```
   FUNCTION FunctionName (variable : VarType) : RecordType;
   ```

   is not allowed.

2. Relational operators cannot be used to compare two records. For instance, in Example 2 statements of the form

   ```
   IF winner84 = winner85 THEN ...
   ```

   or

   ```
   IF winner85 < winner86 THEN ...
   ```

   are illegal.

3. Several fields of the same type can be declared with the same type identifier. For instance, the declaration of the record type NicknameAndCoach in Example 5 also can be written as

   ```
   TYPE NicknameAndCoach = RECORD
                             name, coach : STRING
                           END;
   ```

4. Records can be directly assigned only to records of identical type. For instance, with the following declarations only record variables a, d, and e can be assigned to each other. Individual fields of all records, however, can be assigned.

```
TYPE FirstRecord  = RECORD
                        quantity : Integer;
                        price    : Real
                    END;
     SecondRecord = RECORD
                        quantity : Integer;
                        price    : Real
                    END;
     ThirdRecord  = FirstRecord;

VAR a : FirstRecord;
    b : SecondRecord;
    c : RECORD
           quantity : Integer;
           price    : Real
        END;
    d : FirstRecord;
    e : ThirdRecord;
```

5. As with enumerated types, a shorthand method can be used to declare a variable as a record type. For instance, in Example 1 the TYPE declaration can be omitted and the variable declaration for college replaced with

```
VAR college : RECORD
                 name        : STRING;
                 state       : STRING[2];
                 yearFounded : Integer
              END;
```

The shorthand method cannot be used with parameters of subprograms; therefore it should be avoided.

PRACTICE PROBLEMS 7.2

1. Find the errors in the following program:

```
TYPE CollegeData = RECORD
                      name  : STRING;
                      state : STRING[2]
                   END;

VAR college : CollegeData;

BEGIN
  name := 'Yale';
  state := 'CT';
  Writeln(name, ' is in ', state)
END.
```

2. What will be the output of the following program?

```
PROGRAM SomeNumericFacts;

TYPE FactType = RECORD
                   square  : Integer;
                   cube    : Integer;
                   perfect : (yes, no)  { Is number a perfect square? }
                END;

VAR number : FactType;
    index  : Integer;

BEGIN
  FOR index := 2 TO 4 DO
    WITH number DO
      BEGIN
        square := Sqr(index);
        cube := square * index;
        IF Trunc(Sqrt(index)) = Sqrt(index) THEN
            perfect := yes
          ELSE
            perfect := no;
        Writeln(index:4, square:4, cube:4, (perfect = yes):6)
      END
END.
```

EXERCISES 7.2

In Exercises 1 through 6, determine the output of the program.

1.
```
TYPE QuoteType = RECORD
                    quote : STRING;
                    who   : STRING      { Who said it }
                 END;

VAR quotation : QuoteType;

BEGIN
  quotation.quote := 'The best way out is always through.';
  quotation.who := 'Robert Frost';
  Writeln(quotation.quote);
  Writeln(quotation.who:40)
END.
```

2.
```
TYPE CarType = RECORD
                  year    : Integer;
                  make    : STRING;
                  model   : STRING;
                  mileage : Integer  {in thousands}
               END;
```

```
    VAR myCar        : CarType;
        thisYear, age : Integer;

    BEGIN
      Readln(myCar.year);
      Readln(myCar.make);
      Readln(myCar.model);
      Readln(thisYear);
      age := thisYear - myCar.year;
      IF (age >= 5) OR (myCar.mileage >= 50) THEN
          Writeln('The warranty on your ', myCar.year, ' ', myCar.make,
                  ' ', myCar.model, ' has expired.')
    END.
```

(User response: 1983, Pontiac, 6000, 1990)

3.
```
    TYPE ArtType = RECORD
                    artist : STRING;
                    title  : STRING;
                    price  : Real
                  END;

    VAR art : ArtType;

    BEGIN
      WITH art DO
        BEGIN
          Readln(artist);
          Readln(title);
          Readln(price);
          Writeln(title, ' by ', artist, ' sold for $', price:1:2)
        END
    END.
```

(User response: Van Gogh, Irises, 53.9E6)

4.
```
    TYPE Address = RECORD
                    name   : STRING[40];
                    street : STRING[50]
                  END;

    VAR husband, wife : Address;

    BEGIN
      husband.name := 'George';
      husband.street := '1600 Pennsylvania Ave';
      wife := husband;
      wife.name := 'Barbara';
      Writeln(wife.name, ' lives at ', wife.street)
    END.
```

```
5. TYPE When  = RECORD
                   month : STRING[3];
                   year  : Integer
                END;
       Event = RECORD
                   desc : STRING;
                   date : When
                END;

   VAR watergate : Event;

   BEGIN
     watergate.desc := 'Break-in of Democratic National Headquarters';
     watergate.date.month := 'JUN';
     watergate.date.year := 1972;
     WITH watergate, date DO
       Writeln(desc, ' occurred in ', month, ' of ', year)
   END.

6. TYPE StudentType = RECORD
                         lastName  : STRING;
                         firstName : STRING;
                         major     : STRING
                      END;

   CONST StudentData =
              'Chang|Dom|Film Studies|Brown|Marie|Math|Leonardo| Sal     |'+
              'Business|Torrence|Alvin|Psychology|EOD|EOD|EOD';

   VAR student          : StudentType;
       data, searchName : STRING;
       found            : Boolean;

   FUNCTION NextField (VAR data : STRING) : STRING;
     BEGIN
       NextField := Copy(data, 1, Pos('|', data) - 1);
       data := Copy(data, Pos('|', data) + 1, Length(data))
     END;

   PROCEDURE Output (student : StudentType);
     BEGIN
       WITH student DO
         Writeln(firstName, ' ', lastName, '''s major is ', major)
     END;
```

```
BEGIN
  data := StudentData;
  Readln(searchName);
  WITH student DO
    REPEAT
      lastName := NextField(data);
      firstName := NextField(data);
      major := NextField(data);
      found := (lastName = searchName)
    UNTIL found OR (lastName = 'EOD');
  IF found THEN
      Output(student)
END.
```
(User response: Brown)

In Exercises 7 through 10, find the errors.

7.
```
TYPE ComicStrip  = RECORD
                     title   : STRING[50];
                     creator : STRING[50]


     DayTimeSoap = RECORD
                     title       : STRING[50];
                     favoriteChar : STRING[50]
```

8.
```
TYPE PhraseData = RECORD
                    phrase    : STRING;
                    itsLength : Integer
                  END;

VAR one, two, three : PhraseData;

BEGIN
  Readln(one.phrase);
  one.itsLength := Length(one.phrase);
  Readln(two.phrase);
  two.itsLength := Length(two.phrase);
  three := one + two;
  Writeln(three.phrase, ' has length ', three.length)
END.
```

9.
```
{ Assume the declarations from Exercise 8 have been made }

FUNCTION AddRecords (one, two : PhraseData) : PhraseData;
{ Adds respective fields of a record and returns the record }
  BEGIN
    AddRecords.phrase := one.phrase + two.phrase;
    AddRecords.itsLength := one.itsLength + two.itsLength
  END;
```

10. { Assume the declarations from Exercise 8 have been made }

```
BEGIN
  one.phrase := 'Cat';
  one.itsLength := Length(one.phrase);
  two.phrase := 'Horse';
  two.itsLength := Length(two.phrase);
  Writeln(one < two)
END.
```

In Exercises 11 through 16, define a record having the fields described in (a), declare a variable having that type, and write an assignment statement for the task in (b).

11. (a) Inventory: Name of item, Quantity in stock, Reorder level, price
   (b) Assign "beans" to the name field

12. (a) Bibliography: Author, Title, Publisher, Copyright date
   (b) Assign "The Old Man and the Sea" to the title field

13. (a) States: Area, Population, Capital, Year it joined the union
   (b) Assign "Springfield" to the capital field

14. (a) U.S. Presidents: Name, Date and place of birth and death, Year of inauguration, College attended
   (b) Assign "Coolidge" to the name field

15. (a) Pulitzer prize winners: Name, Literary form, Year
   (b) Use a WITH statement to assign the data "John Steinbeck, Fiction, 1940" to the fields.

16. (a) Weather: Temperature, Pressure, Humidity, Conditions : (Clear, Cloudy, Rain, Snow, Fog) (**Note:** Use an enumerated type for the Conditions field.)
   (b) Use a WITH statement to assign the data "65, 23, 85, Cloudy" to the fields.

17. Write a program that uses a three-field record to store the coordinates and contents of a location on the screen. The type of the column and row fields should be subranges of Integers and the content field should have type Char. A procedure should request the coordinates and content as input from the keyboard, and another procedure should display the character at the specified location. A third procedure should then move the character 10 positions to the right (wrapping around if necessary) with the character moving one position each time the Enter key is pressed.

18. Write a program that requests a word as input from the keyboard, and then displays the number of letters in the word and whether or not the word begins with a capital letter. Use a record with a String, Integer, and Boolean field. Procedures should be used to obtain the input, determine the information to be displayed, and display the information.

    ```
    [sample run]
    Enter word: Pascal
    Number of letters: 6
    Capitalized: TRUE
    ```

19. Write a program to request a secret password and number as input from the keyboard. Use a two-field record to store the input. Compare this record to the record containing the correct secret password and number and inform the user whether he or she has answered correctly. Procedures should be used to obtain the input and determine if the input is correct. Use the UpCase function to convert the input password to uppercase letters before comparing it.

    ```
    [sample run]
    Enter the secret password: Thunder
    Enter the secret number: 99
    Welcome comrade.
    ```

20. Write a menu-driven program to input, alter, and display a person's name, zip code, and area code. The information should be stored in a three-field record and procedures should be used carry out the tasks mentioned above.

    ```
    [sample run]
    1. Input name, zip code, and area code.
    2. Alter information.
    3. Display current information.
    4. Quit.
    Select an option: 1
    Enter name: John Jones
    Enter zip code: 20901
    Enter area code: 301
    Select an option: 2
    Enter data to be altered (N, Z, A): Z
    Enter new zip code: 23456
    Select an option: 3
    John Jones  23456  301
    Select an option: 4
    ```

21. Write a function that accepts as input a four-field record holding a student's three hourly exam grades and final exam grade, and returns a letter grade. The final exam should count as two hourly exams. Use the WITH keyword to access the record's fields.

22. Write a function that accepts as input two records of type CollegeData (see Example 2) and returns True if the records contain the same information in each field and False otherwise.

23. Define a three-field record Phone to hold a home, work, and FAX phone number. Then define a two-field record Client with a string field for a name, and a Phone field for the person's three phone numbers. Write a program that requests a name and three phone numbers as input and then displays the name as it would appear in a card file. Assume that the name has two parts.

```
[sample run]
Enter client's name: Al Adams
Enter home phone number: 123-4567
Enter work phone number: 333-4444
Enter FAX number: 999-1212

Adams, Al
123-4567 (h)
333-4444 (w)
999-1212 (FAX)
```

SOLUTIONS TO PRACTICE PROBLEMS 7.2

1. The variables in the statement part of the program must include both the record variable and the field name. The statement part can be corrected to either

```
BEGIN
  college.name := 'Yale';
  college.state := 'CT';
  Writeln(college.name, ' is in ', college.state)
END.
```

or

```
BEGIN
  WITH college DO
    BEGIN
      name := 'Yale';
      state := 'CT';
      Writeln(name, ' is in ', state)
    END
END.
```

2.
```
2   4    8   FALSE
3   9   27   FALSE
4  16   64   TRUE
```

7.3 SETS   *omit for now!*

A common kind of condition found in IF, WHILE, and UNTIL statements is true if and only if the value of a variable is in a certain list of desired values. An example is

```
IF (myVar = 1) OR (myVar = 3) OR (myVar = 5) OR (myVar = 7) THEN
    statement
```

The longer the list of values, the more unwieldy the conditional statement.

The idea contained in the conditional statement above is simply that given the collection of numbers [1, 3, 5, 7], one would like the condition to be true, if and only if, the value of myVar is in that collection. QuickPascal has a special IN operator which does exactly this. Thus, the conditional statement can be rewritten as follows.

```
IF myVar IN [1, 3, 5, 7] THEN
     statement
```

The IN operator returns the Boolean value True if myVar is one of the numbers 1, 3, 5, or 7 and returns False otherwise. The collection

```
[1, 3, 5, 7]
```

is called a **set** and 1, 3, 5, and 7 are called **elements** of the set. In general, a set is a collection of up to 256 elements of the same type where the allowable types are Integer, Char, or an enumerated type. Only the numbers from 0 through 255 can appear in a set of Integers.

As an alternative to listing the elements of a set each time it is needed, one can define a type with the keyword SET. Then a set variable of this type can be declared in the VAR declaration part of the program and assigned elements with assignment statements. For a numeric set, the following declaration can be made.

```
TYPE IntSet = SET OF 0..255;

VAR mySet : IntSet;
```

Then, after the assignment

```
mySet := [1, 3, 5, 7];
```

the original conditional statement above can be rewritten as

```
IF myVar IN mySet THEN
     statement
```

Ranges can be used to specify the elements of a set. For example, the set [1, 2, 3, 4, 5, 9, 11] can be written [1..5, 9, 11]

EXAMPLE 1 Write a program that requests a person's age and decides whether they get a discount rate at a theater. Assume children up to age 12 and senior citizens 62 and older get the discount rate.

SOLUTION
```
PROGRAM TheaterRate;
{ Decide whether a patron gets a ticket discount }

USES Crt;

TYPE IntSet = SET OF 0..255;
```

```
VAR discountAge : IntSet;
    patronAge   : Integer;

BEGIN
  ClrScr;
  discountAge := [0..12, 62..255];
  Write('Enter the patron''s age: ');
  Readln(patronAge);
  IF patronAge IN discountAge THEN
     Writeln('Discount price')
   ELSE
     Writeln('Full price')
END.

[run]
Enter the patron's age: 18
Full price
```

If a set does not change during execution of the program it may be declared as a constant. The set, discountAge, in the example could have been declared by

```
CONST discountAge = [0..12, 62..255];
```

allowing the TYPE statement, the first declaration in VAR, and the assignment statement in the program to be omitted.

The limitation of 256 elements in any set results from QuickPascal's method of storing sets in memory. Note, however, that since there are only 256 characters in the ASCII character table, one can have a set of Char with as many distinct elements as desired. The following example illustrates how using sets can greatly increase a program's readability.

EXAMPLE 2 Write a program which decides, given any noun, whether it should should be preceded by "a" or "an." Use it in the sentence "A(n) *noun* by any other name would smell as sweet."

SOLUTION
```
PROGRAM SomeSaying;
{ Demonstrate a constant set }

USES Crt;

CONST quote    = ' by any other name would smell as sweet.';
      anLetters = ['a', 'e', 'i', 'o', 'u'];

VAR noun      : STRING;
    firstChar : Char;
```

```
BEGIN
  ClrScr;
  Write('Enter a singular noun: ');
  Readln(noun);
  firstChar := noun[1];
  IF firstChar IN anLetters THEN
      Writeln('An ', noun, quote)
    ELSE
      Writeln('A ', noun, quote)
END.
```

```
[run]
Enter a singular noun: rose
A rose by any other name would smell as sweet.
```

```
[run]
Enter a singular noun: antelope
An antelope by any other name would smell as sweet.
```

Finally, in addition to Integer and Char sets, one may declare a user-defined set. Care must be taken to compare only identifiers of the same type when using the IN operator. This is illustrated in the following example:

EXAMPLE 3 Write a program that tells whether a color is among the additive primary colors and/or the subtractive primary colors.

SOLUTION

```
PROGRAM PrimaryColors;
{ Illustrate a user-defined set }

USES Crt;

TYPE Colors = (red, orange, yellow, green, blue, indigo, violet);
     ColorType = SET OF Colors;

VAR addColors, subColors : ColorType;
    testColor            : Colors;

BEGIN
  ClrScr;
  addColors := [red, green, blue];
  subColors := [red, yellow, blue];
  testColor := green;
  IF testColor IN addColors THEN
    Writeln('Additive primary color');
  IF testColor IN subColors THEN
    Writeln('Subtractive primary color')
END.

[run]
Additive primary color
```

Note in this example that the comparison in the conditional clause was between identifiers of the same type, *Colors*. If *testColor* had been declared to be a String, the compiler would have generated a type mismatch error. The usual restrictions on enumerated types when using Readln and Writeln (as covered in section 7.1) apply to user-defined sets.

Union, Intersection, and Difference of Sets

If set1 and set2 are sets of the same type, then their **union** is the set consisting of those elements either in set1 or in set2 (or both). The **intersection** of set1 and set2 is the set consisting of those elements in *both* set1 and set2. The **difference** of two sets, set1 − set2, is the set consisting of those elements in set1 that are *not* in set2. The QuickPascal operators for union, intersection, and difference of sets are +, *, and −, respectively. These operators are summarized in Table 7.1.

Operation	Notation	Resulting Set
union	set1 + set2	elements in set1 or set2
intersection	set1 * set2	elements in set1 and set2
difference	set1 − set2	elements in set1 but not in set2

Table 7.1   Union, Intersection, and Difference of Sets

EXAMPLE 4   Write a program that accepts two words and lists the letters found in either, both, and neither. Treat upper and lowercase letters as identical.

SOLUTION
```
PROGRAM SetOperations;
{ Demonstrate union, intersection, and difference }

USES Crt;

TYPE CharSetType = SET OF Char;

CONST AllLetters = ['A'..'Z'];

VAR word1, word2 : STRING;
    set1, set2   : CharSetType;

PROCEDURE GetWords (VAR word1, word2 : STRING);
  BEGIN
    Write('Enter the first word:  ');
    Readln(word1);
    Write('Enter the second word: ');
    Readln(word2)
  END;
```

```
PROCEDURE BuildSet (aWord : STRING; VAR aSet : CharSetType);
{ Build a set of all characters occurring in aWord }
  VAR index : Integer;
  BEGIN
    aSet := [];                              { The empty set }
    FOR index := 1 TO Length(aWord) DO
      aSet := aSet + [UpCase(aWord[index])];
  END;

PROCEDURE OutputSet (theSet : CharSetType);
List the letters occurring in theSet }
VAR index : Char;
BEGIN
  FOR index := 'A' TO 'Z' DO
    IF index IN theSet THEN
        Write(index:2);
  Writeln
END;

BEGIN
  ClrScr;
  GetWords(word1, word2);
  BuildSet(word1, set1);
  BuildSet(word2, set2);
  Write('Letters in at least one word: ');
  OutputSet(set1 + set2);                    { union }
  Write('Letters in both words:        ');
  OutputSet(set1 * set2);                    { intersection }
  Write('Letters NOT in either word:   ');
  OutputSet(AllLetters - (set1 + set2))      { difference }
END.
```

```
[run]
Enter the first word:  confusion
Enter the second word: functional
Letters in at least one word:  A C F I L N O S T U
Letters in both words:         C F I N O U
Letters NOT in either word:    B D E G H J K M P Q R V W X Y Z
```

Relational Operators

Two sets are **equal** if they have exactly the same elements. If sets A and B have the same type, then set A is a **subset** of set B if every element of A is in B. The four relational operators for sets are = (equals), <> (not equal), <= (is a subset of), and >= (contains as a subset).

EXAMPLE 5 The following program demonstrates the relational operators for sets.

```
PROGRAM SetRelationalOperators;

VAR letters, vowels : SET OF Char;

BEGIN
  letters := ['a'..'z'];
  vowels := ['a', 'e', 'i', 'o', 'u'];
  Writeln(vowels = letters);
  Writeln(vowels <> letters);
  Writeln(vowels <= letters);
  Writeln(vowels >= letters)
END.

[run]
FALSE
TRUE
TRUE
FALSE
```

Comments:

1. A set containing no elements is called an **empty set**. If the set, mySet, is empty then the condition

   ```
   myVar IN mySet
   ```

   will always be False.

2. A set variable should be initialized before it is used. In the absence of any specific values, a set should be initialized as empty. This can be done by a statement like the following.

   ```
   mySet := []
   ```

   A statement of this sort appears in one of the procedures in Example 4.

3. Although a set variable can be declared directly as shown below,

   ```
   VAR mySet : SET OF 0..255;
   ```

   it is better first to define a type, and then declare the variable to be of that type. Doing this facilitates passing sets to procedures.

PRACTICE PROBLEMS 7.3

1. Determine the output of the following program.

   ```
   PROGRAM Vacation;

   TYPE MonthType = (jan, feb, mar, apr, may, jun,
                     jul, aug, sep, oct, nov, dec);
        MonthSet  = SET OF MonthType;
   ```

```
CONST wholeYear = [jan..dec];
      summer   = [jun..aug];

VAR schoolYear, summerJob, vacationMonths : MonthSet;
    month                                 : MonthType;

BEGIN
  schoolYear := wholeYear - summer;
  summerJob := [jun, jul];
  vacationMonths := wholeYear - (schoolYear + summerJob);
  month := jun;
  IF month IN vacationMonths THEN
     Writeln('Have a good time.')
    ELSE
     Writeln('You cannot go that month.')
END.
```

2. Is the following condition True or False?

```
[bass, trout, salmon] = [trout, bass, salmon]
```

EXERCISES 7.3

In Exercises 1 through 8, what is the value of *newSet* after the statement is executed?

```
TYPE NumSetType = SET OF 0..255;

VAR set1, set2, newSet : NumSetType;

BEGIN
  set1 := [1..5, 7, 9];
  set2 := [1..3, 6, 8];
```

1. newSet := set1 + set2

2. newSet := set1 * set2

3. newSet := set1 - set2

4. newSet := set2 - set1

5. newSet := set1 - set1

6. newSet := (set1 + set2) - (set1 * set2)

7. newSet := (set1 * set2) - set1

8. newSet := (set2 - set1) + (set1 - set2)

In Exercises 9 through 12, find the errors.

9. TYPE Continuum = SET OF Reals;

10. VAR setVar : SET OF Char;

```
BEGIN
  setVar := [];
  setVar := setVar + 'f'
END.
```

11. TYPE CharSet = SET OF Char;

    CONST AllLetters = ['A'..'Z'];

    VAR mySet : CharSet;

    BEGIN
      mySet := AllLetters;
      mySet := mySet + [!]
    END.

12. TYPE IntSet = SET OF Integer;

    VAR mySet : IntSet;
        index : Integer;

    BEGIN
      mySet := [];
      FOR index := 0 TO 5 DO
        mySet := mySet + [index]
    END.

In Exercises 13 through 18, assume the following definitions and declarations have been made. What are the elements of each set after the execution of the program segment?

```
TYPE DecisionType = (no, doubtIt, hmm, maybe, yes);
     CharSet      = SET OF Char;
     DecSetType   = SET OF DecisionType;

CONST Letters = ['A'..'Z'];

VAR decision  : DecSetType;
    someChars : CharSet;
    index1    : DecisionType;
    index2    : Char;
```

13. decision := [no, doubtIt];
    decision := [hmm, maybe, yes] + decision;
    decision := decision - [no, yes]

14. someChars := Letters * ['D'..'G', 'Z'];
    someChars := someChars - ['E'..'Y']

15. decision := [];
    FOR index1 := First(DecisionType) TO Last(DecisionType) DO
      decision := decision + [index1];

16. someChars := [];
    FOR index2 := 'A' TO 'Z' DO
      IF index2 IN ['A'..'E'] THEN
        someChars := someChars + [index2]
       ELSE
        someChars := someChars - [index2]

```
17. decision := [];
    index1 := First(DecisionType);
    REPEAT
      decision := decision + [index1];
      index1 := Succ(index1)
    UNTIL ([no, hmm] <= decision) OR (index1 = Last(DecisionType))

18. someChars := Letters;
    index2 := 'Z';
    WHILE (['A', 'E'] <= someChars) AND (index2 <> 'A') DO
      BEGIN
        someChars := someChars - [index2];
        index2 := Pred(index2)
      END
```

In Exercises 19 through 24, write a subprogram to perform the stated task.

19. Count the number of elements in a set of characters.

20. Given a sentence, construct the set containing the different lengths of words in the sentence. Assume the only punctuation in the sentence is the terminating period. For instance, the sentence "My pencil is on the table." results in the set [2, 3, 5, 6].

21. Given two sets of characters, determine if either is a proper subset of the other. (**Note:** set1 is a proper subset of set2 if set1 is a subset of set2 and set1 is unequal to set2.)

22. Given a set of uppercase letters, determine the highest letter in the set.

23. Given two Integers between 0 and 255, construct the set of all odd numbers between (and possibly including) the two.

24. Consider the following type declarations:

```
TYPE VitaminType = (A, B6, B12, C, D, E, K, Folacin, Niacin,
                      Riboflavin, Thiamin, Choline, Biotin);
     VitaminSet  = SET OF VitaminType;
     Food        = RECORD
                      name : STRING;       { Name of a food }
                      vita : VitaminSet    { Vitamins in the food }
                   END;
```

Write a procedure, with two parameters of type Food, that displays the vitamins present in a meal composed of the two foods and displays the missing vitamins.

25. An anagram is a word formed by reordering the letters of another word. For instance, EDUCATION and CAUTIONED are anagrams of each other. Write a program that requests two words as input, where each word has no duplicate letters, and tells whether the words are anagrams of each other.

26. An employer has a list of eight desirable traits for job applicants: Alert, Brave, Computer literate, Diligent, Experienced in Pascal, First-rate education, Good natured, Humorous. Write a program that requests the letters describ-

ing a job applicant's traits as input from the keyboard and offers a job if the applicant has 6 or more of the desired traits. The traits should be stored in a set.

SOLUTIONS TO PRACTICE PROBLEMS 7.3

1. You cannot go that month. The constant *wholeYear* is a set containing all the elements of the enumerated type, that is, all the months of the year. The constant *summer* contains the months jun, jul, and aug. The assignment statement for *schoolYear* takes the difference of *wholeYear* and *summer*. Thus, *schoolYear* is the set, [jan, feb, mar, apr, may, sep, oct, nov, dec]. The situation is similar for *vacationMonths* as illustrated below.

```
schoolYear              [jan, feb, mar, apr, may, sep, oct, nov, dec]

schoolYear + summerJob  [jan, feb, mar, apr, may, jun, jul, sep, oct,
                         nov, dec].

vacationMonths          [aug]
```

2. The condition is True. The elements of a set are not ordered.

Chapter 7
Summary

1. In addition to the predefined data types (Integer, Real, String, Char and Boolean), an *enumerated* data type consisting of a list of identifiers may be defined with a TYPE statement.

2. An enumerated data type, once defined, determines not only the elements appearing in the data type, but also their order. The left-most element has ordinal number 0, the element immediately to its right has ordinal number 1, and so on.

3. If aVar has an enumerated data type, then Ord(aVar) returns the ordinal number of the value of aVar. Pred(aVar) and Succ(aVar) return the elements immediately preceding and following the value of aVar in the enumerated data type. First(aVar) and Last(aVar) return the left-most and right-most elements of aVar's enumerated data type.

4. Enumerated types, along with Integer, Char, and Boolean types are known as *ordinal types*. Ord, Succ, Pred, Last, and First can be applied to any ordinal data type.

5. A *subrange* type consists of a specified range of an ordinal type.

6. A *record* is a user-defined data type that provides a convenient way of packaging as a single unit several related variables of possibly different types.

7. Once a record has been defined, a variable may be declared to be of that type. Such a variable has one *field* for each field specified in the record definition. If the variable is aVar, and one of the fields is called myField, then that field is accessed by the name aVar.myField.

8. The WITH statement spares the programmer the task of writing the record name and period when referring to a field of a record variable. WITH defines a block within which a record variable's fields may be accessed by specifying only the field.

9. Records may be *nested*, that is, a field of a record may itself be a record.

10. The SET keyword can be used to declare a set variable. A set is a collection of no more than 256 elements of one of the three types Integer (0 through 255), Char, or enumerated. The elements in any one set must have the same type.

11. The expression aVar IN mySet is True if and only if the value of aVar is in the set, mySet. The subset operator <= returns a True value if every element of the set preceding the operator is contained in the set following the operator.

12. The operators, +, *, and − perform set union, intersection and difference, respectively. The *union* of two sets is the set of elements that are in either set. The *intersection* of two sets is the set of elements that are in both sets. The *difference* of two sets, set1 − set2, is the set containing all elements in the first set that are not in the second set.

Chapter 7
Programming Projects

1. In a certain city, police officers receive extra pay for weekend duties. Their hourly rate is increased by 50% for Saturday work and doubled for Sunday. Write a program that requests the name of an officer, the hourly wage, and the number of hours worked each day of the week as input from the keyboard, and returns the wages for the week and the number of hours worked as output. A variable of an enumerated type whose items are the days of the week should be used as the index of a FOR loop requesting the hours worked each day.

```
[sample run]
Enter the officer's name: Richard Tracy
Enter the hourly wage: 23.45
Enter the number of hours worked each day from Sunday to Saturday.
Sunday: 6
Monday: 5
Tuesday: 8
Wednesday: 0
Thursday: 0
Friday: 6
Saturday: 8
Wages for week: Richard Tracy      $1008.35
Number of Hours Worked: 33
```

2. *Rational Arithmetic*. Write a program that requests two positive rational numbers and one of the operations + or * as input, and displays the appropriate sum or product as a rational number. Each rational number should be stored in a record having two Integer fields, one for the numerator and one for the denominator. (Make the simplifying assumption that all numerators and denominators arising are no greater than MaxInt.) The sum or product should be displayed in reduced form. Exercise 28 of Section 6.1 gives the algorithm for finding the greatest common divisor of two integers. The operations + and * should be carried out in procedures and the greatest common divisor should be calculated in a function.

```
[sample run]
Enter numerator of first rational number: 5
Enter denominator of first rational number: 6
Enter numerator of second rational number: 4
Enter denominator of second rational number: 9
Enter the operation ( + or * ): ±
5/6 + 4/9 = 23/18
```

3. The Ford Model T automobile was produced from 1908 to 1927. Jane Edsel, an avid collector of Model T's, owns cars made in 1910, 1912, 1915, 1916, 1920, 1924, and 1927. She is planning an exhibition and hopes to display Model T's from as many years as possible. To complement her collection she will borrow cars from fellow collectors John Escort and James Mustang. John owns Model T's made in 1911, 1915, 1920, and 1923. James owns Model T's made in 1909, 1915, 1920, 1923, and 1926. Write a program to

   (a) request the production years of the cars owned by Jane, John, and James as input from the keyboard and store the information, in an appropriate form, in three sets. (Recall that sets of Integers must range from 0 to 255.)

   (b) display the list of the available production years.

   (c) display the list of the missing production years.

   (d) display the list of cars in both John's and James' collections, but not in Jane's collection. (Jane will choose the better car for each year from this list.)

8

Arrays

8.1 ONE-DIMENSIONAL ARRAYS

A **variable** (or simple variable) is a name to which the computer can assign a single value. An **array variable** is a collection of simple variables of the same type, to which the computer can efficiently assign a list of values.

Consider the following situation. Suppose you want to evaluate the exam grades for 30 students. Not only do you want to compute the average score, but you also want to display the names of the students whose scores are above average. You can accomplish this with the program outlined below.

```
PROGRAM ExamGrades;
{ Analyze exam grades }

VAR student1, student2, ..., student30 : STRING;
    score1,   score2,   ..., score30   : Integer;
    average                            : Real;

PROCEDURE GetStudent (VAR name : STRING; VAR score, total : Integer);
{ Get the data for a single student; increment total by score }
  BEGIN
    Write('Enter a student''s name: ');
    Readln(name);
    Write('Enter the student''s score: ');
    Readln(score);
    total := total + score
  END;

PROCEDURE GetDataAndCalculateAverage
              (VAR student1, student2, ..., student30 : STRING;
               VAR score1,   score2,   ..., score30   : Integer;
               VAR average                           : Real);
{ Get student data and calculate average grade }
  VAR total : Integer;
  BEGIN
    total := 0;
    GetStudent(student1, score1, total);
    GetStudent(student2, score2, total);
    GetStudent(student3, score3, total);
         .
         .
         .
    GetStudent(student30, score30, total);
    average := total / 30
  END;

PROCEDURE ShowIfAboveAverage (name : STRING; score : Integer;
                              average : Real);
  BEGIN
    IF score > average THEN
        Writeln(name, ' is above average')
  END;
```

```
PROCEDURE DisplayTopStudents
             (VAR student1, student2, ..., student30 : STRING;
              VAR score1,   score2,   ..., score30   : Integer;
                  average                             : Real);
  BEGIN
    ShowIfAboveAverage(student1, score1, average);
    ShowIfAboveAverage(student2, score2, average);
    ShowIfAboveAverage(student3, score3, average);
        .
        .
        .
    ShowIfAboveAverage(student30, score30, average)
  END;

BEGIN
  GetDataAndCalculateAverage(student1, student2, ..., student30,
                             score1,   score2,   ..., score30,
                             average);
  DisplayTopStudents(student1, student2, ..., student30,
                     score1,   score2,   ..., score30,
                     average)
END.
```

This program is going to be uncomfortably long. What's most frustrating is that the 30 sets of calls are very similar and look as if they should be condensed into a short loop. A shorthand notation for the many parameters in the procedures would be welcome. It would be nice if we could just write

```
FOR i := 1 TO 30 DO
  BEGIN
    Write('Enter a student: ');
    Readln(studenti);
    Write('Enter the student''s score: ');
    Readln(scorei);
    total := total + scorei
  END;
```

Of course, this will not work. The compiler will treat studenti and scorei as two variable names and display an "undeclared identifier" error message. Even if the variables studenti and scorei were declared, the loop would just keep reassigning new values to them. At the end of the loop they would have the values of the 30th data items.

Pascal provides a data structure called an **array** that lets us do what we tried to accomplish in the loop. The variable names will be similar to those in the Readln statements. They will be

```
student[1], student[2], student[3], . . ., student[30]
```

and

```
score[1], score[2], score[3], . . . , score[30].
```

We refer to these collections of variables as the array variables student and score. The numbers inside the brackets of the individual variables are called **subscripts**, and each individual variable is called a **subscripted variable** or **element**. For instance, student[3] is the third subscripted variable of the array *student*, and score[20] is the 20th subscripted variable of the array *score*.

Array variables have the same kinds of names as simple variables. If *arrayName* is the name of an array variable and *m* and *n* are Integers, then the statement

```
TYPE ArrayTypeName = ARRAY [m..n] OF ElementType;

VAR arrayName : ArrayTypeName;
```

reserves space in memory to hold the values of the subscripted variables *arrayName*[m], *arrayName*[m + 1], *arrayName*[m + 2], . . ., *arrayName*[n]. The spread of the subscripts specified by the type declaration is called the **range** of the array. In particular, the arrays needed for the program above are declared as follows.

```
TYPE ThirtyNames   = ARRAY [1..30] OF STRING;
     ThirtyIntegers = ARRAY [1..30] OF Integer;

VAR student : ThirtyNames;
    score   : ThirtyIntegers;
```

These declarations tell the compiler to set aside a portion of memory for 30 student names and 30 exam grades. See Figure 8.1.

Figure 8.1 The Array *score*

Values can be assigned to individual elements of an array with Read, Readln, or assignment statements and displayed with Write and Writeln statement.

EXAMPLE 1   The following program, along with the proper response to the Readln statement, records the names of the last three Presidents into an array and displays the names. The array is shown in Figure 8.2. The array contain elements with subscripts ranging from 39 through 41.

```
PROGRAM Presidents;
{ Demonstrate arrays }

USES Crt;
```

```
TYPE Names = ARRAY [39..41] OF STRING;

VAR presName : Names;     { Presidents' names }
    presNum  : Integer;   { chronological number of President }

BEGIN
  ClrScr;
  presName[39] := 'Jimmy Carter';
  Write('Enter the name of the 40th President: ');
  Readln(presName[40]);
  presNum := 41;
  presName[presNum] := 'George Bush';
  FOR presNum := 39 TO 41 DO
    Writeln(presName[presNum], ' is President #', presNum)
END.

[run]
Enter the name of the 40th President: Ronald Reagan
Jimmy Carter is President #39
Ronald Reagan is President #40
George Bush is President #41
```

	presName[39]	presName[40]	presName[41]
presName	Jimmy Carter	Ronald Reagan	George Bush

Figure 8.2   The Array presName of Example 1

Write and Writeln cannot display all the elements of an array in a single statement. For instance, the statement

```
Writeln(presName)
```

is not valid and results in the compiler error "Cannot write expressions of this type." Also, Read and Readln cannot input all the elements of an array in a single statement. However, assignment statements do not have this limitation. For instance, in the program above, if a second array of type Names, called anotherPres, is declared, then the statement

```
anotherPres := presName
```

will assign the values of all the elements of presName to the corresponding elements of anotherPres. This is the way entire arrays are copied or duplicated.

An **array constant** can be used to assign values to the elements of an array. The declaration statement of an array constant has the form

```
CONST ArrayConstantName : ArrayTypeName = (valuem, valuem+1, . . . .,
                                           valuen);
```

The type of the constant specified following the colon and the values of the elements of the array are given one after the other. (Every element must be assigned a value.)

EXAMPLE 2   The following program displays the names of the last three Presidents.

```
PROGRAM Presidents;
{ Demonstrate arrays }

USES Crt;

TYPE Names = ARRAY [39..41] OF STRING;

CONST SpecificPres : Names = ('Jimmy Carter', 'Ronald Reagan',
                              'George Bush');

VAR presName : Names;     { Presidents' names }
    presNum  : Integer;   { Chronological number of President }

BEGIN
  ClrScr;
  presName := SpecificPres;
  FOR presNum := 39 TO 41 DO
    Writeln(presName[presNum], ' is President #', presNum)
END.
```

The next example shows how arrays are used to access information.

EXAMPLE 3   The following program stores information about Presidents into arrays and allows the user to request information.

```
PROGRAM AgeOfInauguration;
{ Demonstrate use of arrays for table lookup }

USES Crt;

TYPE Names = ARRAY [39..41] OF STRING;
     Ages  = ARRAY [39..41] OF Integer;

VAR presName  : Names;     { Presidents' names }
    presAge   : Ages;      { Age at inauguration }
    presNum   : Integer;   { Chronological number of President }
    president : STRING;     { Name input by user }
```

```
BEGIN
  ClrScr;
  presName[39] := 'Jimmy Carter';
  presAge[39]  := 52;
  presName[40] := 'Ronald Reagan';
  presAge[40]  := 69;
  presName[41] := 'George Bush';
  presAge[41]  := 64;
  Write('Enter the name of one of the last 3 Presidents: ');
  Readln(president);
  presNum := 39;
  WHILE (presName[presNum] <> president) AND (presNum <= 41) DO
    presNum := presNum + 1;
  IF presNum >= 42 THEN
      Writeln('That name is incorrect.')
    ELSE
      Writeln(president, ' became President #', presNum,
              ' at age ', presAge[presNum])
END.
```

```
[run]
Enter the name of one of the last 3 Presidents: Ronald Reagan
Ronald Reagan became President #40 at age 69
```

The arrays presName and presAge from Example 3 are referred to as **parallel arrays** since elements having the same subscript are related. (See Figure 8.3.) In many applications, a collection of parallel arrays is best converted into a single array of records. (See Figure 8.4.)

	presName[39]	presName[40]	presName[41]
presName	Jimmy Carter	Ronald Reagan	George Bush

	presAge[39]	presAge[40]	presAge[41]
presAge	52	69	64

Figure 8.3 Parallel Arrays

	pres[39]	pres[40]	pres[41]	
pres	Jimmy Carter	Ronald Reagan	George Bush	name
	52	69	64	age

Figure 8.4 Array of Records

EXAMPLE 4   Rewrite the program of Example 3 using a single array of records.

SOLUTION
```
PROGRAM AgeAtInauguration;
{ Demonstrate use of arrays for table lookup }

USES Crt;

TYPE Presidents = RECORD
                    name : STRING;
                    age  : Integer;  { Age at inauguration }
                  END;
     RecentPres = ARRAY [39..41] OF Presidents;

VAR pres      : RecentPres; { Recent Presidents' data }
    presNum   : Integer;    { Chronological # of President }
    president : STRING;      { President name input by user }

BEGIN
  ClrScr;
  pres[39].name := 'Jimmy Carter';
  pres[39].age  := 52;
  pres[40].name := 'Ronald Reagan';
  pres[40].age  := 69;
  pres[41].name := 'George Bush';
  pres[41].age  := 64;
  Write('Enter the name of one of the last 3 Presidents: ');
  Readln(president);
  presNum := 39;
  WHILE (pres[presNum].name <> president) AND (presNum <= 41) DO
    presNum := presNum + 1;
  IF presNum >= 42 THEN
      Writeln('That name is incorrect.')
    ELSE
      Writeln(president, ' became President #', presNum,
              ' at age ', pres[presNum].age);
END.
```

The Integers m and n in the declaration

```
TYPE ArrayTypeName = ARRAY [m..n] OF ElementType;
```

can be literals, constants, or expressions involving constants and literals, but not variables.

EXAMPLE 5   Determine whether each of the following declarations is valid.

(a) `CONST N = 3;`
    `TYPE HorseRace = ARRAY [1..N] OF STRING;`
(b) `VAR n : Integer;`
    `PROCEDURE KentuckyDerby;`
    `TYPE HorseRace = ARRAY [1..n] OF STRING;`

(c) `CONST M = 1;`
`     N = 2;`
`TYPE HorseRace = ARRAY [M - 3..Sqr(N) + 5] OF STRING;`

(d) `CONST R = 1.5;`
`TYPE HorseRace = ARRAY [1..2 * R] OF STRING;`

SOLUTION (a) Valid. One or both of the Integers specifying the range can be given as constants.

(b) Not valid. An Integer specifying the range of an array cannot be the value of a variable. The size of the array is determined at compile time and cannot be altered during runtime.

(c) Valid. Here the range of the array will be $-2..9$. Either M or N can be negative. The only requirement is that $-32768 \leq M \leq N \leq 32767$. Built-in, but not user-defined, functions, can be used in the expressions.

(d) Not valid. Since R has the type Real, so does $2 * R$.

If the range of an array has been declared as a type, then the name of the type can be used in the declaration of the array. For instance, the declaration

```
TYPE Three    = 1..3;
     HorseRace = ARRAY [Three] OF STRING;
```

is valid. That is, an array type declaration can have the form

```
TYPE ArrayType = ARRAY [IndexType] OF ElementType;
```

where *IndexType* is an ordinal type (or a subrange of an ordinal type) and *ElementType* is any type.

```
TYPE Months        = (Jan, Feb, Mar, Apr, May, Jun,
                      Jul, Aug, Sep, Oct, Nov, Dec);
     SummerMonths  = Jun..Aug;
     Days          = 28..31;
     Lengths       = ARRAY [Months] OF Days;
     summerLengths = ARRAY [SummerMonths] OF Days;
```

An array can be used as a checklist or frequency table, as in the next example.

EXAMPLE 6 The following program requests a sentence as input and records the number of occurrences of each letter of the alphabet. An array having the characters from 'A' through 'Z' as subscripts is used to record the number of occurrences of the letters in a natural way.

```
PROGRAM LetterFrequency;
{ Count occurrences of different letters in a sentence }

USES Crt;

TYPE letterCount = ARRAY ['A'..'Z'] OF Integer;
```

```
    VAR count : letterCount;        { occurrences of letters }

  PROCEDURE GetAndCountLetters (VAR count : letterCount);
  { Read and tally the letters of a sentence }
    VAR letter    : Char;
        sentence : STRING;
        charNum  : Integer;
    BEGIN
      FOR letter := 'A' TO 'Z' DO
        count[letter] := 0;
      Writeln('Enter a sentence and hit return.');
      Readln(sentence);
      FOR charNum := 1 TO Length(sentence) DO
        BEGIN
          letter := UpCase(sentence[charNum]);
          IF letter IN ['A'..'Z'] THEN
              count[letter] := count[letter] + 1
        END
    END;

  PROCEDURE ShowLetterCount (VAR count : letterCount);
  { List the tally for each letter of alphabet }
    VAR letter       : Char;
        lettersShown : Integer;
    BEGIN
      lettersShown := 0;
      FOR letter := 'A' TO 'Z' DO
        IF count[letter] > 0 THEN
            BEGIN
              Write(letter:5, count[letter]:3);
              lettersShown := lettersShown + 1;
              IF (lettersShown >= 8) THEN
                  BEGIN
                    Writeln;
                    lettersShown := 0
                  END
            END
    END;

BEGIN
  ClrScr;
  GetAndCountLetters(count);
  ShowLetterCount(count)
END.

[run]
Enter a sentence and hit return.
Oh Auntie Em, there's no place like home.
    A 2    C 1    E 7    H 3    I 2    K 1    L 2    M 2
    N 2    O 3    P 1    R 1    S 1    T 2    U 1
```

In many situations, not every element in an array is assigned data. Under these circumstances it is important to know how many elements hold meaningful data so that processing does not occur on unassigned array entries.

EXAMPLE 7 Write a program to determine the average grade on a exam for a class of 30 students and to list the grades that were above average, where the grades are entered from the keyboard. Assuming some students might miss the exam, use the trailer value −1 to indicate that all the grades have been entered.

SOLUTION An array is needed to store the grades. Since the number of grades is not known in advance, a counter is needed to determine this quantity. The final value of the counter is the array position of the last grade entered.

```
PROGRAM GradesAboveAverage;
{ Find the average grade and list the grades above it }

USES Crt;

CONST MaxClassSize = 30;

TYPE ClassArray = ARRAY [1..MaxClassSize] OF Integer;

VAR student   : ClassArray;
    numGrades : Integer;

PROCEDURE InputGrades (VAR student   : ClassArray;
                       VAR numGrades : Integer);
{ Get the grades for the class }
  VAR grade     : Integer;
      endOfData : Boolean;
  BEGIN
    numGrades := 0;   { Assume no grades initially }
    Writeln('Enter -1 after all grades have been entered.');
    REPEAT
      Write('Grade for student ', numGrades + 1, ': ');
      Readln(grade);
      endOfData := (grade = -1);  { True if trailer entered }
      IF NOT endOfData THEN
          BEGIN
            numGrades := numGrades + 1;
            student[numGrades] := grade
          END
    UNTIL endOfData OR (numGrades >= MaxClassSize)
  END;
```

```
FUNCTION Average (VAR student : ClassArray;
                     numGrades    : Integer) : Real;
{ Returns average of student grades }
  VAR total, number : Integer;
  BEGIN
    total := 0;
    FOR number := 1 TO numGrades DO
      total := total + student[number];
    Average := total / numGrades
  END;

PROCEDURE AboveAve (VAR student : ClassArray;
                      numGrades    : Integer);
{ List all grades above the average grade }
  VAR number   : Integer;
      aveGrade : Real;
  BEGIN
    aveGrade := Average(student, numGrades);
    Writeln('The average grade was: ', aveGrade:1:1);
    Write('The scores above average were: ');
    FOR number := 1 TO numGrades DO
      IF student[number] > aveGrade THEN
          Write(student[number]:4)
  END;

BEGIN
  ClrScr;
  InputGrades(student, numGrades);
  IF (numGrades <> 0) THEN
      AboveAve(student, numGrades)
END.
```

Comments:

1. Subscripts are also referred to as *indices* (singular–index).

2. In practice, the data for an array are usually stored in a file, and a loop is used to assign the data to the elements of the array. This technique will be presented in Chapter 9. For now, we either input the data with Readln statements or store the data in an array constant and assign the array constant to the array variable.

3. If possible, arrays should be passed to procedures or functions by reference, rather than by value. Passing by value requires the computer to create an additional copy of the array.

4. Subscripts outside the range of the array can cause a compiler error message, result in an incorrect output of the program, or generate a run-time error message. For instance, consider the array *derby* declared by

```
TYPE HorseRace = ARRAY [1..3] OF STRING;
VAR derby : HorseRace;
```

The statement

```
Writeln(derby[4])
```

results in an "Out of range" compiler error message. If *n* is a declared Integer variable, the statements

```
n := 4;
derby[n] := 'Secretariat'
```

will compile. The program, however, will either produce a run-time error message (see Comment 5) or act unpredictably.

5. *Range-checking,* that is, checking for out-of-range subscripts, is not normally carried out during run-time; however, run-time range-checking can be invoked by adding the line

```
{$R+}
```

after the program heading line. The dollar sign tells the compiler that this is not an ordinary comment, but rather a *compiler directive.* This directive causes the compiler to add extra code to the EXE file. After debugging, the line can be removed and the program recompiled to created a more efficient EXE file. (**Note:** Compiler directives also can be set from QuickPascal's Options menu.)

6. So far, arrays have been created in a two-part process: First construct an array type and then declare a variable of that type. An array also can be created directly in the variable declaration section without first creating an array type. The general form is

```
VAR arrayName : ARRAY [IndexType] OF ElementType;
```

For instance, the array presName from Example 2 could have been declared with

```
VAR presName : ARRAY [39..41] OF STRING;
```

This nameless type array resulting from the direct declaration has a major drawback; it cannot be passed to procedures or functions. Each parameter of a procedure or function must be followed by a type name; however, directly declared arrays have no type name.

7. The assignment of arrays requires care. To insure the assignment-compatibility of arrays such as pres1 and pres2, create them with declarations such as

```
TYPE Names = ARRAY [39..41] OF STRING;
VAR pres1, pres2 : Names;
```

or

```
VAR pres1, pres2 : ARRAY [39..41] OF STRING;
```

Creating them with either of the following declarations results in assignment incompatibility.

```
TYPE Names = ARRAY [39..41] OF STRING;
VAR pres1 : Names;
    pres2 : ARRAY [39..41] OF STRING;
```

or

```
VAR pres1 : ARRAY [39..41] OF STRING;
    pres2 : ARRAY [39..41] OF STRING;
```

PRACTICE PROBLEMS 8.1

1. (a) Give an appropriate declaration for an array to hold the names of the *Time Magazine* "Man of the Year" awards for the years 1980 through 1989.

   (b) Write a statement to assign to the array element for 1982 the name of that year's winner, "The Computer."

2. The array types used earlier in the discussion of processing student names and exam scores could have been declared with

```
CONST N = 30;

TYPE StudentNames = ARRAY [1..N] OF STRING;
     Studentscore = ARRAY [1..N] OF Integer;
```

What is the advantange of using a constant for the range?

EXERCISES 8.1

In Exercises 1 and 2, give the number of elements in an array declared to be of the following types.

1. `TYPE MyArrayType = ARRAY [0..9] OF STRING;`

2. `TYPE SomeArray = ARRAY [-5..5] OF Integer;`

3. Declare an array of records to hold the following names and their meanings.

First Name	Meaning
Boris	warrior
Wilber	resolute protection
Craig	rock
Adam	red earth
Elvin	elf-friend, wise friend
Stephan	crown, wreath

4. Declare an array of records to hold the following abbreviations and their meanings.

Abbreviation	Latin	Meaning
i.e.	id est	that is
e.g.	exempli gratia	for example
q.e.	quod est	which is
ad. lib.	ad libitum	at pleasure
a.d.	anno domini	in the year of the Lord
et al.	et alii	and others

In Exercises 5 through 12, determine the output of the program.

5.
```
TYPE AnArray = ARRAY [1..20] OF Integer;
VAR myArray : AnArray;

BEGIN
  myArray[5] := 1;
  myArray[10] := 2;
  myArray[15] := 7;
  Writeln(myArray[5] + myArray[10]);
  Writeln(myArray[5 + 10]);
  Writeln(myArray[5 * 2])
END.
```

6.
```
TYPE CharArray = ARRAY [1..6] OF Char;

VAR someVar : CharArray;
    index   : Integer;

BEGIN
  someVar[1] := '!';
  someVar[2] := '@';
  someVar[3] := '#';
  someVar[4] := '$';
  someVar[5] := '.';
  Write('My dear, I don''t give a ');
  FOR index = 1 TO 5 DO
    Write(someVar[index]);
  Writeln('  --Rhett Butler')
END.
```

7.
```
TYPE ArrayType = ARRAY [0..5] OF Integer;

VAR square     : ArrayType;
    index, sum : Integer;

BEGIN
  FOR index := 0 TO 5 DO
    square[index] := index * index;
  sum := 0;
  FOR index := 0 TO 5 DO
    BEGIN
      Writeln(square[index]);
      sum := sum + square[index]
    END;
  Writeln(sum)
END.
```

8. ```
TYPE HorseArray = ARRAY [1..4] OF STRING;

VAR horseman   : HorseArray;
    index, num : Integer;

BEGIN
  FOR index := 1 TO 4 DO
    Readln(horseman[index]);
  Writeln(horseman[4]);
  num := 1;
  Writeln(horseman[2 * num + 1])
END.
```
(Assume the responses are Miller, Layden, Crowley, and Stuhldreher.)

9. ```
CONST First = 65;
      Last  = 71;

TYPE CharArrayType = ARRAY [First..Last] OF Char;

VAR charArray : CharArrayType;
    ascii     : Integer;

BEGIN
  FOR ascii := First TO Last DO
    charArray[ascii] := Chr(ascii);
  Writeln(charArray[(Last + First) DIV 2])
END.
```

10. ```
CONST Max = 5;
      Min = 1;

TYPE ArrayType = ARRAY [Min..Max] OF Real;

VAR someNum : ArrayType;
    index   : Integer;

BEGIN
  FOR index := Max DOWNTO Min DO
    Readln(someNum[index]);
    Writeln(someNum[Min]:5:1)
END.
```
(User responses: 5.4, 3.4, 2.8, 45.23, 98.72)

11. ```
TYPE NameArray  = ARRAY [1..4] OF STRING;
     GradeArray = ARRAY [1..4] OF Integer;

VAR name         : NameArray;
    grade        : GradeArray;
    student, best,
    hiScore      : Integer;
```

```
BEGIN
  best := 0;
  hiScore := -1;
  FOR student := 1 TO 4 DO
    BEGIN
      Readln(name[student]);
      Readln(grade[student]);
      IF grade[student] > hiScore THEN
          BEGIN
            best := student;
            hiScore := grade[student]
          END
    END;
  Writeln(name[best], ' achieved the high score of ', grade[best])
END.
```
(User responses: Bill, 81; Marilyn, 94; Kim, 91; Steve, 76)

12.
```
TYPE Exponent = ARRAY [0..3] OF Integer;

CONST TensElts : Exponent = (0, 10, 100, 1000);

VAR tenToThe : Exponent;

BEGIN
  tenToThe := TensElts;
  Writeln(3 * tenToThe[0]:6);
  Writeln(4.5 * tenToThe[1]:6:0);
  Writeln(0.35 * tenToThe[3]:6:0)
END.
```

For Exercises 13 and 14, suppose an array *river* has been declared to be of type

```
TYPE RiverType = ARRAY [1..5] OF STRING[10];
```

and contains the following data:

river[1]	river[2]	river[3]	river[4]	river[5]
Nile	Ohio	Amazon	Volga	Thames

13. Fill in the empty arrays below to show the progressing status of *river* after each execution of the procedure Mystery.
```
PROCEDURE Mystery (VAR river : RiverType);
  VAR index : Integer;
      temp  : RiverType;
  BEGIN
    temp := river;
    river[1] := temp[5];
    FOR index := 2 TO 5 DO
      river[index] := temp[index - 1]
  END;
```

Mystery(river);

river[1]	river[2]	river[3]	river[4]	river[5]

Mystery(river);

river[1]	river[2]	river[3]	river[4]	river[5]

14. Assuming river is as displayed below, fill in the empty arrays to show the progressing status of *river* after each execution of the procedure AnotherMystery.

river[1]	river[2]	river[3]	river[4]	river[5]
Nile	Ohio	Amazon	Volga	Thames

```
PROCEDURE AnotherMystery (VAR river : RiverType; num1, num2 : Integer);
  VAR temp : STRING[10];
  BEGIN
    temp := river[num1];
    river[num1] := river[num2];
    river[num2] := temp
  END;
```

AnotherMystery(river, 1, 5);

river[1]	river[2]	river[3]	river[4]	river[5]

AnotherMystery(river, 3, 5);

river[1]	river[2]	river[3]	river[4]	river[5]

In Exercises 15 and 16, determine the output of the program.

15.
```
TYPE RecordType = RECORD
        english    : STRING;
        metric     : STRING;
        conversion : Real;    { English unit to metric }
     END;
  ArrayType = ARRAY [1..3] OF RecordType;

VAR measure : ArrayType;
```

```
PROCEDURE FillArray (VAR measure : ArrayType);
  VAR index : Integer;
  BEGIN
    FOR index := 1 TO 3 DO
      BEGIN
        WITH measure[index] DO
          BEGIN
            Readln(english);
            Readln(metric);
            Readln(conversion)
          END
      END
  END;

PROCEDURE ShowOffArray (VAR measure : ArrayType; num : Integer);
  VAR index : Integer;
  BEGIN
    FOR index := 1 TO 3 DO
      WITH measure[index] DO
        Writeln(num, ' ', english, ' = ',
                conversion * num, ' ', metric:4:2)
  END;

BEGIN
  FillArray(measure);
  ShowOffArray(measure, 3)
END.
```

(User responses: inches, centimeters, 2.54, quarts, liters, 0.95, ounces, grams, 28.4)

16.
```
TYPE QuoteType = ARRAY [1..5] OF STRING;
     CodeType  = ARRAY [1..5] OF Integer;

CONST QuoteWords  : QuoteType = ('why', 'every', 'wherefore',
                                 'a', 'hath');
      CodeNumbers : CodeType  = (2, 1, 5, 4, 3);

VAR quote : QuoteType;
    code  : CodeType;
    index : Integer;

BEGIN
  quote := QuoteWords;
  code := CodeNumbers;
  FOR index := 1 TO 5 DO
    Write(quote[code[index]], ' ');
  Writeln('--Shakespeare')
END.
```

In Exercises 17 through 22, identify the errors.

17.
```
TYPE ArrayType = ARRAY [0..4] OF Char;

CONST ArrayData : ArrayType = ('a', 'b', 'c', 'd');

VAR index    : Integer;
    theArray : ArrayType;

BEGIN
  theArray := ArrayData;
  FOR index := 1 TO 4 DO
    Writeln(theArray[index])
END.
```

18.
```
TYPE AnArray = ARRAY ['a'..'c'] OF Integer;

CONST ArrayData : AnArray = (9, 8, 7);

VAR great : AnArray;
    index : Char;
BEGIN
  great := ArrayData;
  FOR index := 'c' DOWNTO 'a' DO
    Writeln(great[index + 1])
END.
```

19.
```
TYPE AnyType = ARRAY [-3..3] OF Real;

VAR index   : Integer;
    myArray : AnyType;

BEGIN
  FOR index := -3 TO 3 DO
    Readln(myArray[index]);
  FOR index := -6 TO 6 DO
    Writeln(myArray[index DIV 2]);
  FOR index := 0 TO 7 DO
    Writeln(myArray[myarray[index]])
END.
```

20.
```
TYPE DeerType = ARRAY [1..9] OF STRING;

CONST DeerData : DeerType = ('Dasher', 'Dancer', 'Prancer', 'Vixen',
                             'Comet', 'Cupid', 'Donder', 'Blitzen',
                             'Rudolph');

VAR index    : Integer;
    reindeer : DeerType;
```

```
BEGIN
  FOR index := 1 TO 9 DO
    IF reindeer[index] = 'Rudolph' THEN
        Writeln('Rudolph was originally named "Rollo"')
      ELSE
        Writeln(reindeer[index])
END.
```

21.
```
TYPE WordsType = ARRAY [1..4] OF STRING;

CONST WordsData : WordsType = ('Et ', 'tu, ', 'Brute?', 'EOD');

VAR word  : WordsType;
    count : Integer;

BEGIN
  {$R+}
  word := WordsData;
  count := 0;
  WHILE word[count] <> 'EOD' DO
    BEGIN
      Write(word[count]);
      count := count + 1
    END
END.
```

22.
```
TYPE IndexType = ARRAY [0..2] OF Real;
     WordType  = ARRAY [1..3] OF STRING;

CONST IndexData : IndexType = (1.0, 2.0, 3.0);
      WordData  : WordType = ('Veni, ', 'Vidi, ', 'Vici.');

VAR count : Integer;
    index : IndexType;
    word  : WordType;

BEGIN
  index := IndexData;
  word := WordData;
  FOR count := 0 TO 2 DO
    Write(word[index[count]]);
END.
```

23. The elements of the array *a* have the following values: a[1] = 6, a[2] = 3, a[3] = 1, a[4] = 2, a[5] = 5, a[6] = 8, a[7] = 7. Suppose $i = 2$, $j = 4$, and $k = 5$. What values are assigned to n when the following statements are executed?

    (a) `n := a[k] - a[i]`
    (b) `n := a[k - i] + a[k - j]`
    (c) `n := a[k] * a[i + 2]`
    (d) `n := a[j - i] * a[i]`

24. The array *month* holds the following three-character strings.

```
month[1]='Jan', month[2]='Feb', . . ., month[12]='Dec'
```

(a) What is displayed by the following statement?

```
Writeln(month[4], month[9])
```

(b) What value is assigned to winter by the following statement?

```
winter := month[12] + ',' + month[1] + ',' + month[2]
```

In Exercises 25 through 32, write a subprogram to complete the stated task.

25. The arrays *arr1* and *arr2* have been declared to have range 1 to 4 and type Char. Characters have been assigned to arr1[1] through arr1[4]. Reverse the order of these characters and store them in *arr2*.

26. Given two arrays, *p* and *q*, of Integer type and range 1 to 20, compute the sum of the products of the corresponding array elements; that is

```
p[1] * q[1] + p[2] * q[2] + . . . + p[20] * q[20]
```

27. Display the values of the array *arr* with range 1 to 30 and type Integer, in five columns as shown below.

```
arr[1]     arr[2]     arr[3]     arr[4]     arr[5]
  .          .          .          .          .
  .          .          .          .          .
  .          .          .          .          .
arr[26]    arr[27]    arr[28]    arr[29]    arr[30]
```

28. Compare two arrays, *arr1* and *arr2*, of range 1 to 10 and type Real to see if they hold identical values; that is, if arr1[j] = arr2[j] for all *j* from 1 through 10.

29. Calculate the sum of the entries with odd subscripts in an array *myArray* of range 1 to 9 and type Integer.

30. Twelve Integer exam grades are stored in the array *grades*. Curve the grades by adding 7 points to each grade.

31. Given the array *arr* of type Real and range 1 to 10, display three columns as follows: Column 1 should contain the original 10 numbers, column 2 should contain the squares of these numbers, and column 3 should contain the averages of the corresponding numbers in columns 1 and 2.

32. Thirty scores, each lying between 0 and 49, are entered by the user. These scores are used to create the array *frequency* as follows:

frequency[1] = # of scores < 10
frequency[2] = # of scores such that $10 <= score < 20$
frequency[3] = # of scores such that $20 <= score < 30$
frequency[4] = # of scores such that $30 <= score < 40$
frequency[5] = # of scores such that $40 <= score < 50$.

Write a procedure to display the results in tabular form as follows:

Interval	Frequency
0 to 10	frequency[1]
10 to 20	frequency[2]
20 to 30	frequency[3]
30 to 40	frequency[4]
40 to 50	frequency[5]

33. Given the following flight schedule,

Flight #	Origin	Destination	Departure Time
117	Tucson	Dallas	8:45 a.m.
239	LA	Boston	10:15 a.m.
298	Albany	Reno	1:35 p.m.
326	Houston	New York	2:40 p.m.
445	New York	Tampa	4:20 p.m.

write a program to load this information into an array of records with fields flightNum, orig, dest, and deptTime, and ask the user to request a flight number. Have the computer find the flight number and display the information corresponding to that flight. Account for the case where the user requests a nonexistent flight.

34. Table 8.1 contains the names and number of stores of the top 10 pizza chains in 1987. Write a program to place these data into an array of records. Compute the total number of stores for these 10 chains, and display a table giving the name and percentage of total stores for each of the companies.

Name	Stores	Name	Stores
1. Pizza Hut	5600	6. Round Table	550
2. Domino's	4148	7. Mr. Gatti's	337
3. Little Caesar's	2375	8. Mazzio's	282
4. Pizza Inn	780	9. Show Biz Pizza Time	274
5. Godfather's	583	10. S'Barro	270

Table 8.1 Top 10 Pizza Chains for 1987 (by number of stores)
Source: Pizza Today magazine

35. A retail store has 5 bins, numbered 1 to 5, each containing a different commodity. At the beginning of a particular day, each bin contains 45 items. Table 8.2 below shows the cost per item for each of the bins and the quantity sold during that day.

Bin	Cost per Item	Quantity Sold
1	3.00	10
2	12.25	30
3	37.45	9
4	7.49	42
5	24.95	17

Table 8.2 Costs of Items and Quantities Sold For Example 28

Write a program to

(a) place the cost per item and the quantity sold from each bin into an array of records having range 1 to 5.

(b) display a table giving the inventory at the end of the day and the amount of revenue obtained from each bin.

(c) compute the total revenue for the day.

(d) list the number of each bin containing fewer than 20 items at the end of the day.

SOLUTIONS TO PRACTICE PROBLEMS 8.1

1. (a) TYPE AnnualAwards = ARRAY [1980..1989] OF STRING;

    VAR manOfTheYear : AnnualAwards;

   (b) manOfTheYear[1982] := 'The Computer'

2. The program can be modified to analyze the scores of any number of students by just altering the constant. Otherwise, several values in the declaration and statement parts of the program would have to be changed.

8.2   SORTING AND SEARCHING

A numeric array is said to be **sorted** if the list of numeric values is in ascending (1, 2, 3, 4) or descending (4, 3, 2, 1) order. An array of strings is said to be sorted if the list of strings is in ascending or descending alphabetical order. Precisely, for all i and $i + 1$ within valid range,

Ascending order: array[i] <= array[i + 1]
Descending order: array[i] >= array[i + 1]

Of the many different techniques for sorting an array, we discuss two: the **bubble sort** and the **Shell sort**. Both sorts require that values of array elements be exchanged. The following example carries out this task in the procedure SwapStr.

EXAMPLE 1   Write a program to alphabetize two words that are input with Readln statements.

SOLUTION
```
PROGRAM DemoSwap;
{ Alphabetize two words }

USES Crt;

VAR first, second : STRING;

PROCEDURE SwapStr (VAR a, b : STRING);
  VAR c : STRING;
  BEGIN
    c := a;
    a := b;
    b := c
  END;
```

```
BEGIN
  ClrScr;
  Write('First word: ');
  Readln(first);
  Write('Second word: ');
  Readln(second);
  IF first > second THEN
      SwapStr(first, second);
  Writeln(first, '  ', second)
END.
```

Bubble Sort

The bubble sort is an algorithm that compares adjacent items and swaps those that are out of order. If this process is repeated enough times, the list will be sorted. Let's carry out this procedure on the list Pebbles, Barney, Wilma, Fred, Dino. The steps for each pass through the list are as follows:

1. Compare the first and second items. If they are out of order, swap them.

2. Compare the second and third items. If they are out of order, swap them.

3. Repeat this pattern for all remaining pairs. The final comparison and possible swap is between the second-to-last and last elements.

The first time through the list, this process is repeated to the end of the list. This is called the first **pass**. After the first pass, the last item (Wilma) will be in its proper position. Therefore, the second pass does not have to consider it and so requires one less comparison. At the end of the second pass, the last two items will be in their proper position. The items that must have reached their proper position have been underlined. Each successive pass requires one less comparison. After four passes, the last four items will be in their proper positions and, hence, the first will be also.

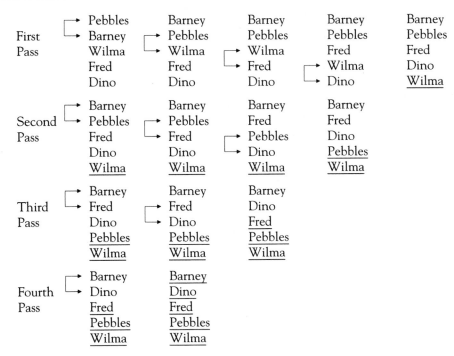

EXAMPLE 2 Write a program to alphabetize the names Pebbles, Barney, Wilma, Fred, Dino.

SOLUTION Sorting the list requires a pair of nested loops. The inner loop performs a single pass and the outer loop controls the number of passes.

```
PROGRAM SortNames;
{ Alphabetize a list of five names }

USES Crt;

CONST NumNames = 5;

TYPE NamesList = ARRAY [1..NumNames] OF STRING;

CONST OrigNames : NamesList = ('Pebbles', 'Barney', 'Wilma',
                               'Fred', 'Dino');

VAR names : NamesList;

PROCEDURE Sort (VAR names : NamesList);
{ Bubble sort names }
  VAR passNum, index : Integer;
  PROCEDURE SwapStr (VAR name1, name2 : STRING);
    VAR temp : STRING;
    BEGIN
      temp := name1;
      name1 := name2;
      name2 := temp
    END;
  BEGIN
    FOR passNum := 1 TO NumNames - 1 DO
      FOR index := 1 TO NumNames - passNum DO
        IF names[index] > names[index + 1] THEN
            SwapStr(names[index], names[index + 1])
  END;

PROCEDURE ShowNames (names : NamesList);
{ Display alphabetized list }
  VAR nameNum : Integer;
  BEGIN
    FOR nameNum := 1 TO NumNames DO
      Write(names[nameNum],'  ')
  END;

BEGIN
  ClrScr;
  names := OrigNames;
  Sort(names);
  ShowNames(names)
END.

[run]
Barney  Dino  Fred  Pebbles  Wilma
```

EXAMPLE 3   Write a program that requests the name and age at inauguration of any five Presidents of the United States and then displays a table listing the Presidents in descending order by their age at inauguration. The table should give the name and age for each President.

SOLUTION

```
PROGRAM SortPresidents;

USES Crt;

CONST NumPrezzes = 5;

TYPE Pres      = RECORD
                     age  : Integer;
                     name : STRING
                   END;
      PresList = ARRAY [1..NumPrezzes] OF Pres;

VAR prezzes : PresList;

PROCEDURE ReadPrezzes (VAR prezzes : PresList);
  VAR presNum : Integer;
  BEGIN
    FOR presNum := 1 TO NumPrezzes DO
      WITH prezzes[presNum] DO
        BEGIN
          Write('Name of President: ');
          Readln(name);
          Write('Age at inauguration: ');
          Readln(age)
        END
  END;

PROCEDURE SortPrezzes (VAR prezzes : PresList);
{ Sorts the Presidents in desc. order by inauguration age }
  VAR passNum, index : Integer;
  PROCEDURE SwapPres (VAR pres1, pres2 : Pres);
    VAR presTemp : Pres;
    BEGIN
      presTemp := pres1;
      pres1 := pres2;
      pres2 := presTemp
    END;
  BEGIN
    FOR passNum := 1 TO NumPrezzes - 1 DO
      FOR index := 1 TO NumPrezzes - passNum DO
        IF prezzes[index].age < prezzes[index + 1].age THEN
            SwapPres(prezzes[index], prezzes[index + 1])
  END;
```

```
PROCEDURE ShowPrezzes (VAR prezzes : PresList);
{ Display the presidents }
  VAR presNum : Integer;
  PROCEDURE InitScreen;
    BEGIN
      ClrScr;
      Writeln('President', 'Age':8);
      Writeln
    END;
  BEGIN
    InitScreen;
    FOR presNum := 1 to NumPrezzes DO
      WITH prezzes[presNum] DO
          Writeln(name, age:17 - Length(name))
  END;

BEGIN
  ClrScr;
  ReadPrezzes(prezzes);
  SortPrezzes(prezzes);
  ShowPrezzes(prezzes)
END.

[run]
Name of President: Buchanan
Age at inaugeration: 65
Name of President: Bush
Age at inaugeration: 64
Name of President: Harrison
Age at inaugeration: 68
Name of President: Reagan
Age at inaugeration: 69
Name of President: Taylor
Age at inaugeration: 64


President      Age

Reagan         69
Harrison       68
Buchanan       65
Bush           64
Taylor         64
```

Shell Sort

The bubble sort is easy to understand and program; however, it is too slow for really long lists. The Shell sort, named for its inventor, Donald L. Shell (see Section 1.4), is much more efficient in such cases. It compares distant items first and works its way down to nearby items. The interval separating the compared items is called the **gap**. The gap begins at one-half the length of the list and is successively halved until eventually each item is compared with its neighbor as in the bubble sort. The algorithm for a list of n items is as follows:

1. Begin with a gap of $g = n$ DIV 2.

2. Compare items 1 and $1 + g$, 2 and $2 + g$, . . ., $n - g$ and n. Swap any pairs that are out of order.

3. Repeat step 2 until no swaps are made for gap g.

4. Halve the value of g.

5. Repeat steps 2 through 4 until the value of g is 0.

EXAMPLE 4   Use the Shell sort to alphabetize the parts of a running shoe. (See Figure 8.5.)

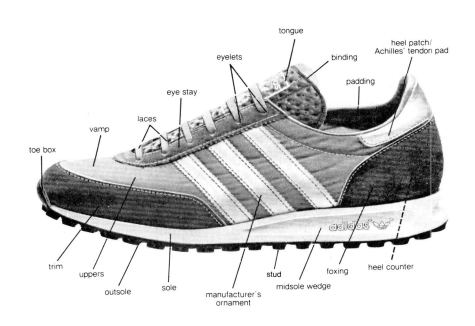

Figure 8.5   Running Shoe

SOLUTION   In the following program a flag is set to tell us if a swap has been made during a pass.

```
PROGRAM ShoeParts;
{ Sort and display parts of running shoe }

USES Crt;

CONST NumParts = 18;

TYPE PartName =  STRING[14];
     PartNames = ARRAY [1..NumParts] OF PartName;
```

```
CONST OrigNames : PartNames =
           ('toe box', 'vamp', 'laces', 'eye stay', 'eyelets',
            'tongue', 'binding', 'padding', 'heel patch',
            'heel counter', 'foxing', 'midsole wedge',
            'mfg''s ornament', 'sole', 'uppers', 'trim',
            'stud', 'outsole');

VAR newNames : PartNames;

PROCEDURE SortData (VAR parts : PartNames);
{ Shell sort shoe parts }
  VAR done       : Boolean;
      index, gap : Integer;
  PROCEDURE SwapPart (VAR part1, part2 : PartName);
    VAR partTemp : PartName;
    BEGIN
      partTemp := part1;
      part1 := part2;
      part2 := partTemp
    END;
  BEGIN
    gap := NumParts DIV 2;
    WHILE gap >= 1 DO
      BEGIN
        REPEAT
          done := True;
          FOR index := 1 TO NumParts - gap DO
            IF parts[index] > parts[index + gap] THEN
                BEGIN
                  SwapPart(parts[index], parts[index + gap]);
                  done := False
                END
        UNTIL done;
        gap := gap DIV 2    { Halve the length of the gap }
      END
  END;

PROCEDURE ShowData (VAR parts : PartNames);
{ Display sorted list of parts }
  VAR partNum : Integer;
  BEGIN
    FOR partNum := 1 TO NumParts DO
      BEGIN
        Write(parts[partNum]:16);
        IF partNum MOD 3 = 0 THEN
            Writeln
      END
  END;
```

```
BEGIN
  ClrScr;
  newNames := OrigNames;
  SortData(newNames);
  ShowData(newNames)
END.
```

[run]

binding	eye stay	eyelets
foxing	heel counter	heel patch
laces	mfg's ornament	midsole wedge
outsole	padding	sole
stud	toe box	tongue
trim	uppers	vamp

Searching

Suppose we had an array of 1000 names in alphabetical order and wanted to locate a specific person in the list. One approach would be to start with the first name and consider each name until a match was found. This process is called a **sequential search**. We would find a person whose name begins with "A" rather quickly, but 1000 comparisons might be necessary to find a person whose name begins with "Z." For much longer lists, searching could be a time-consuming matter. However, whenever the list has already been sorted into either ascending or descending order, then there is a method, called a **binary search**, that shortens the task considerably.

Let us refer to the sought item as **quarry**. The binary search looks for quarry by determining in which half of the list it lies. The other half is then discarded and the retained half is temporarily regarded as the entire list. The process is repeated until the item is found.

The algorithm for a binary search of an ascending list is as follows (figure 8.6 contains the flowchart for a binary search):

1. At each stage, denote the subscript of the first item in the retained list by *first* and the subscript of the last item in the retained list by *last*. Initially, the value of *first* is 1 and the value of *last* is the number of items in the list.

2. Look at the *middle* item of the current list, the item having the subscript *middle* = (*first* + *last*) DIV 2.

3. If the middle item is *quarry*, then the search is over.

4. If the middle item is greater than *quarry*, then *quarry* should be in the first half of the list. So the subscript of *quarry* must lie between *first* and *middle* − 1. That is, the new value of *last* is *middle* − 1.

5. If the middle item is less than *quarry*, then *quarry* should be in the second half of the list of possible items. So the subscript of *quarry* must lie between *middle* + 1 and *last*. That is, the new value of *first* is *middle* + 1.

6. Repeat steps 2 through 5 until *quarry* is found or until the halving process uses up the entire list. In the second case, *quarry* was not in the original list.

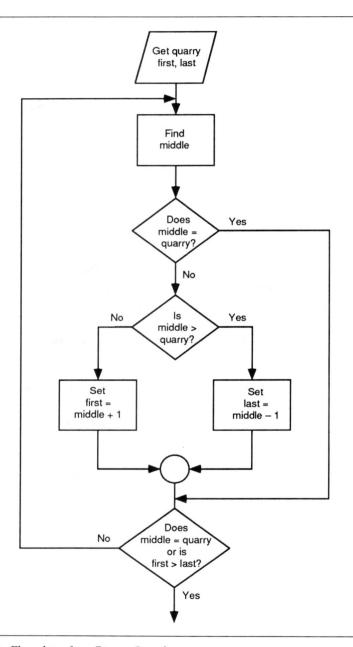

Figure 8.6 Flowchart for a Binary Search.

EXAMPLE 5   Suppose the array *prezzes* in Example 3 has been sorted alphabetically by the *name* field. Write a binary search procedure to locate the data for a President entered from the keyboard.

SOLUTION

```
PROCEDURE FindPres (quarry : STRING; VAR prezzes : PresList);
   VAR first, middle, last : Integer;
       found               : Boolean;
{ Binary search for President name }
  BEGIN
    first := 1;
    last := NumPrezzes;
    REPEAT
      middle := (first + last) DIV 2;
      found := (prezzes[middle].name = quarry);
      IF NOT found THEN
          IF prezzes[middle].name > quarry THEN
              last := middle - 1
            ELSE
              first := middle + 1
    UNTIL found OR (first > last);
    IF found THEN
        WITH prezzes[middle] DO
          Writeln(name:15, age:8)
      ELSE
        Writeln('Incorrect President name.')
  END;
```

Comments:

1. Suppose our bubble sort algorithm is applied to an already sorted list of length n. The algorithm will still make $n - 1$ passes through the list. The process could be shortened for some lists by flagging the presence of out-of-order items, as in the Shell sort. It may be preferable not to use a flag since for greatly disorderd lists the flag would slow down an already sluggish algorithm.

2. The Shell sort will usually outperform the bubble sort by at least a factor of 10 when the number of items is greater than 500.

3. In Example 3, an array of records that was already ordered by one field was sorted by another field. Usually, arrays of records are sorted by the field that is to be searched when accessing the array. This field is called the **key field**.

4. Suppose an array of 2000 items is searched sequentially, that is, one item after another, in order to locate a specific item. The number of comparisons would vary from 1 to 2000, with an average of 1000. With a binary search, the number of comparisons would be at most 11, since $2^{11} > 2000$.

PRACTICE PROBLEMS 8.2

1. The pseudocode for a bubble sort of an array of num elements is given below. Why is the terminating value of the outer loop num − 1 and the terminating value of the inner loop num − j?

```
FOR j := 1 TO num - 1
  FOR k := 1 TO num - j
    IF [kth and (k+1)st items are out of order] THEN swap them
```

2. Complete the table below by filling in the values of each variable after successive passes of a binary search of a list of 20 items, where the sought item is in the 13th position.

First	Last	Middle
1	20	10
11	20	

EXERCISES 8.2

In Exercises 1 through 4, assume the following procedure and function are included in the declarations portion of the program and determine the output.

```
PROCEDURE SwapStr (VAR var1, var2 : STRING);
  VAR temp : STRING;
  BEGIN
    temp := var1;
    var1 := var2;
    var2 := temp
  END;

FUNCTION InAscOrder (word1, word2 : STRING) : Boolean;
  BEGIN
    InAscOrder := (word1 <= word2)
  END;
```

1.
```
VAR str1, str2 : STRING;

BEGIN
  str1 := 'battery';
  str2 := 'test';
  SwapStr(str1, str2);
  Writeln(str1, ' ', str2)
END.
```

2.
```
VAR word1, word2 : STRING;

BEGIN
  Readln(word1);
  Readln(word2);
  IF word1 > word2 THEN
    SwapStr(word1, word2);
  Writeln(word1, ' before ', word2)
END.
```
(User response: beauty, age)

3.
```
VAR word1, word2 : STRING;

BEGIN
  Readln(word1);
  Readln(word2);
  IF NOT InAscOrder(word1, word2) THEN
      SwapStr(word1, word2);
  Writeln(word1, ' before ', word2)
END.
```
(User response: swine, pearls)

4.
```
TYPE NameType = ARRAY [1..4] OF STRING;

CONST NameData : NameType = ('Bach', 'Beethoven', 'Brahms', 'Borodin');

VAR numPass, thisPass : Integer;
    composer          : NameType;

BEGIN
  composer := NameData;
  FOR numPass := 1 TO 3 DO
    FOR thisPass := 1 TO (4 - numPass) DO
      IF InAscOrder(composer[thisPass], composer[thisPass + 1]) THEN
          SwapStr(composer[thisPass], composer[thisPass + 1]);
  FOR numPass := 1 TO 4 DO
    Writeln(composer[numPass]);
END.
```

In Exercises 5 and 6 determine the output of the program assuming the following procedure is in the declaration part.

```
PROCEDURE SwapInt (VAR num1, num2 : Integer);
  VAR temp : Integer;
  BEGIN
    temp := num1;
    num1 := num2;
    num2 := temp
  END;
```

5.
```
VAR num1, num2 : Integer;
    swapFlag   : Boolean;

BEGIN
  Readln(num1, num2);
  swapFlag := (num1 < num2);
  IF swapFlag THEN
      SwapInt(num1, num2);
  Write(num1, ' ', num2);
  IF swapFlag THEN
      Writeln(' They were out of order.')
END.
```
(User response: 75 42)

6.
```
TYPE NumType = ARRAY [1..5] OF Integer;

CONST JumbledNums : NumType = (4, 2, 3, 5, 1);

VAR number           : NumType;
    numPass, thisPass : Integer;

BEGIN
  number := JumbledNums;
  FOR numPass := 1 TO 4 DO
    FOR thisPass := 1 TO (5 - numPass) DO
      IF number[thisPass] > number[thisPass + 1] THEN
          SwapInt(number[thisPass], number[thisPass + 1]);
  FOR numPass := 5 DOWNTO 1 DO
    Writeln(number[numPass])
END.
```

7. Which type of search would be best for the array shown below?

1	2	3	4	5
Paul	Ringo	John	George	Pete

8. Which type of search would be best for the array shown below?

1	2	3	4	5
Beloit	Green Bay	Madison	Milwaukee	Oshkosh

In Exercises 9 and 10, identify the errors.

9.
```
TYPE NameType = ARRAY [1..5] OF STRING[50];

CONST NameData : NameType = ('Snoopy', 'Odie', 'Pluto', 'Marmaduke',
                             'Grimm');
VAR bowWow : NameType;
    index  : Integer;
    found  : Boolean;

BEGIN
  index := 0;
  REPEAT
    index := index + 1;
    found := (bowWow[index] = 'Lassie')
  UNTIL found;
  IF NOT found THEN
      Writeln('Sorry, ma''am.  We couldn''t find your dog.')
END.
```

10.
```
TYPE ListType = ARRAY [1..6] OF STRING;

CONST SomeChars : ListType = ('z', 'a', 'C', 'b', 'q', 'o');

VAR myList          : ListType;
    index1, index2 : Integer;
```

```
[PROCEDURE SwapStr here]

BEGIN
  myList := SomeChars;
  FOR index1 := 1 TO 5 DO
    FOR index2 := 1 TO (6 - index1) DO
      IF myList[index1] < myList[index1 + 1] THEN
          SwapStr(myList[index1 + 1], myList[index1]);
  Writeln('The sorted list is:');
  FOR index1 := 1 TO 6 DO
    Writeln(myList[index1])
END.
```

11. Consider the items Tin Man, Dorothy, Scarecrow, and Lion, in that order. After how many swaps in a bubble sort will the list be in alphabetical order?

12. How many comparisons will be made in a bubble sort of 6 items?

13. How many comparisons will be made in a bubble sort of n items?

14. Modify the program in Example 2 so it will keep track of the number of swaps and comparisons and display these numbers before ending.

15. Rework Exercise 11 using the Shell sort.

16. How many comparisons would be made in a Shell sort of 6 items if the items were originally in decreasing order and were sorted in increasing order?

17. If a list of 6 items is already in the proper order, how many comparisons will be made by a Shell sort?

18. Suppose the array num is declared as follows.

```
TYPE NumsType = ARRAY [1..800] OF Integer;

VAR num : NumsType;
```

The following procedure fills num with values between 0 and 63 that are badly in need of sorting. Write a program that uses the procedure and sorts (in ascending order) the resulting array with a bubble sort. Run the program and time the execution. Do the same for the Shell sort.

```
PROCEDURE FillArray (VAR num : NumsType);
{ Generate numbers from 0 to 63 and place in array }
  VAR index : Integer;
  BEGIN
    num[1] := 5;
    FOR index := 2 TO 800 DO
      num[index] := (9 * num[index - 1] + 7) MOD 64
  END;
```

19. Suppose a list of 5000 numbers is to be sorted, but the numbers consist of only 1, 2, 3, and 4. Describe a method of sorting the list that would be much faster than either the bubble or Shell sort.

20. The bubble sort gets its name from the fact that successive passes cause "lighter" items to rise to the top like bubbles in water. How did the Shell sort get its name?

21. What is the maximum number of comparisons required to find an item in a sequential search of 16 items? What is the average number of comparisons? What is the maximum number of comparisons required to find an item in a binary search of 16 items?

22. Redo Exercise 21 with 2^N items, where N is any positive integer.

In Exercises 23 through 32, write a short program (or partial program) to complete the stated task.

23. Display the names of the seven dwarfs in alphabetical order. Fill the array using the following array constant.

    ('Doc', 'Grumpy', 'Sleepy', 'Happy', 'Bashful', 'Sneezy', 'Dopey')

24. Table 8.3 lists the top 10 most attended exhibits in the history of the National Gallery of Art. Read the data into an array of records and display a similar table with the exhibit names in alphabetical order.

Exhibit	Attendance (in thousands)
Rodin Rediscovered	1053
Treasure Houses of Britain	999
Treasures of Tutankhamun	836
Chinese Archaeology	684
Ansel Adams	652
Splendor of Dresden	617
Wyeth's Helga Pictures	558
Post-Impressionism	558
Matisse in Nice	537
John Hay Whitney Collection	513

Table 8.3 National Gallery of Art's Greatest Hits

25. Table 8.4 presents statistics on ski slopes in the Tahoe Basin area. Read the data into an array of records and display a similar table with the top elevation in descending order.

Area	Top Elevation	Vertical	Lifts
Tahoe Ski Bowl	7,880	1,630	5
Mount Rose	9,700	1,440	5
Heavenly	10,100	3,600	26
Alpine Meadows	8,637	1,800	13
Echo Summit	7,950	550	3
Sierra Ski Ranch	8,852	2,212	10
Homewood	7,990	1,650	9
Kirkwood	9,800	2,000	10

Table 8.4 Ski Slopes

26. Accept 10 words to be input in alphabetical order and store them in an array. Then accept an 11th word as input and store it in the array in its correct alphabetical position.

27. An airline has a list of 200 flight numbers in an ascending sorted array of type Integer, *flgtNum*. Accept a number as input and do a binary search of the list to determine if the flight number is valid.

28. Modify the program in Exercise 18 to compute and display the number of times each of the numbers from 0 through 63 appears.

29. Write a program that accepts a word as input and converts it into Morse code. The dots and dashes corresponding to each letter of the alphabet are as follows:

```
A ._        H ....        O _ _ _        V ..._
B _...       I ..          P ._ _ .        W ._ _
C _._.       J ._ _ _      Q _ _ ._        X _.._
D _..        K _._         R ._.           Y _.__
E .          L ._..        S ...           Z _ _ ..
F .._.       M _ _         T _
G _ _.        N _.          U .._
```

30. Write a program that accepts an American word as input and performs a binary search to translate it into its British equivalent. Use the following list of words for data and account for the case when the word requested is not in the list.

American	British	American	British
attic	loft	ice cream	ice
business suit	lounge suit	megaphone	loud hailer
elevator	lift	radio	wireless
flashlight	torch	sneakers	plimsolls
french fries	chips	truck	lorry
gasoline	petrol	zero	nought

31. Write a program that accepts a student's name and seven test scores as input and calculates the average score after dropping the two lowest grades.

32. Suppose letter grades are assigned as follows:

97 and above	A+	74-76	C
94-96	A	70-73	C–
90-93	A–	67-69	D+
87-89	B+	64-66	D
84-86	B	60-63	D–
80-83	B–	0-59	F
77-79	C+		

Write a program that accepts a grade as input and displays the corresponding letter. (**Hint:** This problem shows that when you search an array, you don't always look for equality. Set up an array of records containing the values 97, 94 ,90, 87, 84, . . ., 59 and their corresponding letters A, A–, B+, . . ., F.)

1. The outer loop controls the number of passes, one less than the number of items in the list. The inner loop performs a single pass, and the jth pass consists of num − j comparisons.

2.
First	Last	Middle
1	20	10
11	20	15
11	14	12
13	14	13

8.3 TWO-DIMENSIONAL ARRAYS

Each array discussed so far held a single list of items. Such array variables are called **single-subscripted variables**. An array can also hold the contents of a table with several rows and columns. Such arrays are called **two-dimensional arrays** or **double-subscripted variables**. Two tables are shown below. Table 8.5 gives the road mileage between certain cities. It has four rows and four columns. Table 8.6 shows the leading universities in three disciplines. It has three rows and five columns.

	Chicago	Los Angeles	New York	Philadelphia
Chicago	0	2054	802	738
Los Angeles	2054	0	2786	2706
New York	802	2786	0	100
Philadelphia	738	2706	100	0

Table 8.5 Road Mileage Between Selected U.S. Cities

	1	2	3	4	5
Business	U of PA	MIT	U of IN	U of MI	UC Berk
Comp Sc.	MIT	Cng-Mellon	UC Berk	Cornell	U of IL
Engr/Gen.	UCLA	U of IL	U of MD	U of OK	Stevens IT

Table 8.6 University Rankings
Source: A rating of Undergraduate Programs in American and International Universities, Dr. Jack Gourman, 1989

Two-dimensional array variables store the contents of tables. They have the same types of names as other array variables. The only difference is that they have two subscripts, each with its own range. The range of the first subscript is determined by the number of rows in the table and the range of the second subscript is determined by the number of columns. The statements

```
TYPE ArrayTypeName = ARRAY [OrdinalType1, OrdinalType2] OF Type;
VAR arrayName : ArrayTypeName;
```

declare an array corresponding to a table having rows labeled with the values of *OrdinalType1* and columns labeled with the values of *OrdinalType2*.

The entry in the row labeled *value1* and the column labeled *value2* is *arrayName*[*value1*, *value2*]. For instance, the data in Table 8.5 can be stored in an array named *rm*. The declarations

```
TYPE MileageTable = ARRAY [1..4, 1..4] OF Integer;
VAR rm : MileageTable;     { road mileage }
```

or

```
VAR rm : ARRAY [1..4, 1..4] OF Integer;
```

will declare the array. The entries of the array are:

rm[1,1]=0	rm[1,2]=2054	rm[1,3]=802	rm[1,4]=738
rm[2,1]=2054	rm[2,2]=0	rm[2,3]=2786	rm[2,4]=2706
rm[3,1]=802	rm[3,2]=2786	rm[3,3]=0	rm[3,4]=100
rm[4,1]=738	rm[4,2]=2706	rm[4,3]=100	rm[4,4]=0

The data in Table 8.6 can be stored in a two-dimensional string array named univ. The declarations

```
TYPE RankingTable = ARRAY [1..3, 1..5] OF STRING;
VAR univ : RankingTable;
```

or

```
VAR univ: ARRAY [1..3, 1..5] OF STRING;
```

will declare the array. Some of the entries of the array are

```
univ[1,1] = 'U of PA'
univ[2,3] = 'UC Berk'
univ[3,5] = 'Stevens IT'
```

Array constants also can be used to store the data for a two-dimensional array. A two-dimensional array constant lists the elements of the first row enclosed in parentheses, followed by the elements of the second row enclosed in parentheses, and so on (parentheses must be placed around this entire list). Improved readability is achieved by aligning the elements to give the appearance of a table.

EXAMPLE 1   Write a program to store and access the data from Table 8.5.

SOLUTION   The actual road mileages are stored in a two-dimensional array constant and assigned to a two-dimensional array.

```
PROGRAM Mileage;
{ Determine road mileage between cities }

USES Crt;

TYPE MileageTable = ARRAY [1..4, 1..4] OF Integer;
VAR row, col : Integer;
    rm       : MileageTable;     { road mileage }

PROCEDURE GetMileages (VAR rm : MileageTable);
{ Assign values to the elements of the array }
  CONST Mileages : MileageTable = ((   0, 2054,  802,  738),
                                    (2054,    0, 2786, 2706),
                                    ( 802, 2786,    0,  100),
                                    ( 738, 2706,  100,    0));
  BEGIN
    rm := Mileages
  END;

PROCEDURE ShowCities;
{ Show possible cities }
  BEGIN
    Writeln('1. Chicago');
    Writeln('2. Los Angeles');
    Writeln('3. New York');
    Writeln('4. Philadelphia');
    Writeln
  END;

PROCEDURE InputCities (VAR row, col : Integer);
{ Input origin and destination cities }
  BEGIN
    Write('Origin: ');
    Readln(row);
    Write('Destination: ');
    Readln(col)
  END;

PROCEDURE ShowMileage (VAR rm      : MileageTable;
                           row, col : Integer);
{ Display mileage between cities }
  BEGIN
    Writeln('The road mileage is ', rm[row, col])
  END;

BEGIN
  ClrScr;
  GetMileages(rm);
  ShowCities;
  InputCities(row, col);
  ShowMileage(rm, row, col)
END.
```

```
[run]
1. Chicago
2. Los Angeles
3. New York
4. Philadelphia

Origin: 3
Destination: 1
The road mileage is 802
```

So far, two-dimensional arrays have only been used to store data for convenient lookup. In the next example, an array is used to make a valuable computation.

EXAMPLE 2 The Center for Science in the Public Interest publishes *The Nutrition Scorebook*, a highly respected rating of foods. The top two foods in each of five categories are shown in Table 8.7 along with some information on their composition. Write a program to compute the nutritional content of a meal. The table should be assigned to an array and then the program should request the quantities of each food item that is part of the meal. The program should then compute the amounts of each nutritional component consumed by summing each column with each entry weighted by the quantity of the food item.

	Calories	Protein (grams)	Fat (grams)	Vit A (IU)	Calcium (mg)
spinach (1 cup)	23	3	0.3	8100	93
sweet potato (1 med.)	160	2	1.0	9230	46
yogurt (8 oz.)	230	10	3.0	120	343
skim milk (1 cup)	85	8	0.0	500	302
wh. wheat bread (1 slice)	65	3	1.0	0	24
brown rice (1 cup)	178	3.8	0.9	0	18
watermelon (1 wedge)	110	2	1.0	2510	30
papaya (1 lg.)	156	2.4	0.4	7000	80
tuna in water (1 lb.)	575	126.8	3.6	0	73
lobster (1 med.)	405	28.8	26.6	984	190

Table 8.7 Composition of Ten Top-Rated Foods

SOLUTION
```
PROGRAM NutritionalValues;
{ Determine the nutritional content of a meal }

USES Crt;

CONST Dishes     = 10;
      Components = 5;

TYPE CompTable      = ARRAY [1..Dishes, 1..Components] OF Real;
     DishQty        = ARRAY [1..Dishes] OF Real;
     DishDesc       = ARRAY [1..Dishes] OF STRING;
     ComponentDesc  = ARRAY [1..Components] OF STRING;
```

```
CONST Comp : compTable =
  (( 23,   3,   0.3, 8100,  93), (160,  2,   1,   9230,  46),
   (230,  10,   3,    120, 343), ( 85,  8,   0,    500, 302),
   ( 65,   3,   1,      0,  24), (178,  3.8, 0.9,    0,  18),
   (110,   2,   1,   2510,  30), (156,  2.4, 0.4, 7000,  80),
   (575, 126.8, 3.6,    0,  73), (405, 28.8, 26.6, 984, 190));
     DishNames : dishDesc =
         ('spinach (1 cup)',          'sweet potato (1 med)',
          'yogurt (8 oz)',            'skim milk (1 cup)',
          'wh. wheat bread (1 slice)', 'brown rice (1 cup)',
          'watermelon (1 wedge)',     'papaya (1 lg)',
          'tuna in water (1 lb)',     'lobster (1 med)');
     CompNames : ComponentDesc =
         ('calories',         'protein (grams)', 'fat (grams)',
          'vitamin A (IU)', 'calcium (mg)');

VAR quantities : DishQty;

PROCEDURE InputAmounts (VAR quantities : DishQty);
{ Request quantities of foods consumed }
  VAR foodNum : Integer;
  BEGIN
    FOR foodNum := 1 TO Dishes DO
      BEGIN
        Write(DishNames[foodNum], ': ');
        Readln(quantities[foodNum])
      END;
  END;

PROCEDURE ShowData (VAR quantities : DishQty);
{ Display amount of each component }
  VAR dishNum, compNum : Integer;
      amount           : Real;
  BEGIN
    Writeln;
    Writeln('This meal contains the following quantities');
    Writeln('of these nutritional components: ');
    FOR compNum := 1 TO Components DO
      BEGIN
        amount := 0;
        FOR dishNum := 1 TO Dishes DO
          amount := amount + quantities[dishNum] *
                    Comp[dishNum, compNum];
        Writeln(CompNames[compNum], ': ', amount:1:1)
      END
  END;

BEGIN
  ClrScr;
  InputAmounts(quantities);
  ShowData(quantities)
END.
```

```
[run]
spinach (1 cup): 1
sweet potato (1 med): 1
yogurt (8 oz): 1
skim milk (1 cup): 2
wh. wheat bread (1 slice): 3
brown rice (1 cup): 0
watermelon (1 wedge): 1
papaya (1 lg): 0
tuna in water (1 lb): 0.5
lobster (1 med): 0

This meal contains the following quantities
of these nutritional components:
calories: 1175.5
protein (grams): 105.4
fat (grams): 10.1
vitamin A (IU): 20960.0
calcium (mg): 1224.5
```

Comments:

1. Three- (or higher) dimensional arrays also can be defined in a similar way as two-dimensional arrays. For instance, a three-dimensional array uses three subscripts, and the assignment of values requires a triple-nested loop. As an example, a weatherman might use a three-dimensional array to record temperatures for various dates, times, and elevations.

2. Each row of a two-dimensional array can be thought of as an array. In this sense, a two-dimensional array is just a one-dimensional array whose elements are one-dimensional arrays. Pascal treats these two as identical. For instance, in Example 2, the array type CompTable could have been declared with

```
TYPE ComponentsQty = ARRAY [1..Components] OF Real;
     CompTable     = ARRAY [1..Dishes] OF ComponentsQty;
```

Consequently, the array consisting of the rth row of comp can be referred to as comp[r] and the element in the rth row, cth column of comp, comp[r,c], also can be written comp[r][c].

PRACTICE PROBLEMS 8.3

1. How many entries will arr have in the following declaration?

```
TYPE ArrayType = ARRAY [0..5, 1..2] OF Integer;

VAR arr : ArrayType;
```

2. Consider a table of 5 columns. When should the information be placed in a two-dimensional array as opposed to a one-dimensional array of five-field records.

EXERCISES 8.3

In Exercises 1 through 8, determine the output of the program.

1.
```
TYPE Table = ARRAY [1..20, 1..30] OF Integer;

VAR arr : Table;

BEGIN
  arr[3, 5] := 6;
  arr[5, 3] := 2 * arr[3, 5];
  Writeln(arr[5, 3])
END.
```

2.
```
TYPE WordTable = ARRAY [1..10, 1..15] OF STRING;

VAR wordT : WordTable;
    avar  : STRING;
    num   : Integer;

BEGIN
  avar := 'Dorothy'
  wordT[1, 1] := avar;
  num := 1;
  Writeln(wordT[num, num])
END.
```

3.
```
CONST P = 2;
      Q = 3;

TYPE Table = ARRAY [1..P, 1..Q] OF Integer;

CONST SomeData : Table = ((4, 1, 6), (5, 8, 2));

VAR row, col : Integer;
    arr      : Table;

BEGIN
  arr := SomeData;
  FOR row := 1 TO P DO
    BEGIN
      FOR col := 1 TO Q DO
        Write(arr[row, col]:2);
      Writeln
    END
END.
```

4.
```
TYPE Table = ARRAY [1..3, 1..3] OF Integer;

CONST VectorData : Table = ((1, 2, 3), (4, 3, 2), (3, 4, 5));

VAR index  : Integer;
    vector : Table;
```

```
  BEGIN
    vector := VectorData;
    FOR index := 1 TO 3 DO
      Write(vector[index, index]:2)
  END.
```

5.
```
TYPE YearType = ARRAY [1..100, 1..50] OF Integer;

VAR year : YearType;
    x, y : Integer;

BEGIN
  x := 7;
  y := 8;
  year[x, y] := 1940;
  Writeln(year[7, 8] + 50)
END.
```

6.
```
TYPE MyArrayType = ARRAY [1..4, 1..5] OF Integer;

VAR myArray  : MyArrayType;
    row, col : Integer;

BEGIN
  FOR row := 1 TO 4 DO
    FOR col := 1 TO 5 DO
      myArray[row, col] := (row - col) * row;
    Write(myArray[2, 1])
END.
```

7.
```
CONST MaxRow = 3;
      MaxCol = 4;

TYPE ArrayType = ARRAY [1..MaxRow, 1..MaxCol] OF Integer;

VAR thisArray : ArrayType;
    row, col  : Integer;

PROCEDURE InitArray (VAR thisArray : ArrayType);
  VAR row, col : Integer;
  BEGIN
    FOR row := 1 TO MaxRow DO
      FOR col := 1 TO MaxCol DO
        thisArray[row, col] := 0
  END;

PROCEDURE FillArray (VAR thisArray : ArrayType);
  BEGIN
    thisArray[1, 1] := 4;
    thisArray[2, 2] := 7;
    thisArray[3, 4] := 6
  END;
```

```
       PROCEDURE DisplayArray (thisArray : ArrayType);
         VAR row, col : Integer;
         BEGIN
           FOR row := 1 TO MaxRow DO
             BEGIN
               FOR col := 1 TO MaxCol DO
                 Write(thisArray[row, col]:2);
               Writeln
             END
         END;

    BEGIN
      InitArray(thisArray);
      FillArray(thisArray);
      DisplayArray(thisArray)
    END.
```

8.
```
   TYPE WeekDays     = (Sun, Mon, Tue, Wed, Thu, Fri, Sat);
        FebruaryType = ARRAY [0..3, Sun..Sat] OF Integer;

   VAR feb  : FebruaryType;
       week : Integer;
       day  : WeekDays;

   PROCEDURE FillMonth (VAR feb : FebruaryType);
     VAR week : Integer;
         day  : WeekDays;
     BEGIN
       FOR week := 0 TO 3 DO
         FOR day := Sun TO Sat DO
           feb[week, day] := week * 7 + (Ord(day) + 1)
     END;

   PROCEDURE OutputCal (VAR feb : FebruaryType);
     VAR week : Integer;
         day  : WeekDays;
     BEGIN
       FOR week := 0 TO 3 DO
         BEGIN
           FOR day := Sun TO Sat DO
             Write(feb[week, day]:3);
           Writeln
         END
     END;

   BEGIN
     FillMonth(feb);
     OutputCal(feb)
   END.
```

In Exercises 9 and 10, identify the errors.

9.
```
PROGRAM Demo;
  { Fill an array }

  TYPE Matrix = ARRAY [1..3, 1..4] OF Integer;

  VAR arr      : Matrix;
      row, col : Integer;

  BEGIN
    FOR row := 1 TO 4 DO
      FOR col := 1 TO 3 DO
        Readln(arr[row, col])
  END.
```

10.
```
PROGRAM Demo;
  { Report individual scores }

  TYPE Matrix = ARRAY [1..3, 1..2] OF Integer;

  CONST StudentData : Matrix = ((80, 85, 90),
                                (72, 80, 88));

  VAR score                 : Matrix;
      row, col, studentNum : Integer;

  BEGIN
    score := StudentData;
    Write('Enter student #(1, 2, 3): ');
    Readln(studentNum);
    Writeln(score[studentNum, 1], score[studentNum, 2]:4)
  END.
```

In Exercises 11 through 14, write a procedure or function to perform the stated task assuming the following declarations have been made.

```
TYPE SomeType = ARRAY [1..10, 1..10] OF Integer;

VAR arr : SomeType;
```

11. Set the entries in the *j*th column to *j*.

12. Assuming values have been previously assigned to each entry, compute the sum of the values in the 10th row.

13. Assuming values have been previously assigned to each entry, interchange the values in the second and third rows.

14. Given an array declared by

```
TYPE AnArray = ARRAY [1..3, 1..45] OF Integer;

VAR arr : AnArray;
```

and assuming values have been previously assigned to each entry, find the greatest value and the locations (possibly more than one) at which it occurs.

In Exercises 15 through 24, write a program to perform the stated task.

15. A company has two stores (1 and 2), and each store sells three items (1, 2, and 3). The tables below give the inventory at the beginning of the day and the quantity of each item sold during that day.

		Item						Item		
		1	2	3				1	2	3
Store	1	25	64	23		Store	1	7	45	11
	2	12	82	19			2	4	24	8
		Beginning Inventory						**Sales for Day**		

(a) Record the values of each table in an array.
(b) Adjust the values in the first array to hold the inventories at the end of the day and display these new inventories.

16. Table 8.8 gives the results of a survey on the uses of microcomputers in four types of businesses. Each entry shows the number of respondents from the category that use the computer for the indicated purpose.

(a) Place the data from the table in an array.
(b) Determine the number of stores using a microcomputer for inventory control.

Applications for Microcomputer	Mass Merchandise	Dept.	Specialty	Combination/ Grocery
Financial Planning	47	47	56	50
Inventory Control	6	0	15	25
Payroll	9	5	4	17
Point-of-Sale	9	0	4	8

Table 8.8 Use of Microcomputers
Source: Stores, August 1985

17. A university offers 10 courses at each of three campuses. The number of students enrolled in each is presented in Table 8.9 below:

						Course					
		1	2	3	4	5	6	7	8	9	10
	1	5	15	22	21	12	25	16	11	17	23
Campus	2	11	23	51	25	32	35	32	52	25	21
	3	2	12	32	32	25	26	29	12	15	11

Table 8.9 Number of Students Enrolled in Courses

(a) Find the total number of course enrollments on each campus.
(b) Find the total number of students taking each course.

18. Table 8.10 gives the amount of money spent for advertising in two years by the leading fast food chains.

(a) Place the data into an array.

(b) Calculate the total increase in advertising expenditures by these five companies.

	1984	1985
1. McDonald's	154	303
2. Burger King	130	154
3. Wendy's	74	84
4. Kentucky Fried Chicken	63	75
5. Pizza Hut	58	63

Table 8.10   Amount Spent on Advertising (in millions of dollars)
Source: Television Bureau of Advertising

19. The scores for the top three golfers at the 1988 U.S. Open are shown in Table 8.11.

(a) Place the data into an array.

(b) Compute the total score for each player.

(c) Compute the average score for each round.

		Round			
		1	2	3	4
Curtis Strange	1	70	67	69	72
Nick Faldo	2	72	67	68	71
Steve Pate	3	72	69	72	67

Table 8.11   1988 U.S. Open Leaders

20. Table 8.12 contains part of the pay schedule for federal employees. Table 8.13 gives the number of employees of each classification in a certain division. Place the data from each table into an array and compute the amount of money this division pays for salaries during the year.

	Step			
	1	2	3	4
GS-1	10,581	10,935	11,286	11,637
GS-2	11,897	12,180	12,574	12,910
GS-3	12,982	13,415	13,848	14,281
GS-4	14,573	15,059	15,545	16,031
GS-5	16,305	16,849	17,393	17,937
GS-6	18,174	18,780	19,386	19,992
GS-7	20,195	20,868	21,541	22,012

Table 8.12   1990 Pay Schedule for Federal White-collar Workers

	1	2	3	4
GS-1	0	0	2	1
GS-2	2	3	0	1
GS-3	4	2	5	7
GS-4	12	13	8	3
GS-5	4	5	0	1
GS-6	6	2	4	3
GS-7	8	1	9	2

Table 8.13   Number of Employees in Each Category

21. Consider Table 8.6, the rankings of three university departments. Write a program that places the data into an array, allows the name of a college to be entered, and gives the categories in which it appears. Of course, a college might appear more than once or not at all.

22. A company has three stores (1, 2, and 3), and each store sells five items (1, 2, 3, 4, and 5). The tables below give the number of items sold by each store and category on a particular day, and the cost of each item.
    (a) Place the data from the left-hand table in a two-dimensional array and the data from the right-hand table in a one-dimensional array.
    (b) Compute and display the total dollar amount of sales for each store and for the entire company.

		Item				
		1	2	3	4	5
	1	25	64	23	45	14
Store	2	12	82	19	34	63
	3	54	22	17	43	35

Number of Items Sold During Day

Item	Cost
1	12.00
2	17.95
3	95.00
4	86.50
5	78.00

Cost per Item

23. Suppose a course has 15 students enrolled and five exams were given during the semester. Write a program that accepts each student's name and grades as input and places the names in a one-dimensional array and the grades in a two-dimensional array. The program should then display each student's name and semester average. Also, the program should display the median for each exam. (For an odd number of grades, the median is the middle grade. For an even number of grades it is the average of the two middle grades.)

24. An n-by-n array is called a **magic square** if the sums of each row, each column, and each diagonal are equal. Write a program to determine if an array is a magic square and use it to determine if either of the arrays below is a magic square. (**Hint:** If at any time one of the sums is not equal to the others, the search is complete.)

(a)
1	15	15	4
12	6	7	9
8	10	11	5
13	3	2	16

(b)
11	10	4	23	17
18	12	6	5	24
25	19	13	7	1
2	21	20	14	8
9	3	22	16	15

SOLUTIONS TO PRACTICE PROBLEMS 8.3

1. The array, *arr*, has six rows numbered 0 through 5 and 2 columns numbered 1 and 2. Thus, it can store 12 entries.

2. Both arrays of records and two-dimensional arrays are used to hold related data. If the data are of different types, then an array of records must be used since all entries of a two-dimensional array must be of the same type. An array of records also should be used if the data will be sorted. In most other cases, two-dimensional arrays are preferable. The common name simplifies the programming, since FOR loops can be used to access data both horizontally as well as vertically.

8.4 A CASE STUDY: CALCULATING WITH A SPREADSHEET

Spreadsheets are the most popular type of software used on personal computers. A spreadsheet is a financial planning tool in which data are analyzed in a table of rows and columns. Some of the items are entered by the user and other items, often totals and balances, are calculated using the entered data. The outstanding feature of electronic spreadsheets is their ability to recalculate an entire table after changes are made in some of the entered data, thereby allowing the user to determine the financial implications of various alternatives. This is called "What if?" analysis.

Figure 8.7 contains an example of a spreadsheet used to analyze a student's financial projections for the four quarters of a year. Column 5 holds the sum of the entries in the other four columns, rows 4 and 10 hold sums of the entries in rows 1 through 3 and 5 through 9 respectively, and row 11 holds the differences of the entries in rows 4 and 10. Since the total balance is negative, some of the amounts in the spreadsheet must be changed and the totals and balances recalculated.

This case study develops a menu-driven program to produce a spreadsheet with the five columns of numbers shown in Figure 8.7, three user-specified categories of income, and five user-specified categories of expenses. The following three tasks are to be selected from a menu:

1. Enter data. The user is prompted for three income categories and five expense categories, and for the amounts in each category for each quarter of the year. Then the program should calculate the amounts for totals and balances, display the complete spreadsheet, and display the menu below it horizontally.

2. Alter data. The user specifies each entry to be altered by giving its row, column, and new amount. After each change is entered, the amounts for the totals and balances should be recalculated and the total spreadsheet and menu displayed. The user is then prompted for further changes until he responds to the request for row, column, and new amount with 0, 0, 0.

3. Quit.

	1 Fall	2 Winter	3 Spring	4 Summer	Total
Income					
1 Job	1000	1300	1000	2000	5300
2 Parents	200	200	200	0	600
3 Scholarship	150	150	150	0	450
4 Total	1350	1650	1350	2000	6350
Expenses					
5 Tuition	400	0	400	0	800
6 Food	650	650	650	650	2600
7 Rent	600	600	600	400	2200
8 Books	110	0	120	0	230
9 Misc	230	210	300	120	860
10 Total	1990	1460	2070	1170	6690
11 Balance	−640	190	−720	830	−340

Figure 8.7 Spreadsheet for Student's Financial Projections

The 55 locations in the spreadsheet that hold amounts are called **cells**. Each cell is identified by its row and column numbers. For instance, the cell 10, 2 contains the amount 1460.

Designing the Spreadsheet Program

In keeping with the top-down approach to problem solving, we break the problem into a small number of basic tasks, each of which will then be broken further. The first task is the setting up of the fixed labels. After that, a menu is presented with the following three options:

1. Create spreadsheet

2. Revise spreadsheet

3. Quit

The first two menu items are broken down into specific subtasks.

1. Create spreadsheet. To form the spreadsheet, we must request the income and expense categories and amounts from the user, calculate the totals and balances, and then display the resulting spreadsheet; that is, task 1 is divided into the following subtasks:

    1.1 Input income and expense categories
    1.2 Input income and expense amounts
    1.3 Calculate totals and balances
    1.4 Display spreadsheet

2. Revise spreadsheet. The user may request a change in just one of the cells by providing its row and column and the new amount. Then the program will recalculate all of the totals and balances and display the revised spreadsheet. That is, task 2 is divided into the following subtasks:

2.1 Input cell (row, column) and new amount
2.2 Calculate totals and balances
2.3 Display spreadsheet

Notice that tasks 2.2 and 2.3 are the same as tasks 1.3 and 1.4. Since the procedure performing tasks 1.3 and 1.4 also can be used for tasks 2.2 and 2.3, respectively, considerable work is saved. Whenever possible, general-purpose procedures such as these should be incorporated in the design of a program.

The next step in designing the program is to examine each of the subtasks identified above and decide which, if any, should be divided further into smaller tasks. The input tasks, 1.1, 1.2 and 2.1, are basic, so we won't divide them any further; but the calculate and display tasks, 1.3 and 1.4, are more involved. These subtasks can be broken down as follows:

1.3 Calculate totals and balances. This subtask requires computing income and expense totals for each of the time periods, computing balances for the time periods, and a "row total" corresponding to each income and expense category of the spreadsheet.

1.3.1 Calculate income totals
1.3.2 Calculate expense totals
1.3.3 Calculate balance
1.3.4 Calculate row totals

1.4 Display spreadsheet. To display the spreadsheet, we need to produce the table in Figure 8.7 that contains labels for the income and expense categories and time periods, and has its data arranged in rows and columns.

1.4.1 Display labels
1.4.2 Display data

The top-down chart in Figure 8.8 shows the stepwise refinement of the problem. The items in the main part of the chart contained in rectangles have continuations below.

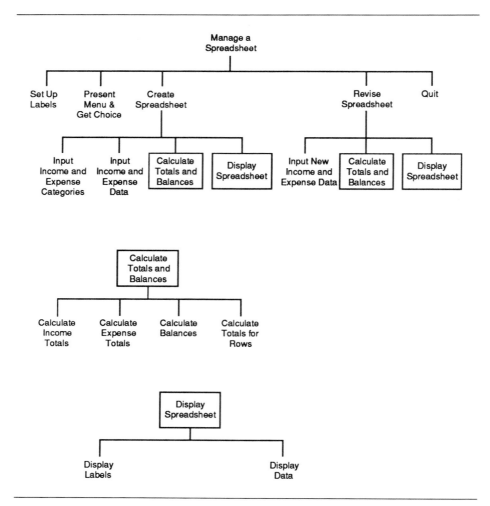

Figure 8.8 Top-Down Chart for Spreadsheet Case Study

Pseudocode for the Spreadsheet Program

The workhorse of the top-down chart is the third row. The following pseudocode shows how these tasks are carried out.

GET INCOME AND EXPENSE CATEGORIES (Procedure InputCategories)
Clear the screen
FOR row counter from 1 TO 3
  Prompt user for income label corresponding to row counter
Display one blank line
FOR row counter from 5 TO 9
  Prompt user for expense label corresponding to row counter

GET INCOME AND EXPENSE DATA (Procedure InputData)
Display two blank lines
FOR row counter from 1 TO 3
  Prompt user for income data corresponding to row counter
Display one blank line
FOR row counter from 5 TO 9
  Prompt user for expense data corresponding to row counter

CALCULATE TOTALS (Procedure CalculateSpreadsheet)
Calculate income totals
Calculate expense totals
Calculate balances
Calculate row totals

DISPLAY SPREADSHEET (Procedure DisplaySpreadsheet)
Display column labels
FOR row counter from 1 TO 11
  IF row counter is 1 THEN
    Display income label
  IF row counter is 5 THEN
    Display blank line and expenses label
  IF row counter is 11 THEN
    Display blank line
  Display row data

GET NEW DATA (Procedure InputNewData)
REPEAT
  Read new data for spreadsheet
UNTIL data okay

Writing the Spreadsheet Program

Three arrays suffice to hold the spreadsheet. (See Table 8.14.) Three of the elements of the array rowLabel, the fourth (Total), 10th (Total), and 11th (Balance), are fixed. The other elements of that array are the categories to be determined by the user. The column labels are all fixed. The data for all rows except 4, 10, and 11 must be entered by the user.

Arrays	Range	Information Held
rowTitles	1 .. 11	Job, Parents, . . ., Balance
colTitles	1 .. 5	Fall, Winter, . . ., Total
userData	1 .. 11, 1 .. 5	Amounts in the 55 cells

Table 8.14 The Arrays that Hold the Spreadsheet

When values have been assigned to the three arrays, the totals are easily calculated with loops containing accumulators. Then the balances are calculated by performing subtractions.

After the user has entered the spreadsheet, he or she is presented with a menu of three options. The user can enter a completely new spreadsheet (with possibly different categories), revise selected data in the current spreadsheet, or quit. The first task is identical to the formation of the original spreadsheet and the last task is trivial.

After selecting the update option, the user is asked for a data entry to alter. The entry is specified by giving the location of the entry, namely its row and column, and the value of the entry. After the three responses are obtained, the program recalculates all of the totals and balances. The user can continue to revise the spreadsheet to his heart's content. The user indicates he or she is finished with the update by responding with 0, 0, 0.

Table 8.15 shows each task discussed above and the procedure that carries out the task. The program follows.

---

1.   Input spreadsheet   InputSpreadsheet
      1.1 Input income and expense categories   InputCategories
      1.2 Input income and expense data   InputData
      1.3 Calculate totals and balances   Calculate
            1.3.1 Calculate income totals   CalculateIncomeTotals
            1.3.2 Calculate expense totals   CalculateExpenseTotals
            1.3.3 Calculate balances   CalculateBalances
            1.3.4 Calculate row totals   CalculateRowTotals
      1.4 Display spreadsheet   DisplaySpreadsheet
            1.4.1 Display labels
            1.4.2 Display data
2.   Revise spreadsheet   ReviseSpreadsheet
      2.1 Input new data   InputNewData
      2.2 Calculate totals and balances   Calculate
      2.3 Display spreadsheet   DisplaySpreadsheet
3.   Quit

Table 8.15 Tasks and their Procedures

```
PROGRAM Spreadsheet;

USES Crt;

TYPE ColTitles  = ARRAY [1..5] OF STRING;
     RowTitles  = ARRAY [1..11] OF STRING;
     RowOfCells = ARRAY [1..5] OF Integer;
     Cells      = ARRAY [1..11] OF RowOfCells;

CONST ColLabels : ColTitles = ('1 Fall','2 Winter','3 Spring',
                                '4 Summer','Total');

VAR choice        : Integer;    { User's main menu choice }
    rowLabels     : RowTitles;  { Row categories entered by user }
    entries       : Cells;      { Numeric data entered by user, totals }
    valuesEntered : Boolean;    { Have the data been given values? }

PROCEDURE CalculateBalances (VAR entries : Cells);
{ Calculate balances }
  VAR col : Integer;
  BEGIN
    FOR col := 1 TO 4 DO
      entries[11, col] := entries[4, col] - entries[10, col]
  END;
```

```
PROCEDURE CalculateExpenseTotals (VAR entries : Cells);
{ Calculate total expenses }
  VAR row, col, total : Integer;
  BEGIN
    FOR col := 1 TO 4 DO
      BEGIN
        total := 0;
        FOR row := 5 TO 9 DO
          total := total + entries[row, col];
        entries[10, col] := total
      END
  END;

PROCEDURE CalculateIncomeTotals (VAR entries : Cells);
{ Calculate total income }
  VAR row, col, total : Integer;
  BEGIN
    FOR col := 1 TO 4 DO
      BEGIN
        total := 0;
        FOR row := 1 TO 3 DO
          total := total + entries[row, col];
        entries[4, col] := total
      END
  END;

PROCEDURE CalculateRowTotals (VAR entries : Cells);
{ Calculate totals for all rows }
  VAR row, col, total : Integer;
  BEGIN
    FOR row := 1 TO 11 DO
      BEGIN
        total := 0;
        FOR col := 1 TO 4 DO
          total := total + entries[row, col];
        entries[row, 5] := total
      END
  END;

PROCEDURE Calculate (VAR entries : Cells);
{ Calculate totals and balances for spreadsheet }
  BEGIN
    CalculateIncomeTotals(entries);
    CalculateExpenseTotals(entries);
    CalculateBalances(entries);
    CalculateRowTotals(entries)
  END;
```

```pascal
PROCEDURE DisplaySpreadsheet (VAR rowLabels : RowTitles;
                             VAR entries   : Cells);
{ Display all spreadsheet information }
  VAR row : Integer;
  BEGIN
    ClrScr;
    Writeln(ColLabels[1]:21, ColLabels[2]:12, ColLabels[3]:10,
            ColLabels[4]:9, ColLabels[5]:11);
    FOR row := 1 TO 11 DO
      BEGIN
        CASE row OF
          1  : Writeln('  Income');
          5  : BEGIN
                 Writeln;
                 Writeln('  Expenses')
               END;
          11 : Writeln
        END;
        Writeln(row:2, rowLabels[row]:12, entries[row, 1]:7,
                entries[row, 2]:10, entries[row, 3]:10,
                entries[row, 4]:10, entries[row, 5]:11);
      END
  END;

PROCEDURE EraseLines;
{ Erase two lines near bottom of screen }
  VAR i : Integer;
  BEGIN
    GotoXY(1, 21);
    FOR i := 1 TO 80 * 2 - 1 DO Write(' ');
    GotoXY(1, 21)
  END;

PROCEDURE GetChoice (VAR choice : Integer);
{ Input user option for main menu }
  BEGIN
    GotoXY(1, 21);
    Writeln('1. Enter data    2. Update data    3. Quit');
    REPEAT
      GotoXY(1, 22);
      Write('Number of choice: ');
      Readln(choice)
    UNTIL choice IN [1..3]
  END;
```

```
PROCEDURE InputCategories (VAR rowLabels : RowTitles);
{ Input category labels }
  VAR row : Integer;
  BEGIN
    ClrScr;
    Writeln('Income category');
    FOR row := 1 TO 3 DO
      BEGIN
        Write('Label: ');
        Readln(rowLabels[row])
      END;
    Writeln;
    Writeln('Expense category');
    FOR row := 5 TO 9 DO
      BEGIN
        Write('Label: ');
        Readln(rowLabels[row])
      END
  END;

PROCEDURE InputCategoryData (VAR rowOfEntries : RowOfCells);
{ Input amounts for one category }
  VAR col : Integer;
  BEGIN
    FOR col := 1 TO 4 DO
      BEGIN
        Write('  ', ColLabels[col]:8, ': ');
        Readln(rowOfEntries[col])
      END
  END;

PROCEDURE InputData (VAR rowLabels : RowTitles;
                     VAR entries   : Cells);
{ Input numeric data for entire spreadsheet }
  VAR row : Integer;
  BEGIN
    Writeln;
    Writeln;
    FOR row := 1 TO 3 DO
      BEGIN
        Writeln('Enter each season''s income from ', rowLabels[row]);
        InputCategoryData(entries[row])
      END;
    Writeln;
    FOR row := 5 TO 9 DO
      BEGIN
        Writeln('Enter each season''s expenses for ', rowLabels[row]);
        InputCategoryData(entries[row])
      END
  END;
```

```
PROCEDURE InputNewData (VAR row, col, newData : Integer);
{ Input row, column, and new amounts for spreadsheet update }
  BEGIN
    REPEAT
      EraseLines;
      Writeln('Enter 0 0 0 to terminate');
      Write('Row Column New data: ');
      Readln(row, col, newData)
    UNTIL (row IN [0..10]) AND (col IN [0..4]);
    EraseLines
  END;


PROCEDURE InputSpreadsheet (VAR rowLabels : RowTitles;
                            VAR entries   : Cells);
{ Input spreadsheet categories and amounts, and display totals }
  BEGIN
    InputCategories(rowLabels);
    InputData(rowLabels, entries);
    Calculate(entries);
    DisplaySpreadsheet(rowLabels, entries)
  END;


PROCEDURE ReviseSpreadsheet (VAR rowLabels : RowTitles;
                             VAR entries   : Cells);
{ Input and change a single spreadsheet entry }
  VAR row, col, newData : Integer;
  BEGIN
    InputNewData(row, col, newData);
    WHILE row <> 0 DO
      BEGIN
        entries[row, col] := newData;
        Calculate(entries);
        DisplaySpreadsheet(rowLabels, entries);
        InputNewData(row, col, newData)
      END
  END;

PROCEDURE SetUpRowLabels (VAR rowLabels : rowTitles);
{ Initialize all pre-set labels }
  BEGIN
    rowLabels[4] := 'Total';
    rowLabels[10] := 'Total';
    rowLabels[11] := 'Balance'
  END;
```

```
BEGIN { Spreadsheet }
  ClrScr;
  SetUpRowLabels(rowLabels);
  valuesEntered := False;
  REPEAT
    GetChoice(choice);
    CASE choice OF
      1 : BEGIN
            InputSpreadsheet(rowLabels, entries);
            valuesEntered := True
          END;
      2 : If valuesEntered THEN
            ReviseSpreadsheet(rowLabels, entries)
          ELSE
            Writeln('The spreadsheet does not contain any values.');
      3 : Writeln('Have a nice day.')
    END
  UNTIL choice = 3
END.  { Spreadsheet }
```

Chapter 8
Summary

1. A list of data is most efficiently processed if stored in an *array*. The *range* of an array is an ordinal data type.

2. *Array constants* provide a convenient device for holding the data to be assigned to an array variable.

3. Related lists of data can be stored in either *parallel arrays* or an *array of records*.

4. Two of the best known methods for ordering (or *sorting*) arrays are the *bubble sort* and the *Shell sort*.

5. Any array can be searched *sequentially* to find the subscript associated with a sought-after value. Sorted arrays can be searched most efficiently by a *binary search*.

6. A table can be effectively stored in a *two-dimensional array*.

Chapter 8
Programming Projects

1. Table 8.16 contains some lengths in terms of feet. Write a program that displays the nine different units of measure, requests the unit to convert from, the unit to convert to, and the quantity to be converted, and then displays the converted quantity. A typical outcome is shown in Figure 8.9.

1 inch = 0.0833 feet	1 rod = 16.5 feet
1 yard = 3 feet	1 furlong = 660 feet
1 meter = 3.2815 feet	1 kilometer = 3281.5 feet
1 fathom = 6 feet	1 mile = 5280 feet

Table 8.16   Equivalent Lengths

1. inch	2. fathom	3. foot
4. furlong	5. kilometer	6. meter
7. mile	8. rod	9. yard

Convert from: 4
Convert to: 6
Length to be converted: 10
Converted length: 2011.68

Figure 8.9   Possible Outcome of Project 1

2. Two ordered arrays of the same type can be *merged* into one ordered array. Write a program to do the following

   (a) Place the names Draper, Kotok, Nelson, Pittman, Stallman, Sullivan, Williams, and EOD in the array, firstList. The last name will serve as a sentinel.

   (b) Place the names Box, Gates, Jewell, Moore, and Willington, along with EOD, in another array, secondList.

   (c) Specify an array masterList of range 1 to 12 and fill it with an alphabetical listing of the preceding 12 names. Accomplish this task by looking at successive names from the other two arrays and selecting the names in order. Since Box precedes Draper, masterList[1] is Box, since Draper precedes Gates, masterList[2] is Draper, and so on.

   (d) Display the names of these 12 renowned computer pioneers in alphabetical order.

   (**Note 1:** Think about how complicated the program would have been if there were no sentinel values in arrays firstList and secondList. **Note 2:** An efficient method for sorting a large list is to split it into two halves, sort each half independently, and then merge the two halves together.)

3. Statisticians use the concepts of **mean** and **standard deviation** to describe a collection of data. The mean is the average value of the items, and the standard deviation measures the spread or dispersal of the numbers about the mean. Formally, if $x_1, x_2, x_3, \ldots, x_n$ is a collection of data, then

$$m = \text{mean} = \frac{x_1 + x_2 + x_3 + \ldots + x_n}{n}$$

$$s = \text{standard deviation} = \sqrt{\frac{(x_1 - m)^2 + (x_2 - m)^2 + (x_3 - m)^2 + \ldots + (x_n - m)^2}{n - 1}}$$

Write a computer program to

(a) Request that up to 40 exam grades be entered from the keyboard.
(b) Calculate the mean and standard deviation of the exam scores.
(c) Assign letter grades to each exam score, ES, as follows:

$$m + 1.5s \leq ES \qquad\qquad\qquad A$$
$$m + 0.5s \leq ES < m + 1.5s \qquad B$$
$$m - 0.5s \leq ES < m + 0.5s \qquad C$$
$$m - 1.5s \leq ES < m - 0.5s \qquad D$$
$$\qquad\qquad ES < m - 1.5s \qquad F$$

For instance, if m were 70 and s were 12, then grades of 88 or above would receive A's, grades between 76 and 87 would receive B's, and so on. A procedure of this type is referred to as **curving grades**.

(d) Display a list of the exam scores along with their corresponding grades.

4. Each team in a six-team soccer league played each other team once. Table 8.17 shows the winners. Write a program to display a listing of the teams giving each team's name and number of games won. The list should be in decreasing order by the number of wins. The entries of the table should be stored in a two-dimensional array *winner* of type Team = (Jazz, Jets, Owls, Rams, Cubs, Zips). Also, each of the two array indices should have the enumerated type Team. For instance, winner[Jazz, Rams] is Rams. (**Note:** The elements on the main diagonal should not be counted as wins since they correspond to the each team playing itself.)

	Jazz	**Jets**	**Owls**	**Rams**	**Cubs**	**Zips**
Jazz	Jazz	Jazz	Jazz	Rams	Cubs	Jazz
Jets	Jazz	Jets	Jets	Jets	Cubs	Zips
Owls	Jazz	Jets	Owls	Rams	Owls	Owls
Rams	Rams	Jets	Rams	Rams	Rams	Rams
Cubs	Cubs	Cubs	Owls	Rams	Cubs	Cubs
Zips	Jazz	Zips	Owls	Rams	Cubs	Zips

Table 8.17   Soccer League Winners

5. The Game of Life was invented by John H. Conway to model some genetic laws for birth, death, and survival. Consider a checkerboard consisting of an N-by-N array of squares. Each square can contain one individual (denoted by 1) or be empty (denoted by −). Figure 8.10(a) shows a 6-×-6 board with four of the squares occupied. The future of each individual depends on the number of his neighbors. After each period of time, called a *generation*, certain individuals will survive, others will die due to either loneliness or overcrowding, and new individuals will be born. Each nonborder square has eight neighboring squares. After each generation, the status of the squares change as follows:

(a) An individual *survives* if there are two or three individuals in neighboring squares.
(b) An individual *dies* if he has more than three individuals or less than two in neighboring squares.

(c) A new individual is *born* into each empty square with exactly 3 individuals as neighbors.

Figure 8.10(b) shows the status after one generation. Write a program to do the following:

(a) Define a constant N to be the length of each row (and column) of the board.

(b) Declare the two-dimensional arrays currentGen with type ARRAY [1..N, 1..N] OF Char to hold the status of each square in the current generation. To specify the initial configuration, have the user input each row as a string of length N, and break the row into 1s or dashes with Copy.

(c) Declare the two-dimensional arrays nextGen with type ARRAY [1..N, 1..N] OF Char to hold the status of each square in the next generation. Compute the status for each square and produce the display in Figure 8.10(b). (**Note:** The generation changes all at once. Only current cells are used to determine which cells will contain individuals in the next generation.)

(d) Assign the next generation values to the current generation and repeat as often as desired.

(e) Display the number of individuals in each generation.

(**Hint:** The hardest part of the program is determining the number of neighbors a cell has. In general, you must check a 3-x-3 square around the cell in question. Exceptions must be made when the cell is on the edge of the array. Don't forget that a cell is not a neighbor of itself.)

Test the program with the initial configuration shown in Figure 8.11. It is known as the figure-eight configuration and repeats after 8 generations.

```
 - - - - - -      - - - - - -            - - - - - - - - - -
 - - - - - -      - - 1 1 - -            - - - - - - - - - -
 - 1 1 1 1 -      - - 1 1 - -          - - - 1 1 1 - - - - -
 - - - - - -      - - 1 1 - -          - - 1 1 1 - - - - -
 - - - - - -      - - 1 1 - -          - - 1 1 1 - - - - -
 - - - - - -      - - - - - -          - - 1 1 1 - - - - -
                                       - - - - - 1 1 1 - -
      (a)              (b)             - - - - - 1 1 1 - -
                                       - - - - - 1 1 1 - -
                                       - - - - - - - - - -
                                       - - - - - - - - - -
```

Figure 8.10 Two Generations   **Figure 8.11** The Figure Eight

9

Files

9.1   TEXT FILES

In previous chapters, data processed by a program were either given as literals in assignment statements, supplied by the user in response to a Readln statement, or stored in named constants. These methods are fine for small quantities of data that are to be used in only one program; however, large amounts of data, data that will be accessed by many different programs, or data that will be updated (such as stock prices and class enrollments) must be kept on a disk. One means of storing data is a **text file**. In this section, we create and use text files. The creation process physically records data onto a disk. These data can then be read from the disk and assigned to variables in much the same way data are read from the keyboard in response to Readln statements.

Figure 9.1 shows what a typical text file looks like on a disk. This particular file holds some people's names and their years of birth. The file has the name YOB.DAT. The two characters ♪ and ◙ stand for carriage return and line feed. The combination "carriage return, line feed" is a standard way of denoting the end of a line. For instance, we press the Enter key to end a line in a QuickPascal program. This sends carriage return and line feed characters to the screen, which cause the cursor to move to the beginning of the next row of the screen.

Barbra♪◙1942♪◙Ringo♪◙1940♪◙Sylvester♪◙1946♪◙

Figure 9.1   Contents of the File YOB.DAT

There are many ways to organize data in a text file. The technique presented in this section is easy to implement. Other techniques are discussed in the comments. A text file can be created with a program or the QuickPascal editor.

Creating a Text File With a Program

1. Choose a DOS file name. A DOS file name is a string consisting of two parts: a base name of at most eight characters followed by an optional extension consisting of a period and at most three characters. Letters, digits, and a few other assorted characters (see Comment 1) can be used in either the name or the extension. Blank spaces are not allowed. Some examples of file names are INCOME.86, CUSTOMER.DAT, and FORT500.

2. Choose an identifier, called the **file variable**, to be used by the program to refer to the file. This identifier must appear in the VAR part of the program with a declaration of the form

   ```
   VAR fileVar : Text;
   ```

3. Execute the statement

   ```
   Assign(fileVar, fileName)
   ```

where *fileVar* is the file variable and *fileName* is the string consisting of the DOS file name. This statement tells the compiler to act on the DOS file *fileName* whenever the file variable *fileVar* is mentioned.

4. Execute the statement

```
Rewrite(fileVar)
```

to open a file on the disk drive for output. It opens a communication line between the computer and the disk drive for storing data *onto* the diskette. It allows data to be output from the computer and recorded in the specified file.

5. Place data into the file with the Writeln statement. If *item* has a value of a predefined type, then the statement

```
Writeln(fileVar, item)
```

places the value of *item* into the file identified by *fileVar* in the same way that the statement, with *fileVar* missing, would display the value on the screen. After the Writeln statement is executed, the characters ♪ and ◙ are placed into the file.

6. After all the data have been recorded into the file, execute

```
Close(fileVar)
```

Executing this statement is called **closing the file**. See Comment 14.

EXAMPLE 1   Write an interactive program to create the file of Figure 9.1. Use "EOD" as a sentinel to indicate that all the data has been entered.

SOLUTION

```
PROGRAM CreateBirthyearFile;
{ Create the file YOB.DAT and record some data into it }

USES Crt;

VAR birthFile : Text;
    name      : STRING;
    year      : Integer;

BEGIN
  ClrScr;
  Assign(birthFile, 'YOB.DAT');
  Rewrite(birthFile);
  Writeln('Enter EOD to finish.');
  Write('Enter a person''s name: ');
  Readln(name);
  WHILE name <> 'EOD' DO
    BEGIN
      Write('Enter the person''s year of birth: ');
      Readln(year);
      Writeln(birthFile, name);
      Writeln(birthFile, year);
      Writeln;
      Write('Enter a person''s name: ');
      Readln(name)
    END;
  Close(birthFile)
END.
```

read before you get into loop

first argument tells where to write it (on the file, not on screen)

very important

```
[run]
Enter EOD to finish.
Enter a person's name: Barbra
Enter the person's year of birth: 1942

Enter a person's name: Ringo
Enter the person's year of birth: 1940

Enter a person's name: Sylvester
Enter the person's year of birth: 1946

Enter a person's name: EOD
```

Creating a Text File With the QuickPascal Editor

1. Press Alt/F/N to open a new program window. (The title bar will contain a file name such as UNTITLD2.PAS.)

2. Type in each item, one item per line. Press the Enter key after each item except the last. (QuickPascal automatically adds the two end-of-line characters when the file is saved.)

3. After all the items have been typed, press Alt/F/S to save the file. When prompted for a DOS file name, either include an extension or follow the base name with a period. This guarantees that the file name on the disk will not have the extension PAS.

EXAMPLE 2 Use the QuickPascal editor to create the file of Figure 9.1.

SOLUTION
1. Press Alt/F/N.

2. Place the following information in the current edit window. (Do not press the Enter key after typing in 1946.)

```
Barbra
1942
Ringo
1940
Sylvester
1946
```

3. Press Alt/F/S and type YOB.DAT when prompted for a name.

Note: Small text files are easier to create with the QuickPascal editor than with a program; however, files are often created from the data of another file. In this event, a program similar to the one of Example 1 must be used.

Reading Information From a Text File

Data stored in a text file can be read in order (that is, sequentially) and assigned to variables with the following steps.

1. Choose an identifier, called the **file variable**, to be used by the program to refer to the file.

2. Execute the statement

   ```
   Assign(fileVar, fileName)
   ```

   where *fileVar* is the file variable and *fileName* is the string consisting of the DOS file name of the file to be read. This statement tells the compiler to act on the DOS file *fileName* whenever the file variable *fileVar* is used.

3. Execute the statement

   ```
   Reset(fileVar)
   ```

   to open a file on the disk drive for input. It opens a communication line between the computer and the disk drive for copying data *from* the disk drive. Data can then be input from the specified file to the variables of the program.

4. Read data from the file with the Readln statement. If *varbl* is a variable of a predefined type, then the statement

   ```
   Readln(fileVar, varbl)
   ```

   assigns data to *varbl* from the indicated file in the same way the statement, with *fileVar* missing, assigns data from the keyboard. Correct use of the Readln statement requires a knowledge of the way the data resides on the disk. The first Readln statement retrieves the first item from the disk, the second Readln statement retrieves the second item from the disk, and so on. The variables in the Readln statements should be of the same types as the values on the disk.

5. After the desired items have been found or all the data has been read from the file, close the file with the statement

   ```
   Close(fileVar)
   ```

   Pascal has a useful Boolean function, Eof, that returns a value of True if the end of a file has been reached. At any time, the value

   ```
   Eof(fileVar)
   ```

   will be True if the end of the file referred to by *fileVar* has been reached, and False otherwise.

EXAMPLE 3   Write a program to display a table showing the ages in 1990 of the people in the text file YOB.DAT.

SOLUTION
```
PROGRAM AgeIn1990;
{ Process data from YOB.DAT file to find ages in 1990 }

USES Crt;

VAR birthFile : Text;
    name      : STRING;
    year      : Integer;
```

```
BEGIN
  ClrScr;
  Assign(birthFile, 'YOB.DAT');
  Reset(birthFile);
  Writeln('Name':9, 'Age in 1990':14);
  Writeln('----':9, '-----------':14);
  WHILE NOT Eof(birthFile) DO
    BEGIN
      Readln(birthFile, name);
      Readln(birthFile, year);
      Writeln(name:9, (1990 - year):14)
    END;
  Close(birthFile)
END.

[run]
     Name    Age in 1990
     ----    -----------
   Barbra             48
    Ringo             50
Sylvester             44
```

The program in Example 3 illustrates the proper way to process a list of data contained in a file. A WHILE loop should be used to test the end-of-file condition at the top. (If the file is empty, no reads from the file should be attempted.) The first collection of data should be read and then the collection should be processed. Figure 9.2 contains the pseudocode and flowchart for this technique.

WHILE there are still data in the file
  Get data from file
  Process the data

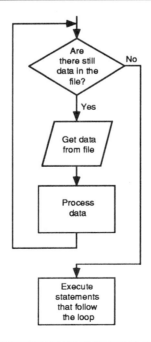

Figure 9.2 Pseudocode and Flowchart for Processing Data From a File

Text files can be quite large. Rather than list the entire contents, we typically search the file for a specific piece of information.

EXAMPLE 4 Write a program to search the file YOB.DAT for the year of birth of a specific person.

SOLUTION
```
PROGRAM LookUpBirthyear;
{ Look up the year of birth of a person requested by the user }

USES Crt;

VAR birthFile    : Text;
    person, name : STRING;
    year         : Integer;

BEGIN
  ClrScr;
  Assign(birthFile, 'YOB.DAT');
  Reset(birthFile);
  Write('Enter name of person: ');
  Readln(person);
  Writeln;
  name := '';
  WHILE (person <> name) AND (NOT Eof(birthFile)) DO
    BEGIN
      Readln(birthFile, name);
      Readln(birthFile, year)
    END;
  IF person = name THEN
      Writeln(person, ' was born in ', year)
    ELSE
      Writeln(person, ' is not in the file YOB.DAT.');
  Close(birthFile)
END.

[run]
Enter name of person: Ringo

Ringo was born in 1940

[run]
Enter name of person: Clint

Clint is not in the file YOB.DAT
```

Passing a Text File to a Subprogram

Parameters of procedures or functions can be of type Text; however, these parameters *must* be VAR parameters.

EXAMPLE 5 Write a program that sorts the items of the file YOB.DAT in a procedure.

SOLUTION

```
PROGRAM SortYOB;
{ Sort the data of the file YOB.DAT by year of birth }

CONST MaxPeople = 50;
      FileName  = 'YOB.DAT';

TYPE PersonRec = RECORD
                   name : STRING;
                   year : Integer
                 END;
     PeopleList = ARRAY [1..MaxPeople] OF PersonRec;

VAR people     : PeopleList;
    numPeople  : Integer;
    peopleFile : Text;

PROCEDURE ReadPeople (VAR people     : PeopleList;
                      VAR numPeople  : Integer;
                      VAR peopleFile : Text);
{ Read the file into an array }
  BEGIN
    Reset(peopleFile);
    numPeople := 0;
    WHILE NOT Eof(peopleFile) DO
      BEGIN
        numPeople := numPeople + 1;
        Readln(peopleFile, people[numPeople].name);
        Readln(peopleFile, people[numPeople].year)
      END;
    Close(peopleFile)
  END;

PROCEDURE SortPeople (VAR people    : PeopleList;
                          numPeople : Integer);
{ Sort the array with a bubble sort }
  VAR passNum, index : Integer;
  PROCEDURE SwapPeople (VAR person1, person2 : PersonRec);
    VAR temp : PersonRec;
    BEGIN
      temp    := person1;
      person1 := person2;
      person2 := temp
    END;
  BEGIN
    FOR passNum := 1 TO numPeople - 1 DO
      FOR index := 1 TO numPeople - passNum DO
        IF people[index].year > people[index + 1].year THEN
          SwapPeople(people[index], people[index + 1])
  END;
```

```
PROCEDURE WritePeople (     people    : PeopleList;
                            numPeople : Integer;
                        VAR peopleFile : Text);
{ Write the contents of the array into a text file }
  VAR personNum : Integer;
  BEGIN
    Rewrite(peopleFile);
    FOR personNum := 1 TO numPeople DO
      BEGIN
        Writeln(peopleFile, people[personNum].name);
        Writeln(peopleFile, people[personNum].year)
      END
  END;

BEGIN
  Assign(peopleFile, FileName);
  ReadPeople(people, numPeople, peopleFile);
  SortPeople(people, numPeople);
  WritePeople(people, numPeople, peopleFile);
  Close(peopleFile)
END.
```

Comments:

1. DOS file names can consist of digits, letters of the alphabet, and the characters & ! _ @ ' ' ~ ( ) { } – # % $.

2. A string variable can be used for the DOS file name in an assign statement. This is advantageous for programs that process data from several different data files. In response to a Readln statement, the user can identify the data file to be processed.

3. The Eof function serves the same role for a file that a trailer value (such as EOD) does for data input from the keyboard. However, there are some important differences. You must first input data from the keyboard before you can check for the trailer value, but you can (and should) use the Eof function before inputing any items from a file. The condition Eof is true if the file is empty or when the last item of the file is read, whereas the trailer value *is* the last item of data.

4. The following program illustrates a common error in reading a text file. The last item in the file will not be processed. Also, if the file is empty, the program will try to read past the end of the file.

```
PROGRAM FortySixers;
{ Erroneous program to display names of people born in 1946 }

USES Crt;

VAR birthFile : Text;
    name      : STRING;
    year      : Integer;
```

```
BEGIN
  ClrScr;
  Assign(birthFile, 'YOB.DAT');
  Reset(birthFile);
  Readln(birthFile, name);
  Readln(birthFile, year);
  WHILE NOT Eof(birthFile) DO
    BEGIN
      IF year = 1946 THEN
          Writeln(name);
      Readln(birthFile, name);
      Readln(birthFile, year)
    END;
  Close(birthFile)
END.
```

5. In this section we assumed that files will be stored on the default drive; that is, the current drive at the time QuickPascal was invoked. To work with a file from another disk drive, precede the name of the file with the letter of the drive and a colon. For instance, if the file YOB.DAT is on a diskette in drive B, then the statement

```
Assign(birthFile, 'B:YOB.DAT');
```

provides access to the file. The combination consisting of the drive letter followed by the colon and file name (including the path) is called the **filespec** of the file.

6. **Caution:** If an existing text file is opened for output with Rewrite, the computer will erase the file and create a new empty file.

7. The extensions of file names often indicate the type of file. For instance, files consisting of QuickPascal programs commonly have ".PAS" as their extensions. The extension ".DAT" is customary for files consisting of data.

8. The text files in this section have only one number per line. Several numbers can be placed on the same line provided they are separated by spaces. If so, the entire line can be read with a single statement of the form

```
Readln(fileVar, numVar1, numVar2, ..., numVarn)
```

9. The statement

```
Writeln(fileVar, item1, item2, ..., itemn)
```

places the values into the file identified by *fileVar* in the same way the statement, with *fileVar* missing, would display the data on the screen. After the Writeln statement executes, the characters ♪ and ◙ are placed into the file.

10. A record cannot be written to or read from a text file as a single unit. Each field must be dealt with separately as in Example 5.

11. A function cannot return a value of type Text.

12. Small files can be modified by Loading them into the QuickPascal editor and using the Search menu in the Menu bar to locate selected items. Large files

are modified by writing a program to create a new file by reading each item from the original file and recording it, with the changes, into the new file. Also, the statement Append(*fileVar*) opens the specified file and permits items to be written at the end of the file. The following code, with the same declaration part as the program of Example 1, adds data to the end of the file YOB.DAT.

```
BEGIN
  ClrScr;
  Assign(birthFile, 'YOB.DAT');
  Append(birthFile);
  name := 'Johnny';
  year := 1926;
  Writeln(birthFile, name);
  Writeln(birthFile, year);
  Close(birthFile)
END.
```

13. Text files use disk space efficiently and are easy to create and use. Their disadvantages are
    (a) often a large portion of the file must be read in order to find one specific item, and
    (b) an individual item of the file cannot be changed or deleted easily by a program. A new file must be created by reading each item from the original file and recording it, with the single item changed or deleted, into the new file.

    Another type of file, known as a **typed** file, has neither of these disadvantages of text files; however, typed files cannot be created or viewed with the QuickPascal editor and are not flexible in the variety and format of the stored data.

14. Data is not actually transferred to the disk each time a Writeln(*fileVar*, . . .) statement is executed. The data is temporarily stored in a portion of memory called a buffer and transferred to the disk when the buffer is full. When a Close statement is executed, the remaining contents of the buffer are transferred to the disk. Therefore, if a program outputting data to a disk does not contain a Close statement, some of the data might never reach the disk.

15. Even when a text file is created with a program instead of with the QuickPascal editor, the file can still be displayed in the editor with Alt/F/O.

16. Text files need not be Closed between Rewrite and Reset statements; QuickPascal will close and reopen the files automatically.

17. The screen and printer can be opened as text files. The following program allows the user to select the device to receive the output.

```
PROGRAM UsersChoice;
{ User greets screen or printer }

USES Crt, Printer;

VAR device   : STRING[4];
    textFile : Text;
```

```
BEGIN
  ClrScr;
  Write('Enter device to receive output (CON or PRN): ');
  Readln(device);
  Assign(textFile, device);
  Rewrite(textFile);
  IF device = 'CON' THEN
      Writeln(textFile, 'Hi, screen.')
    ELSE
      Writeln(textFile, 'Hi, printer.');
  Close(textFile)
END.
```

This feature also is useful for debugging programs that send output to the printer. Have the program initially contain the declaration

```
CONST textFile = CON;
```

and have the Writeln statements send output to textFile. After the program has been debugged, change the constant declaration to

```
CONST textFile = PRN;
```

18. Section 1.3 showed how to rename and erase files in DOS with the commands RENAME and ERASE. QuickPascal also has the capability to perform these operations on closed files. If Str is a string literal or string variable containing a valid DOS file name, the QuickPascal statement

```
Rename(fileVar, Str)
```

changes the DOS file name of the file referenced by *fileVar* to the value of Str, and the statement

```
Erase(fileVar)
```

erases the file reference by *fileVar* from the disk. Both statements require that the file referenced by *fileVar* be closed and the Rename statement requires that the value of Str not be the name of a file already on the disk.

PRACTICE PROBLEMS 9.1

1. Write a program to delete the entire entry for Ringo from the file YOB.DAT.

2. Write a program to add data to the end of the file YOB.DAT in response to user input. Use a trailer value to terminate the addition of data.

EXERCISES 9.1

In Exercises 1 through 6, determine the screen output of the program.

```
1. VAR myFile : Text;
       myVar  : STRING;
```

```
    BEGIN
      Assign(myFile, 'GREETING');
      Rewrite(myFile);
      Writeln(myFile, 'Hello');
      Writeln(myFile, 'Aloha');
      Reset(myFile);
      Readln(myFile, myVar);
      Writeln(myVar);
      Close(myFile)
    END.
```

2.
```
  VAR myFile       : Text;
      myVar, count : Integer;

    BEGIN
      Assign(myFile, 'SOME.DAT');
      Rewrite(myFile);
      FOR count := 1 TO 5 DO
        Writeln(myFile, count + 1);
      Reset(myFile);
      count := 0;
      WHILE NOT Eof(myFile) DO
        BEGIN
          Readln(myFile, myVar);
          count := count + 1
        END;
      Writeln(count);
      Close(myFile)
    END.
```

3.
```
  VAR address : Text;
      street  : STRING;

    BEGIN
      Assign(address, 'ADDRESS.DAT');
      Rewrite(address);
      Writeln(address, '450 Marvin Gardens');
      Writeln(address, '230 Indiana Avenue');
      Writeln(address, '300 Park Place');
      Reset(address);
      WHILE NOT Eof(address) DO
        BEGIN
          Readln(address, street);
          Readln(address, street);
          Readln(address, street)
        END;
      Close(address);
      Writeln(street)
    END.
```

4. Assume the file ADDRESS.DAT has been created by the program in Exercise 3.

```
VAR address : Text;
    street  : STRING;

BEGIN
  Assign(address, 'ADDRESS.DAT');
  Append(address);
  REPEAT
    Readln(street);
    Writeln(address, street)
  UNTIL street = 'EOD';
  Reset(address);
  WHILE NOT Eof(address) DO
    Readln(address, street);
  Writeln(street);
  Close(address)
END.
```

(User responses: 411 Boardwalk, 913 Pacific Avenue, EOD)

5. Assume the file ADDRESS.DAT has been created by the program in Exercise 3.

```
VAR address : Text;
    street  : STRING;
    index   : Integer;

BEGIN
  Assign(address, 'ADDRESS.DAT');
  Append(address);
  FOR index := 1 TO 3 DO
    BEGIN
      Readln(street);
      Writeln(address, Copy(street, 1, Pos(' ', street) - 1))
    END;
  Reset(address);
  WHILE NOT Eof(address) DO
    Readln(address, street);
  Writeln(street);
  Close(address)
END.
```

(User responses: 1313 Kingston, 440 Oak Drive, 250 Donnely Blvd)

6. Assume the file, MYFILE.DAT, contains the following entries:

```
1
4
5
2

VAR dataFile   : Text;
    aVar, count : Integer;
```

```
BEGIN
  Assign(dataFile, 'MYFILE.DAT');
  Reset(dataFile);
  WHILE NOT Eof(dataFile) DO
    BEGIN
      Readln(dataFile, aVar);
      FOR count := 1 TO aVar DO
        Write('*');
      Writeln
    END;
  Close(dataFile)
END.
```

7. What modification of the program in Exercise 4 should be made in order to prevent the trailer value from being written to the file?

8. Assume the file YOB.DAT has been created as in in Example 2. What will be stored in YOB2.DAT after the following program is executed?

```
CONST newName = 'Clint';
      newYear = 1930;

VAR oldFile, newFile : Text;
    name             : STRING;
    year             : Integer;
    foundSlot        : Boolean;

BEGIN
  Assign(oldFile, 'YOB.DAT');
  Assign(newFile, 'YOB2.DAT');
  Reset(oldFile);
  Rewrite(newFile);
  foundSlot := False;
  WHILE NOT Eof(oldFile) DO
    BEGIN
      Readln(oldFile, name);
      Readln(oldFile, year);
      IF (newName < name) AND (NOT foundSlot) THEN
          BEGIN
            Writeln(newFile, newName);
            Writeln(newFile, newYear);
            foundSlot := True
          END;
      Writeln(newFile, name);
      Writeln(newFile, year)
    END;
  Close(oldFile);
  Close(newFile)
END.
```

In Exercises 9 through 14, identify the errors. Assume the files ADDRESS.DAT and YOB.DAT have been created by Exercise 3 and Example 2, respectively.

9.
```
VAR fileVar : Text;
    year    : Integer;
    name    : STRING;

BEGIN
  Assign(fileVar, 'YOB.DAT');
  Append(fileVar);
  Write(fileVar, 'Michael');
  Reset(fileVar);
  WHILE NOT Eof(fileVar) DO
    BEGIN
      Readln(fileVar, name);
      Readln(fileVar, year);
      Writeln(name, ' ', year)
    END;
  Close(fileVar)
END.
```

10.
```
VAR newVar : Text;
    num    : Integer;

BEGIN
  Assign(newVar, 'NEWFILE.DAT');
  Rewrite(newVar);
  FOR num := 1 TO 4 DO
    Writeln(newVar, num * 10);
  Readln(newVar, num);
  Writeln(num);
  Close(newVar)
END.
```

11.
```
VAR aFile : Text;
    aVar  : STRING;
    index : Integer;

BEGIN
  Assign(aFile, 'ADDRESS.DAT');
  Reset(aFile);
  FOR index := 1 TO Eof(aFile) DO
    BEGIN
      Readln(aFile, aVar);
      Writeln(aVar)
    END;
  Close(aFile)
END.
```

12.
```
VAR birthYear : Text;
    name      : STRING;
    year      : Integer;
```

```
BEGIN
  Assign(birthYear, 'YOB.DAT');
  Reset(birthYear);
  WHILE NOT Eof DO
    BEGIN
      Readln(birthYear, name);
      Readln(birthYear, year);
      Writeln(name, ' ', year)
    END;
  Close(birthYear)
END.
```

13.
```
VAR someFile : Text;
    year     : Integer;
    name     : STRING;

BEGIN
  Assign(someFile, 'YOB.DAT');
  Reset(someFile);
  WHILE NOT Eof(someFile) DO
    BEGIN
      Readln(someFile, year);
      Readln(someFile, name);
      Writeln(name, ' ', year)
    END;
  Close(someFile)
END.
```

14.
```
VAR yob : Text;

BEGIN
  Assign(yob, 'YOB.DAT');
  Reset('YOB.DAT');
  Close('YOB.DAT')
END.
```

15. Which of the following are valid file names or filespecs?

(a) ACCOUNTS.REC

(b) B:SALES.87

(c) QUESTION.MRK

(d) 123.DAT

(e) INVENTORY.DAT

(f) A:PRINT

16. Correct the program in Comment 4.

Exercises 17 through 24 are related and use the data in Table 9.1. The file created in Exercise 17 should be used in Exercises 18 through 24.

17. Create the text file COWBOY containing the information in Table 9.1.

Colt Peacemaker	12.20
Holster	2.00
Levi Strauss Jeans	1.35
Saddle	40.00
Stetson	10.00

Table 9.1 Prices Paid by Cowboys for Certain Items in Mid-1800s

18. Write a program to display all items in the file COWBOY costing more than $10.

19. Write a program to add the data Winchester rifle, 20.50, to the end of the file COWBOY.

20. Suppose an order is placed for 3 Colt Peacemakers, 2 Holsters, 10 pairs of Levi Strauss Jeans, 1 saddle, and 4 Stetsons. Write a program to

(a) Create the text file ORDER to hold the numbers 3, 2, 10, 1, 4.

(b) Use the files COWBOY and ORDER to display a sales receipt with three columns giving the name of each item, the quantity ordered, and the cost of that quantity.

(c) Compute the total cost of the items and display it at the end of the sales receipt.

21. Write a program to request an additional item and price from the user. Then create a text file called COWBOY.2 containing all the information in the file COWBOY with the additional item (and price) inserted in its proper alphabetical sequence. Run the program inserting first (Boots, 20) and then (Horse, 35).

22. Suppose the price of saddles is reduced by 20 percent. Use the file COWBOY to create a text file, COWBOY.3, containing the new price list.

23. Write a program to create a text file called COWBOY.4, containing all of the information in the file COWBOY except for the two pieces of data Holster, 2.

24. Write a program to allow additional items and prices to be input by the user and added to the end of the file COWBOY.

25. Suppose the file NAMES contains many names, and that the names are in alphabetical order. Write a program to display all the names in the file. For each letter of the alphabet, display the total number of people having names beginning with that letter. This total should be displayed immediately following the names counted. At the conclusion, display the total number of people in the file. (**Note:** You may need to process the last name separately.)

26. Suppose the file YOB.DAT contains many names and years. Write a program that creates two files called SENIORS and JUNIORS and copies all the data on people born before 1940 into the file SENIORS and the data on the others into the file JUNIORS.

27. A publisher maintains two text files, HARDBACK.INV and PAPERBCK.INV. In each file, each book is recorded on a line and its quantity in stock on the following line. Write a program to access these files. (The program should allow for the case where the book is not in the file.) A sample output of the program should be

```
[run]
Title of book? Gone with the Wind
Hardback or Paperback (H or P)? P
Number of copies in inventory is 6789
```

Exercises 28 through 31 are related. They create and maintain the text file AVERAGE.DAT to hold batting averages of baseball players.

28. Suppose the season is about to begin. Write a program to create a text file containing the name of each player, his times at bat, and his number of hits. The names should be entered by Readln statements and the times at bat and number of hits initially should be set to 0.

29. Each day, the statistics from the previous day's games should be used to update the file. Write a program to read the blocks of information one at a time and allow the user to enter the number of times at bat and the number of hits in yesterday's game for each player in response to Readln statements. The program should update the file by adding these numbers to the previous figures.

30. Several players are added to the team. Write a program to update the file.

31. Write a program to sort the file AVERAGE.DAT with respect to batting averages and display the players with the top ten batting averages. (**Hint:** Assume that the team has at most 60 players.)

Exercises 32 and 33 refer to the sorted file YOB.DAT that contains the names and years of birth of the four people Barbra, Johnny, Ringo, and Sylvester in that order.

32. The file ADD.YOB is similar in format to the file YOB.DAT but contains the following data in the order given: Brooke, 1965; Loretta, 1935; Michael, 1958; Stevie, 1950. Write a program to merge the two files into one file containing all of the information in alphabetical order. After the merge, the new file should have the name YOB.DAT.

33. The file DEL.YOB contains the following names in the order given: Johnny, Loretta, Sylvester. Write a program to create a file consisting of the information in the version of YOB.DAT created in Exercise 32 but with the data for the people listed in DEL.YOB deleted. After the deletions, the new file should have the name YOB.DAT.

34. What are some advantages of files over arrays?

35. Suppose a file must be sorted by a QuickPascal program, but is too large to fit into an array. How can the sort be accomplished?

SOLUTIONS TO PRACTICE PROBLEMS 9.1

1. To delete the entire entry for Ringo, both his name and his year of birth must be deleted. A temporary file is created to hold all the data from YOB.DAT except the entries for Ringo. Then, YOB.DAT is deleted and the temporary file is renamed to YOB.DAT.

```
PROGRAM DeleteRingo;
{ Delete Ringo and his year of birth from the file YOB.DAT }

VAR birthFile, tempFile : Text;
    name                : STRING;
    year                : Integer;
```

```
      BEGIN
        Assign(birthFile, 'YOB.DAT');
        Assign(tempFile, 'TEMP.DAT');
        Reset(birthFile);                    { Open YOB.DAT to read data }
        Rewrite(tempFile);                   { Open a temporary file to hold data }
        WHILE NOT Eof(birthFile) DO
          BEGIN
            Readln(birthFile, name);
            Readln(birthFile, year);
            IF name <> 'Ringo' THEN      { Write all records except Ringo }
              BEGIN
                Writeln(tempFile, name);
                Writeln(tempFile, year)
              END
          END;
        Close(birthFile);                    { Close YOB.DAT before erasing }
        Close(tempFile);                     { Close TEMP.DAT before renaming }
        Erase(birthFile);
        Rename(tempFile, 'YOB.DAT')          { temp file is new YOB.DAT }
      END.
  2. VAR birthFile : Text;
         name       : STRING;
         year       : Integer;

     PROCEDURE GetData (VAR name : STRING; VAR year : Integer);
       BEGIN
         Write('Enter a name (or EOD):   ');
         Readln(name);
         Write('Enter birth year (or 0): ');
         Readln(year)
       END;

     BEGIN
       Assign(birthFile, 'YOB.DAT');
       Append(birthFile);
       GetData(name, year);
       WHILE (name <> 'EOD') AND (year <> 0) DO
         BEGIN
           Writeln(birthFile, name);
           Writeln(birthFile, year);
           GetData(name, year)
         END;
       Close(birthFile)
     END.
```

9.2 TYPED FILES

A typed file is like an array stored on a disk. The entries are numbered 0, 1, 2, 3, and so on, and can be referred to by their numbers. Therefore, a typed file resembles a box of index cards, each having a numbered tab. Any card can be selected from the box without first reading every index card preceding it; similarly, any entry of a typed file can be read without having to read every entry preceding it. The entries can be of any data type; however, records are the most common data type.

The following steps create and access a typed file:

1. Select a data type for the file. The data type can be any of the predefined or user-defined types discussed so far, with the exception of text files and typed files.

2. Specify the file type with a declaration of the form

   ```
   TYPE FileType = FILE OF Type;
   ```

   Of course, if the data type is not of the predefined variety, it must be specified in a TYPE declaration preceding the file type declaration.

3. Choose an identifier, called the **file variable**, to be used by the program to refer to the file. This identifier must appear in the VAR part of the program with a declaration of the form

   ```
   VAR fileVar : FileType;
   ```

   Note: Steps 2 and 3 can be combined in a shorthand declaration for the file variable of the form

   ```
   VAR fileVar : FILE OF Type;
   ```

   The shorthand declaration cannot be used with a parameter of a procedure or function.

4. Execute the statement

   ```
   Assign(fileVar, fileName)
   ```

   where *fileVar* is the file variable and *fileName* is the string consisting of a DOS file name. This statement tells the compiler to use *fileName* whenever the file variable *fileVar* is mentioned.

5. Execute the statement

   ```
   Rewrite(fileVar)
   ```

   to open a file on the disk drive for output. It opens a communications line between the computer and the disk drive both for storing data onto the disk and reading data from the disk.

6. If varbl is a variable of the proper type, then

   ```
   Write(fileVar, varbl)
   ```

   places the value of varbl in the zeroth position of the file identified by *fileVar*. The next such Write statement places a value in the first position of the file. Successive statements place values in positions 2, 3, and so on.

7. At any time, one position in the file is known as the **current position**. When the file is first opened, the **current position** is the zeroth position. After each Write(*fileVar*, . . .) statement is executed, the next position becomes the current position. The value of the function

   ```
   FilePos(fileVar)
   ```

is the number of the current position. If *n* is an Integer literal or expression, the statement

```
Seek(fileVar, n)
```

sets the current position to the value of *n*. The statement

```
Write(fileVar, varbl)
```

places the value of varbl in the current position and then increases the current position by one.

8. Data can be retrieved from the file with a Read statement. The statement

```
Read(fileVar, varbl)
```

assigns the value in the current position to varbl. Therefore, any position can be accessed by a combination of Seek and Read. After a Read statement is executed, the current position is increased by one.

9. After the work on the file is complete, the statement

```
Close(fileVar)
```

closes the DOS file.

10. The next time the file is used, it should be opened with the statement

```
Reset(fileVar, fileName)
```

If Rewrite were used a second time, the existing file would be erased.

11. The total number of positions in the file identified by *fileVar* is given by the value of the function

```
FileSize(fileVar)
```

The number of the last position in the file is FileSize(*fileVar*) − 1 and a new item can be added to the end of the file by first executing

```
Seek(FileSize(fileVar))
```

Unlike text files, typed files cannot be created with the QuickPascal editor. Although often they can be displayed in an edit window via Alt/F/O, only string data will be recognizable. Numeric data is encoded into a condensed form that is difficult to decipher.

EXAMPLE 1   Write a program to create a file called PRES.USA and place the names of the first five presidents in file positions 1 through 5. Then allow the user to request the name of a President by entering the number.

SOLUTION
```
PROGRAM CreatePresFile;
{ Create the file PRES.USA }

USES Crt;

TYPE PresFileType20 = FILE OF STRING[20];
```

```
VAR presFile : PresFileType20;
    pres     : STRING[20];
    num      : Integer;

BEGIN
  ClrScr;
  Assign(presFile, 'PRES.USA');
  Rewrite(presFile);
  pres := '';     { Put something innocuous into position 0 }
  Write(presFile, pres);
  pres := 'Washington';  { Washington goes into position 1 }
  Write(presFile, pres);
  pres := 'Adams';
  Write(presFile, pres);
  pres := 'Jefferson';
  Write(presFile, pres);
  pres := 'Madison';
  Write(presFile, pres);
  pres := 'Monroe';
  Write(presFile, pres);
  Write('Enter a number from 1 to 5: ');
  Readln(num);
  Seek(presFile, num);
  Read(presFile, pres);
  Writeln(pres, ' was President number ', num);
  Close(presFile)
END.

[run]
Enter a number from 1 to 5: 3
Jefferson was President number 3
```

Businesses use typed files of records to keep track of customers and their purchases. Suppose a business issues each customer a numbered courtesy card with numbers 1, 2, 3, and so on, and each customer's courtesy card number serves as his record number. A simplified record might store the following information:

1. Customer's name

2. Date of customer's last visit to the store

3. Total number of times that customer has visited the store.

4. Amount of money spent during the customer's last visit.

5. Total amount of money spent by the customer.

This file could be used to calculate useful data such as:

1. Total number of customers for any given day, month, or year.

2. Amount of money spent in any given day, month, or year.

3. Customers who have visited the business more than 10 times.

4. A listing of all customers and their average purchases per visit.

5. A listing of the customers who have not visited the store in the last year.

EXAMPLE 2   The following program creates a typed file and places information in three positions. The zeroth position holds a record consisting of default data.

```
PROGRAM Shop;

TYPE Shopper = RECORD
                    name       : STRING[34];
                    last       : STRING[10];        {MM-DD-YYYY}
                    visit      : Integer;    {Number of visits}
                    spentLast,         {Amount spent last visit}
                    spentTotal : Real        {Total money spent}
                    END;
        People = FILE OF Shopper;

VAR customers : People;
    client     : Shopper;
    today      : STRING[10];    {MM-DD-YYYY}
    custNum,                     {Customer's courtesy card number}
    count      : Integer;        {Total number of customers today}
    take       : Real;           {Total amount of money spent today}

BEGIN
  Assign(customers, 'CUST.DAT');
  Rewrite(customers);      to create file
  WITH client DO
    BEGIN
      name := '';
      last := '00-00-0000';
      visit := 0;
      spentLast := 0.0;
      spentTotal := 0.0;
      Write(customers, client);
      name := 'Al Adams';
      last := '10-20-1988';
      visit := 2;
      spentLast := 10.0;
      spentTotal := 300.0;
      Write(customers, client);
      name := 'Bob Brown';
      last := '09-22-1988';
      visit := 5;
      spentLast := 20.0;
      spentTotal := 600.0;
      Write(customers, client);
      name := 'Carl Cobbs';
      last := '11-20-1988';
      visit := 20;
      spentLast := 25.0;
      spentTotal := 222.0;
      Write(customers, client)
    END;
  Close(customers)
END.
```

first record is record # 0

very important to close file

EXAMPLE 3 Write a program that updates the file CUST.DAT of Example 2 for a particular day.

SOLUTION The following program uses 0 as a sentinal to indicate that all the data has been entered.

```
PROGRAM UpdateCustomers;

USES Crt;

TYPE Shopper  = RECORD
                   name       : STRING[34];
                   last       : STRING[10];        { MM-DD-YYYY }
                   visit      : Integer;    { Visits to store }
                   spentLast,               { Amt spent last visit }
                   spentTotal : Real;       { Total money spent }
                 END;
     People   = FILE OF Shopper;
     TodayStr = STRING[10];

VAR customers : People;
    client    : Shopper;
    today     : TodayStr; { MM-DD-YYYY }
    custNum   : Integer;  { Customer's courtesy card number }

PROCEDURE CalculateStats(VAR customers : People; today : TodayStr);
{ Calculate and display statistics for today }
  VAR count  : Integer; { Total number of customers today }
      take   : Real;    { Total amount of money spent today }
      recNum : Integer; { Control variable of FOR loop }
  BEGIN
    Seek(customers, 1);
    count := 0;
    take := 0;
    FOR recNum := 1 TO fileSize(customers) - 1 DO
      BEGIN
        Read(customers, client);
        IF client.last = today THEN
            BEGIN
              count := count + 1;
              take := take + client.spentLast
            END
      END;
    Writeln('The number of customers for ', today, ' was ', count);
    Writeln('The take for ', today, ' was $', take:5:2)
  END;
```

```
  BEGIN
    ClrScr;
    Write('Enter today''s date (MM-DD-YYYY): ');
    Readln(today);
    Writeln;
    Assign(customers, 'CUST.DAT');
    Reset(customers);
    Write('Enter customer''s courtesy card number ',
          '(0 to finish): ');
    Readln(custNum);
    WHILE custNum <> 0 DO
      BEGIN
        Seek(customers, custNum);
        Read(customers, client);
        WITH client DO
          BEGIN
            Writeln(name);
            last := today;
            visit := visit + 1;
            Write('Enter amount spent during today''s visit: ');
            Readln(spentLast);
            spentTotal := spentTotal + spentLast
          END;
        Seek(customers, custNum); { Set file position after Read }
        Write(customers, client);
        Writeln;
        Write('Enter customer''s courtesy card number ',
              '(0 to finish): ');
        Readln(custNum)
      END;
    Writeln;
    CalculateStats(customers, today);
    Close(customers)
END.

[run]
Enter today's date (MM-DD-YYYY): 11-08-1990

Enter customer's courtesy card number (0 to finish): 2
Bob Brown
Enter amount spent during today's visit: 75.25

Enter customer's courtesy card number (0 to finish): 1
Al Adams
Enter amount spent during today's visit: 50.00

Enter customer's courtesy card number (0 to finish): 0

The number of customers for 11-08-1990 was 2
The take for 11-08-1990 was $125.25
```

Comments:

1. The data stored in diffent positions of a typed file use the same number of bytes. Integer, Real, STRING, and STRING[*n*] values use 2, 6, 256, and *n* + 1 bytes respectively.

2. Typed files are also known as *direct-access* or *relative* files. Since each position has the same number of bytes, Pascal can calculate where to find a specified position and, therefore, does not have to search for it sequentially.

3. Unlike a text file, a typed file does not require a Reset statement between placing information into the file and reading information from it.

4. Typed file positions do not have to be filled in order. For instance, a new file can be opened and the first item of data written to position 9. In this case, space is allocated for the preceding positions.

5. Writeln and Readln cannot be used to access typed files. Typed files do not make use of line structure.

6. Typed files are more efficient than text files for storing many numbers. For instance, a text file holding the Integers from 10001 to 10010 requires 70 bytes (70 = 10 * 5 digits + 10 cr/lf pairs) whereas a typed file of Integers requires only 20 bytes.

PRACTICE PROBLEMS 9.2

1. Write a program to create the file in Example 1 by storing the data in an array constant and writing it to the file using a FOR loop.

2. Use the file created in Practice Problem 1 to write a program that requests a number from 1 to 5 and displays the name of that president.

EXERCISES 9.2

In Exercises 1 through 8, determine the output of the program segment. Assume PRES.USA has been created by Example 1, assigned to presFile, and opened with Reset.

1.
```
Seek(presFile, 1);
Read(presFile, pres);
Write(pres, ' ');
Read(presFile, pres);
Writeln(pres, ' ');
```

2.
```
Seek(presFile, 0);
Read(presFile, pres);
Writeln(pres);
```

3.
```
Seek(presFile, 0);
FOR num := 0 TO 2 DO
  BEGIN
    Read(presFile, pres);
    Writeln(FilePos(presFile))
  END;
```

4.
```
Seek(presFile, 2);
Reset(presFile);
Read(presFile, pres);
Read(presFile, pres);
Writeln(pres);
```

5.
```
Seek(presFile, 2);
FOR num := 1 TO 3 DO
  BEGIN
    Read(presFile, pres);
    Writeln(pres, num:(20 - Length(pres)))
  END;
```

6.
```
FOR num := (FileSize(presFile) - 1) DOWNTO 1 DO
  BEGIN
    Seek(presFile, num);
    Read(presFile, pres);
    Write(pres, ' ')
  END;
```

7.
```
Seek(presFile, 0);
WHILE FilePos(presFile) <= (FileSize(presFile) - 1) DO
  Read(presFile, pres);
Writeln(pres);
```

8.
```
Seek(presFile, FileSize(presFile) DIV 2);
Read(presFile, pres);
Writeln(pres);
```

In Exercises 9 through 14, assume the following declarations have been made and that the file STUDENT.DAT contains one record for each student in the class.

```
TYPE StudentData = RECORD
                     student : STRING;
                     midterm : Integer;
                     final   : Integer
                   END;
     FileType    = FILE OF StudentData;

VAR studentFile : FileType;
```

9. Write a procedure to open the file, find a student with the highest average score on the two exams and place both items in the VAR parameters *hiStudent* and *hiAverage*, respectively. Do not be concerned about two students having the same score. Be sure to close the file before exiting the procedure.

10. Write a procedure to open the file, request a student's name, and search the file for that student's record. The procedure should place the student's midterm and final scores in the VAR parameters *midterm* and *final*. The value of −1 should be placed in both variables if the student's name is not in the file.

11. Write a Boolean function that takes a student's name as a parameter and deletes his or her entire record from the file. The function should return True if the name was found and deleted, and False otherwise.

12. Write a procedure to add records to the end of STUDENT.DAT. Use 'EOD' as a sentinel value.

13. Write a procedure to output the contents of STUDENT.DAT to the screen in three columns.

14. Write a procedure that performs a bubble sort on the file STUDENT.DAT. The procedure should allow the user to select whether to sort the file in ascending order by name or in descending order by final exam score.

15. Write a program that creates a file of type STRING called NAMES.DAT, and then requests names until 'EOD' is entered. Use the following names as input: Beethoven, Mozart, Haydn, Brahms, Schubert, Bach, Rossini, Borodin. Output the entire file to the screen once all the names are entered.

16. Write a procedure that performs a bubble sort on the file NAMES.DAT. Sort the file directly without first reading it into an array.

17. Write a procedure that performs a Shell sort on the file NAMES.DAT. Sort the file directly without first reading it into an array.

18. Rewrite the program in Example 1 so it does not use an empty string at file position zero; that is, 'Washington' goes in file position 0, 'Adams' in file position 1, and so on. The output should look the same.

SOLUTIONS TO PRACTICE PROBLEMS 9.2

1.
```
PROGRAM BuildFile;

CONST NumOfData = 5;

TYPE List    = FILE OF STRING[20];
     PresType = ARRAY [0..NumOfData] OF STRING[20];

CONST presData : PresType = ('', 'Washington', 'Adams',
                              'Jefferson', 'Madison', 'Monroe');

VAR presidents : List;
    pres       : PresType;
    index      : Integer;

BEGIN
  pres := presData;
  Assign(presidents, 'PRES.USA');
  Rewrite(presidents);
  FOR index := 0 TO NumOfData DO
    Write(presidents, pres[index]);
  Close(presidents)
END.
```

2.
```
PROGRAM GetPresident;

TYPE List = FILE OF STRING[20];

VAR presidents : List;
    onePres    : STRING[20];
    num        : Integer;
```

```
BEGIN
  Assign(presidents, 'PRES.USA');
  Reset(presidents);
  Write('Enter a number from 1 to 5: ');
  Readln(num);
  Seek(presidents, num);
  Read(presidents, onePres);
  Writeln(onePres, ' was President number ', num)
END.
```

9.3 A CASE STUDY: CREATING A SUPERMARKET CHECK-OUT RECEIPT

Many supermarkets have automated check-out counters. Scanners read coded information on each item and send the information to a computer that produces an itemized receipt after all the items have been scanned. This case study develops a program to produce an itemized check-out receipt after all the coded information has been entered.

The standard code is the Universal Product Code (UPC), which consists of a sequence of 10 digits appearing below a rectangle of bars. (See Figure 9.3.) The bars have these digits encoded in a form that can be read by an optical scanner. The first five digits disclose the manufacturer and the second five digits specify the product and the size of the package. The digits 37000 00430 appear on a jar of peanut butter. The string 37000 is the code for Procter & Gamble and 00430 is Procter & Gamble's code for a 22-ounce jar of creamy Jif peanut butter. Of course, the string 00430 will have an entirely different meaning for another manufacturer.

Figure 9.3   Universal Product Code

Suppose a supermarket carries four thousand items and a text file called MASTER.DAT holds the following information for each item: the UPC, the name of the item, the price. Let us also assume the file has been sorted by the UPC for each triplet of lines and that the file ends with a sentinel triplet whose fictitious UPC is greater than any actual UPC. (**Note:** The use of a sentinel is a common practice when an entire file will be read sequentially. The advantage of using a sentinel, as opposed to relying solely on Eof, will become apparent when the program is written.) For instance, the file might contain the following data for three food items.

```
3700000430
22-oz Jif Peanut Butter
1.76
4119601012
19-oz Prog Minn Soup
1.19
7073405307
2.5 oz CS Cinn Rose Tea
1.65
9999999999
Sentinel
0.00
```

We wish to write a program that will accept as input UPC codes entered from the keyboard and produce as output a printed itemized receipt. One way to proceed would be to take each UPC as it is input into the computer and then search for it in the master file to find the item description and price. We then would have to search sequentially through a long file many times. A better way to proceed is to first store the input UPCs in an array and then sort the array in increasing order, the same order as the master file. Then the information can be located in just one sequential pass through the file.

The program must be able to handle the special case in which a UPC code entered is not in the master file. Suppose the first array item, after the array of UPCs has been sorted, is not in the master file. Then its UPC will never equal one of the UPCs in the master file. At some point during the sequential pass through the master file, the array UPC will be less than the most recently read UPC from the master file. This indicates that the UPC is not in the master file, and that the user must be informed of this fact. After the array of UPCs has been sorted, the search algorithm is as follows.

1. Begin with the first (lowest) array item. (It is most likely higher than the first UPC in the master file.)

2. Read the triplets of file data for successive items until the triplet is found whose UPC matches or exceeds the array UPC.

3. If the file UPC matches the array UPC, then print the corresponding description and price of the item from the master file and add the price to the running total. Otherwise, print a message stating that the item is not in the master file.

4. Repeat steps 2 and 3 for each element of the array.

Designing the Supermarket Check-out Program

The major tasks of the program are as follows:

1. Input UPC codes from keyboard (and count number of items). Task 1 uses a loop that requests the UPCs of the items purchased. A counter should keep track of the number of items purchased and a sentinel should indicate that all the UPCs have been entered.

2. Sort the array of UPC codes into ascending order. Task 2 can be accomplished with a bubble sort since the array is small.

3. Create itemized receipt. Task 3 can be divided into smaller subtasks. After the master file is opened, the file is searched sequentially for the triplet holding the first array UPC. If this triplet is found, the item name and price are printed and the price added to the total. Then, the second item is looked for in the same manner. This process continues until all possible items and prices have been printed. Of course, any unlocatable item must be reported. Finally, the total price is printed and the master file is closed. That is, task 3 is divided into the following subtasks:

3.1 Open the master file.
3.2 Search for array UPCs in the master file.
3.3 Print an itemized receipt.
3.4 Close the master file.

Figure 9.4 shows the top-down chart for the program.

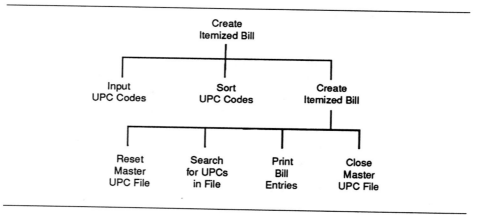

Figure 9.4   Top-Down Chart for the Supermarket Check-out Program

Pseudocode for the Supermarket Check-out Program

INPUT UPC CODES (Procedure InputCodes)
Initialize numItems counter to 0
Prompt user for input
WHILE there are more items to be entered
 Read the UPC into the current array element
 Increment numItems
 Prompt user for more input

SORT UPC CODES (Procedure SortCodes)
FOR passNum = 1 TO numItems − 1
  FOR i = 1 TO numItems − passNum
    IF the ith array UPC is greater than the (i+1)th THEN
      Switch the ith and (i+1)th array elements

CREATE ITEMIZED RECEIPT (Procedure MakeReceipt)
Open the master file
Initialize total to 0
Read first triplet from the master file
FOR i = 1 TO numItems
  WHILE item i's UPC > the current file UPC DO
    Read the next triplet of information from the master file
  IF items i's UPC = the file UPC THEN
    Print the corresponding item description and price
    Increase total by price
  ELSE
    Print that the UPC is not in the master file
Print total
Close the master file

Writing the Supermarket Check-out Program

Table 9.2 shows each of the tasks discussed above and the procedure used to perform the task.

Task	Procedure
1. Input UPCs & count number of items	InputCodes
2. Sort the array of UPCs into ascending order	SortCodes
3. Create itemized receipt	MakeReceipt

Table 9.2 Tasks and Their Procedures

```
PROGRAM CheckOutReceipt;
{ Input the UPCs of purchased items and use the master file to create a
  check-out receipt }

USES Crt, Printer;

TYPE CodesArray = ARRAY [1..100] OF STRING[10];

VAR
    masterFile : Text;          { File of UPCs, descriptions, and prices }
    itemUPC    : CodesArray;    { Array of UPCs for the items purchased }
    numItems   : Integer;       { Counts the number of items purchased }
```

```
PROCEDURE InputCodes (VAR itemUPC : CodesArray;
                      VAR numItems  : Integer);
{ Fill the array with UPC codes for items purchased }
  VAR code : STRING[10];
  BEGIN
    numItems := 0;
    Writeln('Enter * when all items have been entered.');
    Writeln;
    Write('Enter the UPC code of item: ');
    Readln(code);
    WHILE code <> '*' DO
      BEGIN
        numItems := numItems + 1;
        itemUPC[numItems] := code;
        Write('Enter the UPC code of item: ');
        Readln(code)
      END
  END;

PROCEDURE SortCodes (VAR itemUPC : CodesArray; numItems : Integer);
{ Perform bubble sort on the array }
  VAR index, passNum : Integer;
      temp           : STRING[10];
  BEGIN
    FOR passNum := 1 TO numItems - 1 DO
      FOR index := 1 TO numItems - passNum DO
        IF itemUPC[index] > itemUPC[index + 1] THEN
            BEGIN
              temp := itemUPC[index];
              itemUPC[index] := itemUPC[index + 1];
              itemUPC[index + 1] := temp
            END
  END;

PROCEDURE MakeReceipt (VAR masterFile : Text; itemUPC : CodesArray;
                       numItems : Integer);
{ Output store receipt }
  VAR index : Integer;
      total : Real;            { Total cost of all purchases }
      code  : STRING[10];      { UPC at the current file position }
      descr : STRING[30];      { Desc. of item at current position }
      price : Real;            { Price of current item }
  BEGIN
    Assign(masterFile, 'MASTER.DAT');
    Reset(masterFile);
    total := 0;
    Readln(masterFile, code);    { Read first triplet from master file }
    Readln(masterFile, descr);
    Readln(masterFile, price);
```

```
              FOR index := 1 TO numItems DO
                BEGIN
                  WHILE itemUPC[index] > code DO
                    BEGIN
                      Readln(masterFile, code);
                      Readln(masterFile, descr);
                      Readln(masterFile, price)
                    END;
                  IF itemUPC[index] = code THEN
                    BEGIN
                      Writeln(Lst, descr, price:(40 - Length(descr)):2);
                      total := total + price
                    END
                  ELSE
                    Writeln(Lst, '** UPC ', itemUPC[index], ' not listed **')
                END;
              Writeln(Lst, 'Total ======================> $', total:6:2);
              Close(masterFile)
            END;

        BEGIN { CheckOutReceipt }
          ClrScr;
          InputCodes(itemUPC, numItems);
          SortCodes(itemUPC, numItems);
          MakeReceipt(masterFile, itemUPC, numItems)
        END.  { CheckOutReceipt }

        [run]
        Enter * when all items have been entered.

        Enter UPC code of item: 7073405307
        Enter UPC code of item: 3700000430
        Enter UPC code of item: 3700000430
        Enter UPC code of item: 4100034200
        Enter UPC code of item: *


        22-oz Jif Peanut Butter            1.76  ⌉
        22-oz Jif Peanut Butter            1.76  |
        ** UPC 4100034200 not listed **          |   Printed on
        2.5 oz CS Cinn Rose Tea            1.65  |   printer
        Total ======================> $   5.17  ⌋
```

Chapter 9
Summary

1. Each file has a *filespec* that gives the disk drive holding the file and the *file name*. Pascal programs associate a file variable with each file used in a program and refer to the file by that variable.

2. When text files are *opened*, we must specify whether they will be created and either written to, added to, or read from by specifying one of the statements Rewrite, Append, or Reset, respectively. Each statement, once executed, allows a file to be accessed in only one way. Data are written to the file with Writeln statements having the file variable as the first item in the parentheses. Data are read from the file with analogous Readln statements. The Eof function tells when the end of a file has been reached.

3. A text file can be sorted by placing its data in an array, sorting the array, and then writing the sorted data to the file.

4. A typed file of a specified data type stores a collection of entries numbered 0, 1, 2, 3, and so on. Write statements place entries into the file and Read statements retrieve them from the file. The item in any position can be accessed directly with the Seek procedure. At any time, the value of the function FileSize is the number of items in the file.

Chapter 9
Programming Projects

1. Write a rudimentary word processing program. The program should

   (a) Request the text file to hold the document as input from the keyboard.
   (b) Clear the screen and display the symbol > as a prompt at the upper left corner of the screen.
   (c) Request the first line of the file as input from the keyboard and write this line to the file when the Enter key is pressed. (**Note:** Blank lines are acceptable input, but lines exceeding 60 characters in length should not be accepted; the user should be prompted to reenter the line.)
   (d) Display a second prompt at the leftmost position of the second line of the screen and carry out (c) for this line.
   (e) Continue as in (d) with subsequent lines until the user responds with EOD. (EOD should not be written to the text file.)
   (f) Clear the screen and display the complete text file on the screen.

```
[sample run]
Enter the name of the file to create: MYFILE
[ClrScr]
>Of course, the most important feature of a program is that it performs
!!LINE TO LONG!!
>Of course, the most important feature of a program is that
>it performs correctly. This is most likely to occur when
>the solution to the problem is systematically planned.
>EOD
Of course, the most important feature of a program is that
it performs correctly. This is most likely to occur when
the solution to the problem is systematically planned.
```

2. Write a program that counts the number of times a word occurs in a text file. The file name and word should be input from the keyboard. For instance,

opening MYFILE as created in Problem 1 and searching for "is" would produce the output: "is" occurs three times.

3. Table 9.3 gives the leading eight soft drinks and their percentage share of the market. Write and execute a program to read these data from the keyboard and to store them in a text file. Then using the text file, write a second program to request the name of a soft drink brand to be input from the keyboard and to display the brand name along with its percentage share of the market and its gross sales in billions. (The entire soft drink industry grosses about $40 billion.)

Coke Classic	19.8		Dr. Pepper	4.3
Pepsi	18.8		Sprite	3.5
Diet Coke	7.7		7 Up	3.4
Diet Pepsi	4.8		Mountain Dew	2.9

Table 9.3 Leading Soft Drinks and Percentages of Market Share
Source: Beverage Digest (figures through January 1988)

3. *Merge sort.* FILE1 and FILE2 are sorted text files. Write a program that merges FILE1 and FILE2 into a single sorted text file, SORTED.DAT. (Assume that each file ends with a sentinel greater than any regular item in either file.)

4. *Create and Maintain a Telephone Directory.* Write a menu-driven program to create and maintain a telephone directory in a typed file. The following menu options should be available:

   (a) Create a new file and enter new records. (Erase the old file if it already exists.) Each record should have a first name field, a last name field, and a phone number field.
   (b) Add entries to the already created file.
   (c) Find a name in the file. Request a last name and do a sequential search of the file. When the first match is found, display the record and a prompt asking whether the current record is the correct one. If the response is "no," continue the search.
   (d) Delete an entry from the file. The last name should be entered and the record found as in (c). If the response if "yes," delete the record.
   (e) Terminate the program.

   Optional enhancement: Write the program to use a binary search instead of a sequential search in the following way. The file should be sorted before performing the first search. Thereafter, the file should be resorted only if the file has had entries added to it. One method is to use a flag called outOfOrder and to check its value before every search.

5. *Balance a Checkbook.* Write an interactive program to request information (payee, check number, amount, and whether the check has cleared) for each check written during a month and store this information in a typed file. The program should then request the balance at the beginning of the month, display the current balance (beginning balance − sum of cleared checks), and display the payee and amount for each outstanding check.

6. A teacher maintains a typed file GRADES of records containing the following information for each student: name, Social Security number, grades on each of two hourly exams, and the final exam grade. Assume the records have string fields of lengths 25 and 11 (into which the names and Social Security numbers have already been entered) and three Integer fields (that have been initialized to 0). Write a menu-driven program to allow the teacher to do the following:

(a) Enter the grades for a specific exam.

(b) Change a grade of a specific student. The input should be provided from the keyboard.

(c) Print a list of final grades that can be posted. The list should show the last four digits of the Social Security number, the grade on the final exam, and the semester average of each student. The semester average is determined by the formula (exam1 + exam2 + 2 * finalExam) / 4.

10

Graphics

10.1 INTRODUCTION TO GRAPHICS

Note: The programs in this section use functions and procedures from the unit MSGraph; therefore, each program includes MSGraph in the USES declaration part. Also, the files MSGRAPH.QPU and MSGRUTIL.QPU must be available to QuickPascal. These files are on the Utilities disk.

QuickPascal has impressive graphics capabilities. Figure 10.1 shows a graph that can be displayed on the screen and printed by the printer.

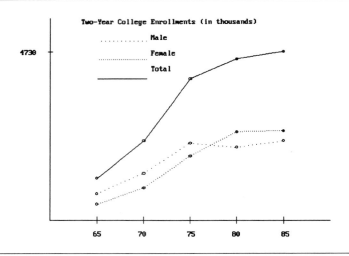

Figure 10.1 A Line Graph
Source: Statistical Abstract of the United States

Most monitors can display graphics (such as points, lines, and circles) if the computer contains the proper monitor adapter card. The most common configurations are a graphics monitor attached to a graphics card or a monochrome display attached to a Hercules card.

Graphics cards provide several different graphics display modes. The modes vary in the width of text characters, the number of points that can be displayed horizontally and vertically, and the number of colors available. We will always use the mode with maximum resolution, that is, with the maximum number of points horizontally and vertically and the most text characters per line. The large number of points allows us to draw figures with precision, and the small text characters are well suited for labeling graphs. Since color is not available with many configurations in a maximum resolution mode, we will use only black and white.

A monochrome display attached to a Hercules graphics card can produce graphics with QuickPascal, provided the program MSHERC.COM is executed from DOS before QuickPascal is invoked. MSHERC.COM can be found on the Utilities diskette. (If your computer has both a Hercules graphics card and a color graphics card, enter MSHERC.COM /H from DOS.)

To determine whether your system can support graphics, execute the following program. If you have graphics capabilities, the program will draw a diagonal line. This program is purely for demonstration purposes; there is no need to understand it at this point. All identifiers in the MSGraph unit begin with the underline character.

```
PROGRAM GraphDemo;

USES MSGraph;

VAR vc : _VideoConfig;    { A record declared in MSGRAPH }

BEGIN
  IF _SetVideoMode(_MaxResMode) > 0 THEN
     BEGIN
       _GetVideoConfig(vc);
       _SetWindow(True, 0, 0, 1, 1);
       _MoveTo_w(0, 0);
       _LineTo_w(1, 1);
       Writeln('The screen is ', vc.numXPixels, ' points wide');
       Writeln('and ', vc.numYPixels, ' points high.');
       Writeln('Each line can contain ', vc.numTextCols,
               ' characters.');
       Writeln('The screen can have ', vc.numTextRows,
               ' lines of text.');
       Writeln(vc.numColors, ' colors are available.')
     END
  ELSE
     Writeln('No graphics mode is available.')
END.
```

The function _SetVideoMode(_MaxResMode) invokes the maximum-resolution graphics mode. Text and graphics can be displayed in the two standard colors of the monitor, which we refer to as black and white. (Depending on the monitor, "white" might be green or amber.)

The DOS diskette contains a program called GRAPHICS.COM that allows you to print graphics for certain configurations of monitors and printers. If you intend to print graphics, you must execute this program (or an equivalent program) before invoking QuickPascal. Then, Shift+PrtSc prints the contents of the screen. The printout is called a **screen dump**. (*Note:* GRAPHICS.COM only does screen dumps from certain IBM-compatible graphics adapters to printers compatible with IBM dot-matrix printers.)

Comments:

1. The unit Crt is not needed in order to use graphics. In this book, we used Crt in order to utilize the ClrScr command. The screen, however is automatically cleared by _SetVideoMode.

2. When both the units Crt and MSGraph are used, Write and Writeln cannot always be used in graphics mode. In these cases, the statement _OutText(*str*) can be used to display a string.

3. The statement GotoXY(x, y) has the counterpart _SetTextPosition(y, x) in MSGraph. Note the reversal of the procedure arguments. For particular values of y and x, _SetTextPosition will not address the same screen location on every monitor. The location depends on the resolution of the graphics card used. The variables vc.numTextRows and vc.numTextCols are useful for consistent screen positioning.

10.2 SPECIFYING A COORDINATE SYSTEM

Suppose we have a piece of paper, a pencil, and a ruler and want to graph a line extending from (2, 40) to (5, 60). We would most likely use the following three-step procedure:

1. Use the ruler to draw an x-axis and a y-axis. Focus on the first quadrant since both points are in that quadrant.

2. Select scales for the two axes. For instance, we might decide that the numbers on the x-axis range from −1 to 6 and that the numbers on the y-axis range from −10 to 80.

3. Plot the two points and use the ruler to draw the straight line segment joining them.

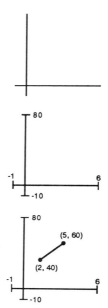

EXAMPLE 1 (a) Draw a coordinate system with the numbers on the x-axis ranging from −2 to 10, and the numbers on the y-axis ranging from −3 to 18.
(b) Draw the straight line from (1, 15) to (8, 6).
(c) Draw the straight line from (−2, 0) to (10, 0).

SOLUTION   (a)

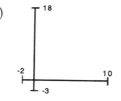

(b)

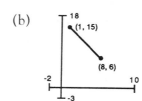

(c) The point $(-2, 0)$ is the left-hand endpoint of the x-axis and the point $(10, 0)$ is the right-hand endpoint; therefore, the line joining them is just the portion of the x-axis we have pictured.

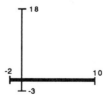

We draw these graphs on the screen with the same three steps that we use with paper, pencil, and ruler. The only difference is that we do step 2 first, then steps 1 and 3. The QuickPascal procedure _SetWindow specifies the range of values for the axes and the pair of procedures _MoveTo_w and _LineTo_w serve as the ruler.

The statement

```
_SetWindow(True, a, c, b, d)
```

specifies that numbers on the x-axis range from a to b and that numbers on the y-axis range from c to d. (See Figure 10.2.) If False is substituted for True in the command, the positive direction of the y-axis will be downward.

Figure 10.2 Result of _SetWindow Procedure

Figure 10.3 Result of _MoveTo_w and _LineTo_w Procedures

QuickPascal remembers the location of a point on the screen known as the **last point referenced**. Initially, this point is the center of the screen. The statement

```
_MoveTo_w(x1, y1)
```

changes the last point referenced to $(x1, y1)$. (The _w tacked on the end indicates that the coordinates used are those defined by the _SetWindow procedure.) The statement

```
_LineTo_w(x2, y2)
```

draws a line segment from the last point referenced to the point with coordinates $(x2, y2)$ and then updates the last point referenced to $(x2, y2)$. Figure 10.3 shows the effect of the pair of statements above.

EXAMPLE 2   Write a program to draw the graph of Example 1, part (b).

SOLUTION   The dummy variable *dummy* is used solely for the purpose of calling the
_SetVideoMode function. The x-axis of the coordinate system specified by
_SetWindow(True, a, c, b, d) extends from (a, 0) to (b, 0), and the y-axis extends
from (0, c) to (0, d).

```
PROGRAM GraphDemo;

USES MSGraph;

VAR dummy : Integer;

BEGIN
  dummy := _SetVideoMode(_MaxResMode);   { Set max-res. mode }
  _SetWindow(True, -2, -3, 10, 18);      { Set coordinate system }
  _MoveTo_w(-2, 0);                      { Prepare to draw x-axis }
  _LineTo_w(10, 0);                      { Draw x-axis }
  _MoveTo_w(0, -3);                      { Prepare to draw y-axis }
  _LineTo_w(0, 18);                      { Draw y-axis }
  _MoveTo_w(1, 15);
  _LineTo_w(8, 6)                        { Draw straight line }
END.
```

EXAMPLE 3   Consider Figure 10.4.

(a) Give the _SetWindow statement that specifies the range for the numbers
on the axes.
(b) Give the statements that draw the axes.
(c) Give the statements that will draw the line.

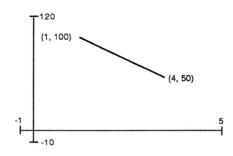

Figure 10.4   Graph for Example 3

SOLUTION   (a) _SetWindow(True, -1, -10, 5, 120)

```
                lowest x-value ┘ │ │  └ highest y-value
                   lowest y-value ┘  └ highest x-value
```

(b) x-axis: _MoveTo_w(-1, 0); { (a, 0) }
                  _LineTo_w(5, 0);   { (c, 0) }

    y-axis: _MoveTo_w(0, -10); { (0, b) }
                  _LineTo_w(0, 120); { (0, d) }

(c) The simplest method is as follows.

    _MoveTo_w(1, 100); { left end of line }
    _LineTo_w(4, 50); { right end of line }

EXAMPLE 4   Write a program to draw a graph of the square root function.

SOLUTION   We will graph the function for values of x from 0 to 100. (See Figure 10.5.)

```
PROGRAM SquareRoot;
{ Graph the Square Root Function }

USES MSGraph;

VAR r, h, dummy : Integer;
    x           : Real;

FUNCTION F (x : Real) : Real;
  BEGIN
    F := Sqrt(x)
  END;

BEGIN
  dummy := _SetVideoMode(_MaxResMode); { Initialize screen }
  r := 100;                            { Largest x-value used }
  h := 10;                             { Largest y-value used }
  _SetWindow(True, -20, -2, 120, 12);  { Set coordinate system }
  _MoveTo_w(-5, 0);
  _LineTo_w(r, 0);                     { Draw x-axis }
  _MoveTo_w(0, -1);
  _LineTo_w(0, h);                     { Draw y-axis }
  x := 0;
  _MoveTo_w(0, 0);                     { Move to starting point for graph }
  WHILE x <= r DO
    BEGIN
      x := x + 0.2;                    { Plot about 500 points }
      _LineTo_w(x, F(x))               { Extend graph to this point }
    END
END.
```

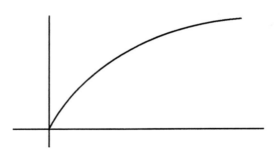

Figure 10.5 Graph of the Square Root Function

The MSGraph unit contains 82 procedures and functions. Among them are procedures that draw a single point and an ellipse. The statement

```
_SetPixel_w(x, y)
```

draws the point with coordinates (x, y). The statement

```
_Ellipse_w(_gBorder, x1, y1, x2, y2)
```

draws an ellipse contained between the x-values $x1$ and $x2$ and the y-values $y1$ and $y2$.

A circle is an ellipse whose width is the same as its height. Two factors have to be considered when drawing a circle.

1. The scales of the axes are most likely different.

2. The height of the screen is different from the width of the screen. If the same scale is used for both axes, then a unit on the x-axis will appear shorter than a unit on the y-axis. In the following discussion, we use a four-to-five ratio of height to width to adjust for common screen dimensions.

One way to obtain a circle is to first select the arguments of the _SetWindow procedure so that the difference in the y-arguments is four-fifths of the difference in the x-arguments. One possibility is

```
_SetWindow(True, -10, -4, 10, 12)
```

since $(12 - (-4)) = (4/5) * (10 - (-10))$. Then, select arguments of the _Ellipse_w procedure with $x2 - x1 = y2 - y1$. One possibility is

```
_Ellipse_w(_gBorder, -5, -2, 5, 8)
```

since $5 - (-5) = 8 - (-2)$.

EXAMPLE 5 Write a program to plot the point (7, 5) and draw a circle of radius 3 about the point.

SOLUTION   The rightmost point to be drawn will have x-coordinate 10 and the highest point
will have y-coordinate 8. Therefore the numbers on the x- and y-axes must range
beyond 10 and 8 respectively. In the following program, we allow the numbers
on the x-axis to range from −2 to 13 and the numbers on the y-axis to range from
−2 to 10. (See Figure 10.6).

```
PROGRAM DrawCircle;
{ Draw circle with center (7, 5) and radius 3 }

USES MSGraph;

VAR dummy : Integer;

BEGIN
  dummy := _SetVideoMode(_MaxResMode);   { Set high-res graphics }
  _SetWindow(True, -2, -2, 13, 10);      { Specify coord. system }
  _MoveTo_w(-2, 0);
  _LineTo_w(13, 0);                       { Draw x-axis }
  _MoveTo_w(0, -2);
  _LineTo_w(0, 10);                       { Draw y-axis }
  _SetPixel_w(7, 5);                       { Draw center of circle }
  _Ellipse_w(_gBorder, 4, 2, 10, 8)      { Draw the circle }
END.
```

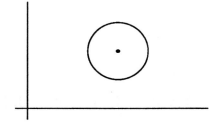

Figure 10.6 Graph for Example 5

Comments:

1. In the examples considered in this section, the range of numbers on the axes
   extended from a negative number to a positive number. Actually, any values
   of *a*, *b*, *c*, and *d* can be used in a _SetWindow procedure. In certain cases,
   however, you will not be able to display one or both of the axes on the screen.
   (For instance, after _SetWindow(True, 1, −1, 10, 10) has been executed,
   the y-axis cannot be displayed.)

2. The following technique can be used to determine a good scale for a
   _SetWindow procedure when graphs with only positive values are to be
   drawn.

   (a) Let *r* be the x-coordinate of the rightmost point that will be drawn by
       any _LineTo_w, _SetPixel_w, or _Ellipse_w procedure.

(b) Let *h* be the y-coordinate of the highest point that will be drawn by any
_LineTo_w, _SetPixel_w, or _Ellipse_w procedure.

(c) Let the numbers on the x-axis range from about −(20% of *r*) to about
r + (20% of *r*). Let the numbers on the y-axis range from about
−(20% of *h*) to about *h* + (20% of *h*). That is, use

```
_SetWindow(True, -0.2 * r, -0.2 * h, 1.2 * r, 1.2 * h)
```

3. If one or both of the points used in the _LineTo_w procedure are off the
screen, the computer only draws the portion of the line that is on the screen.
This behavior is called **line clipping** and is used for the _Ellipse_w procedure
also.

4. A program can contain two _SetWindow statements. Executing the second
statement has no effect on the graphics figures that are already drawn;
however, future graphics statements will use the new coordinate system.

5. Ellipses can be displayed and filled in by replacing _gBorder with
_gFillInterior in the call to the _Ellipse_w procedure.

6. The following procedure will draw a circle of radius *rx* and center (*cx*, *cy*) in
any coordinate system. (The radius *rx* is the horizontal distance from the
center to the boundary.) The parameters *a*, *b*, *c*, and *d* are the dimensions of
the coordinate system.

```
PROCEDURE Circle (rx, cx, cy, a, b, c, d : Real);
  VAR ry : Real;
  BEGIN
    ry := rx * (5 / 4) * ((d - b) / (c - a));
    _Ellipse_w(_gBorder, cx - rx, cy - ry, cx + rx, cy + ry)
  END;
```

PRACTICE PROBLEMS 10.2

Suppose you want to write a program to draw a line from (3, 45) to (5, 80).

1. Use the method of Comment 2 to select an appropriate _SetWindow
statement.

2. Write a program to draw the axes, the line, and a small circle around each
end point of the line. (See Comment 6.)

3. Write the statements that draw a tick mark on the y-axis at height 80 and
label it with the number 80.

EXERCISES 10.2

1. Determine the _SetWindow statement corresponding to the coordinate
system of Figure 10.7.

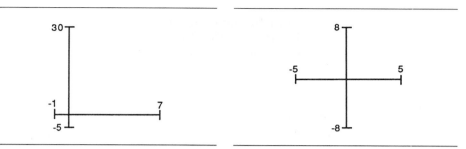

Figure 10.7   Coordinate System for Exercise 1

Figure 10.8   Coordinate System for Exercise 2

2. Determine the _SetWindow statement corresponding to the coordinate system of Figure 10.8.

3. Suppose the statement _SetWindow(True, −1, −8, 4, 40) has been executed. Write down the statements that draw the x-axis and the y-axis.

4. Suppose the statement _SetWindow(True, −3, −0.2, 18, 1) has been executed. Write down the statements that draw the x-axis and the y-axis.

In Exercises 5 through 8, write a program to draw a line between the given points. Select an appropriate _SetWindow statement, draw the axes, and draw a small circle around each end point of the line. (See Comment 6.)

5. (3, 200), (10, 150)

6. (4, 4), (9, 9)

7. (2, 0.5), (4, 0.3)

8. (5, 30), (6, 30)

In Exercises 9 through 20, write a program to draw the given figures. Draw the axes only when necessary.

9. Draw a circle whose center is located at the center of the screen.

10. Draw a tick mark on the x-axis at a distance of 5 from the origin.

11. Draw a tick mark on the y-axis at a distance of 70 from the origin.

12. Draw a circle whose leftmost point is at the center of the screen.

13. Draw four points, one in each corner of the screen.

14. Draw a triangle with two sides of the same length.

15. Draw a rectangle.

16. Draw a square. (**Hint:** Set up a coordinate system using a 5 to 4 ratio.)

17. Draw five concentric circles, that is, five circles with the same center.

18. Draw a point in the center of a circle and a line that is tangent to the circle.

20. Draw two circles that touch at a single point.

In Exercises 21 through 24, consider the following program segment. What would be the effect on the circle if the _SetWindow statement were replaced by the given _SetWindow statement?

```
ClrScr;
dummy := _SetVideoMode(_MaxResMode);
_SetWindow(True, -5, -5, 5, 5);          { Specify coordinate system }
_Ellipse_w(_gBorder, -3, -3, 3, 3)       { Draw ellipse at origin }
```

21. _SetWindow(True, -8, -8, 8, 8)

22. _SetWindow(True, -5, -8, 5, 8)

23. _SetWindow(True, -8, -5, 8, 5)

24. _SetWindow(True, -2, -2, 2, 2)

In Exercises 25 through 27, write a program to perform the given task.

25. Draw a graph of the function $y = x^2$ for x between 0 and 10.

26. Draw a graph of the function $200 / (x + 5)^2$ for x between 0 and 20.

27. Write a program to produce displays such as the one in Figure 10.9. Let the user enter the maximum number (in this display, 8).

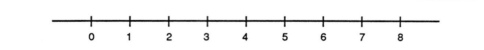

Figure 10.9   Display for Exercise 27

SOLUTIONS TO PRACTICE PROBLEMS 10.2

1. The largest value of any x-coordinate is 5. Since 20% of 5 is 1, the numbers on the x-axis should range from −1 to 6 (= 5 + 1). Similarly, the numbers on the y-axis should range from −16 to 96 (= 80 + 16). Therefore, an appropriate _SetWindow statement is

   ```
   _SetWindow(True, -1, -16, 6, 96)
   ```

2. ```
   PROGRAM GraphLine;

   USES MSGraph;

   VAR dummy : Integer;

   PROCEDURE Circle (rx, cx, cy, a, b, c, d : Real);
   { Draw a circle of radius rx measured along the x-axis
     with center (cx, cy) in the coordinate system
     specified by _SetWindow(True, a, b, c, d) }
     VAR ry : Real;
     BEGIN
     ry := rx * (5 / 4) * ((d - b) / (c - a));
     _Ellipse_w(_gBorder, cx - rx, cy - ry, cx + rx, cy + ry)
   END;
   ```
   ```

```
BEGIN
  dummy := _SetVideoMode(_MaxResMode);
  _SetWindow(True, -1, -16, 6, 96);      { Specify coordinate system }
  _MoveTo_w(-1, 0);
  _LineTo_w(6, 0);                        { Draw x-axis }
  _MoveTo_w(0, -16);
  _LineTo_w(0, 96);                       { Draw y-axis }
  _MoveTo_w(3, 45);
  _LineTo_w(5, 80);                       { Draw the line }
  Circle(0.05, 3, 45, -1, -16, 6, 96);
  Circle(0.05, 5, 80, -1, -16, 6, 96)
END.
```

The radius of the circle about the endpoints was determined by trial and error. As a rule of thumb, it should be about 1 percent of the length of the x-axis.

3. Add the following lines before the END statement of the preceding program. The length of the tick mark was taken to be the diameter of the circle. The row and column for the _SetTextPosition statement, which positions the cursor to print the upper range value, were determined by trial and error. See Figure 10.10 for the output of the entire program.

```
_MoveTo_w(-0.05, 80);
_LineTo_w(0.05, 80);
_SetTextPosition(4, 9);
Write(80);
Readln
```

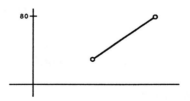

Figure 10.10   Output of Program in Practice Problem 3

10.3 LINE CHARTS

A line chart displays the change of a certain quantity in relation to another quantity (often time). The following steps produce a line chart:

1. Look over the data to be displayed. A typical line chart displays between 5 and 20 items of data corresponding to evenly spaced units of time: years, months, or days. The positions on the x-axis will contain labels such as "Jan Feb Mar Apr..." or "84 85 86 87." These labels can be placed at the locations 1, 2, 3, . . . on the x-axis.

2. Choose a coordinate system based on the number of data items and the size of the quantities. A convenient scale for the x-axis is from −1 to one more than the number of data items. The scale for the y-axis is determined by the largest quantity to be displayed.

3. Draw the line segments. It is a good idea to draw a small circle around the endpoints of each line segment.

4. Draw and label tick marks on the coordinate axes. The x-axis should have a tick mark for each time period. The y-axis should have at least one tick mark to indicate the magnitude of the quantities displayed.

5. Title the chart and give the source of the data.

EXAMPLE 1   Table 10.1 gives enrollment data for two-year colleges taken from the statistical abstract of the United States. Write a program to display the total enrollments for the given years in a line chart. Assume the year and male and female enrollments are stored in the text file COLLEGE.DAT as 1965, 734, 439, 1970, 1317, 906, 1975, etc. (one number per line).

Year	1965	1970	1975	1980	1985
Male	734	1317	2165	2047	2223
Female	439	906	1805	2479	2507
Total	1173	2223	3970	4526	4730

Table 10.1   Two-Year College Enrollments (in thousands)

SOLUTION   Figure 10.11 contains the results of executing the following program. (Explanatory remarks follow the program.)

```
PROGRAM Enrollments1;
{ Line Chart of Total Two-Year College Enrollments }

USES MSGraph;

CONST MaxYears = 10;

TYPE YearQty   = ARRAY [1..MaxYears] OF Integer;
     YearLabel = ARRAY [1..MaxYears] OF STRING;

VAR total              : YearQty;
    lbl                : YearLabel;
    maxEnrollment,
    numYears, dummy    : Integer;
    lf, top, rt, btm   : Real;
    vc                 : _VideoConfig; { For text display }
```

```
PROCEDURE ReadData (VAR lbl                        : YearLabel;
                    VAR total                      : YearQty;
                    VAR numYears, maxEnrollment : Integer;
                        fileName                   : STRING);
{ Read data into arrays & find highest enrollment }
  VAR source        : Text;
      male, female : Integer;
  BEGIN
    Assign(source, fileName);
    Reset(source);
    maxEnrollment := 0;
    numYears := 0;
    WHILE NOT Eof(source) DO
      BEGIN
        numYears := numYears + 1;
        Readln(source, lbl[numYears]);
        Readln(source, male);
        Readln(source, female);
        total[numYears] := male + female;
        IF total[numYears] > maxEnrollment THEN
            maxEnrollment := total[numYears]
      END
  END;

PROCEDURE ShowTitle;
{ Display source and title }
  BEGIN
    _SetTextPosition(vc.numTextRows, 1);
    Write('Source: Statistical Abstract of the United States');
    _SetTextPosition(1, 20);
    Write('Two-Year College Enrollments (in thousands)')
  END;

PROCEDURE DrawAxes (    numYears, maxEnrollment : Integer;
                    VAR lf, top, rt, btm        : Real);
{ Draw axes }
  BEGIN
    btm := -0.2 * maxEnrollment;
    top := 1.2 * maxEnrollment;
    lf := -1;
    rt := numYears + 1;
    _SetWindow (True, lf, top, rt, btm);
    _MoveTo_w(rt, 0);
    _LineTo_w(0, 0);
    _LineTo_w(0, top)
  END;
```

```
PROCEDURE ShowLabels (VAR lbl                           : YearLabel;
                           numYears, maxEnrollment : Integer);
{ Draw axes, labels and tick marks }
  VAR tickDist : Real;
      year     : Integer;
  BEGIN
    tickDist := 80 / (numYears + 2);
    FOR year := 1 TO numYears DO
      BEGIN
        _MoveTo_w(year, -0.02 * maxEnrollment);
        _LineTo_w(year, 0.02 * maxEnrollment);
        _SetTextPosition(vc.numTextRows - 2,
                     Round((1 + year) * tickDist));
        { Write the last 2 digits of the year }
        Write(Copy(lbl[year], Length(lbl[year]) - 1, 2))
      END;
    _MoveTo_w(-0.01 * numYears, maxEnrollment);
    _LineTo_w(0.01 * numYears, maxEnrollment);
    _SetTextPosition(5, 7);
    Write(maxEnrollment)
  END;


PROCEDURE TinyCircle (x, y, lf, top, rt, btm : Real);
  VAR xr, yr : Real;
  BEGIN
    xr := (rt - lf) / 240;
    yr := (top - btm) / 200;
    Ellipse_w(_gBorder, x - xr, y - yr, x + xr, y + yr)
  END;


PROCEDURE LineGraph (VAR total             : YearQty;
                         numYears          : Integer;
                         lf, top, rt, btm : Real);
{ Draw lines connecting data and circle data points }
  VAR year : Integer;
  BEGIN
    _MoveTo_w(1, total[1]);
    TinyCircle(1, total[1], lf, top, rt, btm);
    FOR year := 2 TO numYears DO
      BEGIN
        _LineTo_w(year, total[year]);
        TinyCircle(year, total[year], lf, top, rt, btm)
      END
  END;
```

```
BEGIN
  dummy := _SetVideoMode(_MaxResMode);
  _GetVideoConfig(vc);
  ReadData(lbl, total, numYears, maxEnrollment,
           'COLLEGE.DAT');
  ShowTitle;
  DrawAxes(numYears, maxEnrollment, lf, top, rt, btm);
  ShowLabels(lbl, numYears, maxEnrollment);
  LineGraph(total, numYears, lf, top, rt, btm);
  Readln;
  dummy := _SetVideoMode(_DefaultMode)
END.
```

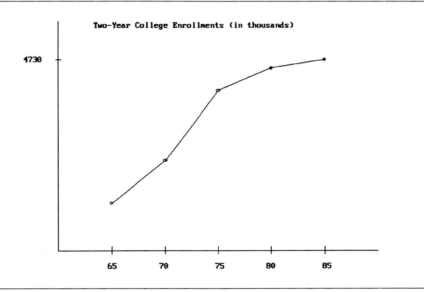

Figure 10.11   Chart for Example 1
Source: Statistical Abstract of the United States

Remarks on the program in Example 1:

1. The value of tickDist in the procedure ShowLabels was determined by subdividing the 80-character row into about n + 2 equal zones. The y-axis appears at the end of the first zone and the labels begin at the end of the second zone. Each zone has length 80 / 7.

2. In the procedure ShowLabels, the lengths of the tick marks and the locations of the text were determined by trial and error.

Line Styling: Patterned, or "styled," lines can be drawn between two points. Some examples are shown in Figure 10.12. Each line has an associated number identifying its style. If *s* is one of the numbers in Figure 10.12, then the statements

```
_SetLineStyle(s);
_MoveTo_w(x1, y1);
_LineTo_w(x2, y2);
```

draws the line from $(x1, y1)$ to $(x2, y2)$ in the style corresponding to the number s. The relationship between style numbers and style lines is discussed in Comment 1.

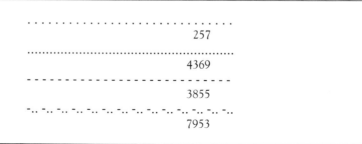

257

4369

3855

7953

Figure 10.12 Line Patterns

Styling is useful when displaying several line charts on the same coordinate system.

EXAMPLE 2 Alter the program in Example 1 so it will draw line charts displaying the male, female, and total enrollments of two-year colleges. Assume the data from Table 10.1 are stored in the text file called COLLEGE.DAT as in Example 1.

SOLUTION The statements must be changed to contain the enrollment figures for males and females and arrays must be created to hold this information. The totals can be computed from the other numbers. The styled lines for male and female enrollments must be drawn. Finally, legends must be given to identify the different line charts. The following program's lines must either replace existing lines or be added to the original program. Figure 10.13 contains the outcome of the modified program.

```
PROGRAM Enrollments2;
{ Line Chart of Male, Female, and Total Two-Year College Enrollments }

USES MSGraph;

CONST MaxYears = 10;

TYPE YearQty   = ARRAY [1..MaxYears] OF Integer;
     YearLabel = ARRAY [1..MaxYears] OF STRING;

VAR male, female, total : YearQty;
    lbl                 : YearLabel;
    maxEnrollment,
    numYears, dummy     : Integer;
    lf, top, rt, btm    : Real;
    vc                  : _VideoConfig; { For text display }
```

```
PROCEDURE ReadData (VAR lbl                    : YearLabel;
                    VAR male, female, total    : YearQty;
                    VAR numYears, maxEnrollment : Integer;
                        fileName               : STRING);
{ Read data into arrays & find highest enrollment }
  VAR source : Text;
  BEGIN
    Assign(source, fileName);
    Reset(source);
    maxEnrollment := 0;
    numYears := 0;
    WHILE NOT Eof(source) DO
      BEGIN
        numYears := numYears + 1;
        Readln(source, lbl[numYears]);
        Readln(source, male[numYears]);
        Readln(source, female[numYears]);
        total[numYears] := male[numYears] + female[numYears];
        IF total[numYears] > maxEnrollment THEN
            maxEnrollment := total[numYears]
      END
  END;

PROCEDURE ShowTitle;
{ Display source and title }
  BEGIN
    _SetTextPosition(vc.numTextRows, 1);
    Write('Source: Statistical Abstract of the United States');
    _SetTextPosition(1, 20);
    Write('Two-Year College Enrollments (in thousands)')
  END;

PROCEDURE DrawAxes (    numYears, maxEnrollment : Integer;
                    VAR lf, top, rt, btm        : Real);
{ Draw axes }
  BEGIN
    btm := -0.2 * maxEnrollment;
    top := 1.2 * maxEnrollment;
    lf := -1;
    rt := numYears + 1;
    _SetWindow(True, lf, top, rt, btm);
    _MoveTo_w(rt, 0);
    _LineTo_w(0, 0);
    _LineTo_w(0, top)
  END;
```

```
PROCEDURE ShowLabels (VAR lbl                        : YearLabel;
                           numYears, maxEnrollment : Integer);
{ Draw axes, labels and tick marks }
  VAR tickDist : Real;
      year     : Integer;
  BEGIN
    tickDist := 80 / (numYears + 2);
    FOR year := 1 TO numYears DO
      BEGIN
        _MoveTo_w(year, -0.02 * maxEnrollment);
        _LineTo_w(year, 0.02 * maxEnrollment);
        _SetTextPosition(vc.numTextRows - 2,
                     Round((1 + year) * tickDist));
        { Write the last 2 digits of the year }
        Write(Copy(lbl[year], Length(lbl[year]) - 1, 2))
      END;
    _MoveTo_w(-0.01 * numYears, maxEnrollment);
    _LineTo_w(0.01 * numYears, maxEnrollment);
    _SetTextPosition(5, 7);
    Write(maxEnrollment)
  END;


PROCEDURE DrawData (VAR male, female, total : YearQty;
                        numYears            : Integer;
                        lf, top, rt, btm    : Real);
{ Draw lines connecting data and circle data points }
  PROCEDURE TinyCircle (x, y, lf, top, rt, btm : Real);
    VAR xr, yr : Real;
    BEGIN
      xr := (rt - lf) / 240;
      yr := (top - btm) / 200;
      _Ellipse_w(_gBorder, x - xr, y - yr, x + xr, y + yr)
    END;
  PROCEDURE LineGraph (VAR qty               : YearQty;
                           numYears          : Integer;
                           lf, top, rt, btm : Real);
    VAR year : Integer;
    BEGIN
      _MoveTo_w(1, qty[1]);
      TinyCircle(1, qty[1], lf, top, rt, btm);
      FOR year := 2 TO numYears DO
        BEGIN
          _LineTo_w(year, qty[year]);
          TinyCircle(year, qty[year], lf, top, rt, btm)
        END
    END;
```

```
  BEGIN
    _SetLineStyle(257);
    LineGraph(male, numYears, lf, top, rt, btm);
    _SetLineStyle(4369);
    LineGraph(female, numYears, lf, top, rt, btm);
    _SetLineStyle(65535);
    LineGraph(total, numYears, lf, top, rt, btm)
  END;

PROCEDURE ShowLegend;
{ Show legend }
  BEGIN
    { Coordinate system to mix graphics & text }
    _SetWindow(False, 0, 0, 80, 25);
    _SetLineStyle(257);
    _MoveTo_w(23, 2.4);
    _LineTo_w(35, 2.4);        { Draw line in row 4; }
    _SetTextPosition(3, 37);
    Write('Male');
    _SetLineStyle(4369);
    _MoveTo_w(23, 4.4);
    _LineTo_w(35, 4.4);        { Draw line in row 6; }
    _SetTextPosition(5, 37);
    Write('Female');
    _MoveTo_w(23, 6.4);
    _SetLineStyle(65535);
    _LineTo_w(35, 6.4);        { Draw line in row 8; }
    _SetTextPosition(7, 37);
    Write('Total')
  END;

BEGIN
  dummy := _SetVideoMode(_MaxResMode);
  _GetVideoConfig(vc);
  ReadData(lbl, male, female, total, numYears,
           maxEnrollment, 'COLLEGE.DAT');
  ShowTitle;
  DrawAxes(numYears, maxEnrollment, lf, top, rt, btm);
  ShowLabels(lbl, numYears, maxEnrollment);
  DrawData(male, female, total, numYears, lf, top, rt, btm);
  ShowLegend;
  Readln;
  dummy := _SetVideoMode(_DefaultMode)
END.
```

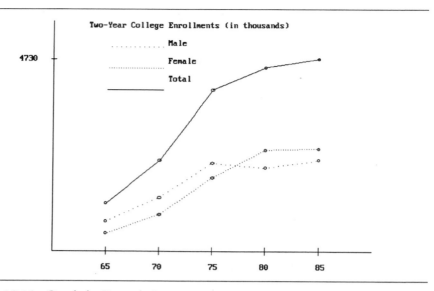

Figure 10.13   Graph for Example 2
Source: Statistical Abstract of the United States

Comments:

1. A line is just a collection of dots on the screen. A style number specifies a pattern for 16 consecutive dots. This pattern is repeated as many times as necessary to draw the line. To obtain the style number for a 16-dot pattern, write down a sequence of 16 0s and 1s (beginning with a 0) to describe the pattern. The 0s correspond to black (unlit) dots and the 1s to white (lit) dots. Convert this binary representation to the corresponding number in decimal form to obtain *s*. For instance, the sequence 0001000100010001 describes the pattern of the second line of Figure 10.13. The binary number 0001000100010001 corresponds to the decimal number 4369. The following program determines the style number for a pattern.

```
PROGRAM StyleNumbers;
{ Determine style numbers for lines }

USES Crt;

VAR binNum        : STRING;
    decNum, place : Integer;

BEGIN
  ClrScr;
  Write('Sequence of 16 zeros and ones: ');
  Readln(binNum);
  decNum := 0;
  FOR place := 1 TO 16 DO
    BEGIN
      decNum := 2 * decNum;
      IF Copy(binNum, place, 1) = '1' THEN
          decNum := decNum + 1
    END;
  Writeln('The style number for this bit pattern is ', decNum)
END.
```

PRACTICE PROBLEMS 10.3

Consider the programs of Examples 1 and 2 that draw the three-line chart of two-year college enrollments.

1. Suppose the enrollment data were given in units of millions instead of thousands and the program modified to accept Real values. How would this affect the appearance of the three-line chart?

2. Why wasn't 1985 (or 85) used in the _SetWindow statement to determine the scale for the x-axis? It is the largest value of x.

EXERCISES 10.3

In Exercises 1 and 2, determine a possible _SetWindow statement that could have been used to obtain the chart.

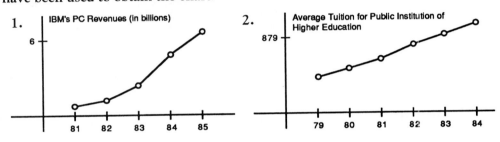

In Exercises 3 through 8, write a program to display the given information in a line chart.

3. The Consumer Price Index is a measure of living costs based on changes in retail prices, with 1967 taken as the base year.

Year	1960	1970	1973	1976	1979	1982	1985
CPI	100.0	116.3	133.1	170.5	217.4	288.7	318.5

Source: Bureau of Labor statistics

4. Workers with Personal Computers (in millions)

Year	1981	1984	1987	1990
Workers	2	6	14	24

Source: Future Computing Incorporated

5. Year End Sales of IBM PCs (in thousands of units)

	Sept	Oct	Nov	Dec
1984	46	57	96	158
1985	60	64	63	91

Source: Future Computing Incorporated ("PC Week", Feb. 18, 1986)

6. Normal Monthly Precipitation (in inches)

	Jan	Apr	July	Oct
Mobile, AL	4.6	5.35	7.7	2.6
Phoenix, AR	0.7	0.3	0.7	0.6
Portland, OR	6.2	2.3	0.5	3.0
Washington, DC	2.8	2.9	3.9	2.9

Source: Statistical Abstract of the United States

7. Dollar Value of Worldwide Computer Shipments (in billions of dollars)

	1980	1983	1986	1989
Large-scale	7	15	20	19
Medium-scale	8	10	15	21
Small-scale	7	8	11	18
PCs	2	12	25	37

Source: International Data Corporation ("PC Week," Jan. 7, 1986)
(Figures for 1986 and 1989 are estimates.)

SOLUTIONS TO PRACTICE PROBLEMS 10.3

1. Not at all. The value of maxEnrollment, 4730, would change to 4.73 but the _SetWindow statement would scale the y-axis with respect to this new value of maxEnrollment and the line charts would look exactly the same as before.

2. If 1985 (or 85) had been used, the line charts would have been unreadable. Line charts are used to illustrate from about 3 to 15 pieces of data. These are best placed at the numbers 1, 2, 3, . . . on the x-axis. In many cases the classifications given below the tick marks will be words (such as Jan, Feb, . . .) instead of numbers.

Chapter 10
Summary

1. Data can be vividly displayed in *line* graphs. These graphs are best drawn in a maximum-resolution graphics mode, specified by calling the function _SetVideoMode(_MaxResMode), that is contained in the MSGraph unit. Screen dumps of line graphs produce printed copy.

2. The programmer can select his or her own coordinate system with the _SetWindow procedure.

3. Lines are drawn with the pair of procedures _MoveTo_w and _LineTo_w, and given a *style* with the procedure _SetLineStyle.

4. The _Ellipse_w procedure draws ellipses and, with care, will produce a circle.

5. The _SetPixel_w procedure turns on a single point on the screen.

Chapter 10
Programming Projects

1. Look in magazines and newspapers for data that is well suited for a line graph and write a program to so display the data.

Programming projects 2 through 5 require rectangles. The statement

```
_Rectangle_w(_gBorder, x1, y1, x2, y2)
```

draws the rectangle with opposite vertices having coordinates (x1, y1) and (x2, y2). Replacing _gBorder with _gFillInterior produces a solid rectangle.

2. Figure 10.14 is called a **horizontal bar chart**. Write a program to produce this chart. (**Note:** If the _SetWindow procedure sets the range on the y-axis from 0 to 25, then the locations for text will be easy to determine.)

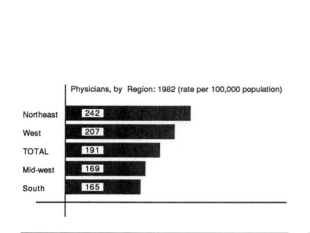

Figure 10.14 Horizontal Bar Chart

Resident Population - Age Distribution (in %)

	1970	1980	1984
65 yrs. and over	9.8	11.3	11.9
18-64 yrs.	55.9	60.6	61.6
Under 18 yrs.	34.3	28.1	26.5

Figure 10.15 Segmented Bar Chart

3. Figure 10.15 is called a **segmented bar chart**. Write a program to construct this chart.

4. Figure 10.16 is called a **range chart**. Using the data in Table 10.2, write a program to produce this chart.

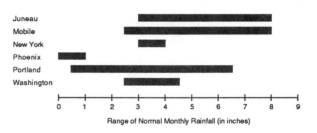

Range of Normal Monthly Rainfall (in inches)

Figure 10.16 Range Chart

	Lowest NMR	Highest NMR
Mobile	2.6	7.7
Portland	5	6.4
Phoenix	1	1.0
Washington	2.6	4.4
Juneau	2.9	7.7
New York	3.1	4.2

Table 10.2 Range of Normal Monthly Rainfall for Selected Cities (in inches)

11

Random Numbers

11.1 GENERATING RANDOM NUMBERS

Consider a specific collection of numbers. We say that a process selects a number at *random* from this collection if any number in the collection is just as likely to be selected as any other and the number cannot be predicted in advance. Some examples are:

Collection	Process
1, 2, 3, 4, 5, 6	toss a balanced die
0 or 1	toss a coin: 0 = tails, 1 = heads
0, 1, . . ., 36, 37	spin a roulette wheel (interpret 00 as 37)
1, 2, . . ., n	write numbers on slips of paper, pull one from hat
Reals from 0 to 1	flip the spinner in Figure 11.1

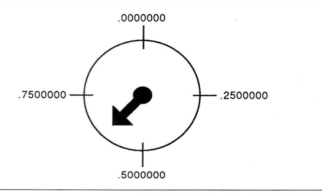

Figure 11.1 Spinner to Randomly Select a Number between 0 and 1

The QuickPascal function Random returns a random number. If *value* is a positive integer, then

```
IntVar := Random(value)
```

randomly assigns an integer between 0 and (*value* − 1) to *IntVar*. A different integer will be assigned each time Random is called in the program and any integer in the range 0, 1, 2, . . ., (*value* − 1) is just as likely to be generated as any other.

EXAMPLE 1 The following program generates five numbers from the set 1, 2, 3, 4, 5, 6. Since Random(6) will return a value from 0 to 5, adding 1 shifts the resulting number into the desired range. (**Note:** The particular sequence of numbers produced by this program will most likely differ on your computer.)

```
PROGRAM PickAnInteger;
{ Generate five integers between 1 and 6 }

USES Crt;

CONST Iterations = 5;
      Range      = 6;
```

```
VAR iterNum : Integer;

BEGIN
  ClrScr;
  FOR iterNum := 1 TO Iterations DO
    Write((Random(Range) + 1):2)
END.

[run]
 5 5 3 6 4
```

Suppose *Iterations* has a much higher value. The integers generated by the program should exhibit no apparent pattern. They should look very much like a sequence of integers obtained from successively rolling a die. For instance, each of the six integers should appear about one-sixth of the time and be reasonably spread out in the sequence. The longer the sequence, the more likely this is to occur.

Random also may be called without arguments. In that case, it acts much like the spinner of Figure 11.1, returning a Real value greater than or equal to 0 and less than 1.

EXAMPLE 2 The following program generates five numbers between 0 and 1.

```
PROGRAM PickReal;
{ Generate five numbers between 0 and 1 }

USES Crt;

CONST Iterations = 5;

VAR iterNum : Integer;

BEGIN
  ClrScr;
  FOR iterNum := 1 TO Iterations DO
    Write(Random:9:5)
END.

[run]
  0.71510  0.68311  0.48214  0.99929  0.64651
```

Random normally generates the same sequence of numbers each time a program is run; however, the QuickPascal procedure

```
    Randomize
```

generates a new basis for the sequence of random numbers. This process is known as **seeding** the random number generator. Calling Randomize at the start of a program will insure that Random generates different values each time the program is executed.

EXAMPLE 3   Write a program to simulate the tossing of a coin. The outcome should tell whether heads or tails was selected.

SOLUTION   Random(2) will be used to select the outcome, with a result of 0 representing heads and a result of 1 representing tails.

```
PROGRAM TossCoin;

USES Crt;

BEGIN
  ClrScr;
  Randomize;
  Write('The coin came up ');
  IF Random(2) = 0 THEN
      Writeln('heads.')
    ELSE
      Writeln('tails.')
END.

[run]
The coin came up heads.
```

EXAMPLE 4   The following program uses the Random function to shuffle a deck of cards and deal five cards from the top of the deck. The 52 cards are initially placed into a "fresh deck" array with the aces coming first, then the twos, . . ., and finally the kings. The cards are numbered from 1 to 52; therefore, cards 1 to 4 will be aces, cards 5 to 8 will be twos, . . ., and cards 49 to 52 will be kings. A string consisting of the denomination and suit identifies each card. The symbols for heart, diamond, club, and spade have ASCII values 3, 4, 5, and 6, respectively, and can therefore be generated by Chr(3), Chr(4), Chr(5), and Chr(6). The cards are shuffled by successively interchanging the card at each position in the deck with a randomly selected card.

```
PROGRAM ShuffleDeck;
{ Shuffle a deck of cards}

USES Crt;

TYPE Deck = ARRAY [1..52] of STRING;

CONST SuitName  : ARRAY [1..4] OF Char =
                    (Chr(3), Chr(4), Chr(5), Chr(6));
      DenomName : ARRAY [1..13] OF STRING[2] =
                    ('A', '2', '3', '4', '5', '6', '7',
                     '8', '9', '10', 'J', 'Q', 'K');

VAR cards : Deck;
```

```
PROCEDURE SetUpDeck (VAR cards : Deck);
  VAR cardNum, cardDenom, cardSuit : Integer;
  BEGIN
    { Set up fresh Deck}
    FOR cardNum := 1 TO 52 DO
      BEGIN
        cardSuit := (cardNum - 1) MOD 4 + 1;  { 1 to 4  }
        cardDenom := (cardNum - 1) DIV 4 + 1; { 1 to 13 }
        cards[cardNum] := DenomName[cardDenom] + SuitName[cardSuit]
      END
  END;

PROCEDURE Shuffle (VAR cards : Deck);
{ Shuffle cards }
  VAR cardNum : Integer;
  PROCEDURE SwapStr (VAR s1, s2 : STRING);
    VAR strTemp : STRING;
    BEGIN
      strTemp := s1;
      s1 := s2;
      s2 := strTemp
    END;
  BEGIN
    Randomize;
    FOR cardNum := 1 TO 52 DO
      SwapStr(cards[cardNum], cards[Random(52) + 1])
  END;

PROCEDURE ShowCards (VAR cards : Deck);
{ Display first five cards }
  VAR cardNum : Integer;
  BEGIN
    FOR cardNum := 1 TO 5 DO
      Write(cards[cardNum], '  ');
  END;

BEGIN
  ClrScr;
  SetUpDeck(cards);
  Shuffle(cards);
  ShowCards(cards)
END.

[run]
7♦  K♥  3♠  A♦  4♣
```

Comments:

1. Each time the function Random appears in a program, it will be reassigned a value. For instance, the task intended (but not accomplished) by the first statement below is achieved by the second set of statements. (Assume r has been declared Real.)

```
{ Generate the square of a randomly chosen number }
Writeln('The square of ', Random, ' is ', Sqr(Random))

{ Generate the square of a randomly chosen number }
r := Random;
Writeln('The square of ', r, ' is ', Sqr(r))
```

Since each Random in the first statement will return a different value, it is highly unlikely that their squares will be equal.

2. We have seen the uses of the Random function in **sampling** (selecting five cards from a deck) and **simulating** (modeling the tossing of a coin). Other uses are

   (a) *Testing of programs for correctness and efficiency.* Selecting randomly chosen data avoids any bias of the tester.
   (b) *Numerical analysis.* In Section 11.3, we use randomly selected points to find the area under a curve.
   (c) *Recreation.* Programs can be written to play games such as blackjack.
   (d) *Decision making.* In Game Theory, a branch of mathematics applied to economics, strategies involve using Random to make decisions. Programming Project 2 discusses Game Theory.

3. Random's apparent flaw is not really a flaw. The fact that in the absence of a Randomize statement the sequence of values produced by successive Randoms will always be the same was intentionally designed into Random. This aspect is useful in debugging simulations in which many random numbers are generated.

4. The sequence of numbers generated by Random is not truly random since, in practice, each number actually determines the next number; however, the sequence has the appearance of a randomly generated sequence. For any subinterval of the interval [0,1), the likelihood of generating a number in that subinterval is the same as for any other subinterval of the same length. The sequence of numbers generated by QuickPascal is said to be **pseudo-random**.

5. The statement Random(*num*) returns an integer from 0 through *num* − 1. The actual data type of its output, however, is not the Pascal type Integer, but the data type Word, which ranges from 0 through 65535. Hence, an expression like Random(3) − 1 should be avoided, since whenever Random(3) has output 0, subtracting 1 produces a number out of the legal range for a Word.

PRACTICE PROBLEMS 11.1

1. Randomly generate 10,000 integers from 1 through 6 and report the number of times the integer 3 occurs in the first thousand numbers, the second thousand, and so on.

2. Modify the program in Example 3 for the case of a biased coin that lands "Heads" three-fourths of the time.

EXERCISES 11.1

In Exercises 1 and 2, determine the output or range of output of the program segment.

1. `Writeln(Random(5) * Random(2))`

2.
```
j := 1;
REPEAT
  Write(j:2);
  j := j + 1
UNTIL j >= Random + 3
```

In Exercises 3 and 4, find the error.

3.
```
WHILE n <> 5 DO
  BEGIN
    n := Random(5);
    Write(n:2)
  END
```

4.
```
n := Random(-5);
IF n = 2 THEN
    Writeln('Two')
```

In Exercises 5 through 8, determine the range of values that can be generated by the given expression.

5. `Random(38) + 1`

6. `Random * Random(10)`

7. `(Random + 1) * (Random + 2)`

8. `2 * Random(5) + 1`

In Exercises 9 through 14, write the expression(s) that will randomly select a number from the given range.

9. An integer from 5 through 10

10. A real number from 2 through 4 (excluding 4)

11. An even integer from 2 through 100

12. A perfect square from 1 through 100

13. Write a program that selects a word at random from among 20 words contained in a constant array.

14. Write a program to simulate the tossing of a coin 100 times and keep track of the number of "heads" and "tails" that occur.

15. Modify the program in Example 4 so that, instead of displaying the first five cards, it determines whether the five cards are of the same suit. Then expand the program to repeat the process 1000 times and count the number of times the first five cards are all the same suit. The program may take quite a while to run.

16. A company has a text file containing the names of people who have qualified for a drawing to win an IBM Personal Computer. Write a program to select a name at random from the file. Assume that the file contains at most 1000 names.

17. A club has 20 members. Write a program to select two different people at random to serve as president and treasurer. (The names of the members should be contained in a text file.)

18. A true-false exam has 10 questions. Write a program to randomly answer the questions in which each answer is equally likely to be "true" or "false".

19. A multiple-choice exam has 10 questions with five possible choices each. Write a program to randomly answer the questions. Each of the five possible choices should have the same likelihood of being selected.

20. Write a program to simulate the tossing of a pair of dice 120 times and record the number of times that the sum of the two numbers is 7.

21. Write a program to select a letter at random from the alphabet.

22. Although tickets for a popular concert will not be sold until nine o'clock, fans start lining up at the box office at eight o'clock. Suppose during each minute, either one or two fans arrive and that the likelihood of just one arriving is four times the likelihood of two arriving. Write a program to simulate the arrival of fans at the box office. For each minute it should report the total number of fans in line.

23. Write a program to simulate 1000 rolls of a die and report the number of times each integer occurs.

24. Write a program to randomly select 30 different people from a group of 60 people whose names are contained in a text file. (**Hint:** Use an array of 60 elements to keep track of whether or not a person has been selected.)

25. Example 4 presented a method for selecting a set of five cards from a deck of 52 cards. This is a special case of the problem of selecting m objects from a set of n objects; or equivalently, of selecting m integers from the integers 1 to n. A brilliant algorithm for accomplishing this task is shown below. (For details see D. E. Knuth, *The Art of Computer Programming*, Volume 2, p. 121, Addison-Wesley Publishing Company, 1969.) This algorithm has the additional feature that the set of m numbers will be ordered. Do a few pencil and paper walkthroughs with small values of m and n to convince yourself that the algorithm does indeed produce the proper output.

```
PROGRAM SelectNums;

USES Crt;

VAR j, select, remaining : Integer;

BEGIN
  ClrScr;
  Write('Enter two numbers(m n): ');
  Readln(select, remaining);
  Randomize;
  FOR j := 1 TO remaining DO
    BEGIN
      IF Random(remaining) < select THEN
          BEGIN
            Write(j:7);
            select := select - 1
          END;
      remaining := remaining - 1
    END
END.
```

26. Use the program in Exercise 25 to select five cards from a deck of 52 cards.

27. *The Birthday Problem.* Given a random group of 23 people, how likely is it that two people have the same birthday? To answer this question, write a program that creates an array of range 23, randomly assigns to each subscripted variable one of the integers from 1 through 365, and checks to see if any of the subscripted variables have the same value. (Make the simplifying assumption that no birthdays occur on February 29.) Now expand the program to repeat the process 100 times and determine the percentage of the time that there is a match. (**Note:** This program may take a few minutes to run.)

SOLUTIONS TO PRACTICE PROBLEMS 11.1

1.
```
PROGRAM DoFreq;
{ Report frequency of integer 3 in each tenth part of a list }

VAR occurrences, numblock, iter, rand : Integer;

BEGIN
  Randomize;
  FOR numBlock := 1 TO 10 DO
    BEGIN
      occurrences := 0;
      FOR iter := 1 TO 1000 DO
        BEGIN
          rand := Random(6) + 1;
          IF rand = 3 THEN
              occurrences := occurrences + 1
        END;
      Write(occurrences:5)
    END;
  Writeln
END.

[run]
168  174  168  183  175  164  152  161  161  164
```

We see that the occurrences of the integer 3 are spread out. In each block of one thousand integers it appeared an average of 167 times, and 167 is close to 1000/6. We expect that in each block of m integers it will occur about m/6 times.

2. The IF block of the program should be changed to

```
IF Random(4) <= 2 THEN
    Writeln('Heads')
  ELSE
    Writeln('Tails');
```

The first line could also have been written as

```
IF Random < 0.75 THEN
```

since the interval from 0 to 0.75 constitutes three-fourths of the interval from 0 to 1, and the value of Random is expected to be in this interval about three-fourths of the time. In general, the likelihood that the value of Random is in a particular subinterval is equal to the length of the subinterval. For instance, the likelihood that the value of Random lies between 0.4 and 0.7 is 0.3. That is, about 30 percent of the time the value of Random can be expected to lie between 0.4 and 0.7.

11.2 GAMES OF CHANCE

The computer can be used to simulate games of chance and analyze various strategies.

Roulette

A roulette wheel contains 38 slots labeled 1 through 36, 0, and 00. (See Figure 11.2). When the wheel is spun, a tiny ball bounces around and comes to rest in a slot. Players wager various types of bets by placing chips on a mat. If a player bets $1 on a number and the ball lands on that number, he receives $36 (including the dollar bet).

Figure 11.2 Roulette Wheel

EXAMPLE 1   Write a program to simulate a spin of a roulette wheel.

SOLUTION   Random(38) evaluates to an integer from 0 through 37. If we associate 37 with 00, then the possible outcomes correspond to the positions on the wheel.

```
PROGRAM OneSpin;
{ Simulate spin of a roulette wheel }

USES Crt;

PROCEDURE OutSpin (spin : Integer);
  BEGIN
    Write('The winning number is ');
    IF spin <> 37 THEN
        Writeln(spin)
      ELSE
        Writeln('00')
  END;
```

```
FUNCTION RouletteSpin : Integer;
  { RouletteSpin = 37 represents a spin of 00 }
  BEGIN
    RouletteSpin := Random(38)
  END;

BEGIN
  ClrScr;
  Randomize;
  OutSpin(RouletteSpin)
END.

[run]
The winning number is 7
```

EXAMPLE 2 A gambler arrives at the roulette table with $100. He decides to bet $1 on the number 7 and continue placing this bet until he either doubles his money or goes broke. Write a program to simulate his experience. After each spin of the wheel, record his current bankroll and the number of times he has played.

SOLUTION The program is straightforward. After each play, the gambler's bankroll will either increase by $35 (if he wins) or decrease by $1. The numbers following "Bankroll:" and "Number of games played:" will change steadily until the session is over.

```
PROGRAM RouletteSession;
{ Program bets EachBet until bankroll is gone or doubled }

USES Crt;

CONST OrigBankroll = 100;    { Starting bankroll }
      EachBet       = 1;      { Amount bet for each play }

VAR bankroll, numSpins : Integer;

PROCEDURE InitSession (VAR bankroll, numSpins : Integer);
{ Randomize, initialize bankroll and number of plays }
  BEGIN
    Randomize;
    bankroll := OrigBankroll;
    numSpins := 0
  END;

FUNCTION RouletteSpin : Integer;
{ RouletteSpin = 37 represents a spin of 00 }
  BEGIN
    RouletteSpin := Random(38)
  END;
```

```
    PROCEDURE AdjustBankroll (VAR bankroll, numSpins : Integer);
    { Adjust bankroll, increment number of plays }
      BEGIN
        IF RouletteSpin = 7 THEN
            bankroll := bankroll + 35 * EachBet
          ELSE
            bankroll := bankroll - EachBet;
        numSpins := numSpins + 1
      END;

    PROCEDURE ShowData (bankroll, numSpins : Integer);
      BEGIN
        GotoXY(1, 12);
        Writeln('Bankroll: ', bankroll:3);
        Writeln('Number of games played: ', numSpins)
      END;

  BEGIN
    ClrScr;
    InitSession(bankroll, numSpins);
    WHILE (bankroll > 0) AND (bankroll < 2 * OrigBankroll) DO
      BEGIN
        AdjustBankroll(bankroll, numSpins);
        ShowData(bankroll, numSpins)
      END
  END.

[run]
Bankroll:    0
Number of games played: 217
```

The output of the program of Example 2 shows that the gambler lost during the session; however, at other gambling sessions he might win. We can estimate how likely he is to end a session as a winner by simulating the play of many sessions and recording the number of wins.

EXAMPLE 3 Simulate the play of 100 sessions of roulette using the strategy of Example 2. Display a running count of the number of wins and losses.

SOLUTION The following program calls most of the program RouletteSession as a procedure to find the outcome of each individual session. To speed up execution, the program does not report the changes in the bankroll during each session, but only the total number of wins and losses.

```
PROGRAM RouletteSessions;
{ Simulate MaxTries sessions of roulette }

USES Crt;

CONST MaxTries = 100;
```

```
VAR tries, gamesWon, gamesLost : Integer;

PROCEDURE Initialize (VAR gamesWon, gamesLost : Integer);
{ Randomize, set games won and lost to 0 }
  BEGIN
    Randomize;
    gamesWon := 0;
    gamesLost := 0
  END;

PROCEDURE OneSession (VAR gamesWon, gamesLost : Integer);
  CONST OrigBankroll = 100; { starting bankroll }
        EachBet      = 1;
  VAR bankroll, numSpins : Integer;
  PROCEDURE InitSession (VAR bankroll, numSpins : Integer);
  { Initialize bankroll and number of spins }
    BEGIN
      bankroll := OrigBankroll;
      numSpins := 0
    END;
  FUNCTION RouletteSpin : Integer;
  { RouletteSpin = 37 represents a spin of 00 }
    BEGIN
      RouletteSpin := Random(38)
    END;
  PROCEDURE AdjustBankroll (VAR bankroll, numSpins : Integer);
  { Adjust bankroll, increment number of plays }
    BEGIN
      IF RouletteSpin = 7 THEN
          bankroll := bankroll + 35 * EachBet
        ELSE
          bankroll := bankroll - EachBet;
      numSpins := numSpins + 1
    END;
  BEGIN
    InitSession(bankroll, numSpins);
    WHILE (bankroll > 0) AND (bankroll < 2 * OrigBankroll) DO
      AdjustBankroll(bankroll, numSpins);
    IF (bankroll > 0) THEN
        gamesWon := gamesWon + 1
      ELSE
        gamesLost := gamesLost + 1
  END;

PROCEDURE ShowData (gamesWon, gamesLost : Integer);
  BEGIN
    GotoXY(1, 12);
    Writeln('Sessions Won:  ', gamesWon);
    Writeln('Sessions Lost: ', gamesLost)
  END;
```

```
BEGIN
  ClrScr;
  Initialize(gamesWon, gamesLost);
  FOR tries := 1 TO MaxTries DO
    BEGIN
      OneSession(gamesWon, gamesLost);
      ShowData(gamesWon, gamesLost)
    END
END.

[run]
Sessions Won:  39
Sessions Lost: 61
```

We expect the gambler to go home a winner about 39 percent of the time and a loser about 61 percent of the time. The gambler might try to increase the likelihood of winning by changing the amount of the individual bet or the size of the bankroll. For instance, two possibilities are

1. Bet $2 on each spin and leave OrigBankroll as $100.

2. Let OrigBankroll equal $200 and bet $1 on each spin.

A computer simulation would show that the likelihoods of winning are about 40 percent and 33 percent, respectively; therefore, doubling the bet is a good idea, but doubling the bankroll is not.

Slot Machines

A slot machine, or "one-arm bandit," is operated by inserting a coin in a slot and pulling a lever. (See Figure 11.3.) This causes three wheels containing pictures of cherries, oranges, plums, melons, bars, and bells to spin around and finally come to rest with one picture showing on each wheel. Certain combinations of pictures, such as three of a kind, produce a payoff to the player.

EXAMPLE 4 Suppose each slot machine wheel contains five cherries, five oranges, five plums, three melons, one bell, and one bar and that the payoff is 10 coins for three-of-a-kind and three coins if any of the pictures is a bar. Simulate 1000 plays and display a running total of the number of games played and the number of coins won.

SOLUTION
```
PROGRAM SlotSpins;
{ Simulate MaxTries spins of a slot machine }

USES Crt;

TYPE Pict     = (cherries, orange, plum, melon, bell, bar);
     WheelPict = ARRAY [1..3] of Pict;

CONST MaxTries = 1000;
```

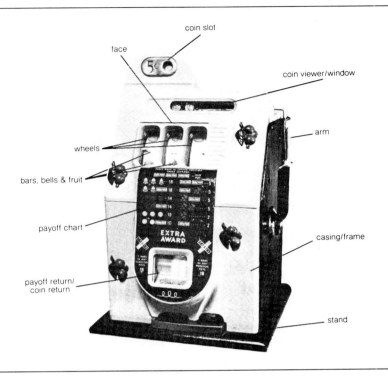

Figure 11.3 Slot Machine

```
VAR tries, numSpins, coinsWon : Integer;
    machine                   : WheelPict;

PROCEDURE Initialize (VAR numSpins, coinsWon : Integer);
{ Randomize, set number of plays and coins won to 0 }
  BEGIN
    Randomize;
    numSpins := 0;
    coinsWon := 0
  END;

PROCEDURE SpinWheels (VAR machine : WheelPict);
{ Spin each of three wheels }
  VAR wheel : Integer;
  PROCEDURE SpinOneWheel (VAR result : Pict);
  { Choose from cherries, orange, plum, melon, bell, or bar }
    BEGIN
      CASE Random(20) OF
        0..4   : result := cherries;
        5..9   : result := orange;
        10..14 : result := plum;
        15..17 : result := melon;
        18     : result := bell;
        19     : result := bar
      END
    END;
```

```
      BEGIN
        FOR wheel := 1 TO 3 DO
          SpinOneWheel(machine[wheel])
      END;

    PROCEDURE ComputePayoff (machine  : WheelPict; VAR coinsWon : Integer);
    { Compute payoff from wheel spins }
      VAR newCoins : Integer;
      BEGIN
        newCoins := 0;
        IF (machine[1] = machine[2]) AND (machine[2] = machine[3]) THEN
            newCoins := 10
          ELSE
            IF (machine[1] = bar) OR (machine[2] = bar) OR
               (machine[3] = bar) THEN
                newCoins := 3;
        coinsWon := coinsWon + newCoins
      END;

  PROCEDURE ShowData (numSpins, coinsWon : Integer);
  { Show number of plays, coins won }
    BEGIN
      GotoXY(1, 12);
      Writeln('Number of plays: ', numSpins);
      Writeln('Total number of coins won: ', coinsWon)
    END;

  BEGIN
    ClrScr;
    Initialize(numSpins, coinsWon);
    FOR tries := 1 TO MaxTries DO
      BEGIN
        SpinWheels(machine);
        ComputePayoff(machine, coinsWon);
        ShowData(tries, coinsWon)
      END
  END.

[run]
Number of plays: 1000
Total number of coins won: 928
```

The simulation shows this slot machine keeps about 7 percent of the amount of money played. The machines vary from casino to casino in the allocation of the pictures and the payoffs. If the specifications of the machine are known, however, then a simulation can be used to determine how profitable the machine is for the casino.

PRACTICE PROBLEM 11.2

Suppose a game of chance has four possible outcomes, called I, II, III, and IV, which are expected to occur 5/12, 1/4, 1/6, and 1/6 of the time, respectively.

1. Write a program to simulate the outcome of the game of chance.

EXERCISES 11.2

In Exercises 1 and 2, determine the percentage of the time that the program segment will produce the output "Red".

```
1. Randomize;
   r := Random;
   IF r < 0.3 THEN
      col := 'White'
    ELSE
     IF r < 0.7 THEN
         col := 'Red'
       ELSE
         col := 'Blue';
   Writeln(col)
```

```
2. Randomize;
   n := Random (148);
   IF n < 37 THEN
      col := 'White'
    ELSE
      col := 'Red';
   Writeln(col)
```

In Exercises 3 and 4, determine why the program segment does not achieve its objective.

```
3. { Simulate toss of a coin }
   Randomize;
   IF Random(2) = 1 THEN
      result := 'Heads';
   IF Random(2) = 0 THEN
      result := 'Tails';
   Writeln(result)
```

```
4. { Simulate 1000 coin tosses }
   heads := 0;
   Randomize;
   n := Random(2);
   FOR j := 1 TO 1000 DO
     IF n = 1 THEN
        heads := heads + 1;
   Writeln('Number of heads: ', heads);
```

In Exercises 5 and 6, subdivide the interval [0,1) to correspond to the given outcomes.

5. Outcome	Likelihood
Yes	1/6
No	1/3
Maybe	1/2

6. Outcome	Likelihood
Go	1/7
Stop	2/7
Caution	4/7

Exercises 7 and 8 simulate the "Big Six" wheel shown in Figure 11.4. The payoff is the number of chips you receive in addition to the one you bet, if your number comes up.

Outcome	Appearances	Payoff
1	23	1
2	15	2
5	8	5
10	4	10
20	2	20
Joker	1	45
Casino	1	45

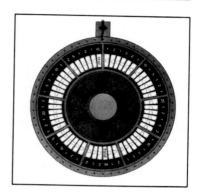

Figure 11.4   Big Six Wheel, Appearances, and Payoffs

7. Write a program to simulate the outcome of the spin of a Big Six wheel so that each item has the appropriate likelihood of occurring.

8. Simulate 10,000 plays of the "5" bet and display the total profit (most likely a negative number).

9. In roulette, a $1 "ODD" bet pays off $1 (in addition to the $1 bet) if the ball comes to rest on an odd number. Simulate 1000 plays of the ODD bet and display a running total of the number of games played and the profit. (A loss will correspond to a negative profit.) This type of bet is typical of most roulette bets. That is, approximately the same amount of money should be lost after 1000 plays. The only exception is the "Five Numbers" bet discussed in Exercise 10.

10. In roulette, a $1 "Five Numbers" bet pays off $6 (in addition to the $1 bet) if the ball comes to rest on 0, 00, 1, 2, or 3. Simulate 1000 plays of the "Five Numbers" bet and display a running total of the number of games played and the profit. (**Note:** This is the worst bet in roulette.)

11. In Monte Carlo and most other European casinos, roulette wheels do not have 00. Also, if you place an ODD bet and the ball rests on 0, then your bet is imprisoned; that is, it stays on ODD for another spin of the wheel. If that spin produces an odd number, you get your dollar back, and if it produces a 0, you get 50 cents back. Simulate 1000 plays of the ODD bet and display a running total of the number of games played and the profit.

12. Consider the program in Example 3. In each session in which the gambler goes broke, he loses exactly $100; however, each time he comes out ahead during a session, he earns anywhere from $100 to $134. Modify the program so it keeps track of his actual earnings and losses. By running the program, you can determine his expected average loss per session.

13. A candy company puts a baseball card in each pack of bubble gum. If each baseball player is as likely to appear as any other. Write a program to request the number of different players and simulate the collection of a complete set of baseball cards. The program should display the number of pictures of each player and the number of packs of bubble gum purchased. (**Note:** Create an array cards, where cards[j] is the number of cards collected with a picture of the jth player.) A possible outcome is as follows:

```
[run]
How many different players are there? 5
4 pictures of player 1
6 pictures of player 2
4 pictures of player 3
1 pictures of player 4
3 pictures of player 5
18 packages of bubble gum were purchased
```

14. Expand the program of Exercise 13 to repeat the process of collecting a set of cards 100 times and report the average number of purchases made to obtain a complete set.

SOLUTION TO PRACTICE PROBLEMS 11.2

```
1. PROGRAM Game;
   { Simulate the game in Practice Problem 1 }

   USES Crt;

   VAR result : STRING;

   BEGIN
     ClrScr;
     Randomize;
     CASE Random(12) OF
       0..4   : result := 'I';
       5..7   : result := 'II';
       8, 9   : result := 'III';
       10, 11 : result := 'IV'
     END;
     Writeln(result)
   END.
```

11.3 MONTE CARLO METHODS

When we solve a problem by repeatedly generating random numbers, we are said to employ **Monte Carlo methods**. In this section, we use Monte Carlo methods to determine the appropriate number of tellers for a bank, evaluate a test-taking strategy, and find the area of a region under a curve.

Bank Tellers

The number of tellers a bank should use depends on several factors: the rate at which customers arrive for service during the time period under consideration, the expected amount of time required to serve each customer, and how much the manager values a short line. Let's first consider the case of a single teller and then expand to the case of any number of tellers.

EXAMPLE 1 Suppose on the average, bank customers arrive at the rate of 36 customers per hour and the amount of time required to serve each customer ranges uniformly from one to six minutes. Assuming there is only one teller, write a program to simulate the operation of the bank for a two-hour period. The program should display a running count of the number of people in line. At the end of the two-hour period, the percentage of time the line had more than three people should be displayed.

SOLUTION Break the two-hour period into one-second slices and monitor the status of the line and the teller every second. Thirty-six customers per hour (3600 seconds), amounts to one customer every 100 seconds. During any 1-second period, therefore the likelihood is 1 percent that a new customer will arrive. The variable lineSize holds the length of the line at any time, and the variable secsLong is increased by one during any second at which there are more than three people in line. When a customer reaches the teller, the Random function determines a number from 60 through 360, call it secsLeft, the number of seconds needed to serve the customer. While a customer is being served, the value of secsLeft decreases by one each second. When the value of secsLeft reaches zero, either a new customer steps forward (if lineSize >= 1) or the teller is idle until another customer arrives. Although the outcome of this program will vary each time it is run, clearly a single teller can't handle the traffic in this bank.

```
PROGRAM Teller;
{ Simulate teller serving a bank line }

USES Crt;

CONST TotalSecs = 60 * 120;  { For 120-minute simulation }

VAR seconds, secsLeft, secsLong, lineSize : Integer;

PROCEDURE Initialize (VAR lineSize, secsLeft, secsLong : Integer);
{ Randomize, initialize variables }
  BEGIN
    Randomize;
    lineSize := 0;      { Length of line }
    secsLeft := 0;      { Secs. remaining to serve customer }
    secsLong := 0       { Secs. line has > 3 customers }
  END;
```

```
PROCEDURE UpdateLine (VAR lineSize, secsLong : Integer);
{ Check for and record new arrivals }
  BEGIN
    IF Random(100) = 0 THEN        { 1 in 100 chance of arrival}
        lineSize := lineSize + 1;
    GotoXY(1, 12);
    Writeln ('Length of line:', lineSize:3);
    IF lineSize > 3 THEN
        secsLong := secsLong + 1
  END;

PROCEDURE UpdateTeller (VAR lineSize, secsLeft : Integer);
{ Update and record status of teller }
  BEGIN
    IF secsLeft >= 1 THEN
        secsLeft := secsLeft - 1;
    IF (secsLeft <= 0) AND (lineSize >= 1) THEN
        BEGIN
          lineSize := lineSize - 1;
          secsLeft := Random(301) + 60   { 60 to 360 secs }
        END
  END;

PROCEDURE ShowData (secsLong : Integer);
{ Show percentage of time line has four or more people }
  BEGIN
    Writeln('Line has more than three people ',
            (100.0 * secsLong / TotalSecs):1:1,
            '% of the time.')
  END;

BEGIN
  ClrScr;
  Initialize(lineSize, secsLeft, secsLong);
  FOR seconds := 1 TO TotalSecs DO
    BEGIN
      UpdateLine(lineSize, secsLong);
      UpdateTeller(lineSize, secsLeft)
    END;
  ShowData(secsLong)
END.

[run]
Length of line: 41
Line has more than three people 85.8% of the time.
```

EXAMPLE 2   Expand the program in Example 1 to support several tellers. The number of tellers should be input by the user.

SOLUTION   The variable secsLeft, seconds remaining to serve current customer, must be replaced by an array secsLeft having one subscripted variable for each teller. The number of tellers will be assumed to be less than 50. The subprogram UpdateTellers must update and record the status of all the tellers.

```
PROGRAM Tellers;
{ Simulate tellers serving a bank line }

USES Crt;

CONST TotalSecs = 60 * 120;  { for 120-minute simulation }

TYPE TellerArray = ARRAY [1..50] of Integer;

VAR lineSize, teller, numTellers, seconds,
    secsLong    : Integer;      { # of secs that lineSize > 3 }
    secsLeft    : TellerArray;  { secs left to serve customer }

PROCEDURE Initialize (VAR lineSize              : Integer;
                      VAR secsLeft              : TellerArray;
                      VAR secsLong, numTellers  : Integer);
{ Randomize, initialize variables }
  VAR teller : Integer;
  BEGIN
    Randomize;
    lineSize := 0;     { Length of line }
    Write ('Number of tellers available: ');
    Readln (numTellers);
    FOR teller := 1 to numTellers DO
      secsLeft[teller] := 0;  { Secs. remaining to serve customer }
    secsLong := 0              { Secs. line has > 3 customers }
  END;

PROCEDURE UpdateLine (VAR lineSize, secsLong : Integer);
{ Check for and record new arrivals }
  BEGIN
    IF Random(100) = 0 THEN   { 1 in 100 chance of arrival}
        lineSize := lineSize + 1;
    GotoXY(1, 12);
    Writeln ('Length of line:', lineSize:3);
    IF lineSize > 3 THEN
        secsLong := secsLong + 1
  END;
```

```
PROCEDURE UpdateTeller (VAR lineSize, timeLeft : Integer);
{ Update and record status of teller }
  BEGIN
    IF timeLeft >= 1 THEN
        timeLeft := timeLeft - 1;
    IF (timeLeft <= 0) AND (lineSize >= 1) THEN
        BEGIN
          lineSize := lineSize - 1;
          timeLeft := Random(301) + 60   { 60 to 360 secs }
        END
  END;

PROCEDURE ShowData (secsLong : Integer);
{ Show percentage of time line has four or more people }
  BEGIN
    Writeln('Line has more than three people ',
            (100.0 * secsLong / TotalSecs):1:1,
            '% of the time.')
  END;

BEGIN
  ClrScr;
  Initialize(lineSize, secsLeft, secsLong, numTellers);
  FOR seconds := 1 TO TotalSecs DO
    BEGIN
      UpdateLine(lineSize, secsLong);
      FOR teller := 1 TO numTellers DO
        UpdateTeller(lineSize, secsLeft[teller])
    END;
  ShowData(secsLong)
END.

[run]
Number of tellers available: 3
Length of line: 2
Line has more than three people 1.5% of the time.
```

By running this program many times and taking the averages of the numbers generated, we can determine the number of tellers necessary to achieve an acceptable output.

Test-Taking Strategies

Suppose a true-false exam has 10 questions and you answer each one by guessing. It's easy to write a program to produce a sequence of 10 "trues" and "falses". Just use Random and guess "true" if its value is less than 0.5. In the long run, this method should produce an average grade of 50 percent. Now, suppose you are given the additional information that 60 percent of the answers are true. How would you proceed to take the exam? You might use a random process that selects "true" 60 percent of the time.

EXAMPLE 3   Analyze the strategy of randomly selecting "true" 60 percent of the time and "false" 40 percent of the time. Suppose the first six correct answers to the exam are true and the rest are false. Simulate taking the test 1000 times and compute the average of the grades.

SOLUTION   Each question is answered by selecting "true" if the value of Random is less than 0.6, and "false" otherwise. Hence, 10 points are earned whenever one of the first six values of Random is less than 0.6, or whenever one of the last four values of Random is greater than or equal to 0.6.

```
PROGRAM TrueOrFalse;
{ Analyze test-taking strategy }

USES Crt;

VAR score : Integer;
    total : Real;

PROCEDURE Initialize (VAR total : Real);
{ Randomize and set total points earned to 0 }
  BEGIN
    Randomize;
    total := 0.0
  END;

PROCEDURE ShowResults (total : Real);
{ Show average score of 1000 tries }
  BEGIN
    Writeln('Average score is ', (total / 1000):1:2)
  END;

PROCEDURE TakeTest (VAR score : Integer);
{ Take exam and report score (from 0 to 100) }
  VAR question : Integer;
  BEGIN
    score := 0;
    FOR question := 1 TO 6 DO
      IF Random < 0.6 THEN
          score := score + 10;
    FOR question := 7 TO 10 DO
      IF Random >= 0.6 THEN
          score := score + 10
  END;

PROCEDURE TryMethod (VAR total : Real);
  VAR tries : Integer;
  BEGIN
    FOR tries := 1 TO 1000 DO
      BEGIN
        TakeTest(score);
        total := total + score
      END
  END;
```

```
BEGIN
  ClrScr;
  Initialize(total);
  TryMethod(total);
  ShowResults(total)
END.

[run]
Average score is 52.26
```

Although the strategy used here is the most obvious one, it's not too good. A better strategy is to answer all questions "true". This strategy guarantees a grade of 60 percent.

Area under a Curve

The areas of regions under certain curves have important interpretations. For instance, the area under the bell-shaped curve in Figure 11.5 gives the percentage of adult males whose height is between 5 and 5.75 feet. The area under the velocity curve in Figure 11.6 gives the total distance traveled by a rocket. One method for determining the area under a curve consists of surrounding the region under consideration by a rectangle, selecting points at random from the rectangle, and counting the percentage falling under the curve. The area is then estimated to be this percentage of the area of the rectangle.

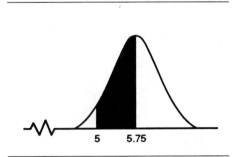

Figure 11.5   Normal Curve   **Figure 11.6**   Velocity of a Rocket

EXAMPLE 4   Figure 11.7 shows a portion of the graph of the curve $x^2 + y^2 = 1$. Use a Monte Carlo method to estimate the area of this region.

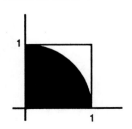

Figure 11.7   Area of a Quarter Circle

SOLUTION   The square drawn in Figure 11.7 completely contains the quarter-circle. Both the x- and y-coordinates of points inside the square have values ranging from 0 to 1. The Random function is used to generate a point inside the square. The point, (x, y), will be inside the circle if $x^2 + y^2 < 1$. Since the area of the square is 1, the percentage of points in the circle approximates the area of the quarter-circle. (**Note:** Since the area of the circle is $\pi*1^2$ or π, the actual area of the quarter circle is $3.141593 / 4$, or 0.7853983.)

```
PROGRAM QuadrantArea;
{ Area of one quadrant of unit circle }

USES Crt;

VAR x, y         : Real;
    total, tries : Integer;

BEGIN
  ClrScr;
  Randomize;
  total := 0;
  FOR tries := 1 TO 1000 DO
    BEGIN
      x := Random;
      y := Random;
      IF Sqr(x) + Sqr(y) < 1 THEN
          total := total + 1
    END;
  Writeln('Approximate area is ', (total / 1000):1:4)
END.

[run]
Approximate area is 0.7869
```

PRACTICE PROBLEMS 11.3

Figure 11.8 shows a shaded region under the graph of the curve $y = x^2$, and a rectangle containing the region.

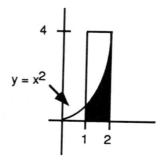

Figure 11.8 Shaded Region

1. Give a pair of formulas using Random to randomly generate the x- and y-coordinates of a point in this rectangle.

2. What relationship must x and y satisfy in order for the point (x, y) to be in the shaded region?

3. Suppose 1000 random points in the rectangle are generated, and 58 percent lie in the shaded region. Estimate the area of the shaded region.

EXERCISES 11.3

Exercises 1 through 4 refer to the bank teller program of Example 1.

1. Suppose whenever the line has seven customers in it, any new customers will leave in disgust. Modify the program in this case and also display the number of customers who give up.

2. Modify the program to compute the total number of minutes that the teller is idle during the two-hour period.

3. Modify the program to compute the average amount of time spent in line by a customer. (**Hint:** The program should keep track of the total number of customers who enter the bank.)

4. Suppose that due to greater computer use in the bank, the amount of time required to serve a customer varies from between a half-minute to five minutes. Modify the program to reflect this change.

5. Use Monte Carlo methods to estimate the area of the quarter-ellipse shown in Figure 11.9(a).

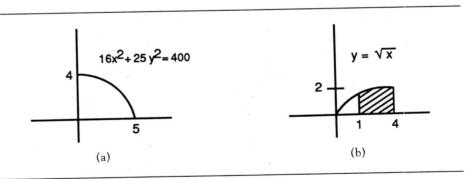

(a)   (b)

Figure 11.9 Regions under Curves

6. Use Monte Carlo methods to estimate the area of the shaded region under the graph of the parabola shown in Figure 11.9(b).

7. Suppose 5 percent of the diskettes manufactured by a certain company are defective, and diskettes are packaged 10 to a box. Simulate the manufacturing of 10,000 boxes of diskettes and display the number of boxes containing one defective diskette, two defective diskettes, . . ., 10 defective diskettes.

8. Airlines overbook flights by between 10 percent and 30 percent of the capacity of the airplane. Suppose for a certain flight with a capacity of 99 passengers, the likelihood of a person with a reservation not showing up for the flight is 25 percent. If less than 99 people show up, the airline loses $150 for each unfilled seat. If more than 99 people show up, however, the airline must "bump" the excess people at a cost of $400 per person. (Hotel fees, meals, and monetary compensation make up the bumping cost.) Do a computer simulation to compute the average estimated loss to the airline when 120 seats are booked. (Use 100 trials to make the estimate.) Repeat the simulation for the case where the airline does not overbook at all.

9. Table 11.1 gives the percentages of the different colors of M&Ms in each of the two types, plain and peanut. Write a program that requests the type of M&Ms as input and then simulates the makeup of a box of 100 M&Ms. The program should list the number of M&Ms of each color.

Color	Percent in Plain M&Ms	Percent in Peanut M&Ms
Brown	30	30
Yellow	20	20
Red	20	20
Orange	10	10
Green	10	20
Tan	10	0

Table 11.1   Percentages of each Color of M&Ms

10. A phone-order software company receives an average of one call per minute, with each call taking between two and nine minutes to process. The company employs six people to answer phones. If all of them are busy, callers are asked to hold until the next available operator is free. If more than five people are on hold, each additional caller is given the option of leaving their name so they can be called back later. About 60 percent of these people accept that option. These people will be called back as soon as an operator is free and no other callers are waiting. Write a program to simulate the processing of the phone calls for a four-hour period. At any time, the program should display the number of people on hold and the number of people waiting to have their calls returned.

SOLUTIONS TO PRACTICE PROBLEMS 11.3

1. The x-coordinates range from 1 to 2 and the y-coordinates from 0 to 4. Therefore, appropriate formulas for generating points are

```
x := Random + 1;
y := 4 * Random;
```

2. If $y < Sqr(x)$, then the point (x, y) will lie below the point $(x, Sqr(x))$, which is on the graph.

3. Since the area of the rectangle is four, the estimate for the area of the shaded region is 0.58 * 4 or 2.32.

Chapter 11
Summary

1. Random(*i*) generates an integer in the range 0 to *i* − 1. When called without arguments, Random returns a real value between 0 and 1 (including 0, but excluding 1). The sequence of values generated by the Random function have the appearance of being chosen at random.

2. Before using the Random function, the Randomize statement should be executed to vary the sequence.

3. The ability to select numbers at random can be applied to sampling, simulation, program testing, numerical analysis, recreation, and decision making.

Chapter 11
Programming Projects

1. *Hangman.* Write a program to play Hangman. A list of 20 words should be placed in a file and one selected at random to be discovered by the user before making 10 incorrect guesses. The program should:
   (a) Use an array to keep track of the letters already guessed
   (b) Display the appropriate number of dashes
   (c) Prompt the user for a letter. If the letter has already been guessed, inform the user and do not count the guess. Otherwise, if the letter is in the word, display all occurrences above the appropriate dashes. (**Hint:** Determine the location to display by a statement such as GotoXY(2 + 4 * (*j* − 1), 12) where *j* is the location of the letter in the word, each dash is three characters long, and a single space separates each pair of dashes.) If the letter is not in the word, decrease the number of misses remaining by one and display the letter in a table of letters guessed. (**Hint:** Use the ASCII value of the letter to determine where to display the letter.)
   (d) Inform the player when either the correct word has been found or the allotment of misses has been used up. (**Hint:** To determine when the entire word has been guessed, keep track of the number of blanks in the word that have been filled.)

2. *Game Theory.* The branch of mathematics called Game Theory is used to maximize gains and minimize losses in business or military problems. As an elementary example of a game theory problem, consider a situation in which you and an opponent each must make choices. Each choice made corresponds to a payoff for you as shown in Figure 11.10. For instance, if you make choice *1*, then you gain $2 if your opponent makes choice *1*, and $14 if your opponent makes choice *2*. Each of you will use a random number generator to make your choice. Suppose your opponent weighs his choices so that 75 percent of the time he chooses *1* and 25 percent of the time he chooses *2*. How should you weight your choices to maximize your expected earnings? Two possibilities are 33 percent, 33 percent, 34 percent, and 45 percent, 10

percent, 45 percent. Write a program that requests you to input the three percentages, and computes the expected earnings for 1000 encounters. Run the program for each of the two triples of percentages mentioned and determine which one is more advantageous to you.

		Opponent	
		1	**2**
	1	2	14
You	**2**	6	12
	3	8	6

Figure 11.10 Game Theory Payoffs

3. *Random Walk.* Figure 11.11 shows a person standing at position 6 on the path to success. Each day he randomly takes one step, either forward or backward. His walk stops when he reaches either end of the path. Write a program that considers each of the nine possible starting positions, simulates the walk 100 times for each starting position, and computes the percentage of walks terminating with success for each starting position. The output should consist of a table displaying the starting positions and the percentages.

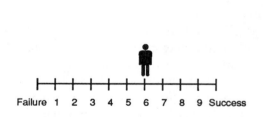

Failure 1 2 3 4 5 6 7 8 9 Success

Figure 11.11 Random Walk **Figure 11.12** Knight's Walk

4. *Knight's Tour.* A knight is placed randomly on a chessboard. On each move the knight takes two steps in a horizontal direction and one step in a vertical direction or two steps in a vertical direction and one step in a horizontal direction. Figure 11.12 shows the eight possibilities. Write a program to do the following:

   (a) Perform the following random tours of the board 100 times and record the number of moves in each tour.

   (1) Randomly place the knight on one of the 64 squares of the chessboard.

   (2) Randomly select one of eight moves for the knight (including possibly a move off the board).

   (3) Repeat step (2) until the knight either moves off the board or occupies a previously occupied position. (First check for the move off the board.)

(b) A tour can theoretically consist of up to 64 moves (one for each square on the board). Produce a 4-column table showing the 64 possible number of moves and the number of tours for each.

5. *Arithmetic Drill.* Write a program that can be used by a child to practice arithmetic skills. The program should contain the following features:

(a) The child should select a level of difficulty (Easy or Hard) and a category (Addition, Subtraction, Multiplication, or Division).

(b) The numbers used should be selected randomly. Easy problems should be stated using single-digit numbers, whereas hard problems can include two-digit numbers. To ensure that division problems always have whole-number answers, generate the answer first and adjust the range of the divisor, y, so *answer* * y is the appropriate size, and let *answer* * y be the dividend.

(c) The child should be told if each answer is correct or not and should have three tries before being told the correct answer.

(d) After working 10 problems, the child should be able to make another selection as in (a).

(e) After giving four consecutive correct answers, the child should randomly receive one of the responses: "Good Work", "Super", "Nice Job", or "Fantastic".

12

Advanced Topics

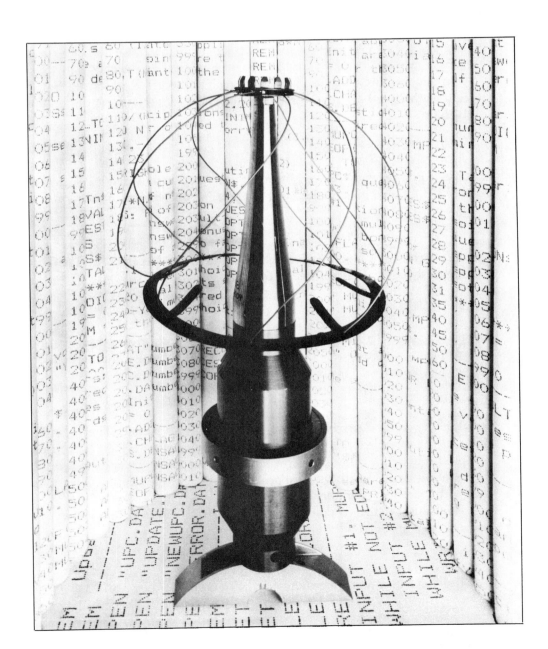

12.1   POINTERS AND LINKED LISTS

The **pointer** data type is simple in appearance and yet is the building block for the most powerful structures of Pascal. In this section, we define pointers and use them to create linked lists. A linked list resembles an array in that it stores a list of data in a specific order. A linked list, however, has two advantages over an array: the length of the list does not have to be specified before the program is executed, and additional items can be inserted easily anywhere in the list.

The variables considered so far that were declared in the VAR part of a program are known as **static variables** and have portions of memory reserved to hold their values. These **fixed** or **static** portions of memory are held for the exclusive use of the declared variables and cannot be used for any other purpose.

Another kind of variable, called a **dynamic variable**, has no portion of memory set aside for it by the compiler. Instead, the memory is allocated at run-time and can be deallocated to free up the memory for other uses. The address of the variable is stored in a special type of variable, known as a **pointer**. The pointer variable is said to point to the dynamic variable. (We do not have to know how memory locations are addressed; Pascal handles the details.)

Dynamic variables can be of any type, such as Integer, Real, String, Set, or Record, with record dynamic variables being the most versatile. A declaration of the form

```
TYPE IntPointer = ^Integer;
```

specifies a pointer type that can be used to define pointer variables. The caret symbol (^) is used in lieu of the word "pointer." A declaration of the form

```
VAR intPtr : IntPointer;
```

specifies intPtr to be a pointer variable that can be used to create and point to an Integer dynamic variable. The statement

```
New(intPtr)
```

creates an Integer dynamic variable by setting aside a portion of memory capable of holding an Integer value and assigning the location of this portion of memory to the variable intPtr. The dynamic variable is referred to by the name

```
intPtr^
```

which is the pointer variable name followed by a caret symbol. That is, intPtr points to the variable intPtr^. The dynamic variable intPtr^ has the same rights and privileges as any other Integer variable. Values can be assigned to intPtr^, its value can be displayed, it can appear in algebraic expressions, and it can be used with relational operators.

The value assigned to a pointer variable is either a location in memory or a special constant called NIL. The assignment statement

```
intPtr := NIL
```

specifies that intPtr points nowhere.

The value of a pointer cannot be displayed on the screen or input from the keyboard. The value can be assigned with "New(intPtr)" or "intPtr := NIL" as mentioned above, or by a statement of the form

```
intPtr := intPtr2
```

where intPtr2 has the same type as intPtr. After this last statement is executed, intPtr and intPtr2 will be two separate pointers, but will point to the same dynamic variable. The statement

```
Dispose(intPtr)
```

frees the portion of memory reserved for intPtr^ and allows the memory to be used for other purposes.

Schematically, a pointer variable can be represented by a small square containing a dot (Figure 12.1(a)). A dynamic variable created by a New statement is depicted by a rectangle and an arrow pointing from the pointer variable to the rectangle (Figure 12.1(b)). Any value assigned to the dynamic variable can be written in the rectangle (Figure 12.1(c)). The Dispose statement removes the rectangle (Figure 12.1(d)), and setting the value of the pointer to NIL is denoted by drawing a diagonal through the square (Figure 12.1(e)).

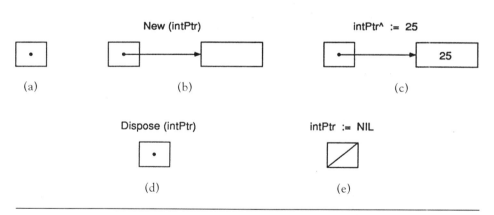

Figure 12.1   Diagrams of Operations on Pointers

EXAMPLE 1   The following program illustrates the material above. Figure 12.2 diagrams the effects of the major statements. Notice the difference between the statements

```
intPtr^ := tempPtr^
```

and

```
tempPtr := intPtr
```

The first statement assigns the value of the variable pointed to by tempPtr to the variable pointed to by intPtr. The second statement causes the pointer tempPtr to point to a different variable, the variable pointed to by intPtr.

```
PROGRAM DemonstratePointers;
{ Demonstrate the creation and use of pointer variables }

USES Crt;

TYPE IntPointer = ^Integer;

VAR intPtr, tempPtr : IntPointer;

BEGIN
  ClrScr;
  New(intPtr);
  intPtr^ := 25;
  New(tempPtr);
  tempPtr^ := 36;
  Writeln(intPtr^, tempPtr^:4);
  intPtr^ := tempPtr^;
  Writeln(intPtr^, tempPtr^:4);
  intPtr^ := 25;
  Writeln(intPtr^, tempPtr^:4);
  Dispose(tempPtr);
  tempPtr := intPtr;
  Writeln(intPtr^, tempPtr^:4);
  tempPtr^ := 81;
  Writeln(intPtr^, tempPtr^:4);
  intPtr := NIL;
  IF intPtr = NIL THEN
      Writeln('nowhere')
END.

[run]
25  36
36  36
25  36
25  25
81  81
nowhere
```

So far, we only have considered Integer dynamic variables, but dynamic variables can be of any data type. For instance, a definition of the form

```
TYPE StrPointer = ^STRING;
```

can be used to declare a pointer to a String dynamic variable. Similar definitions apply for the other variable types.

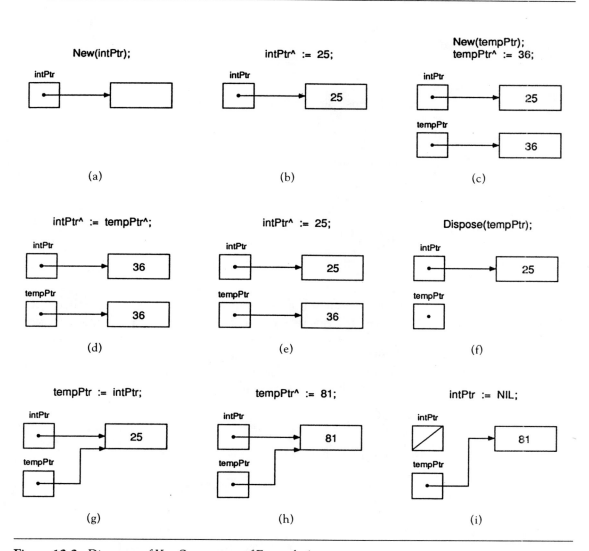

Figure 12.2 Diagrams of Key Statements of Example 1

EXAMPLE 2 The pointer in the following program points to a Record variable.

```
PROGRAM DemoRecordPointer;
{ An example of a pointer to a record }

USES Crt;

TYPE FilmRec    = RECORD
                     name : STRING;
                     year : Integer
                   END;
      FilmPointer = ^FilmRec;
```

```
VAR movie            : FilmRec;
    flickPtr, tempPtr : FilmPointer;

BEGIN
  ClrScr;
  New(flickPtr);
  Write('Enter the most successful movie ever made: ');
  Readln(flickPtr^.name);
  flickPtr^.year := 1982;
  tempPtr := flickPtr;
  Writeln(tempPtr^.name);
  Writeln(tempPtr^.year)
END.

[run]
Enter the most successful movie ever made: E.T.
E.T.
1982
```

The examples considered so far serve solely to illustrate the concept of a pointer. They have little practical use. The real power of a pointer is unleashed when it points to a record having another pointer of the same type as one of its fields. The following is an example of such a declaration. NationPointer is a pointer type to a record dynamic variable of type Nation, and the second field of Nation is a pointer of type NationPointer.

```
TYPE NationPointer = ^Nation;
     Nation        = RECORD
                       name : STRING;
                       next : NationPointer
                     END;
```

This is without doubt a circular definition, but Pascal allows it and with good reason. This declaration allows data to be linked together in a list, called a **linked list**. Figure 12.3 contains a typical linked list.

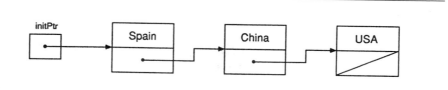

Figure 12.3   A Typical Linked List

The initial pointer, here called initPtr, points to a record variable. This record variable's first field, initPtr^.name, holds the String value 'Spain' and its second field holds a pointer to another record of the same type. This process continues until a record is reached whose pointer points nowhere, that is, whose pointer has the value NIL.

The only limit to the length of such a list is the amount of memory available to Pascal. We will now see how to create and access a linked list. Section 12.2 shows how to create and maintain *ordered* linked lists.

In Figure 12.3, the variables holding the names of the countries Spain, China, and USA can be identified as

```
initPtr^.name
initPtr^.next^.name
initPtr^.next^.next^.name
```

respectively. Fortunately this cumbersome notation is not needed to create and access a linked list.

EXAMPLE 3   The following program builds the linked list of Figure 12.3 by working from the rightmost record to the leftmost. (Section 12.2 gives a technique to form the list from left to right.) Figure 12.4 shows the step-by-step construction. The sequence beginning with initPtr in Figure 12.4(i) is identical with the one in Figure 12.3.

```
PROGRAM BuildList;
{ Build a linked list of countries input by the user }

USES Crt;

TYPE NationPointer = ^Nation;
     Nation        = RECORD
                        name : STRING;
                        next : NationPointer
                     END;

VAR nationName     : STRING;
    initPtr, tempPtr : NationPointer;

BEGIN
  ClrScr;
  initPtr := NIL;
  Writeln('Enter EOD to finish.');
  Write('Enter the name of a country: ');
  Readln(nationName);
  WHILE nationName <> 'EOD' DO
    BEGIN
      New(tempPtr);
      tempPtr^.name := nationName;
      tempPtr^.next := initPtr;
      initPtr := tempPtr;
      Write('Enter the name of a country: ');
      Readln(nationName)
    END
END.
```

```
[run]
Enter EOD to finish.
Enter the name of a country: USA
Enter the name of a country: China
Enter the name of a country: Spain
Enter the name of a country: EOD
```

---

initPtr := NIL;
New (tempPtr);

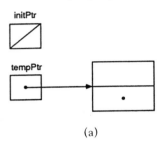

(a)

tempPtr^.name := nationName;
tempPtr^.next := initPtr;

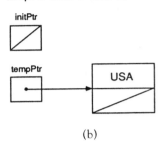

(b)

initPtr := tempPtr;

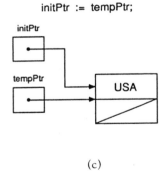

(c)

New (tempPtr);

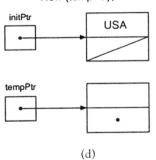

(d)

tempPtr^.name := nationName;
tempPtr^.next := initPtr;

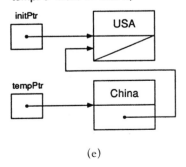

(e)

initPtr := tempPtr;

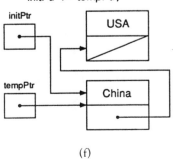

(f)

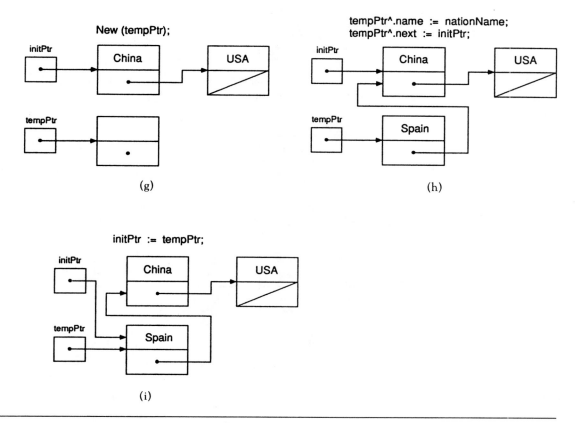

Figure 12.4 Step-by-step Construction of the Linked List of Nations

With slight modifications, the program in Example 3 can be used to construct any linked list. The constructed list can be accessed in several ways.

EXAMPLE 4 A call to the following procedure, with initPtr as argument, can be inserted at the end of the program in Example 3 to display the contents of the list from left to right. Figure 12.5 shows the step-by-step process.

```
PROCEDURE DisplayList (tempPtr : NationPointer);
{ Display the contents of each record in the linked list having tempPtr
  as its initial pointer }
  BEGIN
    WHILE tempPtr <> NIL DO
      BEGIN
        Writeln(tempPtr^.name);
        tempPtr := tempPtr^.next
      END
  END;

[run: continuation from Example 3]
Spain
China
USA
```

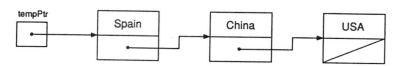

(a) After the procedure is called, tempPtr points to the same record as initPtr, namely Spain's record. Then the value of tempPtr^.name is displayed: Spain.

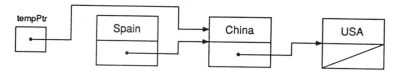

(b) Then tempPtr is assigned the value of tempPtr^.next, and therefore points to China's record. Then the value of tempPtr^.name is displayed: China.

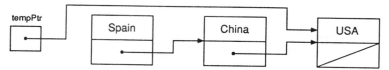

(c) Finally, tempPtr is assigned the value of tempPtr^.next, and therefore points to USA's record. Then the value of tempPtr^.name is displayed: USA.

Figure 12.5 Diagrams of Key Statements of Example 4

EXAMPLE 5 A call to the following Boolean function can be used to determine if a requested country is in the linked list created in Example 3. The call and the interpretation of the function value can be accomplished with a few lines of code appended to the end of the program in Example 3. The steps for carrying out the search are similar to the steps used to display the items of a linked list in Example 4.

```
FUNCTION ItemFound (tempPtr : NationPointer; item : STRING) : Boolean;
{ Search for the occurrence of item in the linked
  list having tempPtr as its initial pointer }
  VAR foundFlag : Boolean;
  BEGIN
    foundFlag := False;
    WHILE (tempPtr <> NIL) AND (NOT foundFlag) DO
      IF tempPtr^.name = item THEN
         foundFlag := True
       ELSE
         tempPtr := tempPtr^.next;
    ItemFound := foundFlag
  END;
```

```
{ Code to be inserted at end of program in Example 3 }
Write('Enter the name of a country: ');
Readln(nationName);
IF ItemFound(initPtr, nationName) THEN
   Writeln(nationName, ' is in the list.')
 ELSE
   Writeln(nationName, ' cannot be found in the list.')
```

```
[run: continuation from Example 3]
Enter the name of a country: Italy
Italy cannot be found in the list.
```

Comments:

1. The thing pointed to by a pointer is sometimes called the *target* of the pointer. A pointer is said to *refer* to its target. The records in a linked list are commonly called *nodes*.

2. Although pointer variables point to dynamic variables, pointer variables themselves are static.

3. A declaration of the form

    ```
    TYPE IntPointer = ^Integer;
    VAR intPtr : IntPointer;
    ```

    can be abbreviated to the shorthand form

    ```
    VAR intPtr : ^Integer;
    ```

    The shorthand form, however, cannot be used for subprogram parameter declarations.

4. The initial pointer of a linked list is not part of the list itself. It points to the first record of the list.

5. Although linked lists resemble arrays in that they hold lists of data, linked lists do not allow random access of data. The 20th record of a linked list can only be accessed by first accessing the preceding 19 records.

6. The circular definition of a pointer type pointing to a record containing a field of the same pointer type is a one-way circle. The pointer type declaration must precede the record definition. The following declaration is illegal:

    ```
    TYPE Nation      = RECORD
                         name : STRING;
                         next : NationPointer
                       END;
         NationPointer = ^Nation;
    ```

7. The Dispose statement does not deallocate the pointer, only the dynamic variable to which it points; thus, if a dynamic variable is the target of only one pointer, be sure to deallocate the dynamic variable before reassigning its pointer. Otherwise the dynamic variable becomes an "orphan." An orphaned variable continues to exist in memory, but cannot be accessed. (See Figure 12.6.)

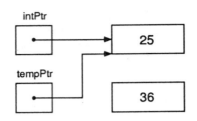

Figure 12.6 An Orphaned Dynamic Variable

8. Be careful when writing subprograms with pointer parameters. Procedures with pointer *VAR* parameters can lose part of a linked list by advancing the the pointer down the list. Procedures with pointer *value* parameters can change the value of the argument's associated dynamic variable.

9. In Figures 12.5(b) and (c) of the program in Example 4, the pointer to the front of the list appears to have been lost. Not so. Since initPtr was passed *by value* to the procedure, initPtr will continue to point to the front of the list after the procedure finishes.

10. In the applications of the next section, a linked list might be empty, that is, consist only of a NIL pointer; therefore, the value of the pointer should be checked for NILity before any attempt to access record fields. In this situation, a statement such as

```
IF initPtr^.name = nationName THEN ...
```

should be replaced by

```
IF initPtr <> NIL THEN
    IF initPtr^.name = nationName THEN
        . . .
```

Actually, QuickPascal allows an alternate method that is not supported by every implementation of Pascal. The statement

```
IF (initPtr <> NIL) AND (initPtr^.name = nationName) THEN ...
```

also can be used since QuickPascal evaluates a compound AND condition by first evaluating the left condition and, if it is false, regarding the compound condition to be false without considering the right condition.

11. Assignment statements of the form varPtr := NIL or varPtr1 := varPtr2, where varPtr1 and varPtr2 have the same type, are valid. A statement of the form Readln(varPtr) is not valid.

12. Since the value of a pointer is a memory location, arithmetic operations may not be performed on pointers. For example, varPtr1 + varPtr2 is invalid. The only valid relational operators for pointers are = and <>. Two pointers are equal if and only if they have the same target or both are NIL.

PRACTICE PROBLEMS 12.1

1. What is the output of the following program?

```
PROGRAM PassPointer;

USES Crt;

TYPE IntPointer = ^Integer;

VAR  intPtr : IntPointer;

PROCEDURE Double (VAR tempPtr : IntPointer);
  VAR myPtr : IntPointer;
  BEGIN
    New(myPtr);
    myPtr^ := 2 * tempPtr^;
    Dispose(tempPtr);
    tempPtr := myPtr;
    Writeln(tempPtr^)
  END;

BEGIN
  Clrscr;
  New(intPtr);
  intPtr^ := 5;
  Double(intPtr);
  Writeln(intPtr^)
END.
```

2. What is the output of the program above if the keyword VAR is removed from the procedure heading?

EXERCISES 12.1

In Exercises 1 through 6, determine the output of the statements for the variables and values in Figure 12.7.

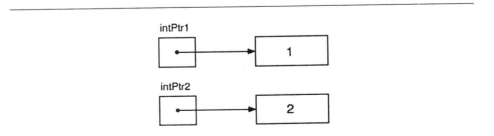

Figure 12.7   Variables and Values for Exercises 1 through 6

1. `Writeln(intPtr1^);`
   `Writeln(intPtr2^)`

2. `intPtr1^ := 3;`
   `Writeln(intPtr1^);`
   `Writeln(intPtr2^)`

3. `intPtr1^ := intPtr2^;`
   `Writeln(intPtr1^);`
   `Writeln(intPtr2^)`

4. `intPtr1 := intPtr2;`
   `Writeln(intPtr1^);`
   `Writeln(intPtr2^)`

5.
```
intPtr1 := intPtr2;
intPtr2 := intPtr1;
Writeln(intPtr1^);
Writeln(intPtr2^)
```

6.
```
intPtr2^:= 4;
intPtr1 := intPtr2;
Writeln(intPtr1^);
Writeln(intPtr2^)
```

In Exercises 7 through 10, determine the output of the program.

7.
```
TYPE StrPointer = ^STRING;

VAR  strPtr1, strPtr2 : StrPointer;

BEGIN
  New(strPtr1);
  strPtr1^ := 'eny';
  strPtr2 := strPtr1;
  strPtr1^ := 'd' + strPtr2^;
  Writeln(strPtr1^)
END.
```

8.
```
TYPE CollegeData = RECORD
                     name  : STRING;
                     state : STRING[2]
                   END;
     RecPointer  = ^CollegeData;

VAR  recPtr1, recPtr2 : RecPointer;

BEGIN
  New(recPtr1);
  recPtr1^.name := 'Princeton';
  recPtr1^.state := 'NJ';
  recPtr2 := recPtr1;
  recPtr2^.name := 'Rutgers';
  Writeln(recPtr1^.name);
  Writeln(recPtr1^.state)
END.
```

9.
```
TYPE IntPointer = ^Integer;

VAR  intPtr : IntPointer;

PROCEDURE Double (VAR tempPtr : IntPointer);
  BEGIN
    tempPtr^ := 2 * tempPtr^;
    Writeln(tempPtr^)
  END;

BEGIN
  New(intPtr);
  intPtr^ := 5;
  Double(intPtr);
  Writeln(intPtr^)
END.
```

10. The program in Exercise 9 with the keyword VAR removed from the procedure heading.

In Exercises 11 through 18, determine the output of the statements for the variables declared below and having the values in the linked list of Figure 12.8.

```
TYPE ListPointer = ^Node;
     Node        = RECORD
                      data : Integer;
                      next : ListPointer
                   END;

VAR initPtr, tempPtr, myPtr : ListPointer;
    num                     : Integer;
```

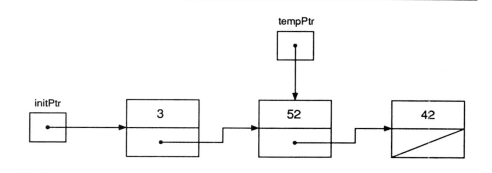

Figure 12.8 Linked List for Exercises 11 through 18

11. `Writeln(initPtr^.data)`

12. `Writeln(tempPtr^.data)`

13. `Writeln(initPtr^.next^.data)`

14. `Writeln(initPtr^.data + tempPtr^.next^.data)`

15. ```
tempPtr := initPtr;
initPtr := tempPtr;
Writeln(initPtr^.data + tempPtr^.data)
```

16. ```
tempPtr^.data := initPtr^.data;
initPtr^.data := tempPtr^.data;
Writeln(initPtr^.data + tempPtr^.data)
```

17. ```
tempPtr := tempPtr^.next;
Writeln(tempPtr^.data)
```

18. ```
myPtr := initPtr;
FOR num := 1 TO initPtr^.data - 1 DO
  myPtr := myPtr^.next;
Writeln(myPtr^.data)
```

In Exercises 19 through 24, identify the errors.

19. TYPE a = ^Integer;

```
BEGIN
  a^ := 52
END.
```

20. VAR letterPtr : ^Char;

```
FUNCTION Duplicate (charPtr : ^Char) : STRING;
  BEGIN
    Duplicate := charPtr^ + charPtr^
  END;

BEGIN
  New(letterPtr);
  letterPtr^ := 'A';
  Writeln(Duplicate(letterPtr))
END.
```

21. TYPE Person   = RECORD
```
                    name  : STRING;
                    socSec : STRING;
                    next  : PersonPtr
                  END;
        PersonPtr = ^Person;
```

22. TYPE Ptr = ^info;
```
      Rec = RECORD
              info : STRING;
              ptr1 : Ptr
            END;
```

23. TYPE ListPtr = ^ListData;
```
      ListData = RECORD
                   entries  : Integer;
                   nextData : ListPtr
                 END;

  VAR listHead : ListData;

BEGIN
  New(listHead);
  listHead^.entries  := 1;
  listHead^.nextData := NIL
END.
```

24. TYPE Ptr = ^Data;
```
      Data = RECORD
               name     : STRING;
               areaCode : Integer;
               next     : Ptr
             END;

  VAR list : Ptr;
```

```
BEGIN
  New(list);
  WITH list DO
    BEGIN
      name      := 'Barney Rubble';
      areaCode := 617;
      next      := NIL
    END
END.
```

In Exercises 25 through 28, assume that a linked list has been created with nodes of type Num defined below and that listPtr points to the first node of the list. Write a procedure or function that accepts listPtr as input and performs the stated task.

```
TYPE NumPointer = ^Num;
     Num        = RECORD
                    number  : Integer;
                    nextNum : NumPointer
                  END;
VAR  listPtr : NumPointer
```

25. [procedure] Display all the numbers in the list.

26. [function] Return the sum of the numbers in the list.

27. [procedure] Delete the fifth node of the list, if it exists.

28. [procedure] Interchange the first and second nodes of the list, if they exist.

29. A local business needs to store the name, address, phone number, and number of purchases of each of its several hundred customers. Write the declarations for a linked list to hold this information.

30. A student needs to store the name, meeting time, and number of credits for all of the courses that she is interested in taking next semester. Write the declarations for a linked list to hold this information.

31. Write a program that requests a positive integer as input from the keyboard and then creates a linked list holding the numbers 1 through N.

32. Suppose a text file contains the information in Table 12.1, with each of the eight items of data on a separate line. Write a program that places the contents of the file in a linked list with each node containing the name and attendance for a monument.

Lincoln Memorial	170
Vietnam Veterans Memorial	346
Washington Monument	130
Jefferson Memorial	108

Table 12.1 Visits to Monuments (in thousands) in April 1989
(*Source:* National Park Service)

33. Suppose a typed file of records contains the information in Table 12.2, with the data on each line comprising a record. Write a program that places the contents of the file in a linked list.

Company	Rooms (1000s)	Properties
Holiday	316	1671
Best Western	159	1758
Marriott	125	487
Quality	122	1060
Ramada	108	665

Table 12.2 Top Hotel Chains
(*Source*: American Hotel and Motel Association)

34. A polynomial of degree n is an expression of the form

$$a_n x^n + a_{n-1} x^n + \ldots + a_1 x + a_0$$

where the coefficients a_n, a_{n-1}, ..., a_1, and a_0 are real numbers, n is a nonnegative integer and $a_n \neq 0$. A polynomial can be represented in a linked list with each node storing the coefficient and degree of a single nonzero term. For instance, the linked list

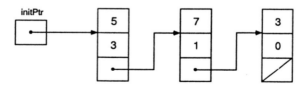

represents the polynomial $5x^3 + 7x + 3$.

Write a program that

(a) requests the coefficients and exponents of a polynomial as input from the keyboard and builds the linked list representing the polynomial.
(b) requests a real number r as input from the keyboard and evaluates the polynomial at r, that is, "plugs in" r for x. (The evaluation should be carried out with a function.)

SOLUTIONS TO PRACTICE PROBLEMS 12.1

1. [run] (See Figure 12.9.)
   10
   10

2. [run] (See Figure 12.10)
   10
   5

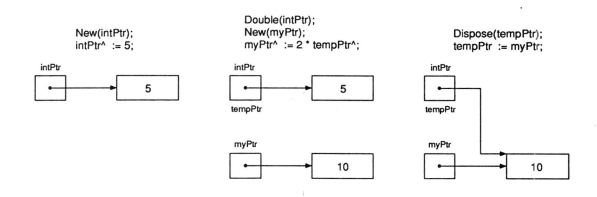

Figure 12.9 Diagrams of Key Statements for Practice Problem 1

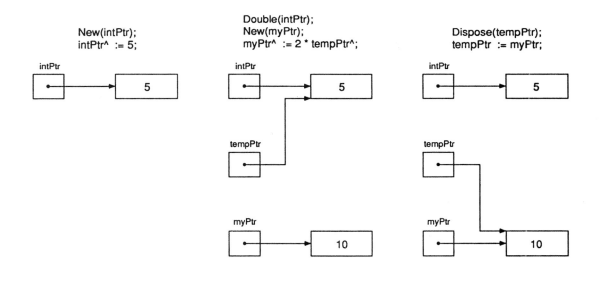

Figure 12.10 Diagrams of Key Statements for Practice Problem 2

12.2 ORDERED LINKED LISTS

In Chapter 9, arrays of records sorted on a field (the key field) of the record type allowed fast searching and the ordered display of data. Linked lists also can be ordered and provide similar benefits. Both sorted storage types have relative advantages and disadvantages. These factors must be weighed when choosing a data representation for a specific application. Sorted arrays can be searched very quickly but cannot be conveniently changed; inserting and deleting entries are time consuming and awkward. While ordered linked lists cannot be searched as quickly as sorted arrays, insertion and deletion operations are easier to implement.

An ordered linked list is a linked list in which the nodes are ordered by one of the fields. This field is known as the **key field**. Figure 12.11 shows an ordered linked list containing the same nodes as the linked list shown in Figure 12.3. The nodes in Figure 12.11, though, are ordered alphabetically by the name field.

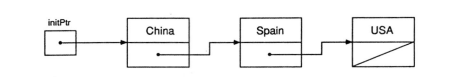

Figure 12.11   An Ordered Linked List

When information is ordered with an array, the data first are placed into the array and then sorted. The records of an ordered linked list, however, can be inserted directly into the list in their proper order. This technique is called an **insertion sort**.

Let's consider algorithms to perform the following tasks for an ordered linked list.

1. Insert an item

2. Delete an item

3. Search for an item

Inserting an Item Into an Ordered Linked List

Figure 12.12 shows the steps and code required to insert Sweden between Spain and USA in the ordered linked list of Figure 12.11.

The technique presented inserts a new node between two existing nodes. Let's now consider inserting nodes at the beginning and the end.

Inserting at the end is essentially the same as inserting in the middle. In this case, assume predPtr points to the last node of the list and curPtr points to NIL.

Section 12.1 gave the process for inserting at the beginning of a linked list. In this case, predPtr is NIL and curPtr points to the first node of the list (or is NIL if the list is empty). Inserting into an empty list (consisting solely of initPtr with value NIL) can be thought of as inserting a node at the beginning of a nonempty list. In both cases, predPtr is NIL and initPtr will finally point to the new node.

1. Assume predPtr and curPtr point to the nodes between which the new country will be inserted. Execute:

```
New(newPtr);
newPtr^.name := 'Sweden';
```

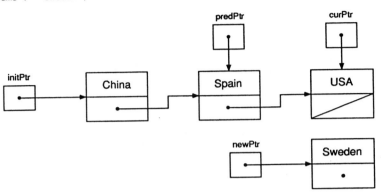

2. Since Sweden will precede USA, set the pointer in Sweden's record to USA. Execute:

```
newPtr^.next := curPtr;
```

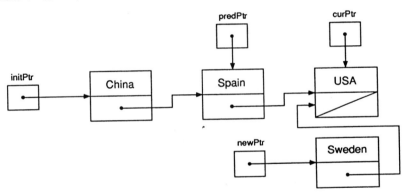

3. To complete the process, make Spain point to Sweden. Execute:

```
predPtr^.next := newPtr;
```

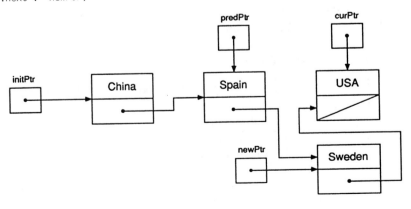

Figure 12.12 Inserting a Node in an Ordered List

1. Assume curPtr points to the node to delete and predPtr points to the preceding node.

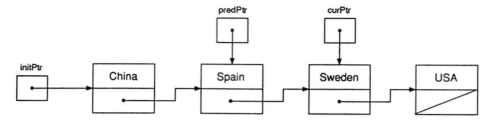

2. To remove Sweden from the list, make USA follow Spain. Execute:

   ```
   predPtr^.next := curPtr^.next;
   ```

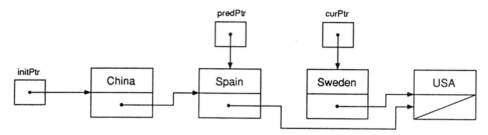

3. Finally, free the memory used to store Sweden. Execute:

   ```
   Dispose(curPtr);
   ```

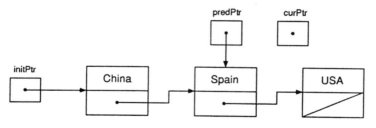

Figure 12.13   Deleting a Node in an Ordered List

Deleting an Item From an Ordered Linked List

Figure 12.13 shows the steps and code required to delete Sweden from the ordered linked list of Figure 12.12(c).

The technique presented deletes a node between two other nodes. Let's now consider deleting nodes at the beginning and the end.

Deleting from the end is essentially the same as deleting from the middle. For this operation, assume curPtr points to the last node of the list and predPtr to the preceding node.

When deleting from the beginning of the list, predPtr points to NIL and curPtr points to the first node of the list. The deletion is carried out by advancing initPtr to the second node of the list and disposing of curPtr. Deleting the node of a one-node list is essentially the same case.

Searching for an Item in an Ordered Linked List

The search procedure is used not only to determine if an item is in a linked list, but to find the proper places for insertions and deletions. The procedure should assign values to three VAR parameters. These are the Boolean parameter *found*, which tells if the item is in the list, and the pointer parameters predPtr and curPtr, which are needed for insertion and deletion. Assume the value of the parameter *quarry* is the item for which to search.

Initially curPtr points to the beginning of the list. Then curPtr is advanced successively, with predPtr immediately following, until curPtr either points to *quarry*, points to the node just past where *quarry* would have been, or is NIL. The pointer predPtr initially is set to NIL (no node precedes the first node). If the value of predPtr is still NIL when the search process ends, *quarry* is, or should precede, the value of the first node. Similarly, when the search ends with curPtr equal to NIL, the *quarry* node is missing and should follow the last node.

```
PROCEDURE OrderedSearch (    quarry              : STRING;
                             initPtr             : ListPointer;
                         VAR predPtr, curPtr : ListPointer;
                         VAR found               : Boolean);
    VAR done : Boolean;      {Is the search complete?}
    BEGIN
      predPtr := NIL;
      curPtr := initPtr;
      found := False;
      done := (curPtr = NIL);
      WHILE NOT done DO
        IF quarry > curPtr^.name THEN
            BEGIN
              predPtr := curPtr;
              curPtr := curPtr^.next;
              done := (curPtr = NIL)
            END
          ELSE
            done := True;
      IF curPtr <> NIL THEN
          found := (quarry = curPtr^.name)
    END;
```

Procedures to insert or delete items from an ordered linked list must begin by calling OrderedSearch to set predPtr and curPtr. The parameter predPtr is not needed just to search. It was included to give OrderedSearch the versatility also to serve the insert and delete processes.

Comments:

1. Linked lists are not random-access structures like arrays, but they have advantages that make them preferable in many situations. Think carefully when selecting the best representation for a set of data. Often the types of operations to be performed on the data must be considered.

2. The difference in design of linked lists and arrays affects the efficiency of essential processes. (See Table 12.3.)

	Insert	Delete	Search
Array	Very Fast	Very Slow	Slow
Linked List	Very Fast	Slow	Slow
Ordered Array	Slow	Slow	Very Fast
Ordered Linked List	Fast	Fast	Fast

Table 12.3 Comparisons Between Arrays and Linked Lists

3. A complete algorithm for insertion should address the possibility that the item to be inserted is already in the list.

PRACTICE PROBLEMS 12.2

1. Why is a search faster with an ordered linked list than with an unordered linked list?

2. Why is a search faster with an ordered array than with an ordered linked list?

EXERCISES 12.2

1. Why is inserting an item into an ordered linked list faster than with an ordered array? (Assume the proper position for the item has been identified.)

2. Why is inserting faster with an unordered linked list than with an ordered linked list?

3. Why is deleting slower with an unordered linked list than with an ordered linked list?

4. After an item has been located, why is deleting faster with an ordered linked list than with an ordered array?

5. Explain why the algorithm for deleting a node from the middle of an ordered linked list is the same as the algorithm for deleting a node from the end.

6. Explain why the algorithm for inserting a node at the beginning of an ordered linked list is different from the algorithm for inserting in the middle or at the end of the list.

In Exercises 7 through 12, assume an ordered linked has been built with records of type **NumberData** as shown below.

```
TYPE ListPointer = ^NumberData;
     NumberData  = RECORD
                     num  : Integer;
                     next : ListPointer
                   END;
```

7. Write the procedure OrderedSearch (initPtr : ListPointer; quarry : Integer; VAR found : Boolean; VAR curPtr, predPtr : ListPointer) to search for the number quarry in the ordered linked list pointed to by initPtr. If quarry is located, then the value of *found* should be True, curPtr should point to quarry's node, and predPtr should point to the preceding node. (If the first node of the list contains quarry, predPtr should be set to NIL.) If quarry is not located, then the value of *found* should be False; and predPtr and curPtr should point to the nodes preceding and following the position where quarry would have appeared. Base your program on the search procedure given in this section.

8. Write the procedure Insert (initPtr : ListPointer; quarry : Integer) to insert the number quarry in the ordered linked list pointed to by initPtr. Use the procedure OrderedSearch from Exercise 7.

9. Write the procedure Delete (initPtr : ListPointer; quarry : Integer) to delete the number quarry from the ordered linked list pointed to by initPtr. Use the procedure OrderedSearch from Exercise 7.

10. Write the Boolean function InOrder (initPtr : ListPointer) : Boolean; that returns True if the numbers in the list pointed to by initPtr are in ascending order, and False otherwise.

11. Write the procedure ReverseOrder (initPtr : ListPointer) that reverses the order of the linked list pointed to by initPtr. The procedure will convert an ascending list to a descending one, and vice versa. (Be sure to Dispose of any unneeded dynamic variables.)

12. Write the procedure DeleteEvens (initPtr : ListPointer) that deletes all even numbers from the ordered linked list pointed to by initPtr. (Test your program by creating a list of the first hundred positive integers and then displaying the list after it is processed by DeleteEvens.)

13. Table 12.4 ranks the states according to their "general healthiness." Assume the states are stored in this order in a text file, with one state per line. Write a program that places the states and their ranking in a linked list ordered by the state name, and then displays the states in alphabetical order along with their ranking.

1 Utah	14 Wisconsin	27 Pennsylvania	40 Rhode Island
2 North Dakota	15 South Dakota	28 Connecticut	41 North Carolina
3 Idaho	16 Iowa	29 Kentucky	42 Alabama
4 Minnesota	17 Maine	30 New Jersey	43 Maryland
5 Hawaii	18 California	31 Missouri	44 Florida
6 Vermont	19 Massachusetts	32 Ohio	45 Georgia
7 Nebraska	20 Alaska	33 Virginia	46 South Carolina
8 Colorado	21 Indiana	34 Arkansas	47 Nevada
9 Wyoming	22 Arizona	35 West Virginia	48 Michigan
10 Montana	23 Oklahoma	36 Illinois	49 Mississippi
11 Washington	24 New Hampshire	37 New York	50 Delaware
12 Oregon	25 Kansas	38 Louisiana	
13 New Mexico	26 Texas	39 Tennessee	

Table 12.4 States Ranked According to "General Healthiness"
Source: Northwest National Life Insurance Company

14. If a linked list is ordered alphabetically, searching for an element can be optimized by creating 26 separate ordered linked lists, one for each letter of the alphabet. The first node in each linked list can in turn be accessed by declaring an array of pointers (indexed with A through Z) where each array element points to the particular ordered linked list that holds data beginning with the same letter as the index of the element. If the items in Table 12.4 are stored in this data structure, then, for example, stateArray[T] points to the node containing "Tennessee", which in turn points to the node containing "Texas", which has a NIL pointer field. On the other hand, stateArray[Z] is the NIL pointer. Write a program using this data structure that builds the ordered linked lists, requests the name of a state, and displays its ranking.

SOLUTIONS TO PRACTICE PROBLEMS 12.2

1. The advantage of an ordered linked list is realized when the sought after item is not in the list. The ordered list need only be searched until the quarry's position is passed, whereas the unordered list must be searched to the end.

2. A binary search can be used with an ordered array, whereas an ordered linked list must be searched with the less efficient sequential search.

12.3 QUEUES, STACKS, AND BINARY TREES

Queues, stacks, and binary trees are important applications of pointers. Queues and stacks are linked lists with restricted access. Binary trees are linked lists for which each record has two pointer fields.

Queues

The word "queue" is used in England as a verb meaning "to form a line," as in "Brits always queue up for a bus." It also is used as a noun meaning "a line," as in "Look at the long queue waiting for the bus." People join the queue at the end, and leave the queue (to board the bus) from the front.

A **queue** can be represented as a linked list in which records are added to the end and removed from the front of the list. Called "first come, first served" or "first in, first out" storage systems, queues bring forth the image of people waiting in a line or marbles rolling through a pipe. Many applications use queues since they preserve the order of the incoming data and thus act as delay devices.

EXAMPLE 1   The registrar at the University of Maryland creates a waiting list for oversubscribed courses. As students DROP courses, waiting students are ADDed on a "first come, first served" basis. The following program uses a queue to process the waiting list for a specific course. Assume a file (possibly empty) has been created for the course.

```
PROGRAM AddCS101;
{ Process the waiting list for a course }

USES Crt;

TYPE StudentList = ^Student;
     Student    = RECORD
                      name : STRING;        { Student name    }
                      next : StudentList    { Points back to  }
                  END;                      {    person behind }
     QueueInfo   = RECORD
                      lineLength : Integer;     { Current length }
                      head       : StudentList; { Next to get in }
                      tail       : StudentList  { Last in line }
                  END;

VAR done     : Boolean;   { True when user selects Quit option }
    choice   : Integer;   { User's choice from menu }
    fileName : STRING;    { File holding line information }
    waitList : QueueInfo; { Record holding line status }

PROCEDURE LoadList (VAR waitList : QueueInfo; VAR fileName : STRING);
{ Build linked list from the information file }
  VAR waitFile : Text;
      listPtr  : StudentList;
  BEGIN
    waitList.lineLength := 0;
    waitList.head := NIL;
    waitList.tail := NIL;
    Write('Enter waiting list file name: ');
    Readln(fileName);
    Assign(waitFile, filename);
    Reset(waitFile);
    WHILE NOT EOF(waitFile) DO
      BEGIN
        New(listPtr);
        Readln(waitFile, listPtr^.name);
        listPtr^.next := waitList.head;
        waitList.head := listPtr;
        waitList.lineLength := waitList.lineLength + 1;
        IF waitList.lineLength = 1 THEN
            waitList.tail := waitList.head
      END;
    Close(waitFile)
  END;
```

```
PROCEDURE GetChoice (VAR choice : Integer);
{ Display menu and get choice from user }
  BEGIN
    REPEAT
      ClrScr;
      Writeln('1. Append student to waiting list');
      Writeln('2. Admit student to course');
      Writeln('3. Display waiting list');
      Writeln('4. Quit');
      Writeln;
      Write('Enter choice: ');
      Readln(choice)
    UNTIL choice IN [1..4];
    ClrScr
  END;

PROCEDURE AppendStudent (VAR waitList : QueueInfo);
{ Add a student to the end of the line }
  VAR name : STRING;
  BEGIN
    Write('Enter name of student: ');
    Readln(name);
    IF name <> '' THEN
      BEGIN
        IF waitList.lineLength < 1 THEN
            BEGIN
              New(waitList.head);
              waitList.tail := waitList.head
            END
          ELSE
            BEGIN
              New(waitList.tail^.next);
              waitList.tail := waitList.tail^.next
            END;
        waitList.tail^.name := name;
        waitList.tail^.next := NIL; { No one is behind tail }
        waitList.lineLength := waitList.lineLength + 1
      END;
    Writeln;
    Write('Student added to list.  Press ENTER to continue.');
    Readln
  END;
```

```
PROCEDURE RemoveStudent (VAR waitList : QueueInfo);
{ First student in line is removed--i.e. gets into the class }
  VAR listPtr : StudentList;
  BEGIN
    IF waitList.lineLength < 1 THEN
       Writeln('No students are on the waiting list.')
     ELSE
       BEGIN
         Writeln(waitList.head^.name,
                 ' was taken from the list');
         waitList.lineLength := waitList.lineLength - 1;
         listPtr := waitList.head;
         waitList.head := waitList.head^.next;
         listPtr^.next := NIL;
         IF waitList.lineLength < 1 THEN
           waitList.tail := NIL;
         Dispose(listPtr);
       END;
    Writeln;
    Write('Press ENTER to continue. ');
    Readln
  END;

PROCEDURE DisplayList (waitList : QueueInfo);
{ Display current status of the line }
  VAR listPtr : StudentList;
  BEGIN
    IF waitList.lineLength < 1 THEN
       Writeln('No students are on the waiting list')
     ELSE
       BEGIN
         Writeln(waitList.lineLength,
                 ' students are waiting:');
         listPtr := waitList.head;
         WHILE listPtr <> NIL DO
           BEGIN
             Writeln('  ', listPtr^.name);
             listPtr := listPtr^.next
           END
       END;
    Writeln;
    Write('Press ENTER to continue.');
    Readln
  END;
```

```
PROCEDURE SaveList (waitList : QueueInfo; fileName : STRING);
{ Save the current list in a text file }
  VAR waitFile : Text;
      listPtr  : StudentList;
  BEGIN
    Write('Saving list...');
    Assign(waitFile, fileName);
    Rewrite(waitFile);
    waitList.tail := NIL;
    WHILE waitList.head <> NIL DO
      BEGIN
        Writeln(waitFile, waitList.head^.name);
        listPtr := waitList.head;
        waitList.head := waitList.head^.next;
        listPtr^.next := NIL;
        Dispose(listPtr);
        Write('.')
      END;
    Close(waitFile);
    Write('Done.')
  END;

BEGIN
  ClrScr;
  done := False;
  LoadList(waitList, fileName);
  REPEAT
    GetChoice(choice);
    CASE choice OF
      1 : AppendStudent(waitList);
      2 : RemoveStudent(waitList);
      3 : DisplayList(waitList);
      4 : done := True
    END
  UNTIL done;
  SaveList(waitList, fileName)
END.
```

Stacks

The **stack** data structure derives its name from the stack of plates commonly found in cafeteria lines. (See Figure 12.14.) The cafeteria staff adds new plates to the top of the pile and each customer also removes a plate from the top of the pile.

In Pascal, a stack can be implemented as a linked list in which records are added to and removed from the front of the list. Thus, it is a "last in, first out" storage structure. Stack operations have special terminology inspired by the model of a spring-loaded stack of plates. Adding an element is referred to as **pushing** the element on the stack, and removing an element is referred to as **popping** it from the stack.

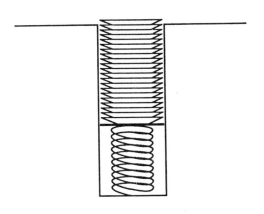

Figure 12.14 A Spring-loaded Stack of Plates

EXAMPLE 2   A **palindrome** is a word or phrase that reads the same from left to right and right to left (ignoring spaces and punctuation). A well-known example is "MADAM I'M ADAM." The following program requests a string as input and determines if it is a palindrome.

```
PROGRAM Palindrome;
{ Decides whether a phrase is a palindrome or not }

USES Crt;

TYPE ListPointer = ^List;
     List        = RECORD
                      oneChar : Char;
                      next    : ListPointer
                   END;

VAR stack  : ListPointer;
    phrase : STRING;

PROCEDURE MakeStack (phrase : STRING; VAR stack : ListPointer);
{ Build a stack using only the letters in the phrase }
  VAR newChar : ListPointer;
      count   : Integer;
  BEGIN
    stack := NIL;
    FOR count := 1 TO Length(phrase) DO
      IF phrase[count] IN ['A'..'Z', 'a'..'z', '0'..'9'] THEN
        BEGIN
          New(newChar);
          newChar^.oneChar := phrase[count];
          newChar^.next := stack;
          stack := newChar;
          newChar := NIL
        END
  END;
```

```
FUNCTION TheSame (VAR phrase : STRING; stack : ListPointer) : Boolean;
{ Compare input phrase to stack }
  VAR oldPtr : ListPointer;
      count  : Integer;
      okay   : Boolean;
  BEGIN
    okay := True;   { Assume the same, try to disprove }
    FOR count := 1 TO Length(phrase) DO
      IF phrase[count] IN ['A'..'Z', 'a'..'z', '0'..'9'] THEN
        BEGIN
          IF UpCase(stack^.oneChar) <> UpCase(phrase[count]) THEN
            okay := False;
          oldPtr := stack;
          stack := stack^.next;
          oldPtr^.next := NIL;
          Dispose(oldPtr)
        END;
    TheSame := okay
  END;

BEGIN
  ClrScr;
  Write('Enter a phrase: ');
  Readln(phrase);
  MakeStack(phrase, stack);
  Write('This phrase is ');
  IF NOT TheSame(phrase, stack) THEN
    Write('not ');
  Write('a palindrome.')
END.

[run]
Enter a phrase: Evil Olive
The phrase is a palindrome.
```

Binary Trees

Trees are studied in "discrete mathematics" courses offered by computer science and mathematics departments. A tree is a special kind of graph consisting of points, called **vertices**, and straight lines, called **edges**. Figure 12.15 shows several examples of trees. The topmost vertex of a tree is called the **root**. A **path** is a sequence of connected edges. (Figure 12.15(b) shows a path from the root to the vertex B.) In a tree, there is a unique path from the root to every other vertex. The vertices immediately connected to the root are called its **children**, and the root is called the **parent** of these vertices. Similarly, each vertex is the parent of the vertices immediately below it. (See Figure 12.16.) A **leaf** is a vertex with no children.

A **binary tree** is a tree in which each vertex has, at most, two children. That is, at most two edges extend from each node. In Figure 12.15, tree (c) is a binary tree. Binary trees are used to store data in hierarchical form or to order information for fast access. In Pascal, a binary tree is implemented as a linked list in which each node is a record having data and *two* pointer fields, a pointer to the

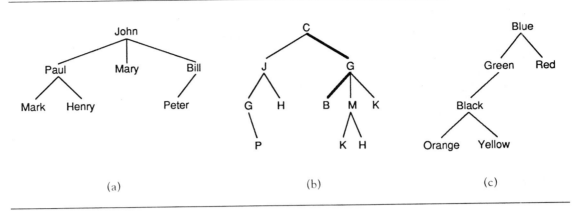

Figure 12.15   Examples of Trees

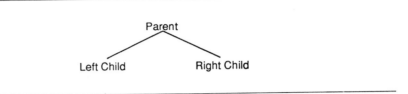

Figure 12.16   A Parent with Two Children

left child and a pointer to the right child. (A NIL pointer indicates the absence of a child.)

Consider the problems of adding and searching for names in a list. If the names are stored in a text file, new names can be added easily to the end of the file; but, searching for a name is time consuming. If the names are stored in alphabetical order in an array, a binary search efficiently locates a name. However, adding a new name is a hassle. Binary trees provide a compromise. Searching for a name in a binary tree is faster than in a text file and new names can be added more easily than with a sorted array.

Figure 12.17 shows a binary tree containing the names of well-known computer languages. Notice that for each language, the left child precedes it alphabetically and the right child follows it alphabetically. A binary tree is created one node at a time; the first name received is placed at the root.

To illustrate the process, let's add the language Logo to the tree in Figure 12.17. First compare Logo with the root, Pascal. Since Logo precedes Pascal alphabetically, consider the left child of Pascal, C. (If Pascal lacked a left child, Logo would be made the left child.) Since Logo follows C alphabetically, consider the right child of C, Forth. (If C lacked a right child, Logo would be made the right child.) Continuing in this manner, Fortran is considered next and then Logo is made the right child of Fortran. (See Figure 12.18.) Names are searched for in the same manner they would be added to the tree. For instance, the name BASIC is searched for by successively comparing it with Pascal, C, and APL until it is located as a child of APL. If the trail ends at a leaf and the sought-after language isn't found, we conclude that the language is not in the tree.

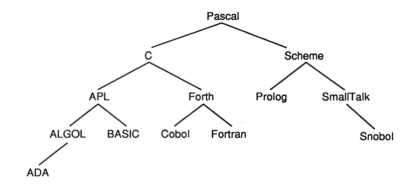

Figure 12.17 A Binary Tree of Programming Languages

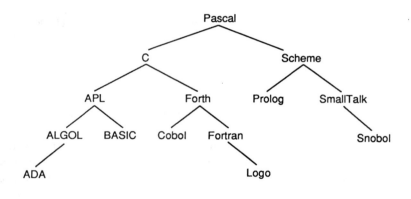

Figure 12.18 A Binary Tree of Programming Languages with Logo Inserted

EXAMPLE 3   Assume a text file contains the names of programming languages in Table 12.5, one per line. The following program builds a binary tree with a node for each language. (The tree in Figure 12.17 will be created.) The user can search for a language and, if it does not exist, choose to add it to the tree.

```
PROGRAM SearchForLanguage;
{ Build and search a binary tree of computer languages }

USES Crt;

TYPE TreePointer = ^Tree;
     Tree        = RECORD
                     name  : STRING;       { Name of language }
                     left  : TreePointer;  { Ptr. to left child }
                     right : TreePointer   { Ptr. to rt. child }
                   END;
```

```
VAR languageTree      : TreePointer;
    language, response : STRING;

PROCEDURE AddLanguage(VAR languageTree : TreePointer;
                          language      : STRING);
{ Put a language into its appropriate position in the tree }
  VAR newNode, oldNode, newEntry : TreePointer;
  BEGIN
    New(newEntry);
    newEntry^.name := language;
    newEntry^.left := NIL;
    newEntry^.right := NIL;
    IF languageTree = NIL THEN
        languageTree := newEntry
      ELSE
        BEGIN
          newNode := languageTree;
          REPEAT
            oldNode := newNode;
            IF language <= oldNode^.name THEN
                newNode := oldNode^.left
              ELSE
                newNode := oldNode^.right
          UNTIL newNode = NIL;
          IF language < oldNode^.name THEN
              oldNode^.left := newEntry
            ELSE
              oldNode^.right := newEntry
        END
  END;

PROCEDURE LoadTree (VAR languageTree : TreePointer);
{ Construct a binary tree from the file of languages }
  VAR languageFile : Text;
      fileName,
      language     : STRING;
      BEGIN
        languageTree := NIL;
        Write('Enter languages file name: ');
        Readln(fileName);
        Assign(languageFile, fileName);
        Reset(languageFile);
        WHILE NOT Eof(languageFile) DO
          BEGIN
            Readln(languageFile, language);
            AddLanguage(languageTree, language)
          END;
        Close(languageFile)
      END;
```

```
      FUNCTION LanguageInTree (languageTree : TreePointer;
                              language    : STRING) : Boolean;
      { Returns True if the language is in the tree }
        VAR searchPtr : TreePointer;
            found     : Boolean;
        BEGIN
          found := False;
          searchPtr := languageTree;
          WHILE (NOT found) AND (searchPtr <> NIL) DO
            IF searchPtr^.name = language THEN
              found := True
            ELSE
              IF language < searchPtr^.name THEN
                searchPtr := searchPtr^.left
              ELSE
                searchPtr := searchPtr^.right;
          LanguageInTree := found
        END;

  BEGIN
    ClrScr;
    LoadTree(languageTree);
    Write('Language to search for (ENTER to quit): ');
    Readln(language);
    WHILE language <> '' DO
      BEGIN
        IF LanguageInTree(languageTree, language) THEN
          Writeln('That language is in the tree')
        ELSE
          BEGIN
            Write('That language is not in the tree.  ');
            Write('Want to add it? ');
            Readln(response);
            IF (response = 'Y') OR (response = 'y') THEN
              BEGIN
                AddLanguage(languageTree, language);
                Writeln(language, ' was added to the language tree.')
              END
          END;
        Writeln;
        Write('Language to search for (ENTER to quit): ');
        Readln(language)
      END
  END.
```

Pascal	Scheme	Prolog	C	SmallTalk	APL	ALGOL
BASIC	Forth	Fortran	Snobol	Cobol	ADA	

Table 12.5 Programming Languages

Comments:

1. A binary tree constructed from a sorted list of items produces an unbalanced tree with just one path. At the opposite extreme is the balanced tree where nearly all the nodes that are not leaves have two descendants. The more balanced the tree, the greater the advantage gained from using the tree for searching. On average, binary trees save a significant amount of time.

2. The computer uses queues and stacks to manage its own affairs. For instance, queues are used for the keyboard and printer buffers and a stack is used to hold temporary results of calculations and information about the state of programs.

3. Stacks also can be implemented with arrays, but implementing queues with arrays is awkward.

4. After the binary tree in Example 3 is built, the languages can easily be displayed in alphabetical order. This task is carried out with recursion in Section 12.4.

PRACTICE PROBLEMS 12.3

1. Suppose the language Formac is added to the binary tree in Fig 12.14. Where will it be stored?

2. If all the statements related to oldPtr are removed in the function TheSame of Example 2, the output of the program will not change. Why are these statements present?

EXERCISES 12.3

In Exercises 1 through 6, determine whether an ordered linked list, a queue, a stack, or a binary tree is the best structure to choose in writing a program to simulate the situation.

1. An alphabetized file cabinet.

2. A bank teller's window.

3. A can of tennis balls.

4. A corporation where the CEO and each employee have at most two immediate subordinates.

5. A stop sign at a busy intersection.

6. A magazine rack at a newsstand.

7. Stacks can be implemented using either linked lists or arrays. Are both structures equally suitable for the implementation of a queue? Explain your answer.

8. If a binary tree is supposed to store a list of names in alphabetical order, why would building the tree from an ordered list defeat the purpose?

9. Much of the data processed in a computer's memory is stored in *buffers*. One type of buffer permits a queue to form until a certain critical length is reached. Once that length is reached, the buffer is *flushed* by removing all or most of the items from the queue. For instance, data to be output to a file often are stored in a buffer until more than 128 bytes accumulate. Then the first 128 bytes are written in succession to the file and the 129th byte becomes first in the queue. When the file is closed, any data remaining in the buffer are flushed into the file from memory.

Write a program that simulates a buffer by successively requesting words from the keyboard and building a queue of characters. The queue should contain successive characters from the words entered. When the queue reaches or exceeds 10 characters, 8 characters should be flushed by removing them from the queue and displaying them on the screen. Allow the user to continue entering words until EOD is entered. At that time, the remaining characters in the queue should be flushed.

```
[Sample run]
Enter phrase: Phineas
Enter phrase: Taylor
PhineasT
Enter phrase: Barnum
aylorBar
Enter phrase: EOD
num
```

10. Write a program to simulate the express line in a grocery check-out by displaying a line of stars showing the current status of the line (one star for each shopper). Assume the register is closed initially and customers are lining up to be serviced. Allow the user to place up to 10 shoppers in a queue by entering the number of items each shopper has in his or her cart (at least 1 and at most 10). Start the simulation either when 10 shoppers are in the queue or when −1 is entered. Assume each customer's purchase takes 3 seconds per item and then an additional 10 seconds (for payment and bagging) after all the items have been processed. The graphic representation of the line should be updated whenever a person leaves the line. When all the customers have been serviced, the simulation is over. (**Hints:** A delay in program execution of num seconds can be produced by the statement Delay(num * 1000). Delay is in the Crt Unit.)

The following declarations can be used to build a stack of Integers. In Exercises 11 through 17, use these declarations to write the following procedures, functions and programs.

```
TYPE StackPointer = ^StackRecord;
     StackRecord  = RECORD
                       num  : Integer;
                       next : StackPointer
                    END;
```

11. Write a procedure Push that adds one Integer to the current stack.

12. Write a function Pop that removes the top item on the stack and returns it as output.

13. Write a Boolean function IsEmpty that returns True if the stack is empty and False otherwise.

14. Write a procedure Exchange that switches the positions of the top two stack elements (if they exist). Use the Push, Pop, and IsEmpty subprograms from previous exercises.

15. Write a procedure ShowStack to display the stack in order from the top element to the bottom element. Use the subprograms from the previous exercises. (**Hint**: Use a temporary second stack.)

16. Write a program that allows the user to maintain a stack by choosing from the following menu items. (The program should use the subprograms from the previous exercises.)

(a) Push: Requests an Integer and adds it to the stack.
(b) Pop: Removes the top item on the stack and displays it.
(c) Exchange: Swaps the top two items on the stack.
(d) Display Stack: Displays the current stack from top to bottom.
(e) Quit: Exits the program.

17. A reverse-polish notation (RPN) calculator accepts commands of the form *<num1> <num2> <operator>*. For example, the sequence 2 3 + on an RPN calculator is equivalent to the standard form 2 + 3. Similarly, the sequence 2 3 + 6 * is the RPN counterpart of (2 + 3) * 6. Expressions are evaluated from left to right through successive simplifications. In this case, 2 3 + is evaluated first and replaced with 5 yielding 5 6 *. The number 30 is returned as the final result. A RPN calculator can be simulated with a stack.

Write a program that accepts a sequence of numbers and operators in valid RPN format as input and evaluates the sequence. Assume the items are entered one at a time from the keyboard, with the equal sign as trailer value. As an item is entered, if it is a number, Push it on the stack. If it is an operator, Pop the top two stack elements, perform the operation on the numbers, and Push the result back on the stack. (The subtraction operator subtracts the number at the top of the stack from the number below it.) For instance, the sequence 4 9 6 1 + − * is valid and is evaluated as 4 * (9 − (6 + 1)) to produce 8.

```
[sample run]
Enter an Integer or operator: 2
Enter an Integer or operator: 5
Enter an Integer or operator: +
Enter an Integer or operator: 3
Enter an Integer or operator: -
Enter an Integer or operator: =
Expression evaluates to: 4
```

Exercises 18 through 20, assume a typed file of records PRES.DAT has been created containing each US President's last name, first name, and the number of his presidency. Assume PRES.DAT is not ordered by either name or number of presidency.

18. Write a program that reads the file and builds a binary tree ordered by the last name and first name of each president. After requesting a President's last name and first name, the program should display his number in the order of Presidents.

19. Write a program that reads the file and builds a binary tree ordered by the presidency numbers. After requesting a presidency number from the keyboard, the name of that President should be displayed.

20. In many database applications, there is too much data in each record to store all the information in the binary tree. In such cases it is common to build a binary tree as if the entire record was being stored, but instead of the record itself, simply storing the file position number of the record. Then, if more data on a specific record is needed from the file, the file position number stored in the binary tree can be used with the Seek statement to get the entire record from the file. Write a program that builds a binary tree from the file PRES.DAT ordered by the presidency numbers. In each node, store only the presidency number and the file position of that president's full record. After requesting the presidency number from the keyboard, the program should find the corresponding node in the binary tree, use the number in the file position field to retrieve the full record from PRES.DAT, and display the President's name.

21. In a "doubly linked" list each node has both a forward and a backward pointer, thus giving bi-directional access to every node in the list. A declaration for a doubly linked list might be as follows.

```
TYPE ListPointer = ^NodeRecord;
     NodeRecord  = RECORD
                      data : STRING;
                      prev : ListPointer;
                      next : ListPointer
                   END;
```

One way to build such a list is to have the last node's *next* pointer be NIL and to have the first node's *prev* pointer be NIL. Pointers to the first and last nodes of the list are needed in order to access both ends.

Write a program that checks a sentence to see if it is a "word palindrome", that is, if the words of the sentence read the same backward and forward (ignoring punctuation and capitalization). An example is, "I am; therefore, am I?" Have the program request a sentence from the user one word at a time. After placing the words into consecutive nodes of a doubly linked list, traverse the sentence from both ends to check whether or not it is a "word palindrome." Test it on the sentence, "You can cage a swallow, can't you, but you can't swallow a cage, can you?"

SOLUTION TO PRACTICE PROBLEMS 12.3

1. Formac will be stored as the right child of Cobol, since it is less than Pascal, greater than C, less than Forth, and greater than Cobol.

2. Although the output will be identical, without oldPtr a dynamic variable will be orphaned at each pass of the loop. This is not serious for small lists, but for long lists or for lists with very large nodes, the program can run out of memory and produce an error message.

12.4 RECURSION

The modular approach to problem solving calls for breaking down a problem into simpler subproblems. In the resulting program, subprograms call other subprograms to perform successively simpler tasks. This idea can be extended to allow subprograms to call themselves. In order for this method to succeed, successive calls to the subprogram must reduce the problem to smaller problems of the same type and must eventually arrive at a base problem with a trivial solution. This process is called **recursion**.

The nth power of a number can be defined iteratively as

$$r^n = \underbrace{r \cdot r \cdots r}_{n \text{ terms}}$$

or recursively as

$$r^1 = r$$
$$r^n = r \cdot r^{n-1}$$

In the recursive definition, the power function is defined in terms of a smaller version of itself. For instance, the computation of r^4 is successively reduced to the computation of r^3, r^2, and finally r^1, a trivial case.

EXAMPLE 1 Define a function based on the iterative definition of a power.

SOLUTION The iterative definition of a power function requires two temporary variables. Also, the code does not resemble the definition.

```
FUNCTION Power (r : Real; n : Integer) : Real;
{ Code the iterative definition of power }
  VAR value : Real;
      term  : Integer;
  BEGIN
    value := 1;
    FOR term := 1 TO n DO
      value := r * value;
    Power := value
  END;
```

EXAMPLE 2 The following function declaration uses the recursive definition of power. It requires no extraneous variables and looks exactly like the definition.

```
FUNCTION Power (r : Real; n : Integer) : Real;
{ Code the recursive definition of power }
  BEGIN
    IF n = 1 THEN
        Power := r
      ELSE
        Power := r * Power(r, n - 1)
  END;
```

Recursive algorithms have two traits.

1. There is a "terminating case" with a direct solution.

2. There is an inductive step reducing the problem to one or more smaller versions of the same problem, with the reduction eventually culminating in the terminating case. This inductive step is called the **reducing step.**

The pseudocode for a recursive solution to a problem has the general form

IF the termination case is reached THEN
  Solve the terminating case directly
  ELSE
  Reduce the problem to one or more versions of the same problem closer to the
  terminating case

Suppose the function Power is called upon to compute Power(r, n), with $r = 2$ and $n = 3$. Figure 12.19 traces the process of evaluation. The value in (a) cannot be calculated right away since $n \neq 1$. Therefore, the recursive step replaces Power(2, 3) with the expression in (b). Similarly, Power(2, 2) in (b) is replaced by the expression in (c). Since $n = 1$ in (c), the termination case has been reached. Power(2, 1) is evaluated directly as 2. Now the recursion process traces backward through (c), (b), and (a), denoted as (c'), (b'), and (a') for the return trip. The value 2 replaces the expression Power(2, 1) in (c) to obtain 4. Then the value 4 replaces the expression Power(2, 2) in (b) to obtain 8. Finally, the value 8 is assigned to Power(2, 3) in (a).

Any subprogram using recursion can be rewritten using iteration, but sometimes the recursive solution is easier to understand and code.

Consider the task of displaying the countries in the linked list of Section 12.1. Since each record has a name field and a pointer field, any name and all the names in subsequent nodes can be displayed by setting the current pointer to the node containing the first desired name, displaying the name, and then advancing the current pointer to the next node. This process is repeated until reaching the NIL pointer.

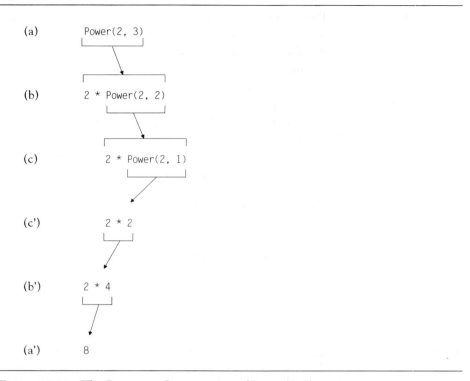

(a)   Power(2, 3)

(b)   2 * Power(2, 2)

(c)   2 * Power(2, 1)

(c')   2 * 2

(b')   2 * 4

(a')   8

Figure 12.19 The Recursive Computation of Power(2, 3)

EXAMPLE 3 Write a recursive procedure to display the countries of the linked list created in Example 3 of Section 12.1.

SOLUTION The initial pointer is passed to the procedure and assigned to tempPtr. The process terminates when the value of the parameter tempPtr becomes NIL.

```
PROCEDURE DisplayList (tempPtr : NationPointer);
{ Display the contents of each node of the linked
  list having tempPtr as its initial pointer }
  BEGIN
    IF tempPtr <> NIL THEN
      BEGIN
        Writeln(tempPtr^.name);
        DisplayList(tempPtr^.next)
      END
  END;
```

The subprograms considered so far could have been written easily with an iterative loop instead of recursion. Some problems, however, are much easier to solve with recursion. (See Examples 4 and 5.)

EXAMPLE 4 The following procedure uses recursion to display the contents of the binary tree of computer languages built in Example 3 of Section 12.3. The algorithm for obtaining the display has four steps. Step (a) is the terminating case and steps (b), (c), and (d) reduce the process to smaller trees.

(a) If the tree has no entries, stop. (terminating case.) Otherwise, do steps (b), (c), and (d).
(b) Display all names in the tree starting with the left child of the root.
(c) Display the item in the root.
(d) Display all names in the tree starting with the right child of the root.

```
PROCEDURE ShowTree (languageTree : TreePointer);
  BEGIN
    IF languageTree <> NIL THEN
      BEGIN
        ShowTree(languageTree^.left);
        Writeln(languageTree^.name);
        ShowTree(languageTree^.right)
      END
  END;
```

EXAMPLE 5 The following program uses recursion to create a magnificent drawing known as a *fractal*. A four-step algorithm creates the fractal.

(a) Specify an intricacy level, a non-negative integer, for the fractal.
(b) Start with a straight line. The line, shown in Figure 12.20(a), is called the level 0 fractal.
(c) To obtain the fractal for the next level, replace each line in the drawing with the sides of an isosceles right triangle having the line as hypotenuse. Figures 12.20(b), (c), and (d) show the level 1, 2, and 3 fractals.
(d) Repeat step (b) until the desired level of recursion is reached. Figure 12.21 shows a fractal of intricacy level 12.

The graphics statements used are explained in Chapter 10.

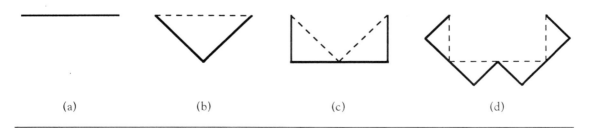

(a)   (b)   (c)   (d)

Figure 12.20 Fractals of Levels 0, 1, 2, and 3

```
PROGRAM Fractal;

USES Crt, Msgraph;

VAR dummy, level : Integer;
```

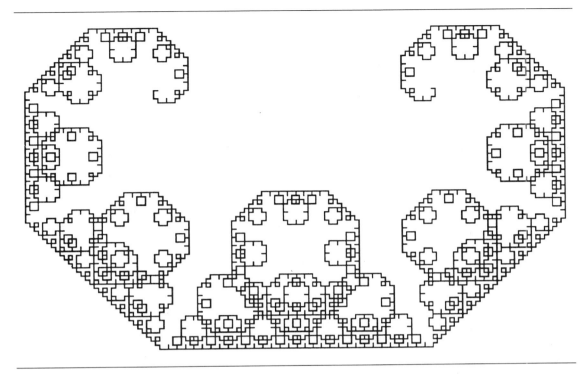

Figure 12.21   Fractal of Level 12

```
PROCEDURE Fract (x1, y1, x2, y2 : Real; level : Integer);
  VAR newX, newY : Real;
  BEGIN
    IF level = 0 THEN
        BEGIN
          { draw the line from (x1, y1) to (x2, y2) }
          _MoveTo_w(x1, y1);
          _LineTo_w(x2, y2)
        END
      ELSE
        BEGIN
          newX := (x1 + x2) / 2 + (y2 - y1) / 2;
          newY := (y1 + y2) / 2 - (x2 - x1) / 2;
          Fract(x1, y1, newX, newY, level - 1);
          Fract(newX, newY, x2, y2, level - 1)
        END
  END;

BEGIN
  ClrScr;
  Write('Enter level of fractal: ');
  Readln(level);
  { invoke graphics mode and specify coordinate range }
  dummy := _SetVideoMode(_MaxResMode);
  _SetWindow(True, 0, 0, 20, 15);
  Fract(6.0, 10.0, 14.0, 10.0, level)
END.
```

Comments:

1. The terminating case of the recursive solution of a problem is also called the *base case* or *stopping case*.

2. If a problem can be solved equally well with either an iterative method or a recursive method, then the iterative method should be used. Usually, iterative methods execute faster and make less of a demand on memory.

3. If a recursive algorithm is coded incorrectly and the terminating case is never reached, the program probably will terminate with the run-time error "Stack overflow."

4. Another kind of recursion, called *indirect recursion* results when two procedures call each other. In the following program, the declaration "PROCEDURE Two; FORWARD" alerts the compiler that procedure *Two* is defined after it is referenced. The variable *counter* is used to prevent an infinite loop.

```
PROGRAM IndirectRecursionDemo;

USES Crt;

VAR counter : Integer;

PROCEDURE Two; FORWARD;

PROCEDURE One;
  BEGIN
    counter := counter + 1;
    IF counter < 5 THEN
        BEGIN
          Write(1:3);
          Two
        END
  END;

PROCEDURE Two;
  BEGIN
    Write(2:3);
    One
  END;

BEGIN
  ClrScr;
  counter := 0;
  One
END.

[run]
   1  2  1  2  1  2  1  2
```

PRACTICE PROBLEMS 12.4

1. If *n* is a positive integer, then n factorial (written *n!*) is the product of the numbers from 1 through *n*. Write a recursive function to calculate *n!*.

2. What is the output of the following program.

```
FUNCTION Alpha (letter : Char) : STRING;
  BEGIN
    IF letter = 'A' THEN
        Alpha := 'A'
      ELSE
        Alpha := letter + Alpha(Pred(letter))
  END;

BEGIN
  Writeln(Alpha('H'))
END.
```

EXERCISES 12.4

In Exercises 1 through 4, determine the output of the program.

1.
```
FUNCTION Sum (n : Integer) : Integer;
  BEGIN
    IF (n = 0) THEN
        Sum := 0
      ELSE
        Sum := n + Sum(n - 1)
  END;

BEGIN
  Writeln(Sum(5))
END.
```

2.
```
PROCEDURE Reverse (n : Integer);
  VAR allButLastDigit : Integer;
  BEGIN
    Write(n MOD 10);
    allButLastDigit := n DIV 10;
    IF allButLastDigit = 0 THEN
        Writeln
      ELSE
        Reverse(allButLastDigit)
  END;

BEGIN
  Reverse(12345)
END.
```

3. PROCEDURE Stars (n : Integer);
```
    BEGIN
      IF n = 0 THEN
          Writeln
        ELSE
          BEGIN
            Write('*');
            Stars(n - 1)
          END
    END;

  BEGIN
    Stars(6)
  END.
```

4. FUNCTION Prod (m, n : Integer) : Integer;
```
    BEGIN
      IF n = 1 THEN
          Prod := m
        ELSE
          Prod := m + Prod(m, n - 1)
    END;

  BEGIN
    Writeln(Prod(5, 4))
  END.
```

In Exercises 5 and 6, find the errors.

5. FUNCTION SkipSum (n : Integer) : Integer;
```
    BEGIN
      IF n = 0 THEN
          SkipSum := 0
        ELSE
          SkipSum := n + SkipSum(n - 2)
    END;
```

6. PROCEDURE HiThere;
```
    BEGIN
      Writeln('Hello');
      HiThere
    END;

  BEGIN
    HiThere
  END.
```

7. The number of subsets of r elements that can be selected from a set of n elements is written $C(n, r)$. $C(n, r)$ is also the coefficient of x^r in the binomial expansion of $(x + 1)^n$. If $r = 0$ *or* n, then the value of $C(n, r)$ is 1. Otherwise, $C(n, r) = C(n - 1, r - 1) + C(n - 1, r)$. Write a program that allows n to be input from the keyboard and displays the coefficients in the expansion of $(x + 1)^n$.

```
[sample run]
Enter a positive integer: 5
1  5  10  10  5  1
```

8. The selection sort of an array proceeds as follows: Find the largest element and exchange it with the last element of the array. The last element remains fixed. Find the largest of the remaining elements and exchange it with the next to the last element. Now the last two elements are in their proper place. Continue this process until the array is sorted. Write a procedure SelectionSort (VAR list : Names; length : Integer) that sorts the elements of the array *list*. Assume the data type Names is declared with TYPE Names = ARRAY [1..100] OF STRING and the array elements are stored with subscripts 1 through *length*.

9. The famous Fibonacci sequence, 1, 1, 2, 3, 5, 8, 13, . . ., begins with two 1s. After that, each number is the sum of the preceding two numbers. Write a recursive function to generate the *n*th term of the Fibonacci sequence.

10. The Greatest Common Divisor of two non-negative integers is the largest integer that divides both numbers. For instance, GCD(6, 15) = 3 and GCD(9, 0) = 9. The standard algorithm for calculating the greatest common divisor of two numbers depends on the fact that GCD(m, n) = GCD(n, m MOD n). Write a program that requests two positive integers as input and displays their greatest common divisor. Use a recursive function (with *n* = 0 as the termination case) to calculate the GCD.

11. The mortgage on a house is paid off in equal monthly payments for a period of years. If *P* is the initial amount of the mortgage, *pmt* is the monthly payment, and *r* is the annual rate of interest; then Balance(*n*), the amount owed after *n* months, can be computed as

```
Balance(n) = (1 + r / 1200) + Balance(P, pmt, r, n - 1)
```

Write a program that requests the amount of the mortgage, the monthly payment, the annual rate of interest, and the number of months elapsed as input, and displays the amount owed.

```
[sample run]
Enter the principal: 37284.45
Enter the monthly payment: 300
Enter the annual rate of interest: 9
Enter the number of monthly payments made: 240
The amount still owed is 23681.85
```

12. Write a recursive procedure to display the elements of an ordered linked list in reverse order (that is, from back to front).

13. Write a program that asks the user to input an arbitrary number of names, and then displays the names in the reverse order they were received. (Do not use arrays, files, or linked lists to store the names.)

14. Write a procedure to display a binary tree from right to left. (Example 4 displays a tree from left to right).

SOLUTIONS TO PRACTICE PROBLEMS 12.4

1. n! = n * (n - 1) * (n - 2) * ... * 3 * 2 * 1

   As written, *n!* can be calculated iteratively with a FOR loop; however, when rewritten as

   n! = n * ((n - 1) * (n - 2) * ... * 3 * 2 * 1) = n * (n - 1)!

   n! is expressed in terms of (n − 1)! and can be calculated recursively. All that is needed is a terminating case. In the original definition above, *n!* is defined for n ≥ 1, but the recursive definition does not make sense when n is 1. Therefore, 1! must be defined separately as the terminating case. Since the value of *n!* exceeds the range for Integers when n ≥8, the value returned by the function should be a Real number.

   ```
   FUNCTION Factorial(n : Integer) : Real;
     BEGIN
       IF n = 1 THEN
           Factorial := 1
         ELSE
           Factorial := n * Factorial(n - 1)
     END;
   ```

2. HGFEDCBA

   Recursive functions needn't have numeric parameters.

Chapter 12
Summary

1. The *pointer* data type allows data to be stored dynamically. The *New* statement allocates a portion of memory as the target of a pointer variable. This memory location can be deallocated with the statement *Dispose*.

2. A *linked list* data structure is a sequence of records, called *nodes*, where each node contains data fields and a pointer to the next node in the sequence. A pointer specifies the first node of the list. The last node points nowhere, that is, it has the value *NIL*.

3. An *ordered linked list* is a device for storing and updating a collection of data. As opposed to arrays, ordered linked lists are sorted as they are built, are easy to update, and do not require their size be known in advance.

4. *Queues* are data structures that can be implemented as linked lists in which data can only be inserted as the last node and only the first node can be deleted.

5. *Stacks* are data structures that can be implemented as linked lists in which data can only be inserted or deleted from one end.

6. A *binary tree* is a dynamic structure in which each node stores data and points to at most two *child* nodes. The data item in each left (right) child node is less (greater) than the data item in its *parent* node. Binary trees are easy to build and efficient to search.

7. A procedure or function that calls itself is said to be *recursive*. Recursive subprograms should have a *terminating* case with a direct solution and an *inductive* step that reduces the problem to one or more smaller problems.

Chapter 12
Programming Projects

1. In Pascal, the Integer data type is limited to values −32,768 through 32,767; however, integers of almost any size can be stored and manipulated with a linked list. Write a program that requests two integers and outputs their sum. Allow the numbers to be input with commas and display their sum with commas. (**Hint:** Input the numbers as Strings, convert the characters to their corresponding numeric digits from 0 through 9, and store them without commas in a linked list.)

   ```
   [sample run]
   Enter first number: 34,867,324,901
   Enter second number: 683,030,512
   Sum = 35,550,355,413
   ```

2. *Airline Reservations.* Write a reservation system for an airline flight. Assume the airplane has 6 seats in each row; use the constant NumRows to hold the total number of rows. The program should maintain two linked lists, a linked list of passenger records ordered by name and a waiting-list queue. Include the following definitions in the declarations part of the program.

   ```
   TYPE SeatArray = ARRAY [1..NumRows, 'A'..'F'] OF (available, reserved);
        PassPointer = ^PassRecord;
        PassRecord  = RECORD                  { Node type for linked list }
                        name : STRING;        { lastname, firstname }
                        row  : 1..NumRows;    { Row number of seat }
                        seat : 'A'..'F';      { 6 seats in each row }
                        next : PassPointer    { Next reserved seat }
                      END;
        QPointer = ^QRecord;
        QRecord  = RECORD                      { Node type for queue }
                     name : STRING;
                     next : QPointer
                   END;
   ```

   SeatArray is used to declare a two-dimensional array storing the current status (available or reserved) of each seat. Assume initially the passenger list is stored in the text file PLANE.DAT and the waiting list in the text file WAIT.DAT. The program should perform the following tasks:

   (a) Initialize the array so that all seats are "available".

   (b) If WAIT.DAT is nonempty, place its contents in a queue.

   (c) If PLANE.DAT is nonempty, place its contents into an ordered linked list with one node for each passenger. As passengers are placed in the list, their seat assignments should be registered in the array.

   (d) Display a three-option menu.

       (1) Add a passenger to the flight or waiting list.

           (a) Request the passenger's name (as lastname, firstname).

           (b) If seats are available, display a chart of available seats in tabular form and let the passenger choose a seat. Add the passenger to the ordered linked list and update the array.

           (c) If no seats are available, place the passenger in the queue.

(2) Remove a passenger from the flight
    (a) Request the passenger's name (as lastname, firstname).
    (b) Delete that passenger's node from the list.
    (c) If the queue is empty, update the array so the seat is "available".
    (d) If the queue is not empty, remove the first person from the queue, and give him or her the newly vacated seat.
(3) Quit (and write the current status into files PLANE.DAT and WAIT.DAT.)

3. *Rudimentary Translator*. Table 12.6 gives English words and their French and German equivalents. Assume these words are stored in a text file with three lines for each triplet of related words. Write a program that places the information in a binary tree, ordered by the English words. The program should then request an English sentence as input from the keyboard and search the binary tree to translate the sentence into French and German.

```
[sample run]
Enter an English sentence: MY PENCIL IS ON THE TABLE.
French translation: MON CRAYON EST SUR LA TABLE.
German translation: MEIN BLEISTIFT IST AUF DEM TISCH.
```

YES	OUI	YA	LARGE	GROS	GROSS
TABLE	TABLE	TISCH	NO	NON	NEIN
THE	LA	DEM	HAT	CHAPEAU	HUT
IS	EST	IST	PENCIL	CRAYON	BLEISTIFT
YELLOW	JAUNE	GELB	RED	ROUGE	ROT
FRIEND	AMI	FREUND	ON	SUR	AUF
SICK	MALADE	KRANK	AUTO	AUTO	AUTO
MY	MON	MEIN	OFTEN	SOUVENT	OFT

Table 12.6 English Words and Their French and German Equivalents

4. *Recursive Binary Search*. Assume intArray is an ordered array of Integers indexed from 1 through 100. Write a recursive function BinarySearch that performs a binary search (see Figure 8.6) on intArray and returns the array index of the sought after item if it is found and returns 0 otherwise. BinarySearch takes as input the value of the sought after item, *quarry*, and also *first* and *last*, the indices specifying the range to be searched. Each call to BinarySearch halves the range of the array in which *quarry* might be located and then calls BinarySearch again with a new range until the termination case is reached. The recursion terminates either when *quarry* equals the value of the item at *middle* or when the bounds collide (*first* > *last*). In the second case, *quarry* is not in the array. Use the following algorithm for the search.

(a) Compute *middle* as (*first* + *last*) DIV 2.
(b) If the array bounds collide, then return 0.
    (1) Otherwise, if the value of *middle* equals *quarry*, then return *middle*.
    (2) Otherwise, if the value of *middle* is greater than *quarry*, then call BinarySearch with range *first* through *middle* − 1.
    (3) Otherwise, call BinarySearch with range *middle* + 1 through *last*.

13

Object-Oriented Programming

13.1   CLASSES AND OBJECTS

> Object-oriented programming will be the major programming development of
> the 1990s, just as structured programming was the major development of the
> 1970s.
>
> Greg Lobdell, Microsoft

Practical experience in the financial, scientific, engineering, and software
design industries has revealed some difficulties with standard program design
methodologies. As programs grow in size and become more complex, and as the
number of programmers working on the same project increases, the number of
dependencies and interrelationships throughout the code increases exponen-
tially. A small change made by one programmer in one place may have many
effects, both intended and unintended, in many other places. The effects of this
change may ripple throughout the entire program, requiring the rewriting of a
great deal of code along the way.

A partial solution to this problem is "data hiding" where, within a module,
as much implementation detail as possible is hidden. Data hiding is an important
principle underlying object-oriented programming. An object is an encapsula-
tion of data and subprograms that act on the data. The only thing of concern to
a programmer using an object is the tasks that the object can perform and the
parameters used by these tasks. The details of the data structures and subprograms
are hidden within the object.

Objects are user-defined data types that are defined similarly to records.
Whereas records have only data fields, objects also have procedures and functions. Objects have their own terminology. Their data types are called **classes**,
their data fields are called **instance variables**, and their procedures and functions
are called **methods**. A class declaration has the form

```
TYPE ClassName = OBJECT
              instVariableName1 : VarType1;        ⎤  Instance
              instVariableName2 : VarType2;        ⎦  variables
                    .
              PROCEDURE ProcName1;                 ⎤
              PROCEDURE ProcName2;                 ⎮
                    .
                                                   ⎬  Methods
              FUNCTION FunctName1 : FunctType1;    ⎮
              FUNCTION FunctName2 : FunctType2;    ⎦
                    .
        END;
```

This declaration is followed by the definitions of the methods. In each
definition heading, the procedure or function is prefixed with the name of the
class and a period to identify it as part of the class. Instance variables and methods
referenced in a method definition must be prefixed by the standard identifier

```
Self.
```

The prefix tells the method that these variables or methods are part of its class.

An **object** is a variable having a class as its type, and is specified with a declaration of the form

```
VAR objectName : ClassName;
```

Classes also are called **object types**. Each object declared to be of the type is referred to as an **instance** of the object type. An object type is a template for creating objects, just as a record type is a template for creating records.

In QuickPascal, objects are dynamic variables, like the targets of pointers, and are created and removed by the statement part of the program with New and Dispose statements. Calls to the methods of objects are called **messages** and have the form

```
objectName.MethodName
```

I have good news and bad news. The good news is that objects simplify the work of the statement part of the program. The statements just bark orders and the objects carry them out. In particular, objects keep track of the data needed to carry out their duties. The bad news is that object implementations often involve many subprograms with small statement parts, which may be tedious to write. The bad news it not really so bad. Once a class has been created, it is easy to reuse in other programs. Also, due to the integration of data and subprograms, the programmer is freed from remembering the details of how the object does its thing.

Objects initially were developed to handle complex graphics routines. Our first example of a program containing an object creates text graphics resembling arcade game animations.

EXAMPLE 1 The following program uses an object called *plane* that is a bomber capable of moving across the screen and releasing bombs. The object keeps track of its position through its instance variables and the methods use the data held in the instance variables to execute messages. The program is analyzed below.

```
PROGRAM BomberAnimation;

USES Crt;

CONST PlaneShape = '>==>';
      BlankPlane = '    ';
      BombShape  = Chr(157);        { ¥ }
      BlankBomb  = ' ';
      Up         = 1;
      Straight   = 0;
      Down       = -1;
```

```
TYPE Airplane = OBJECT
                 position,          {column number of airplane}
                 height    : Integer; {row number of airplane}
                 PROCEDURE Init (initHeight : Integer);
                 PROCEDURE Move (change : Integer);
                 PROCEDURE DropBomb;
                 FUNCTION GetPosition : Integer;
                 FUNCTION GetHeight : Integer
               END;

PROCEDURE Airplane.Init (initHeight : Integer);
  BEGIN
    Self.position := 1;
    Self.height    := initHeight
  END;

PROCEDURE Airplane.Move (change : Integer);
  BEGIN
    GotoXY(Self.position, Self.height);
    Write(BlankPlane);
    Self.position := Self.position + 1;
    Self.height := Self.height - change;
    GotoXY(Self.position, Self.height);
    Write(PlaneShape);
    Delay(150)
  END;

PROCEDURE Airplane.DropBomb;
  VAR altitude : Integer;    { Number of row containing bomb }
  BEGIN
    FOR altitude := Self.height + 1 TO 24 DO
      BEGIN
        GotoXY(Self.position + 2, altitude);
        Write(BombShape);
        Delay(50);
        GotoXY(Self.position + 2, altitude);
        Write(BlankBomb)
      END
  END;

FUNCTION Airplane.GetPosition : Integer;
  BEGIN
    GetPosition := Self.position
  END;

FUNCTION Airplane.GetHeight : Integer;
  BEGIN
    GetHeight := Self.height
  END;

VAR plane : Airplane;
    moves : Integer;
```

```
BEGIN
  ClrScr;
  New(plane);                       {Create dynamic variable plane}
  plane.Init(12);        {Set plane to start at row 12 of screen}
  FOR moves := 1 TO 37 DO
    plane.Move(Straight);
  plane.DropBomb;
  FOR moves := 1 TO 5 DO
    plane.Move(Down);
  plane.DropBomb;
  FOR moves := 1 TO 15 DO
    plane.Move(Up);
  Writeln;
  Writeln('The airplane is on row ', plane.GetHeight,
          ', column ', plane.GetPosition);
  Dispose(plane)
END.
```

Analysis of Program in Example 1

1. **Animation**. The motion of the airplane is achieved by displaying the airplane (>==>) for .15 seconds, erasing the airplane with a string of four blank spaces, and redisplaying the airplane beginning in the next column, possibly shifted one row up or down. The bomb (¥) is dropped straight down from the center of the airplane. Bomb animation is achieved in the same way as airplane animation, but with each display lasting just .05 seconds.

2. **Instance variables**. Each point of the text screen is specified by its column number (1 through 80) and its row number (1 through 25). The variable *position* holds the current column number of the leftmost character of the airplane and the variable *height* holds the current row number of the airplane. Each time the airplane moves, the value of *position* increases by 1 and the value of *height* either stays the same, decreases by 1 (airplane rises), or increases by 1 (airplane descends).

3. **PROCEDURE Init**. This method sets the initial height of the airplane (that is, the value of the instance variable *height*) to row 12 when the message

   ```
   plane.Init(12)
   ```

   is executed.

4. **PROCEDURE Move**. This method moves the airplane one position to the right and either straight, up, or down, depending upon whether the value of *change* is 0, 1, or −1 respectively. The statement Delay(150) causes execution of the program to pause for 150 thousands of a second. Without the Delay statement, the airplane would move so fast it would look like a blur.

5. **PROCEDURE DropBomb**. This method drops a bomb from the center of the airplane. It uses the instance variables *position* and *height* to determine the initial location of the bomb. The bomb falls straight down.

6. FUNCTION GetPosition. This method returns the value of the instance variable *position*.

7. FUNCTION GetHeight. This method returns the value of the instance variable *height*.

8. Statement Part.

 (a) The first three statements clear the screen, create the dynamic object variable *plane*, and tell the object to set the beginning of the 12th row as the initial position of the airplane.

 (b) The first FOR loop tells the object to move the airplane steadily 37 columns to the right, one column at a time. (The argument Straight tells the object to keep the airplane level.)

 (c) The statement "plane.DropBomb" tells the object to drop a bomb. This statement illustrates the advantage of objects over just data and procedures. The passing of the location of the airplane is not necessary. The object always knows the current location. The programmer can just sit back and send a simple message to the object. The object will carry out the task without the programmer thinking about any of the details at this point.

 (d) The second FOR loop tells the object to move the airplane 5 columns to the right, while steadily descending. The argument Down in the message "plane.Move(Down)" reduces the altitude by one unit.

 (e) After the short descent, the statement "plane.DropBomb" drops another bomb.

 (f) The third FOR loop tells the object to make the airplane ascend while moving right 15 positions.

 (g) Finally, the Writeln message uses the two function methods of the object to obtain the final location of the airplane. Again, the object took care of the details.

 (h) The statement "Dispose(plane)" is not strictly necessary since the program is done and so does not need to free the memory set aside for the object. In general though, objects, like pointers, should be Disposed when no longer needed.

Comments:

1. Object-oriented programming is abbreviated as OOP. Table 13.1 relates OOP terms to kindred standard programming constructs.

OOP Term	Standard Construct
Class	Structured data type
Object	Variable having the structured type
Instance variable	Field of a record
Method	Subprogram definition
Message	Subprogram call

Table 13.1   Translation of OOP Terminology

2. The airplane animation object can be rewritten in several ways. For instance, the pair of instance variables *position* and *height* can be combined into a record of two fields. In standard programming, such a change in data structure would be of considerable importance to the person writing the statement part of the program. In OOP, however, the programmer is sheltered from such concerns.

3. Objects can be thought of as actors following directions (messages) from a director (the statement part of a program).

4. Messages tell objects what to do, but not how. The calling of a method is known as a "call-by-desire" invocation. The statement part of the program expresses its desires through messages and leaves the details to the object. The object could have been written at another time or by someone else. Programmers frequently purchase libraries of classes and never see the internal workings of the objects. No matter, the programmer need only know "What," not "How." To paraphrase the famous quotation from John F. Kennedy's inaugural address: Ask not *how* your object does its tasks, rather ask *what* your object can do for you.

5. The instance variables of an object can be assigned values directly by the statement part of the program. For instance, in the program of Example 1, the message

```
plane.Init(12)
```

can be replaced by

```
plane.height := 12
```

This practice is frowned upon since it subverts the purpose of objects, namely, to hide *how* a task is carried out. Good programming style dictates that only messages communicate with objects. This way, the data fields and implementations of the methods can be changed without affecting the programs that use the object.

6. As in records, a WITH statement can be used in method definitions to spare the programmer the job of prefixing instance variables with "Self." A block of the form

```
WITH Self DO
  statement
```

specifies that any instance variable mentioned in the statement will automatically be assumed to have the prefix Self. For example, the definition of PROCEDURE Init in the program of Example 1 can be written as

```
PROCEDURE Airplane.Init (initHeight : Integer);
  BEGIN
    WITH Self DO
      BEGIN
        position := 1;
        height   := initHeight
      END
  END;
```

7. The definitions of the class methods do not have to follow immediately after the class declaration. For instance, if a program has two different classes, their declarations are usually given first, followed by all the method definitions. No ambiguity results since each method is prefixed with the name of its class.

8. The first object-oriented programming language was SmallTalk. Its inventor, Alan Kay, originally imagined objects as separate processing units within a computer system. In order to handle the complexity of large software systems, the computer is divided into an arbitrary number of these units, each with its own specialized memory and specialized processing capabilities. Then objects would talk to one another by sending messages just like a normal computer might request information from the disk drive or send information to a printer or the screen. So programming with objects becomes a process of

   (a) defining the capabilities of objects (defining classes)
   (b) creating instances of objects (declaring variables of the specific class types)
   (c) passing messages to the objects (invoking calls to class methods for specific objects).

9. We now have explored five structured types: arrays, records, sets, files, and objects.

PRACTICE PROBLEMS 13.1

Consider the program BomberAnimation of Example 1.

1. Modify the program so that the statements

```
Writeln;
Writeln('The airplane is on row ', plane.GetHeight,
        ', column ', plane.GetPosition);
```

   can be replaced with

```
plane.DisplayLocation;
```

2. Rewrite the declaration of the instance variables so that the location of the airplane consists of a record with two Integer fields.

EXERCISES 13.1

Consider the program BomberAnimation of Example 1.

1. Although the statement

```
plane.height := 10;
```

   can legally be placed in the statement part of the program, accessing instance variables directly is frowned upon. What statement should be used instead?

2. Rewrite the definition of the method Airplane.Move using "WITH Self DO."

3. Modify the code to create a second airplane and move it to row 4, position 5.

4. Would the program still be valid if the statement Dispose(plane) was deleted?

In each of Exercises 5 through 21, use the class Point and object myPoint declared below.

```
TYPE Point = OBJECT
               p : RECORD
                     x : Real;
                     y : Real
                   END;
               PROCEDURE Init (x, y : Real);
               PROCEDURE Stretch (scale : Real);
               FUNCTION GetX : Real;
               FUNCTION GetY : Real;
               FUNCTION DistOrigin : Real
             END;

PROCEDURE Point.Init (x, y : Real);
  BEGIN
    Self.p.x := x;
    Self.p.y := y
  END;

PROCEDURE Point.Stretch (scale : Real);
  BEGIN
    Self.p.x := scale * Self.p.x;
    Self.p.y := scale * Self.p.y
  END;

FUNCTION Point.GetX : Real;
  BEGIN
    GetX := Self.p.x
  END;

FUNCTION Point.GetY : Real;
  BEGIN
    GetY := Self.p.y
  END;

FUNCTION Point.DistOrigin : Real;
  BEGIN
    DistOrigin := Sqrt(Sqr(Self.p.x) + Sqr(Self.p.y))
  END;

VAR myPoint : Point;
```

5. What is the output of the following main body of the program?

```
BEGIN
  New(myPoint);
  myPoint.Init(3, 4);
  Writeln((myPoint.GetX + myPoint.GetY):1:2);
  Dispose(myPoint)
END.
```

6. What is the output of the following main body of the program?

```
BEGIN
  New(myPoint);
  myPoint.Init(3, 4);
  Writeln('The distance of (', myPoint.GetX:1:2, ', ', myPoint.GetY:1:2,
          ') from the origin is ', myPoint.DistOrigin:1:2, '.');
  myPoint.Stretch(2);
  Writeln('The distance of (', myPoint.GetX:1:2, ', ', myPoint.GetY:1:2,
          ') from the origin is ', myPoint.DistOrigin:1:2, '.');
  Dispose(myPoint)
END.
```

In Exercises 7 through 9, find the error in each statement part.

7.
```
BEGIN
  myPoint.Init(3, 2);
  Writeln('The x-coordinate is ', myPoint.GetX:1:2)
END.
```

8.
```
BEGIN
  New(Point);
  Point.Init(3, 2);
  Writeln('The x-coordinate is ', Point.GetX:1:2);
  Dispose(Point)
END.
```

9.
```
BEGIN
  New(myPoint);
  Init(3, 2);
  Writeln('The x-coordinate is ', GetX:1:2)
  Dispose(myPoint)
END.
```

In Exercises 10 through 15, suppose the following lines are added in the class declaration of Point:

```
PROCEDURE Reflect;    { Reflect current point about origin }
FUNCTION Sum : Real;  { Add x- and y-coordinates }
```

Find the error in the corresponding method definition.

10.
```
PROCEDURE Point.Reflect (x, y : Real);
  BEGIN
    Self.p.x := -x;
    Self.p.y := -y
  END;
```

11.
```
PROCEDURE Point.Reflect;
  BEGIN
    p.x := -p.x;
    p.y := -p.y
  END;
```

12.
```
PROCEDURE Reflect;
  BEGIN
    WITH Self DO
      BEGIN
        p.x := -p.x;
        p.y := -p.y
      END
  END;
```

13.
```
PROCEDURE Point.Reflect;
  BEGIN
    WITH Point DO
      BEGIN
        p.x := -p.x;
        p.y := -p.y
      END
  END;
```

14.
```
FUNCTION Point.Sum : Real;
  BEGIN
    Point.Sum := Self.p.x + Self.p.y
  END;
```

15.
```
FUNCTION Sum : Real;
  BEGIN
    Sum := Self.p.x + Self.p.y
  END;
```

16. (a) Extend the class declaration of Point by adding a method that interchanges the x- and y-coordinates of the point.
(b) Write a main body of a program that requests the coordinates of the point as input from the user and uses this method.

17. (a) Extend the class declaration of Point by adding a Boolean function that is True if the point is in the first quadrant.
(b) Write a main body of a program that requests the coordinates of the point as input from the user and uses this function.

18. (a) Extend the class declaration of Point by adding a function that returns the greater of the x- and y-coordinates of the point.
(b) Write a main body of a program that requests the coordinates of the point as input from the user and uses this function.

19. (a) Extend the class declaration of Point by adding a method that replaces the point by a point the same distance from the origin but on the positive x-axis.
(b) Write a main body of a program that requests the coordinates of the point as input from the user and uses this method.

20. (a) Rewrite the class declaration with the coordinates of the point stored in an array of two elements.
    (b) What changes must now be made to the main body in Exercise 5?

21. Rewrite the definition of the method Point.Stretch using "WITH Self DO" instead of the prefix "Self.".

22. Write a program to request a person's name and age as input and display their name and age after their next birthday. The program should define a class Person with instance variables *name* and *age*, procedure method Increment-Age, and any other required methods.

```
[sample output]
Enter your name: Gabriel
Enter your age: 9
Gabriel, on your next birthday you will be 10.
```

23. Write a program to maintain a list of the senators currently present on the floor of the Senate. The program should define a class Senators with instance variable declarations

```
present : ARRAY [1..100] OF STRING;
total   : 0..100;   { Number of Senators currently on floor }
```

and methods to add a senator to the array, delete a senator from the array, and report the number and names of all senators currently on the floor.

```
[sample run]
A. Add a senator.
B. Delete a senator.
C. Display number of senators on floor.
D. Display names of senators on floor.
E. Quit.
Enter a selection: A
Enter the senator's name: Paul Sarbanes
Enter a selection: A
Enter the senator's name: Paul Simon
Enter a selection: D
The Honorable Paul Sarbanes
The Honorable Paul Simon
Enter a selection: E
```

24. Rewrite the class Senators in Exercise 23 to use an ordered linked list instead of an array to hold the names of the senators.

25. Write a program that requests the slope and y-intercept of a line as input and provides information about the line. The program should define a class Line with instance variable declarations

```
slope : Real;
yIntercept : Real;
```

and methods to translate the line vertically, change the slope, return the y-coordinate corresponding to an x-coordinate input by the user, and return the x-coordinate corresponding to a y-coordinate input by the user.

```
[sample run]
Enter the slope of the line: 2
Enter the y-intercept: 3
A. Translate the line vertically.
B. Change the slope.
C. Find a y-coordinate.
D. Find an x-coordinate.
E. Quit.
Enter a selection: A
Enter the number of units to translate the line: 5
Enter a selection: C
Enter the x-coordinate: 1
The corresponding y-coordinate is 10.00.
Enter a selection: E
```

26. Write a program that requests two complex numbers as input and displays their sum, difference, and product. Use a class having the instance variables *num1*, *num2*, and *result* with a two-field record type. The record fields will hold the real and imaginary parts of the complex number. The class should contain the following methods:

```
PROCEDURE SetNum1 (realPart, imagPart : Real);
PROCEDURE SetNum2 (realPart, imagPart : Real);
PROCEDURE Add;
PROCEDURE Subtract;
PROCEDURE Multiply;
PROCEDURE GetResult (VAR realPart, imagPart : Real)
```

```
[sample run]
Enter a + bi as: a  b
Enter the first complex number: 1  2
Enter the second complex number: 3  4
Sum: 4.00 + 6.00i
Difference: -2.00 + -2.00i
Product: -5.00 + 10.00i
```

SOLUTIONS TO PRACTICE PROBLEMS 13.1

1. The method

```
PROCEDURE DisplayLocation;
```
must be added to the declaration of the class Airplane and the definition

```
PROCEDURE Airplane.DisplayLocation;
  BEGIN
    Writeln;
    Writeln('The airplane is on row ', Self.GetHeight,
            ', column ', Self.GetPosition)
  END;
```
must be added to the method definitions. Notice that "Self.", not "Airplane." is used as the prefix for the methods GetHeight and GetPosition.

Note: The declaration of the method could also have been written

```
PROCEDURE Airplane.DisplayLocation;
```

That is, the prefix "Airplane." is optional in the method declaration but required in the definition heading.

```
2. location : RECORD
              position : Integer;
              height   : Integer
          END;
```

Throughout this book we have favored defining records by first defining a record type and then declaring a record to be an instance of that type. We avoided "shorthand" declarations since they could not be used to declare the types of subprogram parameters. This consideration does not apply to instance variables for two reasons. First, instance variables are never passed to parameters in methods. Methods automatically have access to all instance variables with the "Self." prefix. Instance variables can be thought of as implicitly being passed by reference to every method. Second, a record type cannot be declared inside a class declaration. Declaring the type outside the class definition defeats one purpose of using objects, data hiding.

13.2 INHERITANCE

Section 13.1 presented convincing justifications for object-oriented programming. The true vitality of objects, however, lies in a yet unmentioned feature, **inheritance**. When one class is a specific case of another class, the first can be defined as a **subclass** of the second. The subclass inherits all the instance variables and methods of the parent, then defines new ones of its own.

A subclass declaration differs from an ordinary class declaration in only one way. The name of the parent class appears in parentheses following the keyword OBJECT. If *ClassName1* has been declared as a class, then a declaration of the form

```
TYPE ClassName2 = OBJECT (ClassName1)
              newInstVariableName1 : NewVarType1;     ⎤ New
              newInstVariableName2 : NewVarType2;     ⎥ instance
                 .                                    ⎦ variables
                 .

              PROCEDURE NewProcName1;                 ⎤
              PROCEDURE NewProcName2;                 ⎥
                 .                                    ⎥ New
                 .                                    ⎥ methods
              FUNCTION NewFunctName1 : NewFunctType1; ⎥
              FUNCTION NewFunctName2 : NewFunctType2; ⎥
                 .                                    ⎦
                 .
          END;
```

declares a new class, *ClassName2*, with all the new instance variables and methods mentioned above. In addition, this subclass has all the instance variables and methods of its parent class *ClassName1*.

The following example illustrates inheritance. The parent class is a cash register that allows deposits and withdrawals.

EXAMPLE 1   A tollbooth on the interstate charges \$1 per car and \$2 per truck. Write a program to model a tollbooth operation where both the number of vehicles and the amount of money received are tallied. The base class should be a cash register and the subclass should not only keep a count, but also tally the revenue.

SOLUTION   Table 13.2 gives the tasks to be performed by the cash register, the appropriate type of field for each task, and names for these fields. Table 13.3 does the same for the tollbooth subclass.

Task	Field Type	Field Name
Keep track of balance	Instance variable	balance
Initialize balance	Procedure	Init
Make a deposit	Procedure	Deposit
Make a withdrawal	Procedure	Withdraw
Report balance	Function	CurrentBalance

Table 13.2   Analysis of the Tasks of a Cash Register

Task	Field Type	Field Name
* Keep track of revenue	Instance variable	balance
* Initialize revenue	Procedure	Init
* Increment revenue	Procedure	Deposit
* Report revenue	Function	CurrentBalance
Keep track of number of vehicles	Instance variable	count
Initialize revenue, # of vehicles	Procedure	OpenBooth
Collect from car	Procedure	ServeCar
Collect from truck	Procedure	ServeTruck
Report number of cars	Function	TotalCount

Table 13.3   Analysis of the Tasks of a Tollbooth (Starred tasks are inherited from CashRegister class.)

Let's name the parent class CashRegister and the subclass Toll. The following program defines and uses these classes. Four of the nine fields used by Toll are inherited from CashRegister and therefore, need not be listed in Toll's type declaration. Both CashRegister and Toll have an instance variable named *balance* and methods named *Init*, *Deposit*, and *Withdraw*. Note that though the Withdraw procedure of CashRegister is not used as a task of Toll, it is nevertheless inherited. This is harmless.

In the definition of the procedure CashRegister.Init, CashRegister's instance variable *balance* is set to 0.0. In the procedure Toll.OpenBooth, Toll's instance variable *count* is set to 0 and Toll's Init procedure (inherited from CashRegister) is called to set Toll's *balance* instance variable (also inherited) to 0.0.

```
PROGRAM Tollbooth;

USES Crt;

TYPE CashRegister = OBJECT
                         balance : Real;
                         PROCEDURE Init;
                         PROCEDURE Deposit (amount : Real);
                         PROCEDURE Withdraw (amount : Real);
                         FUNCTION CurrentBalance : Real
                       END;

     Toll        = OBJECT (CashRegister)
                       count : Integer;
                       PROCEDURE OpenBooth;
                       PROCEDURE ServeCar;
                       PROCEDURE ServeTruck;
                       FUNCTION TotalCount : Integer
                     END;

PROCEDURE CashRegister.Init;
  BEGIN
    Self.balance := 0.0
  END;

PROCEDURE CashRegister.Deposit (amount : Real);
  BEGIN
    Self.balance := Self.balance + amount
  END;

PROCEDURE CashRegister.Withdraw (amount : Real);
  BEGIN
    Self.balance := Self.balance - amount
  END;

FUNCTION CashRegister.CurrentBalance : Real;
  BEGIN
    CurrentBalance := Self.balance
  END;

PROCEDURE Toll.OpenBooth;
  BEGIN
    Self.Init;
    Self.count := 0
  END;

PROCEDURE Toll.ServeCar;
  BEGIN
    Self.count := Self.count + 1;
    Self.Deposit(1.00)        { Toll for a car is $1.00 }
  END;
```

```
PROCEDURE Toll.ServeTruck;
  BEGIN
    Self.count := Self.count + 1;
    Self.Deposit(2.00)        { Toll for a truck is $2.00 }
  END;

FUNCTION Toll.TotalCount : Integer;
  BEGIN
    TotalCount := Self.count
  END;


VAR Interstate : Toll;

BEGIN
  ClrScr;
  New(Interstate);
  Interstate.OpenBooth;
  Interstate.ServeTruck;
  Interstate.ServeCar;
  Interstate.ServeTruck;
  Interstate.ServeCar;
  Interstate.ServeCar;
  Interstate.ServeTruck;
  Interstate.ServeCar;
  Writeln('Revenue today: $',
          Interstate.CurrentBalance:1:2);
  Writeln('Vehicles served: ', Interstate.TotalCount);
  Dispose(Interstate)
END.

[run]
Revenue today: $10.00
Vehicles served: 7
```

Not only can a class have several subclasses, but each subclass can have its own subclasses. A subclass of a subclass not only inherits all of its parent's fields, but also its grandparent's. The initial class is called the **base class** and the collection of a base class along with its descendants is called a **hierarchy**.

In practice, considerable work goes into planning and defining the instance variables and methods of the base class. The subclasses are beneficiaries of this effort. Their additional instance variables and methods often can be defined with little effort.

Just as structured programming requires the ability to break complex problems into simpler subproblems, object-oriented programming requires the skill to identify useful hierarchies of classes and subclasses. Both talents are acquired by studying well-designed examples and writing challenging programs.

Software engineers are still working on the guidelines for when and how to establish hierarchies. One useful criterion is the so-called **ISA test**: If one class **is a** more specific case of another class, then the first should be a subclass of the second.

One hypothetical model that communicates the feel of a hierarchy of classes is the taxonomy chart for species. See Figure 13.1.

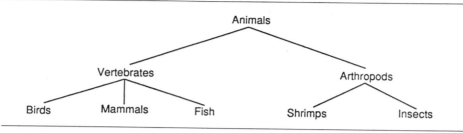

Figure 13.1   Partial Taxonomy Chart for the Animal Kingdom

Every bird is a vertebrate and has all the traits and capabilities common to vertebrates. In addition, birds have some traits and capabilities of their own. The same is true for each of the other classifications and their ancestor classifications. Later, we use the Taxonomy chart to illustrate some subtleties of inheritance.

EXAMPLE 2   Write a program using inheritance and text graphics to draw equilateral triangles and squares.

SOLUTION   A triangle and a square are both polygons; therefore, the polygon is an obvious choice for a class. Equilateral triangles and squares would then be subclasses. Later, other figures could easily be added to the program. We must be able to initialize, define, and draw each polygon. This hints at the methods for the class. Defining the polygon can best be done by consecutively adding vertices to the figure, suggesting an AddVertex routine. Table 13.4 lists the tasks to be performed by the polygon class and Table 13.5 does the same for the equilateral triangle subclass. The entries marked by asterisks are internal to the polygon class; in order to shield the polygon's representation of information, private instance variables should not be referenced outside the class. The procedure DrawLine internal to Draw just draws a straight line between the two vertices passed to it; don't concern yourself with the details of the implementation. The outcome is shown in Figure 13.2.

Task	Field Type	Field Name
Store vertices of the polygon	Instance variable	shape
Store number of vertices	Instance variable	lines
Clear(initialize) the polygon	Procedure	Init
Add vertex to the polygon	Procedure	AddVertex
Draw the polygon	Procedure	Draw

Table 13.4   Analysis of the Tasks of the Polygon Class

Task	Field Type	Field Name
* Store vertices of the triangle	Instance variable	shape
* Store number of vertices	Instance variable	lines
* Clear triangle	Procedure	Init
* Add vertex to the triangle	Procedure	AddVertex
* Draw triangle	Procedure	Draw
Create triangle	Procedure	Make

Table 13.5 Analysis of the Tasks of the Equilateral Triangle Subclass (Starred tasks are inherited from the Polygon class.)

```pascal
PROGRAM Shapes;

USES Crt;

CONST DrawChar = Chr(219);   { a solid block }
      MaxPts   = 10;

TYPE Vertex   = RECORD
                    x : Integer;
                    y : Integer
                  END;
      Polygon = OBJECT
                    shape : ARRAY [1..MaxPts] OF Vertex;
                    lines : Integer;
                    PROCEDURE Init;
                    PROCEDURE AddVertex (newX, newY : Integer);
                    PROCEDURE Draw
                  END;
      EquiTri = OBJECT (Polygon)
                    PROCEDURE Make (x, y, side : Integer)
                  END;

      Square  = OBJECT (Polygon)
                    PROCEDURE Make (x, y, side : Integer)
                  END;

VAR myEquiTri : EquiTri;
    mySquare  : Square;

PROCEDURE PolyGon.Init;
  BEGIN
    Self.lines := 0
  END;

PROCEDURE PolyGon.AddVertex (newX, newY : Integer);
  BEGIN
    Self.lines := Self.lines + 1;
    WITH Self.shape[Self.lines] DO
      BEGIN
        x := newX;
        y := newY
      END
  END;
```

```
PROCEDURE PolyGon.Draw;
  VAR pointNum : Integer;
  PROCEDURE DrawLine (start, finish : Vertex);
    VAR count, dist, xdif, ydif : Integer;
        xinc, yinc              : Real;
    BEGIN
      xdif := finish.x - start.x;
      ydif := finish.y - start.y;
      dist := Round(Sqrt(Sqr(xdif) + Sqr(ydif)));
      xinc := xdif / dist;
      yinc := ydif / dist;
      FOR count := 1 TO dist DO
        BEGIN
          GotoXY(Round(start.x + xinc * count),
                 Round(start.y + yinc * count));
          Write(drawChar)
        END
    END;
  BEGIN
    FOR pointNum := 1 TO Self.lines - 1 DO
      DrawLine(Self.shape[pointNum], Self.shape[pointNum + 1])
  END;

PROCEDURE EquiTri.Make (x, y, side : Integer);
  BEGIN
    Self.Init;
    Self.AddVertex(x, y);
    Self.AddVertex(x + side DIV 2, y + Round(side * Sqrt(3) / 2));
    Self.AddVertex(x - side DIV 2, y + Round(side * Sqrt(3) / 2));
    Self.AddVertex(x, y)
  END;

PROCEDURE Square.Make (x, y, side : Integer);
  BEGIN
    Self.Init;
    Self.AddVertex(x, y);
    Self.AddVertex(x + side, y);
    Self.AddVertex(x + side, y + side);
    Self.AddVertex(x, y + side);
    Self.AddVertex(x, y)
  END;

BEGIN
  ClrScr;
  New(myEquiTri);
  New(mySquare);
  myEquiTri.Make(40, 15, 11);
  mySquare.Make(70, 1, 5);
  myEquiTri.Draw;
  mySquare.Draw;
  Dispose(myEquiTri);
  Dispose(mySquare);
  Readln          { Defer "Press any key" message }
END.
```

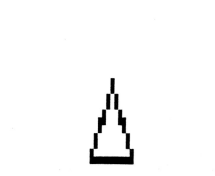

Figure 13.2   Outcome of the Program in Example 2

OVERRIDE and INHERITED

Sometimes, a method in a subclass will perform a task similar to a method in its parent class but with a slight modification. In these cases, there are good reasons for giving the methods the same name. If we try to do this, however, the compiler will complain with the error "Field or Method Already Defined." QuickPascal provides the capability to *override* a method of a parent class. An example is shown below.

```
TYPE Class1    = OBJECT
                    PROCEDURE Init
                 END;
     Subclass1 = OBJECT (Class1)
                    PROCEDURE Init; OVERRIDE
                 END;

VAR classObj : Class1;
    subObj   : Subclass1;
```

In this case, both Class1 and Subclass1 contain methods named Init. Each of the commands classObj.Init and subObj.Init corresponds to the Init procedure in the corresponding object type. The statement part of the main program does not need to know (or care) which version of Init is sent the message.

OVERRIDE requires that the two methods be identical in both name and parameters. The only difference in the two declarations is that the second declaration be followed by OVERRIDE. The parameters must have the same number, the same types, the same order, and even the same names.

Suppose method Init in Subclass1 needs to invoke method Init in Class1. Such a case might arise if Subclass1 performs its initialization by augmenting the initialization of its parent with additional code. Since Init of Class1 was overridden, a call to Self.Init within Subclass1.Init would be recursive. To prevent this and allow inheritance of an overridden method, QuickPascal provides an INHERITED keyword. The following is an implementation of Subclass1.Init that calls Class1.Init.

```
PROCEDURE Subclass1.Init;
  BEGIN
    .
    .
    INHERITED Self.Init;
    .
    .
  END;
```

EXAMPLE 3   The following program uses OVERRIDE and INHERITED to display information about types of animals.

```
PROGRAM Classifications;
{ Gives the characteristics and classifications of types of animals }

USES Crt;

TYPE Animals     = OBJECT
                       PROCEDURE GiveMessage
                   END;
     Vertebrates = OBJECT (Animals)
                       PROCEDURE GiveMessage; OVERRIDE
                   END;
     Mammals     = OBJECT (Vertebrates)
                       PROCEDURE GiveMessage; OVERRIDE
                   END;
     Arthropods  = OBJECT (Animals)
                       PROCEDURE GiveMessage; OVERRIDE
                   END;

VAR myAnimal     : Animals;
    myVertebrate : Vertebrates;
    myMammal     : Mammals;
    myArthropod  : Arthropods;

PROCEDURE Animals.GiveMessage;
  BEGIN
    Writeln('Kingdom: Animals       Can move')
  END;

PROCEDURE Vertebrates.GiveMessage;
  BEGIN
    Writeln('Phylum:  Vertebrates    Has a backbone');
    INHERITED Self.GiveMessage
  END;

PROCEDURE Mammals.GiveMessage;
  BEGIN
    Writeln('Class:   Mammals',
            '          Nurtures young with mother''s milk');
    INHERITED Self.GiveMessage
  END;
```

```
PROCEDURE Arthropods.GiveMessage;
  BEGIN
    Writeln('Phylum:  Arthropods',
            '          Has jointed limbs and no backbone');
    INHERITED Self.GiveMessage
  END;

BEGIN
  ClrScr;
  New(myAnimal);
  New(myVertebrate);
  New(myMammal);
  New(myArthropod);
  myAnimal.GiveMessage;
  Writeln;
  myVertebrate.GiveMessage;
  Writeln;
  myMammal.GiveMessage;
  Writeln;
  myArthropod.GiveMessage;
  Dispose(myAnimal);
  Dispose(myVertebrate);
  Dispose(myMammal);
  Dispose(myArthropod)
END.
```

```
[run]
Kingdom: Animals          Can move

Phylum:  Vertebrates      Has a backbone
Kingdom: Animals          Can move

Class:   Mammals          Nurtures young with mother's milk
Phylum:  Vertebrates      Has a backbone
Kingdom: Animals          Can move

Phylum:  Arthropods       Has jointed limbs and no backbone
Kingdom: Animals          Can move
```

Comments:

1. *Reuse of code.* In practice, traditional language libraries are not always reusable. "My problem is like the one handled by the library routine but a little different. I could modify the source code, but I don't have it. Guess I'll have to write a new routine from scratch." In practice, object-oriented programming has shown that as long as you have the interface to a class, you can extend its capabilities without having the source code.

2. Problem solving with object-oriented programming is a seven-step process.
   (a) Understand the problem.
   (b) Determine the classes (and subclasses) involved in the problem.
   (c) For each class, enumerate the essential methods to be invoked.
   (d) Sketch the main program.

(e) For each class, detail the instance variables.

(f) For each class, code the methods.

(g) Write the main body of the program.

PRACTICE PROBLEMS 13.2

Consider the following class declaration.

```
TYPE Car    = OBJECT
                  maxSpeed : Integer;
                  gasEfficiency : Integer;
                  PROCEDURE SetStats (mph, mpg : Integer);
                  PROCEDURE ShowStats;
                  PROCEDURE ShowCar
              END;
        Ferrari = OBJECT (Car)
                  PROCEDURE SetStats (kph, kpl : Integer); OVERRIDE
              END;
```

1. Why will the method in the subclass Ferrari cause the compiler to display the error message "Header does not match previous declaration."

2. How can the error be corrected?

EXERCISES 13.2

In each of Exercises 1 through 12 use the class Point, its subclass Circle, and the object myCircle declared below. (*Note:* The class Point was discussed in Exercises 13.1.)

```
TYPE Point = OBJECT
                  p : RECORD
                          x : Real;
                          y : Real
                      END;
                  PROCEDURE Init (x, y : Real);
                  PROCEDURE Stretch (scale : Real);
                  FUNCTION GetX : Real;
                  FUNCTION GetY : Real;
                  FUNCTION DistOrigin : Real
              END;
        Circle = OBJECT (Point)
                  radius : Real;
                  PROCEDURE Init (x, y : Real); OVERRIDE;
                  PROCEDURE ChangeRadius (r : Real);
                  FUNCTION GetRadius : Real;
                  FUNCTION Area : Real
              END;
```

```
PROCEDURE Point.Init (x, y : Real);
  BEGIN
    Self.p.x := x;
    Self.p.y := y
  END;

PROCEDURE Point.Stretch (scale : Real);
  BEGIN
    Self.p.x := scale * Self.p.x;
    Self.p.y := scale * Self.p.y
  END;

FUNCTION Point.GetX : Real;
  BEGIN
    GetX := Self.p.x
  END;

FUNCTION Point.GetY : Real;
  BEGIN
    GetY := Self.p.y
  END;

FUNCTION Point.DistOrigin : Real;
  BEGIN
    DistOrigin := Sqrt(Sqr(Self.p.x) + Sqr(Self.p.y))
  END;

PROCEDURE Circle.Init (x, y : Real); OVERRIDE;
  BEGIN
    INHERITED Self.Init(x, y);
    Self.radius := 1.0
  END;

PROCEDURE Circle.ChangeRadius (r : Real);
  BEGIN
    Self.radius := r
  END;

FUNCTION Circle.GetRadius : Real;
  BEGIN
    GetRadius := Self.radius
  END;

FUNCTION Circle.Area : Real;
  BEGIN
    Area := Pi * Sqr(Self.radius)
  END;

VAR myCircle : Circle;
```

1. What is the output of the following code?

```
BEGIN
  New(myCircle);
  myCircle.Init(5, 6);
  Writeln((myCircle.GetX - myCircle.GetRadius):1:2);
  Dispose(myCircle)
END.
```

2. What is the output of the following code?

```
BEGIN
  New(myCircle);
  myCircle.Init(5, 6);
  Writeln('The diameter is ', 2 * myCircle.GetRadius:1:2);
  Dispose(myCircle)
END.
```

3. Add a statement to the code in Exercise 1 to display the coordinates of the center of the circle. The statement should use message calls.

4. Modify the program in Exercise 1 so that the statement

```
Writeln((myCircle.GetX - myCircle.GetRadius):1:2);
```

can be replaced with

```
myCircle.DisplayLeftmostX;    { Display the x- coordinate of the
                                leftmost point of the circle }
```

5. What is the output of the following code?

```
BEGIN
  New(myCircle);
  myCircle.Init(5, 6);
  myCircle.Stretch(0.5);
  myCircle.ChangeRadius(4);
  Writeln('Circle');
  Writeln('  Center: (', myCircle.GetX:1:2, ', '
                       , myCircle.GetY:1:2, ')');
  Writeln('  Radius:  ', myCircle.GetRadius:1:2);
  Writeln('  Area:    ', myCircle.Area:1:2);
  IF myCircle.DistOrigin < myCircle.GetRadius THEN
     Writeln('  The origin is inside the circle.')
   ELSE
     Writeln('  The origin is outside the circle.');
  Dispose(myCircle)
END.
```

6. For the subclass Circle, write a method called PROCEDURE FullInit (x, y, radius : Real) that sets both the center and radius of the circle. Have the method use Point.Init or Circle.Init.

In Exercises 7 through 11, identify the errors.

7.
```
TYPE Ellipse = OBJECT
                  semiMajor : Real;
                  semiMinor : Real;
                  PROCEDURE Init (x, y : Real); OVERRIDE
               END;
```

8.
```
TYPE Ellipse = OBJECT (Point)
                  semiMajor : Real;
                  semiMinor : Real;
                  PROCEDURE Init (x, y : Real); OVERRIDE;
                  FUNCTION Perimeter : Real; OVERRIDE
               END;
```

9.
```
TYPE Ellipse = OBJECT (Point)
                  semiMajor : Real;
                  semiMinor : Real;
                  PROCEDURE Init (a, b : Real); OVERRIDE
               END;
```

10.
```
TYPE Ellipse = OBJECT (Point)
                  semiMajor : Real;
                  semiMinor : Real;
                  PROCEDURE Init (x, y, a, b : Real); OVERRIDE
               END;
```

11.
```
BEGIN
   New(myPoint);
   myPoint.Init(5, 6);
   myPoint.ChangeRadius(3);
   Dispose(myPoint)
END.
```

12. Write a subclass Square of Point. Regard the point *p* as the upper-left corner of the square. Include a procedure method to translate the square horizontally and a function method to return the area of the square.

13. Consider the class Person and subclass Worker declared below. Write a program that uses these classes to figure out how much a young worker will make before retiring at age 65. Assume the worker receives a 5 percent raise each year. See the sample run below.

```
TYPE Person = OBJECT
                  name : STRING;
                  age  : Integer;
                  PROCEDURE Init(name : STRING; age : Integer);
                  FUNCTION GetName : STRING;
               END;

     Worker = OBJECT (Person)
                  salary : Real;                { Current annual salary }
                  PROCEDURE WInit(name : STRING; age : Integer;
                               salary : Real);
                  FUNCTION Earnings : Real    { Earnings until retirement }
               END;
```

```
[sample run]
Enter the person's name: Helen
Enter the person's age: 25
Enter the person's annual salary: 20000
Helen will earn $2415995.48
```

14. Consider the class Stats and subclass CompleteStats declared below. Write a program that uses these classes to process the grades for an exam. See the sample run below.

```
TYPE Stats = OBJECT
              grades : ARRAY [1..50] OF Integer;
              count  : Integer;              { Number of grades entered }
              PROCEDURE Init;                        { Set count to 0 }
              PROCEDURE EntGrade(grade : Integer); { Enter next grade }
              FUNCTION Average : Real          { Return average grade }
           END;

CompleteStats = OBJECT (Stats)
              max : Integer;
              min : Integer;
              PROCEDURE Init; OVERRIDE;  { Set count to 0,
                                           max to 0, min to 100 }
              PROCEDURE EntGrade(grade : Integer); OVERRIDE;
              FUNCTION Spread : Integer   { Return max - min }
           END;

[sample run]
Enter -1 when all grades have been entered.
Enter a grade: 90
Enter a grade: 70
Enter a grade: -1
Average: 80.00
Spread: 20
```

15. Adding machines allow a number to be entered and subsequent numbers to be added or subtracted from a running total. At any time, the running total can be displayed. A calculator can do the same, but also allows multiplication and division. Write a program with a class AddingMachine and a subclass Calculator that simulates the operation of a calculator.

16. Write a program to compute the value at a future date of a certificate of deposit or a savings account. Use a base class Bank with instance variables which are common to the two types of bank account, and subclasses Certificate and SavingsAcct. Certificate should have an instance variable for the number of months to maturity and SavingsAcct should have an instance variable for a sequence of deposits and withdrawals. Assume that all deposits and withdrawals to the savings account are made at the beginning of each month.

1. The parameters in the corresponding method from the class Car have different names.

2. Make the parameter names identical in both methods, or rename the second method FShowStats and delete the word OVERRIDE.

13.3 A CASE STUDY: PLAYING A BOARD GAME

Tic-Tac-Toe, Checkers, and Othello are enjoyable board games familiar to many people. These games and others share several fundamental traits. In each game, there are two players, who have pieces with distinguishing colors or shapes (X and O in Tic-Tac-Toe, for instance). The players alternate placing or moving their pieces on a board, which is a square grid. Each game starts with an initial board configuration and proceeds until some terminating condition signals a win or draw. Table 13.6 lists the characteristics of a typical board game.

1. The game is played on a square grid.
2. There are two players.
3. Each player has a color or shape.
4. The players alternate turns.
5. A piece is added, removed, or moved during each turn.

Table 13.6 Characteristics of a Typical Board Game

Since there are many common attributes, a set of general routines could speed the implementation of the games. Once the programmer writes the shared code, customizations can be added to complete any particular game.

Objects are perfect for this application. The data and routines needed by all the games can comprise a general game class, and the specifics for each implementation can form subclasses. This hierarchical structure is appropriate, since Tic-Tac-Toe, Checkers, and Othello are all specific types of board games.

Careful consideration must be given to selecting the instance variables and methods for the game object. The object should be general enough to be applicable to many games, but not so general that it is cumbersome to use or difficult to specialize. A good rule of thumb is to use the minimum number of instance variables and methods to accomplish the task at hand. In this case, we base the class on the game characteristics found in Table 13.6.

As shown in Table 13.7, the class contains exactly enough instance variables to store necessary information about the players and the state of the game. Similarly, only the methods absolutely essential for a board game are included. The procedures SetBoardSize and SetShapes provide the means to change specifics of a game. Other methods, such as GetMove and SetPiece, perform important tasks involved in actually playing the game. The procedure DrawPiece is used only by methods inside the game object; just like the instance variables of any object, it should not be referenced elsewhere.

542 Object-Oriented Programming

Task	Representation	Name
Store pieces on playing board	Instance variable	board
Store piece shape for player 1	Instance variable	shape1
Store piece shape for player 2	Instance variable	shape2
Store current player	Instance variable	current
Store size of playing board	Instance variable	boardSize
Set size of playing board	Procedure	SetBoardSize
Set piece shapes for players	Procedure	SetShapes
Return current player	Function	CurrentPlayer
Switch current player	Procedure	SwitchPlayer
Draw a piece on screen	Procedure	DrawPiece
Place a piece on board	Procedure	SetPiece
Return piece in a board position	Procedure	Piece
Allow player to select a move	Procedure	GetMove
Initialize and draw playing board	Procedure	Init

Table 13.7 Tasks of the General Game Object

This general game object provides many useful functions, but by itself cannot play a game. A subclass must be added to fill the gaps left free in the game object. We will implement Tic-Tac-Toe to illustrate how this is done.

We start by listing the traits unique to Tic-Tac-Toe (see Table 13.8), just as we listed the traits of a general game earlier. The first two characteristics, the size of the playing board and the player shapes, are set by a single initialize procedure. Each of the other four characteristics corresponds to one procedure or function in the object. The object tasks and their methods are listed in Table 13.9. Note that no extra instance variables are needed, since the entire state of the game is already stored in the general game object.

1. The playing grid is three by three.
2. The player shapes are 'X' and 'O'.
3. The move is made by simply placing a piece.
4. Any unoccupied space is a valid move position.
5. A win occurs when a player has three pieces in a line.
6. A draw occurs when the board is completely filled without any player winning.

Table 13.8 Characteristics Unique to Tic-Tac-Toe

Task	Representation	Name
Initialize and draw playing board	Procedure	Init
Make move by placing a piece	Procedure	MakeMove
Check to see if move is valid	Function	ValidMove
Check for a win	Function	GameWin
Check for a draw	Function	GameDraw

Table 13.9 Tasks Unique to the Tic-Tac-Toe Object (Inherited tasks not included)

Interestingly, almost any game of our general form can be described by different versions of these five methods. Simply by writing alternate Init, MakeMove, ValidMove, GameWin, and GameDraw methods, the programmer can create a different game. Of course, the general game object is needed in each case, but this can be inherited at no expense.

The game and Tic-Tac-Toe objects contain all the necessary routines to play a game, but lack code to sequence the operations. The statement part of the program is responsible for this; it controls the flow of the program. The pseudocode is listed below.

```
Create and Initialize TicTacToe object
REPEAT
  Report which player is to move
  REPEAT
    Get player's proposed move
  UNTIL the move is valid
  Make the move
  Check for a win
  IF nobody won THEN
    Check for a draw
    IF there is no draw THEN
      Switch current player
UNTIL win OR draw
Report win or draw
Free memory occupied by TicTacToe object
```

Most of the lines in the pseudocode correspond to direct calls to object methods. For instance, "Get player's proposed move" is a call to GetMove and "Make the move" is a call to MakeMove. Since the object methods were carefully thought out, the main program almost reads like English. In addition, the program statements are general enough to apply to almost any game. Implementations of Checkers or Othello, for instance, would use similar code; only the specific game methods would need to be rewritten.

So far the discussion has concentrated on what the objects are and what they do, rather than how they do it. The next step in the design process is to decide on the actual representation of data and the implementation of methods of the objects.

First, we plan the game instance variables. The symbols associated with the players' pieces, *shape1*, *shape2*, and *current*, can be of type Char. The dimension of the playing grid, *boardSize*, should be an Integer. The variable *board* stores the pieces on the game grid; for this we use a two-dimensional array of characters. Note that this is only one possible representation. The shapes could be enumerated types instead of characters, for instance.

Most of the procedures and functions of the game class consist of just a few lines. The only difficult procedures are Init and GetMove, which draw the game board and get a player's choice for a move, respectively. The pseudocode for these procedures is shown below.

PSEUDOCODE FOR Init:
 FOR row := 1 TO size
  FOR col := 1 TO size
   Clear board position at (row, col)
 Draw horizontal grid lines for playing board
 Draw vertical grid lines for playing board
 Draw intersection of horizontal and vertical lines for playing board

PSEUDOCODE FOR GetMove:
 Set Done to False
 REPEAT
  Draw the selection cursor at current board position
  Pause a fraction of a second
  Draw the piece at current board position
  Pause a fraction of a second
  IF key pressed THEN
   Read key
   IF key is Space THEN
    set Done to True
   ELSE
    IF key is an arrow key THEN
     Check direction of key
     Move in the appropriate direction if possible
 UNTIL Done

Procedure GetMove allows the player to move a flashing cursor around the playing board and select a position for the player's turn. A few specialized commands are needed for this. KeyPressed is a Boolean function that returns True if a key on the keyboard was pressed. It does not pause program execution as do the Read and Readln commands. This feature allows us to flash the selection cursor. We use the QuickPascal function ReadKey to input the character that was pressed, since this procedure does not echo anything to the screen or require the user to hit Enter.

The only difficult method for the Tic-Tac-Toe object is GameWin, which checks to see if either player has three pieces in a line. The pseudocode and refinements are as follows:

PSEUDOCODE FOR GameWin
 FOR each row and column
  Check for horizontal win at row
  Check for vertical win at column
  Check for diagonal win from upper left to lower right
  Check for diagonal win from lower left to upper right

PSEUDOCODE FOR Check for horizontal win at row
 Look at first piece in row (left-most piece of row)
 IF piece belongs to a player THEN
  Temporarily assume there is a win at row
  FOR each remaining column
   IF piece at row and column does not match left-most piece THEN
    No longer assume there is a win at row

PSEUDOCODE FOR Check for vertical win at column
  Look at first piece in column (upper-most piece of column)
  IF piece belongs to a player THEN
    Temporarily assume there is a win at column
    FOR each remaining row
     IF piece at row and column does not match upper-most piece THEN
      No longer assume there is a win at column

PSEUDOCODE FOR Check for diagonal win
  Look at first piece in starting row (left-most piece of row)
  IF piece belongs to a player THEN
    Temporarily assume there is a diagonal win
    FOR all remaining columns
     Increment or decrement row (depending on direction of search)
     IF piece at row and column does not match left-most piece of
      starting row THEN
      No longer assume there is a diagonal win

GameWin is implemented as a single procedure with three nested procedures, one each for checking horizontal, vertical, and diagonal wins.

At this point, the program should be easy to write. The methods for which no pseudocode was created are simple enough to be coded directly, and the others follow from the pseudocode.

To improve program clarity, a few final thoughts should be given regarding the many fixed values that will appear in the program. Constants should be added to centralize static information and allow a program to be easily modified. The constants appropriate here specify the maximum dimension of the playing grid, the size of the playing grid squares, the characters used to draw the playing grid, the character for the selection cursor, and the keys used to move the cursor.

```
PROGRAM GameObjects;

USES Crt;

CONST Space    = ' ';         { Space character }
      Cursor   = '*';         { Selection cursor }
      Vbar     = Chr(179);    { Vertical grid character }
      Hbar     = Chr(196);    { Horizontal grid character }
      Crossbar = Chr(197);    { Crossbar grid character }
      ArrowKey = Chr(0);      { Indicates arrow key is used }
      Up       = Chr(72);     { Character for move up }
      Down     = Chr(80);     { Character for move down }
      Left     = Chr(75);     { Character for move left }
      Right    = Chr(77);     { Character for move right }
      MaxSize  = 10;          { Maximum dimension of game grid }
      XChars   = 6;           { Horizontal size of grid square }
      YChars   = 4;           { Vertical size of grid square }
```

```
TYPE Game = OBJECT
               board     : ARRAY [1..MaxSize, 1..MaxSize] OF Char;
               shape1    : Char;
               shape2    : Char;
               current   : Char;
               boardSize : Integer;
               PROCEDURE SetBoardSize (size : Integer);
               PROCEDURE SetShapes (player1, player2 : Char);
               FUNCTION  CurrentPlayer : Char;
               PROCEDURE SwitchPlayer;
               PROCEDURE DrawPiece (row, col : Integer; shape : Char);
               PROCEDURE SetPiece (row, col : Integer; shape : Char);
               FUNCTION  Piece (row, col : Integer) : Char;
               PROCEDURE GetMove (VAR row, col : Integer);
               PROCEDURE Init
            END;
    Tic  = OBJECT(Game)
               PROCEDURE Init; OVERRIDE;
               FUNCTION  ValidMove(row, col : Integer) : Boolean;
               PROCEDURE MakeMove (row, col : Integer);
               FUNCTION  GameWin : Boolean;
               FUNCTION  GameDraw : Boolean
            END;

VAR ticTacToe : Tic;
    win, draw : Boolean;
    row, col  : Integer;

PROCEDURE Game.SetBoardSize (size : Integer);
  BEGIN
    Self.boardSize := size
  END;

PROCEDURE Game.SetShapes (player1, player2 : Char);
  BEGIN
    Self.shape1 := player1;
    Self.shape2 := player2
  END;

FUNCTION Game.CurrentPlayer : Char;
  BEGIN
    CurrentPlayer := Self.current
  END;

PROCEDURE Game.SwitchPlayer;
  BEGIN
    IF Self.current = Self.shape1 THEN
        Self.current := Self.shape2
      ELSE
        Self.current := Self.shape1
  END;
```

```
PROCEDURE Game.DrawPiece (row, col : Integer; shape : Char);
  BEGIN
    GotoXY(XChars * (col - 1) + XChars DIV 2,
           YChars * (row - 1) + YChars DIV 2);
    Write(shape)
  END;

PROCEDURE Game.SetPiece (row, col : Integer; shape : Char);
  BEGIN
    Self.board[row, col] := shape;
    Self.DrawPiece(row, col, shape)
  END;

FUNCTION Game.Piece (row, col : Integer) : Char;
  BEGIN
    Piece := Self.board[row, col]
  END;

PROCEDURE Game.GetMove (VAR row, col : Integer);
  VAR colInc : Integer;
      key    : Char;
      done   : Boolean;
  BEGIN
    done := False;
    REPEAT
      Self.DrawPiece(row, col, Cursor);
      GotoXY(80, 25);              { Move cursor out of view }
      Delay(50);
      Self.DrawPiece(row, col, Self.Piece(row, col));
      GotoXY(80, 25);              { Move cursor out of view }
      Delay(50);
      IF keyPressed THEN
        BEGIN
          key := ReadKey;
          done := (key = Space);
          IF key = ArrowKey THEN
            CASE Readkey OF
              Up    : IF row > 1 THEN
                          row := row - 1;
              Down  : IF row < Self.boardSize THEN
                          row := row + 1;
              Left  : IF col > 1 THEN
                          col := col - 1;
              Right : IF col < Self.boardSize THEN
                          col := col + 1
            END
        END
    UNTIL done
  END;
```

```
PROCEDURE Game.Init;
  VAR row, col, x, y : Integer;
  BEGIN
    Self.current := Self.shape1;
    FOR row := 1 TO Self.boardSize DO
      FOR col := 1 TO Self.boardSize DO
        Self.SetPiece(row, col, Space);
    { Draw horizontal bars }
    FOR row := 1 TO Self.boardSize - 1 DO
      FOR x := 1 TO Self.boardSize * XChars - 1 DO
        BEGIN
          GotoXY(x, row * YChars);
          Write(Hbar)
        END;
    { Draw vertical bars }
    FOR col := 1 TO Self.boardSize - 1 DO
      FOR y := 1 TO Self.boardSize * YChars - 1 DO
        BEGIN
          GotoXY(col * XChars, y);
          Write(Vbar)
        END;
    { Draw intersections of bars }
    FOR row := 1 TO Self.boardSize - 1 DO
      FOR col := 1 TO Self.boardSize - 1 DO
        BEGIN
          GotoXY(XChars * col, YChars * row);
          Write(Crossbar)
        END
  END;

PROCEDURE Tic.Init;
  BEGIN
    Self.SetBoardSize(3);
    Self.SetShapes('X', 'O');
    INHERITED Self.Init
  END;

FUNCTION Tic.ValidMove (row, col : Integer) : Boolean;
  BEGIN
    ValidMove := (Self.Piece(row, col) = Space)
  END;

PROCEDURE Tic.MakeMove (row, col : Integer);
  BEGIN
    Self.SetPiece(row, col, Self.CurrentPlayer)
  END;
```

```
FUNCTION Tic.GameWin : Boolean;
  VAR position : Integer;
      tempWin  : Boolean;
  FUNCTION ColumnWin (row : Integer) : Boolean;
    VAR piece : Char;
        col   : Integer;
    BEGIN { Function ColumnWin }
      ColumnWin := False;
      piece := Self.Piece(row, 1);
      IF piece <> Space THEN
        BEGIN
          ColumnWin := True;        { Assume win, try to disprove }
          FOR col := 2 TO Self.boardSize DO
            IF Self.Piece(row, col) <> piece THEN
              ColumnWin := False
        END
    END; { Function ColumnWin }
  FUNCTION RowWin (col : Integer) : Boolean;
    VAR piece : Char;
        row   : Integer;
    BEGIN { Function RowWin }
      RowWin := False;
      piece := Self.Piece(1, col);
      IF piece <> Space THEN
        BEGIN
          RowWin := True;           { Assume win, try to disprove }
          FOR row := 2 TO Self.boardSize DO
            IF Self.Piece(row, col) <> piece THEN
              RowWin := False
        END
    END; { Function RowWin }
  FUNCTION DiagonalWin (row, rowInc : Integer) : Boolean;
    VAR piece : Char;
        col   : Integer;
    BEGIN { Function DiagonalWin }
      DiagonalWin := False;
      piece := Self.Piece(row, 1);
      IF piece <> Space THEN
        BEGIN
          DiagonalWin := True;      { Assume win, try to disprove }
          FOR col := 2 TO Self.boardSize DO
            BEGIN
              row := row + rowInc;
              IF Self.Piece(row, col) <> piece THEN
                DiagonalWin := False
            END
        END
    END; { Function DiagonalWin }
```

```
    BEGIN { Function Tic.GameWin }
      tempWin := False;
      FOR position := 1 TO Self.boardSize DO
        tempWin := tempWin OR ColumnWin(position)
                         OR RowWin(position);
      tempWin := tempWin OR
                  DiagonalWin(1, 1) OR
                  DiagonalWin(Self.boardSize, -1);
      GameWin := tempWin
    END;  { Function Tic.GameWin }

  FUNCTION Tic.GameDraw : Boolean;
    VAR row, col : Integer;
    BEGIN
      GameDraw := True;
      FOR row := 1 TO Self.boardSize DO
        FOR col := 1 TO Self.boardSize DO
          IF Self.Piece(row, col) = Space THEN
              GameDraw := False
    END;

BEGIN { GameObjects }
  ClrScr;
  win  := False;
  draw := False;
  New(ticTacToe);
  ticTacToe.Init;
  REPEAT
    GotoXY(1, 23);
    Write('Player ', ticTacToe.CurrentPlayer, ':  your move');
    row := ticTacToe.boardSize DIV 2 + 1;
    col := row;
    REPEAT
      ticTacToe.GetMove(row, col)
    UNTIL ticTacToe.ValidMove(row, col);
    ticTacToe.MakeMove(row, col);
    win := ticTacToe.GameWin;
    IF NOT win THEN
      BEGIN
        draw := ticTacToe.GameDraw;
        IF NOT draw THEN
          ticTacToe.SwitchPlayer
      END
  UNTIL win OR draw;
  GotoXY(1, 23);
  IF draw THEN
      Writeln('A DRAW.              ')
    ELSE
      Writeln('PLAYER ', ticTacToe.CurrentPlayer, ' WINS!      ');
  Dispose(ticTacToe)
END. { GameObjects }
```

Chapter 13
Summary

1. An *object* is a dynamic structure consisting of *instance variables*, that stores data, and *methods* (procedures and functions), that act on the instance variables. An object offers portability and modifiability by hiding the representation of data. The data that need to be shared by several methods are in a single place where only these methods should alter them. Calling an object method is referred to as *sending a message* to an object.

2. The data type of an object is a *class*. Under a particular class there can be *subclasses*, which *inherit* all the instance variables and methods of the class. A subclass should be a refinement of its parent class.

3. The network of a class and its subclasses (and their subclasses) form an object *hierarchy*. In these cases, the initial class is called the *base class*.

4. Subclasses can OVERRIDE methods declared in "higher" classes. This allows a subclass to duplicate a previously defined method name. The subclass still can call the parent method by preceding the call with the keyword INHERITED.

Chapter 13
Programming Projects

1. (a) Write a program that uses a class Menu to create and display a menu. The class Menu should have instance variables

```
list  : ARRAY [1..10] OF STRING[35];
count : Integer;          { Number of items presently in menu }
```

and methods to place an item in the menu and display the menu.

```
[sample run]
1. Add an item to the menu.
2. Display the menu.
Enter your selection: 1
Enter item: 1. Create a spreadsheet.
Enter your selection: 1
Enter item: 2. Graph data from spreadsheet.
Enter your selection: 2
<screen cleared>
1. Create a spreadsheet.
2. Graph data from spreadsheet.
```

(b) Enhance the program by adding a subclass SpecialMenu enabling placement of the menu at a location specified by the user. Also, allow a title to be placed over the menu and a box to be drawn surrounding the menu.

2. Write a menu-driven program to maintain a stack of integers. The stack should be an object and the menu should include options to push, pop, and display the stack from top to bottom (leaving it intact). Popped numbers should be displayed. Use the following declarations.

```
TYPE StackPointer = ^StackRecord;
     StackRecord  = RECORD
                        data : Integer;
                        next : StackPointer
                    END;
     StackClass   = OBJECT
                        topItem : StackPointer;
                        PROCEDURE Init;
                        PROCEDURE Push (item : Integer);
                        FUNCTION Pop : Integer;
                        FUNCTION IsEmpty : Boolean
                    END;
```

3. A polynomial of degree n is an expression of the form

$$a_n x^n + a_{n-1} x^{n-1} + \ldots + a_1 x + a_0$$

where the coefficients a_n, a_{n-1}, ..., a_1, and a_0 are real numbers, n is a nonnegative integer and $a_n \neq 0$. A polynomial can be represented in a linked list with each node storing the coefficient and degree of a single nonzero term. (See Exercise 34 of Section 12.1.) The derivative and antiderivative of the polynomial above are

$$n a_n x^{n-1} + (n-1)a_{n-1} x^{n-2} + \ldots + a_1$$

and

$$(a_n/(n+1))x^{n+1} + (a_{n-1}/n)x^n + \ldots + (a_1/2)x^2 + a_0 x$$

respectively.

Write a program to request the terms of a polynomial as input and do various calculations. The program should contain a class Polynomial with a pointer instance variable to hold the terms of a polynomial. The class should include the following methods:

(a) Evaluate. Plug in a value of x.
(b) Differentiate. Determine the derivative of a polynomial.
(c) Integrate. Determine an antiderivative of a polynomial.
(d) Slope. Find the slope of the graph of the polynomial at a point whose x-coordinate is input by the user. The slope is calculated by evaluating the derivative of the polynomial at the specified x-value.
(e) Area. Find the (signed) area between the graph of the polynomial from $x = 0$ to a value of x input by the user. The area is calculated by evaluating the antiderivative at the input x-value, evaluating the antiderivative at 0, and subtracting the second quantity from the first.

```
[sample run with 5x³ + 4x]
Enter -1 to signify that all terms have been registered.
Enter the degree of the highest term: 3
Enter the corresponding coefficient: 5
Enter the degree of the next term: 1
Enter the corresponding coefficient: 4
Enter the degree of the next term: -1

A. Specify a value of x, call it a.
B. Calculate f(a).
C. Calculate the slope at x = a.
D. Calculate the area between x = 0 and x = a.
E. Quit

Enter a selection: A
Enter a value for a: 1
Enter a selection: D
The area under the curve from x = 0 to x = 1.00 is 3.25
Enter a selection: E
```

4. A general game class was introduced in Section 13.3. Tic-Tac-Toe was implemented by grouping the methods unique to Tic-Tac-Toe into a subclass of the general game object. The inherited game methods and data, along with the added Tic-Tac-Toe methods, formed an object that could perform all actions associated with Tic-Tac-Toe. Using the same technique, implement the game of Othello, explained below. An Othello object should contain all the methods and data needed for the game.

Othello is a two-player game played on an 8 × 8 grid such as a checkerboard. Every playing piece has a white side and a black side, each corresponding to one of the two players. The players alternate adding pieces of their respective colors (and thereby flipping one or more pieces of the opponent's color) until no further valid plays are available, often because all 64 places are occupied. A player without a valid play must pass and let his opponent make consecutive plays until a valid play is available. The winner is the player with the most pieces on the board at the end of the game. Figure 13.3 shows the starting configuration of the board.

A single piece or a line of pieces of the opponent's color can be flipped when an added piece, along with an existing piece of the player's color, "surround" the pieces to be flipped. Surrounding a line of pieces means having two pieces of one's own color on both ends of the line of opposing pieces or on both sides of a piece. Pieces can be surrounded horizontally, vertically, or diagonally. A play is valid only if it causes at least one piece to be flipped. Note that the corner pieces cannot be flipped, and thus are of strategic importance.

In the initial configuration shown in Figure 13.3, white has four possible plays: E3, F4, C5, and D6. For any play, the surrounded black piece gets flipped to white. After the play, white has four pieces and black has one. Following this, black has three possible plays. (**Hint:** Study the implementation of the method GameWin in the Tic-Tac-Toe object of Section 13.3.)

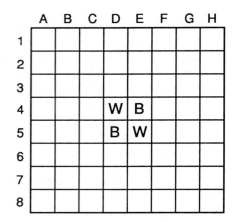

Figure 13.3 Initial Configuration for the Game of Othello

Appendix A

ASCII Values

ASCII Value	Character	ASCII Value	Character	ASCII Value	Character
000	(null)	038	&	076	L
001	☺	039	'	077	M
002	●	040	(	078	N
003	♥	041	)	079	O
004	♦	042	*	080	P
005	♣	043	+	081	Q
006	♠	044	,	082	R
007	(beep)	045	-	083	S
008	■	046	.	084	T
009	(tab)	047	/	085	U
010	(line feed)	048	0	086	V
011	(home)	049	1	087	W
012	(form feed)	050	2	088	X
013	(carriage return)	051	3	089	Y
014	♫	052	4	090	Z
015	☼	053	5	091	[
016	►	054	6	092	\
017	◄	055	7	093	]
018	↕	056	8	094	∧
019	!!	057	9	095	—
020	¶	058	:	096	`
021	§	059	;	097	a
022	▬	060	<	098	b
023	↨	061	=	099	c
024	↑	062	>	100	d
025	↓	063	?	101	e
026	→	064	@	102	f
027	←	065	A	103	g
028	(cursor right)	066	B	104	h
029	(cursor left)	067	C	105	i
030	(cursor up)	068	D	106	j
031	(cursor down)	069	E	107	k
032	(space)	070	F	108	l
033	!	071	G	109	m
034	''	072	H	110	n
035	#	073	I	111	o
036	$	074	J	112	p
037	%	075	K	113	q

ASCII Value	Character	ASCII Value	Character	ASCII Value	Character
114	r	162	ó	210	╥
115	s	163	ú	211	╙
116	t	164	ñ	212	╘
117	u	165	Ñ	213	╒
118	v	166	ª	214	╓
119	w	167	º	215	╫
120	x	168	¿	216	╪
121	y	169	⌐	217	┘
122	z	170	¬	218	┌
123	{	171	½	219	█
124	¦	172	¼	220	▄
125	}	173	¡	221	▌
126	~	174	«	222	▐
127	⌂	175	»	223	▀
128	Ç	176	░	224	α
129	ü	177	▒	225	β
130	é	178	▓	226	Γ
131	â	179	│	227	π
132	ä	180	┤	228	Σ
133	à	181	╡	229	σ
134	å	182	╢	230	µ
135	ç	183	╖	231	τ
136	ê	184	╕	232	Φ
137	ë	185	╣	233	Θ
138	è	186	║	234	Ω
139	ï	187	╗	235	δ
140	î	188	╝	236	∞
141	ì	189	╜	237	Ø
142	Ä	190	╛	238	∈
143	Å	191	┐	239	∩
144	É	192	└	240	≡
145	æ	193	┴	241	±
146	Æ	194	┬	242	≥
147	ô	195	├	243	≤
148	ö	196	─	244	⌠
149	ò	197	┼	245	⌡
150	û	198	╞	246	÷
151	ù	199	╟	247	≈
152	ÿ	200	╚	248	°
153	Ö	201	╔	249	•
154	Ü	202	╩	250	·
155	¢	203	╦	251	√
156	£	204	╠	252	ⁿ
157	¥	205	═	253	²
158	Pt	206	╬	254	■
159	ƒ	207	╧	255	(blank 'FF')
160	á	208	╨		
161	í	209	╤		

Appendix B

Basic Run-Time Error Messages

2 **File not found** A file cannot be Reset or Appended unless it already exists in the place it is expected.

3 **Path not found** The name of a file is not legal. This may mean that the file name includes illegal characters or that a directory specified in the name does not exist.

4 **Too many open files** Results if too many files are opened (with Reset or Rewrite) at the same time. This error can normally be prevented by closing files once they are no longer needed. If necessary, the FILES value can be changed in CONFIG.SYS to allow more files to be used (see a DOS reference manual).

5 **File access denied** An attempt was made to read or write a file that is not opened for the corresponding action, or the file has its access attribute set as read-only. Also, if there is insufficient room on the disk or in a directory, this error may occur.

15 **Invalid drive value** A statement contains an invalid value for a drive. The ChDir and GetDir statements give this error if passed an invalid drive specification.

16 **Current directory may not be deleted** The RmDir statement contained a path that represents the current directory.

17 **Rename must occur on same drive** The Rename statement contained file names with different drive specifications.

100 **File read error** An attempt was made to read past the end of a file.

101 **Disk write error** The disk is full. There is no room to add any more data to the file.

102 **File not assigned** A file cannot be Reset or Rewritten if it has not been Assigned.

103 **File not open** An attempt was made to close, read, or write a file that has not been Reset or Rewritten.

104 **File not open for input** An attempt was made to read a text file that was not Reset. The file must be Reset before it can be read.

105 **File not open for output** An attempt was made to write to a text file that was opened with Reset. The text file should be opened with Rewrite or Append.

106   Invalid numeric format An attempt was made to read a number from a text file and the data did not correspond in format to the variable receiving the data.

150   Disk is write protected An attempt was made to write to a disk that is write protected. (See Appendix I.)

151   Unknown unit An input or output operation was directed to a drive or device that does not exist.

152   Drive not ready An attempt was made to access a drive that is not available or does not contain a disk. Check the latch on the floppy drive.

153   Invalid command DOS does not recognize a command that was passed to it.

154   Data error (CRC) A disk sector contained a Cyclical Redundancy Check error.

157   Non-MS-DOS disk An input or output operation was directed to a disk that is not formatted or is formatted for a different system.

159   Printer out of paper Output was sent to a printer that has no paper.

161   Read fault A hardware error occurred.

162   General failure A hardware or other system error occurred.

160   Device write fault Check that printer is turned on.

180   Object not allocated An object was Disposed without previously being allocated with a New Statement.

181   Invalid object reference A message was sent to an object that was not allocated previously with a New statement.

200   Division by zero Division by zero was attempted by some statement in the program.

201   Range check error This error only arises if the Range Checking compiler option {$R+} is on. It indicates either that an attempt was made to assign a value to a variable or a parameter that is not in its legal range or an attempt was made to access an out-of-range array index.

202   Stack overflow This error only arises when the Stack Checking compiler option is on. It indicates that there is not enough room to store all of the local variables of the subprograms that are in progress. It usually arises during recursion and may indicate that the recursion is infinite, or simply that the stack needs to be larger. The second case may be fixed by increasing the Stack value from the compiler options window (Alt/O/C).

203   Heap overflow The heap is the portion of memory that holds dynamic variables. This error arises when the Heap Checking compiler option is on. It indicates there is not enough room to create any more New pointer records. This may mean a large number of dynamic variables are being orphaned by neglecting to Dispose them, or that the heap is not large enough. If calling Dispose on all records once they are not needed does not solve this problem, then the heap size can be increased from the compiler options window (Alt/O/C).

204 Invalid pointer operation   Disposing a NIL pointer causes this error.

205 Real overflow   A calculation was done with Real values whose result exceeded the legal bounds for Reals, −1.7E+39 through 1.7E+38. This error may arise even if the final value of an expression would have been in bounds. This error can often be corrected by declaring the variable as type Double. (See Appendix F.)

207 Invalid Real operation
   (a) Trunc or Round was called with an argument value that could not be converted to an Integer.
   (b) The Sqrt of a negative number was taken.
   (c) Ln of zero or a negative number was taken.

Appendix C

Compiler Error Messages

(The end of this appendix contains a numerical listing of error messages.)

18 **";" expected** A semicolon must separate statements in a program. TYPE, CONST, and VAR sections and subprogram declarations must also end with a semicolon. Finally, if this error arises at the end of a program (upon the END. statement), it may mean either that a subprogram has been declared without being given a statement part, or a CASE, RECORD, or BEGIN statement in the main body of the program has not been given a matching END.

19 **")" expected** A parenthesis should be added at the indicated position. This may occur if too many parameters are given in a procedure call or if a string literal contains a single quote mark (') in the wrong place. (If it is necessary to use a single quote inside a string, then write two single quotes instead.)

20 **"." expected** A program must end with the statement "END." If this error arises before the last line of the program, then an extra END has been placed somewhere.

30 **"[" expected** Arrays are declared as type ARRAY [*SubRange*] OF Type. Sets are written as [*elements*].

31 **"]" expected** (See above.) A set is written in a format similar to the following: *setName* := [5, 7..13, 99].

35 **"=" expected** Types are defined with equal signs, not colons.

42 **":" expected** Variables are declared by statements of the form

```
VAR variableName : TypeName;
```

and CASE statement value lists are indicated by

```
valueList : statement;
```

47 **"(" expected** This error will result if a type name is given where a value belongs, and QuickPascal therefore expects a type cast, or if a decimal is entered without a zero before it. This may also be caused by omitting the parameters of a subprogram. In particular, this will result if one incorrectly uses a function's value within the function:

74 **":=" expected** Assignment statements must use ":=" instead of "=".

82 **"," expected** This error can arise if too few parameters are passed in a call to a subprogram, or if too few values are included in a typed constant declaration.

21 **BEGIN expected** This may indicate a typographical error. Otherwise, it may indicate a statement where none is expected. Subprograms and the main program must include a BEGIN statement preceding all executable statements.

64 **Boolean expression expected** In conditions, equality is tested with '=', not ':='. Error usually occurs if WHILE, UNTIL, or IF is not followed by a valid condition.

2 **Cannot open file** May indicate that an illegal or unavailable unit name appears in a USES statement. The disk location where the units are stored should match the path specified in the 'Units directories' section of the environment options menu (Alt/O/E).

93 **Cannot read expressions of this type** Read and Readln accept values of type STRING, Char, Integer, and Real. They do not accept Boolean, enumerated, or SET types.

89 **Cannot write expressions of this type** Write and Writeln accept values of type STRING, Char, Integer, Real, and Boolean. They do not accept enumerated or SET types.

115 **Class must be defined at global level** Subprograms cannot define their own object classes. The object classes must be declared in the main program.

116 **Class must be defined in type definition** Object classes must be defined in the TYPE section, not in the VAR section.

51 **Conflicting operands** An operation is being attempted on values of incompatible types. Check that parentheses are used where needed.

36 **Constant expected** Subrange bounds and CASE statement value lists must have constant values. Variables are not allowed in CASE value lists.

81 **Constant value out of range** Arises if a subrange constant or variable is assigned a value outside of its range.

107 **Coprocessor required** In order for the Numeric Processing compiler directive to be allowed, a special chip must be installed. This compiler option can be disabled from the compiler options menu (Alt/O/C).

147 **Directive must be at top of program** Some compiler directives should be placed immediately following the PROGRAM statement.

80 **Disk full** There is no room on the disk for the files that compilation creates.

83 **Division by zero** An expression that the compiler evaluates prior to run-time includes a division by zero.

65 **DO expected** WHILE and FOR statements require the word DO to appear immediately before the body of the loop.

88 **File type expected** This error could be caused by an attempt to Seek on a Text file, which is illegal.

22 **END expected** This error usually occurs in faulty type definitions. A RECORD or OBJECT declaration must terminate with an END statement. Also, keywords appearing in inappropriate places may cause this error.

12 **Error in character constant** An invalid format was used in defining a constant.

50 **Error in expression** This may indicate an arithmetic or string expression has an incorrect format. It also may imply a range was written with three periods (...) instead of two (..).

11 **Error in integer constant** This may indicate that the value is outside the range allowed for Integers (if an integer needs to have a value less than −32768 or greater than 32767 then it should be declared LongInt). It may also indicate that an attempt was made to declare a variable with an illegal character in its name.

106 **Error in real constant** A real constant was defined using an invalid format.

73 **Error in statement** The statement is incomplete or incorrectly written. If this error arises outside of all statement parts of the program, it probably indicates an END is missing somewhere (and so the compiler thinks it is still within a statement part).

112 **Header does not match previous declaration** Occurs in object class declarations when a method declaration differs from the header of its definition. In general, indicates the parameters of a FORWARD declaration of a subprogram do not match the actual declaration of the subprogram. (Once a subprogram has been declared FORWARD, it is not necessary to list the parameters again at all.)

17 **Identifier expected** Elements of enumerated types must be identifiers. (Recall that items such as 5 and 'a' are not identifiers.) Also, literals and expressions cannot be passed to VAR parameters.

25 **Identifier or Label already defined** An identifier cannot be declared twice at the same scope level.

9 **Illegal character** Indicates a character that has no meaning in Quick-Pascal. The only special character allowed in identifier names is the underscore (_) character.

40 **Incompatible subrange types** An assignment was made between values of incompatible subrange types.

150 **Index out of range** An array location has been referenced that is not within the bounds declared for the array. This message can occur only if the {$R+} compiler option is enabled.

61 **Index type is not compatible with the declaration** The array was not declared to accept index values of this type.

85 **Integer expression expected** Functions have specific types for inputs and outputs. Also, Sqrt, Ln, Int, Sin, and certain other functions return Real values regardless of the argument type.

37 Integer or real constant expected (See 85 above.)

94 Integer or real expression expected (See 85 above.)

95 Integer or real variable expected (See 85 above.)

44 Integer constant expected (See 85 above.)

148 Invalid assignment Assignment statements cannot be used with files, objects, or records that contain files or objects.

15 Invalid directive Any comment starting {$ indicates a compiler directive.

91 Invalid file type A file can be of any type that does not include another file. Also, Writeln and Readln can only be called with Text files.

77 Invalid FOR control variable The control variable of a FOR statement must be an ordinal type.

53 Invalid identifier This message may result when a subprogram name is placed where a variable or constant is required.

103 Invalid QPU file The QPU files provided with the copy of QuickPascal are Crt, MSGraph, MSGrUtil, and Printer. In this text, USES statements should only reference these names. (If this error arises with one of those files, get a new copy of the file).

45 Invalid string length The declared length of a string must be in the range of 1 to 255.

54 Invalid type cast Type casts must be from one ordinal type to another, and must produce a value that is inside the range of the destination type.

127 Invalid variable reference This message may be caused by using a constant where a variable is required.

10 Line too long The compiler can only handle lines of up to 127 characters. Any line longer than that should be split.

41 Low bound exceeds high bound The first bound of a range cannot be greater than the second bound in the ordinal type. For enumerated and subrange types, *ident1* is less than *ident2* if *ident1* is listed in the definition of the enumerated type before *ident2*.

60 No such field in this record or object No field with that name was defined in the record or object declaration.

119 Object type expected This will occur if an object is declared as a subclass of something that is not an object class.

120 Object must be defined at global level Subprograms cannot contain their own objects. The objects must be declared in the main program.

116 Object must be defined in type definition Objects must be defined in the TYPE section, not within the VAR section.

28 OF expected CASE statements and ARRAY, FILE, and SET declarations require the keyword OF.

90 **Ordinal expression expected** Ordinal types are Boolean, Char, Integer, enumerated, and subrange types.

38 **Range expected** The situation required a range of values rather than a single value or several values separated by commas.

132 **Real overflow** The value's magnitude exceeded the bounds of Real values (from $-1.7E+38$ to $1.7E+38$).

52 **Right operand is not a set** The IN operator requires a set on the right side.

149 **Set type out of range** This message is generated when a set type is defined with more than 256 elements.

13 **String constant exceeds line** Strings cannot extend beyond one line of a program. If it is necessary to create a string that is longer than this, you should divide it into parts and add them together; such as

```
longString := 'blah blah blah blah blah blah blah blah ' +
              'blah blah blah blah blah blah blah blah'
```

49 **Structure too big** An array or record has been declared that is too large for QuickPascal to accomodate.

39 **Subrange bounds must be scalar** An array must have ordinal bounds.

124 **Syntax error** This is a catch-all error; the marked item does not follow the rules of QuickPascal grammar.

66 **THEN expected** THEN must appear after the condition of an IF statement.

125 **This method has no parent** The INHERITED keyword can only be used if a method of the same name exists in one of the object's ancestors.

27 **This type not allowed here** A file cannot contain another file, files can only be passed to VAR parameters, and the value returned by a function cannot be a record or a file.

114 **Too many parameters** The subprogram being called was not declared to accept this many parameters.

146 **Too many variables** The variables that have been declared require more memory than QuickPascal can create for them. Files can be used instead to store the information, or the data can be stored dynamically using pointers.

79 **TO or DOWNTO expected** A FOR statement must be written

```
FOR var := firstLimit TO (or DOWNTO) secondLimit DO
  statement
```

75 **Type mismatch** Either the wrong type of value is being passed to a parameter of a subprogram, an illegal assignment is being made, or two types are being compared improperly.

14 **Unexpected end of file** Results if no 'END.' statement is present. Check that all comments are closed.

32 Unknown Identifier The identifier (constant, variable, or subprogram) at the cursor has not been declared prior to being used. This error also can occur if an identifier local to a subprogram is used outside the subprogram. Often incorrect spelling is responsible for the error.

159 Unsatisfied forward name reference A name has been used without being defined. Check its spelling.

63 UNTIL expected Either the UNTIL statement corresponding to a REPEAT statement has been omitted, or there are too many ENDs within the REPEAT loop.

43 Unsatisfied forward reference Once a subprogram has been declared FORWARD, it must be defined later at the same scope level. Either the subprogram has not been defined or its scope does not match the scope of the FORWARD declaration.

57 Variable type must be pointer The ^ operator accesses what an identifier points to. (It does not indicate taking a number to a power, as it does in BASIC.) Therefore, ^ can only follow pointers.

58 Variable type must be record Since a period after an identifier name indicates that a field of the identifier is being accessed, periods can only follow RECORD and OBJECT variables.

Numeric Listing of Error Messages

1 Out of memory
2 Cannot open file
3 File too big
4 Too many nested files
5 Cannot read file
6 Cannot close file
7 Cannot seek file
8 Invalid end of line
9 Illegal character
10 Line too long
11 Error in integer constant
12 Error in character constant
13 String constant exceeds line
14 Unexpected end of file
15 Invalid directive
16 End of file expected
17 Identifier expected
18 ";" expected
19 ")" expected
20 "." expected

21 BEGIN expected

22 END expected

23 Label must be in the range 0..9999

24 Label already defined

25 Identifier or Label already defined

26 Error in type definition

27 This type not allowed here

28 OF expected

29 Implementation restriction

30 "[" expected

31 "]" expected

32 Unknown identifier

33 Error in simple type definition

34 Type identifier expected

35 "=" expected

36 Constant expected

37 Integer or real constant expected

38 Range expected

39 Subrange bounds must be scalar

40 Incompatible subrange types

41 Low bound exceeds high bound

42 ":" expected

43 Unsatisfied forward reference

44 Integer constant expected

45 Invalid string length

46 Tag field type must be scalar or subrange

47 "(" expected

48 Too many literals

49 Structure too big

50 Error in expression

51 Conflicting operands

52 Right operand is not a set

53 Invalid identifier

54 Invalid type cast

55 Cannot create file

56 Cannot write file

57 Variable type must be pointer

58 Variable type must be record

59 Variable type must be array or string

60 No such field in this record or object

61 Index type is not compatible with the declaration

62 Routine too big

63 UNTIL expected

64 Boolean expression expected

65 DO expected

66 THEN expected

67 Invalid label

68 Unknown label

69 Label not within current block

70 Label already defined

71 Label expected

72 Undefined label in preceding statement part

73 Error in statement

74 ":=" expected

75 Type mismatch

76 Variable identifier expected

77 Invalid FOR control variable

78 Scalar type expected

79 TO or DOWNTO expected

80 Disk full

81 Constant value out of range

82 "," expected

83 Division by zero

84 Too many local routines

85 Integer expression expected

86 Pointer type cannot be referenced

87 Typed pointer expected

88 File type expected

89 Cannot write expressions of this type

90 Ordinal expression expected

91 Invalid file type

92 Variable parameter expected

93 Cannot read expressions of this type

94 Integer or real expression expected

95 Integer or real variable expected

96 Function not mounted

97 Inline error

98 Label definition not allowed in interface part

99 INTERFACE expected

100 IMPLEMENTATION expected

101 Invalid unit file

102 Field or method already defined

103 Invalid QPU file

104 Duplicate unit name

105 Circular unit reference

106 Error in real constant

107 Coprocessor required

108 Too many nested conditional directives

109 Misplaced directive

110 $ENDIF directive missing

111 Too many conditional symbols

112 Header does not match previous declaration

113 Invalid qualification

114 Too many parameters

115 Class must be defined at global level

116 Class must be defined in type definition

117 Invalid procedure or function reference

118 Procedure or function variable expected

119 Object type expected

120 Object must be defined at global level

121 Object must be defined in type definition

122 Invalid class type

123 Class table overflow

124 Syntax error

125 This method has no parent

126 Type of expression must be pointer

127 Invalid variable reference

128 Symbol table overflow

129 Too many imported units

130 Code cannot exceed 64k bytes

131 Invalid real operation

132 Real overflow

133 Real underflow

134 Undefined external

135 Too many object file names

136 Invalid object file

137 Object file too large

138 Invalid segment definition

139 Invalid segment name

140 Code segment too large

141 Invalid PUBLIC definition

142 Invalid EXTRN definition

143 Too many EXTRNs

144 Invalid fixup

145 Too many opened files

146 Too many variables

147 Directive must be at top of program

148 Invalid assignment

149 Set type out of range

150 Index out of range

151 Object variable expected in MEMBER function

152 Object type expected in MEMBER function

153 Expression too complicated

154 Invalid unit name

155 Line information table overflow

156 Fixup table overflow

157 Source table overflow

158 Unit expected

159 Unsatisfied forward name reference

160 Invalid fixup in iterated data record

161 Include files not allowed here

162 Stack overflow

Appendix D

Debugging Tools

Desk Checking and Writeln Statements

Errors in programs are called *bugs* and the process of finding and correcting them is called *debugging*. Since the compiler does not discover logical errors, they present the most difficulties in debugging. One method of discovering a logical error is by **desk checking**, that is, tracing the value of variables on paper by writing down their expected value after "mentally executing" each line in the program. Desk checking is rudimentary and highly impractical except for small programs.

Another method of debugging involves placing Writeln statements at strategic points in the program and displaying the values of selected variables or expressions until the error is detected. After correcting the error, the Writeln statements are removed. For many programming environments, desk checking and Writeln statements are the only debugging methods available to the programmer.

The QuickPascal Run-Time Debugger

The QuickPascal run-time debugger offers a powerful alternative to desk checking and Writeln statements. The debugger performs automatically the same tasks as desk checking and Writeln statements by allowing the programmer to execute individual statements of a program and to watch the changing values of selected variables and expressions in a special window. The QuickPascal run-time debugger is invoked by selecting the Debug option on the menu bar.

Using the QuickPascal Run-Time Debugger

Tracing and Stepping

The most valuable capability of the debugger is that it allows the programmer to execute single successive statements of a program while pausing in between. This is called **tracing** or **stepping**. Without tracing or stepping, the program would race to its conclusion, and many bugs would remain hidden from the programmer.

To trace through a program, it must first be compiled. When the function key F8 is pressed, the BEGIN in the main statement part of the program is highlighted, and after pressing F8 again, the statement immediately following BEGIN is highlighted. Pressing F8 again executes this statement and highlights the next statement. Each subsequent press of F8 executes the highlighted statement and moves the highlight to the following statement. Tracing provides an excellent way to follow the logical flow of a program through decision structures, procedures, and functions. When a subprogram call is highlighted and F8 is pressed, the highlight bar goes to the first line of the subprogram. After tracing through all the statements in the subprogram, the highlight bar returns to the statement immediately following the original subprogram call. At any time, F4 may be pressed to view the contents of the Output screen.

It may not always be desirable to trace through each subprogram. If a subprogram is highlighted and F10 is pressed rather than F8, the entire subprogram will be executed in a single step, and the statement following the subprogram will be highlighted. It may help to remember that F8 "traces through" a subprogram while F10 "steps over" a subprogram.

Watch Items

While tracing through a program, it is usually desirable to monitor the value of a particular variable. This can be done by designating the variable as a **watch item**. Watch items may be variables, expressions, or conditions, and are displayed in a special window, called the Debug window. As program execution progresses, the values of the watch items appearing in the Debug window change according to their corresponding values in the program.

To create a watch item, press Alt/D/W. A dialog box will appear with the request "Expression: [". Any variable, expression, or condition can be typed into the dialog box. (QuickPascal proposes an expression based on where the cursor was positioned. To use it, simply press Enter.) When the Enter key is pressed, the item will appear in the Debug window. To return to the Edit window press F6. Pressing F6 again will return to the Debug window. To remove an item from the Debug window, press Alt/D/E, use the down arrow key to highlight the item, and then press Tab/Tab/Enter. To remove all items from the Debug window, press Alt/D/W/Tab/Tab/Tab/Enter. By toggling (with F6) between the Edit and the Debug windows, the value of any variable can be monitored throughout the execution of a program.

An alternative to switching between the Edit and Debug windows is to "tile" the screen by pressing Alt/V/T. This splits the screen so both windows may be viewed simultaneously. When the screen is tiled, F6 switches the cursor between the tiled portions of the screen. Pressing Alt/V/A "untiles" the screen.

Value Modification

It may be helpful in debugging to be able to change the value of a variable while execution is suspended. Doing this can be used to escape an infinite loop when otherwise the exit condition for the loop would never be met, or to change the value of a particular variable that has become suspect of problems. QuickPascal makes changing a variable's value in midstream easy. With the program suspended, press Alt/D/M, type in the name of the variable whose value is to be modified, press Tab, type in the new value, and press Enter.

Breakpoints

Breakpoints cause program execution to be suspended when certain events occur. QuickPascal provides three types of breakpoints. Program execution can be suspended when

1. a specific line is reached.

2. a specific line is reached and a given condition is True.

3. a given condition is True.

After a breakpoint causes the execution of a program to be suspended, the values of any watch items in the Debug window may be displayed by pressing F6. New watch items may be specified, causing their current values to be immediately displayed in the Debug window. In addition, the value of any defined variable may be modified. After a program has been suspended at a breakpoint, it can be rerun from the beginning by pressing Shift+F5/F5 or continued from the break-point by pressing F5 alone.

To establish a line as a breakpoint, move the cursor to that line and press F9. The selected line now appears highlighted. When the program is run, execution will be suspended when the highlighted line is reached, but before it is executed.

To establish a line as a breakpoint only when a particular condition is True, move the cursor to that line and then press Alt/D/S/Down-Arrow/Tab/Tab. Type in the condition that must evaluate to True before execution is to stop at that line. Finally, press Enter. When the program is run, execution will be suspended when the highlighted line is reached only if the given condition is True.

To establish a condition alone as the determiner of a breakpoint, press Alt/D/S/Down-Arrow/Down-Arrow/Tab, type in the condition, and press Enter. When running the program, QuickPascal will check the value of the condition before executing each line. If the value is True, program execution will be suspended before the line is executed. **Note:** Programs executed under this type of breakpoint control run slowly. For instance, if the numeric variable myWage is initialized to 0, a condition such as "myWage <= 2" will cause program execution to suspend immediately and at every line of the program until myWage takes on a value greater than 2.

Multiple breakpoints may be set in a program. Whenever any one of the specified breakpoints occurs, program execution is suspended. To remove a breakpoint line, move the cursor to that line and press F9. To remove a break-point condition, press Alt/D/E, use the cursor keys to select the condition, press Tab/Tab and Enter.

A Debugging Walk-Through

The following walk-through uses the debugging tools discussed above.

1. Enter the following program.

```
PROGRAM DebugIt;
{ Demonstrate the debugging tools }

USES Crt;

VAR wage : Real;
```

```
FUNCTION YrIncome (salary : Real) : Real;
{ Estimate yearly income }
  BEGIN
    YrIncome := 2000 * salary
  END;

BEGIN
  ClrScr;
  Write('Hourly wage: ');
  Readln(wage);
  IF wage < 3.35 THEN
      Writeln('Below the minimum wage.')
    ELSE
      Writeln('Ok');
  Writeln('Your approx. yearly income is $', YrIncome(wage):2:2)
END.
```

2. Compile the program. Move the cursor to the statement "Writeln('Ok')", and then press F9. Notice that the line becomes highlighted. The line has been designated as a breakpoint.

3. Run the program by pressing F5 and respond with an hourly wage of 6.50. Notice that the program stops at the breakpoint.

4. Press F4 to look at the Output screen. Notice that the line "Writeln('Ok')" has not been executed. Press F4 again to return to the Edit window.

5. Press Alt/D/W, type wage, and press Enter. Notice that the Debug window has been opened and that the value of the variable has been displayed.

6. Tile the window displays by pressing Alt/V/T. Now the Edit and Debug windows are both visible.

7. Press Alt/D/W, type the condition (wage < 7), and press Enter. Notice that the value of the condition (wage < 7) is displayed as True.

8. Press Alt/D/W, type salary, and press Enter. Notice the error message displayed in the Debug window: <Error P0032 Unknown identifier>. This message appears because the variable salary is only defined when execution occurs within the function YrIncome. If the program is suspended within the function by a breakpoint or tracing, an actual value will be displayed. **Note:** All watch items show this error message before and after the program executes.

9. Press F6 to switch back to the Edit Window.

10. Press F5 to continue running the program to the end. (After viewing the output, press any key to return to the Edit window.)

11. Press F5 to rerun the program from the beginning, but this time respond with the hourly wage of 2.75. Notice that the program ran to the end since the breakpoint was never encountered during the execution of the program. Press any key to return to the Edit window.

12. Remove the one breakpoint previously set by moving the cursor to that line and pressing F9. The line is no longer a breakpoint and is no longer highlighted.

13. Press F8 12 times to execute the program by tracing. Pause between each pressing to observe the values of the variables in the Debug window. Press any key to return to the Edit window.

14. Press F10 nine times to execute the program by stepping. Notice that the function is executed as a single statement. Pause between pushes. Press any key to return to the Edit window.

15. Move the cursor to the line YrIncome := 2000 * salary. Make this a breakpoint by pressing F9.

16. Press F5 to rerun the program. Enter an hourly wage of 5.00.

17. When program execution stops at the breakpoint, press Alt/D/M and type salary, but *do not* press Enter. Press Tab and wait for the current value of 5.00 to be displayed. Modify this value to 3.25, and press Enter.

18. Press F5 to continue execution of the program. Note that the output shows an Ok because the initial input was above the minimum wage, but the annual figure computed (6500.00) corresponds to the subminimum wage of 3.25.

19. To remove all Watch items from the Debug window, press Alt/D/W, then press Tab four times to move the cursor to the <Clear All> option and, lastly, press Enter. Note that the Debug window has closed. Press Alt/V/A to "untile" the screen.

Appendix E

Editing Commands

The charts below summarize the types of editing commands presented in Chapter 1. Some advanced editing commands that use QuickPascal's Clipboard follow these charts.

Commands to Move Cursor

Left one character	Left Arrow
Right one character	Right Arrow
Left to start of word	Ctrl+Left Arrow
Right to start of word	Ctrl+Right Arrow
Left to start of line	Home
Right to end of line	End
Up one line	Up Arrow
Down one line	Down Arrow
Up to first line in program	Ctrl+Home
Down to last line in program	Ctrl+End

Commands to Scroll

Up to a new page	PgUp
Down to a new page	PgDn
Scroll view up one line in program	Ctrl+Up Arrow
Scroll view down one line in program	Ctrl+Down Arrow

Commands to Delete Text

Delete character preceding cursor	Backspace
Delete character at cursor	Del
Delete from cursor to end of word	Ctrl+T
Delete from cursor to end of line	Ctrl+Q/Y
Delete entire line	Ctrl+Y

Using the Clipboard

QuickPascal sets aside a part of memory, called the **Clipboard**, to assist in moving and copying selected portions of text. Whenever the current line is deleted with the command Ctrl+Y or Ctrl+Q/Y, the deleted text is placed in the Clipboard. At any time, pressing Shift+Ins inserts the contents of the Clipboard at the cursor position.

The following steps can be used to move a line of code to a new location.

1. Place the cursor anywhere in the line of code to be moved.

2. Press Ctrl+Y to erase the line of code and place it into the Clipboard.

3. Move the cursor to the desired new location for the line of code. Press Home to be sure the cursor is at the start of the line.

4. Press Shift+Ins to insert the line of code at the cursor position.

(**Note:** After the contents of the Clipboard is copied at the cursor position, the text remains in the Clipboard and can therefore be easily duplicated in several locations.)

Larger portions of contiguous text, called **blocks**, also can be moved into the Clipboard. To select a segment of text as a block, move the cursor to the beginning of the segment, hold down the Shift key, move the cursor to the end of the segment of text, and then release the Shift key. The selected block will be highlighted. The following commands can now be applied to the selected block.

Shift+Del Erases the selected block and places it in the Clipboard.

Ctrl+Ins Places a copy of the selected block in the Clipboard while leaving the block intact.

Del Erases the selected block without placing it in the Clipboard.

Taking any action other than the three actions above, (for instance, moving the cursor) "deselects" the portion of text currently highlighted. Moving a block is described below.

1. Select the block to be moved.

2. Press Shift+Del (or Ctrl+Ins) to erase (or copy) the block and place it into the Clipboard.

3. Move the cursor to the desired new location for the block.

4. Press Shift+Ins to insert the block at the cursor position.

(**Note:** QuickPascal responds to many editing commands familiar to WordStar users. For example, Ctrl+F moves the cursor right to the start of the next word, Ctrl+Q/A invokes find and replace, Ctrl+K/B and Ctrl+K/K select a portion of text as a block, Ctrl+K/n places an invisible marker in the text that can be returned to with Ctrl+Q/n, and so forth.)

Appendix F

Form of QuickPascal Statements

The reference numbers in brackets occurring after some discussions refer to supporting topics presented at the end of the appendix.

System Unit
(Automatically used by QuickPascal programs.)

Abs(*x*)
The function Abs strips the minus sign from negative numbers and leaves other numbers unchanged. If *x* is any number, then Abs(*x*) is the absolute value of *x*.

Addr(*x*)
The value of the function Addr is the address of *x*, where *x* is any variable, typed constant, procedure name, or function name. The values of Addr can only be assigned to pointer variables.

Append(*fileVar*)
The procedure Append attempts to open the existing DOS text file associated with the file variable *fileVar* so that additional text can be appended or written starting at the current end of the file.

ArcTan(*x*)
The trigonometric function arctangent is the inverse of the tangent function. For any number *x*, ArcTan(*x*) is the angle (in radians) between $-Pi/2$ and $Pi/2$ whose tangent is *x*.

Assign(*fileVar, fileName*)
The procedure Assign informs QuickPascal that program references to the file variable *fileVar* are to access the DOS file *fileName*. In general, *fileVar* is an identifier declared in a VAR statement as type Text or FILE OF ..., and *fileName* is the name of a DOS file previously created with the same structure (Text or FILE OF ...). **Note:** Certain DOS devices can be opened and accessed as Text files by using device names as *fileName*.

Device	Can be opened by using *fileName*:
printer	PRN
screen	CON
serial	COM1

BlockRead(*fileVar, bufferVar, n*)
BlockRead(*fileVar, bufferVar, n, unitsRead*)
The procedure BlockRead attempts to read *n* units of data from the DOS file associated with the file variable *fileVar*. The data read is placed into successive memory locations beginning with the first byte of memory reserved for the variable *bufferVar*. (The variable *bufferVar* is often an array or pointer variable.)

577

If the second form of the procedure call is used, then the actual number of units read will be returned in the variable *unitsRead.* (Insufficient amounts of data in the DOS file can cause less than *n* units to be read.) If the contents of successive memory locations are saved in a file with the BlockWrite procedure, then they can later be restored with the BlockRead procedure. This process can be used to save and later restore the contents of the screen and is an efficient way to input large quantities of formatted data.

BlockWrite(*fileVar, bufferVar, n*)
BlockWrite(*fileVar, bufferVar, n, unitsWritten*)
The procedure BlockWrite attempts to store *n* units of data in the DOS file associated with the file variable *fileVar.* The data to be written is read from successive memory locations beginning with the first byte of memory reserved for the variable *bufferVar.* (The variable *bufferVar* is often an array or pointer variable.) If the second form of the procedure call is used, then the actual number of units written will be returned in the variable *unitsWritten.* (Insufficient disk space can cause less than *n* units to be written.)

ChDir(*newDir*)
The procedure ChDir changes the current disk directory on the specified drive to the subdirectory specified by the path *newDir.* For example, the procedure call ChDir('\') specifies the root directory as the current directory of the default drive.

Chr(*n*)
If *n* is a number from 0 to 255, then the function Chr(*n*) returns the character in the ASCII table associated with *n*.

Close(*fileVar*)
The procedure Close closes the DOS file associated with the file variable *fileVar.* Files must be closed before exiting a program and before executing the Rename and Erase procedures.

Concat(*string1, string2*)
Concat(*string1, string2, string3, ...*)
The function Concat joins its string arguments and returns the single concatenated string. Any number of strings can be joined in a single function call. String addition can be used in place of the Concat function: *stringVar* := Concat(*string1, string2*) can be written as *stringVar* := *string1* + *string2*.

Copy(*string, m, n*)
The function Copy returns the substring of *string* beginning with the *m*th character and containing up to *n* characters, if available. No error occurs if *n* is too large for the available characters.

Cos(*x*)
The value of the trigonometric function Cos is the cosine of an angle of *x* radians.

CSeg
The CSeg function returns the value (normally the code segment address) stored in the CS register.

Dec(x)
Dec(x, step)
Executing the procedure Dec is equivalent to executing the statement $x := x - 1$, or $x := x - step$, respectively. The Dec procedure helps the compiler produce more efficient code.

Delete(string, m, n)
The procedure Delete removes n characters from *string* beginning with the mth character. Since Delete is a procedure (not a function like Copy) no assignment needs to be made; the value of *string* is modified. Delete removes no characters if m is greater than the length of *string*. To delete from the beginning of *string* use $m = 1$ (not 0).

Dispose(p)
The procedure Dispose removes the dynamic variable pointed to by the pointer variable p and frees the memory space for reuse. If no other pointer points to p's target, Dispose should be used prior to reassigning p to prevent orphaning its target.

DSeg
The Dseg function returns the value (normally the data segment address) stored in the DS register.

Eof(fileVar)
Eof
The function Eof(fileVar) is True if the end of the file associated with *fileVar* has been reached, and False otherwise. Eof(fileVar) usually should be checked before reading a file. Eof with no arguments is primarily used for .EXE files that will be run from DOS. It checks the status of the "standard input file."

Eoln(fileVar)
Eoln
The function Eoln is True if the end of the current line of the DOS file associated with *fileVar* has been reached, and False otherwise. The end of any line is reached when a carriage return (ASCII 13) is encountered. Eoln with no argument checks the status of the current line in the "standard input file."

Erase(fileVar)
The procedure Erase deletes from the disk the DOS file associated with the file variable *fileVar*. The file must be closed.

Exit
If the procedure Exit is executed in the main program, the program is immediately terminated. If Exit is executed in a function or procedure, no further statements are executed in the function or procedure and program execution returns to the point from which the procedure or function was called.

Exp(x)
The value of the function Exp is e^x, where e (about 2.71828) is the base of the natural logarithm function.

FilePos(fileVar)
The value of the function FilePos is the current position in the open DOS file associated with the file variable *fileVar*. FilePos cannot be used on text files.

FileSize(*fileVar*)

The value of the function FileSize is the number of units (components or records) currently contained in the DOS file associated with *fileVar*. FileSize cannot be used on text files or closed files.

FillChar(*variable, n, character*)

The procedure FillChar places *n* copies of *character* into *n* bytes of contiguous memory starting with the first byte reserved for *variable*. *Character* may be either an ASCII value or a literal character enclosed in single quotes. (Often, an array or pointer variable is used for *variable*.)

Flush(*fileVar*)

Writes to disk the data in the buffer reserved for the text file associated with *fileVar*.

Frac(*x*)

For any real number *x*, the value of the function Frac is the fractional portion of *x*. For example, Frac(2.1055) is 0.1055.

FreeMem(*pointer, n*)

The procedure FreeMem frees *n* bytes of dynamic memory at address *pointer*. FreeMem is used to release memory set aside by GetMem.

GetDir(*drive, path*)

The procedure GetDir assigns to the string *path* the current directory on the disk drive specified by *drive*. *Drive* is an Integer whose value is interpreted as follows: 0 means use the current drive, 1 means use drive A, 2 means use drive B, and so on.

GetMem(*pointer, n*)

The procedure GetMem sets aside *n* bytes of memory on the heap (the portion of memory used for dynamic variables), and assigns the starting address of this memory to the pointer variable *pointer*. The effect is to create a dynamic variable in which *n* bytes of data can be stored.

Halt
Halt(*code*)

The procedure Halt terminates program execution and returns to DOS. If desired, an Integer *code* (program exit code) can be given that will be assigned to the DOS environment variable errorlevel.

Hi(*x*)

If *x* is a Word or Integer, then two bytes of memory (a *low-order* byte followed by a *high-order* byte) are used to store the value of *x*. The value of the function Hi is the contents of the high-order byte. [1]

Inc(*x*)
Inc(*x, step*)

Executing the procedure Inc is equivalent to executing the statement $x := x + 1$, or $x := x + step$, respectively. Using the Inc procedure helps the compiler produce more efficient code.

Insert(*string1, string2, n*)

The procedure inserts *string2* into *string1* starting at position *n* in *string1*. If the resulting string is more than 255 characters long, it is truncated to 255 characters.

Int(*x*)
The value of the function Int is the greatest whole number less than or equal to *x*. Int returns a Real number.

IOResult
The value of the function IOResult is a whole number giving the status of the most recent I/O operation. A status of 0 shows the I/O operation was successful.

Length(*string*)
The value of the function Length is the number of characters in *string*.

Ln(*x*)
If *x* is a positive number, then the value of the function Ln is the natural logarithm (base *e*) of *x*.

Lo(*x*)
If *x* is a Word or Integer, then two bytes of memory (a *low-order* byte followed by a *high-order* byte) are used to store the value of *x*. The value of the function Lo is the contents of the low-order byte. [1]

Mark(*pointer*)
The procedure Mark saves the address of the current top of the heap (the portion of memory used for dynamic variables) in *pointer*.

MaxAvail
The value of the function MaxAvail is the size (in bytes) of the largest continuous block of free memory in the portion of memory used for dynamic variables.

MemAvail
The value of the function MemAvail is the number of bytes of free memory in the portion of memory used for dynamic variables. (This memory is not necessarily contiguous.)

Member(*objectVar, classID*)
The value of the function Member is True if *objectVar* is an instance of the class *classId* or one of its descendants, and False otherwise.

MkDir(*newDir*)
The procedure MkDir creates a new directory with the path given in the string *newDir*.

Move(*source, destination, n*)
The procedure Move copies *n* bytes of memory starting with the first byte used by the variable *source*, and places these bytes in the *n* bytes of memory beginning with the first byte used for the variable *destination*.

New(*pointer*)
The procedure New sets aside space for a new dynamic variable and sets the pointer variable *pointer* to the address of the new variable. The type (Integer, Word, String, etc.) of *pointer* determines how many bytes of memory are set aside. [1]

Odd(*x*)
The value of the function Odd is True if the Integer *x* is odd, and False if *x* is even.

Ofs(x)

The value of the function Ofs is the offset in memory of *x*, where *x* is a variable, typed constant, procedure name, or function name. This offset is given for the segment of memory returned by the function Seg.

Ord(x)

The value of the function Ord is the position of the ordinal value *x* in the definition of the ordinal type. Positions are numbers starting with 0, except for Integers.

ParamCount

The value of the function ParamCount is the number of command-line parameters given when the program was invoked.

ParamStr(i)

The value of the function ParamStr is a string consisting of the *i*th command-line parameter. For DOS versions 3.1 and later, the value of ParamStr when *i* equals 0 is the "program path," that is, the path to the EXE file and the name of the program (e.g. C:\QP\UNTITLED.EXE).

Pi

The value of the constant Pi is 3.14159265358979. The precision of the value varies, depending on the floating-point hardware present.

Pos(subString, string)

The value of the function Pos is the position of *subString* in *string*. If *substring* does not appear in *string*, 0 is returned.

Pred(x)

The value of the function Pred is the predecessor of *x* in the list of values of its ordinal type.

Ptr(seg, off)

The value of the function Ptr is a pointer address with segment *seg* and offset *off*; *seg* and *off* are both of type Word. [1]

Random
Random(limit)

When no parameter is given, the value of the function Random is a psuedo-randomly selected real number from 0 to 1, not including 1. If a whole number *limit* is given, the value of the function is a psuedo-randomly selected whole number between 0 and *limit*−1 inclusive.

Randomize

The procedure Randomize uses the computer's clock to seed the random number generator. It usually is included in any program that uses the function Random.

Read(var1)
Read(var1, var2, ...)
Read(fileVar, var1, var2, ...)

The procedure Read(*var1*) causes the program to pause until the user enters a value to be assigned to *var1*. If several variables are given as parameters to Read, then the user must supply a value for each before program execution will continue. If a file variable *fileVar* starts the Read parameter list, then values for *var1*, etc., will be read from the DOS file associated with *fileVar*; no user input will be required.

Readln(*var1*)
Readln(*var1, var2, ...*)
Readln(*fileVar, var1, var2, ...*)
The procedure Readln first reads in values for *var1*, etc., just as the Read procedure does. After all needed values have been read, Readln skips past any additional values included on the same line as the last value read. As a result, the next time Read or Readln is called, a new line of values will have to be input by the user, or a new line of values will be read from the DOS file associated with the file variable *fileVar*.

Release(*pointer*)
The procedure Release sets the heap-top pointer to *pointer*, a pointer address previously obtained by using the procedure Mark.

Rename(*fileVar, newName*)
The procedure Rename, like the DOS command rename, changes the name of the DOS file associated with the file variable *fileVar* to *newName*. Unlike the DOS command, the QuickPascal procedure Rename allows *newName* to include a new path, thus allowing files to be moved from one directory to another directory on the same disk. The file must be closed before executing Rename.

Reset(*fileVar*)
Reset(*fileVar, size*)
The procedure Reset opens the DOS file associated with the file variable *fileVar* so that information can be read from the file. An Integer *size* may be included to specify a size other than the default for the RAM buffer used with this file.

Rewrite(*fileVar*)
Rewrite(*fileVar ,Size*)
The procedure Rewrite opens the DOS file associated with the file variable *fileVar* so that information can be written to the file. If the DOS file does not already exist, it is created. If the DOS file already exists, its contents are deleted. An Integer *size* may be included to specify a size other than the default for the RAM buffer used with this file.

RmDir(*dir*)
The procedure RmDir removes the subdirectory named in the string *dir*. RmDir can only remove empty subdirectories.

Round(*x*)
The value of the function Round is the whole number nearest to *x*. If *x* ends with .5, then *x* is rounded to the whole number with greatest absolute value.

RunError
RunError(*errorNum*)
The procedure RunError causes program execution to halt and an error message of the form "Runtime error *errorNum* at *program seg:offset*" to be displayed. If *errorNum* is not given, it is taken as 0.

Seek(*fileVar, pos*)
The procedure Seek sets the current file position to *pos* in the DOS file associated with the file variable *fileVar*.

SeekEof
SeekEof(*fileVar*)
The value of the function SeekEof is True if only blanks, tabs, and end-of-line markers remain between the current read position and the end-of-file in the DOS text file associated with the file variable *fileVar*; otherwise the value is False. Calling the procedure SeekEof does not change the current read position in the file.

SeekEoln
SeekEoln(*fileVar*)
The value of the function SeekEoln is True if only blanks and tabs remain between the current read position and the end-of-line marker in the DOS text file associated with the file variable *fileVar*; otherwise the value is False. Calling the procedure SeekEoln does not change the current read position in the file.

Seg(*x*)
The value of the function Seg is the segment of memory in which *x* lies, where *x* is a variable, typed constant, procedure name, or function name.

Self
Instance variables appearing in a method definition must be prefixed with "Self." to identify them as from the method's class.

SetTextBuf(*fileVar, buffer*)
SetTextBuf(*fileVar, buffer, n*)
The procedure SetTextBuf assigns the text file identified by the file variable *fileVar* a buffer of *n* bytes in memory starting at the first byte used by the variable *buffer*. If *n* is omitted, SizeOf(*buffer*) is assumed.

Sin(*x*)
For any number *x*, the value of the trigonometric function Sin is the sine of the angle of *x* radians.

SizeOf(*x*)
The value of the function SizeOf is the number of bytes of memory used by *x*, where *x* is a variable, typed constant, or type identifier.

SPtr
The value of the SPtr function is the value stored in the SP register. This value is the current offset of the stack pointer in the stack segment.

Sqr(*x*)
The value of the function Sqr is $x * x$ (the square of *x*). Sqr returns a value of the same type as *x*.

Sqrt(*x*)
For any non negative number *x*, the value of the square root function Sqrt is the non negative number whose square is *x*. Sqrt returns a Real number.

SSeg
The value of the SSeg function is the value stored in the SS register. This value is the stack segment address of the stack pointer.

Str(*number, stringVar*)
Str(*number:width, stringVar*)
Str(*number:width:decimals, stringVar*)
The procedure Str converts the numeric value *number* to the string *string*Var. The arguments *width* and *decimals* specify the total width and number of decimals places that will appear in the string.

Succ(*x*)
The value of the function Succ is the successor to *x* in the list of values of its ordinal type.

Swap(*x*)
If *x* is any Integer or Word, then the value of the function Swap is the Integer or Word resulting from exchanging the two bytes (high- and low-order bytes) that represent *x* in memory. [1]

Trunc(*x*)
The value of the function Trunc is the whole number obtained by discarding any fractional part of *x*. If *x* is nonnegative, then $Trunc(x) = Int(x)$, otherwise $Trunc(x) = -Int(Abs(x))$. Trunc returns a LongInt value. [1]

Truncate(*fileVar*)
The procedure Truncate deletes beyond the current file position the contents of the DOS file associated with the file variable *fileVar*.

UpCase(*char*)
If *char* is a lowercase letter, then the value of the function UpCase is the corresponding uppercase letter, otherwise the value of UpCase is simply *char*.

Val(*string, number, errorPosition*)
The procedure Val converts the numeric string *string* to its numeric representation *number*. If *string* does not represent a number, *errorPosition* returns the position of the first offending character.

Write(*expression list*)
Write(*fileVar, expression list*)
The procedure Write displays the value of the variable or expression at the current cursor position on the screen or at the current file position in the DOS file associated with the file variable *fileVar*. Several expressions can be placed in the same Write statement, separated by commas. If so, the values will be displayed/written next to each other. (**Note:** Positive real numbers are padded on the left by a single blank.) Any value can be right justified (padded on the left with blanks) by using colons to specify the width (and for a real number, the number of decimal places) of the field in which the value is to be displayed/ written. The general form for formatting an expression is *expression:width:-decimals*.

Writeln
Writeln(*expression list*)
Writeln(*fileVar, expression list*)
The Writeln procedure produces the same output on the screen or in a file as the Write procedure, and then, in addition, moves the cursor to the beginning of a new line on the screen or places an end-of-line marker in the DOS file associated with the file variable *fileVar*. The Writeln statement can be used without any parameters to leave blank lines on the screen or extra end-of-line markers in the DOS file.

Crt Unit

AssignCrt(*fileVar*)
The procedure AssignCrt is used to inform QuickPascal that program references to the file variable *fileVar* are to cause the keyboard or screen to be accessed. For example, after Reset(*fileVar*) is executed, Readln(*fileVar,variable*) is equivalent to Readln(*variable*) and will cause the value for *variable* to be read from the keyboard. If on the otherhand, you Rewrite(*fileVar*), then Writeln(*fileVar,variable*) is equivalent to Writeln(*variable*) and will cause the value of *variable* to be displayed on the screen.

ClrEol
The procedure ClrEol causes the line of text on which the cursor is positioned to be erased from the character at the cursor to the end of the line.

ClrScr
The procedure ClrScr clears the text mode screen and places the cursor at the top left position of the screen. This statement is not needed in graphics mode since the _SetVideoMode statement automatically clears the screen.

Delay(*m*)
The procedure Delay causes the program to pause for *m* thousandths of a second. For example, Delay(1000) pauses the program for 1 second.

DelLine
The procedure DelLine causes the text line on which the cursor is positioned to be deleted, and each text line below the cursor to scroll up one line. The cursor itself is not moved by DelLine.

GotoXY(*x,y*)
The procedure GotoXY cause the cursor to move to column *x* and row *y* on the screen. Columns are numbered across the screen from left to right starting with 1. Rows are numbered down the screen starting with 1.

HighVideo
The procedure HighVideo causes subsequent characters written on the screen to be displayed using the high-intensity (bright) version of the foreground color.

InsLine
The procedure InsLine causes a blank text line to be inserted at the line where the cursor is positioned, and each text line at or below the cursor to scroll down one line. The cursor itself is not moved by InsLine.

KeyPressed

The function KeyPressed is True if a key has been pressed and a character is waiting in the keyboard buffer to be read. Otherwise, KeyPressed is False.

LowVideo

The procedure LowVideo cancels the effect of the HighVideo procedure. Subsequent characters displayed on the screen will have the standard intensity of the foreground color.

NormVideo

The procedure NormVideo ends the effect of any color or attribute changes, so that subsequent characters displayed on the screen will have the colors and attributes that were in effect when the program was started.

NoSound

The procedure NoSound is used to turn off the computer's speaker when it has been turned on by a Sound statement.

ReadKey

The value of the function ReadKey is the next character waiting in the keyboard buffer. If no character is present (KeyPressed is False) then the value of Readkey will be the null character "". ReadKey does not display the character it reads on the screen.

Sound(*f*)

If f is a Word from 19 to 65535, then the statement Sound(f) turns on the computer's speaker with a tone of frequency f cycles per second. The Sound procedure has no effect for f from 0 to 18. [1]

TextBackground(*c*)

The procedure TextBackground causes subsequent characters displayed on the screen to have the background color associated with the color index c. [7]

TextColor(*c*)

The procedure TextColor causes subsequent characters displayed on the screen to have the foreground color associated with the color index c. [7]

TextMode(*mode*)

The procedure TextMode sets the display to the text mode corresponding to *mode*. The following predefined constants may be used for *mode*: BW40, CO40, BW80, CO80, and MONO. In addition, the predefined constant FONT8X8 may be added to these constants to select text modes using an 8 by 8 pixel character block on display adapters that support text modes with 43 display lines. To restore the screen to the text mode that was in effect before going to a graphics mode, use the statement TextMode(lastMode).

WhereX

The value of the function WhereX is the column number (*x*-coordinate) of the location of the cursor.

WhereY

The value of the function WhereY is the row number (*y*-coordinate) of the location of the cursor.

Window(*x1, y1, x2, y2*)

The procedure Window establishes a rectangular portion of the screen as a window in which all subsequent Write's, GotoXY's, ClrScr's, etc., apply, while text outside the window remains unaffected. The window is positioned such that the upper left corner is in column *x1* and row *y1*, while the lower right corner is in column *x2* and row *y2*. (Column and row numbers are relative to the standard screen positions and not to the coordinates resulting from any previous Window statement.) After a Window statement is executed, the cursor is positioned in the upper left corner of the window. All positioning by GotoXY is relative to this new upper left corner, whose position is now considered to be column 1 and row 1.

MSGraph Unit

_Arc(*x1, y1, x2, y2, x3, y3, x4, y4*)

The procedure _Arc draws an arc that is a portion of the ellipse inscribed in the rectangle whose upper left and lower right corners have viewport coordinates (*x1, y1*) and (*x2, y2*), respectively. The arc extends counterclockwise from the intersection of the ellipse with a line from the center of the ellipse through the point with viewport coordinates (*x3, y3*) to the intersection of the ellipse with a line from the center of the ellipse through the point with viewport coordinates (*x4, y4*). The arc is drawn in the current color index. [4], [7]

_Arc_wxy(*wxy1, wxy2, wxy3, wxy4*)

The procedure _Arc_wxy draws an arc that is a portion of the ellipse inscribed in the rectangle whose upper left and lower right corners coordinates are recorded in the _WXYCoord variables *wxy1* and *wxy2*. The arc extends counterclockwise from the intersection of the ellipse with a line from the center of the ellipse through the point recorded in the _WXYCoord variable *wxy3* to the intersection of the ellipse with a line from the center of the ellipse through the point recorded in the _WXYCoord variable *wxy4*. The arc is drawn in the current color index. [7]

_ClearScreen(*area*)

The procedure _ClearScreen clears all or a portion of the screen based on the value of *area*. One of three predefined Integer constants is used for *area*: _GClearScreen to clear the entire screen, _GViewPort to clear the current graphics viewport, or _GWindow to clear the current text window. [4], [6]

_DisplayCursor(*toggle*)

The function _DisplayCursor is used to turn the display of the cursor on or off. If *toggle* is True, the cursor is displayed; if False, the cursor is not displayed. The value of the function is True if the cursor was on when the function was executed; False if the cursor was off.

_Ellipse(*control, x1, y1, x2, y2*)

The procedure _Ellipse draws the ellipse inscribed in the rectangle whose upper left and lower right corners have the viewport coordinates (*x1, y1*) and (*x2, y2*), respectively. If the predefined Integer constant _GBorder is used for *control*, then only the border of the ellipse is drawn, using the current color index. If _GFillInterior is used for *control*, then the ellipse is drawn and its interior filled with the current color index and fill mask. [4], [7], [8]

_Ellipse_w(*control, wx1, wy1, wx2, wy2*)

The procedure _Ellipse_w draws the ellipse inscribed in the rectangle whose upper left and lower right corners have the window coordinates (*wx1, wy1*) and (*wx2, wy2*), respectively. If the predefined Integer constant _GBorder is used for *control*, then only the border of the ellipse is drawn using the current color index. If _GFillInterior is used for *control*, then the ellipse is drawn and its interior filled with the current color index and fill mask. [5], [7], [8]

_Ellipse_wxy(*control, wxy1, wxy2*)

The procedure _Ellipse_wxy draws the ellipse inscribed in the rectangle whose upper left and lower right corners are the window coordinates recorded in the _WXYCoord variables *wxy1* and *wxy2*, respectively. If the predefined Integer constant _GBorder is used for *control*, then only the border of the ellipse is drawn using the current color index. If _GFillInterior is used for *control*, then the ellipse is drawn and its interior filled with the current color index and fill mask. [5], [7], [8]

_FloodFill(*x, y, bcolor*)

The procedure _FloodFill starts at the point with viewport coordinates (*x, y*) and fills the screen in all directions from the starting point with the current color index and fill mask, stopping only when reaching a boundary whose color index is the Integer *bcolor*. If the starting point has a color index of *bcolor*, then no fill will occur. [4], [7], [8]

_FloodFill_w(*wx, wy, bcolor*)

The procedure _FloodFill_w starts at the point with window coordinates (*wx, wy*) and fills the screen in all directions from the starting point with the current color index and fill mask, stopping only when reaching a boundary whose color index is the Integer *bcolor*. If the starting point has a color index of *bcolor*, then no fill will occur. [5], [7], [8]

_GetActivePage

The value of the function _GetActivePage is the number of the current *active* video page. [9]

_GetArcInfo(*start, end, fillFrom*)

After an arc has been drawn, the function _GetArcInfo may be used to obtain the viewport coordinates of the starting and ending points of the arc. The starting and ending points are assigned to the _XYCoord variables *start* and *end*, respectively. The _XYCoord variable *fillFrom* is assigned the viewport coordinates of the point at which a fill of the pie wedge associated with the arc would begin. _GetArcInfo may be used to obtain analogous information after a pie wedge is drawn. The value of the function is True if information on an arc or pie wedge is available, and False otherwise. [4]

_GetBkColor

The value of the function _GetBkColor is a LongInt giving the current background color (in graphics modes) or the current background color index (in text modes). [1], [2], [7]

_GetColor

The value of the function _GetColor is the current graphics color index. The color assigned by default or by the _Remap... procedures to this color index is the color that will be used when graphics are drawn and filled. [7]

_GetCurrentPosition(xy)

The procedure _GetCurrentPosition assigns to the _XYCoord variable xy the current viewport coordinates of the graphics cursor. [4]

_GetCurrentPosition_wxy(wxy)

The procedure _GetCurrentPosition_wxy assigns to the _WXYCoord variable wxy the current window coordinates of the graphics cursor. [5]

_GetFillMask(mask)

The function _GetFillMask assigns to the _FillMask variable mask the current eight-byte fill mask. The value of the function is False if no mask has been set with _SetFillMask, and True otherwise. [8]

_GetFontInfo(fInfo)

The function _GetFontInfo assigns to the _FontInfo variable fInfo information regarding the currently selected font. The value of the function is 0 if information is available, and −1 otherwise. The seven fields of fInfo are fonttype (even = vector, odd = raster), ascent (pixels from top to baseline), pixwidth (0 = proportional font), pixheight, avgwidth, filename, and facename.

_GetGTextExtent(textString)

The value of the function _GetGTextExtent is an Integer giving the width in pixels required by _OutGText to display the characters in the CSTRING textString using the currently selected font.

_GetGTextVector(x, y)

The procedure _GetGTextVector assigns to the pair of Integer variables (x, y) the current graphics text orientation vector set by _SetGTextVector. Although any vector except $(0, 0)$ may be used when setting the graphics text vector with _SetGTextVector, _GetGTextVector always returns a vector of unit length, i.e., $x*x + y*y = 1$.

_GetImage(x1, y1, x2, y2, iBuffer)

The procedure _GetImage saves a copy of the portion of the screen lying within the rectangle whose upper left and lower right corners have viewport coordinates $(x1, y1)$ and $(x2, y2)$, respectively. This image is saved in memory starting with the first byte reserved for the variable iBuffer. Care must be taken that SizeOf(iBuffer) is at least as large as _ImageSize(x1, y1, x2, y2). If the portion of the screen to be saved does not lie completely within the current viewport, then no image will be saved. [4]

_GetImage_w(wx1, wy1, wx2, wy2, iBuffer)

The procedure _GetImage_w saves a copy of the portion of the screen lying within the rectangle whose upper left and lower right corners have window coordinates $(wx1,wy1)$ and $(wx2,wy2)$, respectively. This image is saved in memory starting with the first byte reserved for the variable iBuffer. Care must be taken that SizeOf(iBuffer) is at least as large as _ImageSize_w(wx1,wy1,wx2,wy2). If the portion of the screen to be saved does not lie completely within the current viewport, then no image will be saved. [4], [5]

_GetImage_wxy(*wxy1*, *wxy2*, *iBuffer*)

The procedure _GetImage_wxy saves a copy of the portion of the screen lying within the rectangle whose upper left and lower right corners have the window coordinates recorded in the _WXYCoord variables *wxy1* and *wxy2*, respectively. This image is saved in memory starting with the first byte reserved for the variable *iBuffer*. Care must be taken that SizeOf(*iBuffer*) is at least as large as _ImageSize_wxy(*wxy1*, *wxy2*). If the portion of the screen to be saved does not lie completely within the current viewport, then no image will be saved. [4], [5]

_GetLineStyle

The value of the function _GetLineStyle is the Word currently controlling the line style used by graphic procedures, such as _LineTo and _Rectangle . . ., which draw straight lines. [1], [10]

_GetPhysCoord(*x*, *y*, *xy*)

The procedure _GetPhysCoord translates the viewport coordinates (*x*, *y*) into physical coordinates and assigns the result to the _XYCoord variable *xy*. [3], [4]

_GetPixel(*x*, *y*)

The value of the function _GetPixel is the color index of the pixel with viewport coordinates (*x*, *y*). If the coordinates do not correspond to a point within the current viewport, the value of the function will be −1. [4], [7]

_GetPixel_w(*wx*,*wy*)

The value of the function _GetPixel_w is the color index of the pixel with window coordinates (*wx*, *wy*). If the coordinates do not correspond to a point within the current viewport, the value of the function will be −1. [4], [5], [7]

_GetTextColor

The value of the function _GetTextColor is the current text color index. The color assigned by default or by the _Remap... procedures to this color index is the color that will be used when text is displayed using _OutText or _OutMem. [7]

_GetTextCursor

When using a text video mode, the value of the function _GetTextCursor is a Word giving the current shape of the cursor. [1]

_GetTextPosition(*r*,*c*)

The procedure _GetTextPosition assigns the text cursor's current row and column position, relative to the upper left corner of the current text window, to the Integer variables *r* and *c* respectively. [6]

_GetTextWindow(*r1*, *c1*, *r2*, *c2*)

The procedure _GetTextWindow assigns to the Integer variables *r1*, *c1*, *r2*, and *c2* the number of the top row, leftmost column, bottom row, and rightmost column, respectively, of the current text window. If the procedure _SetTextWindow has not been executed, then *r2* and *c2* give the number of text rows and columns available in the current text mode. [6]

_GetVideoConfig(*vc*)

The procedure _GetVideoConfig assigns to the _VideoConfig variable *vc* data for the current graphics environment. The eleven fields of the *vc* record are numxpixels, numypixels, numtextcols, numtextrows, numcolors, bitsperpixel, numvideopages, mode, adapter, monitor, and memory (Kbs). Mode is one of the predefined Integer constants _MaxResMode, _MaxColorMode, _DefaultMode, _TextBW40, _TextC40, _TextBW80, _TextC80, _MRes4Color, _MResNoColor, _HResBW, _TextMono, _HercMono, _MRes16Color, _HRes16Color, _EResNoColor, _EResColor, _VRes2Color, _VRes16Color, _MRes256Color, and _OResColor. Adapter is one of the predefined Integer constants _MDPA, _CGA, _OCGA, _EGA, _OEGA, _VGA, _OVGA, _MCGA, and _HGC. Monitor is one of the predefined Integer constants _Mono, _Color, _EnhColor, _AnalogMono, _AnalogColor, and _Analog. [2], [9]

_GetViewCoord(x, y, xy)

The procedure _GetViewCoord translates the physical coordinates (x, y) into viewport coordinates, and assigns the result to the _XYCoord variable xy. [3], [4]

_GetViewCoord_w(wx, wy, xy)

The procedure _GetViewCoord_w translates the window coordinates (wx, wy) into viewport coordinates, and assigns the result to the _XYCoord variable xy. [4], [5]

_GetViewCoord_wxy(wxy, xy)

The procedure _GetView_Coord_wxy translates the window coordinates given in the _WXYCoord variable wxy into viewport coordinates, and assigns the result to the _XYCoord variable xy. [4], [5]

_GetVisualPage

The value of the function _GetVisualPage is the number of the current visual video page. [9]

_GetWindowCoord(x, y, wxy)

The procedure _GetWindowCoord translates the viewport coordinates (x, y) into window coordinates, and assigns the result to the _WXYCoord variable wxy. [4], [5]

_ImageSize(x1, y1, x2, y2)

The value of the function _ImageSize is a LongInt giving the number of bytes needed to store the portion of the graphics screen lying within the rectangle whose upper left corner and lower right corner have viewport coordinates $(x1, y1)$ and $(x2, y2)$, respectively. [1], [4]

_ImageSize_w(wx1, wy1, wx2, wy2)

The value of the function _ImageSize_w is a LongInt giving the number of bytes needed to store the portion of the graphics screen lying within the rectangle whose upper left corner and lower right corner have window coordinates $(wx1, wy1)$ and $(wx2, wy2)$, respectively. [1], [5]

_ImageSize_wxy(wxy1, wxy2)

The value of the function _ImageSize_wxy is a LongInt giving the number of bytes needed to store the portion of the graphics screen lying within the rectangle whose upper left corner and lower right corner are recorded in the _WXYCoord variables $wxy1$ and $wxy2$, respectively. [1]

_LineTo(x, y)

The procedure _LineTo draws a straight line from the current graphics cursor position to the point with viewport coordinates (x, y). The _MoveTo procedure may be used before _LineTo to reposition the graphics cursor to the desired starting point for the line. The line is drawn using the current color index, line style, and write mode. If no errors occur, the new graphics cursor position becomes (x, y). [4], [7], [10], [11]

_LineTo_w(*wx, wy*)
The procedure _LineTo_w draws a straight line from the current graphics cursor position to the point with window coordinates (*wx, wy*). The _MoveTo_w procedure may be used before _LineTo_w to reposition the graphics cursor to the desired starting point for the line. The line is drawn using the current color index, line style, and write mode. If no errors occur, the new graphics cursor position becomes (*wx, wy*). [5], [7], [10], [11]

_MoveTo(*x, y*)
The procedure _MoveTo repositions the graphics cursor to the point having viewport coordinates (*x, y*). [4]

_MoveTo_w(*wx, wy*)
The procedure _MoveTo_w repositions the graphics cursor to the point having window coordinates (*wx, wy*). [5]

_OutGText(*textString*)
The procedure _OutGText is used in graphics modes to display the CSTRING *textString* using the current graphics color index and font. The first character in *textString* is displayed with its upper left corner at the current graphics cursor position. The new location of the graphics cursor is the lower right corner of the last character in *textString*. Any tab, carriage return, or line feed characters in *textString* are ignored. The direction in which *textString* is written is control by the graphics text vector set by the procedure _SetGTextVector. The functions _RegisterFonts and _SetFont must be used before calling _OutGText. [7]

_OutMem(*textString*, *n*)
The procedure _OutMem displays the contents of memory starting with the first character of the CSTRING **textString**, and proceeding through consecutive memory locations until *n* characters have been displayed. All low ASCII characters encountered are displayed using their graphic symbol. The procedure _OutMem displays characters using the current text color index and starting at the current position of the text cursor. [7]

_OutText(*textString*)
The procedure _OutText displays the contents of the CSTRING *textString* in the current text color starting at the current position of the text cursor. Low ASCII characters are displayed using their graphic symbol, except carriage return and line feed, which are acted upon rather than being displayed. This procedure may be used in any video mode, but does not provide the formatting available in text modes through the Write procedure.

_Pie(*control, x1, y1, x2, y2, x3, y3, x4, y4*)
The procedure _Pie draws a pie-shaped wedge. The arc of the wedge is a portion of the ellipse inscribed in the rectangle whose upper left and lower right corners have viewport coordinates (*x1, y1*) and (*x2, y2*), respectively. The arc extends counterclockwise from the intersection of the ellipse with a line from the center of the ellipse through the point with viewport coordinates (*x3, y3*) to the intersection of the ellipse with a line from the center of the ellipse through the

point with viewport coordinates (*x4, y4*). The arc is drawn in the current color index. The sides of the pie-shaped wedge are the line segments that connect the center of the ellipse to the starting and ending points of the arc. [4], [7]

_Pie_wxy(*control, wxy1, wxy2, wxy3, wxy4*)

The procedure _Pie_wxy draws a pie-shaped wedge. The arc of the wedge is a portion of the ellipse inscribed in the rectangle whose upper left and lower right corners are the window coordinates recorded in the _WXYCoord variables *wxy1* and *wxy2*, respectively. The arc extends counterclockwise from the intersection of the ellipse with a line from the center of the ellipse through the point recorded in the _WXYCoord variable *wxy3* to the intersection of the ellipse with a line from the center of the ellipse through the point recorded in the _WXYCoord variable *wxy4*. The arc is drawn in the current color index. The sides of the pie-shaped wedge are the line segments that connect the center of the ellipse to the starting and ending points of the arc. [5], [7]

_PutImage(*x, y, iBuffer, action*)

The procedure _PutImage retrieves the rectangular portion of the screen previously saved by _GetImage or _GetImage_w in the memory reserved for the variable *iBuffer*. The retrieved image is placed on the screen so that its upper left corner is at the viewport coordinates (*x1,y1*). The possible values of *action* are identical with and have the same effects as the write mode actions. [4], [11]

_PutImage_w(*wx, wy, iBuffer, action*)

The procedure _PutImage_w serves the same function as _PutImage, but uses window coordinates (*wx, wy*) to specify where the retrieved image's upper left corner is to be placed. [5]

_Rectangle(*control, x1, y1, x2, y2*)

The procedure _Rectangle draws the rectangle whose upper left and lower right corners have the viewport coordinates (*x1, y1*) and (*x2, y2*), respectively. If the predefined constant _GBorder is used for *control*, then only the border of the rectangle is drawn using the current color index, line style, and write mode. If _GFillInterior is used for *control*, then the rectangle is drawn and its interior filled using the current color index and fill mask. [4], [7], [8], [10], [11]

_Rectangle_w(*control, wx1, wy1, wx2, wy2*)

The procedure _Rectangle draws the rectangle whose upper left and lower right corners have the window coordinates (*wx1, wy1*) and (*wx2, wy2*), respectively. If the predefined constant _GBorder is used for *control*, then only the border of the rectangle is drawn using the current color index, line style, and write mode. If _GFillInterior is used for *control*, then the rectangle is drawn and its interior filled using the current color index and fill mask. [5], [7], [8], [10], [11]

_Rectangle_wxy(*control, wxy1, wxy2*)

The procedure _Rectangle_wxy draws the rectangle whose upper left and lower right corners are the window coordinates recorded in the _WXYCoord variables *wxy1* and *wxy2*, respectively. If the predefined constant _GBorder is used for *control*, then only the border of the rectangle is drawn using the current color index, line style, and write mode. If _GFillInterior is used for *control*, then the rectangle is drawn and its interior filled using the current color index and fill mask. [5], [7], [8], [10], [11]

_RegisterFonts(*pathName*)

The function _RegisterFonts reads the font (.FON) file specified in the CSTRING *pathName* and registers (stores) the font header information in memory. The DOS wild card characters * and ? may be used in *pathName*, which allows _RegisterFonts to register a collection of fonts all at once. _RegisterFonts must be called before any of the other font-related routines _GetGTextExtent, _OutGtext, _SetFont, or _UnRegisterFonts are used. The value of the function is an Integer giving the number of fonts registered. A negative value for the function indicates an error: −1 if the file or directory given in *pathName* does not exist, −2 if one or more of the files specified in *pathName* did not have a valid .FON file header, −3 if one or more of the files specified in *pathName* was otherwise invalid, and −4 if insufficient memory exists to register the fonts.

_RemapAllPalette(*newPalette*)

The procedure _RemapAllPalette uses the color values stored in *newPalette* to associate new color values to all the color indices in the palette. *NewPalette* is an array of LongInt with indices ranging from 0 to 15, 63, or 255, depending on the current video mode. Color index 0 is associated with *newPalette*[0], color index 1 with *newPalette*[1], ... Calling _RemapAllPalette without EGA, MCGA, or VGA hardware is an error. [1], [2], [7]

_RemapPalette(*index, value*)

The function _RemapPalette associates the color given by the LontInt *value* to the color index given by the Integer *index*. Any pixels whose color index is *index* will change color immediately to the color represented by *value*. If _Remap-Palette is successful, the value of the function will be the LongInt old color value associated with *index*, otherwise the value of the function is −1. Calling _RemapPalette without EGA, MCGA, or VGA hardware is an error. [1], [7]

_ScrollTextWindow(*n*)

The procedure _ScrollTextWindow scrolls the contents of the text window by the Integer *n* lines. Two predefined constants may be used: _GScrollUp to scroll up one line, or _GScrollDown to scroll down one line. In general, any Integer may be used for *n*, but 0 has no effect, and values whose absolute value is greater than or equal to the number of lines in the text window will clear the window as the procedure _ClearScreen(_GWindow) does. Negative values scroll the screen contents down, positive values up. [6]

_SelectPalette(*number*)

When working in either the _MRes4Color, _MResNoColor, or _OResColor video modes, the function _SelectPalette switches between a collection of predefined palettes. *Number* is an Integer telling which palette is to be made the current palette. In _MRes4Color and _MResNoColor, *number* may range from 0 to 3, while in _OResColor, from 0 to 15. In _MRes4Color and _MResNoColor, each palette has three colors, while in _OResColor, each palette consists of two colors: a black background and the foreground color indicated by *number*. [2]

_SetActivePage(*n*)

The procedure _SetActivePage makes page number *n* the active video page. The maximum value allowed for *n* is numvideopages −1, where numvideopages is a field in the _VideoConfig record returned by the function _GetVideoConfig. [9]

_SetBkColor(*color*)

In text mode, the procedure _SetBkColor changes the background color index to the LongInt *color*. Characters currently on the screen are unaffected, but characters subsequently written will have the background color associated with color index *color*.

In graphics mode, the procedure _SetBkColor changes the background color to the LongInt *color*. The color of all background pixels (color index 0) will immediately change to *color*. LongInt constants for 16 colors are predefined: _Black, _Blue, _Green, _Cyan, _Red, _Magenta, _Brown, _White, _Gray, _LightBlue, _LightGreen, _LightCyan, _LightRed, _LightMagenta, _Yellow, and _BrightWhite. [1], [2], [7]

_SetClipRgn(*x1, y1, x2, y2*)

The procedure _SetClipRgn is used in graphics modes to define a rectangular portion of the screen in which graphics output and font text generated by _OutGText is permitted. Any graphics output that would extend beyond this *clipping region* is discarded. The clipping region is the rectangle whose upper left corner and lower right corner are given by the physical coordinates (*x1, y1*) and (*x2, y2*), respectively. The procedures _SetClipRgn and _SetViewPort do the same thing except that _SetClipRgn does not move the viewport origin. To limit output by _OutText and _OutMem, use the _SetTextWindow procedure. [3], [4]

_SetColor(*color*)

The procedure _SetColor changes the current color index to the Integer *color*. The current color index is used by the _Arc..., _Ellipse..., _FloodFill..., _LineTo, _OutGText, _Rectangle..., _SetPixel..., and _Pie... graphics routines. The default current color index is the highest index allowed in the current palette. If *color* exceeds the default index, then the default index is used. [7]

_SetFillMask(*mask*)

The procedure _SetFillMask sets up the eight bytes stored in the _FillMask variable *mask* as the 8 by 8 pixel pattern used when the screen is filled by _FloodFill... or the graphics routines such as _Rectangle... that allow _GFillInterior as a parameter. When no fill mask has been set by this procedure, all fills are solid, i.e., every pixel in the fill area is set to the current color index. [7], [8]

_SetFont(*options*)

The _SetFont function selects an active font from among the currently registered fonts. Fonts may be selected based on a number corresponding to the order in which they were registered. For example, _SetFont('n1') selects the first font registered, while _SetFont('n2') selects the second font registered, etc. In general, the CSTRING *options* can contain one or more of the following specifications:

Specification	Means to use font that . . .	Example
n*fontnum*	was registered as *fontnum*	_SetFont('n1')
t "*typeface*"	is named by *typeface*	_SetFont('t ''courier''')
h*height*	has char. of height *height*	_SetFont('h15')
w*width*	has char. of width *width*	_SetFont('w10')
f	is fixed spaced	_SetFont('f')
p	is proportionally spaced	_SetFont('p')
v	is a vector font	_SetFont('v')
r	is a raster font	_SetFont('r')
b	is best fit to other specs.	_SetFont('b h15 w10')

Using the **b** specification with at least one font registered will guarantee that a match to *options* is always found. Certain specifications are mutually exclusive and will be ignored if used together: **f** and **p**, **v** and **r**. If a vector font is selected with the n*fontnum*, **t** "*typeface*", or **v** specification, then a character height and width should also be given. When no font exactly matches the specifications in *options* and several close matches exist, the following precedence is used to choose among the close matches: pixel height, typeface, pixel width, fixed or proportional font.

_SetGTextVector(*x, y*)
The procedure _SetGTextVector sets the graphics text vector to the Integer pair (*x, y*). The graphics text vector determines the direction in which font text is written. The default direction is horizontally from left to right, and corresponds to the vector (1, 0). To write text upside down from right to left, use the vector (−1, 0). To write text vertically from bottom to top, use the vector (0, 1). To write text vertically from top to bottom, use the vector (0, −1). In general, if the point (*x, y*) is plotted in a standard xy-coordinate system, and an arrow is drawn from the origin to the point, then this arrow will correspond to the direction in which graphics text is being written. (Only in video modes where the screen aspect is 1:1 will the arrow always point in the exact direction in which text will be written.) Attempts to set the graphics text vector to (0, 0) are ignored.

_SetLineStyle(*style*)
The procedure _SetLineStyle sets up the Word *style* as the current line style mask. The 16 bits in *style* are used to determine which pixels are set to the current color index and which are left unchanged when straight lines are drawn by the routines _Rectangle... and _LineTo. By default the line style mask has the value 65535 ($FFFF), which causes every pixel along the line to be set to the current color index, thereby drawing a solid line. Setting a style of 3855 ($0F0F) is one means of producing dashed lines. [1], [7], [10]

_SetPixel(*x, y*)
The procedure _SetPixel changes the color index of the pixel with viewport coordinates (*x, y*) to the current color index. The procedure _SetPixel is used to color or turn on individual pixels, and may only be used in graphics modes. [4], [7]

_SetPixel_w(*wx, wy*)

The procedure _SetPixel_w changes the color index of the pixel with window coordinates (*wx, wy*) to the current color index. The procedure _SetPixel_w is used to color or turn on individual pixels, and may only be used in graphics modes. [5], [7]

_SetTextColor(*color*)

The procedure _SetTextColor makes the Integer *color* the new color or attribute for text written to the screen using _OutText and _OutMem. Values of *color* from 0 to 15 produce varying colors, or, in Monochrome text mode, one of five attributes: off (0), underlined (1), on normal (7), high-intensity underlined (9), and high-intensity (15). In text modes, adding 16 to a value produces the same color or attribute with the addition that the characters blink.

_SetTextCursor(*shape*)

When working in text modes, the procedure _SetTextCursor changes the shape of the text cursor according to the value of the Word *shape*. The cursor can consist of up to eight line segments (13 in Monochrome text mode). The possible line segments are numbered from 0 to 7 (0 to 12) starting with the bottommost possible segment. If a cursor is desired that begins with line segment *b* and ends with line segment *e*, then a value of $b*256 + e$ must be used for *shape*. For example, if *shape* is 0, then the cursor consists of the single, bottommost line segment, while if *shape* is 7 ($0*256 + 7$), then the cursor is the full character block (use 12 for Monochrome text mode). [1]

_SetTextPosition(*r, c*)

The procedure _SetTextPosition moves the text cursor to row *r* and column *c* in the current text window (*r* and *c* are Integers). Output by _OutText, _OutMem, Write, and Writeln are affected by this repositioning. [6]

_SetTextRows(*rows*)

The function _SetTextRows is used on EGA and VGA adapters to specify the number of text rows to be used in the current video mode. On EGA adapters, the Integer *rows* will be either 25 or 43. On VGA adapters, *rows* will be either 24, 43, or 50, except in _VRes16Color and _VRes2Color modes, where values of 30 and 60 are supported. The value of the function is 0 if the number of rows could not be changed as requested, otherwise it is the actual number of rows set. [2]

_SetTextWindow(*r1, c1, r2, c2*)

The procedure _SetTextWindow defines the text window. The text window is the rectangle whose upper row is *r1*, leftmost column is *c1*, lower row is *r2*, and rightmost column is *c2*, where *r1, c1, r2*, and *c2* are Integers. Once a text window is defined, the upper left corner of the text window is considered row 1 column 1, and all positioning by _SetTextPosition, etc., is done relative to this upper left corner. [6]

_SetVideoMode(*mode*)

The function _SetVideoMode is used to select the desired text or graphics screen mode. The possible predefined Integer constants for *mode* are given in the description of the procedure _GetVideoConfig. If the specified mode is unavailable, the function value will be 0, otherwise the value will be the number of text rows in the selected video mode. [2]

_SetVideoModeRows(*mode, rows*)
The function _SetVideoModeRows combines the operations of _SetVideoMode and _SetTextRows into one function call. The Integer *mode* specifies the desired screen mode, while the Integer *rows* specifies the number of text rows when working with an EGA or VGA adapter. The value of the function is 0 if the *mode* or *rows* is not valid with the current hardware, otherwise the value is the actual number of text rows set. [2]

_SetViewOrg(*x, y, oldOrg*)
The procedure _SetViewOrg moves the origin of the viewport to the location defined by the physical coordinates (*x, y*). The coordinates of all pixels within the viewport are now determined relative to this new origin. The physical coordinates of the previous viewport origin are assigned to the _XYCoord variable *oldOrg*. [3], [4]

_SetViewport(*x1, y1, x2, y2*)
The procedure _SetViewport is used in graphics modes to define a viewport whose upper left corner and lower right corner are given by the physical coordinates (*x1, y1*) and (*x2, y2*), respectively. The procedures _SetClipRgn and _SetViewPort do the same thing, except that _SetViewport moves the viewport origin to the upper left corner of the viewport. To limit output by _OutText and _OutMem, use the _SetTextWindow procedure. [3], [4]

_SetVisualPage(*n*)
The procedure _SetVisualPage makes page number *n* the visual video page. The maximum value allowed for *n* is numvideopages − 1, where numvideopages is a field in the _VideoConfig record returned by the function _GetVideoConfig. [9]

_SetWindow(*fInvert, wx1, wy1, wx2, wy2*)
The procedure _SetWindow is used in graphics modes to specify a coordinate system for the current viewport defined with numbers of type Double. Assume that *wx1* is less than *wx2* and *wy1* is less than *wy2*. Then values along the horizontal axis will range from *wx1* at the left edge of the viewport to *wx2* at the right edge of the viewport. If fInvert is True, then the values along the vertical axis will range from *wy1* at the bottom of the viewport to *wy2* at the top of the viewport. Otherwise, with fInvert False, the values along the vertical axis will range from *wy1* at the top of the viewport to *wy2* at the bottom of the viewport. (**Note:** A viewport always has two independent coordinate systems—a set of Integer coordinates referred to as **viewport coordinates** and a set of Double coordinates referred to as **window coordinates**.) The default window coordinates are identical (except for numeric type) to the current viewport coordinates. If the viewport is changed after window coordinates are set, the new viewport will adopt the same range of window coordinates as the old viewport. [1], [2], [4], [5]

_SetWriteMode(*action*)
The procedure SetWriteMode sets the write mode to *action*, where *action* is _GPSET, _GPRESET, _GAND, _GOR, or _GXOR. [11]

_UnRegisterFonts
The procedure _UnRegisterFonts deletes from memory the header information about all fonts previously registered with _RegisterFonts. Attempting to use _SetFont or _OutGText after calling _UnRegisterFonts is an error.

_WrapOn(*option*)

The function _WrapOn determines whether text written with _OutText or _OutMem is clipped or wrapped to a new line when the text reaches the edge to the current text window. If text is to wrap, use True for *option*, otherwise use False. The value of the function is the previous value of *option*, either True or False. The default for *option* is True. [6]

Dos Unit

(This unit is not used in the text.)

DiskFree(*driveNumber*)

The function DiskFree returns the number of bytes of free space on the specified drive. Drive numbers 1, 2, 3, etc. refer to drives A, B, C, etc. Drive number 0 corresponds to the current drive.

DiskSize(*driveNumber*)

The function DiskSize returns the total capacity in bytes of the specified drive. Drive numbers 1, 2, 3, etc. refer to drives A, B, C, etc. Drive number 0 corresponds to the current drive.

DosExitCode

The function DosExitCode returns the exit code from a child process.

DosVersion

The function DosVersion returns the version number of DOS. The statement Writeln(Lo(DosVersion), '.', Hi(DosVersion)) displays the DOS version number in a recognizable format.

EnvCount

The function EnvCount returns the number of environment variables currently defined in the DOS environment.

Exec(*programPath, commandLine*)

The procedure Exec loads and runs a child process while suspending parent process. The arguments specify the program to be run and the command line to pass to the program.

FExpand(*pathname*)

The function FExpand takes a string expression representing a file name as input and returns a string consisting of a fully qualified DOS path name containing both a drive designator and a root-relative path name.

FindFirst(*searchPattern, attributes, result*)

The procedure FindFirst searches the specified directory for the first file matching the given search pattern and set of attributes. The record variable *result* holds the conclusion.

FindNext(*result*)

The procedure searches the specified directory for the next file matching the search pattern and attributes specified in a previous call to FindFirst.

FSearch(*fileName, directoryList*)

The function searches for a file in a list of directories and returns the directory and file name for the file if found; otherwise, an empty string.

FSplit(*fileSpec, directory, baseName, extension*)
The procedure FSplit separates a file specification into its drive and directory, base name, and extension.

GetCBreak(*breaking*)
The procedure GetCBreak gets the current state of the DOS Ctrl+Break checking. The value of *breaking* is True if DOS checks for Ctrl+Break at each system call.

GetDate(*year, month, day, dayOfWeek*)
The procedure GetDate gets the current system date. The ranges of values of the Word parameters are 1980..2009, 1..12, 1..31, and 0..6, respectively. [1]

GetEnv(*environmentStringLabel*)
The function GetEnv returns the current value of a DOS environment variable.

GetFAttr(*fileVar, attribute*)
The procedure GetFAttr gets a file's attributes.

GetFTime(*fileVar, timeStamp*)
The procedure GetFTime gets the LongInt representing a file's date and time of modification. If a file has been assigned to the variable fileVar and opened, the variable dtVar has been declared to be of type DateTime, and the pair of statements GetFTime(fileVar, timeStamp) and UnpackTime(timeStamp, dtVar) are executed, then the date of the file can be displayed with Writeln(dtVar.month, '/', dtVar.day, '/', dtVar.year) and the time of the file displayed with Writeln (dtVar.hour, ':', dtVar.min,':', dtVar.sec). [1]

GetIntVec(*interruptNumber, address*)
The procedure GetIntVec gets the vector address for a given interrupt number.

GetTime(*hour, minute, second, sec100*)
The procedure GetTime gets the current system time where the parameters have type Word and ranges 0..23, 0..59, 0..59, and 0..99 respectively. [1]

GetVerify(*verifying*)
The procedure GetVerify gets the current state of the DOS verify flag. If *verifying* is True, DOS verifies output to disk.

Intr(*interruptNumber, registerValues*)
The procedure Intr calls a software interrupt, loading and returning register values in a record of type Registers.

Keep(*exitCode*)
The procedure Keep terminates a program but keeps it resident in memory. The parameter passes exit information from the terminated program to the program executing it or to the DOS environment.

MsDos(*registerValues*)
The procedure MsDos calls DOS interrupt $21 and passes register values in a record of type Registers.

PackTime(*dtVar, timeStamp*)
The procedure PackTime converts an unpacked record dtVar, of type DateTime, with six fields named *year, month, day, hour, min,* and *sec* to a packed LongInt *timeStamp*. [1]

SetCBreak(*breaking*)
The procedure SetCBreak turns DOS Ctrl+Break checking on or off by using the values True or False for *breaking*.

SetDate(*year, month, day*)
The procedure SetDate sets the current system date, where the parameters have type Word. [1]

SetFAttr(*fileVar, attribute*)
The procedure SetFAttr sets a file's attributes.

SetFTime(*fileVar, timeStamp*)
The procedure SetFTime sets a file's date and time of file modification record. The value for the parameter timeStamp can be obtained with the procedure PackTime.

SetIntVec(*interruptNumber, vector*)
The Procedure SetIntVec installs a new interrupt handler. If a program changes an interrupt vector, it must restore it before terminating.

SetTime(*hour, minute, second, sec100*)
The procedure SetTime sets the system time where the parameters have type Word. [1]

SetVerify(*verifying*)
The procedure SetVerify sets or clears the state of the DOS verify flag. If *verifying* is True, DOS verifies output to disk.

SwapVectors
The procedure SwapVectors swaps interrupt vectors with previously saved values.

UnpackTime(*timeStamp, dtVar*)
Converts the LongInt timeStamp to an unpacked record dtVar, of type Date-Time, with six fields named *year, month, day, hour, min,* and *sec*. Used with the procedure GetFTime to obtain the date and time for a file. [1]

Supporting Topics

1. *Numeric Data Types:* QuickPascal has the following numeric data types:

Type	Range	Number of Bytes
Byte	0 to 255	1
Integer	-32768 to 32767	2
LongInt	-2147483648 to 2147483647	4
ShortInt	-128 to 127	1
Word	0 to 65535	2
Comp	-9.2E+18 to 9.2E+18	8
Double	-1.7E+308 to 1.7E+308	8
Extended	-1.1E+4932 to 1.1E+4932	10
Real	-1.7E+38 to 1.7E+38	6
Single	-3.4E+48 to 3.4E+48	4

2. *Graphics Screen Modes:*

_MaxResMode	highest resolution graphics mode
_MaxColorMode	graphics mode with most colors
_MResNoColor	320 x 200, 4 gray
_HResBW	640 x 200, BW
_HercMono	720 x 348, BW for HGC
_MRes16Color	320 x 200, 16 color
_HRes16Color	640 x 200, 16 color
_EResNoColor	640 x 350, BW
_EResColor	640 x 350, 4 or 16 color
_VRes2Color	640 x 480, BW
_VRes16Color	640 x 480, 16 color
_MRes256Color	320 x 200, 256 color
_OResColor	640 x 400, 1 of 16 colors(Olivetti)

3. *Physical Coordinates:* The physical coordinates (x, y) identify a point x pixels from the left side of the screen and y coordinates from the top of the screen. The range of x and y depends on the graphics adapter and the screen modes. Some common ranges are $0 \le x \le 639$, $0 \le y \le 199$ (CGA, High-resolution mode) and $0 \le x \le 639$, $0 \le y \le 349$ (EGA, Enhanced resolution mode).

4. *Viewport:* The graphics statement _SetViewport establishes a rectangular portion of the screen as a viewport that will contain all subsequent figures drawn by graphics statements and output by _OutGText. If the physical coordinates of the upper left corner of the viewport are $(x1, y1)$, then figures will be drawn translated $x1$ points to the right and $y1$ points down. Figures are clipped at the boundary of the viewport; only portions inside the viewport are actually drawn. Initially, the viewport is the entire screen. The statement _SetViewOrg specifies a location, not necessarily within the viewport, as the viewport origin. The upper left point of the viewport is the default viewport origin. The viewport coordinates (x, y) identify the point obtained by moving x units horizontally and y units vertically from the viewport origin. (Horizontal displacements are to the right or left depending upon whether x is positive or negative, respectively. Vertical displacements are down or up depending upon whether y is positive or negative.) The two-field record type _XYCoord holds the x and y viewport coordinates of a point.

5. *Window Coordinates:* The window coordinates of a point are the coordinates resulting from the _SetWindow procedure. The default window coordinates are real equivalents of the Integer physical coordinates. The two-field record type _WXYCoord holds the x and y window coordinates of a point.

6. *Text Window:* The text window is the rectangular portion of the screen in which text output is displayed. Any text output that would extend beyond this window is discarded. By default, the entire screen is the text window.

7. *Color index:* Colors on the screen are specified by numbers called **color indices**. Indices range from 0-1, 0-4, 0-16, or 0-255, depending on the hardware configuration. In many situations, the colors associated with these indices can be set by MSGraph procedures and functions. The default correspondences for CGA, EGA, MCGA, and VGA adapter cards are 0, Black; 1, Blue; 2, Green; 3, Cyan; 4, Red; 5, Magenta; 6, Brown; 7, White; 8, Gray; 9, Light blue; 10, Light green; 11, Light cyan; 12, Light red; 13, Light magenta; 14, Yellow; 15, High-intensity white. At any time, a color index is designated as the "current color index." The default current color index is the highest allowable index.

8. *Fill Mask*: A fill mask is an eight-byte array of Byte that determines a rectangular 8 by 8 pixel pattern used to paint the interior of a region bounded by a curve. The default pattern is a solid rectangle of the current color index.

9. *Video Pages*: In many screen modes, video adapter cards can hold the contents of several different screens, called "pages." The pages are numbered 0, 1, ... At any time, the page currently displayed is called the "visual" page and the page currently being written to is called the "active" page. The default active and visual video pages are both page 0. If the active and visual pages are different, a screen full of information can be constructed out of sight and then brought into view by a change in the visual page.

10. *Line Style*: Lines can be drawn in various patterns or "styles." For instance, the pattern can be sequence of dots and/or dashes. The default style is a solid line.

11. *Write Mode*: The current write mode determines how new lines drawn on the screen with _Rectangle... and _LineTo will interact with what is already on the screen. The default write mode is the predefined Integer constant _GPSET which causes each pixel being changed by the new line to be assigned the current color index, regardless of what is already on the screen. (The line style mask determines which pixels on the new line are subject to being changed.) Other possible write modes are _GPRESET, _GAND, _GOR, and _GXOR. In general, if *oldci* is the current color index of a pixel that is being overwritten by the new line, *lineci* is the color index of the new line at this pixel, and *action* is the write mode, then the new color index, *newci*, of this pixel is determined as follows:

action	newci
_GAND	*oldci* AND *lineci*
_GOR	*oldci* OR *lineci*
_GXOR	*oldci* XOR *lineci*
_GPRESET	NOT *lineci*
_GPSET	*lineci*

Appendix G

Guide to Keywords

ABSOLUTE
Used to access memory locations directly by specifying the precise memory location of a variable.

AND
The compound condition obtained by combining two conditions with the logical operator AND is True if both of the two conditions are True. Also used as a bitwise operator for Bytes or Integers. A bit in the resulting Byte or Integer has value 1 if both bits in the same position in the original two Bytes or Integers have value 1.

ARRAY
Defines an array data type.

BEGIN
Indicates the start of a block of statements.

CASE
A control structure that branches based on the value of a variable called the selector.

CONST
Specifies the start of the constant definition section of a program or subprogram.

CSTRING
Defines a data type consisting of a series of up to 255 characters ending in a null byte, as in the C programming language. CSTRING[n] limits the number of non-null characters to n.

DIV
The Integer division operator. m DIV n is the quotient when the Integer n is divided into the Integer m by long division.

DO
Used with WHILE, FOR, and WITH to introduce the statement block.

DOWNTO
Indicates that the control variable of a FOR loop should be decremented through the specified subrange.

END
Indicates the end of block of statements.

ELSE
Used with IF to introduce the second statement block.

EXTERNAL
Identifies a separately compiled procedure or function written in assembly language.

FILE
Defines a file data type.

FOR
A loop structure that uses an ordinal control variable to execute a statement once for each element in a specified subrange of an ordinal type.

FORWARD
Declares a procedure but omits its definition until a second declaration. This permits mutually referencing procedures.

FUNCTION
Specifies the start of a function definition section of a program or subprogram.

GOTO
Transfer control to a location specified by a label.

IF
A control structure that branches based on whether a condition is True or False.

IMPLEMENTATION
Indicates the beginning of the unit section that defines the unit's procedures and functions.

IN
The set inclusion operator. The condition *element* IN *setVar* is True if *element* is a member of *setVar*.

INHERITED
Modifies a message of an object class to refer to the parent method.

INLINE
Defines machine code that is inserted into the program.

INTERFACE
Indicates the beginning of the unit section that declares the variables, constants, procedures, and functions available to the calling program.

INTERRUPT
Declares a procedure as an interrupt procedure. Interrupt procedures may handle program interrupts.

LABEL
Specifies the start of the label declaration part of a program or subprogram. Labels are the destinations of GOTO statements.

MOD
The Integer remainder operator. *m* MOD *n* is the remainder when the Integer *n* is divided into the Integer *m* by long division.

NIL
Constant pointer that points nowhere.

NOT
The condition obtained by preceding a condition with the logical operator NOT has the opposite truth value of the original condition. Also used as a bitwise operator for Bytes or Integers. A bit in the resulting Byte or Integer has value 1 if the bit in the same position in the original Byte or Integer has value 0.

OBJECT
Specifies the start of the definition of an object data type.

OF
Separates ARRAY, FILE, or SET from its desired type. Also, used with CASE to introduce the value lists.

OR
The compound condition obtained by combining two conditions with the logical operator OR is True if either or both of the two conditions is True. Also used as a bitwise operator for Bytes or Integers. A bit in the resulting Byte or Integer has value 1 if one or both bits in the same position in the original two Bytes or Integers have value 1.

OVERRIDE
Declares a method in an object class definition to be distinct from a ancestor's method having the same heading.

PACKED
Instructs the compiler to store arrays, files, records, or sets in a compressed form. Only needed with other Pascal compilers since the QuickPascal compiler always uses compressed form.

PROCEDURE
Specifies the start of a procedure definition section of a program or subprogram.

PROGRAM
Specifies the start of a program.

RECORD
Specifies the start of the definition of a record data type.

REPEAT
A loop structure that executes a statement at least once, and until a specified condition becomes True.

SET
Defines a set data type.

SHL
The bitwise shift-left operation that shifts the bits of an integer value a specified number of places to the left.

SHR
The bitwise shift-right operation that shifts the bits of an integer value a specified number of places to the right.

STRING
Defines a data type consisting of a series of up to 255 characters. STRING[n] limits the number of characters to n.

THEN
Used with IF to introduce the first statement block.

TO
Indicates that the control variable of a FOR loop should be incremented through the specified subrange.

TYPE
Begins a type definition section of a program or subprogram.

UNIT
Identifies and names the code that follows as a unit.

UNTIL
Contains the terminating condition of a REPEAT loop.

USES
Begins the unit specification section of a program. This section makes the subprograms in the listed units available for use in the program.

VAR
Specifies the start of a variable declaration section of a program or subprogram. Also declares a parameter of a procedure or function to be a reference (or variable) parameter.

WHILE
A loop structure that executes a statement as long as a specified condition is True.

WITH
Used with records and objects to eliminate the need for prefixes.

XOR
The compound condition obtained by combining two conditions with the logical operator XOR is True if exactly one of the two conditions is True. Also used as a bitwise operator for Bytes or Integers. A bit in the resulting Byte or Integer has value 1 if exactly one of the bits in the same position in the original two Bytes or Integers has value 1.

Appendix H

Handling a Mouse

Preliminaries

To use a mouse with QuickPascal, the program MOUSE.COM must be executed from DOS to load the mouse driver. After executing it, the message "Mouse is enabled" will appear. In addition, a compatible mouse must be properly installed. The specifics of the mouse and mouse driver may vary. Consult the documentation included with your mouse for details.

If the mouse driver is loaded, the mouse is installed properly, and Quick-Pascal is invoked, then a small rectangle should appear near the middle of the screen. This is the *mouse cursor* and its position on the screen should correspond to the motion of the mouse on the desktop. The mouse cursor is usually referred to simply as "the mouse." No confusion should result since the actual mouse and the mouse cursor on the screen move together.

If the mouse is visible, move it to a menu name and press the left button. Pressing the button in this way is called "clicking on the option." The menu should pull-down and its options should appear. These in turn can be selected by moving the mouse and clicking on the desired option. To remove a pull-down menu, move the mouse cursor to a blank area of the screen and click on nothing.

If the mouse is not visible when QuickPascal is first invoked, then it possibly is the same color as the screen background. Try moving the mouse around the screen. If the mouse becomes visible in non-background regions of the screen, move the mouse to the Options menu, click the (left) button to get a pull-down menu, and then click the (left) button on Display. Select a background region that makes the mouse visible by pressing the down-cursor and up-cursor keys to change the color selection until the mouse becomes visible in the background region. Save this configuration by clicking on Save.

Another way to select an item is by "dragging." Dragging refers to holding down the mouse button while moving the cursor. Dragging can be used with menus to produce a highlight in the menu rather than a mouse cursor. A menu option is selected by dragging until the option is highlighted and then releasing the button.

Using the Mouse (Refer to Figure H.1.)

Select a Menu Item
Click on the menu name, and then click on the desired item in the pull-down menu that appears.

    -or-

Move to the menu name and drag downward until the selection bar reaches the item of choice. Then release the button to select the item.

Cancel a Selected Menu
Click anywhere outside the menu.

Select an Action from the Reference Bar
Click on the action name. For example, to run the program in the Edit window, click on <F5=Run>.

Close an Open Window
Click on the close (upper-left) button.

Size a Window
Click on View and then on Size in the pull-down menu. Now move the mouse until the "phantom" window is of the desired size, and then click. To cancel the size change, press Esc before clicking.
-or-
Move the mouse to the sizing (lower-right) corner of the window, and then drag the phantom window until it is of the desired size.

Move a Window
Click on View and then on Move in the pull-down menu. Now move the mouse until the phantom window is in the desired location, and then click. To cancel the move, press Esc before clicking.
-or-
Move the mouse to the title bar, and then drag the phantom window to the desired location.

Open an Existing File
Click on File and then on Open in the pull-down menu. In the resulting dialog box, click once on the desired file name, and once on OK.
-or-
"Double-click" on the file name; that is, click twice in rapid succession.

Select an Edit Block
Move the mouse to one end of the block and then drag to the other end of the block.

Scroll Vertically
Move the mouse to the vertical elevator, and then drag the mouse in the appropriate direction.
-or-
Move the mouse to the appropriate arrow at the end of the scroll bar at the right of the screen, and then hold down the button.

Scroll Horizontally (Pan)
Move the mouse to the horizontal elevator and then drag the mouse in the appropriate direction.
-or-
Move the mouse to the appropriate arrow at the end of the scroll bar at the bottom of the screen, and then hold down the button.

Move Text Cursor in Edit Window
Move the mouse to where you want the text cursor, and then click.

Change Active Windows
Click in any visible part of the window to be activated.

Fill Screen with Current Window

Click once in the maximize (upper-right) button.

    -or-

Double-click anywhere in the title bar.

Return Current Window to Normal Size

Click once in the maximize (upper-right) button.

    -or-

Double-click anywhere in the title bar.

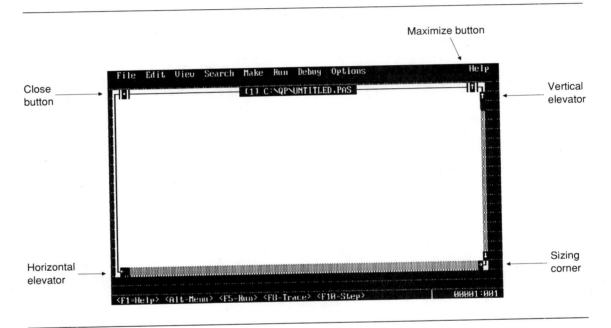

Figure H.1   Buttons Used with a Mouse

Appendix I

Installing QuickPascal

Using Diskettes

Diskettes store data and programs in a magnetic format, much in the same way that cassette tapes store sounds. Figure I.1 shows a standard type of diskette known as a 5¼-inch diskette. The diskette drive records and reads data through the read/write window. When the write-protect notch is covered with a piece of tape, no file can be erased or recorded on the diskette. The diskette drive grips the diskette through the spindle hole and uses the index hole to locate sectors on a round plastic disk inside the jacket.

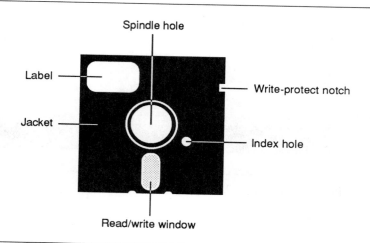

Figure I.1 5 1/4" Diskette

When handling a diskette, be careful not to touch the exposed surface in the read-write window. Other recommendations for the care of a diskette include:

(a) Use a felt-tip pen to write on the label.
(b) Do not bend or apply pressure to the diskette.
(c) Protect the diskette from extremes of temperature.
(d) Shield the diskette from dust by keeping it in its envelope when not in use.
(e) Do not remove the diskette from the diskette drive while the red light is on.
(f) Turn the computer off during a thunderstorm. Electrical surges can destroy data on the diskette.

To insert a diskette into a diskette drive, hold the diskette with the label facing up and the read/write window pointing toward the diskette drive. Insert the diskette and pull down the lever on the diskette drive to secure the diskette.

Some computers use a smaller, plastic covered diskette known as a 3½-inch diskette (See Figure I.2). This type of diskette is sturdier and is inserted by just pushing it into the drive. When the write-protect notch is open, no file can be erased or recorded on the diskette.

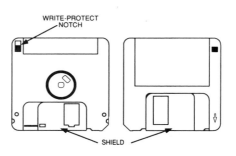

Figure I.2   3 1/2" Diskette

DOS

Each computer comes with a set of DOS (Disk Operating System) diskettes. The DOS programs carry out diskette operations.

If the computer has a hard disk, the contents of the DOS diskettes are usually placed on the hard disk when the computer is first readied for use. Then, every time the computer is turned on, a program containing the most basic DOS procedures is copied into memory.

For two-diskette systems, the drives are called the A drive and the B drive. The A drive is usually on the left (when the drives are side by side) or on the top (when the drives are one above the other). The DOS Startup diskette should be placed in the A drive before the computer is turned on. Then, the core DOS program will automatically be copied into memory when the computer is turned on. (For a one-diskette system, the single A drive is used for startup.) A red light indicates that the disk drive is reading or writing to the diskette. Do not touch the drive until the light goes out.

After the computer has been turned on with access to DOS, we say that the computer is in the DOS environment. After QuickPascal has been invoked, we say that the computer is in the QuickPascal environment.

Creating Working QuickPascal Diskettes

What is needed?

1. An IBM or compatible computer with at least 448K of memory and one of the following configurations of disk drives.
   (a) two 360K 5 1/4" diskette drives
   (b) a hard disk (and a diskette drive)

(c) a 720K 3 1/2" diskette drive

(d) a 1.2MB high-density 5 1/4" diskette drive

(e) a 1.44MB 3 1/2" high-density diskette drive

(f) an arrangement equivalent or exceeding the capacity of one of the above

(**Note:** QuickPascal will not run on a system with only a single 360K 5¼" diskette drive.)

2. The two 5¼" 360K diskettes, Program Diskette and Utilities Diskette, included with this book. (If your computer uses only 3½" diskettes, find a computer with diskette drives of both sizes and copy the contents of the two diskettes onto a 3½" diskette. See Section 1.3 for the details of formatting and copying diskettes.) For systems without a hard disk, a DOS Startup disk and formatted blank diskettes are also needed.

Two Diskette System

Working copies of the supplied diskettes must be prepared. The working Program diskette will be an exact copy of the supplied Program diskette. The working Utilities diskette will contain only those files currently needed from the supplied Utilities diskette. The working Utilities diskette will have free space for storing your QuickPascal programs. The following steps create the working diskettes:

1. Insert the DOS diskette into the A-drive. The A-drive is usually on the left (when the drives are side by side) or on the top (when the drives are one above the other).

2. Turn on the computer by flipping the power switch to the ON position. You also may have to turn on the monitor by pulling or turning a knob on the monitor. There will be a delay while the computer performs some internal tests.

3. The computer may prompt you to type in the date and time. Each of these items is entered by typing it and then pressing the Enter key. (The Enter key is the key with the hooked arrow.) You may decline supplying the date and/or time by pressing the Enter key without entering the date and/or time.

(**Note:** Carrying out steps 1 through 3 is called **booting the system**.)

4. When the A-prompt appears, type FORMAT B: and press the Enter key. (If you get an error message that says "Bad command or filename," either you have misspelled FORMAT or your DOS system diskette does not contain the program FORMAT.COM. In the latter case, locate a diskette with this program, place it into the A-drive, and enter the command FORMAT B: again.)

5. When you are prompted to put a diskette in the B-drive, do so using one of the two blank diskettes. Press the Enter key to start the formatting. When the question FORMAT ANOTHER (Y/N)? appears, press Y and the Enter key. You will then be prompted to put another diskette into drive B. Remove the diskette that has just been formatted from drive B and insert the other blank diskette. Press Enter to start the formatting. When the FORMAT ANOTHER question reappears, press N and the Enter key. Remove the

newly formatted diskette from the B-drive. Remove your DOS system diskette from the A-drive and store it in its sleeve.

(**Note:** Some recent versions of DOS request a volume label as part of the formatting process. You can decline by pressing the Enter key.)

6. Label one of the newly formatted diskettes "Working Program Diskette" and the other "Working Utilities Diskette."

7. Place the Program Diskette from this book into the A-drive and the diskette labeled "Working Program Diskette" into the B-drive. Following the A-prompt, type COPY A:*.* B: and press the Enter key. All the files on the diskette in the A-drive will now be copied onto the diskette in the B-drive. When the A-prompt returns, remove the Program Diskette from the A-drive and store it in a safe place. Remove the Working Program Diskette. (If your Working Program Diskette is ever damaged, you can format a new diskette as in steps 4 and 5 above, and then repeat this step to obtain a new Working Program Diskette.)

8. Place the Utilities Diskette from this book into the A-drive and the diskette labeled "Working Utilities Diskette" into the B-drive. Following the A-prompt, enter the following, one at a time.

```
COPY A:SYSTEM.QPU B:
COPY A:CRT.QPU B:
COPY A:PRINTER.QPU B:
```

The SYSTEM, CRT, and PRINTER files on the diskette in the A-drive will now be copied onto the diskette in the B-drive.

9. The extra space on the Working Utilities Diskette will hold your programs. Since space is limited, you should copy only necessary files to the diskette.

10. If you have a mouse and plan to use it, copy MOUSE.COM. When you reach Chapter 10, "Graphics," copy MSGRAPH.QPU and MSGRUTIL.QPU. (If you are doing graphics on a Monochrome Display with a Hercules card, also copy MSHERC.COM.)

One Diskette System

We assume that the single diskette drive uses high-density 5¼" diskettes or 3½" diskettes, and the contents of the two supplied diskettes have been copied onto the single diskette. This single diskette will be referred to as the "master diskette."

A working diskette containing the files currently needed must be prepared from the master diskette. The working diskette will have free space for storing your QuickPascal programs. The following steps create the working diskette.

1. Insert the DOS Startup diskette into the drive.

2. Turn on the computer by flipping the power switch to the ON position. You also may have to turn on the monitor by pulling or turning a knob on the monitor. There will be a delay while the computer performs some internal tests.

3. The computer may prompt you to type in the date and time. Each of these items is entered by typing it and then pressing the Enter key. (The Enter key

is the key with the hooked arrow.) You may decline supplying the date and/or time by pressing the Enter key without entering the date and/or time.

(**Note:** Carrying out steps 1 through 3 is called **booting the system.**)

4. When the A-prompt appears, type FORMAT A: and press the Enter key. (If you get an error message that says "Bad command or filename," either you have misspelled FORMAT or your DOS system diskette does not contain the program FORMAT.COM. In the latter case, locate a diskette with this program, place it into the drive, and enter the command FORMAT A: again.)

5. When you are prompted to put a diskette into the A-drive, *remove the DOS diskette* and replace it with a blank diskette. Press the Enter key to start the formatting. When the question FORMAT ANOTHER (Y/N)? appears, press N and the Enter key. A message will appear instructing you to insert a diskette with COMMAND.COM in drive A. Do this by removing the newly formatted diskette from the drive and replacing it with the DOS Startup diskette.

(**Note:** Some recent versions of DOS request a volume label as part of the formatting process. You can decline by pressing the Enter key.)

6. Label the newly formatted diskette "Working Diskette."

7. Place the master diskette into the drive. Following the A-prompt, type COPY A:*.* B:, press the Enter key, and follow the instructions given by the computer. You will repeatedly be told to insert various diskettes. The phrase "diskette for drive A:" refers to the master diskette and "diskette for drive B:" refers to the working diskette.

8. Place the working diskette in the drive and execute

       ERASE MS*.*

   These files are not needed until Chapter 10 and can be copied onto the working diskette at that time.

9. If you do not plan to use a mouse, enter ERASE MOUSE.COM.

Hard Disk System

The process of placing QuickPascal onto a hard disk consists of creating a subdirectory QP of the root directory and copying the contents of both supplied diskettes into the QP directory. This process need only be carried out once. QuickPascal will remain on the disk even after the computer is turned off. The detailed steps are as follows:

1. Turn on the computer by flipping the power switch to the ON position. You also may have to turn on the monitor by pulling or turning a knob on the monitor. There will be a delay while the computer performs some internal tests.

2. The computer may prompt you to type in the date and time. Each of these items is entered by typing it and then pressing the Enter key. (The Enter key is the key with the hooked arrow.) You may decline supplying the date and/or time by pressing the Enter key without entering the date and/or time.

(*Note:* Carrying out steps 1 and 2 is called **booting the system**.)

3. Type MD \QP and press the Enter key.

4. Type CD \QP and press the Enter key.

5. Insert the QuickPascal Program diskette into the A-diskette drive.

6. Type COPY A:*.* and then press the Enter key.

7. Remove the QuickPascal Program diskette from the A-drive and store it in a safe place. This diskette should not be needed again unless an accident causes files on your hard disk to be erased or become otherwise unusable.

8. Repeat steps 5, 6, and 7 with the QuickPascal Utilities diskette.

Invoking QuickPascal

The discussion below assumes QuickPascal has been copied onto working diskettes or a hard disk.

Two Diskette System

To invoke QuickPascal:

1. Boot your system.

2. Place the working copy of the Program diskette into the A-drive.

3. Place the working copy of the Utilities diskette into the B-drive.

4. At the prompt, type B: to change to the B-drive.

5. At the B-prompt, type A:QP and press the Enter key.

One Diskette System

To invoke QuickPascal:

1. Boot your system.

2. Place the working diskette into the drive.

3. At the A-prompt type QP and press the Enter key.

Hard Disk System

To invoke QuickPascal:

1. Boot your system. (Make sure no diskette is in drive A.)

2. At the prompt, type CD \QP to change to the directory containing Quick-Pascal and then press the Enter key.

3. Type QP and press the Enter key.

Appendix J

Jewels of the QuickPascal Menus

File

New
Open a new Edit window for the creation of a separate program.

Open
Load an existing program from a disk into a new Edit window.

Merge
Load an existing program from disk and insert it at the cursor position in the current Edit window.

Save
Save the contents of the current Edit window on a disk under the name currently displayed in the title bar. The saved version overwrites any previous version with that name.

Save As
Change the name of the disk file associated with the current Edit window, and save the contents of the current Edit window under a new name. Any old file retains its old name.

Save All
Save the program in each Edit window to its associated disk file if the program has been modified. The names of all programs appear at the bottom of the View menu. The programs that have been modified since they were last saved are preceded by asterisks.

Print
Print a hard copy of the selected text or the complete contents of the current Edit window.

DOS Shell
Suspend QuickPascal and return to the DOS prompt by loading a second copy of DOS. (Typing EXIT at the DOS prompt will resume QuickPascal at the exact point from which it was suspended.)

Exit
Terminate this QuickPascal session and return to DOS.

Edit

Undo
Return the current line to the form it had before the last set of edits (to the form it had when the cursor was most recently moved back to the line). Undo has no effect after the cursor is moved off the line.

Cut
Remove the selected block of text from the Edit window and place it in the clipboard.

Copy
Place a copy of the selected block of text into the clipboard. The copied text will still be in the Edit window.

Paste
Insert, at the Edit window cursor, a copy of the contents of the clipboard.

Clear
Remove the selected text from the Edit window without saving it in the clipboard. (Clipboard contents remain unaltered.)

Read Only
Toggle the current Edit window between standard edit status and read-only status. (Read-only status is used to prevent accidental editing.)

Pascal Syntax
Toggle the current Edit window between displaying or not displaying Pascal keywords, comments, and string literals in highlighted form.

View

Close
Close (remove) the current Edit window. If editing has occurred, a query to save contents will be made. (Same as Ctrl+F4)

Move
Move the current Edit window (with the cursor keys) to a new location on the screen.

Size
Change the number of rows and/or columns in the current Edit window.

Duplicate
Open a new window whose contents are a copy of the current Edit window.

Cascade
Arrange multiple windows on the screen so that successive windows fill the whole screen except for the portion needed for the title bars of earlier windows.

Tile
Arrange multiple windows on the screen so that each window is of equal size and occupies a separate rectangular portion of the screen. In debugging, the Edit window can be tiled with the Debug window to have watch items on the screen during program tracing.

Output Screen
Toggle to and from the display of the output screen. The same function is performed by the F4 key.

Debug Window
Switch to or open the Debug window.

Help Window
Switch to or open the help window. The help feature is not available with the textbook version of QuickPascal.

Search

Find
Beginning at the cursor, find the first occurrence of a specified symbol, word, or phrase.

Selected Text
Find the next occurrence of the text currently selected as a block.

Repeat Last Find
Look for the next occurrence of the text most recently searched for.

Change
Beginning at the cursor, find the first occurrence of specified text or a block of text, and replace it with new text.

Toggle Tag
Tag or untag the current line. Tags allow quick return to specific lines in a program.

Next Tag
Move the cursor down to the next tagged line.

Prev Tag
Move the cursor up to the previous tagged line.

Clear All Tags
Untag all tagged lines in the current Edit window.

Make

Compile File
Compile the contents of the current Edit window.

(**Note:** The following four commands in this menu are not needed for the types of programs discussed in this text.)

Build Main File
Compile the file specified as the main file of a multi-module program.

Rebuild Main File
Compile all the files associated with the multi-module program whose main file is in the Edit window.

Set Main File
Specify the main file (file containing the main program) in a multi-module program.

Clear Main File
Clear (make blank) the name of the main file.

Run

Restart
Use when a program has been suspended before completion, so that the next call for execution of the program will restart the program from the beginning.

Go
Start/continue execution of the program in the current Edit window. F5 performs the same function.

Continue To Cursor
Start/continue execution of the program in the current Edit window, suspending the program before executing the line on which the cursor lies.

Trace Into
Execute a single line of the current program and then suspend execution. If that line involves a procedure or function call, branch to the procedure or function so that its lines can be executed individually. The same function is performed by F8.

Step Over
Execute a single line of the current program and then suspend execution. If that line involves a procedure or function call, execute the entire procedure or function at once, regardless of how many lines it contains, so that the next line to be executed will be the line below the current line. F10 performs the same function.

Animate
Toggle on or off animation. With animation on, each line of the program is highlighted as it is about to be executed, with a momentary display of the output screen occurring only when output is generated.

Debug

Calls
When program is suspended, display (from most recent to least recent) the names of any procedures or functions that have been called and not yet completed. In other words, show the nesting of procedure and function calls used to reach the current program line.

Set Breakpoint
Define a specific line, condition, or both which when reached and/or True is to cause program execution to be suspended. F9 toggles the current cursor line as a breakpoint.

Edit Breakpoint
Add, remove, or modify breakpoints in the current program.

Watch Value
Add, remove, or modify expressions whose values are to be displayed in the Debug window.

Modify Value
During the suspension of program execution, change the value of any defined variable.

Options

Display
Change the foreground and background colors used in the display of different types of text on the screen. Select between 25 and 43/50 display lines depending on the capability of your video adapter. Change the spacing of tab stops.

Mouse
Control the function of the right mouse button.

Compiler
Toggle on or off 10 compiler related options, including range checking and stack checking. Specify stack size and minimum and maximum heap size.

Run/Debug
Specify a value for ComStr (command line parameters), select animation speed, control whether or not screens are swapped for the display of output.

Environment
Specify the directory(s) in which QuickPascal is to look for source files, include files, unit files, etc.

Short Menus
Toggle between full menus and short menus.

Answers

To Selected Odd-Numbered Exercises

CHAPTER 1

Exercises 1.2

1. The Edit window
3. The backspace key removes the character preceeding the cursor while the delete key removes the character at the cursor.

5. UNTITLED.PAS	7. The internal program name followed by a semicolon.		9. Ctrl+Y
11. Backspace	13. Del	15. Home	17. Alt/M/C
19. Up Arrow	21. Alt/F/X	23. Ctrl+End	25. Esc
27. Tab	29. End+Enter	31. Esc	33. Alt/F/N

35. Remove the ClrScr statement. 37. The Hello's are written under one another rather than side by side.
39. Edit window [5].   41. Another copy of the program appears below the one at the top.
43. MYPROGRAM has more than the maximum eight characters.
45. The PROGRAM statement appears in the wrong place.

Exercises 1.3

1. COPY	3. RENAME	5. DIR	7. DISKCOPY
9. 22,875 bytes			

CHAPTER 3

Exercises 3.1

1. 12	3. 1	5. 2	7. 4
9. 0	11. −21	13. 40	15. 10
17. −5	19. 1	21. −8	23. 0
25. 100.0	27. 0.035	29. −501230.0	31. 3
33. $2.53000000000000E+0001$	35. $-7.00000000000000E+0000$	37. $2.00100000000000E+0003$	39. $1.49200000000000E-0004$
41. 2	43. 1500	45. $6.00000000000000E+0000$	47. $1.00000000000000E+0000$
49. $5.00000000000000E+0000$	51. Valid	53. Not valid	55. Valid
57. Not valid	59. Valid	61. valid	63. 5
65. 5	67. 7:2	69. 10:3	71. 10:6
73. 10	75. 12	77. 15	

79.

Statement Part	m	n
BEGIN		
m := 2;	2	—
n := 3 * m;	2	6
m := n + 5;	11	6
Writeln(m + 4);	11	6
n := n + 1	11	7
END.		

81. 6   **83.** 1 2 3 411   **85.** 14.91

87. Variable to be assigned is not on the left side of the assignment. The correct form is m := j + k.

89. Real numbers cannot be preceded by a dollar sign nor include a comma.

91. Variables in assignment statement are not of the same type.

93. The variable *two* is undeclared, and a colon should appear in the declaration.

95.
```
PROGRAM EarthConstants;

CONST Radius = 6.378E06;

VAR diameter, circumference, volume : Real;

BEGIN
  diameter := 2 * Radius;
  circumference := diameter * Pi;
  volume := (4 / 3) * Pi * Radius * Radius * Radius;
  Writeln(diameter:10:0, circumference:10:0, volume:25:0)
END.
```

97.
```
PROGRAM Corn;

CONST Acres     = 30;
      CornPerAcre = 18;

BEGIN
  Writeln('Total output = ',
         (Acres / CornPerAcre):5:2, ' tons of corn.')
END.
```

99.
```
PROGRAM CarTrip;

CONST Start = 2;
      Finish = 7;
      Distance = 233;

BEGIN
  Writeln('Average speed = ',
         (Distance / (Finish - Start)):5:2, ' miles per hour.')
END.
```

101.
```
PROGRAM WaterUsage;

CONST GallonsPerPerson = 1600;
      People          = 240000000.0;
      DaysInYear      = 365;

BEGIN
  Writeln('People use ',
         (GallonsPerPerson * People * DaysInYear):0:0,
         ' gallons of water every year.')
END.
```

Exercises 3.2

1. Tom and Jerry   **3.** That's life.   **5.** Moscow, USSR   **7.** 10 plus 10

9. concatenation   **11.** Q: How long is a mile? A: 6   **13.** I♥NY   **15.** ?

17. The ASCII value of 'B' is 66   **19.** 11   **21.** 11   **23.** Hello
1234

25. 1212Twelve   **27.** A ROSE IS A ROSE IS A ROSE   **29.** 10 Downing Street

31. "We're all in this alone." Lily Tomlin
"We're all in this alone." Lily Tomlin

33. abcdef
abcdef
abcdef abcdef

35. I r s

37. The ballgame isn't over, until it's over. Yogi Berra

39. i) Not valid
ii) Valid
iii) Valid

41. A string cannot be assigned to a character.

43. A string cannot be surrounded by double quotes.

45. A constant string cannot have a character extracted.

47. Chr(77) + Chr(129) + Chr(110) + Chr(99) + Chr(104) + Chr(101) + Chr(110)

49.
```
PROGRAM VolumeOfEarth;

  VAR radius, volume : Real;

  BEGIN
    radius := 6170.0;
    volume := (4 / 3) * Pi * radius * radius * radius;
    Writeln('The volume of the Earth is ', volume:0:0,
            ' cubic kilometers.')
  END.
```

Exercises 3.3

1. 16

3. 3
5
2

5. unbearable

7. IQ is 120

9.
```
VAR num : Integer;

  BEGIN
    Write('Enter the number to cube: ');
    Readln(num);
    Writeln(num, ' cubed is ', num * num * num)
  END.
```

11. Cannot Readln an expression. **13.** The quantity (80 - Length(saying)) / 2 is not an Integer.

15.
```
PROGRAM Thunder;

  VAR seconds, distance : Real;

  BEGIN
    Write('How many seconds between lightning and thunder? ');
    Readln(seconds);
    distance := seconds / 5;
    Writeln('The storm is ', distance:0:1, ' miles away.')
  END.
```

17.
```
PROGRAM CaloriesBurned;

  CONST CalBike = 200;
        CalJog  = 475;
        CalSwim = 275;
        CalFat  = 3500;
  VAR bikeHours, jogHours, swimHours : Real;
      totalCalories, poundsBurned    : Real;

  BEGIN
    Write('How many hours spent biking? ');
    Readln(bikeHours);
    Write('How many hours spent jogging? ');
    Readln(jogHours);
    Write('How many hours spent swimming? ');
    Readln(swimHours);
    totalCalories := (bikeHours * CalBike) + (jogHours * CalJog) +
                     (swimHours * CalSwim);
    poundsBurned := totalCalories / CalFat;
    Writeln(poundsBurned:0:1, ' pounds of fat were burned.')
  END.
```

19.
```
PROGRAM HandleGrade;

  VAR grade : Integer;

  BEGIN
    Write('Enter grade: ');
    Readln(grade);
    grade := grade + 5;
    Writeln(grade)
  END.
```

Exercises 3.4

1. 10	**3.** 0.5	**5.** 6.0	**7.** Z
9. 7	**11.** 1	**13.** 0	**15.** 7
17. e	**19.** 0.5	**21.** 16	**23.** 45.0
25. 101	**27.** 7.0	**29.** 3	**31.** −1

33. 4

35. aby

37. 4

39. 0

41. Lul

43. ullaby

45. 16.0

47. 0.25

49. 0.33

51. 7
3

53. The year is 1990

55. J C

57. You each owe 5.08

59. Quick a
as a w
The average wink lasts .1 seconds.

61. Copy cannot be used on an Integer.

63. The Real value of function Int cannot be assigned to Integer variable num1.

65.
```
PROGRAM RoundNumber;

VAR number : Real;
    places : Integer;

BEGIN
  Write('Enter a number: ');
  Readln(number);
  Write('How many places to round? ');
  Readln(places);
  Writeln('The rounded number is ', number:0:places)
END.
```

67.
```
PROGRAM Quarters;

VAR amount : Real;
    qtr    : Integer;

BEGIN
  Write('Enter amount: ');
  Readln(amount);
  qtr := Trunc(100 * Frac(amount)) DIV 25;
  Writeln(qtr, ' quarters')
END.
```

69.
```
PROGRAM ConvertDecHrs;

VAR decHrs   : Real;
    hrs, min : Integer;

BEGIN
  Write('Enter a time in decimal hours: ');
  Readln(decHrs);
  hrs := Trunc(decHrs);
  min := Round((Frac(decHrs) * 60));
  Write(hrs, ' hours, ', min, ' minutes.')
END.
```

CHAPTER 4

Exercises 4.1

1. It isn't easy being green.
Kermit the frog

3. Why do clocks run clockwise?
Because they were invented in the northern
hemisphere where sundials move clockwise.

5. 7

7. Keep cool, but don't freeze.
Source: A jar of mayonnaise.

9. 88

11. It was the best of times.
It was the worst of times.

13. Your name has 7 letters.
The first letter is G

15. abcde

17. 144 items in a gross

19. 30% of M&M's Plain Chocolate Candies are brown.

21. 1440 minutes in a day

23. t is the 6th letter of the word.

25. According to a poll in the May 31, 1988 issue of PC Magazine,
75% of the people polled write programs for their companies.
The four most popular languages used are as follows.
22% of the respondents use BASIC
16% of the respondents use Assembler
15% of the respondents use C
13% of the respondents use Pascal

27. Yoko Izumi, you were born in 1965

29. The Statue of Liberty weighs 250 tons

31. You will receive a BA degree at age 22

33. All's well that ends well.

35. There is no argument in the procedure call.

37. The parameter and local variable of LengthName cannot have the same name.

39.
```
PROGRAM ShowLuckyNum;

  VAR num : Integer;

  PROCEDURE Lucky (num : Integer);
    BEGIN
      Writeln(num, 'is a lucky number.')
    END;

  BEGIN
    num := 7;
    Lucky(num)
  END.
```

41.
```
PROGRAM TreeInfo;

  PROCEDURE Tallest;
    VAR tree   : STRING;
        height : Integer;
    BEGIN
      Readln(height, tree);
      Writeln('The tallest ', tree, ' in the U.S. is ',
                 height, ' feet.')
    END;

  BEGIN
    Tallest;
    Tallest
  END.
```

43.
```
PROGRAM Survey;

  PROCEDURE ShowInfo (perc0:1: Real; major : STRING);
    BEGIN
      Writeln(perc0:1, ' percent said that they intend to major in ', major);
    END;

  BEGIN
    Writeln('According to a 1986 survey of college freshmen');
    Writeln('taken by the Higher Educational Research Institute:');
    Writeln;
    ShowInfo(26, 'business');
    ShowInfo(2, 'computer science')
  END.
```

45.
```
PROGRAM FavoriteNumber;

  VAR favorite : Integer;

  PROCEDURE Traits (favorite : Integer);
    BEGIN
      Writeln('The sum of your favorite number with itself is ',
               favorite + favorite);
      Writeln('The product of your favorite number with itself is ',
               favorite * favorite)
    END;

  BEGIN
    Write('What is your favorite number? ');
    Readln(favorite);
    Traits(favorite)
  END.
```

47.
```
PROGRAM Farm;

  VAR animal, sound : STRING;

  PROCEDURE Verses(animal, sound : STRING);
    BEGIN
      Writeln('Old McDonald had a farm. Eyi eyi oh.');
      Writeln('And on his farm he had a ', animal, '. Eyi eyi oh.');
      Write('With a ', sound, ' ', sound,', here');
      Writeln(' and a ', sound, ' ', sound, ' there.');
      Write('Here a ', sound, ', there a ', sound);
      Writeln(' everywhere a ', sound, ' ', sound, '.');
      Writeln('Old McDonald had a farm. Eyi eyi oh.')
    END;
  BEGIN
    Write('Enter an animal: ');
    Readln(animal);
    Write('Enter a sound: ');
    Readln(sound);
    Verses(animal, sound)
  END.
```

Exercises 4.2

1. 9

3. Can Can

5. 5

7. Less is More

9. Gabriel was born in the year 1980

11. Ohio Buckeyes

13. 121
    35

15. 1
    1

17. de Leon discovered Florida

19. 7
    0

21. The variable var3 was not declared.

23.
```
PROGRAM SalesTax;

  VAR price, tax, cost : Real;

  PROCEDURE GetPrice (VAR price : Real);
    BEGIN
      Write('Enter the price of the item: ');
      Readln(price)
    END;

  PROCEDURE Compute (price : Real; VAR tax, cost : Real);
    BEGIN
      tax := 0.05 * price;
      cost := price + tax
    END;

  PROCEDURE ShowBill (price, tax, cost : Real);
    BEGIN
      Writeln('Price: ', price:10:2);
      Writeln('Tax:   ', tax:10:2);
      Writeln('       -----------';
      Writeln('Cost:  ', cost:10:2)
    END;

  BEGIN
    GetPrice(price);
    Compute(price, tax, cost);
    ShowBill(price, tax, cost)
  END.
```

25.
```
PROGRAM RectangeArea;

  VAR length, width, area : Real;

  PROCEDURE GetData (VAR length, width : Real);
    BEGIN
      Write('Enter the length and width: ');
      Readln(length, width)
    END;

  PROCEDURE ComputeArea (length, width : Real; VAR area : Real);
    BEGIN
      area := length * width
    END;

  PROCEDURE ShowArea (area : Real);
    BEGIN
      Writeln('The area of the rectangle is ', area:0:3)
    END;

  BEGIN
    GetData(length, width);
    ComputeArea(length, width, area);
    ShowArea(area)
  END.
```

27.
```
PROGRAM Initials;

   VAR first, last      : STRING;
       firstInit, lastInit : Char;

   PROCEDURE InputName (VAR first, last : STRING);
     BEGIN
       Write('What is the person''s first name? ');
       Readln(first);
       Write('What is the person''s last name? ');
       Readln(last)
     END;

   PROCEDURE CalculateInitials (    first, last      : STRING;
                                  VAR firstInit, lastInit : Char);
     BEGIN
       firstInit := UpCase(first[1]);
       lastInit := UpCase(last[1])
     END;

   PROCEDURE ShowInitials (firstInit, lastInit : Char);
     BEGIN
       Writeln(firstInit, ' ', lastInit)
     END;

   BEGIN
     InputName(first, last);
     CalculateInitials(first, last, firstInit, lastInit);
     ShowInitials(firstInit, lastInit)
   END.
```

31.
```
PROGRAM Baseball;

   VAR name       : STRING;
       atBat, hits : Integer;
       average     : Real;

   PROCEDURE InputData (VAR name : STRING; VAR atBat, hits : Integer);
     BEGIN
       Write('Input the player''s name: ');
       Readln(name);
       Write('Input the times at bat: ');
       Readln(atBat);
       Write('Input the hits: ');
       Readln(hits)
     END;

   PROCEDURE ComputeAverage (atBat, hits : Integer; VAR average : Real);
     BEGIN
       average := atBat / hits
     END;

   PROCEDURE ShowData (name : STRING; average : Real);
     BEGIN
       Write(name, '''s batting average is ', average:0:3)
     END;

   BEGIN
     InputData(name, atBat, hits);
     ComputeAverage(atBat, hits, average);
     ShowData(name, average)
   END.
```

29.
```
PROGRAM Merchandise;

   VAR cost, price, markup : Real;

   PROCEDURE InputData (VAR cost, price : Real);
     BEGIN
       Write('Enter the cost: ');
       Readln(cost);
       Write('Enter the selling price: ');
       Readln(price)
     END;

   PROCEDURE ComputeMarkup (cost, price : Real; VAR markup :
   Real);
     BEGIN
       markup := ((price - cost) / cost) * 100
     END;

   PROCEDURE ShowMarkup (markup : Real);
     BEGIN
       Writeln('The markup is ', markup:0:2, '%')
     END;

   BEGIN
     InputData(cost, price);
     ComputeMarkup(cost, price, markup);
     ShowMarkup(markup)
   END.
```

Exercises 4.3

1. pup

3. You can park about 500 cars.   **5.** 400

7. The day is Wed

9. 15
3

11. No type is specified for the function result.

13.
```
PROGRAM Convert;

VAR centigrade : Integer;

  FUNCTION Fahrenheit (centigrade : Integer) : Integer;
    BEGIN
      Fahrenheit := Round(centigrade * (9 / 5) + 32)
    END;

  BEGIN
    Writeln('Input a temperature in centigrade: ');
    Readln(centigrade);
    Writeln('The temperature in Fahrenheit is ', Fahrenheit(centigrade))
  END.
```

15.
```
FUNCTION RoundXToN (x : Real; n : Integer) : Real;
  VAR tenToTheN : Real;
  BEGIN
    tenToTheN := Round(Exp(n * Ln(10)));  { value of 10 to the N }
    RoundXToN := Round(x * tenToTheN) / tenToTheN
  END;
```

17.
```
PROGRAM PopcornPrices;

VAR popcorn, butter, bucket, total : Real;

PROCEDURE InputCost (VAR popcorn, butter, bucket, total : Real);
  BEGIN
    Write('Input the cost of the popcorn: ');
    Readln(popcorn);
    Write('Input the cost of the butter: ');
    Readln(butter);
    Write('Input the cost of the bucket: ');
    Readln(bucket);
    Write('Input the customer cost: ');
    Readln(total)
  END;

FUNCTION Profit (popcorn, butter, bucket, total : Real) : Real;
  BEGIN
    Profit := total - popcorn - butter - bucket
  END;

BEGIN
  InputCost(popcorn, butter, bucket, total);
  Writeln('The profit is $',
          Profit(popcorn, butter, bucket, total):4:2)
END.
```

19. (a)
```
FUNCTION Min (num1, num2 : Integer) : Integer;
    BEGIN
      Min := num1 + num2 - Max(num1, num2)
    END;
```

(b)
```
PROCEDURE Order (VAR num1, num2 : Integer);
    VAR temp : Integer;
    BEGIN
      temp := Max(num1, num2);
      num1 := Min(num1, num2);
      num2 := temp
    END;
```

(c)
```
PROGRAM ThreeInOrder;

  VAR num1, num2, num3 : Integer;

  [ PROCEDUREs Min, Max, and Order here ]

  BEGIN
    Write('Enter three numbers separated by spaces: ');
    Readln(num1, num2, num3);
    Order(num1, num2);
    Order(num2, num3);
    Order(num1, num2);
    Writeln('The numbers in order are: ', num1, ' ', num2, ' ', num3)
  END.
```

CHAPTER 5

Exercises 5.1

1. True

3. True

5. False

7. True

9. False

11. False

13. Invalid. Should have (4 < m) AND (m < 7).

15. Valid

17. Valid

19. Valid

21. Invalid. Integer cannot be OR'd nor compared with Boolean.

23. Valid

25. True

27. True

29. False

31. False

33. False

35. True

37. False

39. Not equivalent

41. Equivalent

43. Not equivalent

45. Not equivalent

47. Not equivalent

49. (a <> b) AND (a <> d)

51. a >= b

53. b1 <> b2

55.
```
FUNCTION Implies (cond1, cond2 : Boolean) : Boolean;
  BEGIN
    Implies := (cond2 OR (NOT cond1))
  END;
```

Exercises 5.2

1. Less than ten

3. Tomorrow is another day.

5. 3

7. The cost of a call is $11.26

9. The number of vowels is 2

11. positive

13. One
Three

15. Incorrect form of Boolean expression.
Should be: (1 < num) AND (num < 3).

17. Incorrect form of Boolean expression.
Should be: (major = 'Business') OR
(major = 'Computer Science')

19. Integer cannot be compared to a String.

21. Intended form is (j = 4) OR (k = 4)

23. a := 5

25.
```
IF j = 7 THEN
    b := 1
  ELSE
    b := 2
```

27.
```
Write('Is Alaska bigger than Texas'
    ' and California combined? ');
Readln(answer);
IF answer[1] = 'Y' THEN
    Writeln('Correct' )
  ELSE
    Writeln('Wrong');
answer := ''
```

29.
```
IF j * 2 > 7 THEN
    m := n + 2
```

31.
```
IF (m >= 5) OR (d < 'H') THEN
    n := j + k
  ELSE
    b := False
```

33.
```
IF (d = '#') AND (NOT b) THEN
    j := j + 1
```

35.
```
IF (j > k) AND (2 * c = m) AND (d = 'L') THEN
    Writeln(c)
  ELSE
    Writeln(d)
```

37.
```
IF (j + m > n) AND (c = d) THEN
    BEGIN
      t := s;
      Writeln(c)
    END
    ELSE
      n := Sqr(j)
```

39.
```
IF (d > 'M') AND (m > 5) AND (n = 7) THEN
    b := True
  ELSE
    IF n < 7 THEN
      n := 8
```

41. PROGRAM GiveTip;

```
CONST TipPercent = 0.15;
      MinimumTip = 1.00;

VAR bill, tip : Real;

BEGIN
  Write('Input bill amount: ');
  Readln(bill);
  tip := bill * TipPercent;
  IF tip < MinimumTip THEN
      tip := MinimumTip;
  Writeln('The tip is $', tip:0:2)
END.
```

45. PROGRAM SavingsWithdrawal;

```
VAR oldBalance, newBalance, withdrawal : Real;

BEGIN
  Write('What is the current balance? ');
  Readln(oldBalance);
  Write('What is the withdrawal amount? ');
  Readln(withdrawal);
  IF withdrawal <= oldBalance THEN
      newBalance := oldBalance - withdrawal
    ELSE
      newBalance := oldBalance;
  Writeln('New balance: $', newBalance:0:2);
  IF withdrawal > oldBalance THEN
      Writeln('Withdrawal denied');
  IF newBalance < 150.00 THEN
      Writeln('Balance below $150')
END.
```

49. PROGRAM PigLatin;

```
VAR word, pigWord : STRING;

FUNCTION Consonant (letter : Char) : Boolean;
  BEGIN
    Consonant := NOT ((letter = 'a') OR (letter = 'e') OR
                      (letter = 'i') OR (letter = 'o') OR
                      (letter = 'u'))
  END;

BEGIN
  Write('Enter a word: ');
  Readln(word);
  IF Consonant(word[1]) THEN
      pigWord := Copy(word, 2, Length(word) - 1) + word[1] + 'ay'
    ELSE
      pigWord := word + 'way';
  Writeln('The pig latin equivalent is ', pigWord)
END.
```

43. PROGRAM DiskOrder;

```
CONST UnitPrice = 1.00;
      BulkPrice = 0.70;
      BigOrder  = 25;

VAR disks : Integer;
    cost  : Real;

BEGIN
  Write('Enter number of disks ordered: ');
  Readln(disks);
  IF disks < BigOrder THEN
      cost := disks * UnitPrice
    ELSE
      cost := disks * BulkPrice;
  Writeln('The total cost for the order is $', cost:0:2)
END.
```

47. PROGRAM Lottery;

```
VAR digit1, digit2, digit3 : Integer;

FUNCTION BothSeven (a, b : Integer) : Boolean;
  BEGIN
    BothSeven := ((a = 7) AND (b = 7))
  END;

BEGIN
  Write('Input three digits separated by spaces: ');
  Readln(digit1, digit2, digit3);
  IF BothSeven(digit1, digit2) OR
     BothSeven(digit2, digit3) OR
     BothSeven(digit1, digit3) THEN
      Writeln('Lucky seven')
END.
```

51. PROGRAM NJStateTax;

```
VAR income, tax : Real;

BEGIN
  Write('Enter income: ');
  Readln(income);
  IF income <= 20000.00 THEN
      tax := 0.02 * income
    ELSE
      IF income <= 50000.00 THEN
          tax := 400.00 + 0.025 * (income - 20000.00)
        ELSE
          tax := 1150 + 0.035 * (income - 50000.00);
  Writeln('The tax for this amount is $', tax:0:2)
END.
```

Exercises 5.3

1. Output for 6.5: 3.75
Output for 17: 3.75

3. Output for apple: Begins with a lowercase letter.
Output for Zebra: Begins with an uppercase letter.
Output for ?anonymous?: Does not begin with a letter.

5. Output for 2: The less things change, the more they remain the same.
   Output for 3: Time keeps everything from happening at once.
   Output for 5: Less is more.

9. A variable cannot be used in the value list.

13. A String type is not valid for the selector.

17. Valid

19. Valid

23.
```
CASE num OF
    1        : Writeln('one');
    6..MaxInt : Writeln('two')
END
```

27.
```
PROGRAM CloudCover;

VAR percentage : Integer;

BEGIN
  Write('Enter the percentage of cloud cover: ');
  Readln(percentage);
  CASE percentage OF
     0..30 : Writeln('clear');
    31..70 : Writeln('partly cloudy');
    71..99 : Writeln('cloudy');
    100    : Writeln('overcast')
  END
END.
```

29.
```
PROGRAM Shapes;

VAR shapeLetter : Char;
    area        : Real;

PROCEDURE GetShape (VAR shapeLetter : Char);
  BEGIN
    Writeln('C = Circle');
    Writeln('P = Parallelogram');
    Writeln('K = Kite');
    Writeln;
    Write('Enter the letter of the desired shape: ');
    Readln(shapeLetter)
  END;

FUNCTION CircleArea (radius : Real) : Real;
  BEGIN
    CircleArea := Pi * Sqr(radius)
  END;

PROCEDURE DoCircle (VAR area : Real);
  VAR radius : Real;
  BEGIN
    Write('Enter radius: ');
    Readln(radius);
    area := CircleArea(radius)
  END;

FUNCTION ParallelogramArea (length, height : Real) : Real;
  BEGIN
    ParallelogramArea := length * height
  END;
```

7. Output for 0: True.
   Output for 3: False.

11. Invalid entry in valid list: 3 <= num <= 10

15. The action associated with the second value list will never be executed.

21. Not valid

25.
```
CASE num OF
    1         : Writeln('lambs');
    3, 4      : Writeln('eat');
    5, 8..MaxInt : Writeln('ivy')
END
```

```
PROCEDURE DoParallelogram (VAR area : Real);
  VAR length, height : Real;
  BEGIN
    Write('Enter the length and height: ');
    Readln(length, height);
    area := ParallelogramArea(length, height)
  END;

FUNCTION KiteArea (length, width : Real) : Real;
  BEGIN
    KiteArea := (length * width) / 2
  END;

PROCEDURE DoKite (VAR area : Real);
  VAR length, width : Real;
  BEGIN
    Write('Enter the length and width: ');
    Readln(length, width);
    area := KiteArea(length, width)
  END;

BEGIN
  GetShape(shapeLetter);
  CASE UpCase(shapeLetter) OF
    'C' : DoCircle(area);
    'P' : DoParallelogram(area);
    'K' : DoKite(area)
  END;
  Writeln('The area of the figure is ', area:0:1)
END.
```

31.
```
PROGRAM IRSrewards;

CONST Full10 = 7500.00; { Maximum is 10 percent on first 75000 }
      Full5  = 1250.00; { Maximum is 5 percent on next 25000 }

VAR recovered,           { The amount recovered by the IRS }
    reward     : Real;   { The reward for the informant }

BEGIN
  Write('Enter the amount recovered: ');
  Readln(recovered);
  CASE Round(recovered/1000) OF
    0..75   : reward := recovered * 0.10;
    75..100 : reward := Full10 + ((recovered - 75000) * 0.05)
    ELSE      reward := Full10 + Full5 +
                        ((recovered - 100000) * 0.01)
  END;
  IF reward > 50000 THEN
    reward := 50000;
  Writeln('The reward is $', reward:1:2)
END.
```

CHAPTER 6

Exercises 6.1

1. 17

3. worship oatmeal

5. 2

7. 23 sKIDOO

9. Infinite loop

11. Condition should read: UNTIL answer = 'Y'

13.
```
n := 0;
REPEAT
  n := n + 1;
  Readln(num);
  Write(num)
UNTIL n = 3
```

15.
```
PROGRAM Cel_To_Fahr;

VAR  Celsius, Fahrenheit: Real;

BEGIN
  REPEAT
  Write('Enter a temperature in Celsius (0 - 100): ');
    Readln(Celsius)
  UNTIL (Celsius >= 0) AND (Celsius <= 100);
  Writeln('The temperature in Fahrenheit is ',
          ((9/5) * Celsius + 32):0:0)
END.
```

17.
```
PROGRAM Product;

VAR num, sum, maxnum : Integer;

BEGIN
  sum    := 0;
  num    := 0;
  maxnum := 0;
    WHILE (sum * num) < 400 DO
    BEGIN
      Write('Enter a positive integer : ');
      Readln(num);
      IF num > maxnum THEN
          maxnum := num;
      sum := sum + num
    END;
  Writeln('The greatest integer entered was ', maxnum)
END.
```

19.
```
PROGRAM MexicanPopulation;

VAR population : Real;
    years      : Integer;

BEGIN
  years := 0;
  population := 14.0;
  WHILE population < 20 DO
    BEGIN
      population := population * 1.03;
      years := years + 1
    END;
  Writeln('It will take ', years ,' years.')
END.
```

21.
```
PROGRAM StringManipulation;

VAR aWord      : STRING;
    posR, posN : Integer;
    first      : Char;

BEGIN
  REPEAT
    Write('Enter a word containing the two characters r & n: ');
    Readln(aWord);
    posR := Pos('r', aWord);
    posN := Pos('n', aWord)
  UNTIL (posR <> 0) AND (posN <> 0);
  IF posR < posN THEN
      first := 'r'
    ELSE
      first := 'n';
  Writeln('The letter ', first, ' appeared first.')
END.
```

23.
```
PROGRAM SavingsAccount;

VAR balance : Real;
    years   : Integer;

BEGIN
  years := 0;
  balance := 15000;
  WHILE balance > 0 DO
     BEGIN
        balance := balance * 1.05 - 1000;
        years := years + 1
     END;
  Writeln('The account will be depleted in ', years, ' years.')
END.
```

25.
```
PROGRAM SavingsAccount2;

VAR balance : Real;
    years   : Integer;

BEGIN
  years := 0;
  balance := 1000;
  WHILE balance < 1000000 DO
     BEGIN
        balance := balance * 1.08 + 1000;
        years := years + 1
     END;
  Writeln('The account will reach a million dollars in ',
          years, ' years')
END.
```

27.
```
PROGRAM FlowChart;

VAR f, n : Integer;

BEGIN
  Write('Enter an integer: ');
  Readln(n);
  f := 2;
  WHILE n > 1 DO
    IF (n MOD f) = 0 THEN
       BEGIN
         Writeln(f);
         n := n DIV f
       END
    ELSE
       f := f + 1
END.
```

Exercises 6.2

1. Pass #1
Pass #2
Pass #3
Pass #4

3. 5678910111213

5.
```
1  4  7  10
2  5  8  11
3  6  9  12
```

7. Average = 90.00

9. DDDDD
aaaaa
ttttt
aaaaa

11. ABCDE

13. DOWNTO should be used instead of TO

15. An infinite loop

17.
```
FOR num := 1 TO 9 DO
  IF Odd(num) THEN
      Writeln(num)
```

19.
```
PROGRAM RowOfStars;

VAR col : Integer;

BEGIN
  FOR col := 1 TO 10 DO
    Write('*')
END.
```

21.
```
PROGRAM Stars;

VAR rows, columns : Integer;

BEGIN
  FOR rows := 1 TO 10 DO
    BEGIN
      FOR columns := 1 TO 10 DO
        Write('*');
      Writeln
    END
END.
```

23.
```
PROGRAM Sums;

VAR i   : Integer;
    sum : Real;

BEGIN
  sum := 0;
  FOR i := 1 TO 100 DO
     sum := sum + (1 / i);
  Writeln('The sum is ', sum:1:2)
END.
```

25.
```
PROGRAM CountSibilants;

  VAR sentence : STRING;

  FUNCTION CountSibs (sentence : STRING) : Integer;
    VAR index, total : Integer;
        theChar      : Char;
    BEGIN
      total := 0;
      FOR index := 1 TO Length(sentence) DO
        BEGIN
          theChar := UpCase(sentence[index]);
          IF (theChar = 'S') OR (theChar = 'Z') THEN
              total := total + 1
        END;
      CountSibs := total
    END;

  BEGIN
    Write('Enter a sentence: ');
    Readln(sentence);
    Writeln('The total number of sibilants is ',
            CountSibs(sentence) ,'.')
  END.
```

29.
```
PROGRAM Decay;

  VAR cobalt60 : Real;
      years    : Integer;

  BEGIN
    cobalt60 := 10;
    FOR years := 1 TO 5 DO
      cobalt60 := cobalt60 - (cobalt60 * 0.12);
    Writeln('There will be ', cobalt60:0:2, ' grams left.')
  END.
```

27.
```
PROGRAM Bank;

  VAR years   : Integer;
      balance : Real;

  BEGIN
    balance := 800;
    FOR years := 1 TO 10 DO
        balance := balance * 1.07 + 100;
    Writeln('The final balance after 10 years is ', balance:0:2)
  END.
```

31.
```
PROGRAM HollowRectangle;

  VAR num, i, j : Integer;

  PROCEDURE HorizLine (num : Integer);
    VAR i : Integer;
    BEGIN
      FOR i := 1 TO num DO
        Write('*');
      Writeln
    END;

  BEGIN
    Write('Enter a number greater than 3: ');
    Readln(num);
    HorizLine(num);
    FOR i := 1 TO num - 2 DO
      BEGIN
        Write('*');
        FOR j := 1 TO num - 2 DO
          Write(' ');
        Writeln('*')
      END;
    HorizLine(num)
  END.
```

33.
```
PROGRAM MultTable;

   VAR m, n, x, y : Integer;

   BEGIN
     m := 0;
     REPEAT
       Write('Enter 2 integers from 2 TO 12: ');
       Readln(m, n)
     UNTIL ((m > 2) AND (m < 12)) AND ((n > 2) AND (n < 12))
     FOR x := 1 TO m DO
       BEGIN
         FOR y := 1 TO n DO
           Write(x * y:4);
         Writeln
       END
   END.
```

37.
```
PROGRAM Words;

   VAR p, q : Char;

   BEGIN
     FOR p := 'a' TO 'z' DO
       FOR q := 'a' TO 'z' DO
         IF (p = 'a') OR (p = 'e') OR (p = 'i') OR (p = 'o') OR
            (p = 'u') OR (p = 'y') OR (q = 'a') OR (q = 'e') OR
            (q = 'i') OR (q = 'o') OR (q = 'u') OR (q = 'y') THEN
           Writeln(p, q)
   END.
```

35.
```
FUNCTION IntPower (base, exponent : Integer) : Integer;
   VAR sum, index : Integer;
   BEGIN
     sum := 1;
     IF exponent <> 0 THEN
       FOR index := 1 TO exponent DO
         sum := sum * base
     ELSE
         sum := 1;
     IntPower := sum
   END;
```

Exercises 6.3

1. 13

3.
```
pie
cake
melon
EOD
```

5.
```
    A
Apple
Apricot
Avocado

    B
Banana
Blueberry

    G
Grape

    L
Lemon
Lime
```

7. 90

9. counters

11. −1 is added to the total

13. EOD will be displayed

15.
```pascal
PROGRAM Average;

   VAR num, sum, i : Real;

   BEGIN
      sum := 0;
      i   := 0;
      Write('Enter first number in list ( -1 to quit ): ');
      Readln(num);
      WHILE num <> -1 DO
         BEGIN
            sum := sum + num;
            i := i + 1;
            Write('Next: ');
            Readln(num)
         END;
      IF i <> 0 THEN
            Writeln('The average is ', (sum / i):3:0)
   END.
```

19.
```pascal
PROGRAM FollowOrders;

   VAR num, passes : Integer;

   BEGIN
      passes := 0;
      Write('Enter a positive integer less than 400: ');
      Readln(num);
      WHILE num <> 1 DO
         BEGIN
            IF NOT Odd(num) THEN       { If num even divide it by 2 }
                  num := num DIV 2
               ELSE
                  num := 3 * num + 1;
            passes := passes + 1
         END;
      Writeln('It took ', passes ,' passes.')
   END.
```

21.
```pascal
PROGRAM StatePop;

   VAR currPop, projPop, sum : Real;

   PROCEDURE Calculate (projPop : Real; VAR sum : Real; state : STRING);
      VAR temp, currPop : Real;
      BEGIN
         Write('Enter the current population of ', state, ': ');
         Readln(currPop);
         temp := 100 * (projPop - currPop) / currPop;
         Writeln('The state of ', state,
                  ' will have a growth of ', temp:3:2, '%');
         sum := sum + temp
      END;

   BEGIN
      sum := 0;
      Calculate(33.5, sum, 'California');
      Calculate(20.2, sum, 'Texas');
      Calculate(18, sum, 'New York');
      Calculate(15.4, sum, 'Florida');
      Calculate(11.6, sum, 'Illinois');
      Writeln('The average % population growth is ', (sum / 5):3:2, '%')
   END.
```

17.
```pascal
PROGRAM GradeOfEggs;

   VAR weight : Real;

   BEGIN
      REPEAT
         Write('Enter the weight of an egg (-1 to quit): ');
         Readln(weight);
         CASE Round(weight * 100) OF
            250..MaxInt : Writeln('The grade is Jumbo.');
            225..249    : Writeln('The grade is Extra Large.');
            200..224    : Writeln('The grade is Large.');
            175..199    : Writeln('The grade is Medium.');
            150..174    : Writeln('The grade is Small.');
            0..149      : Writeln('Send it to the Bakery.')
         END;
      UNTIL weight = -1
   END.
```

23.
```
PROGRAM TwoHighestScores;

   VAR hi1, hi2, num : Integer;

   PROCEDURE Check (VAR num, hi1, hi2 : Integer);
   { Checks if num is greater than hi1 or hi2 }
     BEGIN
       IF num > hi1 THEN
           BEGIN
             hi2 := hi1;
             hi1 := num
           END
         ELSE
           IF num > hi2 THEN
               hi2 := num
     END;

   BEGIN
     num := 0;
     hi1 := -1;
     hi2 := -1;
     WHILE num <> -1 DO
       BEGIN
         Write('Enter score (-1 to quit): ');
         Readln(num);
         Check(num, hi1, hi2)
       END;
     IF (hi1 = -1 ) OR (hi2 = -1) THEN
         Writeln('At least two scores must be entered.')
       ELSE
         Writeln('The two highest scores were ', hi1, ' and ', hi2)
   END.
```

25.
```
PROGRAM RemoveContents;

   VAR index       : Integer;
       sentence    : STRING;
       current     : Char;       { Current string position }
       insideParens : Boolean;   { True if current string position is
                                   between parentheses in sentence }
   BEGIN
     insideParens := False;
     Writeln('Enter a sentence: ');
     Readln(sentence);
     FOR index := 1 TO Length(sentence) DO
       BEGIN
         current := sentence[index];
         IF ( current = '(' ) OR ( current = ')' ) THEN
             insideParens := ( current = '(' )
           ELSE
             IF NOT insideParens THEN
               Write(current)
       END
   END.
```

CHAPTER 7

Exercises 7.1

1. Not valid.   **3.** Not valid.   **5.** Not valid.   **7.** Not valid.

9. Pisces   **11.** Taurus   **13.** Pisces   **15.** Gemini

17. 0   **19.** 1   **21.** 'a', 'b', 'c', 'd', 'e', 'f'

23. 'A', 'B', 'C', 'D', 'E', 'F', 'G', 'H'

25. TYPE Months31 = (January, March, May, July, August, October, December)

27. TYPE Planets = (Mercury, Venus, Earth, Mars, Jupiter, Saturn, Uranus, Neptune, Pluto)

29. TYPE Directions = (North, East, South, West)

33. Incompatible types in comparison.

37.
```
FUNCTION NewEngland (state : Original13) : Boolean;
   BEGIN
      NewEngland := ((state = MA) OR (state = CT) OR
                     (state = RI) OR (state = NH))
   END;
```

31. 6 5 4 3 2 1 0

35. Improper subrange in CASE statement; 'a' is greater than 'Z'.

39.
```
PROGRAM RockPaperScissors;

   TYPE Choice = (Rock, Paper, Scissors);

   VAR player1, player2 : Choice;
       response         : Char;

   FUNCTION Convert (response : Char) : Choice;
      BEGIN
         CASE UpCase(response) OF
            'R' : Convert := Rock;
            'P' : Convert := Paper;
            'S' : Convert := Scissors
         END
      END;

   BEGIN
      Write('Enter choice of player 1 (R, P, S): ');
      Readln(response);
      player1 := Convert(response);
      Write('Enter choice of player 2 (R, P, S): ');
      Readln(response);
      player2 := Convert(response);
      CASE ord(player1) - ord(player2) OF
         0     : Writeln('Tie.');
         1, -2 : Writeln('Player 1 wins.');
        -1,  2 : Writeln('Player 2 wins.')
      END;
   END.
```

Exercises 7.2

1. The best way out is always through.
                    Robert Frost

5. Break-in of Democratic National Headquarters occurred in JUN of 1972

7. There are no END statements terminating the RECORD blocks.

9. A function cannot return a record.

11. (a)
```
TYPE Inventory = RECORD
                    name     : STRING;
                    quantity : STRING;
                    level    : Integer;
                    price    : Real
                 END;
VAR inv : Inventory;
```

13. (a)
```
TYPE States = RECORD
                 area       : Real;
                 population : Real;
                 capital    : STRING;
                 year       : Integer
              END;
VAR illinois : States;
```

15. (a)
```
TYPE Pulitzer = RECORD
                   name    : STRING;
                   litForm : STRING;
                   year    : Integer
                END;
VAR prizeWinner : Pulitzer;
```

3. Irises by Van Gogh sold for $53900000.00

(b) inv.name := 'beans'

(b) illinois.capital := 'Springfield'

(b)
```
WITH prizeWinner DO
   BEGIN
      name := 'John Steinbeck';
      litForm := 'Fiction';
      year := 1940
   END
```

17.
```
PROGRAM ScreenPoint;

USES Crt;

TYPE ValidCols     = 1..80;
     ValidRows     = 1..25;
     ScreenLocation = RECORD
                        column : ValidCols;
                        row    : ValidRows;
                        blip   : Char
                      END;

VAR screenChar : ScreenLocation;

PROCEDURE GetInput (VAR screenChar : ScreenLocation);
  BEGIN
    Write('Enter screen column: ');
    Readln(screenChar.column);
    Write('Enter screen row: ');
    Readln(screenChar.row);
    Write('Enter character: ');
    Readln(screenChar.blip)
  END;

PROCEDURE DisplayChar (screenChar : ScreenLocation);
  BEGIN
    GotoXY(screenChar.column, screenChar.row);
    Write(screenChar.blip)
  END;

PROCEDURE MoveChar (VAR screenChar : ScreenLocation);
  VAR moves : Integer;
  BEGIN
    DisplayChar(screenChar);
    GotoXY(1, 1);
    Writeln('Hit Return once for every character move');
    FOR moves := 1 TO 10 DO
      BEGIN
        GotoXY(1, 2);
        Readln;
          WITH screenChar DO
            IF column < 80 THEN
                column := column + 1
              ELSE
                column := 1;
          DisplayChar(screenChar)
      END
  END;

BEGIN
  ClrScr;
  GetInput(screenChar);
  MoveChar(screenChar)
END.
```

```
19. PROGRAM Security;

    USES Crt;

    TYPE Password = RECORD
                      name   : STRING;
                      number : Integer
                    END;

    VAR user, secret : Password;

    PROCEDURE Initialize (VAR secret : Password);
      BEGIN
        secret.name := 'Antler';
        secret.number := 47
      END;

    PROCEDURE GetInput (VAR user : Password);
      BEGIN
        Write('Enter the secret password: ');
        Readln(user.name);
        Write('Enter the secret number: ');
        Readln(user.number)
      END;

    PROCEDURE Compare (secret, user : Password);
      BEGIN
        IF (secret.name = user.name) AND (secret.number = user.number) THEN
            Writeln('Welcome comrade.')
          ELSE
            Writeln('Denied!')
      END;

    BEGIN
      ClrScr;
      Initialize(secret);
      GetInput(user);
      Compare(secret, user)
    END.

23. PROGRAM KeepInformation;

    USES Crt;

    TYPE Phone  = RECORD
                    home : STRING;
                    work : STRING;
                    fax  : STRING
                  END;
         Client = RECORD
                    name      : STRING;
                    telephone : Phone
                  END;

    VAR newClient : Client;
```

```
21. TYPE Grades = RECORD
                    exam1 : Integer;
                    exam2 : Integer;
                    exam3 : Integer;
                    final : Integer
                  END;

    VAR work : Grades;

    FUNCTION LetterGrade (work : Grades) : Char;
      BEGIN
        WITH work DO
          CASE Round((exam1 + exam2 + exam3 + 2 * final) / 5) OF
            90..100 : LetterGrade := 'A';
            80..89  : LetterGrade := 'B';
            70..79  : LetterGrade := 'C';
            60..69  : LetterGrade := 'D';
            ELSE      LetterGrade := 'F'
          END
      END;
```

```
PROCEDURE GetInput (VAR newClient : Client);
  BEGIN
    WITH newClient DO
      BEGIN
        Write('Enter client''s name: ');
        Readln(name);
        WITH telephone DO
          BEGIN
            Write('Enter home phone number: ');
            Readln(home);
            Write('Enter work phone number: ');
            Readln(work);
            Write('Enter FAX number: ');
            Readln(fax)
          END
      END
  END;

FUNCTION LastName (name : STRING) : STRING;
  VAR spacePos : Integer;
  BEGIN
    spacePos := Pos(' ', name);
    LastName := Copy(name, spacePos + 1, Length(name) - spacePos)
  END;

FUNCTION FirstName (name : STRING) : STRING;
  VAR spacePos : Integer;
  BEGIN
    spacePos := Pos(' ', name);
    FirstName := Copy(name, 1, spacePos - 1)
  END;

PROCEDURE ShowInfo (newClient : Client);
  BEGIN
    WITH newClient DO
      BEGIN
        Writeln(LastName(name), ', ', FirstName(name));
        WITH telephone DO
          BEGIN
            Writeln(home, ' (h)');
            Writeln(work, ' (w)');
            Writeln(fax, ' (FAX)')
          END
      END
  END;

BEGIN
  ClrScr;
  GetInput(newClient);
  ShowInfo(newClient)
END.
```

Exercises 7.3

1. [1..9]   **3.** [4, 5, 7, 9]   **5.** []   **7.** []

9. Since Real is not an ordinal type, it is not valid in a set.

11. Singletons of character sets are denoted ['!'], not [!]. Also, ! is out of the set range as defined.

13. decision = [doubtIt, hmm, maybe]

15. decision = [no, doubtIt, hmm, maybe, yes]

17. decision = [no, doubtIt, hmm]

19.
```
FUNCTION Cardinality (aSet : CharSet) : Integer;
    VAR count     : Integer;
        character : Char;
    BEGIN
      count := 0;
      FOR character := Chr(0) TO Chr(255) DO
        IF character IN aSet THEN
            count := count + 1;
      Cardinality := count
    END;
```

23.
```
PROCEDURE OddSet (num1, num2 : Integer; VAR numSet : IntSet);
    VAR index : Integer;
    BEGIN
      numSet := [];
      IF (num1 >= 0) AND (num2 <= 255) THEN
          FOR index := num1 TO num2 DO
            IF Odd(index) THEN
                numSet := numSet + [index]
    END;
```

21.
```
FUNCTION ProperSubset (set1, set2 : IntSet) : Boolean;
    BEGIN
      ProperSubset := ((set1 <= set2) OR (set2 <= set1))
                          AND (set1 <> set2)
    END;
```

CHAPTER 8

Exercises 8.1

1. 10

3.
```
TYPE NameDefn = RECORD
                  name    : STRING;
                  meaning : STRING
                END;
     NameArray = ARRAY [1..6] OF NameDefn;

VAR names : NameArray;
```

5. 3
7
2

7. 0
1
4
9
16
25
55

9. D

11. Marilyn achieved the high score of 94

13.

river[1]	river[2]	river[3]	river[4]	river[5]
Thames	Nile	Ohio	Amazon	Volga

river[1]	river[2]	river[3]	river[4]	river[5]
Volga	Thames	Nile	Ohio	Amazon

15. 3 inches = 7.62 centimeters
3 quarts = 2.85 liters
3 ounces = 85.20 grams

17. ArrayType holds 5 elements, indexed 0..4. The constant was declared with only 4 elements.

19. Elements of myArray are Real, while the indicies of myArray are Integer, so elements of myArray cannot be used as index values in the program's last statement.

21. Count is set to 0, so the first time the WHILE loop runs, it checks word[0] <> 'EOD', producing a range error.

23. a) 2   **b)** 7   **c)** 10   **d)** 9

25.
```
PROCEDURE Reverse (VAR arr1, arr2 : CharArray);
    VAR i : Integer;
    BEGIN
      FOR i := 1 TO 4 DO
        arr2[i] := arr1[5-i]
    END;
```

27.
```
PROCEDURE ShowTable (VAR arr : IntArray);
   VAR row, col : Integer;
   BEGIN
     FOR row := 0 TO 5 DO
       BEGIN
         FOR col := 1 TO 5 DO
           Write(arr[row * 5 + col]:10);
         Writeln
       END
   END;
```

31.
```
PROCEDURE ShowStuff (VAR arr : RealArray);
   VAR index : Integer;
       item  : Real;
   BEGIN
     FOR index := 1 TO 10 DO
       BEGIN
         item := arr[index];
         Writeln(item:10:4, Sqr(item):10:4,
                ((Sqr(item) + item) / 2):10:4)
       END
   END;
```

29.
```
PROCEDURE CalculateOdds (VAR myArray : IntArray;
                         VAR sum : Integer);
   BEGIN
     sum := 0;
     FOR index := 1 TO 9 DO
       sum := sum + myArray[index];
     Writeln('The sum is ', sum)
   END;
```

33.
```
CONST NumFlights = 5;
   TYPE RecordType = RECORD
                       flightNum : STRING[20];
                       orig      : STRING[20];
                       dest      : STRING[20];
                       deptTime  : STRING[20];
                     END;
       FlightType = ARRAY [1..NumFlights] OF RecordType;
       DataType   = ARRAY [1..NumFlights * 4] OF STRING[20];

   CONST FlightData : DataType =
     ('117', 'Tucson',   'Dallas',   '8:45 a.m.',
      '239', 'LA',       'Boston',   '10:15 a.m.',
      '298', 'Albany',   'Reno', '   1:35 p.m.',
      '326', 'Houston',  'New York', '2:40 p.m.',
      '445', 'New York', 'Tampa',    '4:20 p.m.');

   VAR flight : FlightType;
       flNum  : STRING[20];
       i      : Integer;
       found  : Boolean;

   PROCEDURE FillArray (VAR flight : FlightType);
     VAR index : Integer;
     BEGIN
       FOR index := 1 TO NumFlights DO
         WITH flight[index] DO
           BEGIN
             flightNum := FlightData[(index - 1) * 4 + 1];
             orig      := FlightData[(index - 1) * 4 + 2];
             dest      := FlightData[(index - 1) * 4 + 3];
             deptTime  := FlightData[(index - 1) * 4 + 4]
           END
     END;

   BEGIN
     FillArray(flight);
     Write('What is the flight number? ');
     Readln(flNum);
     i := 0;
     REPEAT
       i := i + 1;
       found := (flight[i].flightNum = flNum)
     UNTIL (i = NumFlights) OR found;
     IF found THEN
         WITH flight[i] DO
           Writeln('Flight: ', flightNum, 'Origin: ':10, orig,
                  'Destination: ':16, dest, 'Departing ':13,
   deptTime)
       ELSE
         Writeln('That flight number does not exist.')
   END.
```

```
35. CONST NumBins  = 5;

    TYPE  BinRecord = RECORD
                        unitPr : Real;
                        sold   : Integer
                      END;
          BinArray  = ARRAY [1..NumBins] OF BinRecord;
          DataType  = ARRAY [1..NumBins * 2] OF Real;

    CONST BinData : DataType = ( 3.00, 10,  12.25, 30,
                                 37.45, 9,  7.49, 42, 24.95, 17);

    VAR bin : BinArray;

    PROCEDURE FillArray (VAR bin : BinArray);
      VAR index : Integer;
      BEGIN
        FOR index := 1 TO NumBins DO
          WITH bin[index] DO
            BEGIN
              unitPr := BinData[(index - 1) * 2 + 1];
              sold   := Round(BinData[(index - 1) * 2 + 2])
            END
      END;

    PROCEDURE ProduceTable (VAR bin : BinArray);
      VAR num     : Integer;
          revenue : Real;
      BEGIN
        revenue := 0;
        Writeln('Item':4, 'Inventory':12, 'Revenue':12, '  Less than 20');
        FOR num := 1 TO NumBins DO
          WITH bin[num] DO
            BEGIN
              revenue := revenue + (sold * unitPr);
              Write(num:3, (45 - sold):8, (sold * unitPr):15:2);
              IF (45 - sold) < 20 THEN
                  Writeln('*':10)
               ELSE
                  Writeln
            END;
        Writeln('Day''s total revenue: ', revenue:1:2)
      END;

    BEGIN
      FillArray(bin);
      ProduceTable(bin)
    END.
```

Exercises 8.2

1. test battery

3. pearls before swine

5. 75 42

7. A Shell sort requires seven comparisons and four swaps. A full bubble sort requires ten comparisons and six swaps. Therefore, the Shell sort is better for the data.

9. The REPEAT loop will not terminate since the search string is not is the array; *index* will be incremented to exceed the maximum array index.

11. Four swaps are required.

13. The number of comparisons for a bubble sort of n items is $n(n-1)/2$.

15. Three swaps are required.

17. 8

19. Traverse the list, counting the number of occurances of each element (1, 2, 3, and 4). Then form a sorted array consisting of the appropriate number of each element. The sorting involves no comparisons.

21. The maximum number of comparisons required to find an item in a sequential search of 16 items is 16. The average number of comparisons is 8. The maximum number of comparisons required to find an item in a binary search of 16 items is 4.

23.
```
PROGRAM SevenDwarfs;

  USES Crt;

  CONST NumDwarfs = 7;

  TYPE Names = ARRAY [1..NumDwarfs] OF STRING;

  CONST Dwarfs : Names = ('Doc', 'Grumpy', 'Sleepy', 'Happy',
                          'Bashful', 'Sneezy', 'Dopey');

  VAR dwarfNames     : Names;
      index1, index2 : Integer;

  PROCEDURE Swap (VAR str1, str2 : STRING);
    VAR temp : STRING;
    BEGIN
      temp := str1;
      str1 := str2;
      str2 := temp
    END;


  BEGIN
    ClrScr;
    dwarfNames := Dwarfs;
    FOR index1 := 1 to NumDwarfs - 1 DO
      FOR index2 := 1 TO NumDwarfs - index1 DO
        IF dwarfNames[index2 + 1] < dwarfNames[index2] THEN
          Swap(dwarfNames[index2 + 1], dwarfNames[index2]);
    FOR index1 := 1 TO NumDwarfs DO
        Writeln(dwarfNames[index1])
  END.
```

25.
```
PROGRAM TahoeBasinSki;

  USES Crt;

  CONST MaxSlopes = 8;

  TYPE OneSlope  = RECORD
                     area     : STRING;
                     topElev,
                     vertical,
                     lifts    : Integer
                   END;
     AllSlopes = ARRAY [1..MaxSlopes] OF OneSlope;

  VAR skiSlopes : AllSlopes;
   PROCEDURE InputData (VAR skiSlopes : AllSlopes);
   VAR slopeNum : Integer;
   BEGIN
     FOR slopeNum := 1 TO MaxSlopes DO
       WITH skiSlopes[slopeNum] DO
         BEGIN
           Writeln('Enter data for slope #', slopeNum);
           Write('      Area name: ');
           Readln(area);
           Write('  Top Elevation: ');
           Readln(topElev);
           Write('       Vertical: ');
           Readln(vertical);
           Write('          Lifts: ');
           Readln(lifts);
           Writeln
         END
   END;
```

```
PROCEDURE Swap (VAR slope1, slope2 : OneSlope);
  VAR temp : OneSlope;
  BEGIN
    temp := slope1;
    slope1 := slope2;
    slope2 := temp
  END;

PROCEDURE Sort (VAR skiSlopes : AllSlopes);
  VAR index1, index2 : Integer;
  BEGIN
    FOR index1 := 1 TO MaxSlopes - 1 DO
      FOR index2 := 1 TO MaxSlopes - index1 DO
        IF skiSlopes[index2 + 1].topElev > skiSlopes[index2].topElev THEN
            Swap(skiSlopes[index2 + 1], skiSlopes[index2])
  END;

PROCEDURE Show (skiSlopes : AllSlopes);
  VAR slopeNum : Integer;
  BEGIN
    Writeln('Area':20, 'Top Elevation':20, 'Vertical':15, 'Lifts':15);
    Writeln('----':20, '-------------':20, '--------':15, '-----':15);
    FOR slopeNum := 1 TO MaxSlopes DO
      WITH skiSlopes[slopeNum] DO
        Writeln(area:20, topElev:20, vertical:15, lifts:15)
  END;

BEGIN
  ClrScr;
  InputData(skiSlopes);
  Sort(skiSlopes);
  Show(skiSlopes)
END.
```

27.
```
PROCEDURE FindFlight (VAR flgtNum : Flights);
  VAR first, middle, last, quarry : Integer;
      found                       : Boolean;
  BEGIN
    Write('Enter flight number to search for: ');
    Readln(quarry);
    first := 1;
    last := 200;
    REPEAT
      middle := (first + last) DIV 2;
      found := (flgtNum[middle] = quarry);
      IF NOT found THEN
          IF flgtNum[middle] > quarry THEN
              last := middle - 1
            ELSE
              first := middle + 1
    UNTIL found OR (first > last);
    IF found THEN
          Writeln('Flight is valid')
      ELSE
          Writeln('Flight is not valid')
  END;
```

29.
```
PROGRAM Encode;

USES Crt;

TYPE MorseCode  = STRING[4];
     MorseArray = ARRAY ['A'..'Z'] OF MorseCode;

CONST Morse : MorseArray = ('._',    '_...',  '_._.',  '_..',
                            '.',     '.._.',  '__.',   '....',
                            '..',    '.___',  '_._',   '._..',
                            '__',    '_.',    '___',   '.__.',
                            '__._',  '._.',   '...',   '_',
                            '.._',   '..._',  '.__',   '_.._',
                            '_.__',  '__..');

VAR word   : STRING;
    letter : Integer;

BEGIN
  ClrScr;
  Write('Enter a word: ');
  Readln(word);
  FOR letter := 1 TO Length(word) DO
    Write(Morse[UpCase(word[letter])], ' ');
  Writeln
END.
```

31.
```
PROGRAM AverageScore;

  USES Crt;

  CONST NumScores = 7;
  TYPE ScoreArray = ARRAY [1..NumScores] OF Integer;

  VAR name   : STRING;
      scores : ScoreArray;

  PROCEDURE InputData (VAR name : STRING; VAR scores : ScoreArray);
    VAR scoreNum : Integer;
    BEGIN
      Write('Enter student''s name: ');
      Readln(name);
      FOR scoreNum := 1 TO NumScores DO
        BEGIN
          Write('Enter score for test number ', scoreNum, ': ');
          Readln(scores[scoreNum])
        END
    END;

  PROCEDURE Swap (VAR score1, score2 : Integer);
    VAR temp : Integer;
    BEGIN
      temp := score1;
      score1 := score2;
      score2 := temp
    END;

  PROCEDURE Sort (VAR scores : ScoreArray);
    VAR index1, index2 : Integer;
    BEGIN
      FOR index1 := 1 TO NumScores - 1 DO
        FOR index2 := 1 TO NumScores - index1 DO
          IF scores[index1 + 1] < scores[index1] THEN
              Swap(scores[index1 + 1], scores[index1])
    END;

  PROCEDURE ShowAvg (name : STRING; scores : ScoreArray);
    VAR scoreNum, total, average : Integer;
    BEGIN
      total := 0;
      FOR scoreNum := 3 TO NumScores DO
        total := total + scores[scoreNum];
      average := Round(total / (NumScores - 2));
      Writeln('The average score for ', name, ' is ', average)
    END;

BEGIN
  ClrScr;
  InputData(name, scores);
  Sort(scores);
  ShowAvg(name, scores)
END.
```

Exercises 8.3

1. 12

3. 4 1 6
5 8 2

5. 1990

7. 4 0 0 0
0 7 0 0
0 0 0 6

9. The array indicies are out of bounds; *row* can only range from 1 to 3.

11.
```
FOR row := 1 TO 10 DO
   arr[row, j] := j
```

13.
```
FOR col := 1 TO 10 DO
   BEGIN
     temp := arr[2, col];
     arr[2, col] := arr[3, col];
     arr[3, col] := temp
   END
```

15.
```
PROGRAM KeepInventory;

USES Crt;

CONST Items  = 3;
      Stores = 2;

TYPE ItemData = ARRAY [1..Stores, 1..Items] OF Integer;

CONST BegInv : ItemData = ((25, 64, 23), (12, 82, 19));
      Sales  : ItemData = ((7, 45, 11), (4, 24, 8));

VAR inventory : ItemData;

PROCEDURE Initialize (VAR inventory : ItemData);
  BEGIN
    inventory := BegInv
  END;

PROCEDURE Recalculate (VAR inventory : ItemData);
  VAR store, item : Integer;
  BEGIN
    FOR store := 1 TO Stores DO
      FOR item := 1 TO Items DO
        inventory[store, item] := inventory[store, item] - Sales[store, item]
  END;

PROCEDURE Show (inventory : ItemData);
  VAR store, item : Integer;
  BEGIN
    FOR store := 1 TO Stores DO
      BEGIN
        Writeln('Store number ', store, ':');
        FOR item := 1 TO Items DO
          Writeln('  Item #', item, ' =', inventory[store, item]:3);
        Writeln
      END
  END;

BEGIN
  ClrScr;
  Initialize(inventory);
  Recalculate(inventory);
  Show(inventory)
END.
```

17.
```
PROGRAM University;

USES Crt;

CONST Campuses = 3;
      Courses  = 10;

TYPE Enrollments = ARRAY [1..Campuses, 1..Courses] OF Integer;

CONST Enroll : Enrollments = (( 5, 15, 22, 21, 12, 25, 16, 11, 17, 23),
                              (11, 23, 51, 25, 32, 35, 32, 52, 25, 21),
                              ( 2, 12, 32, 32, 25, 26, 29, 12, 15, 11));
```

```
      VAR campus, course, totalEnroll, totalCourse : Integer;

    BEGIN
      ClrScr;
      totalEnroll := 0;
      FOR campus := 1 TO Campuses DO
        FOR course := 1 TO Courses DO
          totalEnroll := totalEnroll + Enroll[campus, course];
      Writeln(totalEnroll, ' students enrolled.');
      FOR course := 1 TO Courses DO
        BEGIN
          totalCourse := 0;
          FOR campus := 1 TO Campuses DO
            totalCourse := totalCourse + Enroll[campus, course];
          Writeln('  Course', course:3, ':', totalCourse:4)
        END
    END.
```

19.
```
PROGRAM Golf;

USES Crt;

CONST Players = 3;
      Rounds  = 4;

TYPE PlayerNames = ARRAY [1..Players] OF STRING;
     GolfScores  = ARRAY [1..Players, 1..Rounds] OF Integer;

CONST Names  : PlayerNames = ('Curtis Strange',
                             'Nick Faldo',
                             'Steve Pate');
      USOpen : GolfScores  = ((70, 67, 69, 72),
                             (72, 67, 68, 71),
                             (72, 69, 72, 67));

VAR player, round, totalScore, totalRound, averageRound : Integer;

BEGIN
  ClrScr;
  FOR player := 1 TO Players DO
    BEGIN
      totalScore := 0;
      FOR round := 1 TO Rounds DO
      totalScore := totalScore + USOpen[player, round];
      Writeln('Total score for ', Names[player],
              ' is ', totalScore)
    END;
  Writeln;
  FOR round := 1 TO Rounds DO
    BEGIN
      totalRound := 0;
      FOR player := 1 TO Players DO
        totalRound := totalRound + USOpen[player, round];
      averageRound := totalRound DIV Players;
      Writeln('Average score for round ', round, ' is ', averageRound)
    END
END.
```

21.
```
PROGRAM UniversityRankings;

USES Crt;

CONST Categories = 3;
      Places     = 5;
```

```
TYPE Divisions = ARRAY [1..Categories] OF STRING;
     Schools   = ARRAY [1..Categories, 1..Places] OF STRING;

CONST Fields     : Divisions = ('Business', 'Comp Sc.', 'Engr/Gen.');
      TopSchools : Schools   = (('U of PA', 'MIT', 'U of IN',
                                 'U of MI', 'UC Berk'),
                                ('MIT', 'Cng-Mellon', 'UC Berk',
                                 'Cornell', 'U of IL'),
                                ('UCLA', 'U of IL', 'U of MD',
                                 'U of OK', 'Stevens IT'));

VAR fieldNum, rankingNum : Integer;
    schoolName           : STRING;
    found                : Boolean;

BEGIN
  ClrScr;
  Write('Enter the name of a school: ');
  Readln(schoolName);
  Writeln;
  found := False;
  FOR fieldNum := 1 TO Categories DO
    FOR rankingNum := 1 TO Places DO
      IF TopSchools[fieldNum, rankingNum] = schoolName THEN
      BEGIN
        found := True;
        Writeln('Ranked #', rankingNum, ' in ', Fields[fieldNum])
      END;
  IF NOT found THEN
      Writeln(schoolName, ' is not ranked among the top ',
              Places, ' schools')
END.
```

23.
```
PROGRAM StudentScores;

USES Crt;

CONST Students = 1;
      Exams    = 6;

TYPE NameData   = ARRAY [1..Students] OF STRING;
     ExamScores = ARRAY [1..Exams] OF Integer;
     ExamData   = ARRAY [1..Students] OF ExamScores;

VAR names  : NameData;
    scores : ExamData;

PROCEDURE InputData (VAR names : NameData; VAR scores : ExamData);
  VAR student, exam : Integer;
  BEGIN
    FOR student := 1 TO Students DO
      BEGIN
        Write('Enter name for student number ', student, ': ');
        Readln(names[student]);
        Writeln('Enter exam scores for ', names[student]);
        FOR exam := 1 TO Exams DO
          BEGIN
            Write('  Score #', exam, ': ');
            Readln(scores[student, exam])
          END
      END
  END;
```

```
    FUNCTION Average (studentScores : ExamScores) : Real;
      VAR exam, examTotal : Integer;
      BEGIN
        examTotal := 0;
        FOR exam := 1 TO Exams DO
          examTotal := examTotal + studentScores[exam];
        Average := examTotal / Exams
      END;

    PROCEDURE Swap (VAR num1, num2 : Integer);
      VAR temp : Integer;
      BEGIN
        temp := num1;
        num1 := num2;
        num2 := temp
      END;

    PROCEDURE SortScores (VAR studentScores : ExamScores);
      VAR index1, index2 : Integer;
      BEGIN
        FOR index1 := 1 TO Exams - 1 DO
          FOR index2 := 1 TO Exams - index1 DO
            IF studentScores[index2 + 1] < studentScores[index2] THEN
                Swap(studentScores[index2 + 1], studentScores[index2])
      END;

    FUNCTION Median (studentScores : ExamScores) : Real;
      BEGIN
        SortScores(studentScores);
        IF Odd(Exams) THEN
          Median := studentScores[(Exams DIV 2) + 1]
          ELSE
          Median := (studentScores[Exams DIV 2] +
                    studentScores[(Exams DIV 2) + 1]) / 2
      END;

    PROCEDURE ShowStatistics (names : NameData; scores : ExamData);
      VAR student, exam : Integer;
      BEGIN
        FOR student := 1 TO Students DO
          BEGIN
            Writeln(names[student], ':');
            Writeln('  Average = ', Average(scores[student]):4:1);
            Writeln('  Median  = ', Median(scores[student]):4:1)
          END
      END;

BEGIN
  ClrScr;
  InputData(names, scores);
  ShowStatistics(names, scores)
END.
```

CHAPTER 9

Exercises 9.1

1. Hello

3. 300 Park Place

5. 250

7. The REPEAT loop should be replaced with these lines.

```
Readln(street);
WHILE street <> 'EOD' DO
  BEGIN
    Writeln(address, street);
    Readln(street)
  END
```

11. Eof returns a Boolean value, not an Integer. So the FOR statement is illegal. The loop should begin with WHILE NOT Eof(aFile) DO, instead.

15. a, b, c, d, f

17.
```
CONST NumItems = 5;
          price : ARRAY [1..NumItems] OF Real =
                    (12.2, 2.0, 1.35, 40.0, 10.0);
          name  : ARRAY [1..NumItems] OF STRING [30] =
              ('Colt Peacemaker', 'Holster', 'Levi Strauss Jeans',
              'Saddle', 'Stetson');

VAR cowFile : Text;
    item    : Integer;

BEGIN
  Assign(cowFile, 'COWBOY');
  Rewrite(cowFile);
  FOR item := 1 TO NumItems DO
    BEGIN
      Writeln(cowFile, name[item]);
      Writeln(cowFile, price[item]:0:2)
    END;
  Close(CowFile)
END.
```

21.
```
VAR cowFile, cowFile2 : Text;
    name, newName     : STRING;
    price, newPrice   : Real;
    inserted          : Boolean;
BEGIN
  Write('What is the item called? ');
  Readln(newName);
  Write('What is the price of the item? ');
  Readln(newPrice);
  Assign(cowFile2, 'COWBOY.2');
  Rewrite(cowFile2);
  Assign(cowFile, 'COWBOY');
  Reset(cowFile);
  inserted := False;
  WHILE NOT Eof(cowFile) DO
    BEGIN
      Readln(cowFile, name);
      Readln(cowFile, price);
      IF (newName < name) AND NOT inserted THEN
        BEGIN
          Writeln(cowfile2, newName);
          Writeln(cowfile2, newPrice:0:2);
          inserted := True
        END;
      Writeln(cowFile2, name);
      Writeln(cowFile2, price:0:2)
    END;
  Close(cowFile);
  Close(cowFile2)
END.
```

9. The name Michael was added without including a birthdate. The WHILE loop at the end of the program will read Michael's name and then create an error when it hits the end of the file instead of finding his birthdate.

13. The name precedes the birthdate in YOB.DAT, so the program should also read the data in that order.

19.
```
VAR cowFile : Text;

BEGIN
  Assign(cowFile, 'COWBOY');
  Append(cowFile);
  Writeln(cowFile, 'Winchester rifle');
  Writeln(cowFile, 20.50:0:2);
  Close(cowFile)
END.
```

23.
```
VAR cowFile, cowFile4 : Text;
    name              : STRING;
    price             : Real;
BEGIN
  Assign(cowFile4, 'COWBOY.4');
  Rewrite(cowFile4);
  Assign(cowFile, 'COWBOY');
  Reset(cowFile);
  WHILE NOT Eof(cowFile) DO
    BEGIN
      Readln(cowFile, name);
      Readln(cowFile, price);
      IF name <> 'Holster' THEN
        BEGIN
          Writeln(cowFile4, name);
          Writeln(cowFile4, price:0:2)
        END
    END;
  Close(cowFile);
  Close(cowFile4)
END.
```

25.
```
VAR namesFile           : Text;
    name                : STRING;
    total, frequency    : Integer;
    lastLetter, curLetter : Char;
    firstPass           : Boolean;
BEGIN
  Assign(namesFile, 'NAMES');
  Reset(namesFile);
  total := 0;                    { Prime counters }
  total := 0;
  firstPass := True;             { Allows WHILE loop to prime values }
  WHILE NOT Eof(namesFile) DO
    BEGIN
      Readln(namesFile, name);
      IF firstPass THEN
        BEGIN
          curLetter := name[1];
          firstPass := False
        END;
      total := total + 1;
      lastLetter := curLetter;
      curLetter := name[1];
      IF curLetter = lastLetter THEN
          BEGIN
            Writeln(name);
            frequency := frequency + 1
          END
      ELSE
        BEGIN
          Writeln(lastLetter:10, ': ', frequency);
          Writeln(name);
          frequency := 1
        END;
    END;
  Writeln(curLetter:10, ': ', frequency); { Treat last name }
  Writeln ('Total Names: ', total);
  Close(namesFile)
END.
```

27.
```
VAR bookFile           : Text;
    booktype           : Char; { 'H'ardback or 'P'aperback }
    readName, targetName : STRING;
    qty                : Integer;

BEGIN
  Write('Title of book? ');
  Readln(targetName);
  REPEAT
    Write('Hardback or Paperback (H or P)? ');
    Readln(booktype);
    booktype := UpCase(booktype)
  UNTIL (booktype = 'H') OR (booktype = 'P');
  IF booktype = 'H' THEN
      Assign(bookFile, 'HARDBACK.INV')
    ELSE
      Assign(bookFile, 'PAPERBCK.INV');
  Reset(bookFile);
  readName := '';
  WHILE (NOT Eof(bookFile)) AND (readName <> targetName) DO
    BEGIN
      Readln(bookFile, readName);
      Readln(bookFile, qty)
    END;
  IF (readName = targetName) THEN
      Writeln('Number of copies in inventory is ', qty)
    ELSE
      Writeln('Book is not in the file.');
  Close(bookFile)
END.
```

31.
```
CONST maxPlayers = 60;

TYPE PlayerRec = RECORD
                   name  : STRING;
                   atBats : Integer;
                   hits  : Integer
                 END;
     PlayerArray = ARRAY [1..maxPlayers] OF PlayerRec;

VAR playerFile  : Text;
    player      : PlayerArray;
    numPlayers  : Integer;

PROCEDURE LoadData (VAR player : PlayerArray; VAR numPlayers : Integer;
                    VAR playerFile : Text);
{ Load names, times at bat, and hits for all PlayerRecs }
  BEGIN
    Reset(playerFile);
    numPlayers := 0;
    WHILE NOT Eof(playerFile) DO
      BEGIN
        numPlayers := numPlayers + 1;
        WITH player[numPlayers] DO
          BEGIN
            Readln(playerFile, name);
            Readln(playerFile, atBats);
            Readln(playerFile, hits)
          END
      END
  END;
```

29.
```
VAR statFile, newFile                    : Text;
    name                                 : STRING;
    atBats, hits, gameAtBats, gameHits : Integer;

BEGIN
  Assign(newFile, 'AVERAGE.TMP');
  Rewrite(newFile);
  Assign(statFile, 'AVERAGE.DAT');
  Reset(statFile);
  WHILE NOT Eof(statFile) DO
    BEGIN
      Readln(statFile, name);
      Readln(statFile, atBats);
      Readln(statFile, hits);
      Write(name, '''s times at bat in yesterday''s game: ');
      Readln(gameAtBats);
      Write(name, '''s hits in yesterday''s game: ');
      Readln(gameHits);
      Writeln(newFile, name);
      Writeln(newFile, atBats + gameAtBats);
      Writeln(newFile, hits + gameHits)
    END;
  Close(statFile);
  Close(newFile);
  Erase(statFile);
  Rename(newFile, 'AVERAGE.DAT')
END.
```

```
    PROCEDURE SortData (VAR player : PlayerArray; numPlayers : Integer);
    { Bubblesort arrays by batting average }
      VAR passNum, index : Integer;
      PROCEDURE SwapPlayers (VAR player1, player2 : PlayerRec);
        VAR playerTemp : PlayerRec;
        BEGIN { Procedure SwapPlayers }
          playerTemp := player1;
          player1 := player2;
          player2 := playerTemp
        END; { Procedure SwapPlayers }
      BEGIN { Procedure SortData }
        FOR passNum := 1 TO numPlayers - 1 DO
          FOR index := 1 TO numPlayers - passNum DO
            IF (player[index].hits / player[index].atBats ) <
                (player[index + 1].hits / player[index + 1].atBats) THEN
                  SwapPlayers(player[index], player[index + 1])
      END; { Procedure SwapData }

    PROCEDURE SaveData (VAR player : PlayerArray; numPlayers : Integer;
                          VAR playerFile : Text);
    { Copy array back into file }
      VAR i : Integer;
      BEGIN
        Rewrite(playerFile);
        FOR i := 1 TO numPlayers DO
          WITH player[i] DO
            BEGIN
              Writeln(playerFile, name);
              Writeln(playerFile, atBats);
              Writeln(playerFile, hits)
            END
      END;

    PROCEDURE ShowBest (VAR player : PlayerArray; numPlayers : Integer);
    { Display top 10 players }
      VAR i : Integer;
      BEGIN
        Writeln('Player      AVG');
        Writeln;
        IF numPlayers > 10 THEN
          numPlayers := 10;
        FOR i := 1 TO numPlayers DO
          WITH player[i] DO
            Writeln(name, (hits / atBats):13:3)
      END;

    BEGIN
      Assign(playerFile, 'AVERAGE.DAT');
      Reset(playerFile);
      LoadData(player, numPlayers, playerFile);
      SortData(player, numPlayers);
      Rewrite(playerFile);
      SaveData(player, numPlayers, playerFile);
      Close(playerFile);
      ShowBest(player, numPlayers)
    END.
```

33.
```
VAR nameFile, delFile, newFile : Text;
    name, delName             : STRING;
    year                      : Integer;

PROCEDURE ReadData (VAR inFile : Text; VAR name : STRING;
                    VAR year   : Integer);
  BEGIN
    Readln(inFile, name);
    Readln(inFile, year)
  END;

PROCEDURE WriteData(VAR outFile : Text; name : STRING; year : Integer);
  BEGIN
    Writeln(outFile, name);
    Writeln(outFile, year)
  END;

BEGIN
  Assign(nameFile, 'YOB.DAT');
  Assign(delFile, 'DEL.YOB');
  Assign(newFile, 'NEW.DAT');
  Reset(nameFile);
  Reset(delFile);
  Rewrite(newFile);
  WHILE NOT Eof(delFile) DO
    BEGIN
      Readln(delFile, delName);
      ReadData(nameFile, name, year);
      WHILE (name < delName) DO
        BEGIN
          WriteData(newFile, name, year);
          ReadData(nameFile, name, year)
        END
    END;
  WHILE NOT Eof(nameFile) DO
    BEGIN
      ReadData(nameFile, name, year);
      WriteData(newFile, name, year)
    END;
  Close(newFile);
  Close(delFile);
  Close(nameFile);
  Erase(nameFile);
  Rename(newFile, 'YOB.DAT')
END.
```

Exercises 9.2

1. Washington Adams

3. 1
2
3

5. Adams
Jefferson
Madison

7. Monroe

```
9. PROCEDURE GoodStudent (VAR hiStudent : STRING; VAR hiAverage : Real);
     VAR tempFile : FileType;
         tempRec  : StudentData;
         tempAve  : Real;
     BEGIN
       hiAverage := -1;
       Assign(tempFile, 'STUDENT.DAT');
       Reset(tempFile);
       WHILE NOT Eof(tempFile) DO
         BEGIN
           Read(tempFile, tempRec);
           tempAve := (tempRec.midterm + tempRec.final) / 2;
           IF tempAve > hiAverage THEN
               BEGIN
                 hiStudent := tempRec.student;
                 hiAverage := tempAve
               END
         END;
       Close(tempFile)
     END;
11. FUNCTION FindAndDelete (name : STRING) : Boolean;
      VAR newFile, studentFile : FileType;
          tempRec              : StudentData;
          position             : Integer;
      BEGIN
        Assign(studentFile, 'STUDENT.DAT');
        Assign(newFile, 'NEW.DAT');
        Reset(studentFile);
        Rewrite(newFile);
        FindAndDelete := False;
        WHILE NOT Eof(studentFile) DO
          BEGIN
            Read(studentFile, tempRec);
            IF tempRec.student <> name THEN
                Write(newFile, tempRec)
              ELSE
                FindAndDelete := True;
          END;
        Close(newFile);
        Close(studentFile);
        Erase(studentFile);
        Rename(newFile, 'STUDENT.DAT')
      END;
13. PROCEDURE DisplayFile;
      VAR tempRec     : StudentData;
          studentFile : FileType;
      BEGIN
        Assign(studentFile, 'STUDENT.DAT');
        Reset(studentFile);
        Writeln('Student        Midterm               Final');
        WHILE NOT Eof(studentFile) DO
          BEGIN
            Read(studentFile, tempRec);
            WITH tempRec DO
              Writeln(student, midterm:(20 - Length(student)),
                      final:20)
          END;
        Close(studentFile)
      END;
```

15.
```
TYPE StringFile = FILE OF STRING;

VAR composerFile : StringFile;

PROCEDURE AddNames (VAR composerFile : StringFile);
  VAR composer : STRING;
  BEGIN
    Write('Enter a name: ');
    Readln(composer);
    WHILE composer <> 'EOD' DO
      BEGIN
        Write(composerFile, composer);
        Write('Enter a name: ');
        Readln(composer)
      END
  END;

PROCEDURE DisplayFile (VAR composerFile : StringFile);
  VAR composer : STRING;
  BEGIN
    Seek(composerFile, 0);
    WHILE NOT Eof(composerFile) DO
      BEGIN
        Read(composerFile, composer);
        Writeln(composer)
      END
  END;

BEGIN
  Assign(composerFile, 'NAMES.DAT');
  Rewrite(composerFile);
  AddNames(composerFile);
  DisplayFile(composerFile);
  Close(composerFile)
END.
```

17.
```
PROCEDURE SortFile (VAR composerFile : StringFile);
  VAR first, last, gap, index : Integer;
      comp1, comp2            : STRING;
      newGapNeeded            : Boolean;
  BEGIN
    first := 0;
    gap := FileSize(composerFile) DIV 2;
    last := FileSize(composerFile) - 1;
    WHILE gap <> 0 DO
      BEGIN
        REPEAT
          newGapNeeded := True;
          FOR index := first TO (last - gap) DO
            BEGIN
              Seek(composerFile, index);
              Read(composerFile, comp1);
              Seek(composerFile, index + gap);
              Read(composerFile, comp2);
              IF comp1 > comp2 THEN
                BEGIN
                  Seek(composerFile, index);
                  Write(composerFile, comp2);
                  Seek(composerFile, index + gap);
                  Write(composerFile, comp1);
                  newGapNeeded := False
                END
            END
        UNTIL newGapNeeded;
        gap := gap DIV 2
      END
  END;
```

CHAPTER 10

Exercises 10.2

1. `_SetWindow(True, -1, -5, 7, 30)` **3.**
```
_MoveTo_w(-1, 0);
_LineTo_w(4, 0);
_MoveTo_w(0, -8);
_LineTo_w(0, 40)
```

5.
```
USES MsGraph;

VAR dummy : Integer;

PROCEDURE Circle (rx, cx, cy, a, b, c, d : Real);
  VAR ry : Real;
  BEGIN
    ry := rx * (5 / 4) * ((d - b) / (c - a));
    Ellipse_w( gBorder, cx - rx, cy - ry, cx + rx, cy + ry)
  END;

BEGIN
  dummy :=  SetVideoMode( MaxResMode);
  SetWindow(True, -2, -30, 12, 220);
  MoveTo_w(-2, 0);
  LineTo_w(12, 0);
  MoveTo_w(0, -30);
  LineTo_w(0, 220);
  MoveTo_w(3, 200);
  LineTo_w(10, 150);
  Circle(0.12, 3, 200, -2, -30, 12, 180);
  Circle(0.12, 10, 150, -2, -30, 12, 180)
END.
```

7. [Assume declarations from Exercise 5.]
```
BEGIN
  dummy := _SetVideoMode(_MaxResMode);
  _SetWindow(True, -1, -0.1, 5, 0.6);
  _MoveTo_w(-1, 0);
  _LineTo_w(5, 0);
  _MoveTo_w(0, -0.1);
  _LineTo_w(0, 0.6);
  _MoveTo_w(2, 0.5);
  _LineTo_w(4, 0.3);
  Circle(0.05, 2, 0.5, -1, -0.1, 5, 0.6);
  Circle(0.05, 4, 0.3, -1, -0.1, 5, 0.6)
END.
```

9. USES MsGraph;
```
VAR dummy : Integer;

BEGIN
  dummy := _SetVideoMode(_MaxResMode);
  _SetWindow(True, -5, -4, 5, 4);
  _MoveTo_w(0, 0);
  _Ellipse_w(_gBorder, -1, -1, 1, 1)
END.
```

15. USES MsGraph;
```
VAR dummy : Integer;

BEGIN
  dummy := _SetVideoMode(_MaxResMode);
  _SetWindow(True, -5, -4, 5, 4);
  _MoveTo_w(-3, -2);
  _LineTo_w(-3, 2);
  _LineTo_w(3, 2);
  _LineTo_w(3, -2);
  _LineTo_w(-3, -2)
END.
```

21. The ellipse will be smaller.

23. The x-dimension of the ellipse will contract.

27. USES MsGraph;
```
VAR i, max, dummy, col : Integer;

BEGIN
  Write('What is the maximum value on the ruler? ');
  Readln(max);
  dummy := _SetVideoMode(_MaxResMode);
  _SetWindow(True, -1, -12, max + 1, 12);
  _MoveTo_w(-1, 0);          { Draw the axis }
  _LineTo_w(max + 1, 0);
  FOR i := 0 TO max DO
    BEGIN
      _MoveTo_w(i, 0.5);
      _LineTo_w(i, -0.5);
      col := (80 * (i + 1) DIV (max + 2)) + 1;
      _SetTextPosition(17, col);
      Write(i)
    END;
  Writeln
END.
```

Exercises 10.3

1. _SetWindow(True, 79, -1, 86, 7);

3. USES MsGraph;
```
TYPE YearType = ARRAY [1..7] OF Integer;
     CPIType  = ARRAY [1..7] OF Real;

CONST YearData : YearType = (1967, 1970, 1973, 1976, 1979, 1982, 1985);
      CPIData  : CPIType  = (100.0, 116.3, 133.1, 170.5, 217.4, 288.7, 318.5);
VAR dummy, num : Integer;
```

```
BEGIN
  dummy := _SetVideoMode(_MaxResMode);
  _SetWindow(True, 1960, -60, 1990, 340);
  _MoveTo_w(1960, 0);
  _LineTo_w(1990, 0);
  _MoveTo_w(1965, -10);
  _LineTo_w(1965, 340);
  _SetTextPosition(5, 15);
  Write('Consumer Price Index (1960 base year)');
  _SetTextPosition(16, 8);
  Write(100);
  FOR num := 1 TO 7 DO
    BEGIN
      _MoveTo_w(YearData[num], -6);
      _LineTo_w(YearData[num], 6);
      _SetTextPosition(23, (num * 8) + 10);
      Write(YearData[num]);
      _MoveTo_w(YearData[num], CPIData[num]);
      IF num <> 7 THEN
          _LineTo_w(YearData[num + 1], CPIData[num + 1])
    END;
  Writeln;
  Write('Source: Bureau of Labor Statistics');
  Readln
END.
```

CHAPTER 11

Exercises 11.1

1. An integer from zero to four.   **3.** Random(5) returns one of 0, 1, 2, 3, and 4, so the WHILE loop never ends.

5. Integers from 1 to 38   **7.** Real values greater than or equal to 2 and less than 6.   **9.** Random(6) + 5

11. 2 * (Random(50) + 1)

13.
```
CONST words : ARRAY [0..19] OF STRING[20] =
    ('A', 'Be', 'Cat', 'Do', 'Em', 'Fa', 'Go', 'He', 'I', 'Jab', 'Kit',
     'La', 'Me', 'No', 'Or', 'Pi', 'Quit', 'Re', 'So', 'To');
  BEGIN
    Randomize;
    Writeln(words[Random(20)])
  END.
```

15.
```
TYPE Suit = (club, heart, diamond, spade);
     Deck = ARRAY [1..52] OF Suit;

CONST NumOfShuffles = 1000;

VAR card        : Deck;
    flushes, try : Integer;

PROCEDURE SetUpDeck (VAR card : Deck);
  VAR cardNum : Integer;
  BEGIN
    FOR cardNum := 0 TO 12 DO
      BEGIN
        card[cardNum * 4 + 1] := club;
        card[cardNum * 4 + 2] := heart;
        card[cardNum * 4 + 3] := diamond;
        card[cardNum * 4 + 4] := spade
      END
  END;
```

```
    PROCEDURE Shuffle (VAR card : Deck);
      VAR cardNum : Integer;
      PROCEDURE SwapCards (VAR s1, s2 : Suit);
        VAR temp : Suit;
        BEGIN { Procedure SwapCards }
          temp := s1;
          s1 := s2;
          s2 := temp
        END;  { Procedure SwapCards }
      BEGIN { Procedure Shuffle }
        Randomize;
        FOR cardNum := 1 TO 52 DO
          SwapCards(card[cardNum], card[Random(52) + 1])
      END;  { Procedure Shuffle }

    FUNCTION IsAFlush (VAR card : Deck) : Boolean;
      VAR i : Integer;
      BEGIN
        IsAFlush := True;
        FOR i := 2 TO 5 DO
          IF card[i] <> card[1] THEN
              IsAFlush := False
      END;

  BEGIN
    SetUpDeck(card);
    flushes := 0;
    FOR try := 1 TO NumOfShuffles DO
      BEGIN
        Shuffle(card);
        IF IsAFlush(card) THEN
            flushes := flushes + 1
      END;
      Writeln('There were ', flushes, ' flushes in ',
              NumOfShuffles, ' shuffles.')
  END.
```

17.
```
    VAR presNum, treasNum, thisNum : Integer;
        members                    : Text;
        thisName                   : STRING;

    BEGIN
      Randomize;
      presNum := Random(20) + 1;
      { The treasurer is one of the 19 besides the president }
      treasNum := Random(19) + 1;
      IF treasNum >= presNum THEN
          treasNum := treasNum + 1;
      Assign(members, 'MEMBERS.DAT');
      Reset(members);
      thisNum := 1;
      WHILE NOT Eof(members) DO
        BEGIN
          Readln(members, thisName);
          IF (thisNum = presNum) THEN
              Writeln(thisName, ' is president.')
            ELSE
              IF (thisNum = treasNum) THEN
                  Writeln(thisName, ' is treasurer.');
          thisNum := thisNum + 1
        END;
      Close(members)
    END.
```

19. `VAR probNum, choiceNum : Integer;`

```
BEGIN
  Randomize;
  FOR probNum := 1 TO 10 DO
    BEGIN
      Write(probNum, '. ');
      choiceNum := Random(5);
      Writeln(Chr(choiceNum + 97))  { Character from 'a' to 'e' }
    END
END.
```

21.
```
BEGIN
  Randomize;
  Writeln(Chr(Random(26) + 97))
END.
```

23. `VAR freq : ARRAY [1..6] OF Integer;`
```
      try, roll : Integer;
BEGIN
  Randomize;
  FOR roll := 1 TO 6 DO
    freq[roll] := 0;
  FOR try := 1 TO 1000 DO
    BEGIN
      roll := Random(6) + 1;
      freq[roll] := freq[roll] + 1
    END;
  FOR roll := 1 TO 6 DO
    Writeln(roll, ' came up ', freq[roll], ' times.')
END.
```

27. `TYPE PersonArray = ARRAY [1..23] OF Integer;`
```
CONST NumTrials = 1000;

VAR person              : PersonArray;
    num, another, trial : Integer;
    totalMatches        : Integer;
    match               : Boolean;

BEGIN
  Randomize;
  totalMatches := 0;
  FOR trial := 1 TO NumTrials DO
    BEGIN
      FOR num := 1 TO 23 DO
        person[num] := Random(365) + 1;
      match := False;
      FOR num := 1 TO 23 DO
        FOR another := 1 TO 23 DO
          IF (person[num] = person[another])
            AND (num <> another) THEN
              match := True;
      IF match THEN
        totalMatches := totalMatches + 1;
    END;
    Writeln('Percent of trials producing a match: ',
            (totalMatches / NumTrials) * 100:0:0, '%')
END.
```

Exercises 11.2

1. About 40%

3. Using Random twice is like flipping the coin twice. An ELSE statement should be used for the Tails condition.

5. 0.166667, 0.333333, 0.5

7. `VAR num     : Integer;`
```
      outcome : STRING[10];

BEGIN
  Randomize;
  num := Random(54) + 1;
  CASE num OF
     1..23 : outcome := '1';
    24..38 : outcome := '2';
    39..46 : outcome := '5';
    47..50 : outcome := '10';
    51..52 : outcome := '20';
    53 : outcome := 'Joker';
    54 : outcome := 'Casino'
  END;
  Writeln('The outcome is ', outcome, '.')
END.
```

9. `VAR profit, games, num : Integer;`
```
BEGIN
  Randomize;
  profit := 0;
  FOR games := 1 TO 1000 DO
    BEGIN
      num := Random(38);
      IF Odd(num) AND (num <> 37) THEN
        profit := profit + 1
      ELSE
        profit := profit - 1
    END;
  Writeln('profit: ', profit)
END.
```

```
11. VAR profit      : Real;
        num, games : Integer;

    PROCEDURE ProcessOdd (VAR profit : Real);
      BEGIN
        profit := profit + 1
      END;

    PROCEDURE ProcessEven (VAR profit : Real);
      BEGIN
        profit := profit - 1
      END;

    PROCEDURE ProcessZero (VAR profit : Real);
      BEGIN
        num := Random(37);
        IF num = 0 THEN
            profit := profit + 0.5
          ELSE
            IF Odd(num) THEN
                ProcessOdd(profit)
      END;

    BEGIN
      Randomize;
      profit := 0;
      FOR games := 1 TO 1000 DO
        BEGIN
          num := Random(37);
          IF num = 0 THEN
              ProcessZero(profit)
            ELSE
              IF Odd(num) THEN
                  ProcessOdd(profit)
                ELSE
                    ProcessEven(profit)
        END;
      Writeln('profit : ', profit:1:1)
    END.
```

CHAPTER 12

Exercises 12.1

1. 1
   2

3. 2
   2

5. 2
   2

7. deny

9. 10
   10

11. 3

13. 52

15. 6

17. 42

19. *a* is a pointer type and not itself a pointer variable.

21. ^Person must be defined before it can be used in the record definition.

23. Since listHead was declared as a record, not a pointer, New cannot be used on it.

25.
```
PROCEDURE DisplayList (listPtr : NumPointer);
  BEGIN
    WHILE listPtr <> NIL DO
      BEGIN
        Writeln(listPtr^.number);
        listPtr := listPtr^.nextNum
      END
  END;
```

27.
```
PROCEDURE DeleteFifth (VAR curPtr : NumPointer);
  VAR nodeNum : Integer;
      deleted : Boolean;
      predPtr : NumPointer;
  BEGIN
    nodeNum := 0;
    deleted := False;
    WHILE (curPtr <> NIL) AND NOT deleted DO
      BEGIN
        nodeNum := nodeNum + 1;
        IF nodeNum = 5 THEN
          BEGIN
            predPtr^.nextNum := curPtr^.nextNum;
            deleted := True
          END
        ELSE
          BEGIN
            predPtr := curPtr;
            curPtr := curPtr^.nextNum
          END
      END
  END;
```

29.
```
TYPE ListPointer = ^StoreRecord;
     StoreRecord = RECORD
                     name            : STRING;
                     address         : STRING;
                     phone           : STRING;
                     numOfPurchases  : Integer;
                     nextCustomer    : ListPointer
                   END;
```

31.
```
PROGRAM MakeNumberList;

TYPE NumPointer = ^NumRecord;
     NumRecord  = RECORD
                    number : Integer;
                    next   : NumPointer
                  END;

VAR  listPtr : NumPointer;        { Points to current list position }
     num     : Integer;           { Size of list }

PROCEDURE BuildList (VAR listPtr : NumPointer; num : Integer);
{ Build a list from back to front leaving listPtr at the front }
VAR node   : Integer;
    curPtr : NumPointer;
BEGIN
  FOR node := num DOWNTO 1 DO
    BEGIN
      New(curPtr);
      curPtr^.number := node;
      curPtr^.next := listPtr;
      listPtr := curPtr
    END
  END;

BEGIN
  New(listPtr);
  listPtr := NIL;
  Write('Enter a positive integer: ');
  Readln(num);
  BuildList(listPtr, num)
END.
```

```
33. PROGRAM HotelInfo;

    TYPE ListPointer = ^HotelRecord;
         HotelRecord = RECORD
                           company : STRING;      { Company name }
                           rooms   : Integer;     { Rooms in 1000s }
                           prop    : Integer;     { Properties owned }
                           next    : ListPointer  { Next node in list }
                       END;
         InputRecord = RECORD                      { File record format }
                           company : STRING;
                           rooms   : Integer;
                           prop    : Integer
                       END;

    VAR inputFile : FILE OF InputRecord;   { File containing hotel data }
        initPtr,                           { Beginning of list }
        predPtr,                           { Previous node holding data }
        curPtr    : ListPointer;           { Current node position }
        fileRec   : InputRecord;           { Data from file position }

    BEGIN
      Assign(inputFile, 'HOTEL.DAT');      { Typed file holding data }
      Reset(inputFile);
      New(curPtr);                    { Create first node }
      initPtr := curPtr;             { Save position of beginning of list }
      WHILE NOT Eof(inputFile) DO
        WITH curPtr^ DO
          BEGIN
            Read(inputFile, fileRec);
            company := fileRec.company;
            rooms := fileRec.rooms;
            prop := fileRec.prop;
            predPtr := curPtr;   { Save current node containing data }
            New(curPtr);         { New node to hold data if any left in file }
            predPtr^.next := curPtr  { Link new node into list }
          END;
      Dispose(curPtr);                   { WHILE loop left this target empty }
      predPtr^.next := NIL     { This is the end of the list }
    END.
```

Exercises 12.2

1. Inserting in an ordered array requires that a space be opened up in the proper array position by moving all the position's successive elements one position toward the end of the array. With an ordered linked list, all the elements remain intact except the item immediately preceeding the position where the insertion occurs.

3. In an unordered linked list, searching for an item requires every item in the list be examined. With an ordered list, one only need search until locating the list position where the sought after item should be.

5. If predPtr points to the second to the last item and curPtr points to the last item (which in turn has a NIL *next* field), then the same algoritm may be used for deleting from the middle. The NIL pointer will be assigned to predPtr's *next* field and the deletion will be complete after disposing curPtr.

```
7. PROCEDURE OrderedSearch (initPtr : ListPointer; quarry : Integer;
                            VAR found : Boolean;
                            VAR curPtr, predPtr : ListPointer);
   VAR done : Boolean;
   BEGIN
     predPtr := NIL;
     curPtr := initPtr;
     found := False;
     done := (curPtr = NIL);
     WHILE NOT done DO
       IF quarry > curPtr^.num THEN  { Haven't reached quarry yet }
           BEGIN
             predPtr := curPtr;
             curPtr := curPtr^.next;
             done := (curPtr = NIL)
           END
         ELSE                        { Either reached or exceeded quarry }
           done := True;
     IF curPtr <> NIL THEN
         IF quarry = curPtr^.num THEN
             found := True
   END;
13. PROGRAM SortStates;

    TYPE ListPointer = ^StateRec;
         StateRec   = RECORD
                        name : STRING;
                        rank : Integer;
                        next : ListPointer
                      END;

    VAR stateFile : Text;
        state     : STRING;
        listPtr   : ListPointer;
        ranking   : Integer;

    PROCEDURE FindSlot (   state : STRING; listPtr : ListPointer;
                        VAR predPtr, curPtr : ListPointer);
      VAR found : Boolean;
      BEGIN
        found := False;
        predPtr := NIL;
        curPtr := listPtr;
        WHILE (curPtr <> NIL) AND NOT found DO
          IF curPtr^.name < state THEN
              BEGIN
                predPtr := curPtr; curPtr := curPtr^.next
              END
            ELSE
              found := True
      END;
```

```
  PROCEDURE AddNode (    state : STRING; ranking : Integer;
                     VAR listPtr : ListPointer);
    VAR newPtr, predPtr, curPtr : ListPointer;
    BEGIN
      New(newPtr);
      newPtr^.name := state;
      newPtr^.rank := ranking;
      FindSlot(state, listPtr, predPtr, curPtr);
      IF predPtr = NIL THEN    { Insert at beginning of list }
          BEGIN
            newPtr^.next := curPtr;
            listPtr := newPtr
          END
        ELSE                    { Insert in middle of list }
          BEGIN
            predPtr^.next := newPtr;
            newPtr^.next := curPtr
          END
    END;

  PROCEDURE DisplayList (listPtr : ListPointer);
    BEGIN
      WHILE listPtr <> NIL DO
        WITH listPtr^ DO
          BEGIN
            Writeln(name, rank:(30 - Length(name)));
            listPtr := next
          END
    END;

  BEGIN
    Assign(stateFile, 'STATE.DAT');
    Reset(stateFile);
    listPtr := NIL;
    ranking := 1;
    WHILE NOT Eof(stateFile) DO
      BEGIN
        Readln(stateFile, state);
        AddNode(state, ranking, listPtr);
        ranking := ranking + 1
      END;
    DisplayList(listPtr);
    Close(stateFile)
  END.
```

Exercises 12.3

1. Ordered linked list

5. Queue

3. Stack

7. If a queue is implemented as an array, adding an item to the queue involves first shifting the current elements toward the end to open a gap. This is inconvenient and doesn't correspond to the intuitive idea of a queue. In addition, an array always has a fixed maximum length unlike most real queues. Thus, a linked list is usually preferable.

11.
```
PROCEDURE Push (VAR topItem : StackPointer; item : Integer);
  VAR newPtr : StackPointer;
  BEGIN
    New(newPtr);
    newPtr^.num := item;
    newPtr^.next := topItem;
    topItem := newPtr
  END;
```

13.
```
FUNCTION IsEmpty (topItem : StackPointer) : Boolean;
  BEGIN
    IsEmpty := (topItem = NIL)
  END;
```

```
15. PROCEDURE ShowStack (topItem : StackPointer);
      VAR tempItem : StackPointer;
      BEGIN
        tempItem := NIL;
        WHILE NOT IsEmpty(topItem) DO
          BEGIN
            item := Pop(topItem);
            Writeln(item);
            Push(tempItem, item)
          END;
        WHILE NOT IsEmpty(tempItem) DO
          Push(topItem, Pop(tempItem));
        Write('Press Enter.');
        Readln
      END;
```

Exercises 12.4

1. 15

3. ******

5. No terminating case if n is odd.

```
7. PROGRAM BinomialCoefficients;

   VAR n, r : Integer;

   FUNCTION C (n, r : Integer) : Integer;
     BEGIN
       IF (n = 0) OR (r = 0) OR (n = r) THEN
         C := 1
       ELSE
         C := C(n - 1, r - 1) + C(n - 1, r)
     END;

   BEGIN
     Write('Enter a positive integer: ');
     Readln(n);
     FOR r := 0 TO n DO
       Write(C(n, r), ' ')
   END.
```

```
9. FUNCTION Fib (n : Integer) : Integer;
   BEGIN
     IF (n <= 2) THEN
       Fib := 1
     ELSE
       Fib := Fib(n - 1) + Fib(n - 2)
   END;
```

```
11. VAR n, intRate : Integer;
        prin, pmt  : Real;

    FUNCTION Balance(prin, pmt : Real; intRate, n : Integer) : Real;
      BEGIN
        IF n = 0 THEN
          Balance := prin
        ELSE
          Balance := (1 + intRate / 1200) *
          Balance(prin, pmt, intRate, n - 1) - pmt
      END;

    BEGIN
      Write('Enter the principal: ');
      Readln(prin);
      Write('Enter the monthly payment: ');
      Readln(pmt);
      Write('Enter the annual rate of interest: ');
      Readln(intRate);
      Write('Enter the number of monthly payments made: ');
      Readln(n);
      Writeln('The amount still owed is ', Balance(prin,pmt,intRate,n):1:2)
    END.
```

```
13. PROGRAM ReverseOrder;

    VAR aWord : STRING;

    PROCEDURE GetWord (aWord : STRING);
      BEGIN
        Write('Enter a word (or EOD): ');
        Readln(aWord);
        IF aWord <> 'EOD' THEN
          BEGIN
            GetWord(aWord);
            Writeln(aWord)
          END
      END;

    BEGIN
      GetWord(aWord)
    END.
```

CHAPTER 13

Exercises 13.1

1. `plane.Init(10);`

3. [Declarations should be]
```
VAR plane, plane2 : Airplane;
    moves        : Integer;
[Add the following lines in the statement part]
New(plane2);
plane2.Init(4);
FOR moves := 1 TO 5 DO
  plane2.Move(Straight);
Dispose(plane2);
```

5. 7.00

7. New was not used to create the object myPoint.

9. The object name must be specified for each message.

11. "Self." must preceed each instance variable.

13. Self should replace Point in the WITH statement.

15. The object class name should be included in the method heading.

17. (a)
```
FUNCTION Point.InFirstQuad : Boolean;
    BEGIN
      InFirstQuad := (ABS(Self.p.x) = Self.p.x) AND
                     (ABS(Self.p.y) = Self.p.y) AND
                     (Self.p.x <> 0) AND (Self.p.y <> 0)
    END;
```

(b)
```
BEGIN
    New(myPoint);
    Write('Enter the coordinates of a point: ');
    Readln(x, y);
    myPoint.Init(x, y);
    IF myPoint.InFirstQuad THEN
        Writeln('The point is in the first quadrant.')
      ELSE
        Writeln('The point is not in the first quadrant.');
    Dispose(myPoint)
END.
```

23.
```
PROGRAM SenateProgram;

TYPE SenateClass = OBJECT
                     senator : ARRAY [1..100] OF STRING;
                     total   : 0..100;
                     PROCEDURE Init;  PROCEDURE AddSenator (name : STRING);
                     PROCEDURE RemoveSenator (name : STRING);
                     PROCEDURE DisplaySenate;
                     PROCEDURE NumOfSenators
                   END;

PROCEDURE SenateClass.Init;
  BEGIN
    Self.total := 0
  END;

PROCEDURE SenateClass.AddSenator (name : STRING);
  BEGIN
    Self.total := Self.total + 1;
    Self.senator[Self.total] := name
  END;

PROCEDURE SenateClass.RemoveSenator (name : STRING);
  VAR index : 1..100;
      found : Boolean;
  BEGIN
    index := 1;
    found := False;
    WHILE (index <= Self.total) AND NOT found DO
      BEGIN
        IF Self.senator[index] = name THEN
            BEGIN
              Self.senator[index] := Self.senator[Self.total];
              Self.total := Self.total - 1;
              found := True
            END;
        index := index + 1
      END
```

```
PROCEDURE SenateClass.DisplaySenate;
  VAR index : 1..100;
  BEGIN
    FOR index := 1 TO Self.total DO
      Writeln(index:4, ' The Honorable ', Self.senator[index])
  END;

PROCEDURE SenateClass.NumOfSenators;
  BEGIN
    Writeln('There are ', Self.total, ' senators on the floor.')
  END;

VAR senate : SenateClass;
    name   : STRING;
    done   : Boolean;

FUNCTION MenuChoice : Char;
  VAR choice : Char;
  BEGIN
    REPEAT
      Writeln('A   Add a senator.');
      Writeln('B   Delete a senator.');
      Writeln('C   Display number of senators on floor.');
      Writeln('D   Display names of senators on floor.');
      Writeln('E   Quit');
      Write('Enter a selection: ');
      Readln(choice);
      choice := UpCase(choice)
    UNTIL choice IN ['A'..'E'];
    MenuChoice := choice
  END;

BEGIN
  New(senate);
  senate.Init;
  done := False;
  REPEAT
    CASE MenuChoice OF
      'A' : BEGIN
              Write('Enter the senator''s name: ');
              Readln(name);
              senate.AddSenator(name)
            END;
      'B' : BEGIN
              Write('Enter the senator''s name: ');
              Readln(name);
              senate.RemoveSenator(name)
            END;
      'C' : senate.NumOfSenators;
      'D' : senate.DisplaySenate;
      'E' : done := True
    END;
  UNTIL done;
  Dispose(senate)
END.
```

Exercises 13.2

1. 4.00

5. Circle
```
    Center: (2.50, 3.00)
    Radius: 4.00
    Area:   50.27
    The origin is inside the circle.
```

9. The header of Ellipse.Init must match the header from Point. Init exactly. In this case the parameter names do not match.

3. `Writeln('The center is at: (', myCircle.GetX:0:2, ', ', myCircle.GetY:0:2, ').');`

7. No ancestor of Ellipse is specified in parentheses so there is nothing to OVERRIDE.

11. ChangeRadius is not a method of Point, and myPoint is a Point.

```
13. TYPE Person = OBJECT
                   name : STRING;
                   age  : Integer;
                   PROCEDURE Init (name : STRING; age : Integer);
                   FUNCTION GetName : STRING
                END;

        Worker = OBJECT (Person)
                   salary : Real;
                   PROCEDURE WInit (name : STRING; age : Integer;
                                        salary : Real);
                   FUNCTION Earnings : Real { Earnings til retirement }
                END;

    PROCEDURE Person.Init (name : STRING; age : Integer);
      BEGIN
        Self.name := name;
        Self.age := age
      END;

    FUNCTION Person.GetName : STRING;
      BEGIN
        GetName := Self.Name
      END;

    PROCEDURE Worker.WInit (name : STRING; age : Integer; salary : Real);
      BEGIN
        Self.Init(name, age);
        Self.salary := salary
      END;

    FUNCTION Worker.Earnings : Real;
      VAR annualSal, sum : Real;
          index          : Integer;
      BEGIN
        annualSal := Self.salary;
        sum := 0;
        FOR index := Self.age TO 64 DO
          BEGIN
            IF index <> Self.age THEN           { Since 5% increase   }
                annualSal := annualSal * 1.05; {   starts second year }
            sum := sum + annualSal
          END;
        Earnings := sum
      END;

  VAR WorkerObj : Worker;
      name     : STRING;
      age      : Integer;
      salary   : Real;

  BEGIN
    New(WorkerObj);
    Write('Enter the person''s name: ');
    Readln(name);
    Write('Enter the person''s age: ');
    Readln(age);
    Write('Enter the person''s annual salary: ');
    Readln(salary);
    WorkerObj.WInit(name, age, salary);
    Writeln(WorkerObj.name, ' will earn ', WorkerObj.Earnings:1:2);
    Dispose(WorkerObj)
  END.
```

Index

Microsoft QuickPascal 1.0 requires the following hardware:

1. An IBM PC Personal Computer or "compatible" that runs MS-DOS or PC-DOS Version 2.1 or later

2. 448K of installed memory

3. One of the following disk configurations:
   (a) Two 360K 5¼-inch diskette drives
   (b) A hard disk (and a diskette drive)
   (c) A 720K 3½-inch diskette drive
   (d) A 1.2MB high-density 5 1/4-inch diskette drive
   (e) A 1.44MB 3½-inch high-density diskette drive
   (f) An arrangement equivalent to or exceeding the capacity of one of the above

MICROSOFT SOFTWARE LICENSE

READ THIS FIRST. Your use of the Microsoft software (the "SOFTWARE") is governed by the legal agreement below.

BY OPENING THE SEALED DISKETTE PACKAGE YOU ARE AGREEING TO BE BOUND BY THE TERMS AND CONDITIONS SET BELOW. IF YOU DO NOT AGREE WITH SUCH TERMS AND CONDITIONS, YOU SHOULD RETURN THE UNOPENED DISKETTE PACKAGE TO-GETHER WITH THE BOOK TO THE PLACE YOU OBTAINED THEM FOR A REFUND.

1. **GRANT OF LICENSE**. Microsoft grants to you the right to use one copy of the enclosed SOFTWARE on a single terminal connected to a single computer (i.e. with a single CPU). You must not network the SOFTWARE or otherwise use it on more than one computer or computer terminal at the same time.

2. **COPYRIGHT**. The SOFTWARE is owned by Microsoft or its suppliers and is protected by United States copyright laws and international treaty provisions. Therefore, you must treat the SOFTWARE like any other copyrighted material (e.g. a BOOK or musical recording) **except** that you may either (a) make one copy of the SOFTWARE solely for backup or archival purposes, or (b) transfer the SOFTWARE to a single hard disk provided you keep the original solely for backup or archival purposes. You may not copy the written materials.

3. **OTHER RESTRICTIONS**. You may not rent or lease the SOFTWARE, but you may transfer the SOFTWARE and written materials on a permanent basis provided you retain no copies and the recipient agrees to the terms of the Agreement. You may not reverse engineer, decompile or disassemble the SOFTWARE.

DISCLAIMER OF WARRANTY AND LIMITED WARRANTY

THE SOFTWARE AND ACCOMPANYING WRITTEN MATERIALS (INCLUDING IN-STRUCTIONS FOR USE) ARE PROVIDED "AS IS" WITHOUT WARRANTY OF ANY KIND. FURTHER, MICROSOFT DOES NOT WARRANT, GUARANTEE, OR MAKE ANY REPRESEN-TATIONS REGARDING THE USE, OR THE RESULTS OF THE USE, OF THE SOFTWARE OR WRITTEN MATERIALS IN TERMS OF CORRECTNESS, ACCURACY, RELIABILITY, CUR-RENTNESS, OR OTHERWISE. THE ENTIRE RISK AS TO THE RESULTS AND PERFORMANCE OF THE SOFTWARE IS ASSUMED BY YOU. IF THE SOFTWARE OR WRITTEN MATERIALS ARE DEFECTIVE YOU, AND NOT MICROSOFT OR ITS DEALERS, DISTRIBUTORS, AGENTS, OR EMPLOYEES, ASSUME THE ENTIRE COST OF ALL NECESSARY SERVICING, REPAIR OR CORRECTION.

The diskettes in this book were reproduced by Dellen Publishing Company under a special arrange-ment with Microsoft Corporation. For this reason, Dellen Publishing Company is responsible for the product warranty and for support. If your diskettes are defective, please return them to Dellen Publishing Company, which will arrange for their replacement. In no event shall Microsoft's liability and your exclusive remedy as to defective software, written materials, and disks be other than either (a) return of the purchase price or (b) replacement of the disk which is returned to Microsoft with a copy of the receipt. If failure of the disk has resulted from accident, abuse or misapplication, Microsoft shall have no responsibility to replace the disk or refund the purchase price. Any replacement disk will be warranted for thirty (30) days.

NO OTHER WARRANTIES. MICROSOFT DISCLAIMS ALL OTHER WARRANTIES, EITHER EXPRESS OR IMPLIED, INCLUDING BUT NOT LIMITED TO IMPLIED WARRANTIES OF MERCHANTABILITY AND FITNESS FOR A PARTICULAR PURPOSE, WITH RESPECT TO THE SOFTWARE AND ANY ACCOMPANYING HARDWARE. THIS LIMITED WARRANTY GIVES YOU SPECIFIC LEGAL RIGHTS. YOU MAY HAVE OTHERS, WHICH VARY FROM STATE TO STATE.

NO LIABILITY FOR CONSEQUENTIAL DAMAGES. IN NO EVENT SHALL MICROSOFT OR ITS SUPPLIERS BE LIABLE FOR ANY DAMAGES WHATSOEVER (INCLUDING WITHOUT LIMITATION DAMAGES FOR LOSS OF BUSINESS PROFITS, BUSINESS INTERRUPTION, LOSS OF BUSINESS INFORMATION, OR OTHER PECUNIARY LOSS) ARISING OUT OF THE USE OR INABILITY TO USE THIS MICROSOFT PRODUCT EVEN IF MICROSOFT HAS BEEN ADVISED OF THE POSSIBILITY OF SUCH DAMAGES. BECAUSE SOME STATES DO NOT ALLOW THE EXCLUSION OR LIMITATION OF LIABILITY FOR CONSEQUENTIAL OR INCI-DENTAL DAMAGES, THE ABOVE LIMITATION MAY NOT APPLY TO YOU.